Eight Miles High

folk-rock's flight
from Haight-Ashbury
to Woodstock

by Richie Unterberger

**Backbeat
Books**

San Francisco

Published by Backbeat Books
600 Harrison Street, San Francisco, CA 94107
www.backbeatbooks.com
email: books@musicplayer.com

An imprint of the Music Player Network
Publishers of *Guitar Player, Bass Player, Keyboard,* and other magazines
United Entertainment Media, Inc.
A CMP Information company

CMP
United Business Media

Distributed to the book trade in the US and Canada by
Publishers Group West, 1700 Fourth Street, Berkeley, CA 94710

Distributed to the music trade in the US and Canada by
Hal Leonard Publishing, P.O. Box 13819, Milwaukee, WI 53213

Cover Design by Doug Gordon
Text Design and Composition by Leigh McLellan
Front Cover Photos: Crosby, Stills, Nash & Young; Joni Mitchell; Donovan: ©Michael
    Ochs Archives.com. Simon & Garfunkel: ©Paul Ryan/Michael Ochs Archives.com

Library of Congress Cataloging-in-Publication Data

Unterberger, Richie, 1962–
    Eight miles high : folk-rock's flight from Haight-Ashbury to Woodstock/
    by Richie Unterberger.
        p. cm.
    Includes discography (p.), bibliographical references (p.), and index.
    ISBN 0-87930-743-9 (alk. paper)
    1. Folk-rock music—History and criticism. I. Title: 8 miles high. II. Title.

    ML3534.U55 2003
    781.66—dc21

                                                        2003040440

Printed in the United States of America

03 04 05 06 07   5 4 3 2 1

contents

6

Folk-Rock Superstars and Supergroups   *203*

Veterans from Buffalo Springfield and the Byrds form Crosby, Stills, Nash & Young, folk-rock's first supergroup. Folk-rock superstars Judy Collins, Joni Mitchell, Simon & Garfunkel, and James Taylor see out the '60s with sounds that stray further still from their folk roots. The record business gets slicker and more corporate as the singer-songwriter boom brings in more money, while the artists manage to balance commercialism with social consciousness and rebellion.

7

Liege & Lief: A Truly British Folk-Rock   *233*

Enigmatic British singer-songwriters like Nick Drake, Roy Harper, and Al Stewart make their first important recordings, giving a new hue to the American-dominated singer-songwriter movement. Britain hosts the last major, and most traditionally based, branch of folk-rock to flower in the 1960s as Fairport Convention, Steeleye Span, and others electrify specifically English traditional folk songs.

8

Folk-Rock from Newport to Woodstock   *265*

Folk and folk-rock audiences merge and metamorphose in the interim between the 1965 Newport Folk Festival (where Dylan was so stormily received) and the end of the 1960s, when massive crowds attend events such as Woodstock to see and hear folk-rock and hard rock performers mix freely.

epilogue

Folk-Rock's Legacy   *289*

A look at the enduring influence of 1960s folk-rock, from the 1970s to the early twenty-first century, as the originators matured, died, or survived to preserve the form and help keep the folk-rock wheel turning.

introduction

In the summer of 1965, the arrival of folk-rock could have scarcely been greeted with more excitement, surprise, bewilderment, and even fearful outrage than the landing of aliens from outer space.

Folk purists clashed with the new guard of electric rockers, sometimes explosively, most famously at Bob Dylan's first concert with a rock 'n' roll band at the Newport Folk Festival. The Byrds had taken a Dylan song to the top of the singles charts with their electric reinvention of "Mr. Tambourine Man"; before the year was out, they would do the same with Pete Seeger's "Turn! Turn! Turn!" *Billboard* magazine ran headlines like "Folk+Rock+Protest=An Erupting New Sound." Barry McGuire's "Eve of Destruction" inspired denunciations from clergymen and fellow pop stars alike even as it bulldozed its way to #1. The Byrds and Dylan were followed by fellow ex-folk troubadours the Lovin' Spoonful, the Mamas & the Papas, Donovan, Simon & Garfunkel, and others in an en masse rush to electrify. Their music had changed unrecognizably from the acoustic sounds they were making just a couple of years earlier. And with their long-haired visages and flamboyant wardrobes, those performers had themselves changed unrecognizably from the short-haired, relatively clean-cut beatniks who had grinned from the sleeves of obscure folk albums in 1963 and 1964.

At the end of the 1960s, folk-rockers were selling just as many records, and were if anything shaggier and more provocatively dressed and opinionated than they had been five years earlier. Yet folk-rock was no longer the tinder for debate, controversy, and squabbling over who was entitled to play folk-influenced music and how it could and should be played. Folk-rock was now a firmly embedded pillar of popular music. And it was no longer just "an erupting new sound." Folk-rock had sprouted into *several* erupting new sounds, some of which had already run their course, some of which were just starting to boil. Taken together, they helped set the course of popular music for the rest of the twentieth century.

The birth and initial frenzy of folk-rock, from the early-'60s folk revival to its teetering on the brink of psychedelia in mid-1966, was covered in my previous book, *Turn! Turn! Turn!: The '60s Folk-Rock Revolution* (Backbeat Books, 2002). The remaining years of the decade would be just as exciting for folk-rock, even as the music became progressively more difficult to pigeonhole, spinning and splintering into psychedelic folk-rock, singer-songwriters, country-rockers, and the inventors of an idiosyncratically British blend of rock and traditional folk music. These are the years that brought folk-rock to both new peaks and, at the beginning of the 1970s, the ultimate and inevitable close of the revolution's first and most exciting phase. And these are the years covered by

Eight Miles High: Folk-Rock's Flight from Haight-Ashbury to Woodstock, the sequel to *Turn! Turn! Turn!*, just as the song "Eight Miles High" was the Byrds' next hit single after "Turn! Turn! Turn!"

"Eight Miles High" is often and justly acclaimed as one of the first psychedelic rock songs. It might have seemed—might *still* seem, more than 35 years later—a radical break from both the folk and rock music that had preceded it. It might even seem a radical break from the folk-rock the Byrds had steered to perfection on "Turn! Turn! Turn!" To the guardians of the radio airwaves, it was alien and futuristic enough—and subject to such far-fetched (mis)interpretation—that it was banned from many playlists. Yet, as Byrds leader Roger McGuinn enjoys explaining, it is in some ways still very much a folk song.

It's impossible to understand how the Byrds took such an unexpected detour without examining their prior recordings. Likewise, it's impossible to understand how folk-rock could arrive at this brave new frontier—and smash into numerous equally unexpected offshoots throughout the rest of the '60s—without examining the folk-rock that was created before "Eight Miles High" and other records propelled the music from the jet age into hyperspace. This book's "prequel" extensively details the initial marriage between folk and rock. Before launching into this second volume, though, a summary of the key events, happy accidents, and artistic/commercial hothouses on the folk-rock road prior to our mid-1966 starting point is in order.

The large majority of the musicians who pioneered folk-rock in the mid-'60s started their career as acoustic performers in the early-'60s folk revival. The early-'60s folk boom was actually the crest of a folk revival that had been underway for several decades, but truly began to pick up steam in the latter part of the 1950s, with the popular success of the Kingston Trio and some other folk acts. The Kingston Trio and similar groups have been seen as (or accused of) cleaning up folk for mass consumption. But even the rootsiest forms of American (and sometimes non-American) folk music were gaining in popularity with the energetic touring and political activism of veteran performers like Pete Seeger, the work of folklorists and collectors such as Alan Lomax and Harry Smith, and the growth of independent labels with large folk catalogs, such as Folkways, Elektra, and Vanguard.

In the early '60s, folk music was attracting a larger, and more youthful, American audience than it ever had or ever would. There was an explosion of folk music venues, particularly in coffeehouses in large cities and college towns; the institution of several well-attended folk festivals, most prominently the ones held at Newport; the superstardom of Joan Baez and Peter, Paul & Mary; the widening readerships of the folk music magazines *Sing Out!* and *Broadside*; and the burgeoning careers of artists such as Judy Collins. There was also the cultivation of young topical and protest folk songwriters championed by Bob Dylan, including Buffy Sainte-Marie, Tom Paxton, and Phil Ochs. Peter, Paul & Mary took Dylan's "Blowin' in the Wind" into the Top Ten, and folk music was an integral building block of socially progressive activism, particularly within the civil rights movement.

Yet folk music was also being commercialized to an ungainly degree by wholesome, sterile folk-variety combos and mainstream exposure on the 1963 television show *Hootenanny*. There was some restlessness with the homogenization of mainstream folk, as well as the narrow-minded political/artistic parameters of hard-line purist folk and its dry, minimal acoustic accompaniment. Some of that restlessness began to manifest itself with more flexible songwriting and more rhythmic, denser arrangements on albums by Judy Collins, Ian & Sylvia, Judy Henske, and others. But the true impetus shoving young American musicians from acoustic folk to electric rock was supplied by the Beatles, who overwhelmed both the record industry and the entire country with the phenomenal success of their first Stateside visit in February 1964.

Many of the younger folkies had never really abandoned their love of the classic rock 'n' roll they grew up on in the 1950s. The Beatles—and the legion of British Invasion bands that followed them in 1964 and 1965, like the Rolling Stones, the Animals, the Kinks, the Yardbirds, Them, the Searchers, and the Zombies—reignited their passion for the music. But what they devised when they started to buy and play electric guitars wasn't quite the same as quasi-Merseybeat, though some were trying their hardest to sound like the Beatles. It was a new hybrid that didn't have a name yet, the British Invasion mixing with the folk-bred harmonies and folky guitar picking and strumming styles that the musicians had perfected on the folk circuit. The musicians that would form the Byrds, the Lovin' Spoonful, and the Mamas & the Papas spent much of 1964, and some of 1965, coming to grips with amplified rock in small clubs in Greenwich Village and Hollywood. British Invasion groups the Animals and the Searchers were already electrifying some folk-based material in 1964, though not with the conscious intent of creating a new blend of the styles.

At the same time, Bob Dylan himself had been mightily impressed by the Beatles, although it would take him a good year or so to start recording with electric musicians. In the meantime he'd composed a startling new song, "Mr. Tambourine Man," which like many of his 1964 compositions broke away from the protest idiom into more poetic, sometimes abstract realms of personal expression. When an unreleased version of his first pass at the song in the studio made its way to the Byrds, the mixture of folk and rock that the group was tentatively exploring had its essential final ingredient: lyrical intelligence, beyond what other rock groups—the Beatles included—had ever attempted.

In early 1965, the Byrds were starting to draw overflow crowds on Sunset Strip even before they released a record; Dylan made his first all-out rock 'n' roll recordings, without diminishing his lyrical ambitions; and other songwriters such as Richard Fariña, Donovan, and Fred Neil were beginning to electrify, albeit lightly, songs of similar lyrical depth. It finally came to a flashpoint when the Byrds' debut single, "Mr. Tambourine Man," reached #1 on the American charts in June 1965.

The music industry was quick to label the new sound "folk-rock"—a term that the musicians themselves were rarely comfortable with, but the one that's endured, all the way into the twenty-first century. The Byrds' success, with both the "Mr. Tambourine Man" single and the Top Ten *Mr. Tambourine Man* album, made them America's counterparts to the Beatles, led by their wondrous harmonies and the jingle-jangle of Roger McGuinn's electrified 12-string guitar. Almost immediately, the folk-rock boom was on, as more commercially oriented groups raced on the Byrds' heels in the next few months, such as the Turtles, the We Five, and Sonny & Cher.

Folk-rock's passage from fad to something more enduring gained exponentially greater weight when Bob Dylan scored his first massive electric rock hit, "Like a Rolling Stone," also in the summer of 1965. By that point he'd outraged folk purists by "going electric" at the 1965 Newport Folk Festival, in a brief but cataclysmic performance that sparked about as many diametrically opposed reactions as any live set of music ever has. It, and Dylan's likewise stormily received electric sets throughout the rest of 1965, formed the focal point of a firestorm of controversy, particularly within the folk community. The purist-vs.-rocker divisions have been exaggerated by some historians. Yet certainly there was a significant and vocal segment of the folk audience that viewed electrified folk-rock (and Dylan's folk-rock in particular) as not just a commercial sellout, but a betrayal of the traditional folk and socially progressive values that many longtime folkies held dear.

Still, the folk-rock juggernaut was by this point unstoppable. If some of the links to the folk traditions that had inspired the musicians to pick up a guitar to begin with were being diluted, much more was being gained. Put simply, folk-rock was more interesting and exciting than the simpler acoustic folk music on which they'd cut their teeth. Put specifically, folk-rock was far more powerful music that could make you dance as well as think, and lent itself to far more memorable melodies and textural possibilities, both in the boost in amplification and the greater diversity of instruments. Put in terms of "dollars and sense," folk-rockers reached far more listeners—and made far more money—than acoustic guitar-and-harmonica-driven troubadours could ever envision.

The expansion of their target market of college and high school students was in 1965 bigger than at any other point in history, and just at the point when that audience's social consciousness had begun to expand and become receptive to the folk-rockers' musical messages. These were messages that could, for the first time, introduce almost any subject into rock music: frank sexual expression, antiwar sentiments, oblique drug references, baroque romanticism, or apolitical depictions of inner states of mind. The beat, the tunes, the electricity, the words, the blend of the best attributes of folk and rock—all combined to take popular music into a place that neither folk nor rock could have gotten to on their own.

Throughout the rest of 1965, other acts made a big folk-rock splash, whether with gravelly protest (Barry McGuire's "Eve of Destruction"), good-time celebratory sounds that owed much to folk jug bands (the Lovin' Spoonful), smoothly harmonized romantic folk-rock (the Mamas & the Papas), or folk-rock at its most cerebral (Simon & Garfunkel). Sometimes it was made by veterans who'd been kicking around the underbelly of the record business for nearly a decade. Sometimes it was by groups who seemed to have gotten their big shot only by happenstance, as with Simon & Garfunkel, whose original acoustic version of "The Sound of Silence" was overdubbed with electric instruments in absentia, and the Mamas & the Papas, who got their big break as backup vocalists at a McGuire session. And sometimes it was by rock artists who'd been drawn into folk-rock's slipstream from the electric rock side, rather than the acoustic folk one. The absorption of folk-rock into the Beatles' 1965 recordings, particularly their late-1965 album *Rubber Soul*, was the ultimate validation of folk-rock's influence and importance.

Although the brouhaha over folk-rock and whether musicians were selling out by electrifying was starting to subside by early 1966, the music's creativity and constant reinvention were not. In 1966 the Lovin' Spoonful, Simon & Garfunkel, the Mamas & the Papas, and Bob Dylan all consolidated their superstardom with huge hits. Most young acoustic folk singers of note either took all-out plunges into folk-rock, including Tim Hardin, Judy Collins, and Tom Rush, or at least made their first tentative ventures into folk-rock waters, as did Phil Ochs and Ian & Sylvia. On Sunset Strip, Love and Buffalo Springfield rose to challenge the Byrds for Hollywood folk-rock supremacy. The Byrds themselves, fresh from the chart-topping triumph of "Turn! Turn! Turn!" that had ended 1965, incorporated Indian raga, improvisational jazz, and exotic imagery into their sound and hurtled into psychedelic rock with "Eight Miles High." Elektra, Vanguard, and Verve/Folkways, all labels known for strong folk rosters, began to shift their emphasis to electric folk-rock. Elsewhere folk-rockers infiltrated the rosters of labels from the biggest, like Columbia, to the most avant-garde independents, like ESP, whose Fugs cracked the Top 100.

At times it seemed that virtually every important folk-rock act was rising from the streets of Greenwich Village and Sunset Strip, but in fact it was a worldwide phenomenon. Donovan was Britain's chief folk-rock ambassador, particularly when he shed his Dylan imitator tags with the kaleidoscopic folk-psychedelic-rock of 1966's "Sunshine Superman" hit, and his album of the same name. In fact he was the British Isles' *only* folk-rock ambassador to match the feats of America's greatest masters of the form in the mid-'60s, though other British folk-rockers would rise to the challenge later in the decade and British Invasion rock groups continued to effectively incorporate folk-rock into their songwriting and records from time to time.

Elsewhere in the United States, countless teenage garage bands mimicked aspects of the Byrds and other leading folk-rock groups, occasionally coming up with something quite respectable. The odd band based far from New York or L.A., like the Blue Things in Kansas, made records nearly on a par with the best sounds of either the East or West Coast. Weird one-off folk-rock experiments and novelties surfaced by numerous acts known for styles far removed from folk-rock, or from future stars years away from making national headway. Older folk revival veterans from Pete Seeger to Ramblin' Jack Elliott made little-noticed folk-rock outings in the studio, sometimes with acceptable results, though more often with embarrassing or inconsequential ones. Folk-rock's tentacles had extended to every level of popular music, even if some die-hard purists continued to boo Bob Dylan's electric sets with future members of the Band during his world tour in the spring of 1966.

Folk-rock might not have been the magnet for quite as much attention in 1966 as it had the previous year, but it could still stir up quite a hubbub. Dylan's "Rainy Day Women #12 & 35" and, to a far greater extent, the Byrds' "Eight Miles High" met roadblocks in radio airplay due to suspicions over drug allusions in the lyrics. Other songs and recordings were affected as well, adding to a growing establishment backlash against the newfound freedom of the folk-rock revolution. Hunger for record sales usually wins out over fear of the moral majority, however. Record companies, including some of America's biggest, continued to avidly sign and promote folk-rockers bearing words of love, dissent, and imagination, often charged by sex and drugs as well as rock 'n' roll.

This was the precarious position in which folk-rock found itself in mid-1966—a head-spinning world of expanding possibilities, albeit a frightening one, hemmed in by commercial pressures, record label expectations, media censorship, and the rising clamor of internal strife in the United States over the war in Vietnam and racial relations. One major figure would largely retreat from the folk-rock battlefield for about 18 months, at the peak of his powers. On July 29, 1966, Bob Dylan, fresh off his world tour and the release of his best album yet, was injured in a mysterious motorcycle accident near his home in Woodstock, New York. There would be no new album for a year and a half, an eternity by 1960s release schedules.

Some would claim that without Dylan around to set the ultimate standard, folk-rock, and even rock music as a whole, would pass its peak. But in fact even before his temporary withdrawal from the music business, folk-rock was starting to head down unpredictable and thrilling roads that had little to do with Dylan's hand on the steering wheel. Jefferson Airplane had released its first single, one which, though not a hit, had already received special attention in a July 1, 1966, *Time* article on the connection between sex, drugs, and rock 'n' roll—something lead singer Marty Balin readily owned up to in the article. The group was but the vanguard of a posse of San Francisco bands that would swiftly usher folk-rock into the psychedelic age. Much of that ground had already been broken for them in Los Angeles by the Byrds, both with the "Eight Miles High" single and their *Fifth Dimension* album, issued just 11 days before Dylan's motorcycle accident.

It is at this point that *Turn! Turn! Turn!: The '60s Folk-Rock Revolution* ended. The revolution, however, was far from over. It would take the next few years of folk-rock, as documented here, to make this particular wheel turn, turn, turn. Not full circle, perhaps. Yet certainly to a point where it was not just unrecognizable from the folk revival that had sparked it, but also far more multihued, expansive, and eclectic from what it had been, even in 1966.

Is *he* folk-rock? Is *she* folk-rock? Are *they* folk-rock?" Substitute any number of 1960s recording artists for the pronouns in those sentences and you get questions with which I was pelted like a dartboard throughout the writing of both *Turn! Turn! Turn!* and *Eight Miles High*. The precise definition of what constitutes a folk-rocker was the matter of much discussion in 1965 and 1966, and continues to be today. Yet if anything, the discussion would become even more contentious when evaluating the course folk-rock would take throughout the rest of the decade, which made the innovations of the mid-'60s seem like a relatively orderly path in comparison.

In the latter part of the decade, the singer-songwriter school owed its birth directly to the folk-rock movement. So did country-rock, though that assertion might draw a few uneasy grunts. You'll get far more howls of protest by noting that much psychedelic rock was an outgrowth of folk-rock—indeed, some might find the very notion incomprehensible. Yet the evidence is there to hear, not just in the folk and folk-rock roots of many psychedelic rockers (particularly Californians), but also in the traces, strong to blatant, of folk-rock in many of their best recordings. Arcane subgenres of '60s rock such as acid folk and sunshine pop, popularized many years later by obsessive collectors, were similarly rooted in the folk-rock blend. And much of the late-blooming heyday of British folk-rock at the tail end of the decade was perhaps folk-rock in its purest form: a traditional folk song or original composition in the trad-folk vein, livened up with electric rock instruments. It's pure enough, indeed, that some stuffed shirts view folk-rock itself as primarily or even exclusively a British idiom, though such narrow-mindedness runs counter to the very expansion of possibility that was folk-rock's greatest gift to popular music.

All these offshoots were happening all at once and at rapid yet subtly different paces. It must have been exciting to live through; having been born in 1962, it wasn't something I really experienced. It's *still* exciting to hear the recorded evidence today, as many who weren't even born when the decade ended continually discover. It's also undeniably difficult to document in an evenly distributed chronological fashion. That's not only because everything was happening all at once, but because so many performers were difficult to slot into just one style, and influences crisscrossed like crazy between genres and even continents.

Like its predecessor, *Eight Miles High* does follow a rough chronological progression, from the "Eight Miles High" single itself to Woodstock and a little beyond. And to make folk-rock's increasingly dense web of interconnectiveness fathomable, this book is, for the most part, separated into sections on different branches of the folk-rock tree. One should be wary, though, of too rigorously categorizing and segregating folk-rock's different strains. Many, maybe most, of its important performers crossed boundaries all the time. Artists known primarily as straightforward singer-songwriters laid down some downright weird psychedelic freakouts; feedback-addled psychedelic bands did some hushed acoustic ballads; British groups who made epics out of ancient folk ballads had sometimes covered American folk-rock singer-songwriters just a year previously; and regardless of subgenre, it seems that almost everyone recorded a little to a lot of country-rock at one time or another, whether in London, Los Angeles, or Nashville. Precious tunesmiths known for melancholic romantic ballads let loose unexpectedly with antiwar screeds. Hippie folk-rockers-gone-psychedelic interspersed delicate love songs with calls for revolution and drug-inspired improvisation.

Even within individual careers, or certain albums, a loosey-goosey unpredictability often ruled the day. What was Bob Dylan—a hard bluesy rocker or a laidback country squire? Were the Byrds determined to push the outer limits of electronic experimentation, or content to retreat to gentle country-rock, or masterful interpreters of Dylan (and Gerry Goffin–Carole King) songs—or all this at once? Kaleidoscope was a pre-worldbeat band, a Cajun outfit, a blues group, or straightahead jangly folk-rockers depending on what track was spinning around the turntable at the moment. Tim Buckley—folk-rock crooner, psychedelic clairvoyant, or defiantly inaccessible jazz-avant-gardist? And could Neil Young ever decide whether he wanted to play on his own with an acoustic guitar, or blister his listeners with cranked-to-eleven guitar noise—then, or now?

Yet somehow all of these performers retained a folk-rock base at the core of their appeal. There was more that united these performers than separated them, in general approach if not in specific content. The common thread was, frequently, the same hunger for trying something new that had led them from rock to folk music as teenagers, and then back to folk-rock as young (usually) adults. So much territory was explored, so many angles mined for both novelty and genuine experimentation, that by the time the '60s ended, a return to the roots of the basic acoustic folk music that had set the whole shebang off would itself be embraced as a radical innovation.

Along the way, many major folk-rock talents made their recording debuts and rose to varying levels of stardom—Joni Mitchell, Leonard Cohen, Linda Ronstadt, Arlo Guthrie, the Band, Jefferson Airplane, and the Youngbloods; and in the UK, Fairport Convention, the Pentangle, and the Incredible String Band. Several who had already attained stardom by mid-1966 maintained, more or less, the same level of quality: Dylan, Donovan, Simon & Garfunkel. Several of the best bands to form in the mid-'60s fractured or changed almost beyond recognition: the Byrds, Buffalo Springfield, Love, the Lovin' Spoonful, and the Mamas & the Papas. Some veterans of those squabbles would form folk-rock's (and indeed American rock's) ultimate supergroup: Crosby, Stills, Nash & Young.

Several battled their own contrary impulses and personal demons to such an uncompromising degree that sustained commercial success became impossible: Tim Buckley, Phil Ochs, Tim Hardin. Some would pass virtually unnoticed even in the underground, yet rise phoenix-like to unimaginably widespread acclaim 20 and 30 years later: Nick Drake, Skip Spence. Some similar cult acts have yet to undergo such a renaissance, despite the undeniable brilliance of some of their records, like Dino Valenti, Blackburn & Snow, and the Holy Modal Rounders. Some would make tentative, almost unnoticed baby steps, but not find their true audience until the 1970s, like Jackson Browne. And many artists who didn't make folk-rock their main diet borrowed notably and impressively from the form, ranging from the Beatles and Pink Floyd to the Grateful Dead. At the end of the 1960s, folk-rock had to a large degree become such a part of rock's mainstream that people were often not bothering to even call it folk-rock anymore.

ight Miles High portrays all this and more in its exploration of late-'60s folk-rock, a genre that became an even more slippery fish to bottle in those years than it had been when people started arguing about it in 1965 and '66. At its most pop-informed, this music offers polished harmonizers like the Mamas & the Papas; in its most strictly interpreted and traditional definition, Fairport Convention in their late-1969 phase; and at its center, the musicians who comprised the Byrds, Buffalo Springfield, and, later, Crosby, Stills, Nash & Young. There's room for artists more commonly categorized as psychedelic, such as Jefferson Airplane and the Grateful Dead. There are some, like Joni Mitchell or the Incredible String Band, who didn't even use electric guitars or rock rhythm sections in their early albums, although their material and delivery was geared toward a folk-rock aesthetic and a rock audience. There are also a host of folk-rock performers that many would rather classify as singer-songwriters, even if their 1960s work was strongly planted in folk-rock's soil. I'd rather be generously inclusive than stingily exclusive, particularly when the music is good.

By the same token, I have discussed, sometimes in depth, work by folk-rock musicians who did not owe strict allegiance to folk-rock conventions, whether their psychedelic recordings or their more pop-oriented ones. One of the prime distinctions between folk-rock musicians and their traditional folk ancestors was their willingness to blend different musics, even if some of those ingredients were not folk *or* rock, strictly speaking. If that upsets some purists who want to stick to a much more enclosed framework, so be it. Upsetting purists was one of the few things most branches of folk-rock *did* have in common.

Some have argued—in books that have nothing to do with music—that the 1960s actually didn't stop until Richard Nixon's re-election in 1972 or his resignation from presidential office in 1974. But by most common measures, the '60s did stop at the end of 1969. And although some particularly fine or significant folk-rock recordings from the very early '70s are discussed here (especially those strongly echoing late-'60s folk-rock), this book does, for the most part, stop at the end of 1969: the end of folk-rock's golden era.

Of course folk-rock continues to be performed, recorded, and reissued today, occasionally selling great numbers of records, and occasionally still evolving, though at a much slower rate than in the '60s. In closing the book on the first phase of folk-rock's revolution, though, you've got to stop somewhere. Naturally, as in most things folk-rock, the point where the last landmark of 1960s-rooted folk-rock blurs into the first signpost of 1970s folk-rock can be debated endlessly. Is it Joni Mitchell's *Blue*, James Taylor's *Sweet Baby James*, the departure of Richard Thompson from Fairport Convention, or the breakup of Crosby, Stills, Nash & Young? It's any number of such things. Like the beginning of folk-rock half a decade previously, its shift into a new era can be ascribed to many people in general, yet no one in particular.

Eight Miles High, like *Turn! Turn! Turn!*, puts much weight on the memories and perspectives of those who were there, drawing from more than 100 interviews, principally with musicians but also with producers, record label executives, club owners, and journalists. Many of the voices that appear in *Turn! Turn! Turn!* reappear in this volume to discuss a slightly later era: Roger McGuinn, Donovan, Judy Collins, John Sebastian, Janis Ian, Arlo Guthrie, Richie Furay, Chris Hillman, and Elektra Records founder/president Jac Holzman are only some of them. (See the list of "dramatis personae" for brief recaps of the pre-1967 careers of the key figures covered in both *Eight Miles High* and *Turn! Turn! Turn!*) There are also new voices who did not enter folk-rock's main stage until after the mid-'60s, such as Robin Williamson, Iain Matthews, Jim Messina, Melanie, and Jerry Jeff Walker.

Reminders of people and places that had plowed the folk-rock field were again omnipresent as I traveled during my research, not just in the libraries holding faded reports on the Isle of Wight festivals and the like, but also in the most out-of-the-way, untouristed spots—albeit ones you have to make a pretty dedicated, conscious effort to stumble across. There was, for instance, the grave of the greatest British folk-rock singer, Sandy Denny, in Wimbledon, London, apparently the recipient of few fans or visitors these days. Or Rishikesh, India, where I strolled through swinging monkeys and roving goats and cows in the now-deserted compound where the Beatles and Donovan studied with the Maharishi, and Donovan influenced the construction and composition of the Beatles' folkiest numbers on *The White Album*.

At such moments it struck me that the era in which the two volumes comprising this history of folk-rock took place is now more than three decades behind us, and might seem as far off and ghostly as a gravestone or the decomposing poster of the Maharishi at the Rishikesh compound's crumbling lecture hall. At a time when the world is noisier than ever—and, unfortunately, just as troubled and violent as it was in the turbulent '60s, in many respects—one occasionally wonders whether the folk-rock of yore is in danger of getting lost and forgotten. But again, at the most unexpected places, its songs live on and even thrive, and not just on commercial-ridden oldies stations. At its most upmarket, you could hear it in the Los Angeles Staples Center sports arena. During their 2002 reunion tour there, Crosby, Stills, Nash & Young encored not with one of their own oldies, but a surprise rendition of "Eight Miles High"—a folk-rock classic that still sounds like a blast from the future in the twenty-first century. At roughly the same time but in a much different place, there was the corner outside my Haight-Ashbury post office where a street musician bleated through the most tuneless guitar-harmonica desecration of "Mr. Tambourine Man" imaginable during the spring I was bringing *Eight Miles High*—the book—to completion.

Folk-rock's golden age might have ended at the end of the 1960s, but several decades later, its legacy lives in a way its originators might have appreciated most: It's no longer the next new thing. It's a revered folk music, played and listened to in all levels of the Western, and sometimes non-Western, world. It's just as revered as the traditional folk music that kicked the whole thing off in the first place, long before "Eight Miles High" kicked off its flight from Los Angeles and Haight-Ashbury to Woodstock and beyond.

Richie Unterberger
May 2003
San Francisco

the story so far

dramatis personae

The following "dramatis personae" played key roles in folk-rock's story both before and after the mid-1966 launching point of *Eight Miles High: Folk-Rock's Flight from Haight-Ashbury to Woodstock*. Below is a recap of their most crucial contributions in the early phases of folk-rock, prior to those covered in this book. (For a full account of their early careers, see this book's prequel, *Turn! Turn! Turn!: The '60s Folk-Rock Revolution*.)

Lou Adler: Producer for the Mamas & the Papas and Barry McGuire.

Eric Andersen: One of the very first folk-rock singer-songwriters to be pegged as a "new Dylan," though his style was gentler. He had just begun to go electric in mid-1966 with his second album, *'Bout Changes & Things*, subsequently re-recorded in its entirety with full electric rearrangements as *'Bout Changes & Things Take Two*.

Peter Asher: Half of the folky pop-rock British Invasion duo Peter & Gordon, prior to his second career as successful manager and producer.

Joan Baez: The biggest solo superstar of the folk boom, and an early interpreter and booster of Bob Dylan, though she never fully embraced the folk-rock sound of the 1960s with major commercial or artistic dividends.

The Band aka the Hawks: Originally the Toronto-based backup group for rock 'n' roller Ronnie Hawkins, the Hawks became Bob Dylan's backing band for his live shows from late 1965 through mid-1966, sometimes recording with him as well. The Hawks—guitarist Robbie Robertson, bassist Rick Danko, pianist Richard Manuel, organist Garth Hudson, and drummer Levon Helm—would by 1968 be renamed the Band, although Helm dropped out of the group from late 1965 through late 1967.

The Beatles: The group that was the single biggest influence on young folkies going electric, via both the compositions of principal singer-songwriters John Lennon and Paul McCartney, and the electric 12-string guitar playing of George Harrison. After their successful invasion of America in early 1964, the Beatles themselves began to absorb the influence of folk and folk-rock, particularly on their late-1965 album *Rubber Soul*.

The Beau Brummels: Although they never thought of themselves as a folk-rock group or as overtly influenced by folk music, they made some of the finer folk-rock-shaded music of the mid-'60s, including their hits "Laugh, Laugh" and "Just a Little." They were also the first San Franciscan folk-rock-aligned act of note.

David Blue: Idiosyncratic singer-songwriter whose self-titled 1966 debut on Elektra was the most blatant aping of Bob Dylan's *Highway 61 Revisited/Blonde on Blonde* phase ever waxed.

The Blue Things: Perhaps the most overlooked mid-'60s folk-rock group, based in Kansas and recording material reminiscent of the Byrds and the Beau Brummels in Nashville.

Joe Boyd: Production manager of the 1965 Newport Folk Festival, head of Elektra Records' UK division, and a budding record producer.

Buffalo Springfield: The best Los Angeles folk-rock group other than the Byrds, formed in Hollywood in early 1966 by guitarist Stephen Stills, guitarist Richie Furay, guitarist Neil Young, bassist Bruce Palmer, and drummer Dewey Martin. Their self-titled first album, split between Stills and Young compositions and blending folk, country, and all-out rock 'n' roll, was issued near the end of 1966.

The Byrds: The top folk-rock group, formed in Los Angeles in 1964 by guitarist Roger McGuinn, guitarist Gene Clark, guitarist David Crosby, bassist Chris Hillman, and drummer Michael Clarke. With their gorgeous harmonies and McGuinn's spine-tingling mastery of the electric 12-string guitar, they had the first major folk-rock hit with a cover of Bob Dylan's "Mr. Tambourine Man" in mid-1965, and another #1 single with Pete Seeger's "Turn! Turn! Turn!" at the end of that year. Noted for both their excellent Bob Dylan interpretations and a growing body of good original material, primarily from the pen of Gene Clark at their outset.

Judy Collins: Although she began her recording career at the beginning of the 1960s as a traditional folk singer, she changed the focus of her repertoire to interpretations of contemporary folk singer–songwriters beginning with 1963's album *#3*, which featured accompaniment and arrangements by the pre-Byrds Roger McGuinn. By the mid-'60s she was starting to move into folk-rock, and into orchestrated baroque folk-rock with the 1966 LP *In My Life*.

Bobby Darin: Although far more a mainstream pop star than a folk or folk-rock musician, he was a surprisingly influential mentor to folk-rockers-in-the-making like Roger McGuinn, who played with Darin on stage, and Jesse Colin Young, whom he helped get signed to Capitol Records.

Jim Dickson: The original manager (with Eddie Tickner) of the Byrds, and crucial in bringing the group together and bestowing them with studio rehearsal time, electric equipment, an acetate of an unreleased Bob Dylan song called "Mr. Tambourine Man," and ultimately a contract on Columbia. Also a producer, and also worked with the Dillards, the Modern Folk Quartet, and Hamilton Camp.

The Dillards: A top bluegrass group of the folk boom, who shared management with the Byrds, and whose Dean Webb had helped the Byrds work out the vocal harmonies on "Mr. Tambourine Man."

Dion: Pop-rock and doo wop star of the late '50s and early '60s who had moved into blues and folk-rock on neglected, commercially unsuccessful mid-'60s sessions for Columbia.

Donovan: Britain's only major mid-'60s folk-rock artist, who was accused of being a Bob Dylan imitator when he had his first hits in 1965 with acoustic-centered love and protest songs like "Catch the Wind" and "Universal Soldier." In 1966 he shed the Dylan comparisons with the eclectic, psychedelic-tinged folk-rock of the *Sunshine Superman* album and the big hits "Sunshine Superman" and "Mellow Yellow."

Bob Dylan: The top protest folk songwriter of the early-'60s folk boom, and then the top folk-rock songwriter of the mid-'60s. Dylan had massive single hits with "Like a Rolling Stone," "Positively 4th Street," and "Just Like a Woman" after "going electric" on the 1965–66 albums *Bringing It All Back Home*, *Highway 61 Revisited*, and *Blonde on Blonde*. He was the single biggest focal point of controversy between folk purists and rock fans, particularly after he started playing electric rock live in mid-1965, and touring the world with future members of the Band as his backing group.

Cyrus Faryar: A member of the Modern Folk Quartet, who moved from folk to folk-rock in the mid-'60s without coming close to the fame of their friends in the Lovin' Spoonful, the Mamas & the Papas, and the Byrds.

The Fugs: The most underground and lyrical taboo-breaking of mid-'60s rock groups, who started as a chaotic jug band–like ensemble on Folkways Records, but by 1966 had developed into a reasonably tight rock band. Centered around singer-songwriters Ed Sanders and Tuli Kupferberg, their second album, released in 1966 by the avant-garde ESP label, somehow crept into the Top 100 despite overt references to sex, drugs, and radical subversive politics.

Arthur Gorson: Producer/manager who worked with Phil Ochs, Tom Rush, David Blue, Eric Andersen, and Jim & Jean.

Vern Gosdin: Member of the bluegrass band the Hillmen, which had also included his brother Rex and a pre-Byrds Chris Hillman.

Davy Graham: Astonishingly versatile British folk guitarist who helped open acoustic folk to jazz, world music, and rock influences in the UK, adding some accompaniment from a rhythm section on his groundbreaking mid-'60s LP *Folk, Blues & Beyond*.

Albert Grossman: Admired, feared, and powerful manager of folk and folk-rock singers Bob Dylan, Ian & Sylvia, Peter, Paul & Mary, the Paul Butterfield Blues Band, and others.

Roy Halee: Engineer/producer for Simon & Garfunkel.

Tim Hardin: A singer-songwriter with a sorrowful voice, first-class original material, and major personal and professional problems. After making some of the first attempts at electric folk-rock with blues-oriented songs in 1964, he hit his stride on his official debut album for Verve in 1966.

Judy Henske: The husky-voiced folk singer who'd recorded perhaps the most important pre-1964 almost-folk-rock track, "High Flying Bird." In the late '60s, she was a close friend of Phil Ochs, wife of ex-Modern Folk Quartet and late-'60s Lovin' Spoonful member Jerry Yester, and half of the unclassifiable psychedelic-hued duo Judy Henske & Jerry Yester.

Carolyn Hester: Noted early-'60s folk singer, on whose first Columbia album Bob Dylan had played harmonica in 1961, and who moved into folk-rock herself with some obscure recordings for Columbia in 1966.

The Holy Modal Rounders: The eccentric, sometimes zany folk duo of Peter Stampfel and Steve Weber, both of whom would also play with the Fugs in their early days.

Jac Holzman: The founder and president of Elektra Records, a top independent folk label of the folk boom. It would become the top album-oriented independent rock label of the 1960s as it started to move into the rock field with the Paul Butterfield Blues Band and folk-rockers like Love, Judy Collins, Tom Rush, and Tim Buckley.

Janis Ian: The youngest folk-rocker bar none to have a hit, with "Society's Child." The controversial song about interracial dating had been recorded and unsuccessfully shopped to numerous labels long before it became a hit in 1967.

Ian & Sylvia: The husband-wife harmonizing team of guitarist singer-songwriters Ian & Sylvia Tyson, who did much to expand the boundaries of folk arrangements on their early-'60s Vanguard albums. After Sylvia's "You Were on My Mind" was covered for a huge folk-rock hit by the We Five in 1965, the duo started to move into folk-rock themselves, with erratic though sometimes fine results.

Erik Jacobsen: Producer for the Lovin' Spoonful and Tim Hardin.

Jefferson Airplane: Probably San Francisco's most celebrated and successful psychedelic group, but one which had started as a bunch of folk-rockers when it formed in 1965. Only one flop single had been issued by mid-1966, but the band was already starting to attract national attention, not only via a mention in *Time* magazine, but also a lyrical reference in Donovan's *Sunshine Superman* track "The Fat Angel."

Bob Johnston: Producer of most of Bob Dylan's *Highway 61 Revisited* and all of Dylan's *Blonde on Blonde*; also did some production for Simon & Garfunkel.

Bruce Langhorne: Folk-rock session guitarist supreme, who played on Bob Dylan's *Bringing It All Back Home* and mid-'60s albums by Richard & Mimi Fariña, Tom Rush, Joan Baez, Buffy Sainte-Marie, Gordon Lightfoot, and others.

Murray Lerner: Director of the film documentary *Festival*, comprised of footage from the 1963–66 Newport Folk Festivals, including part of Bob Dylan's appearance with an electric band at the 1965 event.

Gordon Lightfoot: Top country-influenced Canadian folk singer-songwriter, just starting to achieve recognition as a solo artist with his first album in 1966 after a misbegotten attempt to cover Bob Dylan's "Just Like Tom Thumb's Blues" on a single.

Bob Lind: One of the first folk-rock singer-songwriters to record with orchestration, most notably on his 1966 hit "Elusive Butterfly."

Love: The first all-out rock band on Elektra Records, and a heavily (though not exclusively) folk-rock-influenced one. Their self-titled debut album in 1966 mixed the Byrds with influences from tough British Invasion bands like the Rolling Stones, paced by the enigmatic songs of principal singer-songwriter Arthur Lee and the lighter, more romantic compositions of Bryan MacLean.

The Lovin' Spoonful: The top happy-go-lucky folk-rock group, formed in New York around the end of 1964 by guitarist and principal songwriter John Sebastian, guitarist Zal Yanovsky, bassist Steve Boone, and drummer Joe Butler. Their 1965–66 hits "Do You Believe in Magic," "Daydream," "You Didn't Have to Be So Nice," "Rain on the Roof," and "Did You Ever Have to Make Up Your Mind" were folk-rock's links to the good-time eclecticism of the jug bands, though they rocked real hard on their #1 hit "Summer in the City."

The Mamas & the Papas: Formed from remnants of wholesome acoustic folk groups by guitarist and principal songwriter John Phillips, his wife Michelle Phillips, Denny Doherty, and Cass Elliot. Based in L.A., they were the top male-female romantic folk-rock-pop harmonizers, and for a time the most successful, with the hits "California Dreamin'," "Monday, Monday," "I Saw Her Again," and others.

Charlie McCoy: Esteemed Nashville session musician who played on Bob Dylan recordings in the mid-'60s.

Barry McGuire: Formerly of the New Christy Minstrels, he had his only big hit in 1965 with P.F. Sloan's protest folk-rock song "Eve of Destruction," and helped the Mamas & the Papas get their recording contract when they sang backup on some of his sessions.

Terry Melcher: Producer of the first two albums by the Byrds, and producer of fellow Columbia folk-rockers the Rising Sons, whose lineup featured Taj Mahal, Ry Cooder, Jesse Kincaid, Gary Marker, and future Byrds drummer Kevin Kelley.

Frazier Mohawk aka Barry Friedman: Early semi-manager of Buffalo Springfield and producer of sides by the Paul Butterfield Blues Band.

Mickie Most: Producer for Donovan.

Fred Neil: The majestically low-voiced singer-songwriter, more admired among fellow musicians than the general public. With his 1965 album *Bleecker & MacDougal*, he tread lightly into electric folk-rock on whimsical yet haunting original songs combining folk, pop, country, and blues.

Mike Nesmith: The most accomplished musician of the Monkees, and the singer-songwriter of their most folk- and country-influenced material.

Nico: Before joining the Velvet Underground in 1966 and singing a few songs on their first album, she did a little-noticed folk-rockish single in England in 1965, a cover of Gordon Lightfoot's "I'm Not Sayin'."

Michael Ochs: Manager of his brother, Phil Ochs.

Phil Ochs: The most celebrated acoustic folk protest singer-songwriter other than Bob Dylan, even though he made just one electric folk-rock recording prior to 1967—an impressive remake of his famed "I Ain't Marching Anymore."

Tom Paxton: Respected singer-songwriter of both protest and love tunes, the most famous of those being "The Last Thing on My Mind," "Ramblin' Boy," "Bottle of Wine," and "I Can't Help But Wonder Where I'm Bound." Famously resistant to and critical of folk-rock in its early stages, although his attitude would soften and his own late-'60s records would include some electric backing and orchestration.

D.A. Pennebaker: Director of *Don't Look Back*, a documentary of Bob Dylan's 1965 British tour, and cinematographer for *Eat the Document*, a documentary of Dylan's 1966 British tour.

Peter, Paul & Mary: Ultra-successful folk trio of the early '60s who brought covers of songs by Pete Seeger ("If I Had a Hammer") and Bob Dylan ("Blowin' in the Wind") to the Top Ten.

Peter Yarrow, Noel "Paul" Stookey, and Mary Travers ventured mildly into folk-rock in the last half of the decade, most notably on their hit "I Dig Rock & Roll Music."

Shawn Phillips: Expatriate American folk singer living and recording in Britain in the mid-'60s, and an important sideman to Donovan in the recording of *Sunshine Superman*.

Tim Rose: Singer-songwriter who was in the folk-boom trio the Big Three with Cass Elliot before going solo and recording for Columbia, where he helped popularize the songs "Hey Joe" and "Morning Dew."

Paul Rothchild: The most important producer for Elektra Records during the label's mid-'60s transition from folk to folk-rock, working on records by the Paul Butterfield Blues Band, Love, Fred Neil, Tom Rush, and Tim Buckley.

Tom Rush: Respected Cambridge folk singer who announced his conversion to folk-rock by filling the first side of his 1966 Elektra LP *Take a Little Walk with Me* with early rock 'n' roll and rhythm and blues covers.

Buffy Sainte-Marie: The Canadian-born Native American singer-songwriter who authored the standards "Universal Soldier," "Until It's Time for You to Go," and "Codine."

Jerry Schoenbaum: Head of Verve/Folkways records and its spinoff Verve/Forecast, labels which released mid-'60s folk-rock records by Tim Hardin, Janis Ian, Jim & Jean, and the Blues Project.

Pete Seeger: Probably the most venerated veteran of twentieth-century American folk music, both as an interpreter of countless folk songs and the composer of standards like "Turn! Turn! Turn!" and "Where Have All the Flowers Gone." Like folklorist Alan Lomax, he would contend with criticism for his reaction to electric folk-rock at the 1965 Newport Folk Festival all the way into the twenty-first century, although Seeger actually would record some music with electric backing later on in the decade.

Simon & Garfunkel: The duo of singer-songwriter-guitarist Paul Simon and singer Art Garfunkel, who had been recording since the late '50s when they had a rock hit as Tom & Jerry. By 1964 they were folk singers, and in late 1965 they became folk-rockers when "The Sound of Silence" made #1, followed by the 1966 hits "Homeward Bound," "I Am a Rock," and "Hazy Shade of Winter."

Howard Solomon: Owner of the Cafe Au Go Go club in Greenwich Village, New York City.

Maynard Solomon: Co-founder of Vanguard Records, the most successful independent label of the folk boom, particularly with Joan Baez and Ian & Sylvia. In the mid-'60s, Vanguard moved into folk-rock territory with electrified records by Baez, Ian & Sylvia, Eric Andersen, Buffy Sainte-Marie, Richard & Mimi Fariña, and others.

Happy Traum: Early-'60s folk-boom musician who had recorded with the New World Singers and Bob Dylan prior to a brief mid-'60s stint in the electric rock band the Children of Paradise.

The Turtles: Los Angeles band who were among the first groups to enter commercial folk-rock with their 1965 Top Ten cover of Bob Dylan's "It Ain't Me Babe," though they quickly moved into more mainstream, good-time pop-rock.

Dino Valenti: Mercurial singer-songwriter and composer of the folk-rock standard "Get Together," whose emotional nasal vocals and furious guitar strumming influenced folk-rockers-in-the-making on both the East and West Coasts. His own recording opportunities in the early and mid-'60s were minimal, in part due to a stretch in prison, though he did cut some rare early folk-rockish sides for Elektra in 1964.

Frank Werber: Producer/manager for the Kingston Trio and the We Five.

Jerry Yester: A member of the Modern Folk Quartet, one of several clean-cut folk combos that morphed into an electric folk-rock group, although the band only recorded a few electric singles before splitting.

Jesse Colin Young: The most noted singer-songwriter in the Youngbloods, and one who had already made some little-noted solo folk albums that strayed toward early folk-rock before the Youngbloods formed in the mid-'60s.

prologue

·····················

fifth dimension

*"'Eight Miles High' is a folk song.
There's no question in my mind about that."*
—Roger McGuinn

The legend goes that while the Byrds were in the midst of a grueling Dick Clark's Caravan of Stars bus tour in late 1965, a coal train passed in front of them as their vehicle was stopped at a railroad crossing. As it happened, a tape of John Coltrane was playing at the time, as it was in the Byrds' rolling quarters throughout the tour. The passage of a coal train while John Col-trane took off on his wild improvisations might have seemed like nothing less than a heaven-sent blessing of approval for the Byrds' next flight plan.

The Byrds had only been together for a year and a half or so, but in many respects their career had seemed as serendipitous as the appearance of a coal train at the exact same moment as John Coltrane was supplying their personal soundtrack. The group had barely known its way around amplified instruments when it formed in mid-1964. At the beginning of the summer of 1965, the Byrds were sitting at #1 with their classic electric rock interpretation of Bob Dylan's "Mr. Tambourine Man." That same summer, they toured Britain as America's answer to the Beatles. And they closed the year with another #1 hit and all-time folk-rock classic with their cover of Pete Seeger's "Turn! Turn! Turn!"

For all their success, though, there were some doubts as to whether they could sustain their momentum. The British tour had been troubled—plagued by illness, mixed audience reaction, and harsh criticism from a press with unrealistically high expectations of a group that had been playing live before an audience for less than a year. The band's second album, *Turn! Turn! Turn!* (released at the end of 1965), would have been considered a major triumph by most other acts, but wasn't quite up to the magnificence of their debut LP, *Mr. Tambourine Man*. Gene Clark's compositions remained compellingly brooding, and he showed signs of developing an abstract Dylanesque lyricism in "Set You Free This Time." But Roger McGuinn and David Crosby were yet to develop into composers of that order, still devising above-average Beatlesque songs, and the LP's Dylan covers weren't nearly as remarkable as those on *Mr. Tambourine Man*. There were still lingering accusations that the group wouldn't have gotten anywhere as far as it did without plundering the Dylan catalog. McGuinn, Clark, and Crosby had an extraordinary collaboration in waiting, however, that would advance not just their own music but all of rock into an unimagined brave new world.

Crosby had for some time been feeding McGuinn large doses of both the Indian music of Ravi Shankar and the free-jazz improvisations of John Coltrane. When the Beatles stayed in a Benedict

Canyon mansion above Beverly Hills during an American tour in August 1965, McGuinn, Crosby, John Lennon, and George Harrison sat in a large bathtub, flying on acid and playing 12-string guitars. McGuinn and Crosby showed the others what they knew about Shankar; McGuinn has said that Lennon and Harrison hadn't even heard of the Indian sitar virtuoso. When it came time to embark on the Dick Clark package, McGuinn made a tape of Shankar material and Coltrane's *Impressions* and *Africa/Brass* albums, which the Byrds played, over and over, in their mobile home during the lengthy tour. "We had a cassette player, and a tape of Ravi Shankar on one side, and John Coltrane on the other," said McGuinn in Mike Jahn's *Rock*. "We played that damn thing 50 or 100 times, through a Fender amplifier that was plugged into an alternator in the car."

The band, and particularly McGuinn, applied those lessons to a new Clark-McGuinn-Crosby composition, "Eight Miles High." The song was by itself an impressive diary of their disoriented sensations during their 1965 tour of England. With all the members making heroic contributions, however, it was turned into something entirely alien when the Byrds had finished with it in the studio. Chris Hillman pushed it into gear with a pulverizing, ominous unaccompanied bassline that remains one of rock's all-time great intros. McGuinn uncorked three mesmerizing solos that put Coltrane's fractured free jazz and Shankar's ragas onto the electric 12-string, with a fury and speed that perfectly complemented the song's flight metaphors. The Byrds' harmonies were never more ghostly and uplifting than they were during the verses, evoking a mysterious land both seductive and menacing. It all came to a crashing end as the tempos accelerated and the keys rose, easing to a finale much like an airplane cruising onto a landing strip.

"I was trying to emulate the music of John Coltrane," explained McGuinn on the 1995 PBS television series *Rock & Roll*. "I believe it was 'India,' and there was a repetitive line"—here he broke off to mimic the devious four-note introductory riff of "Eight Miles High"—"in that. And I wanted to get the, almost the valves closing on the . . . try to emulate that on the 12-string. So the sustain made that possible. It breathes out like a wind instrument, as opposed to a string instrument."

Like "Mr. Tambourine Man," the masterpiece "Eight Miles High" was the result of some painstaking hours in the studio that had seen some failed attempts and misfires. The first version (as well as an early version of its B-side "Why") had been recorded on December 22, 1965 at RCA Studios in Hollywood, produced by Byrds manager Jim Dickson. Although certainly impressive, it was rawer than the take that was ultimately released, and would have run into insurmountable problems had they and Dickson tried to put it out as a single. For one thing, Dickson was not the band's Columbia-assigned producer; Terry Melcher was, though he was about to be ousted. More crucially, it had not been recorded at Columbia's own studios, which ran counter to company policy. The upshot was that "Eight Miles High" and "Why" had to be redone at Columbia Studios a month later, the RCA version lying in the vaults for 20 years. Crosby insisted in interviews that the RCA version was considerably better, and more in line with the sound the Byrds wanted; McGuinn, more restrained in his enthusiasm, felt that the guitar solo on the RCA version might have been more spontaneous.

As is often the case with unreleased recordings that build up a mystique by virtue of both their enthusiastic word-of-mouth and inaccessibility in the vaults, it was actually a letdown when the recording was finally included on an archival compilation in the late '80s. Although the Byrds might have been justifiably frustrated in not being able to record and release "Eight Miles High" where and when they wanted, the officially released Columbia version was in every way superior. Even McGuinn's solos were markedly better, particularly in the positioning of the magically fluttering notes that ended his improvisations with exclamation points. The RCA version frankly sounds more ragged, far less impeccable in its timing, and far less spectacular in its conclusion. Interestingly, yet another take has circulated on a bootleg that, while extremely similar to the one on the single, contains a middle solo that's almost twice as long. This perhaps is the truest expression of the spontaneous free jazz–Indian 12-string flight that McGuinn and his cohorts were striving for with "Eight Miles High," though it was simply way too long to be released on a 45 rpm disk. As it was, the break, outlandishly experimental in and of itself, lasted about 45 seconds in the version chosen for release, which was outrageously long for a single in early 1966.

What was most important, though, was not so much the process as the end achievement. By that measure "Eight Miles High" was a total triumph, not just musically, but also in the context of the group's own stormy career. There had already been friction over creative roles in the band: guitarist Clark penned the lion's share of the original songs for the first two albums while early Crosby efforts like "Stranger in a Strange Land" and "Flower Bomb Song" failed to make the cut; Clark's instrumental contributions were usually relegated to the tambourine, in part due to pressure from Crosby; and Hillman and drummer Michael Clarke were not even signed to the Columbia contract—or allowed to play on the record—when "Mr. Tambourine Man" was recorded. As Dickson explains, "I thought 'Eight Miles High' was the first time that all members contributed a great deal, and I was very proud of them."

Much as they had with their early folk-rock in late 1964 and early 1965, the Byrds were so far ahead of the curve that they were playing music that had yet to be named. It was psychedelic rock, and for the song's title alone, many assumed it was drug-inspired. For that reason *Bill Gavin's Record Report* opined in April that the single implied "encouragement and/or approval of the use of marijuana and LSD," and thus could not be recommended for airplay.

The Byrds, particularly McGuinn, always denied this. They repeatedly emphasized that the song's title referred to the altitude of an airplane in flight, such as the plane they had flown to England. Six miles high, they admitted, would have been the more aeronautically correct altitude for a jet in flight, but Clark lobbied for "Eight Miles High" as it sounded better and more poetic. (Adding further credence to the flight metaphors, Clark told a Huntsville, Alabama, audience in 1987 that the song was written in Huntsville, nicknamed "Rocket City" and "Aerospace Capital of the World" owing to its status as a center for rocket research and production; the Byrds did play at Huntsville's Madison County Coliseum in the mid-'60s.) Dickson and Byrds co-manager Eddie Tickner even had lawyer Marshall L. McDaniel send a letter to *Bill Gavin's Record Report* explaining that "Eight Miles High" referred to flight altitude and not drugs, demanding that a correction be published and reserving the right to seek compensation for damages.

Gavin did print the letter, without apologizing for his magazine's recommendation that the song not be broadcast. The damage was done, though. "Eight Miles High" rose no higher than #14, and the Byrds never had another Top 20 hit. Bob Dylan's 1966 single "Rainy Day Women #12 & 35," with its incessant chorus "Everybody must get stoned!," was also un-recommended by the publication, though it suffered far less fallout, reaching #2 in the charts. The singles' roadblocks were not limited to the US, with Birmingham Councilor Colin Beardwood demanding that the British home secretary ban both songs in the UK as well. "Don't get me wrong—I'm not a fuddy duddy and, in fact, I'm a Dylan fan," he claimed to *Disc*. "But both these songs have a subtle message encouraging drug taking and influence of this kind can't be particularly good for young people."

"We could have called the song '42,240 Feet,'" an exasperated Roger McGuinn told the British music weekly *New Musical Express* (commonly abbreviated as *NME* in the UK). "But somehow this didn't seem to be a very commercial song title and it certainly wouldn't have been scanned . . . . It seems extraordinary that a very pretty lyric about an intriguing city should be condemned because the phrases are couched in some sort of poetry." Almost 30 years later, on the *Rock & Roll* series, McGuinn made allowances for a slightly more flexible interpretation: "Well, I think the word 'high' was a double meaning, and we all knew it. Everyone at that time had experimented with drugs, and there was a tongue-in-cheek thought about the word 'high.' But it wasn't the main thrust of the song."

Interviewed in 2001, McGuinn insists that, underneath all the psychedelic frenzy, "Eight Miles High" is "a folk song. It tells a story like a folk song. It's the story of the Byrds going to England in '65, of experiencing cultural shock. 'The signs on the street that say where you're going'—street signs in America are always on posts and they're at corners and intersections. In England, they're up on the second or third floor story of a side of a building, and they're big rectangular things. And some of them have fallen off, and you really can't tell where you are a lot. So [there's the line] 'signs on the street that say where you're going are somewhere just being their own.'

"'Rain gray town, known for its sound' is London," he continues. "'In places, small faces unbound' are the audiences we encountered. 'Eight miles high, and when you touch down, you'll find that it's stranger than known'—that's the airplane ride to England . . . when you get there, it's different. 'Nowhere is there warmth to be found, among those afraid of losing their ground'—that was the bands and the press and the people who had kind of a chip on their shoulder about, 'What do you mean, you're America's answer to the Beatles?' It's a folk song, there's no question in my mind about that." Furthermore, McGuinn views with approval how the folk process itself has shaped radically different subsequent cover versions of the song by acoustic guitar virtuoso Leo Kottke and '80s punk band Hüsker Dü, who "did it with a lot of anger and clashing chords."

After "Eight Miles High" there was no weight (not that there ever had been) to detractors' accusations that the group was merely riding on Dylan's coattails. Dylan couldn't have come up with "Eight Miles High," and nor could anyone else. The Byrds were now in a league of their own. They would continue to take folk-rock into the stratosphere throughout 1966 and 1967, their mid-1966 *Fifth Dimension* (issued a few months after the "Eight Miles High" single) marking the first album by major early folk-rockers to break away from folk-rock into folk-rock-psychedelia. And where they flew, many would follow.

he sudden influx of Indian influences into the Byrds' sound was even more apparent on the single's B-side, "Why," bearing the McGuinn-Crosby songwriting credit (though Crosby would later maintain that he was entirely responsible for its composition). Although not nearly as strong a song as "Eight Miles High," it too had a Shankar-ish drone and an extended raga-like instrumental break so Indian in flavor that some mistook it for a sitar. Actually it was McGuinn's customary 12-string Rickenbacker, the sound distorted by a battery-run device he constructed from an amplifier of a portable record player and a two-and-a-half-inch loudspeaker from a walkie-talkie, placed in a wooden cigar box. The guitarist's well-known love of electronic gadgetry had paid off again (and is, incidentally, heard to far better effect on the original B-side version than the tamer one re-recorded for inclusion on their 1967 album *Younger Than Yesterday*). The misconception that McGuinn had played sitar on the recording was reinforced by a 1966 press conference at which the group discussed its new directions and McGuinn was photographed playing the instrument. In fact the sitar had been rented for the photo session by CBS, and McGuinn didn't actually know how to play it.

"I first heard Ravi Shankar back in 1964, when Jim Dickson played some of the stuff that they'd been recording over at World Pacific [Studios], where he worked, and Ravi was one of their artists," McGuinn noted on the *Rock & Roll* series. "And we loved it. I'd never heard anything like Indian music before. And Crosby and I got into it on the 12-strings. We started playing"—by way of illustration, McGuinn uncurled a snatch of "Why"—"trying to emulate the sound of the sitar on a 12-string."

These explorations into raga, improvisation, and electronic distortion would be amplified and diversified on the aptly titled *Fifth Dimension* album, released in July. Although the Byrds were still a young group—this being their third LP after forming only two years earlier—they were already in the throes of tumultuous changes, and not all of them were as pleasant or easy to handle as adding new musical influences. *Fifth Dimension* would be recorded without their first producer or (for the most part) the input of the Byrd who had been the band's chief songwriter.

Hard as it might be to fathom of a group that released three albums and several singles in just two years (all still revered to varying extents in the twenty-first century), the Byrds were thought by some to be floundering in mid-1966. The debacle of "Eight Miles High"'s suppression in some territories for supposed drug references had pushed them well behind the Mamas & the Papas, the Lovin' Spoonful, and Simon & Garfunkel in sales. Far more worrisome was the departure of Gene Clark shortly after the release of "Eight Miles High" for various personal reasons, among them his tragically ironic fear of flying. McGuinn may have been the group's leader and primary musical voice, both vocally and instrumentally, but Clark was still its primary songwriter, and the member most adept at expressing romantic sentiments. It was also he who had been most responsible for penning "Eight Miles High," though McGuinn and David Crosby collaborated in its composition.

"Gene was a very prolific writer," says Chris Hillman. "I mean, this guy would write five or six songs a week, and three of 'em were great. Really, really good ones! This guy was not a well-read man. But it was like he would pull these beautiful poetic phrases out of nowhere." In an early 2002 interview with Sean Egan for *Goldmine*, Hillman contested speculation that jealousy over Clark's wealth of songwriting credits (and consequent greater publishing income) was a factor in Gene's exit from the Byrds. But he did speculate that the Byrds' management had thoughts of making money on both the Byrds and Gene Clark as a solo act, which Jim Dickson says was not the case: "We worked with him to keep him available to come back to the Byrds. In fact Chris and Mike both played on his solo album."

Whatever the reasons, however, Clark left to begin a solo career that never saw him rise above cult status. His first album, *Gene Clark and the Gosdin Brothers* (1967), sounded much like a 1966 Byrds record with more ordinary material and lesser ambition, the comparisons to his former band secured by the use of Hillman and Clarke as the rhythm section. In the meantime, for their third album, the Byrds faced the enormous challenge of coming up with quality original material minus Clark, as well as selecting covers that would not find them accused of milking Bob Dylan and Pete Seeger dry. It is to their enormous credit that they did so, creating an album that would anticipate the exploding eclecticism of folk-rock in the last four years of the 1960s, from psychedelia and country-rock to utter reinventions of traditional folk songs for the electronic age.

Terry Melcher, the Columbia producer who'd been at the helm for their first two albums, was no longer in the picture. Even before the *Fifth Dimension* sessions had started, he'd been replaced by Columbia vice president Allen Stanton, who'd produced the "Eight Miles High"/"Why" single. When manager Jim Dickson is asked whether it might not have made more sense for him to take the reins, given his prior production of both unreleased Byrds songs and albums by the Dillards, Hamilton Camp, the Modern Folk Quartet, and others, he demurs: "I did not feel that I needed to produce them in spite of what others have said. There were things I would have tried to do differently and some songs I would have tried to prevent. Terry Melcher was OK with me, but I wasn't ready to give him publishing as he had insisted. It was the Byrds that all signed a note instructing us to get rid of Terry that made that happen. CBS did not allow other than staff producers at that time, so my producing was never an option."

There are few albums in the history of rock as erratic as *Fifth Dimension*. Its highs, no pun intended, were high indeed. McGuinn's "5D (Fifth Dimension)" was like a psychedelicized sea shanty, its lilt embellished by Van Dyke Parks's cathedral-toned organ, its knowingly intoned lyrics intimating psychic entry into an alternate, more loving universe. "Mr. Spaceman," another McGuinn original, was embryonic country-rock—a term that had yet to be coined—yet with a cosmic bite, like those of bluegrass cowboys metamorphosed into space cowboys. The McGuinn-Crosby joint effort "I See You" was another ride on the astral plane of "Eight Miles High," with its jagged raga-jazz-rock 12-string patterns and shape-shifting harmonies and lyrics. "Eight Miles High" itself was included, though it had come out four months earlier on the single, and was the only song recorded while Gene Clark was still aboard.

Fifth Dimension was not wholly a journey into an alternate sonic universe, however. As McGuinn says, "I used to regard the Byrds' albums as kind of electronic magazines. You wanted a little bit of this, a little bit of that." The "electronic magazine" component of McGuinn's vision for the

The Byrds, around the time Gene Clark flew the nest.
Left to right: David Crosby, Roger McGuinn, Michael Clarke, and Chris Hillman.

LP format was given its more earthly dimension by some of the group's best traditional covers, which also served as the strongest links to the more conventional folk-rock of its 1965 recordings. "John Riley" had been one of the most done-to-death chestnuts of the folk revival, based on a seventeenth-century British ballad that was retooled by Ricky Neff and Roger's old mentor Bob Gibson. On *Fifth Dimension* it was reinvented top-to-bottom by McGuinn's spinning 12-strings and some of the Byrds' best harmonies, tastefully overlaid with some real strings (as was another folk standard, "Wild Mountain Thyme," on the same LP). The medieval-sounding lyric of a man returning from seven years of roaming to find his woman has stayed true to him, sweeping her in his arms after she's failed to recognize him upon his return, may have seemed anachronistic at the dawn of the era of free love. The Byrds' beauty was in making the ancient tale seem entirely contemporary in its drama.

Even more radical was "I Come and Stand at Every Door," a poem by Nazim Hikmet told in the voice of a seven-year-old killed by the Hiroshima blast. Translated by Pete Seeger, it was set to the melody of the folk ballad "Great Selchie of Shule Skerry" (which has also been titled "Silkie"). Both Judy Collins and Joan Baez, among others, had recorded "Silkie"/"Great Selchie of Shule Skerry" and "John Riley" back in the early '60s. The Byrds' "I Come and Stand at Every Door," midwifed by Seeger's translation, was thus a more direct continuation of the folk process than most of the young buyers of *Fifth Dimension* realized at the time. Updated to the present with Hikmet's horrifying description of nuclear decimation and urge to fight for peace, it was taken even further from its origins by the Byrds' hypnotic electric chime-drone arrangement. As a further testament to the ongoing folk process in the psychedelic/nuclear age, the Misunderstood, a largely American band based in England, did its own turbo-charged psychedelic version of "I Come and Stand at Every Door" in 1966, using the same Seeger/Hikmet lyrics, yet an entirely different melody.

On the other hand, increased group democracy was not always a good thing. "Hey Joe," recorded after much insistence by lead singer Crosby, was disappointingly unimaginative and rushed by the Byrds' high standards (and not as good as the hit version by their fellow Sunset Strip denizens the Leaves). "Captain Soul" was nothing more than a blues jam; "What's Happening?!?!" unveiled Crosby's propensity for tedious philosophizing, lifted by McGuinn's inimitably strangled electronic 12-string guitar phrases; and "2-4-2 Fox Trot (The Lear Jet Song)"'s whooshing jet effects, cockpit dialog, and keening peels of proto-acid rock guitar could not disguise its utter lack of a substantial tune and lyrics. The shift into higher electronic gear was too much for some to take: "Several nice songs are almost completely overpowered by the electronics of this group, which parlayed Dylan and Seeger tunes to chart heights in times past, and which seems to be on an electronic Scottish bagpipe kick at this session," chided *Sing Out!* in its review of the album.

Does McGuinn see the Byrds' migration from folk-rock to psychedelia as a logical progression? "Sure. Basically, we were all taking acid. So . . ."—he laughs heartily—"it's only natural that the kind of music that would come out of it would be that." He's quick to clarify, however, that impressions of acid trips were not the sole dimension to "5D (Fifth Dimension)," seeing it as "more of a spiritual song than an acid song. But the two kind of combine. You have to understand, we were taking acid not just to get high, but for spiritual enlightenment. If anybody will believe it, that was our motivation. We thought we could kind of understand the universe better, and be more one with God, if we took this stuff. It was more like the Indian tribes that did mescaline and peyote as part of their religious rituals. They experienced a spiritual side of life that they didn't see otherwise."

In a November 1970 interview with *Creem*, McGuinn went to further lengths to simultaneously clarify the spiritual sphere of "5D (Fifth Dimension)" and diminish the drug inferences that were read into the song: "It's really painful to think you've got a really hip audience, a mass of them. And so you write this real hip song, '5D,' and they don't like it, don't understand it all, think it must be about dope. '5D' was an ethereal trip into metaphysics, into an almost Moslem submission to Allah, an all-mighty spirit, free floating, the fifth dimension being that mesh that Einstein theorized about. He proved theoretically—but I choose to believe it—that there's an ethereal mesh in the universe, and probably the reason for the speed of light being what it is is because of the friction encountered going through that mesh."

Here McGuinn broke off to quote an excerpt of the song's lyric: "'How is it, that I can come out to here and be still floating, and never hit bottom and keep falling through, just relaxed and paying attention.' We were talking about a way of life, sort of a submission to God or whatever you want to call that mesh, that life force. In order to get it, you have to understand what it is and how to do it to some extent. It takes some experience, and most people haven't encountered that, our culture being so dogmatically oriented, with everything cut-and-dry, and black-and-white, and no gray. These days, the only way you're going to get it is through your own head."

McGuinn also emphasized the continuity of such spiritual concerns in the Byrds, predating *Fifth Dimension*'s explorations and reaching back all the way to their first recordings. "After '5D' I was discouraged—at least, as to putting out spiritual data to a record-buying public for AM radio consumption," he confessed. (Perhaps some of the discouragement was engendered by the song's relatively poor performance as a single; it had reached only #44 in the charts.) "Now you'll have to understand, I was also spiritually involved in 'Tambourine Man' and 'Turn! Turn! Turn!' Like my interpretation of 'Mr. Tambourine Man,' whether Dylan meant it or not, the tambourine man was Allah, the eternal life force, and 'take me for a trip upon your magic swirling ship' was just like let my soul go where you want it to, and I promise to go under it. It was sort of an Islam concept. Perhaps I got too intellectual with '5D,' because the other two had a heavy sugar-coating over the spiritual message that was in there. I think the vibrations in my voice sort of telepathically conveyed it."

These were indeed pretty cerebral and spiritual concepts for a pop single of 1966 (or indeed of any era). But the pop audience was catching up to them very fast, with the increasing aid, real or imagined, of psychedelic drugs to open doors of perception. LSD in particular was rising in popularity around the time of *Fifth Dimension*'s release, which as it happened was just months before the drug was made officially illegal in America in October 1966. Drugs would fuel part of the inspiration for taking folk-rock into its next phase, as a foundation for psychedelia, and California would be its crucible. But the next big leap forward for both folk-rock and the counter-culture would be concentrated not in New York or Los Angeles, the cities that had cultivated the overwhelming majority of folk-rock's innovations since the birth of the music. It would be in San Francisco, whose vanguard folk-rock band, Jefferson Airplane, would issue its debut album on *Fifth Dimension*'s heels in August.

1

folk-rock to acid rock

the san francisco sound

he term "psychedelic rock" is guaranteed to generate as much heated discussion as the term "folk-rock" when it comes to defining what it really means. To some, it's rock with long, distortion-ridden guitar solos and improvisation. To others, it's whimsical, arty pop littered with special effects. There are those who see its unpredictable collision of disparate elements as a mirror of the drug experience, specifically the LSD one. Others point to the integration of Indian and Middle Eastern influences and the spontaneous verve of free jazz into a rock setting. Another camp might stress the melodic invocation of free love and a utopia-'round-the-bend ethos. Many would say that psychedelic music is a mix of all of the above.

What *is* beyond a doubt, if not often noted, is that many of the musicians pioneering psychedelic rock came from folk and folk-rock backgrounds. That was certainly the case in America, and especially in California, and most especially in the San Francisco Bay Area, the region that would become the leading beachhead of acid rock. Jefferson Airplane, Big Brother & the Holding Company, the Grateful Dead, Quicksilver Messenger Service, Country Joe & the Fish—all boasted ex-folkies, who sometimes comprised the majority of the lineups. The folk melodies, harmonies, and lyrical perspectives that had colored their initial forays into rock sometimes seemed all but buried in a blitz of feedback and interminable jamming by the end of the decade. Yet those elements would nonetheless periodically reassert themselves with vigor, sometimes leaping to the forefront, sometimes even beyond the 1960s, particularly in the work of the Grateful Dead, the one band from the preceding list to endure as a popular institution for the rest of the twentieth century.

Not until Jefferson Airplane took "Somebody to Love," "White Rabbit," and its *Surrealistic Pillow* album into the Top Ten in mid-1967 did California acid rock sweep the United States. The path from folk to folk-rock to psychedelia had been accelerating in California for a couple of years, however, and not just in San Francisco. As with so many of folk-rock's innovations, the trailblazers of folk-to-freakout were the Byrds. "Eight Miles High" had been psychedelia's signpost. At its root, as McGuinn notes, it was a folk song, changed into something else entirely by the free-flight 12-string guitar solos that welded the spirit of John Coltrane and Ravi Shankar to rock music. Those explorations into raga, improvisation, and electronic distortion would be amplified and diversified on the aptly titled *Fifth Dimension* album, released in July 1966. And while the Byrds remained based in Los Angeles, it would be the San Francisco bands that would amplify that blueprint to its nth degree.

T he San Francisco folk-rock (and subsequent psychedelic) sound, however, was rooted in the same kind of forces that had given birth to the folk-rock hybrid in other cities, even if it was a tad late in catching up to New York and Los Angeles. The city, a haven for freethinkers and adventurers since it was founded around the time of the gold rush in the mid-1800s, also had a long tradition of both folk music and radical politics. The first noncommercial, listener-supported radio station in the United States, KPFA, was founded there by pacifists and conscientious objectors just after the conclusion of World War II, and remains one of the five affiliate stations in the Pacifica Network of community radio stations today.

Teacher Phil Elwood had a slot on KPFA every Sunday spinning jazz, folk, and blues releases. By the mid-'60s he had become a popular music critic for the *San Francisco Examiner*. "Recognition of folk music as a music of the people was a very strong movement in the Berkeley that I grew up in," he says. "Before the war, maybe 1941, '42, I saw Pete Seeger and Leadbelly and Guthrie out on a pier in San Francisco, protesting for the Harry Bridges Labor Union. We all bought the record albums that were put out by Moe Asch, later of Folkways." Harry Smith did much of his rooting around for rarities that he assembled for his *Anthology of American Folk Music* series, the first archival reissues of folk music from the 1920s and 1930s (issued by Folkways in 1952), in Berkeley. Barbara Dane and Malvina Reynolds, two of the most dedicated left-wingers of the folk revival, were based in the Bay Area, and the Kingston Trio rose to fame with their residency at the Purple Onion in San Francisco.

By the early '60s there were numerous other folk venues in San Francisco, across the bay in Berkeley, and down the peninsula in San Jose and Palo Alto. There were regular folk festivals at San Francisco State University and in Berkeley, and, a couple hours' drive south, in coastal Monterey. German immigrant Chris Strachwitz had set up one of America's leading folkloric labels, the still-running Arhoolie, doing many of its blues, Cajun, and Tex-Mex field recordings himself. Janis Joplin and future members of the Grateful Dead were among several young musicians who appeared on KPFA's folk programs. Elwood even remembers Creedence Clearwater Revival's John Fogerty performing on KPFA "when he was in high school, as a folk guitarist, playing his own songs." Fogerty's mother, the singer told *Goldmine* in 1997, "took me to all the festivals and the barbecues and that was great exposure and a big influence on me."

Nevertheless, by music industry standards, San Francisco was still the provinces. Like Toronto and Boston—both homes to many folk musicians moving in the direction of rock—it lacked the recording facilities to compete with those in Los Angeles, New York, and London. And it would lack these for some time, years past the Summer of Love, with much classic San Francisco '60s psychedelic rock being recorded in Los Angeles or New York. Jefferson Airplane, for instance, recorded in L.A. until their fifth studio album, 1969's *Volunteers*, the first the band did in their San Francisco hometown. There was also not yet a concentrated hip/club community to rival those in Cambridge, Greenwich Village, and the Sunset Strip.

Perhaps as a consequence, some future folk-rock musicians who based themselves in the region briefly, including several of the Byrds, ended up living elsewhere to take their shots at the brass ring. San Francisco was a place to hang out in—not to get ahead. By the same token, many of the folk musicians who would become mainstays of the San Francisco sound drifted around for a while before settling in the Bay Area. Paul Kantner of Jefferson Airplane, David Freiberg of Quicksilver Messenger Service, and Sherry Snow of Blackburn & Snow had all been in the same proto-commune with David Crosby in Venice next to L.A. Janis Joplin had flitted between Texas, San Francisco, and New York for three years before taking the position of lead singer for Big Brother & the Holding Company in 1966.

Much of the San Francisco scene's fertilization actually took place around 1964 in the South Bay, then (as now) much less hip than the big city. Several colleges were there, though, which gave young bohemian musicians both a place to study while waiting out the real world, and an audience of like-minded budding hippies to play for. Jerry Garcia played bluegrass and taught guitar at Dana Morgan's Music Store in Palo Alto, where he joined Ron "Pigpen" McKernan and Bob Weir to form the jug band Mother McCree's Uptown Jug Champions (a July 1964 performance was actually issued on CD in 1999). Jorma Kaukonen, the Santa Clara University graduate then still sometimes billed as "Jerry" Kaukonen, taught guitar in San Jose and played acoustic folk and blues in local clubs, sometimes accompanying Janis Joplin (a couple of recordings from this association, complete with clattering typewriter in the background, show up on the *Janis* box set). Paul Kantner, another one-time Santa Clara University student, and David Freiberg helped run the Offstage folk club in San Jose, at which Joplin, Garcia, and Kaukonen played. Also floating around the South Bay scene was Canadian-born Skip Spence, later of the Airplane and Moby Grape but then a folk singer, and San Jose State student Sherry Snow. "That whole group of us hung around San Jose State," says Snow, "and then a lot of us moved up to San Francisco and Berkeley. That's where everything germinated."

In the first half of 1965, San Francisco may have still been a sleepy burg by Hollywood music industry standards, but things were already starting to happen, in both rock and the general counterculture. A local label, Autumn, was recording just-about-folk-rock national hits with the Beau Brummels. The We Five, whose harmonies were overlooked precursors to the yearning male-female vocal blends of Jefferson Airplane, had one of the first major folk-rock hits with "You Were on My Mind." The Haight-Ashbury, until recently a rather rundown neighborhood, was becoming a key flagship of hippiedom with influxes of students and artists taking advantage of the low rents in large Victorian houses, bringing with them considerable quantities of drugs. This is the district where the Grateful Dead, Big Brother & the Holding Company, the Charlatans, and other burgeoning San Francisco bands lived for important stretches as they struggled to make the transition from motley conglomerations of ex-folkies and rock/blues/jazz journeymen to out-and-out electric rock bands.

In the subsequent decades, it's sometimes been fashionable among historians to put down the Beau Brummels and the Autumn roster as a teenybopper scene that was necessary for the hipper outfits to counteract and render obsolete. This revisionism does a great disservice to the Beau Brummels, who did so much to set the standards for the melancholy melodies and harmonies that would remain integral to the appeal of San Francisco acts like Jefferson Airplane, Quicksilver Messenger Service, and some other local bands well into the acid rock era. Usually remembered only for their two hits "Laugh, Laugh" and "Just a Little," the group continued to develop as performers and composers throughout 1965. Their unimaginatively titled *Volume 2* album contained the nearly unsurpassed gems of yearning romantic folk-rock romanticism "I Want You" and "Sad Little Girl," even if their single "Don't Talk to Strangers" copped too liberally from the Byrds' 12-string licks and harmonies. A hoard of outtakes, to be issued in dribs and drabs over the next few decades—there was enough for a three-CD box set in 1996!—testifies not just to their prolific productivity, but also to their artistic maturation. Like other folk-rock acts from San Francisco and elsewhere, the Beau Brummels were starting to write about not just love but also states of mind, as well as anticipate some aspects of country-rock.

Autumn Records, too, did not limit itself to lightweight pop-rock, even if some of its early output was low-level British Invasion imitation. The Vejtables did a few respectable pop-folk-rock singles, including a cover of Tom Paxton's "The Last Thing in My Mind," featuring the vocals of Jan Errico, one in a line of strong, strident Bay Area female folk-rock singers. Autumn also recorded a single by the Great Society, the dynamic, underrated proto-psychedelic band featuring future Jefferson Airplane star Grace Slick, with an early version of "Somebody to Love" on the A-side. The label did demos with the Charlatans, Dino Valenti, and, under the short-lived name the Emergency Crew, the Grateful Dead.

But by 1966, the company went kaput, torpedoed by the poor organizational skills of partners Tom Donahue and Bob Mitchell, who rumor had it were spending much of their time and money at Bay Meadows racetrack. (Donahue would subsequently launch KMPX, the first widely heard underground-oriented FM rock station in the US.) The entire Autumn roster was transferred to Warner Brothers. No one was screwed worse by the deal than the Beau Brummels, who in 1966 were coerced by their new label into recording an entire album of Top 40 covers at a time when they should have been establishing themselves as an important, original band. The musicians would bounce back to make a couple of decent albums for the label before the decade closed, expanding into dream fantasy–tinged lyrics on 1967's *Triangle*, but their career never recovered.

Jefferson Airplane had more in mind than a parochial setup like Autumn when the group formed in 1965. Over the next five years half a dozen members would assert themselves as strong musical personalities within the band. But at its outset, there's no doubt that the founder/visionary was singer Marty Balin, owner of the most heart-tugging vocal sob in rock music. Balin's resume was similar to those of so many primal folk-rockers: a near-buried failed attempt at rock 'n' roll via a couple early-'60s singles on the Challenge label; a stint with folk vocal group the Town Criers, who never released anything while Balin was in the band (although a live track appeared on an obscure anthology many years later); immersion in the Beatles' *A Hard Day's Night* film; and the realization, with the Byrds' out-of-the-blue stardom, that the time for matching folk with rock was right. He got the backing to open a club on Fillmore Street, the Matrix, and needed to put together a band, including himself, naturally, to play it. His first recruit was singer-guitarist Paul Kantner, whom he met at the San Francisco folk club the Drinking Gourd. An obvious choice was Jorma Kaukonen, well known throughout the Bay Area as a guitar virtuoso, even if he wasn't particularly angling for a place: "I was totally uninterested in rock or popular music at the time," he says. "Kantner convinced me to try playing in the band and I was totally seduced by the whole thing."

"Basically, why they got together was the Byrds," says Peter Albin of Big Brother & the Holding Company. "They said, 'There's this great group down in Los Angeles, man, and we just hope that we can do a little bit of what they're doing, and I hope you like it' kind of thing. So a lot of their early stuff [was material by people like] Fred Neil, they did a couple of his songs, and I think they did a Dino Valenti song. [They also covered the Byrds' "I'll Feel a Whole Lot Better," as well as a Dylan song that the Byrds did on their second album, "Lay Down Your Weary Tune," as evidenced by the earliest available live Airplane bootleg, from January 1966.]

"Marty Balin designed that group: not only put it together, but he had an image, he had a concept, and he auditioned people. One of the people he auditioned was a gal named Joanie Simms. [She] dragged me over there with my guitar and I backed her up on some song," recalls Albin. "She was a very loud, red-haired Jewish blues singer, belter. I knew that she wasn't gonna get in any group. She was just too brash and wild and weird." Big Brother & the Holding Company, as it happens, would get the brashest, wildest, and weirdest female singer of all; Balin would select Signe Anderson, a more restrained but quite capable belter that he'd heard at the Drinking Gourd.

"The night I heard them at the Matrix, the band couldn't have been more than a few months old," remembers Steve Lalor, soon to help form Seattle's best folk-rock group, the Daily Flash. "They still had the old string bass player who did Al Jazzbo Collins bits while Paul struggled to keep his electrified acoustic 12-string in tune. They had a terrible time staying in tune. Marty, who I knew loosely from the folk scene, seemed very proud of the fact that the band did a very accomplished job of 'Midnight Hour.' It seemed to mean a lot to him that his ragtag bunch of white folkies could 'get down.' I liked the look of the acoustic bass, but the sound didn't cut it. I don't remember who was drumming, but it was overpowering the bass. Paul and Marty were still trying to control their guitar and amp sounds. I asked Marty how solid he was on all the band personnel, hoping for a potential opening. Marty said he was very happy with everybody in the band."

Actually, he wasn't. Original bassist Bob Harvey and drummer Jerry Peloquin were let go. Harvey was critical of Balin's leadership in a 1999 interview he gave to Greg Gildersleeve for the Web site "A Jefferson Starship Airplane Site," saying "there wasn't even one original song in the whole repertoire," and that the unreleased David Crosby composition "Flower Bomb Song" was "turned down coldly by Marty." Harvey added, "After saying the band had to be unique, which was the reason for being acoustic and electrified, all that went out the window the minute RCA said they would sign us if we went all electric—all rock & roll. Paul and Marty both say they weren't looking for stardom or for big money, and I say bullshit. Stardom and money were about the only things that meant anything."

Harvey and Peloquin's replacements were determined by the kind of offhand decisions so common to the head-hunting process of major folk-rock bands. Jack Casady, another guy who'd played rock as a teenager before moving into folk and blues, was teaching bass in Washington, DC, before an unexpected phone call from his old friend Kaukonen lured him to San Francisco. Skip Spence, like Michael Clarke of the Byrds, was selected by Marty Balin just 'cause he *looked* like a drummer. It didn't matter that Balin had never heard him play, or that guitarist Spence didn't even play drums, unless you counted his high school marching band. He was in. Fortunately, it turned out that unlike Clarke he was a good songwriter as well, even if his flight with the Airplane would be a short one.

Way ahead of the local competition in storming the citadels of major-labeldom, the Airplane made its first recordings for RCA in December 1965. Although its debut single, "It's No Secret" (which Balin hoped would be covered by Otis Redding), came out in February 1966, it wasn't until August that *Jefferson Airplane Takes Off* hit the shops. By that time, the band and the city had started moving on to wilder, louder thoughts and expressions. But *Takes Off* was still a fetching portrait of the group in its straightforward folk-rock phase, with Balin still the dominant force as both lead singer and songwriter.

If the sound was much like a tentative early Byrds, the musicians differed from their inspirations in the male-female harmonic blend and a romantic idealism. No one oozed more sincerity than Balin, on both rockers like "It's No Secret" and tender ballads such as "Don't Slip Away" and "Come Up the Years." The cover of Dino Valenti's "Let's Get Together," probably the most respected rock version of the song prior to the hit rendition by the Youngbloods, foretold a communal idealism that transcended boy-girl relationships. The moody "Blues from an Airplane" (co-written by Balin and Spence) hinted at the more oblique, inscrutably optimistic wordplay the band would delve into on subsequent albums.

Even if *Takes Off* was mostly about love, it was love of a young adult kind, couched in hip language not as immediately accessible to either elders or slightly younger teenagers. "RCA's conservative," Balin told *San Francisco Chronicle* writer Ralph J. Gleason in an interview included in Gleason's book *The Jefferson Airplane and the San Francisco Sound*. "It's run by older men who really don't have anything going in rock and they were so desperate to get into it, that's why they took us.... Then when we started doing our material, they were very confused by the lyrics, you know. And we had a lot of discussion between them and what we were saying in our music. They used to ask us about all the lyrics. Like on the first album, all the material is about love.... One song is about a guy and a girl making love in outer space. And it's symbolic, the language of it. We had to explain it to them, almost every song we did.... Teenyboppers don't know what we're doing. They think we're weird.... My age group, I never have to explain my songs to."

ew other first-wave-style folk-rock records were recorded by San Francisco bands before psychedelic elements started to shift the scene into interstellar overdrive. There was one other act, Blackburn & Snow, that cut similar material, of similar quality and quantity, for We Five producer Frank Werber's Trident production company in 1966 and 1967. Only two little-heard singles on

Blackburn & Snow, the duo of Jeff Blackburn (with guitar) and Sherry Snow.

Verve were released, however, leaving the duo of guitarist-singer Jeff Blackburn and vocalist Sherry Snow to sink unnoticed when their romance ended and the couple broke up. An entire CD's worth of tracks finally saw the light of day in 1999, containing ample evidence of a pair that could and should have been serious competition for the Airplane and their ilk. Blackburn & Snow had so much going for them: captivating, unusual male-female harmonies with bittersweet, slightly dissonant overtones; strong original material that zigzagged entrancingly between minor and major keys; and crystal-clear studio arrangements that drew from not just the Byrds, but also the Everly Brothers and country music. Their photogenic young-couple-in-love presence was a genuinely hippie alternative to the more manufactured Sonny & Cher.

What they didn't have, for reasons that remain somewhat inexplicable, was a regular release schedule. No Blackburn & Snow album appeared at the time, despite an abundance of quality songs, such as their first single, "Stranger in a Strange Land." An exultant folk-rocker, it was written by Snow's friend David Crosby under a pseudonym, and stronger than anything Crosby wrote on the first three Byrds albums (although the Byrds did get as far as cutting the song's unissued instrumental backing track, subsequently released on the expanded *Turn! Turn! Turn!* CD). While comparisons to the early Airplane were inevitable, they were at the same time different enough from the Airplane to have carved their own niche. But by the time their last single did get issued, the moment for upbeat, no-frills folk-rock had passed. Other than Kansas's Blue Things, there were no more unjustly overlooked folk-rockers of the 1960s than Blackburn & Snow (though at least the Blue Things had the satisfaction of managing to release an entire album while they were still around).

Snow, who now goes by the name Halimah Collingwood, is diffident as to whether Blackburn & Snow deserved a place among folk-rock immortals. She does agree that the pair had something that set them apart. "Because of the kind of melodies that [Blackburn] wrote, I could hear all this harmony everywhere. It's much more dissonant than, I think, any of the other groups. I liked to stretch notes, so I was stretching the sound, going up and coming back, dissonant and then resolving it. The harmonics, when you get those sounds so close together, they create all these overtones and undertones. That's what I was always listening for, that kind of resonating energy."

In some ways Blackburn & Snow were victims of times that were not a-changin' quite fast enough, being just a bit in advance of the hit-hungry commercial mindset that subsequent Bay Area bands would do a little to ameliorate. "We very much wanted to perform our own sound," says Snow. "Neither of us wanted to compromise what we were doing to become commercial. Some of the other groups, maybe they were willing to do that. And Trident, Frank Werber, wanted us to, to some extent. They wanted to get us to do a comedy act and that kind of stuff, kind of like a Sonny & Cher. We were not into that at all. We were naturally funny when we were on, but we didn't want to have to learn any lines and anything. We considered ourselves purists—pure to what was our music, and who we were.

"That's why it was so hard for us to work with Trident. They did a lot of things to the sound that we would never have done. But what can you do? They were paying us, and we were under contract. They wanted singles, like We Five had their one single. That's not the market that we were in. That wasn't important to us. Blackie was not sitting there trying to write a hit." Indeed Blackburn & Snow's talents would have been far better served by the LP format than the 45. But it wasn't until a year or two later, in large part due to San Francisco groups, that rock artists would be seen as capable of sustaining a profitable career via the album market rather than the singles one. Werber, it must be stressed, was also frustrated that more Blackburn & Snow material wasn't released, maintaining, "It isn't like I didn't try. There was not a lot of interest. From anybody."

"I think if it had been marketed well, and it had come out early enough, it would have done something," Snow continues. "Certainly there could have been some underground popular attention to it. It was that much different from the Byrds and from some of the other groups. A duo that are in love, it's hard to keep that going under all those stresses. Because we were not business savvy at all. We were singers and artists."

Beyond the outstanding harmonies and melodies, there was a more intangible quality to the folk-rock of Blackburn & Snow and the early Jefferson Airplane that separated them from most rock artists, folk-rock and otherwise, outside of the Bay Area. Even if many of the songs were ostensibly about love, it was not solely a love between two people that was being extolled, but a love among *all* people—between friends, among the community, between performance and audience. A love that, as naive as it sounds, could through collective force change the world that so many folk-rockers were protesting against, through action and example.

"When we would sing, there was a tremendous love that was coming between us," says Snow of her collaboration with Blackburn. "That's pretty magical, when you see that on stage. Most of those other groups weren't like that. We were singing the music that was about what we believed in. A lot of the motivating force at that time was to become a more real human being, and to have a deeper experience of life, a more open consciousness. I think the music really reflected that, because we were trying to reflect on more than just love: [also] about everyday life and what was affecting you, and what affected society. A lot of people could not understand what Blackie was saying at all in his lyrics. Some of his songs have a vagueness to them that weren't so commercial. But I think there was a lot of beauty in his words and some of the melodies."

David Crosby's "Stranger in a Strange Land," covered by the duo on one of their singles and inspired by Robert A. Heinlein's science fiction classic of the same name, was very much in that spirit. A call to free love among brothers and sisters and others, it would be heartily expounded upon in several of his post-1966 songs for the Byrds and Crosby, Stills, Nash & Young. "We all read *Stranger in a Strange Land*," confirms Snow, who'd already lived in a communal situation with Crosby and other future folk-rockers in Venice before any of them had gone electric. "Everybody talked about 'grokking' and 'fullness.' That was THE BOOK."

This could be viewed as an extension of the all-for-one, humanitarian ethos that had first sparked the left-wingers so crucial to launching the folk revival decades earlier. The difference, beyond the obvious ones of electrified instruments, was that this generation was not going to focus so much on systematic change of the capitalistic system through union organizing, education of the masses in Marxist-Leninist ideology, and the like. The alterations they were advocating had more to do with changes in everyday behavior, and in putting more loving values into direct, sometimes sexual practice, rather than working for more abstract, theoretical collective action. If it was perhaps less avowedly politically radical than the all-for-one-and-one-for-all hymns of yore, it was undeniably a hell of a lot more fun.

Musicians made this clear not just in their songs, but also in some of their public statements. "There's not enough love in the world nowadays," gushed David Crosby in a strange interview disc— including only Crosby and McGuinn's answers, leaving radio DJs to voice the questions—to promote the *Fifth Dimension* album. "And the groups give them [listeners] love, the good ones. And I think they know it . . . and you gotta love the kids and the music both to play it right, so that it will excite them. There is definite love going on between the kids and the performers, and it's both ways."

That did not rule out the possibility, naturally, that one-to-one, brother-to-sister, or performer-to-audience love couldn't indeed change the larger world. On the 1967 Leonard Bernstein–hosted CBS special *Inside Pop: The Real Revolution*, Graham Nash, still in the Hollies and a couple of years away from teaming up with David Crosby in Crosby, Stills & Nash, proclaimed, "What Donovan's trying to put over will stop war dead." On the same program, the more taciturn McGuinn put in his pitch for peaceful change through vibes in more all-encompassing, symbolic terms: "Emotions are stronger than fists."

Like much of folk-rock, it was a sentiment that could be mass-marketed by the system to which it was posing an alternative. "Jefferson Airplane Loves You" read the promotional bumper stickers that RCA printed shortly after it signed the band. At first, there was not a tidal wave of reciprocation. *Jefferson Airplane Takes Off* reached only #128 in the charts, tallying much of its sales in the San Francisco Bay Area. It would take the band's next album, *Surrealistic Pillow*, to break the San

Francisco sound nationally, peaking at #3 in the LP charts and spawning the hit singles "White Rabbit" and "Somebody to Love."

While still just about grounded in folk-rock, the Airplane's ride had now taken on a psychedelic hue. Jorma Kaukonen had developed a snaky, squalling echo-laden sound that set him apart from the Byrds, which was something of a conscious decision. "Paul was enamored with Roger McGuinn's sound and encouraged me to get a Rickenbacker 12-string just like his," he says. "It wasn't really me and I gravitated back to the six-string, alternating instruments on different songs, and then finally recycling the Rick. The Echoplex just opened a door to a fun universe. It would be some time before I would get involved with experimenting with effects and the like."

But the biggest change was one of personnel. Signe Anderson had been replaced in late 1966 by Grace Slick (interestingly, Sherry Snow had been approached about taking the position too, but declined, preferring to stay with Jeff Blackburn). Slick and Balin formed one of rock's great male-female harmony teams, passionately weaving around and sparking off each other both in the studio and onstage. Unlike Anderson, though, Slick was not steeped in folk music, as either a singer or a songwriter. Her steely, sexy vocals took the band in another direction, as did songs like "White Rabbit," with drug allusions both menacing and alluring, set to a bolero-like beat. The pure folk-rock sound was combining with other technological and musical streams to lift the Airplane's music to another, and higher, level, much as Shankar and Coltrane had done with the Byrds. Unlike the Byrds, however, the Airplane would not retain folk and folk-rock as nearly as much of a base for their subsequent work.

That's not to say that there wasn't some great folk-rock on *Surrealistic Pillow* that was just as important to putting it over in Middle America as the album's psychedelic hits. The Balin-Kantner collaboration "Today" was the best romantic folk-rock ballad bar none, and a hit single in the waiting that was never issued on 45. Marty's customarily teary vocal and melody built to a crescendo embodying the cup-runneth-over-with-love of his lyrics, decorated by steel guitar flicks from guest Jerry Garcia. His "Comin' Back to Me" was folk-rock at its most pastoral, while Kaukonen's solo instrumental showcase "Embryonic Journey" was a stunning flashback to his virtuosic folk roots. "My Best Friend," donated by now ex-drummer Skip Spence (who had been replaced by Spencer Dryden after the first album), was far closer to an underproduced Mamas & the Papas than anyone seems to have been prepared to admit. So was "How Do You Feel," donated by friend Tom Mastin (of obscure L.A. folk-rockers Mastin & Brewer). Kantner's "D.C.B.A. 25," just as tuneful and imbued with shades of light and dark harmony as any of the album's songs, departed from those other songs in its enigmatic lyrics, evoking the sensations of both love and head trips without referring to them in specific terms.

There were other songs the Airplane recorded and/or performed live around this time that were similarly uplifting folk-rock with an acid edge: their cover of "High Flying Bird" (an outtake from their first sessions in December 1965, and regularly performed live in 1967 even after Slick had entered the lineup), the pleading-yet-stern "Go to Her," and the gentle afterhours folk-rock of "J.P.P. McStep B. Blues," another Skip Spence castoff. Yet such material largely retreated from Jefferson Airplane's recorded repertoire beginning with its third album, *After Bathing at Baxter's*.

Jefferson Airplane circa 1967. Front row, left to right: Paul Kantner, Grace Slick, and Jorma Kaukonen. Back row, left to right: Marty Balin, Spencer Dryden, and Jack Casady.

In hindsight, this was for two reasons. One was that the musicians were diversifying at a furious rate, exploring distorted modal jams, jazzy improvisation, hard blues-rock, and off-the-wall subject matter (particularly in Slick's songs).

The other was that Marty Balin, responsible for both founding the band and penning more material than any other member on the first two LPs, withdrew from the group's creative forefront. He only wrote half a song on *After Bathing at Baxter's*, and Slick, understandably, was now the visual and media focus of the group. Kaukonen and Casady in particular wanted to steer the Airplane away from Balin's sentimental love songs. If the result was to diminish his songwriting input, that had no major effect on the group's popularity; Paul Kantner was there to pick up the songwriting slack. It did mean, however, that no post-1967 Airplane records would feature nearly as much heart-on-its-sleeve folk-rock as the first two had.

By the time *After Bathing at Baxter's* hit the shops at the end of 1967, several other major San Francisco Bay Area bands had followed the Airplane's journey from folk to folk-rock and psychedelia, both live and, increasingly, on record. The Charlatans have often been tagged as the first San Francisco psychedelic band. That comes as a surprise to some listeners, if they do manage to locate the Charlatans' sparse body of recording work, as they'll hear an outfit that sounds much more like an electrified jug-cum-blues-cum-good-time rock ensemble than like the Airplane or the Grateful Dead. The Charlatans' primary contribution to Haight-Ashbury rock was not sonic innovation, but outlandish image. They dressed in clothing right out of the Western saloon era, took the requisite drugs, and were generally far more interested in having a good time than becoming recording stars. Their best lineup only issued one single, a 1966 effort for Kapp whose Robert Johnson and Coasters covers were poor representations of their best wares.

Nearly a couple of dozen cuts from 1965–68 did emerge 30 years later on *The Amazing Charlatans*, and do show a quirky if somewhat quaint band that has its place in San Francisco's folk-to-psychedelic evolution. Its most talented musicians, guitarist Mike Wilhelm and drummer/guitarist Dan Hicks, were both electrified folkies, while George Hunter's autoharp added a tinge of old-world balladry. Over the course of numerous demos (including some for Kama Sutra and Autumn), they took a cornucopia of Americana into a time-warped hybrid of Haight-Ashbury haze and nineteenth-century barroom fare. "East Virginia," "Alabama Bound," and "Jack of Diamonds" were among the traditional folk numbers mashed through their juicer, along with Buffy Sainte-Marie's standby "Codine." Hicks, their sole songwriter of note, spun ironocomic tales with hints of good-time Tin Pan Alley and Western swing. "It was funkier," responds Hicks when asked to compare the group to other folk-rockers in the area. "It wasn't quite as arranged. But also, we had songs that were, you could call, old-timey, that went into pop of the '30s or something sometimes. We'd play 'Sweet Sue,' 'Somebody Stole My Gal,' or something, where these other bands weren't doing that."

The result was something like an undernourished Lovin' Spoonful that had baked in the sun for too long, with all the good and bad that entails. At times there were flashes of genuine excellence. Hicks's "We're Not on the Same Trip" was a lost treasure of early psychedelia, with its diving autoharp, squiggly crossfires of distorted guitar, and droll yet melodic wordplay. "I Saw Her," taught to them by their friend and occasional guest member Lynne Hughes from *The Coffee House Songbook* (issued by *Sing Out!* publishers Oak Publications), was folk-rock in the truest sense, in that it placed a compellingly mournful English madrigal of indeterminate origin into a rock context. But the group never could corral its inconsistent assets into a viable recording career. By the time of its one and only album, 1969's pleasant but inconsequential *The Charlatans*, Hicks had left to start his whimsical solo career, the time for good-time folk-rock had passed, and the time for psychedelia was passing.

The fried Lovin' Spoonful ambience on some of their recordings may have been no accident, as the Kama Sutra demos were produced by Erik Jacobsen. The Lovin' Spoonful producer hails Hicks as "one of the greats, for sure. And another guy who squandered his potential, I hate to say. Dan could sing, but he was much flatter then, all the time. He kind of subsequently harnessed that kind of flat singing, but then he was truly flat, pitchwise. And he wasn't the world's greatest drummer. George really couldn't play anything. He was more like the image-maker, and sang 'Alabama Bound,' and had long hair. And Wilhelm, who could kind of sing and kind of play . . . we're doing vocals, and I remember him pulling his lips back onto his cheek like it was white, this tension just oozing out, grinding his jaw. He just couldn't relax. They came in the studio, they were so uptight, and they really didn't have that edge of togetherness, when you put all the microphones on. I couldn't get anything, and nobody really liked them. Nobody saw it. They were just too far out, and too crazy. And when you met 'em, they came across strange and sarcastic. But I tried, several times. They made some nice things, but they were kind of contentious [with] each other and bickering.

"They didn't have any original songs, outside of Dan Hicks's, and they didn't want him to be the frontman. So there was no consensus as far as material. I guess maybe that was one of our major problems with the Charlatans, that there was just no unified musical direction, and no real output of pop songs. I know they always have snippy comments they make about me, [that] I didn't think they were good enough or something. I *don't* think they were good enough. They were not good enough to live in musical history, unfortunately, in a big way." Remarks Hicks, "I don't know if they had an idea to make us anything like this Lovin' Spoonful. I think they were hoping that, because we played old-timey stuff also, like they did, maybe there would be a connection there, and we could kinda push that and make a success out of that. The tunes came out as good as they could."

Hicks amplified his punning humor and Western swing influences in his subsequent, still-running solo career. The short gap between the Charlatans and Dan Hicks & His Hot Licks was filled by unissued, sparsely produced 1967–68 recordings that bridged the good-timey barely-psychedelia of the Charlatans with his more old-timey solo career. Finally released in 1998, these are some of the wittiest folk-psychedelic excursions, branching out into all manner of goofy, unpredictable verbal and melodic directions, reinforcing his stature as the Bay Area's leading cosmic screwball. Like the recordings of Blackburn & Snow and the Charlatans, it's another body of work that was barely or never heard at the time, unfairly consigned to the ears of a tiny corner of rock collectordom.

ig Brother & the Holding Company rose from about as informal, humble roots in Haight-Ashbury as the Charlatans did, and also boasted a number of ex-folkies in the lineup. Bassist Peter Albin had played bluegrass and old-timey music in bands with his brother around San Mateo, about 20 miles south of San Francisco. James Gurley had played folk-blues in coffeehouses in Detroit before moving to San Francisco. "His style was basically the fingerpicking style," says Albin. "He said that one time he got into John Lee Hooker's music, and just locked himself in a room and learned how to play that way. For like about three days, he didn't eat or drink, he just plain played these records and played this music on an acoustic guitar."

Gurley was another one of the folkies who made the awkward changeover to electric music by putting a DeArmond pickup into his acoustic, as some of the first L.A. folkies to go electric had in tiny clubs circa 1964–65. "I think he had a mahogany-bodied Martin," continues Albin. "Really, he hadn't played electric guitar before then. I remember propping it up, getting kind of a weird sound. We'd put pennies and scotch tape on the thing, and eventually he got a Gibson Les Paul Junior." Sam Andrew, far more experienced on electric guitar, rounded out a bunch that had formed out of jam sessions at 1090 Page Street, where Albin's brother Rodney let out a 25-room Victorian for a total of $675 a month, a bargain even in those days.

Big Brother vaulted to a leading position in the Haight-Ashbury rock race with the addition of Janis Joplin on most lead vocals. Joplin's salacious image and ear-shattering soul-rock singing has made it difficult for subsequent generations to detect her folk influences. But it's crucial to appreciate that she was very much a folk-blues singer before 1966, with years of experience in folk clubs in Texas and San Francisco. Albin had come across her on her first stay in San Francisco, where "I first saw her at a round-robin session at KPFA called 'Midnight Special.' Everybody would sit around this one microphone in a circle and just do one song. She played guitar and sang. She was basically just doing Bessie Smith–type stuff. She didn't really need a microphone. She was extremely loud."

Live and home recordings predating her entry into Big Brother came out on some anthologies after her death, attesting to her acoustic folk-blues roots. Albin remembers how one night, shortly after Janis had joined Big Brother and the band had moved into a house together in Marin County, "I'm up in my room, and someone turns on this record player, and it's Joan Baez, real loud. I'm pissed off, so I walk down the stairs, and I found that it's *not* the record player. It's Janis doing 'Silver Dagger' or something like that. It sounds exactly like Joan Baez. I couldn't fucking believe it. So she had the ability to do much different kinds of voices." She also sang some Dixieland jazz with Dick Oxtot, and took advantage of her first stay in the Bay Area, says Phil Elwood, to hear some of his Ma Rainey records, after Barbara Dane had advised him to expose Janis to the early jazz blueswoman.

By 1966 Joplin had started to outgrow her trad roots and entertained thoughts of joining the 13th Floor Elevators, Austin's top rock group and psychedelic pioneers in their own right, who later would spend some time playing the developing acid rock ballroom circuit in San Francisco. She ended up, however, returning to San Francisco, joining Big Brother shortly after her arrival in mid-1966. Interestingly, not long after she had gotten into Big Brother, Elektra producer Paul Rothchild tried to put together a band featuring Joplin, Taj Mahal, blues-folk guitarist Stefan Grossman, and guitarist Steve Mann. According to Grossman, Rothchild and Elektra wanted something to compete with the Mamas & the Papas, even to the extent of using the same session dudes (bassist Joe Osborn and drummer Hal Blaine) as the studio rhythm section. "We actually had a rehearsal in Berkeley, with just me, Taj, Janis, and Steve, and it was all go," says Grossman. "I went back to New York to get the money, 'cause they said they wanted to set us up in L.A. in a house and then we would record. I went to the Elektra office and they said, 'Oh no, it couldn't happen,' because of contracts." Joplin was left in Big Brother for good, at least for a couple of years.

Much of Big Brother's early repertoire was taken from old folk and blues songs. Its first album included updates of the spiritual "Blindman"; "Down on Me," which Andrew had heard on a recording by a gospel group in the 1930s; and "All Is Loneliness," from New York City's genre-defying, folk-jazz-avant-garde blind street musician, Moondog. "Bye, Bye Baby" had been written by Powell St. John, who had played harmonica with Joplin in the Austin folk group the Waller Creek Boys back in the early '60s (and would later sing with Bay Area band Mother Earth). "Coo Coo" (recorded at the sessions but initially released only on a single), a contender for one of the most overdone standards of the folk revival, had been learned by many musicians from Clarence Ashley's rendition on *Anthology of American Music*.

Big Brother's debut was recorded in a hurry in December 1966 in a shady deal that had hastily been cut with Mainstream Records to raise emergency funds when the band went broke on the road. Hence the playing was unrefined, yet the reckless San Francisco risk-taking came through strong on imaginative reinventions of the folk-based material, in both Joplin's raunchy moan-shriek and the group's loose, loud guitar interplay. Nowhere was that more apparent than on "Coo Coo," where the tempo verged on manic, the lead guitar (by Albin on this occasion) wound up into a vibrant raga-rock frenzy, and Joplin's vocals conveyed an urgent desperation missing from more resigned, pat folk interpretations of the tune.

"It's psychedelic, if only in the terms of very long, extended soloing," agrees Albin. "It was kind of folky, still, that type of solo. When we did it for Mainstream Records, they wouldn't let the song go on much more than three minutes, so we felt we got a little cheated there. On stage, it would go like for five minutes or more. I would really try to get into a lot of single-string, hammering-on stuff." The liberal recastings of old folk songs was not limited to instrumental improvisation, but also extended to the lyrical rewriting that had been an established part of the folk process long before folk-rock or psychedelia. "When Janis came into the band, we had been doing 'Down on Me' with more tradi-tional lyrics, but she said, 'That's old hat, you know.' So she wrote some new lyrics to that song. That's part of the folk tradition, anyway, changing things around to meet your own desires of what you want to say. 'Down on Me' was kind of a religious song, and she did use, still, some religious lyrics, but she made it kind of like a peacenik song too. I still sing 'Blindman,' and I always try to change the lyrics with that one—wherever I'm playing, I'll try to find out the history of the area and put partic-ular people into the song."

In at least one instance, an original practitioner expressed distaste for what these hippies were doing to the material. Moondog asked if the band did his "All Is Loneliness" in 5/4 time, remem-bers Albin, and "I said, no we do it in 4. He says, 'Uch. You lost the whole essence of it.' We said, 'We tried to do it in 5, Mr. Moondog, but we couldn't do it. We're just not that good.' He says, 'Uoh [grunts].' That was a tough song to do. You listen to his rounds, he's doing all these different time signatures and phew, [it's] tough." Moondog aka Louis Hardin, speaking in 1998 shortly before his death, was slightly more charitable: "It wouldn't be the way I would do it, but she [Joplin] liked it, and it was very thoughtful of her to do it. But I'm very fussy about arrangements and that sort of thing, and when people record my things, they're not too careful about the technical side of it. Some-times it doesn't sound the way I would hope it would sound. But anyway, it's a compliment."

Big Brother, like Jefferson Airplane and others, would quickly spin off into a multitude of ad-mixtures, from heavy blues-rock to soul to free-flight jazzy electric improvisations. What folk-rock had done—as it had in so many other contexts—was to give musicians an opportunity that they might not have otherwise conceptualized. For Joplin, it lay in finding that fronting a rock band was far more suitable for her loud voice than working in folk clubs. For Gurley, it was a chance to mix his earthy folk and John Lee Hooker influences with inspiration from freakier favorites John Cage, Moondog, John Coltrane, and Miles Davis. In Albin's case, he saw his opening by discovering that "a lot of groups that came around to 1090 Page to these jam sessions that we had in '65 didn't have bass players. That's basically when I made my move to electric and why I made it, because there was just not too many bass players." For the entire band, he emphasizes, it was a chance "to do jazz-type things, but within our frame of reference, blues and folk music and rock 'n' roll. We would take a song like 'Hall of the Mountain King,' which was classical music, and turn it into kind of a jazz thing, with this extended [jam]. We did lots of experimental-type music. We incorporated all sorts of different, weird shit, from Moondog, Coltrane to John Cage to Betty Boop cartoons."

cross the bay in Berkeley, another band made a quick hop, skip, and jump from ragtag folkies to psychedelic stars. Country Joe McDonald and Barry Melton were the only two guitarists, and the only two musicians involved to play on later Country Joe & the Fish records, when their ad hoc jug band recorded "I-Feel-Like-I'm-Fixin'-to-Die Rag" and "Superbird" in June 1965. The session, recorded by Chris Strachwitz of Arhoolie Records, was do-it-yourself in the purest sense, for use as a record to sell at the first Teach-In against the Vietnam War held at the University of California at Berkeley campus. It was a sort of audio edition of the *Rag Baby* folk magazine that McDonald ran with ED (pronounced "Ed," spelled in caps) Denson.

"Our first EP has a duet where Joe's playing acoustic and I'm playing an electric, and it's sort of transitional," says Melton. "But it's not really rock music. It's a full jug band on one tune, and one of the guitars electrified on the other cut." Backing the pair were musicians on washboard, kazoo, and washtub bass; the other two songs on the four-track EP were conventional topical folk tracts by forgotten singer-guitarist Peter Krug. The melody to "I-Feel-Like-I'm-Fixin'-to-Die Rag" was based on "Muskrat Ramble" by New Orleans traditional jazz trombonist Kid Ory.

It seemed highly improbable that "I-Feel-Like-I'm-Fixin'-to-Die Rag" would ever evolve into the most famous antiwar folk-rock-psychedelic song of the 1960s. Even this first record was done as something of a street protest rather than a commercial enterprise. "We even had a table for the express purpose of selling our first batch of records right in [UC Berkeley's] Sproul Plaza during the Teach-In," says Melton. "We alternated between playing the record over a speaker system and playing the song live to whoever came by. There were many tables there, but I think ours was the only one selling records." Adds Phil Elwood, who saw McDonald when Joe was just another guy busking folk songs on street corners near campus on Berkeley's Telegraph Avenue, "I was astonished that Country Joe became anything more. He was the perfect street-rocking protest man."

Melton was not angling to become a rock star either. Like so many of the musicians electrifying in the mid-'60s, he was even in early 1965 still a folkie, playing with others in hootenannies and as opening acts for featured performers at the Jabberwock in Berkeley. Melton, in fact, shared an apartment next door to the club, his roommates including future Country Joe & the Fish bassist Bruce Barthol, who had first met Melton in a high school folk music club. Another roommate was folk guitarist Robbie Basho, who experimented with eerie dissonance, tunings, and world music influences on his obscure recordings. "Bruce and I lived mostly on white bread, peanut butter, powdered skim milk, and whatever food we could forage from the Jabberwock," confesses Melton. "After the customers ate, we came down and scoured the leftovers." The janitor at the Jabberwock was then teenage Jef Jaisun, who a few years later would cut the folk-hippie satire "Friendly Neighborhood Narco Agent," eventually to become a staple on Dr. Demento's radio show.

As had happened only slightly earlier in Los Angeles clubs like the New Balladeer, the acoustic coffeehouse innocence would soon get transmogrified by electric music and an entry into commercial rock that no one was anticipating. As for many other incipient folk-rockers, it happened almost by accident, the bonds strengthened by musical and political interests deeply grounded in the folk revival and even pre-rock Leftism. "Sometime during the summer, I got a phone call out of the blue from some guy named Joe McDonald asking me if I wanted to make a record with him," remembers

Melton. "Joe and I had a kind of instant communication. Both of us were 'red diaper babies' and had astoundingly similar backgrounds. His dad was from Oklahoma, mine from Texas, and both of our mothers were East Coast Jews. We shared a mutual fondness for Woody Guthrie—Woody and his family had actually been neighbors of mine in early childhood, and my dad was a friend of Woody's—and all things Left in folk music.

"I should note Joe was, in a word, kind of 'straight' when I first met him, and I elected not to pull any of my carefully rolled joints out of my guitar case when we met for our first rehearsal. After all, he was still in the Navy reserves, married, and while he seemed to be a very political guy, I could tell he wasn't a 'head.' But I brought Joe over to our house, introduced him to the Jabber-wock group of folks, and eventually he began to become a regular in our scene and a regular in the Instant Action Jug Band. This is the band that gets its own chapter title ('The Frozen Jug Band') in the Tom Wolfe book *Electric Kool-Aid Acid Test*."

However, Melton and McDonald were, like other folkies, converted to the power of electricity after seeing the Paul Butterfield Blues Band (who often played in the Bay Area) in concert. En-thuses Melton, "It had all the excitement of electric music, and it had all the intellectual cachet of folk music." Within months, Country Joe & the Fish evolved at the unbridled pace of an acid rush, almost as if the musicians were being willingly swept along by cultural undertows out of their direct control, rather than shaping their destiny by themselves. Melton and McDonald, who as a folk duo had toured around colleges in the Northwest on behalf of the Students for a Democratic Society, got a fuller band together after McDonald moved into Melton's house, in which bassist Bruce Barthol was also residing. As all this was happening, according to Barry, "We turned Joe on to acid. He needed it, or so we thought.

"Once we hit into the electric medium and into the rock medium, we were pandering to the public taste," Melton continues. "We became extraordinarily popular. The little folk club where we used to play once every two weeks, we played every single night for a month, or something like that, and filled it. And after a while we filled *two* shows a night every single night."

Still, the transformation from that first recording to their second EP, released on the Rag Baby label in mid-1966, was nothing short of astonishing. Although there were still a couple of lineup changes to come before the band did its first album for Vanguard, the EP was, as Melton aptly notes in comparing it to the debut Fish full-length LP, "much more weirdo wacko kind of Middle-Eastern Japanese, San Francisco raga-influenced stuff." Blues, disquieting minor keys, vibro-distorto elec-tric guitar, and Farfisa organ swirled around each other in one of rock's most convincing early fac-similes of an acid trip. It all came to a head on the six-minute instrumental "Section 43," re-recorded in a somewhat less exciting version on the Fish's first Vanguard LP. Its Asiatic guitar, tribal maracas, devious organ, floating harmonica, and ethereal mid-sections of delicate koto-like guitar picking rivaled the Paul Butterfield Blues Band's "East West" as the finest psychedelic instrumental ever.

But was it folk-rock? Melton thinks so. "Rock music is the garbage can of music, or the melt-ing pot, depending on what your attitude is," he laughs. "You can throw anything in the soup, and it becomes a big stew. You can keep throwing things in all day, and it will absorb it, and still be edible. So in a band like Country Joe & the Fish, we could absorb jazz, Japanese music, Middle Eastern music,

Indian music, blues music, country music—it all fit in there somewhere. It was okay to do that. And for a lot of folk musicians, particularly guys like me from fairly urban areas, here was a chance to throw in all the stuff that we knew, everything from Pete Seeger and the Weavers to John Coltrane, in one place."

Also influential on the Fish was guitarist John Fahey, nominally a folk musician but too avant-garde to be confined to that category, who devised all sorts of interesting dissonances with his acoustic compositions. "Joe was a great admirer of John Fahey, as was I," explains Melton. "Our manager, ED Denson, was from Takoma Park, Maryland, grew up with John Fahey, and later co-founded the Takoma label with John. ED, I think more than Joe, had the idea that we could use Fahey-like compositional structures, which had discrete sections and/or movements, and incorporate them into electric music. Hence the four or five discrete movements of 'Section 43.'"

Two more musicians with folk and folk-rock experience—folk-blues guitarist David Cohen (who also played organ in the Fish) and Gary "Chicken" Hirsh, who'd drummed with Blackburn & Snow—were aboard by the time the group started recording for Vanguard. Country Joe & the Fish's first album, 1967's *Electric Music for the Mind and Body*, could be viewed as the most psychedelic extension of the jug band aesthetic. There was raga-rock ("Section 43"), apocalyptic blues-rock ("Death Sound Blues"), good-time country-folk-rock ("Sad and Lonely Blues"), organ-driven hard rock ("Love"), and weird minor-key-driven organ instrumentals ("The Masked Marauder"). Just as importantly, there were all kinds of lyrical viewpoints: political protest (the anti-President Lyndon Johnson diatribe "Superbird," initially heard on the first EP and re-recorded in a full rock arrangement), drug songs ("Flying High"), love songs about women ("Not So Sweet Martha Lorraine"), and love-everybody love songs ("Love").

"Our records could be a real schizophrenic experience, 'cause we didn't have an overall sound sometimes," admits Melton. "We went from sort of ragtime to blues to jug band to blah blah blah. You could call us a jack of all trades and a master of none, in some respects. But we really *had* sets where we played ten songs, none of which had any real musicological relationships to the one that preceded [it]. So I think we weren't looking for a sound, although we had this sort of Farfisa organ semi-psychedelic sound that ultimately became a niche."

Although Country Joe & the Fish's second album was not as strong as *Electric Music for the Mind & Body*, it did contain a newly electrified "I-Feel-Like-I'm-Fixin'-to-Die Rag." Anti-Vietnam War sentiment was much higher when it was released in late 1967 than it had been at the outset of the folk-rock era in mid-1965. The war was on a never-ending ramp of escalation, and its end looked as far away as ever. But far from merely being scared about getting killed in Vietnam, young men (and young women, even though they were not subject to the draft) were not buying the very morality of killing people halfway around the globe who had never done them harm. Virtually no one who bought a Country Joe & the Fish record had to be convinced that the Vietnam War was a bad thing.

The genius of the Fish's "I-Feel-Like-I'm-Fixin'-to-Die Rag" was in how it projected those sentiments with equal doses of savage sarcastic humor and genuine outrage. The absurdity of the war and its addled reasoning was mimicked by the hurdy-gurdy organ, super-jaunty tempo and kazoo blasts, and wiseass vocal delivery recruiting soldiers for dispatch to Vietnam and their heavenly makers for no discernible purpose, ending with bursts of gunfire. The song passed from FM radio hit to mythic legend when McDonald, minus the original Fish, gave a rousing solo acoustic performance of the song at the Woodstock festival, later featured in the *Woodstock* movie, substituting his infamous "F-U-C-K" cheer for the original "F-I-S-H" one. It was a long way from its roots in McDonald's Guthrie-Seegerite solo folk days, Chris Strachwitz's Arhoolie Records, and Kid Ory's "Muskrat Ramble."

And repercussions of those roots followed the song around. A cover by Pete Seeger in 1970 was included on a single that was pressed in small quantities as advance DJ copies, but never released. Seeger once commented that distributors refused to handle it; he was also prohibited from singing it on Spanish TV. (As of late 2002, the single could be heard on McDonald's Web site.) Folklorist Strachwitz retained 50% of the song's publishing rights, which brought him a considerable windfall after its use on the *Woodstock* soundtrack, helping him to keep his still-active Arhoolie label going. In 2001, McDonald was sued by Kid Ory's daughter, who claimed that the melody was "68 percent similar" to that heard in her father's 1924 recording of "Muskrat Ramble." McDonald was warned that singing "Fixin' to Die" in public would subject him to a $150,000 fine.

Early Fish manager ED Denson, who'd already done important work in the folk revival by helping to locate old country bluesmen and revive their careers, agrees that Country Joe & the Fish were like a West Coast counterpoint to the East Coast's most radical folk-rock band, the Fugs. "They were similar in that both were essentially political in focus. However, the Fugs were from

Country Joe & the Fish. Clockwise from top center: Barry Melton, Bruce Barthol, Country Joe McDonald, David Cohen, and Chicken Hirsh.

a longer tradition of direct action protest than anyone in the Fish, and they had that proto-punk Lower East Side attitude from the onset, while the Fish were fundamentally innocent (vs. worldly)."

Nor were the Fish intent on using music as a vehicle for preaching to the masses. "We were all 'stoners' back then, and one of the first realizations borne of psychedelic insight is the inadequacy of language," feels Melton. "In fact, I think every member of my band and any of the other bands called upon to play at political events was a bit angered at the fact that the politicos would use our music as a shill to lure crowds and then talk to them endlessly. And there is nothing more grating to a stoned audience than a bunch of people talking. Somehow, I believe what we all sensed was that whatever it was that was 'high' about our music wasn't to be found in the words. Rather, it was in the improvisational interplay between the musicians and those magic moments when we really got into the 'zone,' that magical place of near-enlightenment, approaching pure experience, when we truly escaped the smallness of who we were into a place far more expansive and reflective of an altered state or other reality. And I truly believe that's why the audiences came to hear our music—for the same reasons they later flocked to see the Grateful Dead—to see if we'd 'get there' that night."

Melton remains proud, however, that songs such as "I-Feel-Like-I'm-Fixin'-to-Die Rag" "had to do with the mission of Country Joe & the Fish. We were interested in stopping the war. Our thing was political action. And somehow, it became manifest to us at some point in time that we'd have a bigger voice if we stepped into a popular idiom. This perception proved correct. We were glad we were there, because it made us more relevant. For a minute there in time, we were *bigger* than Pete Seeger." Denson seconds the benefits of playing rock to circulate messages to much bigger audiences than would have been available to folk performers by the late '60s: "I think it made all the difference in the world. If you are going to swim in the ocean of the masses you have to look like you belong there, or else the fish will not recognize you as one of their own."

"It wasn't simply political commentary," continues Melton. "Other bands alluded to drugs; we talked about them, straight-up. The Grateful Dead didn't have any songs that actually directly talked about drugs. 'Driving that train, high on cocaine'—that's later on. If you listen to what's on the first record, there's some stuff there that's fairly shocking for its time. We were talking about weed right on the first record, getting high. By the second record, we were singing the LSD commercial. So we were overt. Not simply politically overt, sociologically overt. In other words, we said it. We also said 'fuck,' you know. We were the guys who said what other people alluded to. It was right there in the lyric content. Everybody else had the message coded in there."

Melton remains a little disappointed, though, in the sound of the Fish's Vanguard recordings, produced by Sam Charters. Charters was a pioneering folklorist who had produced numerous folk, blues, and jug band recordings for Prestige during the folk revival, and by the late '60s was making exciting electric blues recordings for Vanguard with Chicago greats like Junior Wells and Buddy Guy. But, thinks Melton, "Sam didn't know how to record rock 'n' roll. Our recordings are drier than a lot of the rock recordings of the period. They have a sort [of] almost classic finish. Those records don't sound the way we sounded. Because we were playing louder, at a more distorted pace, than other people seemed to be able to capture on vinyl. They made us turn down for it."

No musicians had a more vexing time capturing their essence on record than the Grateful Dead. They would over time play to more concertgoers than any other rock band, but they were far from being established album-sellers in the 1960s. Their evolution on record was a long, strange trip, as the cliché goes, but also a painful one at times for both musicians and listeners. More than any band before or since, the Dead were an amorphous hodgepodge of influences, from down-home R&B and traditional folk to bluegrass and Stockhausen. It was hard for those outside their large cult of devoted live followers and drug ingesters (who were often one and the same) to get a handle on the music. Determining whether their fabled space jams or easygoing folk-country-rock tunes were more central to their appeal would be opening as many fights as a debate at the 1965 Newport Folk Festival over folk vs. rock.

The less lysergically inclined listener, however, will almost always find the Dead's most folk-oriented material their most accessible. Their figurehead, both in image and music, was Jerry Garcia, who not coincidentally was the member most schooled in folk music, having played bluegrass banjo and folk guitar throughout the first half of the 1960s. He even traveled through the South in 1964 to tape bluegrass bands. "But the more I got into it [folk], the more it became obvious to me that it was kind of a closed circle," he told Ralph J. Gleason in *The Jefferson Airplane and the San Francisco Sound*. But bluegrass would remain a factor in much of the Dead's music, Garcia translating the fluidity and jazz-folk synthesis of bluegrass runs to electric psychedelia, the band's harmonies bearing the stamp of high, lonesome multipart bluegrass vocal parts.

Folk-rock was a part of the Dead's arsenal from their very first studio recordings for Autumn Records in November 1965, six of which are now available on the box set *The Golden Road*. Those demos included a rocked-up "I Know You Rider" (done by many folk revival acts and by the Byrds in a brazen 1966 electric version that wasn't released until the 1980s), and an off-kilter take on Gordon Lightfoot's "Early Morning Rain" that added characteristic exotic mutated melodic/vocal harmonic tangents in latter parts of the verses. Yet even then the musicians were flying all over the place, with inscrutable stoned, fractured originals like "Mindbender (Confusion's Prince)" and gruff Them-like R&B on "Caution (Do Not Stop on Tracks)." Throughout the rest of the 1960s the Dead remained an exasperatingly frustrating proposition on record, not just due to the infinite canvas of stylistic dabblings, but also due to their erratic qualities as interpreters, songwriters, and musicians. Deadheads would find it heretical, but for more objective listeners, on the early Dead albums there is no getting around the oft-mediocre R&B covers; their severe limitations as lead vocalists; their shortage of first-class original tunes; and the impenetrability of their more free-form jams, reaching an apex on 1968's *Anthem of the Sun*.

Yet the Grateful Dead were resourceful in their excavation of interesting source material to cover, at a time when that art was largely backseated by leading rock bands in favor of original compositions. Their first album alone, a rushed-sounding debut, included fairly radical reworkings of jug band blues like "Viola Lee Blues" (originally by Cannon's Jug Stompers, led by "Walk Right In" composer Gus Cannon) and "Sitting on Top of the World" (by the Mississippi Sheiks); "Cold Rain and Snow," learned by Garcia from traditional banjo player Obray Ramsey; and "Morning Dew," one in a long line of folk-rock covers of the song first recorded by Bonnie Dobson. By 1969's *Auxomoxoa*, the Dead were proving capable of turning out some affecting, first-class gentle, coun-trified folk-rock with a mystical halo on originals like "St. Stephen" and "China Cat Sunflower."

The Dead would not make the best of either the studio or the possibilities inherent in their folk-rock synthesis until 1970, on the *Workingman's Dead* and *American Beauty* albums. Here the focus was, for the first time, on real *songs* that organically blended nineteenth- and twentieth-century Americana, rather than on a vaguer all-paths-are-one sensibility. Garcia's newfound love for pedal steel guitar gave the songs a country-rock edge. The Crosby, Stills & Nash–indebted har-monies of familiar Dead standbys like "Uncle's John Band" wisely emphasized the vocalists' abil-ities as country-folk-rock harmonizers instead of highlighting their disabilities as lead singers.

Frequent lyrical input from Robert Hunter gave many of the songs a narrative old West qual-ity. "It was a surprise to us, as it was to everyone else, that this machine-eating monster psyche-delic band is suddenly putting out sweet, listenable material," he said while discussing this era in the Grateful Dead video documentary *Anthem to Beauty*. As in the late-'60s work by the Band, while many of the musical and lyrical references dated back to before 1900, the counterculture could nonetheless find in the Grateful Dead's skewed Americana elements that mirrored its own struggles and joys in the present. The Dead may have been behind every other major band of the 1960s in perfecting their brand of folk-rock, but in one respect the slowest tortoise won the race, as their popularity continually expanded over the next 25 years, when most of their original com-petitors had long disbanded.

But the Dead, other than on (arguably) *Workingman's Dead* and *American Beauty*, never were a folk-rock band. As with some of the major British rock bands of the 1960s, they and other San Francisco groups used folk-rock as an influence, or just one of a range of possible approaches. The difference, however, was that folk music was a much greater influence in Bay Area psychedelia than it was in British rock. Quicksilver Messenger Service is most remembered as a jammin' psy-chedelic band, taking off for extended blues-rock gallops on the back of John Cippolina's distinctly quivering guitar. Yet it also made some sturdy, no-nonsense harmony folk-rock, particularly on the grab bag of songs that ex-folkie David Freiberg brought into its set, such as "Codine," "Babe I'm Gonna Leave You," and Hamilton Camp's "Pride of Man." Rogue folkie Dino Valenti might have been in the band when it started in the mid-'60s, in fact, but got busted for drugs before even rehearsing with the other musicians once. The group kept the flame burning for him by putting Valenti's "Dino's Song" on its first album, and Valenti would eventually join (and in fact take over leadership of) the group at the end of the '60s.

Elsewhere in the San Francisco scene, Moby Grape, with ex-Airplane drummer Skip Spence as one of its songwriters and three guitarists, seamlessly wove country and folk traces into its en-ergetic, slightly psychedelicized roots rock. When the folk elements were at their most ascendant, this band crafted some of its best work, with the spine-tingling melodies of songs like "Sitting By the Window," "Bitter Wind," and "It's a Beautiful Day Today" disguising a sober melancholy. Cree-dence Clearwater Revival, the premiere roots-rock band of all time, always made everything sound like rock, rather than blues-rock, country-rock, folk-rock, or what have you. Still, it's worth mentioning that the group's *Willy and the Poor Boys* album (from late 1969) included two songs, "Cotton Fields" and "The Midnight Special," that must have been in the early repertoire of uncounted musicians—folk and rock, from both sides of the ocean—in the days when they were first mastering their instruments.

Behind the Bay Area front lines, Mad River, the obscure but interesting Berkeley band that released two Capitol albums in the late '60s, put odd, glistening dissonances into its guitars and bad-trip lyrics into its best material. Yet its leader, Lawrence Hammond (whose quavering, sorrowful vocals made Marty Balin's lovelorn ballads sound like Happy Hour in comparison), was a transplanted Midwestern folkie. Downcast folk effectively contrasted with clashing pyrotechnic guitars in Mad River's "Orange Fire," one of the great overlooked anti-Vietnam songs (only available in the 1960s on a self-released EP), and closed its somewhat chaotic debut album with a brief but eerie acoustic piece, "Hush Julian," highlighting Hammond's ghostly Aeolian singing.

And even if San Francisco bands left purer folk-rock territory for psychedelic extemporizing, they usually both revisited their folk roots effectively from time to time and deployed them to color their overall scheme. Grace Slick's "Lather" was certainly a ballad in the best storytelling tradition, albeit given a psychedelic sheen by judicious sound effects and its bizarre tale of an adult mired in childhood. The Airplane's cover of Fred Neil's "The Other Side of This Life," with extended psychedelic guitar solos and rousing ensemble harmonies, was a mainstay of its live shows, as captured on its concert album *Bless Its Pointed Little Head*. And while the Airplane's *Volunteers* 1969 album is most remembered for the antiestablishment manifesto of the title track and the Paul Kantner–David Crosby–Stephen Stills collaboration "Wooden Ships," one of its highlights was the adaptation of the traditional gospel-blues song "Good Shepherd," with some of Jorma Kaukonen's best bee-stinging guitar. "Certainly the harmonies always betrayed the folkie roots," says Kaukonen of the band's post-*Surrealistic Pillow* output. "And of course, 'Good Shepherd' was in my repertoire for many years before the band."

On the same LP, even "We Can Be Together" and "Volunteers" itself had spun their principal riffs off a bluegrass lick that Kantner got from David Crosby. The same lick grounds the Grateful Dead's "St. Stephen," though no one seems to know the actual bluegrass or folk song from which it arose. In that sense, even late-'60s psychedelic rock could still, on occasion, evince strong links to the folk process at the core of the folk tradition, building new songs out of sources whose exact origins and authors had become lost to time.

After the dust had cleared for historical inspection, the question lingered: How was it that so many San Francisco folkies made the near-lightning dash to psychedelic rock, pausing for barely a breath at the folk-rock junction? The most prosaic reason is that the folk-rock stopover was not as well documented on record in San Francisco as it was in other regions. Jefferson Airplane was the only leading Bay Area folk-rock-to-psychedelia band to release an album before 1967, and that LP, *Jefferson Airplane Takes Off*, remains its only pure folk-rock statement. Not until the Airplane,

Country Joe & the Fish, Big Brother & the Holding Company, the Grateful Dead, Quicksilver Messenger Service, and the Steve Miller Band played at the Monterey Pop Festival in June 1967 did the media pay serious attention to the region's rock scene.

Not only were big labels slower to pick up on the San Francisco scene than they were on similar bursts of activity in New York and L.A., but the musicians were less eager to get involved with the record companies, and indeed with the whole commercial stardom trip. They were less concerned with making it big than with having fun, hanging out, and making the music they wanted. So it was that the Grateful Dead's debut LP didn't appear until 1967; Quicksilver's not until 1968; and the Charlatans' sole, little-noticed album not until 1969. Some didn't even get that far. Blackburn & Snow didn't even have an LP release. Transplanted Northwesterners PH Phactor Jug Band, hailed by Kaleidoscope's Chris Darrow as "the best jug band ever," did just one obscure jug band-into-folk-rock single, 1967's "Minglewood Blues," which was indeed just about the most convincing cross between jug band folk and blues-rock ever issued.

As Phil Elwood wrote in *Billboard* in May 1967, "The rock scene here is folk-based music with virtually no connections with old-fashioned show business." There were few other cities where bands regularly played their music for nothing in outdoor spaces like the Panhandle of Golden Gate Park, adjoining Haight-Ashbury, which saw free shows by the likes of the Dead and Big Brother. "When we came to Boston, we had to practically break the law and go up against all kinds of crap to set up in a park and play for free," says Banana of the Youngbloods, who would move from the East Coast to San Francisco in part to plug into the more easygoing and generous Haight-Ashbury spirit. "And we'd get sued by the club owner because we did that. Massachusetts is much more uptight."

Even some independent labels had trouble grokking the Bay Area's different way of doing things. Country Joe & the Fish were Vanguard Records' only major success in signing a West Coast rock band, and Barry Melton thinks "they never really understood, appreciated, or wanted to be, really, in the rock music business." He agrees with more conventional folk and folk-rock Vanguard artists that the company was actually more focused on classical music than pop, "because they considered it to be a safer bet, more revenue-producing, and a better investment over the long run." Yet he does realize a label like Vanguard probably afforded more freedom to record the Fish's controversial lyrics than even some other indies might have allowed. "They were very much moved by the Left, had very principled ideals, and very much stood by our political stance. I don't think they understood the drug thing *at all*. But they backed us up politically. And I *know* that would not have been possible on one of the major labels. I'm not sure it would have been possible with Elektra. So maybe we were where we were supposed to be, based on the content of what we were doing.

"It was the biggest company we could go to who would afford us that level of freedom, and still have unrestricted content. Although not everything was unrestricted. Like, our second album cover is totally retouched, 'cause it offended [Vanguard executives] Maynard [Solomon] and Seymour [Solomon]'s father, who was in the art department. In reality, on the second cover, I'm wearing a full-dress Nazi uniform with a swastika on the sleeve, and Gary Hirsh was wearing a pope outfit with a real pope hat. But that offended them. It would be a depiction of a real Catholic priest, and a real Nazi officer. To us, though, the symbolism had a lot of shock value."

Still, like the Sunset Strip folk-rock stars, some of the Haight-Ashbury big shots would eventually use the establishment to promote their product in ways that seem contrived or even ludicrous now. Dick Clark interviewed Jefferson Airplane about hippie life on *American Bandstand*, and on *The Smothers Brothers*, the Airplane played snatches of the Rascals' "People Got to Be Free" during a never-ending, not-so-funny comic variety sketch based around the song. Even more memorable was the sight of Jerry Garcia and Hugh Hefner bantering about Haight-Ashbury at the bar in early 1969 on *Playboy After Dark*. The Airplane also did honest-to-god radio commercials for Levi's jeans. (Not that such an endeavor was rare among supposedly antiestablishment acts; the Rolling Stones had done a jingle for Rice Krispies in 1964, and even Tom Paxton wrote the unforgettable "My Dog's Bigger than Your Dog" jingle for a TV commercial for Ken-L-Ration dog food.)

"A lot of the groups were not focused on being real popular, like pop stars, except for maybe the Jefferson Airplane," says Peter Albin. "Initially, they started out wanting to be a group that would make some money. Just from the standpoint of, here's a guy [Balin] who's auditioning, trying to find people who will fit into his concept. Big Brother didn't really do that, and a lot of other groups didn't. They were people who were friends together. I didn't audition people. It just kind of fell together. I don't remember listening to, like, three or four guitar players. It was the guy who came over and started playing with us.

"Basically, Big Brother was all from the people either who lived in the same house or hung around the same house. We weren't calculating. I think that the Airplane, particularly Marty Balin, was: 'What kind of musician, what type of musician will work well within my idea, my concept of a rock group.' And he was definitely basing it on the Byrds. They definitely got into the psychedelic stuff a lot more than people expected. I mean, talk about long solos and things. Jorma took as long solos as Garcia did, along with Casady too. *I* never took solos that long."

T he rapid evolution of live music in the Bay Area was another spark igniting its quick journey from folk to psychedelia. By 1967, the live rock circuit—in San Francisco, but all over, really—had expanded from clubs and just-ex-coffeehouses to ballrooms and auditoriums such as San Francisco's vaunted Fillmore and Avalon. More volume was needed to project to larger audiences; more crazed energy was needed to keep pace with the audience's drug intake, wilder behavior, and accompanying light shows that were often used as a backdrop. This couldn't help but be reflected in the music. "I've played acoustic guitar in the modern Fillmore auditorium, and it fills up the whole place," says Barry Melton. "But if I had stepped on that stage in 1967 and tried to play acoustic guitar, you wouldn't have hardly been able to hear it. The sound system just couldn't deal with it. So the only way you were going to impress anybody is to have a stack of amplifiers, and then you could make the place rock. The only way that you could propel music to a really big crowd, in the '60s, was with amplified music."

Other obvious catalysts toward psychedelicization were, of course, drugs. It's easy for pie-eyed, tie-dyed young Deadheads to ascribe much or even most of the brilliance of San Francisco acid rock to the properties of acid itself. Nothing memorable would have come of the movement if it hadn't been crowded with talented songwriters, singers, and instrumentalists. But drug-taking did fuel new musical and lyrical patterns, a practice dating back to before Haight-Ashbury and folk-rock, not just in jazz but also in folk music. Drugs had entered the rock scene with a vengeance right around the time that folk-rock broke. "I recall that a jazz musician friend of mine who had been drafted and sent to Germany returned on leave a year later—in the summer of '65—and I took him to hear the Byrds," recalls Gary Marker of the Rising Sons. "Hanging with the newer generation of rock musicians, he was absolutely stunned that in just 12 short months grass had made the leap from being something only jazz musicians did to a much broader youth/rock 'n' roll culture."

"A lot of the people that were into folk were also into other kinds of music and very eclectic," points out Albin. "I think most of 'em were fairly well-educated, liked all different kinds of music, and allowed themselves to experiment with music while they were experimenting with drugs. I think drugs does have a part to play here. You talk to anybody from New York, and when they came out from New York and would find some hippies here in San Francisco and we'd give 'em a joint, they couldn't fucking believe the joints. They were twice the size, twice the power. It would zonk you out on a whole different kind of level."

Drugs could, though not necessarily did, go hand in hand with the absorption of nonrock and nonfolk influences into folk-rock. Barry Melton characterizes psychedelic rock as "a folk-rock idiom borrowing from jazz's ability to incorporate improvisation. Folk musicians improvised anyway. The only thing 'psychedelic' music did was, it jazz-ized folk music. Musicologically speaking, it was logical at a time when Miles Davis and Doc Watson existed on the same plane. You have a time when there's all these elements coming together, because of the power of the media, and the intermixing of people from different backgrounds.

"In the early days, I think it fair to say that the Dead, Fish, Airplane, Quicksilver, and Big Brother had one thing in common: Any of those bands might get up on stage and do ten songs for an hour, or they might do one song for ten hours! Well, one song for ten hours is no doubt an exaggeration, but it was not uncommon for us to get up on the stage so loaded that we did one song for an hour and a half, or two hours, after which a bunch of really anxious management types began drawing lines with their fingers across their throats and we somehow ended in some manner. Why would anyone do one song for two hours, you ask? Simple: We were all so loaded we had no sense of time whatsoever. Recording, of course, 'cured' us all of our ramble-on tendencies."

World music also played a significant part, as did experimental acoustic folk-based musicians such as John Fahey, whose influence on Country Joe & the Fish was already noted, and Sandy Bull, who drew from Middle Eastern, Indian, Latin, Spanish, blues, gospel, and other styles on his mid-'60s Vanguard albums (sometimes using electric guitar, and even a rock rhythm section on his cover of Chuck Berry's "Memphis"). Feels Melton, "If you listen to 'Eight Miles High,' [the] solo in there, that stuff is close" to what Bull did. He adds, "I was a big Hamza El Din fan. Kimio Eto mixed the traditional Japanese koto with a sort of American influence. I learned from both of them, 'cause I heard both of them play a lot in Southern California when I was growing up. So I brought that with me, that sort of Japanese and Middle Eastern influence, and Indian ragaesque thing." Occasionally such all-purpose eclecticism could work against the musicians; numerous otherwise fine early folk-rock albums suffered from what seemed liked an unspoken obligation to throw on a weak jug band novelty or straight blues tune, almost as if to prove that the groups could do everything, though not do everything well. But at its best, the same spirit led musicians to hit thrilling peaks that folk and rock alone—and not even folk-rock itself—could not have scaled.

If the square root of why so many folk-rock musicians dove into psychedelia might seem apparent when the entire folk-rock revolution is taken into account, it's rarely been cited. For ultimately, in expanding from folk-rock to psychedelia, the musicians were only continuing to feed the same hunger that had led them into folk music in the first place. The voracious acquisition of folkloric ballads, contemporary protest tracts from *Sing Out!* sheet music, traditional American folk songs from Alan Lomax– and Harry Smith–assembled collections, and even more exotic recordings and songbooks was the same restless, self-actualizing impulse that had led so many into folk-rock. The subsequent admission of influences from free jazz, Indian music, and drugs was essentially a continuation of the same eclecticism that had been driving the musicians since they were teenagers in the late '50s. Barry McGuire had seen this coming in *Melody Maker* in late 1965, where he predicted, "The folk-rock controversial songs are just the beginning. Soon there'll be sounds that people have never dreamed of—the integration of Eastern and Western music. The Eastern scales and quarter tones will integrate well with rock 'n' roll music. The Byrds, the Beatles and others are already doing it."

Nat Hentoff was one of the critics to pick up on it at the time, presciently writing in *The American Folksong Revival* book in 1967: "The message of the new folk music can only be fully apprehended through the total medium—instrumental textures and ways of singing as well as the lyrics themselves. It is, therefore, all the more essential for the new folk performers to construct instrumental colors and rhythms and new singing voices that can be corollaries for the new expanded verbal language. And that construction, still inchoate, has begun. The use of Indian instruments by the Beatles, the Byrds and Donovan. The experimenting with more complex metrical patterns. The increasingly venturesome play with electronic possibilities. The kind of open listening that leads Paul Simon to say: 'I'm learning to play the sitar and I'm fascinated by the singing in intervals of seconds by those Bulgarians. You see, the new pop music can incorporate all those influences, and more.'"

The difference between the new folk-rock-psychedelic musicians and previous folk-based artists was that, having found one style that stoked their simultaneous urges for musical and social stimulation, they didn't feel bound to stay there and both play and defend it to death. That applied not just to acoustic folk, but also to folk-rock. They felt no obligation to either establish or adhere to rigorous party-line boundaries within folk-rock, or even to remain folk-rock artists. And, just as vitally, they had a new, younger audience that wasn't hung up on purist dedication as were the folk revivalists. These new listeners were as anxious as the artists to investigate new directions and combinations. Very few folk-rock fans were going to feel betrayed by a folk-rock act's branching into areas other than folk-rock, as long as the music was good.

The folk-rock-to-psychedelia syndrome may have been more prevalent and rapid in San Francisco than anywhere else, but it was hardly limited to the Bay Area. In Los Angeles, the city's three best folk-rock bands—the Byrds, Buffalo Springfield, and Love—all made some of their greatest music in 1967 by widening their periscopes into all manners of psychedelic rock, orchestral rock, country-rock, and more. For the Byrds, it was an especially interesting and troubled year, yielding some of their greatest recorded music, most embarrassing live performances, and the ultimate cracking of the core that had thrust them to folk-rock's forefront.

2

forever changes

folk-rock psychedelicized,
from sunset strip to outer space

On October 7, 1966, a poker-faced CBS press release announced "The Byrd's [sic] Million Dollar Insurance Policy" against abduction by aliens. "Tickner-Dickson, the management representatives of the Byrds, recently revealed that they have taken extreme precautionary measures in the interest of their clients," it solemnly began. "Eddie Tickner reports that he has taken out a US $1,000,000 insurance policy with Lloyds of London against the loss of the Byrds to outer space." After all the group had, soberly explained the release, invited aliens to take them on a tour of the galaxies in its new single "Mr. Spaceman," taken from mid-1966's *Fifth Dimension* album. In a way it was a logical extension of Roger McGuinn's pleas to be taken on a trip inside Mr. Tambourine Man's magic swirling ship on the band's first hit single.

The Byrds, needless to say, never did make that physical journey to the cosmos. Even as they did their best to take that trip in mind and spirit, they did not survive the journey intact, becoming prey to the kind of all-too-earthly personality conflicts and artistic clashes that have broken up many a rock band. But in their first incarnation's last year in orbit, their fourth and fifth albums would take their listeners as close to the outer limits as could be done with a mere phonograph record.

Other than a couple of misfires, *Younger Than Yesterday*, released in early 1967, was their best album besides *Mr. Tambourine Man*, and more progressive in many ways. David Crosby had finally blossomed into a first-class composer with "Renaissance Fair" (a collaboration with Roger McGuinn, but more David's song), a beatific report on an early flower child gathering of the same name, and his jazzy, brooding "Everybody's Been Burned," garnished by a typically outstanding McGuinn 12-string solo. Chris Hillman had suddenly developed into a singer-songwriter of note, contributing both straightforward and Beatlesque folk-rock (although "Thoughts and Words" included a spellbinding backwards guitar solo). He was also responsible for the groundbreaking proto-country-rock on "Time Between" and "The Girl with No Name," both of which featured ex-Kentucky Colonels picker and soon-to-be-Byrd Clarence White.

McGuinn indulged his space cowboy fixation with "C.T.A.-102," with extraterrestrial voice effects and electronic blips counterpointing a lyric of hope that musical messages from earth could be heard by aliens. He's come closer to his wish than most in his place: The song was referred to by Dr. Eugene Epstein in *The Astrophysical Journal*, and "Mr. Spaceman" was eventually used to wake up astronauts on the space shuttle. Underneath the cosmic messages in both "Mr. Space-man" and "C.T.A.-102," though, were solid country-influenced folk-rock tunes that could have easily been adapted by bluegrass bands.

Younger Than Yesterday also contained the Byrds' final pair of Top 40 singles. "So You Want to Be a Rock & Roll Star" was, again, evidence of an unsurpassed eclecticism with the recruitment of esteemed South African jazzman Hugh Masekela to play the song's distinctive scat trumpet lines during the instrumental break. The witty, wry McGuinn-Hillman lyric betrayed a disillusionment with the star-making machinery of the rock biz (which they had been a part of themselves, albeit more on their own terms than most bands were allowed), and McGuinn's guitar once again effectively brought a jazz lilt to the 12-string.

"My Back Pages," ironically considering its lyric about turning a back on the past, was a retreat to the device that had brought them the stardom they mocked in "So You Want to Be a Rock & Roll Star": an electrified cover of an acoustic Bob Dylan song. Whether it signified a regression was irrelevant, though, as the result was a magnificent reinterpretation that transformed a Dylan dirge to a sparkling mid-tempo rocker. McGuinn cooked up yet another classic opening 12-string line and solo, while the Byrds' harmonies on the chorus both gave it commercial clout and added much-needed tenderness to the song's key declarations of finding renewed youth by abandoning the too-earnest philosophizing of the past. The song had been suggested for the album by Jim Dickson, on his way out as the Byrds' co-manager (he would officially leave in mid-1967). He had urged McGuinn to record it from his car window when he and Roger, in separate cars, happened to pull up alongside each other in traffic.

Younger Than Yesterday and its follow-up album, *The Notorious Byrd Brothers* (issued in the first week of 1968), are now revered as two of the great 1960s albums by historians and fans. At the time, though, the Byrds were considered by many to be waning. Their albums and singles weren't selling nearly as well as they had in 1965 and early 1966, and they were not rated highly as a live band. Particularly notorious was their haphazard set at the Monterey Pop Festival, where Crosby heartily endorsed LSD onstage, and preceded "He Was a Friend of Mine" with a rant decrying the conspiracy to cover up the truth behind the Kennedy assassination. "I want to say it anyway, even though they will edit it out," Crosby announced, referring to the documentary D.A. Pennebaker was making of the festival. And sure enough, the Byrds didn't make the *Monterey Pop* movie, but for musical reasons, according to Pennebaker: "I wanted to fly the whole way. I thought that kind of grounded us."

"It's funny," muses Hillman. "We went from being better live in the early days to better in the studio later on, and became too lackadaisical on stage. We were a better studio band as the years went by. We made some good records, we made some silly ones. But everybody else does, too." Dean Webb of the Dillards, who supported the Byrds on some shows during their mid-'60s peak, remembers how their volume, which had so profoundly affected their original audience at the Ciro's club in Los Angeles in early 1965, did not always translate well to large concerts: "I'd see people get up and leave, because it was so loud they couldn't stand it. A lot of times, they'd have their amplifiers on stage behind them so loud they were drowning out their own vocals. There was a little competition between them. Somebody'd turn up, and somebody next to 'em would notice, and they'd turn their thing up another notch or two, or whatever. It was competitive. And that's crazy, 'cause once you drowned out your own singing, that's absurd. You got a wall of noise going up there." And the lackadaisical attitude Hillman admits to did not go unnoticed in late 1967, when Tracy Thomas groused in *NME*, "Why they continue to do 'Eight Miles High' without learning the harmony remains a mystery."

Crosby sat in for an absent Neil Young in Buffalo Springfield's set at Monterey Pop Festival, and the Byrds were beginning to feel that they might be better off without the temperamental singer-songwriter for good. He did make important contributions to *The Notorious Byrd Brothers* as a principal writer on three of its best songs, but was becoming more vocal in rancorous disputes over what material to record. Some of his compositions, such as the ménage à trois ballad "Triad" (later recorded by Jefferson Airplane), were being passed over; Crosby in turn was uninterested in participating in some sessions he thought inappropriate, such as those for their cover of Gerry Goffin and Carole King's song "Goin' Back." McGuinn and Hillman had had enough, and fired him in late 1967, leaving a wounded Crosby to take leave of the music business for a while before helping to found a group that would be much bigger than the Byrds ever were.

"He was becoming insufferable," McGuinn told *Goldmine* almost 35 years later. "He really didn't like us anymore. He was angry with all the rest of The Byrds. He would say things like, 'You guys aren't good enough musicians to be playing with me.' Stuff like that. We just went, 'Well who needs this?'" In the same piece, Crosby admitted, "I don't think I was easy to get along with or work with then. I think I was young and egotistical and wanting more space for myself—more writing and more credit. It's very unfortunate. I think it was one of the best musical chemistries ever."

Drummer Michael Clarke also drifted away in late 1967, and McGuinn and Hillman were left to complete much of *The Notorious Byrd Brothers* on their own, with help from some session men like Clarence White and drummer Jim Gordon. Clarke has been dismissed as a pretty-boy thumper who only got the drum seat because he looked right, but though he was the least creative of the original Byrds, his contribution wasn't superfluous. "When Michael Clarke first got in the Byrds, he didn't know how to play drums," says future Byrds drummer Gene Parsons, who just a year later would be in Clarke's place. "He had his cardboard box. So for him to have done what he did . . . he actually ended up with a sound that you could hear him play and go, 'Hey, there's Michael playing.' It's rare for a drummer to actually have a distinctive sound playing that kind of music. My hat's off to him."

Although the album was very good, the devastating consequences of the breakup of the original Byrds lineup cannot be overstated. The Byrds were folk-rock's central figures, in much the same way as the Beatles were the British Invasion's guiding lights. The loss of Gene Clark in 1966 had been papered over without significant damage. But Crosby, for all his peccadilloes, was a different matter.

In addition to his musical assets, imagewise he and McGuinn were the ultimate complementary opposites of L.A. rock, with Crosby the irascible grinning socialite, McGuinn the stoic epitome of cool. Roger's Ben Franklin glasses were now gone, having blown off while he was on a motorcycle. But his eccentric image as the ultimate rock 'n' roll scientist was maintained by a confession to *Flip* magazine that his ambition was to plug his Rickenbacker 12-string into a color TV and watch the patterns change, and a demonstration of his voice-activated one-foot-tall home robot for one inquisitive reporter. (Back in 1965, when an *NME* scribe had asked about a slide rule in McGuinn's jacket pocket, he responded cryptically, "I always carry it, just in case.")

Actor/screenwriter/producer Peter Fonda even told Roger that McGuinn and Crosby were the role models for Fonda and Dennis Hopper's respective parts in the 1969 film *Easy Rider*. One wonders if the Byrds' beneficent view of outer space aliens—as heard in "Mr. Spaceman" and "C.T.A.-102," and expounded upon quite directly by McGuinn and Crosby on their *Fifth Dimension* promo interview disc—influenced the scene in *Easy Rider* in which Jack Nicholson tells Fonda and Hopper about similarly benign outer-space onlookers. At any rate, the yin-yang between McGuinn and Crosby was irreplaceable, even after the Byrds drafted in Gene Clark to take Crosby's place; Clark, still not up to flying or touring, left after just three weeks.

But the Byrds were not the tightest of friends, and had not known each other that well or that long before they had formed in 1964. "The Byrds were five very different people that would have probably not hung out together without the common interest," believes Dickson. "The plus was that there was someone for everyone. The minus, lack of a sense of unity of purpose. Everyone tried to politic for what they thought was the right way to go."

Hillman now acknowledges that the loss of Dickson (whose exit was accompanied by the loss of more business-oriented Byrds co-manager Eddie Tickner) was more important than they might have realized at the time. "It got a little personal, as things do, and things didn't always roll as smoothly as they should. Dickson gets a lot of credit for this whole deal. He set this thing on track. And we derailed it ourselves. When we didn't listen to him, we cut a couple of stupid things on the records. We didn't have the schoolteacher leading us into the classroom. It started to splinter." The inclusion of a vicious argument in the studio as a bonus track on the expanded CD of *The Notorious Byrd Brothers* is a convincing document of the tension, with Michael Clarke the target of particularly cruel taunts.

The band was, says Hillman, "just starting its descent into hell then. And there was Roger and I in the breach, having had our fallout with David, in finishing this record with [producer] Gary Usher. Roger and I got more as a team in *Notorious Byrd Brothers*, when we started to play around in the studio with stuff. McGuinn's always been a real joy to work with. He's a real professional in the studio. Roger has impeccable time as a musician." And fortunately, there was enough professionalism and cessation of hostilities to ensure that *The Notorious Byrd Brothers* was worthy of the band's name, even if the Byrds were essentially down to a duo by the time it was released.

Notorious was, like all previous Byrds albums, an extension of McGuinn's "electronic magazine" concept of full-length recordings, but now with a more savvy electronic sheen than ever. "Tribal Gathering" was, like "Renaissance Fair," another enticing portrait of a major countercultural event, this time inspired by the 1967 Human Be In at San Francisco's Golden Gate Park. McGuinn took another ingenious trick out of his bag by creating the dolphin sounds of "Dolphin's Smile" with his fingernails on the neck of his Rickenbacker, leading into another playful, engaging Crosby-dominated collaboration. The then-new Moog and Red Rhodes's steel guitar made for a typical optimal Byrdsian blend of rustic past and electronic future on the Hillman-penned "Natural Harmony."

"Old John Robertson" gave a preview of the Byrds' subsequent jaunt into country-rock, and they proved their mettle at translating Goffin-King songs into pure folk-rock with "Wasn't Born to Follow" and "Goin' Back," the latter gifted by yet another great 12-string solo. "Draft Morning" was the Byrds' gentle, understated contribution to the folk-rock anti-Vietnam protest canon. (It was also the source of considerable annoyance to Crosby, angered by McGuinn and Hillman's addition of lyrics after his departure.) "Space Odyssey" was the Byrds' furthest-reaching electronic voyage, with a McGuinn-R.J. Hippard song that could have been mistaken for a sea shanty taken to 2001 by exotic synthesizer overwashes. No other Byrds track reached at once so far back to the past and so far into the future. McGuinn had notions of taking that concept even further with the Byrds' next album. But "Space Odyssey" was as far as he ever got, due in part to the fashion in which Hillman and newcomer Gram Parsons would become co-captains of the group's ship in 1968.

As the Byrds were imploding, their close rivals Buffalo Springfield had also plowed through a particularly fractious year that saw some of its best music and sowed the seeds for its demise. It had begun splendidly, with Stephen Stills's "For What It's Worth" giving the group its only Top Ten hit, and making a fair bid for the title of best protest rock song of the 1960s. Motivated by youth riots on Sunset Strip as police cracked down on the Hollywood counterculture by enforcing a curfew, its cause might seem trivial when compared to, say, tens of thousands of young American soldiers (and many times more Vietnamese soldiers and civilians) getting killed half a world away. Yet struggles against authority for the right for youth to enjoy and express themselves were important too, even for the relatively privileged youth of Beverly Hills and Hollywood. Folk-rock giants were in the forefront of the struggle, politically if not literally, with Byrds co-manager Jim Dickson organizing CAFF (Community Action For Facts And Freedom) to fight and demonstrate against police brutality and the rampant pro-development forces who wanted youth venues off the Strip. The Byrds played a benefit concert in support of CAFF in February 1967, and ultimately the more rabid schemes to harass youth and overdevelop the Strip were halted.

Stills was actually in San Francisco, not L.A., when these riots took place, but still captured the essence of the conflict well. What lifted it above similar missives of the period, though, was a considered ambiguity that both described and cast a critical eye on the actions of both the police and the protesters. That and, of course, an immediately memorable call-and-response chorus, and Neil Young's inimitable sustained ringing harmonic notes throughout the track.

Barry Friedman aka Frazier Mohawk, who had roadied for the early Byrds and acted as early manager/mentor of Buffalo Springfield, sees songs such as "For What It's Worth" embodying a form of folk-rock protest very specific to the era. "What was interesting about that time was that there were so many people doing kind of protest songs, but nobody was really pissed off," he points out.

Buffalo Springfield. Left to right: Stephen Stills, Bruce Palmer, Dewey Martin, Neil Young, and Richie Furay.

"It was a time when they felt that the song itself, that the song that they wrote, could be the weapon against the invader, or the establishment, the status quo. Yet the song would have an effect. It actually had power. I think you don't see much of that, except maybe in some of the rap stuff now. It's political, but it still isn't moving large numbers of people.

"People who stand for somebody else's beliefs, stand for your beliefs, so you associate with the cause; there *aren't* a lot of those folks now. But they said what we couldn't say ourselves, for us. They weren't really *angry*. Earlier, at the beginning [of folk-rock, the Byrds'] 'He Was a Friend of Mine,' 'Turn! Turn! Turn!,' all of those—they weren't *angry* songs. But they certainly were protest songs."

Buffalo Springfield was unable to build on the single's success as well as it should have, due to a series of calamities and internal strife. Bassist Bruce Palmer was deported for several months in early 1967 after a drug bust. Neil Young quit and returned to the group on more than one occasion, including a couple months in the middle of the year that saw him out of the lineup that played the Monterey Pop Festival. Ken Koblun (from Young's old Winnipeg band the Squires), Jim Fielder, and the Daily Flash's Doug Hastings all served brief tours of duty before being unceremoniously discarded. In the studio, songwriters were lobbying for space for their own compositions, sometimes at the expense of working as a team. Some of the tracks ended up as, essentially, solo vehicles with contributions by bandmates. Out of this messy confusion emerged the group's finest record, *Buffalo Springfield Again*.

It could be fairly argued that *Buffalo Springfield Again* is not either folk-rock or psychedelic. It was all over the place, reflecting the rapidly eclectic widening of their tastes and influences, beyond folk and rock to country, jazz, and soul. In an interview with *Hit Parader* shortly after the album's release, Stills cited a rather breathless resume of current favorite influences, including Jimi Hendrix,

Eric Clapton, bluesman Albert King, Moby Grape, the Beach Boys, Judy Collins, Ian & Sylvia, Arlo Guthrie's "Alice's Restaurant," and jazz greats Miles Davis, Horace Silver, and Dave Brubeck. While not as lengthy, Young's list was similarly diverse, taking in country pianist Floyd Cramer, British instrumental legends the Shadows, the Doors, the Youngbloods, Moby Grape, and the still-undisputed titans of rock, the Beatles and the Rolling Stones. Indeed, Young's "Mr. Soul," which led off the album, was rather too blatant in its cop of the main riff from the Stones' "(I Can't Get No) Satisfaction."

But when you came down to it, folk-rock was still at the heart of *Buffalo Springfield Again*'s strength and attraction. Stills's "Bluebird" might have been a smoky hard rock tune, but the arc of its harmonies and the sparkle of its acoustic guitar runs were folk-fried, and the drumless banjo-led section that ends the track is pure bluegrass. His "Rock & Roll Woman," which cried to be a hit single but somehow stalled outside the Top 40, was a classic of folk-rock harmonizing and 12-string guitar riffs. Stills came up with the tune after jamming at David Crosby's house, and Crosby sang harmony on a lyric (inspired by Grace Slick) deftly echoing the freewheeling spirit of '67.

Young offered his most poignant abstract love song with "Expecting to Fly," in reality a solo piece with epochal psychedelic-orchestral production by Jack Nitzsche, given a folk flavor by his distinctive reverbed country-folk licks and a quasi-classical touch with a full choir of female soul singers. His six-minute "Broken Arrow" ran through almost as many genres and sections as minutes in its suite-like structure and epic sweep, but did bear a convoluted fable-telling feel that was not inimical to the folk tradition. Richie Furay, emerging as a songwriter of note after failing to place any compositions on the group's debut, offered lighthearted proto-country rock with "A Child's Claim to Fame," featuring dobro by famed Ricky Nelson session guitarist James Burton. Furay's "Sad Memory," on the other hand, was suitable for coffeehouses predating the folk-rock big bang, with his All-American vocal timbre exuding habitual nice-guyness.

While still a few months shy of his twentieth birthday, Jim Messina began to work with Buffalo Springfield as an engineer on much of *Buffalo Springfield Again*, and had an up-close look at the principal songwriters' varied musical approaches. "Neil was more relaxed, more methodic," he remembers. "Stephen was more impetuous, the kind of guy that when he came into the studio, he wanted to work immediately, if not sooner. I knew that I needed to have things set up and ready to go, and then try to anticipate what he was going to do. 'Cause he didn't really tell me what he was going to do when he came into the studios. He just said, 'I got this idea, I want to put this down.' I made sure machines were patched in and microphones ready in the studio so that I had to do the least amount possible to get him rolling."

And this time around, the group was determined to get a better sound in the studio than it had with their 1966 debut *Buffalo Springfield*, whose production (by then, managers Charlie Greene and Brian Stone) was repeatedly slagged in the ensuing decades. The rich acoustic-electric guitar textures on cuts like "Rock & Roll Woman," "Hung Upside Down," and "Bluebird" had little parallel in previous rock music in their sheer density. The band acknowledged as much in the original LP credits, which billed the guitars on "Bluebird" to Young, Stills, and Furay—"all 11,386 of 'em." Messina attributes part of this to the group's eagerness to explore the full limits of the technical capabilities at the Hollywood studio it favored, Sunset Sound. "We had great tools at Sunset Sound," he explains. "Great Neumann microphones; great pre-amps, all tube; Fairchild limiters. I had lots of experience working with limiters long before they became popular, making fuzztones and compressed sounds long before they started becoming popular. We could squeeze that stuff and make it sound good. That's why it was interesting to work with the Springfield, because I could do some of that stuff, and it was okay. They liked it. Whenever you get creative people together in a positive situation, great things can happen."

By this time, the group's studio expertise had graduated to the point where it was crafting studio tracks that would be difficult if not impossible to approximate in live performance, particularly Young's "Expecting to Fly" and "Broken Arrow." The latter song, feels Messina, "was about recording three or four different tunes, and actually editing them together. The problem was it felt too cut-and-dried in terms of the patchwork. It would have been nice to try to actually record all, if not most, of it live so that the transitions felt better. But that's really up to the artist, who sees and feels how it should be, not up to the producer to decide whether it's right or wrong. What Neil heard is what you have there; that's how he wanted to do it, and that's the way we did it."

But if tracks like "Expecting to Fly" and "Broken Arrow" were pinnacles of psychedelic folk-rock, they were also symptomatic of a growing desire among the group's individual songwriters to work on their own, even on tracks credited to Buffalo Springfield. On the group's third and last album, 1968's *Last Time Around*, the musicians had further splintered to the point where they were often not recording together on the same track, the songwriter at times using just one or no other members, as well as session musicians like Buddy Miles and Gary Marker. Musically they were splintering off further from folk-rock too, with Stills getting into hard rock and Latin beats.

The quality still remained high, and the folk-rock melodies and vocals still played a strong part in highlights like Stills's "Pretty Girl Why"; Young's "I Am a Child" (based in part on one of the songs he had auditioned at Elektra back in 1965, "The Rent Is Always Due"); and Furay's beautiful ballad "Kind Woman," one of the earliest and greatest country-rock songs, with Rusty Young on pedal steel. Messina, who'd joined on bass in the beginning of 1968, co-produced the record with Furay for posthumous release, to little thanks from their colleagues. Young called it a "miserable job" in late 1969 on a radio interview with KSAN in San Francisco, singling out Stills's "Four Days Gone" as a particular example, and feeling as if the result sounded "more like a Pogo [sic] album than a Buffalo Springfield album."

Messina remains, understandably, puzzled by the criticism, considering that Young and Stills did little to help complete the album in its final production stages, despite having opportunities to do so. "When I got the call from Ahmet Ertegun asking me if I'd consider producing the band, I asked why, and he says, 'Well, it appears that you're the only one that they all trust.' I look back at what I had to work with and was given to work with, with one or two guys in the studio at a time, plus them giving me stuff to put together, and I think I did the best with what I had to work with. Certainly Ahmet didn't object.

"I can see now that the group obviously had some problems in that they just weren't working together as much," he continues. "I would have preferred to have a lot of those sessions happen where they were playing together. But quite honestly, with the tapes I got from CBS that I believe [Atlantic Records executive Ertegun] had produced, I mean, I barely heard three instruments on those things. So obviously it wasn't the first time that this was happening, where everybody wasn't playing at the same time. But I didn't take that so much as a negative, because there've been other acts that liked to record with just a click track and a bass and a drum. So it wasn't like, 'Oh my god, this is a metaphor for a problem here.' A lot of people were recording like that, 'cause they thought the Beatles recorded like that. Maybe the reason Stephen didn't always show up to a Neil date, or Neil didn't always show up to a Stephen date, is they respected each other enough to give [each other] the space to work."

Nonetheless, Messina adds, "There was a distant feeling going on. Neil quite often brought in stuff alone. Richie, on the other hand, I kind of had to get his stuff organized for him, 'cause he's not really a producer and not really an arranger. He really didn't know that many people. That's when I leaned on Leon Russell's crew to help me out with [drummer] Jimmy Carstein playing, some players to get Richie's stuff recorded. But as a producer, that's what a person does.

"Nothing appeared to me to be that much that it would break a group up. I had more fights with my surf bands than I saw going on in Buffalo Springfield! Whatever it was, they didn't bring it around me. Maybe that was a conscious effort, but maybe they knew that if it got into the studio like that, they wouldn't get their work done."

Buffalo Springfield disbanded in May 1968, though, even before the album came out. Much more would be heard from its front line of singer-songwriters, and the group's influence proved immense considering its brief livelihood and modest sales, its songs and harmonies influencing future star Californian rock bands such as the Eagles. But its potential as a unit was criminally unrealized. Its two figurehead singer-songwriters wasted no time moving on to solo careers, with Stills recording on his own as early as June 7, 1968, when he did an unreleased cover of Traffic's "Dear Mr. Fantasy" with the kind of Latin rhythms he'd begun exploring on some of the Springfield's final recordings. Young soon signed as a solo recording artist with Reprise. Unbelievably, within a year, Stills and Young would be playing together again in Crosby, Stills, Nash & Young, although on far different terms than they had with Buffalo Springfield. Furay and Messina, for their parts, founded their own influential country-rock band, Poco.

ooking back, it seems unrealistic for one band to accommodate the songs and ambitions of Stills and Young. Stills has been slammed for being too much of a control freak, Young for being not enough of a team player, and bassist Bruce Palmer for being generally careless in putting himself into situations that brought on drug and legal problems. Stills, like Young, would eventually begin recording some Springfield tracks essentially on his own, but not after doing as much as anyone to try and make the band thrive as a working unit. "I was trying to be Boss Cat and trying to keep the thing in order," he admitted to *Rolling Stone* a few years later. "You gotta dig that part of my upbringing in the South was very militaristic. I was in this military school and being taught how to be an *officer*. Wow, I was like, 11, and that stuff can't help but stick way down. Anyway, a lot of the ways I relate to situations like that is to simply take command. Because someone has to, because that is the only thing that will work and of course somebody like Neil or Bruce is instantly going to rebel. So there was chaos."

The emergence of a third talented songwriter, Furay, made it yet harder to find leeway for everyone. The many unreleased demos and outtakes by all three writers on 2001's *Buffalo Springfield Box Set*—many of them very good and just as stylistically varied as the Springfield's albums—prove just how intense the crunch was to find enough room for all the quality material. "There was a lot of creativity in the band, and certainly the competition between Steve and Neil had its impact," says Furay. "It was hard to maintain a sense of balance when it comes to egos. When you think you're what makes the whole thing happen and lose sight of the big picture, it's gonna create problems that many times are insurmountable. I believe if we would have had the management to handle the ego, it could have gone on a long time, but we didn't.

"We were a group of many faces. That is, as much as we came out of the folk-rock era, we would not allow ourselves to be boxed into someone's preconceived idea of what they wanted us to be. There was too much creativity. Some groups are one-dimensional, and what you hear is what you get. The Springfield would not allow ourselves to be boxed in. As you listen to the music you can hear so many different influences. We blended them together to make a unique sound that the music critics said"—here he quotes from the lyrics of "For What It's Worth"—"'There's something happenin' here, what it is ain't exactly clear'—but it's real special! We were, and continued to be, innovators throughout our musical journey. What we brought to the table, we left many times for others to feed upon, missing out on the financial success (at least in my case) but rewarded with the fact others made it commercially accessible, copying it and in essence saying, 'This is good!' What direction we would have taken—I think all you have to do is listen to the music we all made in the ten years following and that would give you a pretty good idea."

Messina, who in the first half of 1968 was not only producing Buffalo Springfield but also playing with the group onstage and socializing with his bandmates, insists that the conflicts between Stills and Young—played up into a white-hot intense love-hate relationship by some journalists—have been overstated. "You would think that if they fought or hated each other as much as [some say] they did, they'd have buried a hatchet in one of each other's skulls. I never saw them fight. I never saw a disrespectful thing go on between the two of them in my presence. There were no drugs." As to the legendary live one-upmanship between the two guitarists, Messina laughs, "Onstage, they would have little duels in terms of playing solos and stuff. But gee, we used to do that all the time in surf bands, to create some excitement." That guitar-dueling aspect of the band, incidentally, was rarely reflected on its disciplined studio recordings, with the exception of an extended nine-minute version of "Bluebird" that showed up on a 1973 anthology, and beyond Springfield in the live 1970 version of Young's "Southern Man" on Crosby, Stills, Nash & Young's *4 Way Street*.

"There was *nothing* going on in that studio that gave me the impression that these guys were at each other's throat," he emphasizes. "Quite honestly, if that had been going on in front of me, I don't think I'd have wanted to stick around. I can't be around crazy people, and I didn't feel that they were crazy. I thought they were frustrated. I did not experience conflict between personalities; I experienced frustration, the excitement or desire to get things done quickly, or want to make a record. Those are things that, as also a songwriter, singer, and artist, are feelings I experience every time I make a record. Those guys were pretty nice people to work with. I've worked with a hell of a lot worse, seen a lot worse."

Yet Messina can see how forces built that made it impossible for the band to continue. "I've learned over the years that the more you can keep a group working on its own music and the musicians playing together, the better the music is going to feel. The moment you start going to outside players and hiring pros—I have nothing against pros, I love 'em—but when it comes to making a group record, it should be the group. The band, to me, has to be there to make the music work.

"Stephen was a very passionate Latin rhythm melodic player, writer. Very blues-, Latin-oriented. Stephen *was* the Buffalo Springfield, as far as I was concerned. When I look back with 20/20 hindsight, it's very clear that Stephen would do what he did with Crosby, Stills & Nash. Stephen needed to go in that direction. He needed people who could hear that, who could feel it, who were excited about it. I don't, quite honestly, know whether he was getting that in Buffalo Springfield. I think he did a lot of work on his own to try to get his music to be the best that it could.

"Neil was a little more folky, trying to take that music and make it more sophisticated. It certainly had a passion, but a different quality to the passion, focused on the lyric more. And also a little more country. There was a lot of Floyd Cramer kind of licks in his guitar playing, which was very attractive. Neil became more of a rocker after he left the band. His first album, which I played on, surprised me because it seemed to be a lot stronger. He seemed to be a little more hesitant, or trying to go in a different direction, when he was in Springfield. Maybe that was because he didn't want to conflict his styles with Stephen, I don't know. Neil, I think, benefited greatly from the group busting up. We're not talking about success, I'm just talking about what he started doing with his guitar and voice, and songs like 'Down By the River.' He really blossomed as a writer.

"Then there was Richie, whose real passion was he loved George Jones, he loved country music. 'Kind Woman' is a perfect example of the beginning of his solo writings, that kind of gave you the feeling of where his heart was a lot in music. He needed to have the right to write more songs. Richie needed to go someplace where people would like his songs, and like his voice, and could have more than one or two songs. From that standpoint, it would have had to change.

"Stephen and Neil were very, very prolific, and certainly shooting for getting as much of their material on each record as they could. I was there, unconsciously, trying to make sure that Richie was represented, that Stephen was represented, that Neil was represented. Stephen was also looking out for Richie to make sure that he did get his best stuff on the record. During *The Last Time Around*, Stephen asked me, 'Are you gonna be working with Richie on getting his stuff recorded?' I said 'Yes,' and he says, 'Well, make sure you hear a song called 'Kind Woman,' because it's one of his best.'

"I've seen this happen before, that sometimes people have to come together to get attention. But the talent is just so great that it's frustrating for them to work together. I think they needed more attention that the Buffalo Springfield just couldn't give them."

The instability of groups like the Byrds and Buffalo Springfield sets in relief one of the drawbacks of the rather loose, make-up-the-rulebook-as-we-go-along way many of the West Coast folk-rock groups formed. Long-lived British groups like the Beatles and the Who had largely known each other since their teen years and grown up in close proximity to each other. The Byrds and Buffalo Springfield came from all over North America and had not known each other too well even by the time they were hot Hollywood bands. This unfamiliarity no doubt enhanced their unpredictable innovations, but made it harder to work out personal disagreements and artistic differences. Too, their backgrounds as folk and solo musicians might have made it more difficult to share the spotlight in a group situation.

"That's a good thought, that the folk solo background was to blame for that to some extent," comments Roger McGuinn. "It never occurred to me. I know the Beatles had a very stick-together kind of brotherhood. It was kind of amazing. I mean, if you'd ask one of them a question, they'd go, 'Oh, we don't know about that yet.' It was a gestalt. They were four people with a common mind, and they would stick up for each other, in ways that I was envious of. Like, if somebody would insult me in front of David Crosby, he'd agree with them. Every time," he laughs. "And if you insulted George [Harrison] in front of John [Lennon], he would punch 'em in the nose. It was like a different mentality. Crosby could go off on his own any second and do a solo gig."

At least members of the Byrds and Buffalo Springfield had the satisfaction of continuing to make important, acclaimed music in subsequent group and solo projects. For Love, its third album was both a mountaintop and the end of the road as the band's major force in rock. Its second album, *Da Capo* (released at the beginning of 1967), had seen the band veer off crazily but effectively in a number of directions, from the atomic garage rock of their sole Top 40 hit "7 and 7 Is" to flamenco, jazz-rock, and a side-long jam. Folk-rock was still evident in the guitar riffs of pretty songs like "The Castle" and "She Comes in Colors," and Bryan MacLean later admitted he based his sole composition on the LP, "Orange Skies," on McGuinn's guitar break in the Byrds' "The Bells of Rhymney." But as a whole the group's folk-rock connection was becoming tenuous.

Acoustic folk-rock flavorings would resurface with a vengeance on late 1967's *Forever Changes*, a classic fusion of seductive melodies and gentle, shimmering guitar strums with opaque psychedelic lyrics and Arthur Lee's choked Johnny Mathis–with–an–intellect crooning. The Latin-influenced fox-hunting horns and brass added to the seductive oddity of a dreamy folk-rock masterpiece. Every listening revealed new shades of good and evil struggling for the soul of Arthur Lee and Sunset Strip hippiedom. Lee songs like "Andmoreagain" and "The Good Humor Man He Sees Everything Like This" were so heartbreakingly pretty on the surface that it took a while to get to the sad, questioning, sometimes bitter observations underneath. The words had a surrealistic ambience quite different from that of Dylan's, but rewarding and intriguing for those who took up the challenge of mulling over their meaning.

Bryan MacLean, whose more florid, tiptoeing compositions were sometimes elbowed aside to make room for Lee's, trumped the leader with one of his two songs on the album, "Alone Again Or." Its bright yet ominous layers of acoustic guitars, key-shifting melody, flamenco guitar break, and ambiguous lyrics of love-for-everyone and loneliness became the album's most famous track, if not

Love with the lineup that recorded Forever Changes.
Left to right: Michael Stuart, Ken Forssi, Arthur Lee, Bryan MacLean, and Johnny Echols.

indeed Love's most renowned recording. "Love was really the two writers, Arthur and Bryan," says Bruce Botnick, who co-produced the album with Arthur Lee (and worked as an engineer on many 1960s Elektra Records sessions). "Bryan brought another sensibility to it, as deep as what Arthur was writing, but coming from a different direction. He was very sensitive." (Even more sensitive, heart-of-glass MacLean ballads from the time can be heard on acoustic solo demos assembled for the Sundazed CDs *ifyoubelievein* and *Candy's Waltz.*)

Love was in such bad shape at the outset of the album that Botnick had to shock the musicians into getting serious by using session musicians to back Lee on two songs. A shaken, tearful band got it together to play on the rest of the album. As for the Tijuana Brass–on–hallucinogens sound of the orchestral arrangements, Botnick admits, "I brought the stuff in. You gotta look at music in that period. Radio wasn't narrow like it is today. In those days, you would hear Love followed by

Frank Sinatra, going into Herb Alpert & the Tijuana Brass. There was an amalgamation, a synergy, between all the different styles.

"I brought in this arranger [David Angel]. I think I might have found him through my mother, who was a music copyist working for Sinatra and Nelson Riddle at the time. He sat down with Arthur, and Arthur really warmed to it. He sang all the lines to Angel—all the string lines and all the brass lines, everything. It's a really weird mix of Tijuana Brass and the rock 'n' roll he was coming from. At that time, it was the thing to do, to legitimize yourself in some respects, to have strings on your record—[to show] that you'd grown up, and to make rock 'n' roll legal in some respects." Interestingly, there was some thought of getting Neil Young involved in the album's production (Botnick had engineered some of Buffalo Springfield's sessions), but "the more he got into it, he was realizing that he had things he wanted to say and he wanted to do, and producing wasn't one of them."

Forever Changes was not a huge seller at the time, peaking at #154 in the charts. In fact Love never did become very big outside of California, in part due to its refusal to tour; it wasn't until May 1968 that the band played New York for the first time. The Lee/MacLean-led lineup of Love broke up in 1968 after just one more single. Although Lee recorded other Love albums with different musicians over the next few years, almost always in a hard rock rather than folk-rock style, absolutely nothing he wrote or released in subsequent years came close to the madcap greatness of his work on Love's first three LPs.

Middle age was not kind to Love. Several of the original members spent time in jail, and Bryan MacLean died unexpectedly on Christmas in 1998. Lee, a victim of California's "three strikes you're out" rule for repeat criminal offenders, started serving a lengthy jail sentence in the mid-'90s (he was released in late 2001 after almost six years in confinement). Yet *Forever Changes*, in spite of its modest impact at the time of its 1967 release, became the biggest cult album of all time, its following just growing and growing through subsequent decades and generations. Several great folk-rock-psych records are discussed in this chapter and the preceding one, such as *Surrealistic Pillow*, *Younger Than Yesterday*, and *Buffalo Springfield Again*. But *Forever Changes* might be the greatest of them all.

Of the three Love albums he played on, Bryan MacLean told Phil Nee in an interview for WRCO radio in Wisconsin in early 1998, "*Forever Changes* was the most symmetrical. In the first album, we were just trying to get the hang of it. In the second album, for some reason we got derailed and put that big, huge, long song on the other side, which is a shame. There's a lot of other stuff we could have done that would have been better. Then by the time *Forever Changes* came along, we were beginning to get at ease with what we were doing. If I had it to do over, I wouldn't have quit. I was kind of lured away and it was not a smart decision." If the band had stayed together, feels producer Botnick, "It's kind of hard to say where they would have gone. But the band had gotten to the end of the road. *Forever Changes* was really Arthur's record, Arthur and Bryan's record. The [other] guys were just sidemen." As to the inability of these still-young men to come up with anything of the same order again, he waxes philosophical: "Some of us have a short run, some of us have a long run. Some of us have something to say in a very short period of time."

Kaleidoscope. On roof, from left to right: Chris Darrow, Solomon Feldthouse.
Below roof, from left to right: David Lindley, Chester Crill, and John Vidican.

Another interesting Southern Californian folk-rock-psychedelic band that emerged slightly after the mighty triumvirate of the Byrds, Buffalo Springfield, and Love was Kaleidoscope. Forget folk-rock—Kaleidoscope, as its name portended, was more eclectic than any other rock band of the '60s, period. Multi-instrumentalists David Lindley and Chris Darrow had already played traditional folk together in the Mad Mountain Ramblers and the Dry City Scat Band. Other multi-instrumentalists were Chester Crill and Solomon Feldthouse, who was playing both flamenco and Leadbelly-styled tunes in folk clubs. Like the Byrds and Buffalo Springfield, most of them really had no significant background in rock music, although Darrow had been in an R&B/rock band, the Floggs (who sounded rather like the Animals with somewhat more of a folk-rock influence, as some unreleased demos reveal), shortly before Lindley recruited him for Kaleidoscope.

Teenage drummer John Vidican was selected on flimsier grounds, as Michael Clarke and Skip Spence had been for the Byrds and Jefferson Airplane. He was picked, admits Darrow, because "he was an 18-year-old hippie who looked pretty good, kind of the high school marching band drummer. He was the only one that had any kind of pop charisma in our band. These folk music guys, they'd never worked with drummers, so they just figured all drummers were the same. And if you could find one that looked cool, that's pretty much what we all wanted. A lot of these guys, I think, did get picked on kind of how handsome they were, whether or not they could play the drums." In all other respects, the group made virtually no concessions to the commercial image-making factory. As Crill laconically notes regarding Feldthouse's raspy melismatic vocals, often heard on the band's Middle Eastern excursions in particular, "Only that particular period of time would have even *tolerated* somebody who sang like that."

In its late-'60s albums, Kaleidoscope mixed old-time folk, British folk, Byrds-like folk-rock, jug band, R&B, blues, jazz, Middle Eastern, Cajun, Appalachian, comedy, flamenco, and feedback-riddled psychedelic jams on the same LP, and sometimes in the same track. There were relatively short, concise Byrds-type songs ("Pulsating Dream"), antiwar folk-raga-rock protest ("Keep Your Mind Open"), ten-minute-plus workouts combining Middle Eastern music with psychedelic improvisation ("Seven-Ate Sweet"), banjo instrumentals, droning Celtic folk-rock ("Greenwood Sidee"), and a lengthy jam built around Howlin' Wolf's "Smokestack Lightning" ("Beacon from Mars"). The group even did a soul-psychedelic single with Larry Williams and Johnny "Guitar" Watson, "Nobody," featuring Lindley's harp guitar and Feldthouse's saz (a Turkish lute). The records were erratic but exhilarating, even if they didn't sell much.

Live Kaleidoscope took the multi-instrumentalist folk approach of the New Lost City Ramblers into the psychedelic era, as all the members except Vidican could play several instruments, including (for rock) exotic ones like mandolin, harmonium, viola, harpsichord, oud, saz, and clarinet. Lindley played guitar with a violin bow, as did Darrow on bass, an approach that might have influenced one of their big fans, Jimmy Page (who called Kaleidoscope "my favorite band of all time" in a *ZigZag* interview). "It was very entertaining to watch, because it wasn't just five hippies who looked alike," says Crill. "It was five very *ugly*-looking hippies who had entirely different ways of approaching things. A lot of our early live concerts, the only problem was the timing of throwing the instruments around the stage." There was a more mundane advantage to their versatility too. "All of the other bands that we watched being recorded in the same space we were occupying, that they were giving major promotion to, [Columbia] had studio guys play all their albums. One of the things David particularly concocted was, we would get stuff that they couldn't do that [to]."

If Kaleidoscope's transmutation of traditional folk to the outer limits of world music fusion might not have sat well with some purists, at least one esteemed folk scholar was paying attention. "D.K. Wilgus, who was the head of the ethnomusicological department at UCLA, came to see us play at the Ash Grove, and heard our records," says Darrow. "He said that our version of 'Oh Death' [a much-performed traditional folk lament heard on *Anthology of American Folk Music*, among numerous other sources] was the perfect, ultimate [example] of a[n] evolutionary folk thing, using [it] from the standpoint of its inception as a death ballad, and having it now be a 'pop' song, with drums, and still holding the tradition of that stuff. Which I took as a great compliment."

Kaleidoscope, like other folk-rock outfits, might have had too many individual talents to be contained in one place. Darrow left the band after its first two, and best, albums, *Side Trips* and *A Beacon from Mars*. According to Darrow, "We wanted to have original material that reflected somewhat the psychedelic/Middle Eastern/metaphysical kind of area that seemed so important at that time. Even when we did interpretive stuff, our rule was to always make it our own. When I was brought in, I was told that this was going to be a leaderless band, and each one of these guys could lead their own band their own way. But when it was my song or my turn to do it, I'd be the one to be able to tell everybody what to do. I just didn't want to be so heavily influenced by the Middle Eastern stuff. I wanted to go more folk-rock probably, and a little more country-rock, and a little bit more popular music-oriented stuff, because I was one of the major writers in the band. I felt like I had something I wanted to say, and wanted to do it. And it wasn't going in that direction, so that was why I ultimately left."

The band's third album, *Incredible!*, still had some high points, such as "Seven-Ate Sweet." But by the end of the decade and after several lineup changes, the best of its truly kaleidoscopic energy had dissipated, with David Lindley moving on to a career as a major session musician (particularly with Jackson Browne). "In terms of all that stuff coming out of one band, it was almost too hard for some people to take," summarizes Darrow. "We always expected everybody to get it, but it was hard to even find *musicians* that could get it. I'm starting to realize in retrospect that it was maybe silly for us to assume that we were going to be some kind of huge commercial success, because it was hard enough to find musicians that could play the stuff, let alone people that knew how to listen to it. We were a lot more effective on musicians than on the populace. It's been a long time coming in terms of our appreciation; now we've been termed, in too many articles, the first worldbeat band, which I think we probably were."

While the folk-rock-psychedelic shuffle was largely a West Coast affair it was not limited to California's high-profile bands, spreading around the world and filtering down into groups barely known outside of their stomping grounds. Donovan, as discussed in the book *Turn! Turn! Turn!*, started doing it in 1966 with *Sunshine Superman*, and continued to at times over the next few years, particularly on his "Hurdy Gurdy Man" single. His American chum and *Sunshine Superman* sideman Shawn Phillips had moved to Italy and, in the absence of a record deal, gotten perhaps even further out: "I did some experimental work with sitar, changing tape speed, turning the tape over backwards and playing to it, just generally trying to develop something other than what I was hearing in the commercial field. About two weeks before they landed on the moon, I wrote a poem called 'Anonymous Astronomous,' and had that experimental sitar stuff behind it."

From Texas, the 13th Floor Elevators had ties to the Austin folk scene, both via some material written for them by Powell St. John and the crazy up-and-down electric jug runs of Tommy Hall, which were even heard on the band's bone-crunching garage-rock classic "You're Gonna Miss Me." "Splash 1," from their debut album, is a lost melodic folk-rock gem of incandescent radiance with eerily trippy yet romantic lyrics alluding to mind-melding and reincarnation. In the course of their brief career they got sucked into a psychedelic vortex from which they never returned, their songs growing ever-more unfathomable and drug-drenched. Chicago's best psychedelic group, H.P. Love-craft, was led by folkie George Edwards, and put fine Jefferson Airplane–style harmonies on both original material and radically restructured covers of folk songs like "High Flying Bird," "Way-faring Stranger," and Fred Neil's "That's the Bag I'm In" and "Country Boy & Bleecker Street." Back in Los Angeles, Dr. West's Medicine Show & Junk Band, who had a minor novelty jug band hit with "The Eggplant That Ate Chicago," zoomed through a brief folk-rock phase straight to the goofball psychedelia of their 1968 single "Jigsaw." "Crazy questions aren't so crazy when you can't remem-ber who you are," it wailed over distorted raga-riffs that bisected snake-charming flutes and over-amped fuzz guitars. The band's leader, Norman Greenbaum, would ride crunchier meltdown fuzz guitar hooks and distorted glissandos to #3 in 1970 with his solo hit "Spirit in the Sky," produced by former Lovin' Spoonful aide de camp Erik Jacobsen.

In New York, the Fugs, having left ESP for Reprise after a deal with Atlantic fell through, fol-lowed the lukewarm *Tenderness Junction* with 1968's impressive *It Crawled into My Hand, Hon-est*. Here their psychedelia was more a matter of a wild juxtaposition of styles than special effects: A Gregorian chant about "Marijuana" bumped against maudlin profane satirical country tunes, the psychedelic-folk-rock send-up "Crystal Liaison," the honest-to-God tuneful folk-rock of Tuli Kupferberg's "Life Is Strange," and a side-long suite that wasn't far behind the Mothers of Inven-tion's similarly constructed *We're Only in It for the Money* in the intelligent rock comedy sweep-stakes. The Fugs, however, were wearied by years of personnel comings and goings, and by battles at the forefront of American radicalism—they and Phil Ochs were the only noted folk-rock artists with a presence at the 1968 Democratic Convention protests. They disbanded in 1969, following a dispirited, burnt-out final studio album.

From Kansas, the Blue Things, having done some of the finest neglected straightforward mid-'60s folk-rock, did some of the finest neglected early psychedelia on three songs from Sep-tember 1966 sessions that were used on a couple RCA singles. Guitarist Mike Chapman coaxed a violin-like tone out of his axe with fuzztone and pickups, and the songs detailed a Dylanish sense of psychological overload and confusion. Snake-charming organ, backwards vocals, and a simu-lated nuclear explosion were all fair game for use in the studio. "The Orange Rooftop of Your Mind," the best of these, had its roots as a folk song by Val Stecklein, as heard on a home demo that surfaced in 1987, arranged into full-blast psychedelic rock by Chapman in the studio. Another, "You Can Live in My Tree," was co-written by Stecklein and underground cartoonist S. Clay Wilson.

Blue Things bassist Richard Scott sees these tracks as a natural extension of what they had done by making folk material sound bigger on their earlier folk-rock outings. With psychedelic singles such as "Orange Rooftop," he feels, "the higher volume levels, the sustained guitar, the feedback, the fuzztone, and stereo bass" were, likewise, "ways of making our sound larger." At the time, in the group's fan club booklet, he described "Orange Rooftop" as "about a girl caught up in the rat race of today, she is trying to be like and do like everyone else and can't take the pressure so her mind is slowly snapping"; "One Hour Cleaners" concerned "a psychiatrist whose only hold on sanity is provided by his patients." It was too far-out, perhaps, to catch on in the 45 market. A bigger blow than their failure was the departure of principal singer-songwriter Stecklein after these singles had been cut. The group, according to Scott, "told him that he needed to take a couple of months off, get his head back together, and come back. And he just chose not to." The Blue Things' recording career came to an end soon afterward.

Back in California, some folkies even made the jump to hard rock and psychedelia without stopping at folk-rock's junction at all. John Kay went from taunting David Crosby at L.A.'s New Balladeer folk club in the mid-'60s to leading Steppenwolf. Sean Bonniwell, who'd been in the sterile folk group the Wayfarers, had met Roger McGuinn back when the Byrds were the Jet Set. A couple of years later he'd founded the Music Machine of "Talk Talk" fame, who made some highly underrated garage psychedelia. Alan Wilson and Bob Hite had formed a jug band before electrifying and becoming one of America's few successful '60s blues-rock bands, Canned Heat, which differed from many others of that sort in taking much of its repertoire from pre–World War II acoustic rural blues.

Then there were psychedelic stars with no folk or folk-rock past who borrowed from folk-rock. While few people would count Jimi Hendrix as a folk-rocker, and justifiably so, there can be no doubt that he was heavily influenced by Bob Dylan. Hendrix covered several Dylan songs, most famously "All Along the Watchtower" and "Like a Rolling Stone," but also less iconic compositions like "The Drifter's Escape" and "Can You Please Crawl Out Your Window." (Just prior to forming the Jimi Hendrix Experience, he'd been making waves on the Greenwich Village scene as guitarist in the band of John Hammond, one of the first acoustic folk-blues revivalists to record with electric backing. Around the same time, Hendrix even worked briefly as an accompanist to folk singer Ellen McIlwaine.) Dylan's biggest contribution to Hendrix's mindset, though, was probably conceptual. The wide acceptance of a singer-songwriter with such unusual lyrics and such an unconventional voice helped give Hendrix the courage to break out of the restrictions of his own R&B background, writing odd songs and singing in a voice that was not deemed to be especially tuneful but which overcame its limitations with its sheer force of personality.

Hendrix wasn't listening only to Dylan, as far as folk-rock was concerned; his first hit was "Hey Joe," with a tempo similar to the version on Tim Rose's 1966 single. Chas Chandler was touring the States with the Animals in the summer of 1966, he recalled in John McDermott and Eddie Kramer's *Hendrix: Setting the Record Straight*, when "someone played me Tim Rose's version of 'Hey Joe,' which had been out for about nine months in America. [Chandler no doubt got the chronology wrong; Rose's "Hey Joe" was not recorded until April 1966.] I was so taken by it that I vowed, 'As soon as I get back to England, I'm going to find an artist to record this song.'" The next day, Chandler claimed, he was watching Hendrix perform at the Cafe Wha? in the Village, where the first song Jimi played was "Hey Joe." That was enough to pique his interest in the guitarist, whom he ended up taking to England to manage and produce.

At the other end of the scale from the likes of Hendrix, there were unlikely singers whose recognition had peaked in the early-'60s folk revival, yet made some wholly unexpected plunges into strange psychedelic rock. Alex Hassilev of the Limeliters produced Elektra's weird astrological concept LP *The Zodiac: Cosmic Sounds*, which featured some of the first Moog synthesizer ever heard on record. The twelve tracks, one devoted to each sign of the Zodiac, were graced with spoken narration by fellow folk revival veteran Cyrus Faryar, formerly of the Modern Folk Quartet. Carolyn Hester, who had met Ravi Shankar way back in 1963 at the Edinburgh Folk Festival, did (with Shankar in attendance) an uncategorizable cover of Shankar's "Majhires" in late 1966 in which sitar and Eric ("Deliverance") Weissberg's banjo backed her Bengali vocals. (Unissued at the time, it appeared on her 1994 *Dear Companion* compilation.) As the singer of the Carolyn Hester Coalition, she made a couple of obscure psychedelic-shaded albums in the late '60s and early '70s that included rock updates of material that would have been familiar to coffeehouse regulars a decade or so earlier, such as "East Virginia" and Ed McCurdy's antiwar song "Last Night I Had the Strangest Dream." "I felt that contemporary folk music had led us to question authority, and that had led to our questioning boundaries of all kinds . . . political, social, musical," says Hester of her move into psychedelic rock. "The flower-power generation had questioned authority of all kinds, especially in the realm of Vietnam and civil rights. Senator Robert Kennedy was assassinated during these sessions, which led to the song 'Sir Robert, the Lost Knight.' I feel that these records tell the story of the time."

More notable was Judy Henske and Jerry Yester's *Farewell Aldebaran* on Frank Zappa's Straight label. Henske and Yester had both played important peripheral roles in folk-rock's birth. But *Farewell Aldebaran* was something else again in its odd song-poems about mean-spirited churches, flaming stars, and medieval knights, wrapped in crunching blues-rock, warped country-folk, bubblegum satire, and early synthesizer experiments. Yester, who had established himself as a producer of note with a couple Tim Buckley albums, pulled out all the stops in arrangements pocked with zithers, pipe organs, delicate strings, and mandolins, while Henske swooped between low bluesy moans, gothic drones, and sweet, high harmonies. It was one of the most unjustly ignored albums of the late '60s, though it didn't have too much to do with folk or folk-rock. It was as if the musicians, ignited by the zeitgeist that had stretched so many of their old folk friends beyond recognition, found something in themselves they didn't even know they possessed.

There was also the odd spectacle of brief psychedelic detours by folk musicians who would become more known for the folk music they did *after* folk-rock and psychedelia had passed from fashion. Peter Rowan and David Grisman were in Earth Opera, the Boston Elektra psychedelic band most remembered for their antiwar epic "The American Eagle Tragedy"; David Bromberg and fellow folk vet Rusty Evans did brain-damaged-sounding psych with the Deep; and Jerry Jeff Walker, prior to establishing himself as a storytelling singer-songwriter with "Mr. Bojangles," was in New York's Circus Maximus, famous for the eight-minute "Wind," a staple of early free-form FM radio. Stefan Grossman played with the Fugs for a few months, but found his true calling as a virtuosic acoustic folk guitarist, particularly after electric blues-rock guitar-slinger Mike Bloomfield "went up to me and said, 'You play incredible acoustic guitar, but you're really shit at electric.' So I just stopped playing electric guitar."

If Tom Paxton sat out the psychedelic revolution in the studio, he could get some vicarious pleasure from a shrieking, Doors-like makeover of his plaintive portrait of authoritarian control, "Mr. Blue," into a psychedelic rave-up by Clear Light (on his label, Elektra, and like the Doors, produced by Paul Rothchild). Far from being offended, Paxton was downright tickled. "I was up at Elektra," he recounts, "and Paul Rothchild said, 'Listen. Come back in the engineering room. I want to play something for you, I want your reaction to it.' So I went back with him, and he put on this tape, and out came this ominous kind of drum thing and a voice saying, 'Good morning, Mr. Blue.' He was genuinely concerned about how I'd take it. But *I* thought it was just fabulous! Great! I wouldn't call it a hit, but it got quite a bit of airplay. I *love* hearing people do different approaches to my songs to suit their own sensibilities, as long as you can tell that they love the song and they're trying to do it the best they can."

These neat little cubbyholes of folk-rock-psych niches and oddities still fail to contain some acts whose styles elude convenient confinement to any region or subgenre. The best illustrations are the Youngbloods, who in their prime straddled New York good-time folk-rock and San Francisco psychedelia. When the band formed in the mid-'60s, Jesse Colin Young and Jerry Corbitt had woken up Lowell "Banana" Levinger in the middle of the night to ask him to move from Boston to New York to play electric piano with them. It didn't matter that Levinger, a multi-instrumentalist who'd already moved from folk to rock with the Trolls, didn't have an electric piano. He got a spare one from Boston rock band Barry & the Remains, playing his first gig with the Youngbloods at Gerde's Folk City on the table in the booth next to the stage.

On their first two albums, 1967's *The Youngbloods* and *Earth Music*, the Youngbloods were quite like the Lovin' Spoonful in their mixture of blues covers, good-time electrified extensions of the jug band sound, and reflective, melodic folk-rock ballads. It was the last of these that were their strongest suit, particularly when sung and written by Jesse Colin Young, whose vocals had the most effective cross between tender restraint and soulfulness in all of rock. Banana agrees there were similarities with the Spoonful, but adds, "There was a bigger than usual jazz influence in the Youngbloods. The electric piano sound was unique. And then there was Jesse's voice; there never has been anything like it." Young ended up on bass after they'd failed to recruit Felix Pappalardi (they also tried to get fellow top New York folk-rock sessioneer Harvey Brooks), though Pappalardi did become friends with the Youngbloods, ending up producing their first two LPs after their failed entreaties.

But the Youngbloods were finding that the California audiences and lifestyle suited them better than the more stifling New York scene, decamping to the Bay Area by the time of their third and best album, *Elephant Mountain*. "We came out here and everybody thought we were fantastic," Banana observes. "We couldn't believe it! We were banging heads against this brick wall in New York City, and came out here, and people went nuts. So it only took us twice before we figured out, 'You know, maybe we should move.' By the time we got to San Francisco, one of the things that distinguished us is that we were able to engage an audience without being real powerful, loud and crunchy, like

The Youngbloods. Left to right: Jesse Colin Young, Jerry Corbitt, Joe Bauer, and Banana Levinger.

Blue Cheer and that type of scene. There'd be three or four acts at the Fillmore and the Family Dog or something, and all of them except us would just be *insanely* loud and powerful and ferocious. And then we would come on with this gold-throated guy and this wimpy-sounding electric piano, jazz drum set, and improvise."

1969's *Elephant Mountain* was their best synthesis of mellow folk-rock with jazzy, psychedelic-inflected improvisation, offering several of Young's best compositions: "Darkness, Darkness," "Ride the Wind," "Smug," and, above all, "Sunlight," his finest moment as a romantic folk-rock balladeer. "Our best record, in my opinion, is *Elephant Mountain*, by far," says Banana. "It's a whole album that's kind of sewn together as one piece." But it wasn't what was getting the Youngbloods their most attention in 1969. A single from their first album that had been a minor hit in 1967, "Get Together," became another in a line of folk-rock songs that were fluke nationwide smashes due to circumstances totally beyond the artists' control. In 1969, it was re-released after use in a television public service ad promoting unity, and shot to #5.

Dino Valenti's infectious peace-and-love anthem had been recorded by several artists, including Jefferson Airplane (who recorded the song as "Let's Get Together") and the We Five, and was performed live by many others, including Judy Collins and Joni Mitchell (who would also do it live with Crosby, Stills, Nash & Young in 1970). The Youngbloods, thinks Banana, learned it by seeing it done at the Cafe Au Go Go in New York by Buzzy Linhart, who "had a really cool snaky, modal version of it, that in my opinion, we never quite captured." As with "Hey Joe," the folk-rock song of murky origins that had been covered by several bands on Sunset Strip before the Leaves had the hit single with it in 1966, the best version won. The Youngbloods' rendition, with rousing harmonies and a vocal by Young that radiated compassion, was the definitive interpretation—and the definitive optimistic hippie statement of the 1960s.

The best mid-'60s good-time folk-rock stars, the Lovin' Spoonful and the Mamas & the Papas, were not as capable of bridging the gap from the folk-rock boom to psychedelia. This was due as much or more to spiraling personal difficulties as any lack of musical acumen. The Spoonful's career never recovered from Steve Boone and Zal Yanovsky's bust for marijuana in San Francisco. Yanovsky was threatened with deportation, and the source for the pot was named. Although the band offered to pay for an attorney for the source, he refused the offer and ended up serving a brief jail sentence. The underground press came down hard on the Spoonful when they learned what had happened.

The castigation was ironic considering that, according to Spoonful producer Erik Jacobsen, the group had done much to get the San Francisco live psychedelic scene going at a Family Dog dance they played with the Charlatans at the Longshoremen's Hall in late 1965: "That whole idea of going and listening to music and getting high started there." Yanovsky left the group in mid-1967, to be replaced by his friend Jerry Yester, but things were never the same. Jacobsen was gone too, "which was fine by me, because we had kind of run our course. We were falling apart."

There were still some nice, gentle folk-rock hits to fall from Sebastian's pen in 1967 before Yanovsky left, including "Darling Be Home Soon" and "Six O'Clock." On the country-twanged satire "Nashville Cats," Sebastian—in keeping with the band's determination to play all of their immense arsenal of instruments—played the pedal steel part after a mere 45 minutes of experience. But the Spoonful might have lost momentum even without the irritation of the pot bust crisis.

"John [Sebastian] started thinking of himself more as a solo," says Yester, "and wanted to have more to do with how the records were done, and had Zally playing just chinks on rhythm and stuff, which really kind of was frustrating for him. Up to the point where doing 'Darling Be Home Soon' on *Ed Sullivan*, Zally was, like, bouncing a rubber frog in front of John's face for the whole thing. It was kind of embarrassing, and really not cool. It was certainly funny, but funny was not what they wanted right then. It did change, and it had a lot to do with John trying to take a lot of the control away from what used to be a band venture." Adds Boone, "The Spoonful succeeded as a group far beyond its reach as individual members in their solo careers. I think we had a strength when we were together that none of us achieved again, as performers anyway." Still, Sebastian was on his way out, leaving in mid-1968 to go on his own, the Spoonful struggling on for half a year as a trio before breaking up.

The Mamas & the Papas, like the Spoonful, were fading but still quite popular in 1967. John Phillips made a vast contribution to 1960s rock by, with Lou Adler, acting as a co-producer of the Monterey Pop Festival. He'd also given the whole flower power scene its contrived unofficial anthem by writing "San Francisco (Be Sure to Wear Flowers in Your Hair)" (which he and Adler also produced) for Scott McKenzie, who had played with Phillips back in the early '60s in the Journeymen.

"I went to a party at Judy Collins's place, and I sang the song there and it was not at all the same kind of version as the Mamas & the Papas, with Hal Blaine on drums and Larry Knechtel on piano, Joe Osborn on bass and me playing sort of rhythm," Phillips told L.A. Johnson in a 1995 interview on Gary Hartman's Scott McKenzie Web site. "It was finger picking, Carter Family style. Everyone liked it very much and it was a nice song. Then we got to California with it and I guess it was [producer] Lou Adler's influence, really, because he got Joe and Larry and myself into that mode of playing that country-folk-rock. The feeling of the song changed from sort of a lament and just sort of a, you know, I don't know what to call it—a dreaming song, that kind of thing." The AM pop appeal of the single was in part driven by the tinkling noises, a cross between a xylophone and a music box, supplied by a baby's toy played by Michelle Phillips at the very beginning of the song.

McKenzie's recording history, like those of many folk-rockers, dated back to the beginning of the 1960s, and "San Francisco" was not his first venture into rock, having been preceded by a couple of flop pop-rock singles. Yet he was to be remembered as one of folk-rock's ultimate flash-in-the-pan one-hit wonders, hastily cobbling together a follow-up album consisting mostly of covers of songs by Phillips, Donovan (who played guitar on McKenzie's version of his "Celeste"), the Lovin' Spoonful, and Tim Hardin. His 1967 recordings would be produced by Phillips and Mamas & Papas producer Lou Adler, shapers of the ultimate commercial distillation of Los Angeles folk-rock. "I had never worked with Adler before, and was impressed with the way he would let the musicians play what they would gravitate to," says fellow ex-Journeyman Dick Weissman, who played banjo and guitar on the album. "Then he would zero in on getting us to condense our ideas into a more coherent (and commercial) form."

The album didn't even make the Top 100, and McKenzie never had another hit. Weissman agrees that McKenzie was surprised at the single's success and wasn't much of a self-starter when it came to building upon it: "Scott had two operations for pre-cancerous nodes in his throat when the Journeymen were active, and I also have the impression that he wasn't really prepared to go and sing his lungs out for two hours. There's a funny story about Scott and the Mamas & the Papas being in Paris, and hundreds of French teenagers gathering under Scott's hotel room, seeking 'the word' from their guru. Scott refused to talk to them, and John kept coaxing him, saying that he could make up something appropriate for his fans." McKenzie wasn't quite done, coming back in 1970 with an album of entirely self-penned songs, *Stained Glass Morning*, that had to be one of the sleepiest country-rock albums ever made, at once dull and perversely fascinating in its low-energy torpor.

Back in 1967, the Mamas & the Papas themselves were barely surviving John and Michelle Phillips's rocky marriage. They eked out a quartet of hit singles that year, including "Creeque Alley," the bouncy winding tale of the group's formation that was real-life folk-rock storytelling at its best, and "Twelve Thirty (Young Girls Are Coming to the Canyon)," which evoked the lure of circa-'67 L.A. as much as Michelle Phillips's flower power–poster child beauty. But as Denny Doherty notes, "What people were seeing on the outside and hearing from this supergroup was one thing, but what was going on inside was *As the World Turns*, *All My Children*, and *General Hospital* eventually. To keep all those balls in the air, keep the public persona going, keep your contractual recording things going, and then to be creative on top of that . . . it was an intolerable situation.

"We were dragged along with the momentum of our success for three years, whether we wanted to or not. It was like, 'my god, you're in paradise, but you've got AIDS. You'll have fun for a while here, but you know this is doomed.' 'Really? Well, why don't we just get out now, before it gets too . . .' 'No, no, no, we can't. You got a contract, two albums a year, product, product, product, product,

product.' So it was just madness. We couldn't get together any more, as a quartet of people that were creative. And you had to be together to be creative, and that's what created all the problems, us being together so much, so closely, 24 hours a day, seven days a week. Familiarity breeds contempt."

"Everyone, especially me," John Phillips told *Melody Maker* in 1970, "just got bored . . . I felt as though we'd gone as far as we could go. You take our first album and the Beatles' first album, ours is so much more polished and refined, we just didn't have that far to go to reach our full potential. We didn't play our own instruments, so it was difficult, I hated the idea of repeating ourselves over and over again." In *Rolling Stone* the same year, he elaborated, "The last album was torture to make, just torture. We couldn't rehearse, and I think it contains some of the best songs but we couldn't do them properly, everything's a little flat. We didn't really have the interest. I was really glad to see the Mamas and Papas go. I didn't want to be the Brothers Four, working off a hit for the next ten years."

Adler is more succinct: "The dynamics of their personalities is what made them the Mamas & Papas from a social and a cultural sense. And it's also what was their downfall. But also during the two-year time, we did four very successful albums. We were churning 'em out."

The Mamas & the Papas got off the merry-go-round by breaking up in 1968, the Phillips's marriage falling by the wayside soon after that. Cass Elliot was playing the Circus Maximum room at Caesar's Palace in Las Vegas by October of that year, and had some subsequent success with a straight pop career. Her entry into the world of mainstream all-around entertainment would permanently obscure, to some degree, the considerable role she played as a facilitator of significant folk-rock connections. She was particularly influential on the Lovin' Spoonful (whose John Sebastian and Zal Yanovsky met at her apartment in early 1964 at a gathering to watch the Beatles on *Ed Sullivan*) and Crosby, Stills & Nash (whom she helped bring together and had hopes of singing with in their earliest formative days). Under contractual obligation, the Mamas & the Papas reunited one last time for an ignored early-'70s album, by which time their greatest contributions to folk-rock had long been history.

As the foremost good-time folk-pop-rock bands began to break up, the breach would be filled by the brigade of sunshine pop acts, mostly from Southern California. Sunshine pop was not so much folk-influenced rock as folk-rock-influenced pop, sometimes very much in an easy listening, Mamas-&-the-Papas mold, such as Spanky & Our Gang (who did actually have some folk experience) oozed on their hits. Peter, Paul & Mary had their sole genuinely folk-rocking hit, 1967's "I Dig Rock & Roll Music," in this style, although the single, with lovingly-intended impersonations of the Mamas & the Papas and Donovan, was often misinterpreted as a mean-spirited swipe at the electric folk-rock that had severely dented the trio's sales after 1964.

Minor sunshine pop groups with more guts like the Sunshine Company, who took Steve Gillette's "Back on the Street Again" into the Top 40, had to sandwich its folk-rock covers and originals around happy-face material supplied to them by outside songwriters. Some of the other groups working around the fringes of good-time Southern California folk-rock, like the Rose Garden (famous for the one-shot hit "Next Plane to London") and the Peanut Butter Conspiracy, put some of the most studied imitations of Roger McGuinn's 12-string guitar solos on their discs without coming near the brilliance of the Byrds' songs. (The Rose Garden, in fact, was produced by early Buffalo Springfield manager-producers Charlie Greene and Brian Stone (with Pat Pipolo), and included a couple of otherwise unrecorded Gene Clark songs on its sole, obscure album.) Only occasionally would a real folk-rock gem emerge from this sea of non-hits, such as the Ashes' 1966 single "Is There Anything I Can Do?" Co-written by early L.A. folk-rock pioneer Jackie DeShannon, its mesmerizing 12-string guitar jangle and hauntingly fetching lead female vocal came close to fusing the best of the early Byrds and the Mamas & the Papas.

And what of groups like the Turtles and the Association who had started with folk-rock, and were getting big pop hits in the late '60s without dabbling much in psychedelia? Turtle Howard Kaylan has no regrets about leaving the folk-rock track, dating the band's change in direction to the time it saw "Happy Together" composers Garry Bonner and Alan Gordon onstage in New York as part of the Magicians: "We saw these happy guys having a wonderful time onstage with music that made us smile, and we all knew that we would protest no longer. We were now a good-time group, and from that night on, we changed to a poppier sound that suited our image and personality much better than our former one." Even with so much folk-rock and psychedelic music hogging the scene, there still remained a huge segment of the listening audience that wanted nothing more than (or so much as) to be entertained, almost as if the folk-rock revolution had never taken place.

If sunshine pop was the most ridiculously optimistic, commercial outgrowth of folk-rock that could be imagined, acid folk—a term that, like sunshine pop, only circulated among avid historians and collectors years after the 1960s—was folk-rock's quirkiest, *least* commercial manifestation. Essentially, acid folkers could have usually played their songs on streets and subways as acoustic buskers. Their compositions, however, had a skewed, oft-troubled vision of fracture and disorientation that was just as acid-dipped in its weirdness as the longest Grateful Dead jam. In the studio, the acoustic guitar backbones were overlaid with off-the-wall confluences of special effects and exotic instruments that could never have been conceived in any other era than the late '60s and the very early '70s. In a sense, the acoustic mid-'60s folk recordings by the pre-electric Holy Modal Rounders and their friend Michael Hurley (on his Folkways album *Blueberry Wine*) were important antecedents of the form, mixing a solid grounding in traditional folk with screwball, at times deranged lyrics and vocals. Indeed the Holy Modal Rounders' "Hesitation Blues," from their 1964 debut album, might have contained the very first use of the word "psychedelic" on a musical record. But acid folk was wilder and far more electric than even the weirdest pre-electric Rounders-Hurley yowlfest.

Although the term "acid folk," like "sunshine pop," is rarely deployed outside the rock record collecting world, it was used prominently as early as 1969 in Lillian Roxon's *Rock Encyclopedia*, the first serious rock music reference book. "We already know about acid rock," she wrote in her entry for Pearls Before Swine. "What the underground group called Pearls Before Swine sings is acid *folk*, that is, folk music affected by the discoveries of an LSD-influenced generation."

Like the Fugs, Pearls Before Swine started at ESP Records, about as wacky an independent record label as there was in the 1960s. But ESP was far from the least successful of such companies; like the Fugs, Pearls Before Swine actually had some not-bad sales despite limited to non-existent airplay. Where the Fugs were often scathingly direct in their satirical diatribes and romantic poems about sex and protest politics, Pearls Before Swine was more oblique and inscrutable, like the panel from Hieronymous Bosch's "Garden of Earthly Delights" painting that adorned their debut album, *One Nation Underground*. Tom Rapp's lisping vocals were as weird as the music, which spanned rusty Dylan soundalikes and vicious antiwar protest to more characteristic fragile, dreamy numbers suggesting a mind on the lookout for a more poetically surrealistic place than the battleground that was late-'60s Manhattan. As with the Fugs, there was a raw auteur-amateur vibe to their ESP recordings, though Pearls Before Swine was more conscious of integrating odd combinations of instruments and electronic oscillation that could be nightmarish, mystical, or just confused. Its second album, *Balaklava*, even used actual tapes of Florence Nightingale and the man who sounded the trumpet call for the Charge of the Light Brigade, as well as recordings of animals in a swamp for "Images of April."

Completing the cloudy obscurity of the music was the fog-shrouded public profile of the band, who did just one show (in early 1968) in its original incarnation. After its first album, Pearls Before Swine was pretty much a nom de plume for Rapp and a revolving door of accompanists, though the LPs continued to bear the Pearls Before Swine billing. The first album, reported *The New York Times*, was done in four days; the second, *Balaklava*, took 18 months. It was hardly a conventional formula for building a following, even a cult one. Rapp has estimated that *One Nation Underground* nonetheless managed to sell a quarter of a million copies, primarily through the nation's actual underground, though it didn't make the *Billboard* charts.

For all the strangeness of his songs, principal Pearls singer-songwriter Rapp had come to folk-rock from a more or less typical path. He'd learned tunes from *The Joan Baez Song Book*, become a Beatles fan, and was to his recollection "one of the few people, in Florida at least, at that time who had heard Bob Dylan's 'Tambourine Man.' I remember hearing [the Byrds] for the first time; the first thing they did was 'Tambourine Man' on, I think, *Hullaballoo*. As soon as they started playing it, I said, 'This is gonna be a hit, and this is gonna change everything.' And it *did*, in fact."

Yet Rapp "always felt most of the other folk-rock groups were folk done as rock. It was mostly Bob Dylan with drums. Our material was a lot more psychedelic, even from the word go. It was less about folk tunes amplified. A lot of the songs were almost folky, in a sense that it's a story and here's verse one-two-three-four-five-six-seven-eight. [But] the songs are different because they come from someplace strange. I don't think we [were] real explicit and overly literal about everything, which was one of the drawbacks of some of the music, like 'Eve of Destruction.'" In *The New York Times* in 1968, Rapp even attempted to name a different genre into which to put the group than "acid folk": "We want our material to transcend the ordinary and the mundane. I like to write about the old things—old myths and legends, Valhalla, elves and dwarfs, magic rings—and magic men. If you really want to give our sound a name, how about 'transcendental rock'?"

Pearls Before Swine, formed by high school friends in Melbourne, Florida, didn't even have a performing band when it got its deal with ESP by submitting a tape in late 1966. ESP owner Bernard Stollman, according to Rapp, put Pearls Before Swine up at his parents' house because he couldn't afford to put the group up at a hotel when it came to New York to record *One Nation Underground*. In keeping with ESP's generally bizarre modus operandi, this particular family lived in digs with a doorman in the upscale neighborhood of 90th & Riverside in the same building as Judith Crist and Roy Lichtenstein, and likely plusher than any hotel most labels would have offered. When it came time to record, says Rapp, "We had to go in there and put down all the tracks and overdubs, and do all the mixing, in just a few days. The first record cost about $1,500, and it was mostly for the tape cost, I guess.

"But ESP always had this idea: 'art for the artist.' They would never interfere, as long as you did it quick and cheap, like Roger Corman movies. You could do anything you want, as long as you did it under budget, you know?" Which explains, to some degree, the simultaneously shambling homemade and near-avant-garde feel of ESP's other, yet more obscure folk-rock ventures of the time, like the Holy Modal Rounders' unholy cacophony on *Indian War Whoop* (with playwright Sam Shepard on drums) and the label's sole album with singer-songwriter Bruce MacKay. It also explains how Pearls Before Swine were able to get away with putting a chorus that spelled "fuck" in Morse code on "(Oh Dear) Miss Morse." Famed New York DJ Murray the K didn't get away with it when he played it on his show, drawing the wrath of Morse code–schooled Boy Scouts and Boy Scout Masters.

Despite the limitations of time and money, Rapp is full of praise for Richard Alderson, the label's house engineer of sorts, who also worked on ESP albums by the Fugs and the Rounders: "They put us in [engineer Richard Alderson's] care, and he was a genius," adds Tom. "The way the studio was set up, there'd always be a million instruments from other bands, coming through doing various things. There'd be an oud, tabla, celeste, all kinds of things you didn't even know existed. We were able to do our stuff with all those odd instruments, and under Richard's sense of how they could sound on a budget."

Something like Pearls Before Swine could only be marketed by word of mouth and packaging that, while it might have been considered commercial suicide in corporate boardrooms, worked to the group's advantage in the rapidly expanding hippie underground of 1967 and 1968. ESP's devil-may-care attitude allowed bands to get away with album covers that would have likely never gotten a thumbs-up at bigger companies. Even the Beatles and the Rolling Stones, after all, fought losing battles to put out albums in controversial sleeves showing the Beatles as baby butchers (the original artwork for *Yesterday...And Today*) and a graffiti-covered toilet stall (the original artwork for the Stones' *Beggars Banquet*). By contrast Pearls Before Swine encased its very first album in a Hieronymous Bosch hellscape, and the second in Pieter Breughel's similarly horrific painting "The Triumph of Death."

"I always thought that probably more people bought the records for the covers than the music," guesses Rapp. "Though usually, if they liked the covers, they would like that music too. Other folk-rock albums mostly had the group on the front. We always thought, who needs another album with four white guys on it? The first album had a pullout of the whole Bosch print that was on the cover, and you used to see that in people's apartments all over the place. It was really underground; no one formally went around hawking us. But people would just sort of [find out] by word of mouth or because of that wacky cover, which is part of the attraction. Once you buy an album that has a certain kind of cover, you hear the music through that cover in a way. And expect it to be not whatever you expected it to be."

As underground as Pearls Before Swine was, the band was far better known than most of the acid folk oddballs. Jeff Monn, John Braheny, Billy Joe Becoat, Sixto Rodriguez, and Chris Lucey aka Bobby Jameson (whose sole album, actually released back in early 1966, was about the most early Arthur Lee and Love-like recording of the '60s) were just some of the names that made LPs in this tributary of music styles, selling in microscopic quantities and eventually auctioned to collectors for astronomic prices on eBay. As is often the way with radical new trends, it took a while for psychedelia to permeate all corners of the young generation, and many obscure acid folk albums didn't come out until the tail end of the '60s or very beginning of the early '70s, when the progenitors of psychedelic folk-rock had usually long since moved on to other things. Perry Leopold even titled side two of his 1970 LP *Experiment in Metaphysics* "ACID FOLK," although the album itself (pressed in a run of just 300 copies) was pretty unexceptional.

Not all of the acid folk albums were done by no-names who managed to fire only one or two blips across the radar screen before vanishing into the Goodwill bins. There was Jake Holmes, whose "Dazed and Confused," originally a tortuous acoustic ballad overlaid with dabs of screeching distorted electric guitar, was adapted by Led Zeppelin into a much heavier blues-rocker on its debut album. His stranger-than-fiction resume included a stint with noted folk-rock singer Tim Rose in the mid-'60s group the Thorns, and future fame as the author of the US Army's inescapable "Be All You Can Be" jingle. And there was a strange detour to the fringe of acid folk by Keith Jarrett. Better known as a major jazz pianist-composer, he did a little-known, has-to-be-heard-to-be-believed 1968 album, *Restoration Ruin*, alternating between wheezing son-of-Dylanisms and sub-Love/Tim Buckley baroque folk-rock flute. The maestro also played all of the instruments, including strings, flamenco guitar, bleating harmonica, and woefully unsynced drums, as well as tapping into acid-fried lyrics on numbers like "Sioux City Sue New."

Given how idiosyncratic and slightly, or very, deranged most of the acid folkies sounded—like the work of loners liable to get institutionalized, overdose, or open gunfire on the establishment at a drop of a hat—it's not a surprise that many of them recorded for small labels, or even private pressings. Some of them never even made albums, like the Ron-de-Vous. Their sole single, "Trip So Wild" (on the tiny Mastertone label), was a despondent gem of morose acid damage, with its arresting minor-keyed melody, drumless guitar-bass busk, and visions-of-spiders-crawling-on-the-wall vocal. "Don't look at me, I'm in a bad way, I took a trip so wild today," sang-moaned the lead vocalist by way of introduction. "I'm lost and I can't find the way; if you color me, color me gray." And it only got creepier and gloomier from there. Could anyone have reasonably expected it to have gotten played on AM radio even once, let alone become a hit?

The stories behind these records' creation, usually untold for 20 or 30 years (or never told), often turn out to be as strange as the music itself. Two of the more intriguing tales were those of Linda Perhacs and Satya Sai Maitreya Kali (aka Craig Smith), whose strange journeys went against all unwritten music industry rulebooks of the time. Perhaps because of this, they led to highly personal enterprises that would have been unlikely to have been sanctioned by any prominent record executive, and today stand as some of the best lost acid folk relics.

Linda Perhacs, a contrast to many acid folkies in both her gender and the loving optimism of her songs, nevertheless sounded rather like a skewed Joni Mitchell on her lone release, 1970's *Parallelograms*. The largely acoustic album was jolted out of genteel coffeehouse territory by lyrics such as "I'm spacing out, I'm seeing silences between the leaves," swirling double-tracked voices, and phrasing that can make the songs seem more like windblown leaves of sound than commercial endeavors. The title track was acid folk minimalism, consisting of exactly eight words and a round-like vocal that dissolves into eerie, disquieting waves of electronically distorted voices, flutes, and rattles.

Perhacs got her deal with Kapp Records almost by accident when she met film composer Leonard Rosenman and his wife, who were patients at a clinic where she worked. They asked her what she did with her personal time; she told them she traveled and wrote songs; they asked to hear them; she gave them a homemade tape. They called her at 8:00 A.M. the following morning (a Saturday) and asked her to start working with them immediately; Rosenman produced *Parallelograms*. It was indeed easier to cut through the red tape of record company bureaucracy then, as Perhacs notes, "I never knocked on a door. Leonard opened doors all over the Los Angeles music world then because he knew everyone. He was experimenting with some of the earliest attempts at modulation of tones and vocals for his serious compositions and when I heard them, it sparked a jump in my creativity.

"In those days, we did not have the massive computers to help us create music. But that is what I was reaching for when I wrote *Parallelograms*. I wanted it to be like a Japanese air painting in motion, with the sounds moving through space creating the shapes of the words being spoken or sung, and for the shapes caused by the throwing of sound and tones from speaker to speaker to do what we now can do with 'surround sound.' Or, if performed live, to throw the sounds as shapes of moving music around the room with the words and shapes visible via lighting in motion. We only had one piece of equipment to help us do this then. I believe it was called a voice modulator; all else was live musicians," including noted jazzman Shelly Manne on drums.

"I brought the 'score' into the recording room on a very long piece of graph paper like a scroll that unwound. It was not music notation—it was picture graphs with timings noted under the pictures. The musicians were top professionals and really enjoyed the sessions. But we were limited due to [having] an idea before the use of computers for composing. The melodic part is only the frame that encloses the experimental center; the central part is the most creative area to express and recreate and enjoy from a musician's viewpoint. The album is a result of this one idea, because it opened the door to the finances to do the entire album." For all its experimental ambitions, the songs were still at their core melodic folk with tinges of pop, rock, and jazz, like Joni Mitchell's, to again use the obvious reference point. And few heard *Parallelograms* at the time— even those who are aware of it now are likely to have first come across it within the last few years, after it was excavated for CD reissue on a tiny independent.

Of the acid folk small label/vanity pressings known almost exclusively to collectors, the best are the two albums credited to one Satya Sai Maitreya Kali, otherwise known as Craig Smith. Released in the early '70s, but in large part recorded in the second half of the 1960s, the LPs mix quite good intersections of the Monkees and Buffalo Springfield with weirder, hollower arrangements featuring eerie, disembodied vocals. These muse upon religion and the cosmos with a forlorn desperation suggesting a man unable to find a place for himself anywhere on earth, or in the entire universe.

In a way, the until-recently virtually unknown saga of Satya Sai Maitreya Kali is a microcosm of both the acid folk underworld and the weird journey of Southern California folk-rock itself in the last half of the 1960s, from the sunniest to the darkest ends of the street. It turns out that the schizophrenic flavor of those albums was more than a faint echo of real-life schizophrenia in the featured artist. It isn't easy to explain how Smith went from, roughly speaking, the Monkees to Manson-like mumbo-jumbo, funded in part by Glen Campbell and Andy Williams. It sounded like a daft Hollywood movie. But just as similar scenarios happened to several figures circulating in Hollywood rock circles at the time, it actually happened to Smith, though on a low-level budget that made his journey a sort of B-movie version of the ones undergone by the likes of David Crosby, Neil Young, and the Beach Boys.

There is a mundane reason why the Satya Sai Maitreya Kali records sound half-normal and half-insane. Half the material was not recorded in the early '70s by Smith, but around 1967 by Smith's group the Penny Arkade, an engaging and hugely Buffalo Springfield–influenced band. Smith had previously been part of the duo Chris and Craig, who did an obscure folk-rock-psych single on Capitol. Smith and "Chris," aka Chris Ducey (not to be confused with Chris Lucey), would be the two singer-songwriters in the Penny Arkade, bouncing off and complementing each other much like a promising minor-league Stephen Stills and Neil Young. Like so many noted L.A. folk-rockers, they had migrated from New York, where they had known a pre-Monkees Mike Nesmith, and even did a pilot for a TV series about a rock band trying to make it big while living in Greenwich Village, *The Happeners*. *The Happeners* didn't happen, and Nesmith, coincidentally, got a role in a hit series about a California band that existed somewhere between reality and fiction, *The Monkees*. And it was Nesmith who funded and produced a wealth of demos by the Penny Arkade.

"Mike was a Monkee then," remembers Penny Arkade bassist Don Glut. "He came to California out of Texas as a serious musician songwriter-singer. And suddenly nobody took him seriously. People would call him 'old wool hat' and all this sort of thing. He wanted to demonstrate his real musical abilities by producing another band, which was us." In fact the Penny Arkade sounded better, and certainly more like an organic actual group, than the Monkees did on their studio recordings of the same era. Songs like "Country Girl," "Swim," "Lights of Dawn," and "Color Fantasy" successfully emulated the melodic, occasionally country-tinged folk-rock of Buffalo Springfield, though without approaching the Springfield's magnificence. The 12-minute "Knot the Frieze" could even be taken as the Penny Arkade's counterpart to "Broken Arrow," as it too was a suite strung together from pieces that could have on their own been solid folk-rock songs.

"Mike was shopping our things around to various record companies," resumes Glut, "and no sooner would we get the demos to the record company when our music didn't sound anything like that anymore. He said, 'I want a record company where you guys can grow, where you can keep doing new things.' And he never signed a contract with anybody; he kept looking for better deals. Then, I guess, his finances drastically took a turn for the worse. *The Monkees* got canceled. Suddenly he couldn't afford producing a band." The Penny Arkade were left in the lurch and broke up shortly afterward, leaving behind about two albums' worth of unreleased material that seemed destined to molder in the closet. But Smith's story wasn't quite finished.

Several Smith songs had been recorded by unlikely pop artists, with Glen Campbell covering "Country Girl," Andy Williams doing "Holly," and the Monkees themselves cutting "Salesman." "Craig made a lot of money with the songs that were recorded by other people, and used that money to travel around the world," says Glut. "He got real heavily into drugs, and immersed in a lot of unusual philosophies and religions which changed him mentally. When he came back here, he wasn't Craig anymore. He was Maitreya, which he told me once meant 'I love.' I don't know which language. But that's what he said it meant. [As an aside, there seemed to be some of this particular weirdness going around L.A. in the 1960s, as the aforementioned Bobby Jameson aka Chris Lucey also called himself "Maitreya" for a time.]

"Craig basically went off the deep end. He started to do a lot of weird things to a lot of people. Apparently he blinded his father. You couldn't really have a conversation with him. He was, like, staring off into space. He shaved his head so he was like Lex Luthor. I finally realized that, 'Hey, I don't really want to be connected with Craig anymore.'" He wasn't so far gone, though, as to be unable to record anymore, putting together about an album's worth of old Penny Arkade tracks and (without telling anyone else in the band) combining them with more recent, far spookier solo acoustic recordings. "Love and pain are the same," he crooned on "Ole Man," echoing the similarly creepy sentiments in Charles Manson's deranged songs of a very slightly earlier era, though with far greater melodicism and musical skill. (As a side note, Manson had fancied himself a singer-songwriter and even made demo tapes in an unsuccessful bid to get signed by ex-Byrds producer Terry Melcher; as is well known, several of the Manson family murders took place at Melcher's former house.)

The Penny Arkade–Smith cuts were jumbled up and issued on the crudely packaged Satya Sai Maitreya Kali LPs. Their artwork, a collage of snapshots from his world travels, hand-drawn religious and celestial symbols, and liner notes of an impenetrable syntax, seemed more a flyer for an insane asylum than a sleeve for a commercial release. A negative of a grim skull-like head glared out from one cover, its forehead plastered with a tattoo of a spider. "What was interesting to me was that when he did all those post–Penny Arkade songs, Craig seemed so far off the deep end," says Glut. "His music was getting stranger and stranger. [Yet] he would recycle something from the early days of the Penny Arkade, put new lyrics on it, as a new song. It's like he hadn't gotten too far off the beaten track to realize that some of the old stuff he did was really good.

"The last I had any contact with Craig, I got a phone call around 1971 or '72," Glut finishes. "He said, they're gonna play 'Knot the Frieze' on a radio station at a certain time that night. I turned on the radio, they played 'Knot the Frieze,' and [the DJ] got maybe five minutes into it, and he stopped it—'Well, enough of that.' That's the last I heard of Craig." Had Smith not surreptitiously put the Penny Arkade songs on his homemade albums, though, the world would have likely never known of their existence. Demand among collectors, due both to the rarity and the unusually high quality for a vanity pressing, eventually led to a double-CD release of the Satya Sai Maitreya Kali albums in Germany, and perhaps the second-most remarkable risen-from-the-dead story in acid folk. The first-most remarkable resurrection, that of Skip Spence, would command national media attention that made Satya Sai Maitreya Kali's renaissance seem like small potatoes.

S ome acid folk albums did manage to escape on big labels in the late '60s, the best of them crafted by the Holy Modal Rounders, Dino Valenti, and Skip Spence. Their very existence was, in each case, something of a miracle considering the instability of the performers and the profit-minded watchfulness of their companies. All had extremely admirable track records as cult folk-rock pioneers, and all made records that, while finding them at an artistic peak, could not have possibly appealed to more than a handful of listeners, even in an era when the psychedelic audience was at its most adventurous.

The Moray Eels Eat the Holy Modal Rounders, that group's sole effort for Elektra, was similar to the Mothers of Invention's *We're Only in It for the Money* and the Fugs' *It Crawled into My Hand, Honest* in its collages of bits and pieces forming side-long psychedelic suites. The Mothers and the Fugs, though, were careful craftsmen in their songwriting, if a bit loony in their lyrical preoccupations. *The Moray Eels Eat the Holy Modal Rounders* sounded like the work of old-timey folk musicians who had gone into the studio without rehearsing immediately following a massive

The Holy Modal Rounders, with Peter Stampfel in the center.

acid test, laying down blues, ragtime, and country extemporizations as their brains fried to a crisp. For all that, the record was highly enjoyable, oft-inspired zaniness, like that of a jug band caught in a funhouse mirror separating the third and fourth dimensions. The vocals sounded like either snide parodies of Appalachian hillbillies or those of drug addicts who could barely mumble a phrase before nodding off. The words often seemed like first-person accounts of the narrator's psyche falling to pieces, made clear enough by track titles like "My Mind Capsized," "Half a Mind," and "The STP Song." But it was all funny, and it just toed the precarious line between inspiration and insanity.

The unrehearsed, incoherent quality of the LP is an audio verité document of how things actually were, according to the Rounders' Peter Stampfel. He feels the reason their previous album, *Indian War Whoop*, "sounds so crappy is that Weber [Steve, the other main Rounder] wouldn't rehearse." He then recalls telling producer Frazier Mohawk (the former Barry Friedman, after a name change), "'The reasons this sounds so crappy is because Weber wouldn't practice, blah blah blah. You want a record to sound good, ya gotta stand there with a gun pointed at his crotch, cock the trigger, and say practice, motherfucker!' He said he would. Then when it was time to actually rehearse, when we all got to California, he said, 'Okay, everything's fine, I talked to Weber, he'll be great. I'm gonna get some coffee—go practice.' Of course, Weber didn't want to do that. So again, we went into the studio absolutely cold. Both of the engineers decided it would be a cool thing to make the records without any grooves between the songs, 'cause it would be more psychedelic or something."

Mohawk, who had already gotten into the folk-psych trip as producer of Kaleidoscope's first album, has more positive memories of the record. "I was the company freak, so I got all the freak groups. All of those things that I thought in [Stampfel's] music were quirks, I realized 30 years later, in fact were very well constructed and planned. He knows exactly what he's doing. There's very little randomness in his randomness. The problem was, everybody was *so* stoned in the making of that that there isn't one tune that has an ending, or that is complete. Nothing ever got finished in the recording of that. On [one] song, I was so stoned I played guitar on it when we were mixing it, and I'd never played guitar in my life! I took all of the pieces and thought it would be interesting to put them all together." For his part, Stampfel contends that only one song has missing words, and then only because "Mohawk insisted the song was sufficiently done as to require no more lyrics when we had done only two verses."

"Peter was the most stoned person I'd ever met in my life, he and his wife," counters Mohawk. "We went to take album cover pictures that never saw the light of the day at this cheap Hollywood motel, where they were staying. His wife got up out of bed, walked to the middle of the room where there was a chair, pulled her pants down, sat down, and took a piss. And thought it was the bathroom, thought she'd gone to the toilet. These were *really* stoned people." Stampfel again puts a different spin on the story, noting that the band was exhausted after having been up for several days, and "although I got her out of bed, she was still asleep. When I sat her down on a chair, she unconsciously thought it was the toilet and peed."

"The first time I'd ever been over to Peter's house, he offered me a cookie, and a roach carried it across the counter and took it away before I could get to it," continues Mohawk. "*Two* roaches.

The reason he invited me over was because he said he could change the songs on the radio. They would just sit there, decide what songs were gonna play, and then they would play." *The Moray Eels Eat the Holy Modal Rounders* does actually sound like a radio dial being flipped between stations, albeit stations playing music that would have never been broadcast by all but the most devil-may-care underground ones. As to why the group never released another album on Elektra, company president Jac Holzman has only these words: "It just never seemed to come up again."

According to Stampfel, though, "There was a follow-up recording, authorized by Holzman. This time I stayed away from speed, however Mohawk brought a bunch of heroin to the session, which was used by [three fellow Holy Modal Rounders] and himself. This left the three former too comatose to record, and caused Mohawk to freak out and shut himself in a closet. When I found him there he looked like he was hiding from the Nazis. Naturally, he blamed the session's failure on us to David Anderle, the man in charge under Holzman. When I explained what happened to David, he said my version made more sense than Mohawk's had.

"The upshot was that the other guy (name slips away) was put in charge of us. He said the only way he would record us was if Sam Shepard wrote some sort of comedy musical piece which would comprise an entire album. I said I wanted to record twelve songs, with spaces between them. He said his way or nothing. Nothing it was, although in retrospect, it would have been interesting and worthwhile to have had Sam write a whatever-he-would-have-written for us all to do."

Over at Columbia, Dino Valenti's sole album, 1968's *Dino Valente* (sic), was a far more placid affair. The singer-songwriter responsible for "Get Together" had influenced a great number of aspiring folk-rockers in the first half of the 1960s, but never gotten it together to record an album on his own. *Dino Valente* was Columbia's shot at capturing the man known as the "underground Dylan" in the studio, and artistically, it succeeded. For the most part the arrangements highlighted just him and his 12-string guitar, bathed in reverb and multitracked voices. He didn't sound much different than he had when he'd sung "Wayfaring Stranger" back in the early '60s, but to a 1961 audience, the songs would have seemed beamed in from outer space. The lyrics were stream-of-consciousness hippie conversations, most apparently aimed at convincing distraught nubile young beauties that only Valenti was capable of understanding them and dissipating their confusion through the power of blissful love. It was fragile, beautiful acid folk, with a glisten and otherworldly echo that softened the bluntness of Valenti's pinched, nasal voice. But it barely sold anything, due to the rather fraught circumstances of its production.

According to Valenti's close friend, Quicksilver Messenger Service guitarist Gary Duncan (who played on some of *Dino Valente*), Valenti first cut an album with Jack Nitzsche of "well-produced little nuggets of radio stuff." Valenti didn't like it, though, and went into the studio to do things more on his own agenda. In the process he managed to alienate studio musicians like Carol Kaye, who calls her session with Valenti "really a chore, the worst record date," and Columbia executives, whom Valenti would call in the middle of the night to insult. Says producer Bob Johnston, "You had to bring him back into check because he'd start a song, and 25 minutes later he'd be playing the same song. When we first started, I told him that we had to pick songs for the album. He said, 'Well, let me do these two.' Two of them were about an hour, and I said 'OK, need to cut one of them off, Dino.' He said, 'What do you mean? I've only got two songs.' I said, 'I don't care. If you want to make an hour record, that's fine. But otherwise, you'll have one song.' He said, 'Oh man, you can't do that. What can I do?' I said, 'You don't have to ask me. Chop 'em up. I don't want to chop your songs up.'"

"Bob, at that time, from what I understand, was sort of like Epic Records' troubleshooter," says Duncan. "He was the producer they sent in for acts they couldn't really deal with. Bob Dylan. Johnny Cash. Dino Valenti. Guys that were temperamental. His job was to go in and make the artist feel comfortable, and get a performance out of him that they could sell. And that's what he did with Dino. He made Dino happy. He let him do what he wanted.

"There was a couple of days straight that we didn't do anything in the studio but fly paper airplanes. 'Cause Dino was in a bad mood. So Johnston came in with this international paper airplane book. It had all these paper airplanes that you could put together and fly. We spent two days in the studio—I don't know what it cost, but it wasn't cheap—to sit around and just fly airplanes. We didn't do any music at all. But that's the way Johnston did things. He made him feel like he was a king. And they got a record out of him that made Dino happy. He loved it." But the public hardly got to hear it, as Columbia, not eager to work with an artist that had proved more trouble than he was worth, barely promoted the record. Valenti would record several LPs in the 1970s with Quicksilver, but never made another album as a soloist.

All other acid folk horror stories pale, however, next to the genesis of Skip Spence's *Oar*. In 1968 Spence, the victim of bad acid, was committed to Bellevue Hospital in New York for six months after brandishing a fire axe midway through the sessions for Moby Grape's second album. According to Moby Grape producer David Rubinson, "When he got out, he wanted a motorcycle and to go down to Nashville and record an album. And Columbia generously at that time, considering what had happened, said okay. They gave him a budget, and he went on down to Nashville, I believe by motorcycle, and went to work in the studio." In the space of about a week, acting as his own producer, he recorded the songs and played all the instruments on *Oar* (credited to Spence under his given name, Alexander Spence, although it's commonly referred to as a Skip Spence album).

Miraculously, considering the circumstances, *Oar* was a magnificent if nutty fusion of gutbucket acoustic blues, country, and folk music with the lyrics of one who has seen the afterlife and returned to share his revelations. Spence's wraithlike vocals, from a Johnny Cash–like gutter to an ethereal wispy howl, were ideal vehicles for wonderfully punning, off-the-wall paeans to the joys of sex, Biblical morality tales, ethereal goddesses, circus-like characters with muscles in their eyes, and "Lawrence of Euphoria." It was as if a dying Delta bluesman had been handed a guitar on the corner of Haight-Ashbury in 1968, given a final sacramental sugar cube, and recorded his final impressions as his spirit escaped his body. The one-man-alone-in-a-hotel-room ambience was imbued with a guileless honesty that cut down the barrier between song and performer as well as any ancient folkloric recording ever had.

"At that time *Sgt. Pepper* had come out," says Rubinson, who helped mix the record. "Even Moby Grape wanted things backwards on their albums and orchestras and stuff. What was happening [on *Oar*] was totally against [that] grain. It was completely from the heart and completely raw. It was like sitting down and listening to an authentic blues recording, a field recording almost. There was nothing between him and his art, there was no 'Gee, I'm going to try and make a hit record, I hope the critics like this, I bet I could make some money if I do it this way, what's the budget like, are we over budget, do we have enough this time?' There was no 'How do I do this, what's the best chord here?' It was totally intuitive.

"He was, in his earlier incarnation, a very witty, whimsical, lighthearted guy, full of laughter. And not a poet of darkness. The drugs took that. But this album is very personal and *very* witty." Peter Lewis of Moby Grape concedes that *Oar* "was scary to me, when I heard it . . . not that it wasn't organized. It was. But there was this part of it that delved into the darkness of the soul." Columbia, a label that had way too large a roster to promote each and every act with the attention it deserved, "had no aspirations for this commercially," according to Rubinson. "They didn't think it was going to sell, and they barely pressed it up and basically buried it. They never really serviced it properly, and it was never promoted." *Oar*, according to one estimate, sold only 700 copies, a tally that a major label has to work to *keep* at such a low level.

If drugs had spurred Spence and others on to some new creative heights, some, like Spence (and in England, Syd Barrett), would also become the '60s rock generation's prime acid casualties. "If every snowflake is different, every human is metabolically different," cautions Banana Levinger. "The way they react to LSD is all different. To some people, it's a rollicking good time. To other people, it is a confirmation of all the spiritual bases that they have always believed in, but now it kind of is elucidated and put into more concrete thought that can actually be expressed. To other people, it throws them out of phase, and they're out of phase for the rest of their life. LSD and marijuana play a big role in intensity, creativity, and research, and the other drugs play a big role in tragedy, decay, sorrow, and anguish. It's tragic, in a lot of cases."

Spence, beset by mental and chemical difficulties, was one such case. He never made another album. By the 1990s he was living in a San Jose residential care home, a diagnosed paranoid schizophrenic taking antipsychotic drugs, given to hearing voices and talking to himself. To some moralists, that might seem like the final payback for the indulgences of the acid rock era, and proof positive that folk's path from folk-rock to psychedelia exacted a horrible cost. But fate had a final card to play as Spence was passing from this world to the next in the early spring of 1999.

Oar, partly as the result of a couple low-key reissues in the late '80s and early '90s, had by the end of the twentieth century attracted such a fanatical cult following that Skip Spence was no longer a cult, exactly. Beck, Tom Waits, Robyn Hitchcock, and Robert Plant were among those who recorded a tribute album to the ailing mad genius. There was a feature on National Public Radio. And the 1999 CD reissue of *Oar*, topped with bonus tracks of course, sold about 50 times as many copies as the original LP had in 1969. Skip Spence, once a tree fallen in a deserted forest, was now the greatest equivalent to Vincent Van Gogh not only in all of folk-rock, but in all of rock music. *Oar* had been resurrected in much the same manner as young revivalists had dug up old folk songs and rediscovered bluesmen in the early '60s, when the slang terms "folk-rock" and "acid" had not even entered the English language. As much as anything by the Byrds or Bob Dylan, Spence's *Oar* demonstrated that the best of 1960s folk-rock was timeless, in ways that transcended the lively, troubled, and jumbled psychedelic era that made it possible.

3

folk-rock grows up

the singer-songwriters

I

f folk-rock seemed in danger of floating into the ether or vanishing under a cloud of drugs and loud electric guitars after Haight-Ashbury got hold of it, there were just as many forces tugging it back to earth in the final years of the 1960s. There would always be an audience for music that put the priority firmly on songs and their singers, rather than wild and unpredictable experimentation and risk. And by the late '60s, there was room to do so in a folk-rock context without drawing nearly as much wrath from purists.

Although still largely devoted to traditional folk music, *Sing Out!*, whose editorship had transferred to Happy Traum in 1967, was by now printing songs by Joni Mitchell and the Incredible String Band, and even the Band's "The Weight." These were symbols that *Sing Out!* and the purists in its readership were coming to peace with folk-rock, accommodating the parts of it they liked instead of fulminating about whether it had any right to exist at all. The late '60s also found the magazine doing major interviews with Country Joe McDonald, Roger McGuinn, and Bob Dylan, though the last of these in particular may have been motivated by the publication's dire need to dig itself out of a financial crisis. (Which it helped do; the *Sing Out!* with Dylan on the cover sold, in Traum's estimation, about 50,000 copies, and although circulation had dropped down to 12,000 by 1971, the magazine is still going today.)

Sing Out!'s broadening focus was an acknowledgment that contemporary songwriting was now about much more than current news events; by 1971, Traum admitted to *Rolling Stone* that there were "less politics than there have ever been" in the magazine. "Suddenly people who had started out in the folk world—Tim Buckley, Eric Andersen, James Taylor, the Spoonful, Youngbloods—were writing some pop songs," says Traum now. "That became the scene, and the political singer-songwriter, like Phil Ochs, kind of got left hanging out to dry. Although he tried to do his own version of folk-rock, of course."

Now that the debate over whether folk musicians were entitled to use electric instruments and write about all kinds of contemporary issues had largely died out, folk-rock singer-songwriters were free to refine their sound and work their love of roots music into a more flexible framework than solo acoustic arrangements had allowed. The continued expansion of the album market as young people accounted for a larger and larger portion of total record sales; the proliferation of FM radio stations willing to play albums by artists who didn't have hit singles; the ongoing growth of their target demographic as teenagers matured into college students and graduates: all made it easier for folk-rock artists to survive and even thrive. As the singers grew further into adulthood, the songs reflected more mature concerns, the tempos slowed down, and the time for a renewed appreciation for their earlier ties to country, blues, and folk had come. With the birth of two new branches of folk-rock—the singer-songwriter movement and country-rock—folk-rock itself grew up into adulthood by the end of the decade.

art of the increased maturity of folk-rock and singer-songwriting was due to changes in the industry itself, which was becoming less driven by insatiable thirst for singles hits, and more inclined to hunt for album sales. "LP Perils Single in Bowing Acts" announced an August 18, 1967 headline on the front page of *Billboard*, as a sort of corporate acknowledgment of a trend that had actually been building throughout the decade. "The LP is threatening the single's long-held dominance in the launching of pop artists," began the report. "Record company executives have discovered that the new type of groups being launched on disks don't need single hits to sell albums." By mid-1968, according to *Forbes* magazine, LPs accounted for more than 75% of the revenues earned by popular records.

Just as crucially, the explosive growth of FM radio in the late '60s gave such product far much more exposure than it had in the past. Many of the new FM stations were targeted toward the underground or at least open-minded young adult rock listenership. They and their listeners not only tolerated but encouraged airplay for more than one or two songs from an LP; long cuts that could not fit into the strict time limitations of AM commercial radio programming; new and/or somewhat unfamiliar artists; and playlists that could reflect the individual, and often adventurous, taste of the DJs rather than the dictates of the market. All of rock music, and much nonrock music, benefited from this. But it was certainly a specific boon for singer-songwriters who wanted to create a serious mood over the course of an album, rather than knock your socks off with a catchy tune. It was also a boon for labels that specialized in the same. "Underground stations like WNEW in New York, WBZ in Boston, and a few others—we had four, five, six artists always being played on those stations," says Verve/Forecast chief Jerry Schoenbaum. "It was very helpful."

On occasion FM radio even helped break artists who hadn't recorded yet, as Pacifica affiliate WBAI in New York did by playing tapes of Arlo Guthrie's "Alice's Restaurant" and Jerry Jeff Walker's "Mr. Bojangles," creating demand for those records before they even existed. (As retribution that was likely more coincidental than cosmic, another Pacifica affiliate, Houston's KPFT, had its transmitter bombed and signal cut in 1970 while broadcasting "Alice's Restaurant," at the precise moment when Guthrie and the Army psychiatrist scream "kill, kill" together.) In Philadelphia, Joni Mitchell's live broadcasts on the FM programs of Gene Shay and others (which are still bootlegged today) had done an enormous amount to build her following between 1966 and 1969. In Boston, WBZ's broadcast of an unreleased coffeehouse tape of Tom Rush's cover of Mitchell's "Urge for Going" was heard by country star George Hamilton IV, who had Gordon Lightfoot put him in touch with Joni. She sent him a demo tape, and Hamilton's recording of the song in Nashville was the first release of a Mitchell song to enjoy substantial commercial success. Going beyond the strictly singer-songwriter branch of folk-rock, KPPC DJ B. Mitchell Reed made an unreleased nine-minute version of Buffalo Springfield's "Bluebird" an underground airplay hit of sorts in the Los Angeles area in 1967. This extended version, unearthed when Reed discovered the tape while house-sitting for Stills, would appear on the posthumous *Buffalo Springfield* compilation about five years later.

The FM stations played a huge role, still not fully acknowledged by history, in creating and sustaining a buzz over singer-songwriter albums that were widely influential, and/or instrumental in launching artists to eventual stardom, despite selling relatively few copies at the time. *Joni Mitchell* and *Songs of Leonard Cohen* are just two of the better examples. "That's the thing that's so amazing about those times," says David Anderle. As a producer and director of Elektra's West Coast office, Anderle was closely involved with first-rate albums by several artists who relied almost totally upon FM radio for any airplay they got, including Tim Buckley, Love, Joni Mitchell, and even Judy Collins (who had little AM radio exposure other than for "Both Sides Now"). "That's gone, the fact that a record can come out, not sell that many records, and cause that much energy. You can't even think of that nowadays."

Some have seen the singer-songwriter movement's overall toning down of folk-rock's earlier, wilder years—reflected quite strongly in the low-volume arrangements of albums like *Joni Mitchell* and *Songs of Leonard Cohen*, as it happens—as a stripped-down, back-to-basics backlash against psychedelic excess. It's advisable to keep in mind, though, that the boundaries between psychedelic warriors and singer-songwriters were, like so many artificial divisions between folk-rock camps, not solid and exclusionary. Singer-songwriters may have gotten mellow and introspective, but were often reaching into new instrumental directions with their use of orchestras and exotic tunings. Perhaps their confessional styles seemed solipsistic, but they still made room for trenchant social commentary and even social protest. Sometimes the confessional troubadours dallied with psychedelic effects; some of those most responsible for groundbreaking psychedelia pioneered country-rock. If some of the early excitement and sense of discovery in playing electric instruments for the first time was lost, a greater consistency and firmer handle on more personal lyrical expression was gained.

The origin of the term "singer-songwriter," to describe folk-based composer-vocalists aiming for the popular audience, is even vaguer than the origin of the term "folk-rock." Even more than folk-rock, it's a term used by critics and aficionados, rather than in everyday conversation. The phrase was certainly used as early as 1965, when Elektra released a compilation LP, *Singer Songwriter Project*, with cuts by four newly emerging folk-based composer-vocalists (Richard Fariña, Patrick Sky, Dave Cohen aka David Blue, and Bruce Murdoch).

Just as *Billboard* had been to a large degree responsible for popularizing the term "folk-rock" itself in mid-1965, it might have been another widely read, nationally circulated publication that made "singer-songwriter" a catchphrase for a new trend. On July 5, 1968, Robert Shelton—who had already done a great deal to make the folk boom and folk-rock legitimate in the eyes of the mainstream media as a *New York Times* music critic—penned a piece for the paper headlined "Singer-Songwriters Are Making a Comeback." While it wasn't quite clear where they were coming back from or if they'd ever been away, the subhead made the subtext explicit: "Developing Trend Indicated at the Bitter End by Jerry Walker and Joni Mitchell."

"After two years of the dominance of electric pop groups, the singer-songwriter with the pre-Edison guitar is making a comeback," announced Shelton. "Trends in Greenwich Village night haunts are mercurial, but all indications are that a return to folk-style performances is well on the way. [Village club] The Bitter End, long on a heavy rock diet, is presenting two of the most interesting folk-oriented talents to emerge since Arlo Guthrie and Janis Ian were strumming in the Village two years ago. The Gaslight, long an incubator for folk talent, has reopened on Macdougal Street. Gerde's Folk City is pondering a move to the West Village while two former centers of electric pop, the Night Owl [where the Lovin' Spoonful had honed their sound] and the Generation, remain closed.

"Part of the reason for the drift from the band to the single performer or small group is economics. The cost of booking an electric band can be prohibitive. Part of the change, however, is the cyclical nature of pop taste, indicating the high-frequency rock 'n' roar may have reached its zenith."

Although the hyphenated label "singer-songwriter" didn't start to widely circulate until the early '70s, the style was clearly rooted in the late '60s, when singer-songwriters such as Leonard Cohen and Joni Mitchell started to record, and others like Fred Neil and Tim Hardin made important records that cultivated the form. To the uninitiated, it sounds ludicrously broad: Isn't everyone who sings and writes songs a singer-songwriter, whether Paul McCartney, Patti Smith, or Robert Johnson? As it's been applied, however, it refers to performers, the bumper crop of them from the late '60s and early '70s, who recorded personal and poetic songs that could have been (and sometimes were) performed solo on guitar, harmonica, and piano.

As one of the two performers spotlighted by Shelton in that *Times* piece points out, of course its roots also went way back to the folk boom. Explains Jerry Jeff Walker (despite the article's headline, he's been known as Jerry Jeff Walker since he started recording, not "Jerry Walker"): "There was a real movement [in the early '60s] to collect authentic folk music. We probably took 200 years of music and swallowed it up in six months. Everybody's trying to play it more traditionally than anybody else. It was too analytical, too studied—you know, 'the back hammer claw forward hammer-on by such-and-such' was the only way to play 'Little Darlin'' or something.

"I wanted my music to be alive. I didn't want to go up there all night long and say, 'This is a song Woody Guthrie wrote [when] he was in a car going on to the Dust Bowl.' I wasn't a folkologist; I was tired of explaining. Really the shortcut became, if you couldn't be [traditional folk multi-instrumentalist] Mike Seeger, you might as well be Tom Paxton or Bob Dylan or Phil Ochs, because you could kind of cut across the gap and write your own. I wrote about what *my* existence was, so pretty soon I didn't have to say, 'This is somebody...' I just played 'em, and sort of became a person singing the song. A *believable* person.

"Early friends of mine said when I came hitchhiking through Dallas in '62, I had an old road bag that'd been with me a couple years. I was beat up. My clothes had road grime on 'em and I was slowly becoming what I was trying to become. So we'd sing a song about a guy he met in a jail cell in New Orleans"—as Walker did in his most famous composition, "Mr. Bojangles"—"they might believe you. They wouldn't have much of a stretch.

"In a sense, that's what Dylan was doing in the early years. He was going from being a folk singer onstage trying to copy what all these guys were doing in [Minneapolis's bohemian district] Dinkytown to a fact where he could just be something believable when he sang it. Show business has always been partly creating an image onstage. But we were trying to create an image that wasn't much different from who we were off and on." As for the singer-songwriter label itself, Walker whimsically speculates, "We had to put *something* down. 'What are you?' 'I sing, and I'm a song-writer. Yeah, that's it.'"

Folk singers had already started to write and record their own material in their own personas a year or two before folk-rock came along. The so-called singer-songwriters of the late '60s differed markedly, though, in the far greater depth, flexibility, and electricity of their musical accompaniment. "You're trying to write your songs, and get your songs accompanied in a way that enhances it with-out running over it too much," elaborates Walker. "If you can get it done with three instruments, fine. If it takes you five or seven—whatever you need. But you're trying to bring this feeling to it. So it works best if you can get a band that you can play with, live with, and be with—an expensive luxury. It takes whoever you're playing with to do it. If you can do it with acoustics, it's fine. If you can do it with electric, *that's* fine."

Some would have it that the schism between folk purists and the rock crowd would have made folkies disinclined to pay attention to the new breed of singer-songwriters. In reality, however, many of the new singer-songwriters' devotees were listeners who had first become folk enthusiasts during the much more tradition-based early-'60s revival. "They were really folk singers who just happened to be writing songs," says Gene Shay, host of influential folk programs on WHAT (and later WDAS) in Philadelphia throughout the 1960s. "Many of them were still doing some traditional material, or some covers of folk tunes. So the distinction wasn't that wrenching. I often thought of [them] as just people who were taking folk music into a more contemporary orchestration, a different dimension, more acceptable for a young group of people who were interested in musical chops, and not quite as old-fashioned. The new audience were getting a more contemporary story about people like them.

"I always just thought of it as an extension. At the time, we just considered Joni [Mitchell] a folk singer. She was playing the folk circuit, playing all the clubs, [including Philadelphia's] the Main Point, the Second Fret, and the same thing with Jerry Jeff Walker. When he played 'Mr. Bojangles' with [David] Bromberg backing him up, I used to think, 'Hey, this is just high-powered folk music,' very much the way that bluegrass was high-powered country music." Indeed, while Shay's programs were identified as folk shows, he gave plenty of airtime for live sets by breaking folk-rock songwrit-ers passing through Philly like Mitchell, Walker, Richie Havens, Tim Buckley, Arlo Guthrie, and James

Taylor. Shay doesn't remember much of a fallout, either from his radio listeners or among folk purists offended by the addition of instruments, orchestration, electricity, and other aspects of pop and rock: "I found the audiences very accepting. There have always been some purists or traditionalists who turned their nose up at anything that wasn't played on an acoustic instrument, and any song that didn't have a ballad structure or wasn't based on some traditional material."

Folk-rock's breakthroughs gave the new breed of folk-rock singer-songwriters license to record with other musicians on their albums for a greater range of complementary sounds. It also enabled them to write idiosyncratic sung monologues and dialogs that might have simply baffled or even angered folk revival audiences in their direct candor or literary symbolism. They were solo performers, not ones given to collaborating as members of full rock bands. They often didn't have permanent bands for their live tours, and sometimes didn't even play with bands onstage. All that considered, it's no surprise that the new breed's records relied heavily on session musicians, and were mostly recorded in Los Angeles and New York. (Most of the prominent singer-songwriters were based in or near those cities too, with a handful of Canadian expatriates among their ranks.) Sometimes, though not always, they had expressive yet unorthodox voices and visages that would have made it difficult for them to get contracts before the mid-'60s, or would have consigned them to behind-the-scenes songwriting for other artists. Indeed, it was often through other voices that these writers were first heard.

As she had been since 1963, Judy Collins would remain instrumental to giving important songwriters their first exposure through the end of the 1960s. *In My Life*, from 1966, was her first album to bring in pop and rock influences (though she had previously recorded a cover of Bob Dylan's "I'll Keep It with Mine" on a non-LP folk-rock single). Actually, there was relatively little straight-up "rock" on *In My Life*, its hard-charging cover of Richard Fariña's "Hard Lovin' Loser" notwithstanding. There was, far more often, a combination of folk with classical-styled arrangements on covers of songs by contemporary writers like Leonard Cohen, Donovan, the Beatles, and Randy Newman, as well as some theatrical art songs by the likes of Jacques Brel and Brecht-Weill. It was dubbed "folk-baroque" by some in the press, a hybrid created to a large degree on *In My Life* and its successor *Wildflowers* by the collaboration between the singer, producer Mark Abramson, and arranger/conductor Joshua Rifkin. Rifkin had been in the Even Dozen Jug Band with young folk musicians like John Sebastian and Stefan Grossman, and then had some success with classical interpretations of Beatles songs on the Elektra album *The Baroque Beatles Book*. He was one of a parade of unlikely characters who somehow fell into important ancillary roles in folk-rock, both at Elektra and throughout the business.

"What you had with Judy and myself were people who had both folk and classical background," says Rifkin, who after the 1960s became a musicologist, conductor, and pianist, esteemed for his research in Renaissance and baroque music. "Virtually none of us doing that stuff then had an actual rock background. Folk, perhaps, was the link. I think they brought me in because they were interested in trying something new with her. My response was, when [Elektra] asked me about arranging for her, 'I've never arranged before. So of course I'd love to.' It is really extraordinary that they

Judy Collins, around the time of her Wildflowers *album.*

took these chances on me and several other people. They were ready to try practically anything, or try what appealed to them, and I for one am eternally grateful for their having done so.

"Everybody was open to and looking for new possibilities; people were very, very eager to try different things, and see what would happen. There were, I think, at the same time new possibilities for recognition and success that folk musicians had not had before. Pop music now was changing, and it opened up possibilities of folk-derived music being part of a sort of broader pop scene. That was tantalizing, fascinating, challenging, and so forth. The other thing—I think everybody was, to be honest, attracted by the notion of a higher level of success."

Wildflowers (released in late 1967) had three Leonard Cohen songs and two by Joni Mitchell, before either of those Canadians had released albums of their own. Interestingly this record, which many would classify as folk-rock without a second thought, and which contained one of the biggest folk-rock hits of the 1960s, actually had no guitars. Even more than *In My Life*, it was an art song record, the arrangements dominated by string parts. "This was an even stronger move away from folk stuff," agrees Rifkin. "Although this was categorized as folk or folk-rock or whatever, largely because of what Judy had been doing in her career and because of the nature of some of the songs, it was a very decisive move away from all the basic suppositions of folk, and even commercialized or classicized folk music. It was definitely going towards what was sometimes called art pop in those days. There was a lot of that kind of stuff about, or at least hints in that direction. It's no accident that Van Dyke Parks's first LP came out at about the same time, and there were lots of string quartets on Beatles and Stones tracks. That too was in air, and we took the consequences fairly extreme."

So where was the folk, and the rock, in this particular folk-rock album? As Rifkin sees it, "They're not standard pop songs, they're neither blues, nor are they the normal structure of pop songs. They were strophic, the way folk songs traditionally were. And they were written by songwriters who had come out of what was loosely defined as the folk tradition, or the folk scene. Joni Mitchell was a singer in folk clubs. It was obviously not country-folk, not traditional folk. It was modern, urban folk; literate folk, if you will. In that way it was already straddling lines, and we were pushing it still farther."

That extended to taking material by writers who were not only pretty unknown, but also not connected to the folk scene at all. "In Hollywood when we were doing *Wildflowers*, a very unprepossessing man came to thank me very warmly for the arrangement on *In My Life* of a tune of his," remembers Rifkin. "And not thinking at all, I just sort of thanked him politely, and said, 'Yes, well, I was very happy to do it,' etc., didn't really think anything more of it. It was, in fact, Randy Newman. He wasn't heard of. I tell that story with a lot of embarrassment today." As an intriguing aside that itself indicates how Elektra employees were opening their ears to the pop market, prior to working on Newman's "I Think It's Going to Rain Today" on *In My Life*, Rifkin had indeed heard one of Randy's songs without recognizing the composer. He came across it on, of all things, a 1965 single by Liverpudlian pop singer Cilla Black that never even made the American charts, "I've Been Wrong Before." Although Black is now regarded as a lightweight by most critics, and the Elektra crowd as the hip cutting edge, as Rifkin reveals, "We all thought [it] was one of the great singles of the '60s. At parties at Mark Abramson's house, we used to play that thing 20, 40 times in a row, just wearing out the vinyl."

One of the Joni Mitchell covers on *Wildflowers*, "Both Sides Now," was a monumental breakthrough for both the singer and the composer. It gave Judy Collins a Top Ten hit, and Elektra Records its biggest hit of the 1960s (after a special single remix, a year after it had first appeared on LP) other than its smashes by the Doors. If folk-baroque could be said to be a style in its own right, "Both Sides Now" was its crowning moment, with harpsichord tinkles rather than guitars providing the main hooks, and Joshua Rifkin's full orchestral arrangement heightening Collins's crisp, crystal-clear delivery rather than diluting it. The song was a superb elucidation of life's ambiguity, inspired by a passage in Saul Bellow's book *Henderson the Rain King*. It was put in more storybook imagery (and given a much stronger melody) than Dylan and his acolytes would have usually used, but no less effective for that.

"I had been introduced to a number of Joni songs by a producer who was interested in having me arrange for her, about the time we were setting up the project that became *In My Life*," recalls Rifkin. "I remember hearing 'Circle Game' and a few other of Joni's songs on a demo tape, being very impressed by them, and then losing sight of her, but then hearing Judy say when we were planning *Wildflowers* that she had some marvelous new songs by Joni Mitchell. 'Both Sides Now' was not in the original batch. I think it came to Judy after we'd already done a lot of the recording out on the [West] Coast. I think Judy already had it from Joni and was playing around with it in part at the guitar, and in part on piano. The harpsichord lick on 'Both Sides Now' is derived from something that Judy was doing at the piano.

"By that time, already Judy had given it a very different groove from what Joni had, as I later learned when I heard Joni sing it. The sort of soft rock rhythm that we have was kind of in Judy's take on the song when she first presented it to me. Doing these albums was in many ways a very collaborative enterprise. The first song on the album, [Mitchell's] 'Michael from Mountains,' is dominated by that kind of harp riff that starts the thing off, and then keeps coming back at various points. That, again, grew out of something that Judy was doing on a 12-string guitar when she first played it for me.

"I got feedback once from Joni, who was not happy with 'Both Sides Now.' She wasn't angry, she didn't dislike it. But she did feel we made a very, very different song out of it, and that it was not the song that she knew and felt. That's certainly a reasonable point." But, as with some other classic folk-rock covers, there was no way it would have reached as many ears or have had any chance at all on AM radio in the version Mitchell was singing in folk clubs, accompanied only by her acoustic guitar. It took not only a much more varied and textured multi-instrumental arrangement to put it over to singles-buyers, but also an artist such as Collins who was not afraid to put her own interpretive stamp on the song.

It would not be until about a year after *Wildflowers* was issued that "Both Sides Now" would become a huge hit. In the intervening time, the country had been shaken by the assassinations of Martin Luther King, Jr. and Robert Kennedy, plus the riots at the 1968 Democratic Convention in Chicago. "From the beginning I thought 'Both Sides Now' was a potential single but I wasn't sure about the timing," wrote Elektra president Jac Holzman in his oral history-cum-autobiography, *Follow the Music*. "The world needed to settle down a bit for these wise and gentle words to be heard. Almost a year later there were rumors of an English group coming out with the song so I moved quickly." A competing version by an Irish group recording in London, the Johnstons, actually did bubble under the Top 100 on the heels of the Collins single. But as Nat Joseph, who ran the Transatlantic label for which the Johnstons recorded, puts it: "Jac had a thing about breaking Judy Collins. Jac put *fortunes* in to ensure that Judy beat the Johnstons out."

Wildflowers was a Top Five album as well, and taken with *In My Life* endures as a peak of the folk-baroque movement, if there was such a thing. "Those albums did have a very substantial influence," believes Rifkin. "We were about the first to make this move, and within the next couple of years, everybody had their orchestral album. In some ways, we really set a standard with it. These albums did something, A, that hadn't really been done, and B, was quite beautiful. Very few of the albums I heard that took off into the direction impressed me very much."

Not every memory of Elektra is golden, and in a discouraging footnote, it was not a sound that Rifkin himself would get to cultivate on many other outings within the rock world. While Rifkin harbors generally glowing impressions of Elektra, as he remembers, "I, with [Judy Collins's] *Wildflowers*, was a fairly desirable property in this narrow segment of the pop world. There were a lot of people who wanted sort of imitations of the kind of stuff I'd been doing. And who better, after all, to imitate me than myself? So I got quite a number of feelers and quite a number of offers. Jac [Holzman], being the very canny businessman that he always was, decided to protect his investment in me and put me under exclusive contract. I, as a young kid growing up in the traditional record world, thought this was marvelous because in those days, it was a mark of a great artist to have an exclusive contract. It was a bad mistake, because in fact I had to turn away work that came to me from elsewhere, and this involved some work I really would have wanted to do. Meanwhile, Elektra gave me virtually nothing."

nother Elektra artist who followed Collins both into selecting nuggets by emerging songwriters and employing symphonic production was Tom Rush. *The Circle Game*, from early 1968, was almost a preview of the early '70s singer-songwriter explosion. There were three songs by his friend Joni Mitchell, one of which, "Urge for Going," Elektra had vainly tried to break as a national hit single after it had been given a strong push by WBZ in Boston back in 1966. There were also two songs by James Taylor, yet to record his debut for Apple Records, and one by young Californian Jackson Browne, still years away from his first album. Rush, like Collins, was also developing his own songwriting, and the result was an extremely varied if low-key and lushly orchestrated set (conducted by Paul Harris, a familiar mainstay of NYC folk-rock sessions).

"The songwriters hadn't really come to the forefront yet," says Rush. "In fact, *Rolling Stone* said that the *Circle Game* album was the beginning of the singer-songwriter phenomenon. Joni was sending me tapes of new songs as she wrote them. I had a tape from her with about five really nice tunes on it, many of which she has since recorded. But at the end she sticks on this tune, and she said, 'I just finished writing this. It really sucks. You're gonna hate it. I don't know why I'm even bothering to put it on here.' And it was 'The Circle Game,' which reinforced my thought that the artist is the last one to know when they've got something good.

"In the case of Jackson, he was being published by Elektra. So I had access to his demos, and he I think later sent me some tapes that he made for me. James, I met actually through Paul Rothchild, who said, 'This is a kid who you oughta hear.' These three writers in my mind were very much kindred spirits, although I don't think they'd ever met, and they weren't aware of each other. They were writing tunes with a folk sensibility, but they were at the same time musically more sophisticated and lyrically more literate than the traditional folk stuff. It was a large but logical step in my mind.

"If I helped to bring Joni, Jackson, and James a little sooner to the public eye, that was worth doing, because they became very important artists," Rush concludes. "*Circle Game* I like a lot, but I think if I were to do it again, I would not use the strings and horns to the extent that they were used there. It felt good at the time, but it feels a bit overproduced now." Producer Arthur Gorson, on the other hand, thinks the end result was a little restrained in that respect: "The goal was to make a commercial record, except Tom was a very astute judge of his audience, and was afraid to push too far in terms of how much orchestration would go on it. He limited the amount of production that we could do, because he was afraid of alienating his more purist audience."

It was in keeping with a facet of the Elektra house sound that was briefly dubbed "symphonic folk" by the British press, and would occasionally even be heard in a live setting, as when Buffy Sainte-Marie was accompanied by an orchestra on a few songs at an October 1967 concert at New York's Philharmonic Hall. It was also adopted, in a daintier manner than on Collins's and Rush's records, on Tom Paxton's late '60s albums. "When the Beatles started using acoustic instruments, and then when they added string quartets, all the bets were off," Paxton told *Melody Maker* in 1967. "Well, this attitude has filtered down to your humble servant, and I will be using up to a full orchestra on my next album ... the ballad form, which has been the basis for folk music for hundreds of years, just will not sustain itself in 1967. I think we've got to learn from the orchestral form. A song needs to be put together like a symphony, with several different sections—movements, if you like .... It was Judy Collins's last album that really showed me what could be done in the field."

He never approximated a symphony more than on the epic 15-minute "The Iron Man" on 1969's *The Things I Notice Now*, which recalled the mammoth ambitious poems Phil Ochs set to orchestration on his slightly earlier A&M albums. Both Paxton and Ochs were here delving not so much into folk-rock as art song, although Paxton's compositions were not as melodic or biting as Ochs's and his voice not nearly as powerful or singed with character and passion as the likes of Judy Collins. Still, the orchestral form might have suited Paxton's strengths more than the standard load-on-the-electric-guitars approach, as he readily acknowledges, "I never really got very interested in electric guitars or anything like that. It just wasn't what my sensibility was, that's all."

Paxton had been one of the topical folk singers most resistant to electric folk-rock in the mid-'60s, most infamously in his "Folk Rot" article for *Sing Out!* It was a sign of the times that he'd not only broadened his musical outlook, but also his lyrical one, in turn indicating that the more doctrinaire flames of the folk-based contemporary songwriter had virtually been extinguished. "I got the feeling when I was a protest singer that people were agreeing with the sentiment of a song, not because it was a good song," he admitted to *NME*. "That got to be boring. Now I feel the same way, politically, about things but my approach is different. I write songs ... not preach sermons or tell people how they should live their lives. Like all honest changes it came gradually. I began to tire of specific preaching songs and one by one dropped them from my repertoire to replace them with more honest ones."

Elektra's most adventurous singer-songwriter of the late '60s, Tim Buckley, had by the end of his tenure with the label trampolined outside of the boundaries not just of folk-rock, but of anything that could be considered reasonably accessible popular music. At the outset, though, he was Southern Californian folk-rock's great teenage hope. His beautiful tenor voice essayed naive but gorgeous folk-baroque on his self-titled 1966 debut album, often buttressed with assistance from his close friend and frequent lyricist Larry Beckett. Jack Nitzsche, the arranger who floated in and out of some of the most inventive Los Angeles folk-rock recordings throughout the '60s, did the string arrangements; Van Dyke Parks added harpsichord, piano, and celeste; and guitarist Lee Underwood contributed shimmering, fluid lead guitar, as he would on several of Buckley's subsequent albums. Both the structures and settings echoed jazz and classical music, yet folk-rock formed most of the foundation. The spookily reverbed guitars of "Song of the Magician" and "Song Slowly Song" added some quasi-psychedelic mystery, though the more standard compositions were almost mainstream tuneful folk-rock. Particularly when Beckett supplied the lyrics, the words could be obtuse reflections of altered states of mind, without totally obscuring the more precious romanticism that dominated the songs Buckley wrote alone.

Buckley went into more psychedelic modes on his greatest record, 1967's *Goodbye and Hello*, which caromed among spooky Moroccan-flavored incantations to lost love ("Hallucinations"); an epic suite of the schizophrenic tension in American society in "Goodbye and Hello"; beautiful elegiac ballads of weathered experience ("Morning Glory" and "Once I Was"); circus-like surrealism ("Carnival Song"); and one of the 1960s' great underappreciated antiwar songs, "No Man Can Find the War," opening and concluding with atomic bomb blasts (the last one backwards). Beckett's lyrics, Beckett himself observes, are "more literary, and use more literary devices. [Tim's] persisted in being personal sort of surrealistic statements of his own love life. It forms a nice balance, actually, when we have albums with both of our things on it."

"No Man Can Find the War" served as proof that antiwar protest was not dying out with the dawn of the singer-songwriter era, but taking on more subtle dimensions. Explains Beckett, "The whole country was obsessed [with Vietnam], especially our idealistic generation, that was really honestly against war, and then [had] it thrust on us. The imagery has a kind of quick-cut quality, like you would see on network TV portrayals of the war—even now!—are we going to beat Belgrade down or not?

"But that's not the *real* war. The real war is, where does this stuff come from? Where do these people come from that can treat other people so? That's the real war, inside, that nobody even *addresses*. They never talk about it on the network news. All they talk about is how many people were killed on each side, and those numbers are usually falsified anyway. It was part of my frustration that now, and back then, people are 'end the war and cure the symptoms,' and the disease flourishes."

Elektra may have pioneered the folk-baroque form with Judy Collins's *In My Life*, but as *Goodbye and Hello* producer Jerry Yester relates, Jac Holzman's appetite for symphonic folk did know some bounds. As the track "Goodbye and Hello" was being prepared, "Holzman called up as I was going over the score with the orchestra and said, 'So, I hear you have an orchestra. If there's any way I can cancel that session, I would. Why didn't you call me?' I said, 'Well, it just happened kind of fast, I didn't think I needed to call you.' 'Well...if I could cancel it, I would.' Then he slammed the phone down. The next time I saw him was when we were mixing it, and he said, 'This is the greatest piece I've ever heard,' just giving me all kinds of praise."

Goodbye and Hello was Buckley's first chart album (albeit at a lowly #171), and the photogenic singer seemed destined for some sort of stardom. He was blessed by a muse that respected no musical boundary, however, and made him hard to sell as his music cartwheeled off into all sorts of surprising tangents. *Happy Sad*, his third album, turned him into a jazz-folk-rock singer, as influenced by Miles Davis as much as it was by Bob Dylan or Fred Neil. Buckley was extremely adept at this, and *Happy Sad*'s results were mostly happy, both in the high quality of the languid music and its entry into the Top 100. It would be, startlingly, his only Top 100 record, as he began a trail of releases that would lead him away from not only folk-rock, but also from virtually all of the popular music audience.

lektra would show reasonable patience with Buckley before letting him go; his final release for the label, 1970's *Lorca*, remains one of the least commercial albums by any significant artist of the time. But some were starting to wonder whether the label, important to the development of folk-rock in the singer-songwriter arena and other areas, was beginning to abandon its folk roots. As Tom Rush's *The Circle Game* was by far his highest-selling Elektra LP, it was surprising that the label did not renew its contract with the singer, who signed on with Columbia instead. Rush, and some other Elektra artists, feel that the label's commitment to folk and folk-rock was waning in the wake of its surprising mega-success with the Doors, whose "Light My Fire" made #1 in 1967 and made them Elektra's first bona fide superstars.

"When I first signed on with Elektra, it was a very small label," says Rush. "I remember being struck by the idea that people would buy a Tom Rush record, never having heard of this guy, simply because the record was on Elektra, and they trusted Elektra. Jac [Holzman] was really dedicated to making high-quality records, with high-quality artwork and high-quality pressing and printing and all the rest. He was doing stuff that he really enjoyed himself. Then they did at some point decide that there's more to it than this, and decided to go after a really big market.

"I do remember, when I switched to Columbia from Elektra, Elektra actually chose not to renew my contract. They were willing to renew on the same terms, but they weren't willing to sweeten the pot at all. It could be that they were trying to conserve their resources to develop the Doors and artists that they thought could go down that road. I think Jac's feeling was that that was the future. He was fond of Ochs and the rest of us, but the rock 'n' roll route was the future of the label. *The Circle*

Tim Buckley in the late 1960s.

Game did head and shoulders above either of its predecessors. We seemed to be moving in the right direction here. So why not keep it rolling? The fact that Jac wasn't willing to up the ante puzzled me."

Holzman says he would have liked to have done another record with Rush, but adds, "I had a feeling that [*The Circle Game*] was as good as it was gonna get with Tom. As [Arthur]Gorson says in the book [Holzman's autobiography *Follow the Music*], the singer-songwriters and the folkies weren't the kings of the castle anymore." Elektra didn't abandon folk-rock; it still had Judy Collins, after all, who was not only its biggest folk-rock artist, but its most profitable artist of any sort besides the Doors. Still, it had already let go of Fred Neil and Phil Ochs before Rush, and was putting a growing percentage of its energy behind psychedelic and hard rock acts, from the MC5 and the Stooges to Clear Light and veteran blues-rock guitarist Lonnie Mack. It should also be noted that Elektra had never been an exclusively folk or folk-rock label, also issuing numerous sound effects records and (on its Nonesuch subsidiary) classical music to help keep up the cash flow. Nor, for that matter, were the other indies that had been crucial in '60s folk and folk-rock: Vanguard had its large classical line, and even in England, Transatlantic Records (covered more thoroughly in chapter four) launched with a sex education record.

On the other hand, emphasizes Tom Paxton, "I never felt any pressure from Jac to change what I was doing. When we did *6* [in 1970], that was fairly fully produced. But then we did the live album, and I had acoustic instruments on that. However, I think my failure to go in that [electric] direction more probably damaged, in the end, their eagerness to work with me. It's hard to know, because Jac sold Elektra about the time I was wrapping up the live album. I could have stayed at Elektra, but I felt a lack of enthusiasm there by then."

Underlying complaints about the success of the Doors in particular may have been an uneasy realization that poetic, intelligent songwriting in rock was no longer limited to folk-rooted artists. Jim Morrison was a big Dylan fan, and Doors guitarist Robbie Krieger's bottleneck style was heavily influenced by folk-blues guitarists (he had even been in a jug band, the Back Bay Chamberpot Terriers). Yet Billy James, who signed the Doors to Columbia (where they did not release anything) and later worked with them at Elektra, says of Morrison's muse, "You couldn't trace it to Tin Pan Alley, and you couldn't trace it to Dylan either—another tributary had begun." It was a tributary that was getting filled by dozens of other psychedelic and hard rock groups without folk backgrounds or to-the-fore folk influences, yet featuring lyrics of literary quality and social import. These included the Beatles, of course, but also the Who, Procol Harum, the Velvet Underground, Pink Floyd, Traffic, the Mothers of Invention, and Sly & the Family Stone, to name just a few. The competition for listeners searching for meaning in music was that much more intense, and elbowing into a market that folk-rockers had for a while dominated.

It's also evident in retrospect that some people, not just artists but also fans, might have been expecting too much of Elektra. Its integrity was held in unparalleled respect by both eclectic folk and underground rock fans. "Elektra at the time had this great credibility," says Elton John lyricist Bernie Taupin, then a fanatical teenage record collector buying Elektra folk-rock LPs such as Love's *Forever Changes* in London import bins. "Anything that came out on Elektra you knew was going to be good." This reverence was not just due to the quality of its LPs, but also in recognition of a president who was actually in touch with the grass roots of its fan base. Holzman advertised in piddly-dink folkzines that could have had no chance of affording his product great exposure, apparently more as a gesture of support than profit-driven marketing; wrote personal missives to the letters section of tiny-circulation periodicals like the *Little Sandy Review*; and personally befriended young folk-turned-rock journalists like Paul Nelson and Paul Williams. "Elektra was a very small outfit by today's standards," Joshua Rifkin reminds us. "I don't know if there were even 20 people working at the main office. It was a kind of place where you could drop by in the afternoon and say, 'Is Jac in?,' and he was, and you could go into his office and chat with him for an hour. I don't imagine it's like that these days."

When Phil Ochs complained in *Broadside* about Elektra "reaching out for the commercial market" with acts like the Doors, Holzman took the time to fire off a five-paragraph letter to the magazine. He defended the label's commitment to both its folk and rock components, noting, "Phil should remember that it was the open-mindedness of both Vanguard and Elektra that caused him to be heard on records at all, *and without censorship of any kind!*" (Actually, buried in a lengthy previous Ochs interview in *Broadside*, the singer had said that Elektra cut out a part of his sleeve notes on one of his LPs out of concern that it would hurt his image.) Numerous musicians interviewed for this book—not just singer-songwriters with folk origins, but musicians from rock groups as well—often punctuated horror stories of their careers with comments to the effect of, "If only we had signed with a label like Elektra..."

But Elektra was a business, too. Its license for expression did not always extend to permission for the artists to choose their own LP sleeve artwork, which might sound like a relatively minor restraint, but had in fact discouraged both Pearls Before Swine and Joni Mitchell (who would design and often paint her own covers) from signing with the company. It couldn't sign every worthy act, both because of financial considerations—it had fervently courted the Lovin' Spoonful and Buffalo Springfield, but lost out to larger offers—and because, as an independent company, it just couldn't put out more than 20 or so albums a year.

Nor was its judgment infallible. There were turkey one-shots, both at the sales register and on the ear, by slight, underdeveloped singer-songwriters like Pat Kilroy, Steve Noonan, and Diane Hildebrand. It had chances to sign Neil Young (after he'd recorded demos at its New York branch in late 1965) and Janis Ian that didn't result in deals, and had only signed Jackson Browne to a publishing contract, not a recording one (although in fairness he wasn't ready to record as a singer in the late '60s). Tom Rush had unsuccessfully tried to sell Holzman on his friend Joni Mitchell: "I took some of her stuff to Jac, and he said she sounded too much like Judy Collins, which in fact she probably did. But so what?! C'mon, Jac! Listen to the songs! I thought the songwriting was so strong that it didn't matter. Then I tried to get [Elektra's] Judy [Collins] to do some of her stuff, and Judy wasn't biting either until 'Both Sides Now.'"

Another missed opportunity is bewailed by producer Frazier Mohawk, who says James Taylor "was the first guy who came in and auditioned for me. I went into Jac, and I said, 'I got a guy, I want to sign him.' He said, 'We already have a folk singer. Why don't you produce Tom Rush instead?' Tom and I didn't get along so good, so I never did that. But it broke my heart. [Taylor] was the first guy who walked in the door, the first day I went to work." At the same time, he praises Elektra's overall vision: "Jac understood what artist development was, and he had patience. He was an incubator, and very few labels understood that. Very few *people* understood that."

Two of the more mercurial ex-Elektra folkies, Fred Neil and Phil Ochs, would do some of their finest work for other labels in the second half of the 1960s. Neil, after putting just a bit of electric guitar on his 1965 album *Bleecker & MacDougal*, had played live at the Night Owl in the Village with backup by the Seven Sons, who included Buzzy Linhart on vibes. That phase of his development was never documented on record, but he did make his full entry into folk-rock on Capitol with *Fred Neil*, issued at the beginning of 1967.

Few singer-songwriters made a more graceful dive into folk-rock than Neil did with his opening track, "The Dolphins." Its plangent waves of electric guitar were perfectly complemented by its wondrous melody and lyrics, in which observations of dolphin life intermingled with sorrow over failed romance. As his friend Jerry Jeff Walker heard it, the shaky, watery guitar reverb came about through the unplanned serendipity that guided many of folk-rock's finer moments: "They said they were running through the song, they all smoked a joint, and the guy was so stoned he'd just watch Freddie's hands whenever Freddie played the chord. He would just play the downbeat; the thing would go, 'whum-whum-whum-whum.'

"They came back to see if everything was sounding like they wanted, and somebody said, 'Hey man, that's cool what you're doing on that guitar. Keep doing it. Don't worry about the rest of us. You just keep doing that.' It was still new in the session, and the guy was a little stoned and couldn't keep up the speed. So instead of playing a busy thing, he played less. The reverb filled in the gap. And as they began to listen, [they] said, 'Okay, that works.'"

Elsewhere on *Fred Neil*, there were more outstanding songs in which Neil did not, like so many other mid-'60s folk-rock authors, adopt the posture of the man in the street. He was much more the man in the hammock, watching the world go by with an oxymoronic good-time regret to his low moan-hummed vocals. "Everybody's Talkin'" would become a standard, particularly via Harry Nilsson's hit cover, and deft colors were filled in on some of the arrangements with harmonica (by Al Wilson of Canned Heat) and bouzouki.

Guitarist John Forsha was one of several outstanding instrumentalists on the album, along with Wilson, Cyrus Faryar, and Peter Childs. He gives producer Nik (sometimes spelled Nick) Venet credit for putting Neil in a comfort zone for the singer's first full rock sessions: "The amplified instruments were mixed right in with the acoustic wash. Even when we got 'funky,' there was never a feeling in the studio of heavy electricity. Our amp volumes were way down. There was no heavy edge to anything in the room. You had a feeling, often, that there was a little too much guitar, when you get me and Cyrus and Pete and Freddie going all at once. Nik never really stepped in and said, 'Don't do that.' He got what he wanted. The results were quite tidy, and we hadn't a clue how he was going to arrive at that."

Adds Larry Beckett, who visited the sessions with Tim Buckley, "The album *Fred Neil*, [Buckley] and I and all of our friends think of as one of the four or five albums of the '60s. I don't care

The mysterious Fred Neil.

what-all lists or sales charts anybody wants to throw up. To me, it's like the *Kind of Blue* of the '60s. [Miles Davis's classic jazz album] *Kind of Blue* is a disc you can listen to over and over, you never get tired of it, it's eternally fresh. And so is that *Fred Neil* album."

Neil, however, was fated to be a songwriter's songwriter, admired hugely by his peers. His profound low blues-pop vocals also made him, to an unappreciated extent, a singer's singer for folkrockers not blessed with the widest of ranges. As Walker puts it, "For [those] of us that didn't sing like Dion or Sting or Paul McCartney, we had our hero in a *low* singer." But he would never be well known to the general public, and even when his work got a wide hearing, it was only through covers of his songs (like Nilsson's "Everybody's Talkin'" and Jefferson Airplane's "The Other Side of This Life").

It didn't help that he had utter disregard for the usual machinations of the record business, not touring or even giving interviews, aside from one given to *Hit Parader* in 1966. The album market created by the rise of FM radio in the late '60s was just beginning, and he couldn't coast off of that for a living, in the way other, similar artists were starting to do without the benefit of hit singles. His prospects were further hindered by a meandering second album for Capitol, *Sessions*, in which the raga element that had pleasantly tinged some of his work started to overwhelm it, and the takes often sounded like spontaneous jams rather than focused, concise songs.

Offers John Sebastian, "I've always felt like the Capitol recordings were a real letdown, a real 'oh, let's just give up and let Fred have his head and underachieve.' That Capitol material really didn't have that tautness created by having [Felix] Pappalardi and I bugging the hell out of him about these arrangements and things [as they had on Neil's Elektra recordings]. I think it was inferior to the Elektra body of work, simply because it did not have the effort. Venet, when he writes about Fred and those sessions, makes it sound like this was a real accomplishment to kind of let Fred have his way. But in fact, I thought it was a lazy man's approach." (A bemused Jerry Jeff Walker remembers asking Sebastian, "How did Freddie ever play a 12-string? He didn't have discipline." [John] said, 'When Freddie'd go smoke a joint, I'd go tune the 12-string.' 'Cause John also had to play harmonica with it, and he wanted to sound in tune.")

If Neil's problem was an inability to handle fame, Phil Ochs had almost the opposite predicament: Fame wasn't coming quickly enough. In particular, he couldn't match the fame of Bob Dylan, the competitor whose discarded topical song torch he was bearing, and who ruthlessly put Ochs down as a singing journalist. Although he remained an active performer in 1966 and 1967, Ochs sat out the folk-rock tempest for about a year-and-a-half as his Elektra contract expired and he shopped for another deal, moving to Los Angeles from New York. Aside from his fine, virtually unheard UK-only single with an electric version of his protest classic "I Ain't Marching Anymore," he hadn't released a single electric folk-rock recording on Elektra. (Intriguingly, however, Lee Mallory had a minor hit in 1966 with an elaborately produced harmony sunshine pop-rock version of a song written by Ochs and folkie Bob Gibson, "That's the Way It's Gonna Be.") "Phil Ochs was beset by a devil that was very difficult for me to deal with, and that was his Dylan fixation," says Holzman. "We did great records with Phil. But he didn't feel we were doing enough for him. When a person doesn't feel that we're doing enough, the right thing to do is give them their release, and let 'em go elsewhere."

Eventually he hooked up with A&M, for whom he finally went decisively not just electric, but orchestral, with grandiose flamboyance. *Pleasures of the Harbor* (1967) and *Tape from California* (1968) were among folk-rock's most wide-ranging ventures, with erratic if generally worthy results. From *Pleasures*, "Outside of a Small Circle of Friends," Ochs's most celebrated song, was inspired by the murder of Kitty Genovese in New York, which eyewitnesses did nothing to stop. It proved the art of the topical song was far from dead, its jaunty mock-Dixieland-tack piano arrangement contrasting magnificently with Ochs's deadpan account of apathetic bystanders refusing to intervene in crimes to justice and morality. It probably would have been a hit single if not for a reference to marijuana, and although two subsequent edited versions were released, it became another victim of unofficial blacklist by AM radio.

Producer Larry Marks put Ochs's songs in settings that were sometimes ideal counterpoints for the lyric, as on "Outside of a Small Circle of Friends" and "The Party," a cinematic eight-minute skewering of a socialite gathering with cocktail jazz backup. At other times, however, the rococo baroque-classical arrangements smothered the lyrics; the L.A. session-rock playing fell flat; or caution-to-the-wind experimentalism actually worked against the songs, as on "The Crucifixion," which fought against dissonant electronic treatments by arranger Joseph Byrd. Live, however, like several folk-rock singer-songwriters who'd already gone electric on record, Ochs usually continued to play solo acoustic. For those who felt songs such as "Crucifixion" were ill-served by their overambitious studio arrangements, the archival CD *There & Now: Live in Vancouver, 1968* is a recommended alternative, featuring solo acoustic versions of "Crucifixion" and other songs from his late-'60s albums.

Ochs was now dividing his time between topical songs and ever-more abstract poetry, leading *Tape from California* to change lanes as often as the L.A. traffic. "The War Is Over" was one of the great antiwar songs, with its martial fife-and-drums slamming home Ochs's reports of one-legged veterans whistling as they mowed their lawns; the 13-minute "When in Rome" was interminable, impenetrable, and dripping with syrupy strings. His greatest wish was for these albums to lift him into pop stardom. Yet although they were admired and sold more than most mid-'60s folk LPs had, they didn't come close to being hits. Ochs wanted fame and wide sociocultural influence, but seemed inherently unable to make the artistic compromises that might have gotten him more of it. The contradiction in shooting for high sales with highly literate, controversial anti-establishment manifestos that would have sailed over the heads of much of the great unwashed and been greeted with hostility by major radio outlets does not seem to have been one that he fully comprehended.

"When I took over managing him in '67, he wanted to make his *Sgt. Pepper* album," says his brother, Michael Ochs. "Having grown up in the movie theaters, he wanted to make *Pleasures of the Harbor* the John Wayne movie *Long Voyage Home*. He wanted to do it full orchestral. When he wrote songs like 'Pleasures of the Harbor' and 'Crucifixion,' he wanted to do more *with* the songs. He wasn't, like, thinking about going into folk-rock. He wanted to be the Beatles. He wanted to be mixing every form of music, from classical to Hollywood-type to rock to you-name-it."

Ochs also had made the leap, as Dylan had before him, of moving beyond protest songs to personal ones, although Phil differed in that he blended sociopolitical songs with introspective poetic ones rather than abandoning topical songwriting altogether. That widening of his repertoire actually dated back to the most popular song on his final Elektra album, the lovely romantic tune "Changes," which in Michael's view "surprised him [Phil]. It was like, 'Oh, this is totally different than anything else I've ever written.' Phil did not think this out. If he would still buy the news, and still get most of his material from that, he would have been just as happy.

"But what happened was, the muse changed within him. He started writing more personal stuff, and that's something he'd never done before. When he wrote 'Changes,' he went, 'Boy, this is great stuff.' Then he opened himself up for more of that type of stuff. But I think it was also the hardest thing for him to do, 'cause emotionally, he played everything very close to the vest. It was very hard for him to get in touch with his emotions." By the end of the 1960s that difficulty and other psychological problems would begin to short-circuit his career as he came up against writer's block, though in 1968 he still seemed as prolific as ever.

Another artist whose personal demons made the second half of the 1960s tough going was Tim Hardin. His "If I Were a Carpenter," from his April 1967 album *Tim Hardin 2*, had already been a Top Ten hit for Bobby Darin in late 1966. Darin was then in the midst of remolding himself as the mildest of folk-rock singers with torpid covers of songs by Hardin and John Sebastian on his albums *If I Were a Carpenter* and *Inside Out*, and writing some of his own songs in a style heavily indebted to Hardin. This was apparently much to Hardin's displeasure, as he called Darin's

"If I Were a Carpenter" a "carbon copy" in *Disc*, complaining, "I have nothing in common with Darin. I suppose he tried to get as close to my sound as he could, but I don't like other people covering my songs. Using them as a vehicle for commercial success. If I had my way, my songs would not be available for anyone else to sing. I don't care about so-called chart success. I'm not interested in the pop market."

"He did a demo of 'If I Were a Carpenter,'" contends Verve executive Jerry Schoenbaum. "His managers ran to Atlantic Records and gave it to Bobby Darin. Darin did the exact same arrangement, imitated the voice, and I was really pissed at his management. I said, 'I'm trying to break this artist. You take one of his great songs and give it to Bobby Darin. Why don't we do it with him?' I think they had a piece of the publishing, and that was why they gave it to Darin. It's a little bit of Enron all over again."

Tim Hardin 2 had augmented his typically head-hanging, what's-the-use persona with tasteful strings on a strong set that also featured standouts like "Black Sheep Boy" and "Lady Came from Baltimore." Typically, he pissed and moaned about that in *Disc* as well, claiming, "When I heard *Tim Hardin 2* I wept. They had added backing after I'd finished the tracks and my voice sounded so terrible because I was very very sick when I cut that album." Producer Erik Jacobsen casts a suspicious eye on Hardin's comments: "He knew all about that. He never came to me and said, 'I don't want you to put those on.' He liked those things, as far as I knew. [It made] a nice musical effect. They were kind of classy-sounding songs, they had the beautiful chords, and the strings sounded great on them. And they were sentimental songs, very sentimental. I don't doubt that later on he was high and said, 'I never should have put the fucking strings on.'" Left more to his own devices after Jacobsen resigned from the producer's seat, Hardin would never again record work on par with those of his first two Verve albums, and indeed never even record another studio album for Verve.

Janis Ian.

he rock/pop division of Verve, the label where Hardin had done his best work, would lose much of its innovative impetus by the end of the 1960s. In the final years of the decade, however, it continued to issue some commendable product by other folk-rock singer-songwriters. Janis Ian didn't have a follow-up to her hit single "Society's Child," but produced four intermittently interesting albums in which she integrated soul, jazz, pop, and blues into her mix. Her words were often overly busy, preachy, or self-preoccupied, but did delve into some areas seldom touched by pop music, such as the neglect of the elderly in "Shady Acres" (another song that, like "Society's Child," had been recorded in an acoustic solo folk version for *Broadside*). Underripe composition was understandable in light of her tender age; she was still in her teens at the end of the 1960s, after all. Her underrated bluesy, soulful voice was not dissimilar in some respects to another singer-songwriter who started on Verve, the more pop-oriented Laura Nyro. Ian doesn't agree with the Nyro comparison, but does think "we had much in common from growing up, particularly the jazz influences and love of orchestration."

Richie Havens, unlike most of the other singer-songwriters signed by Verve (and other labels of the era for that matter), was at least as noted for his interpretive skills as his songwriting ones. A popular Village folk performer since the early '60s, he once claimed (in *The New York Times*) to have done a dozen sets a night for 40 minutes each in the Macdougal Street basket houses, where the money was made in tips thrown into baskets passed among the crowds. No doubt that helped build a wide interpretive repertoire, which he would still draw from well after he began his recording career, even as late as his legendary appearance at Woodstock, where he updated the moss-covered folk revival standard "Handsome Johnny." "I've never seen anything like it," famed San Francisco rock promoter Bill Graham raved about Havens's bond with his audience, in a 1967 piece in *Newsweek*. "Our sound has always been big and raucous. People come here to dance. But they lie down like lambs for Richie."

Havens also hit upon a novel open tuning bar chord style, in part to compensate for his inability to master more traditional ways of guitar playing with as much acumen as many of his competitors. By tuning his guitar to an open chord and using his thumb to cover most of the six strings in each guitar fret, he was able to create basic progressions that enabled him to both change chords rapidly and strum at a furious rate. "His guitar playing was always incredibly strong rhythmically," says Bruce Langhorne, who worked as a guitar accompanist and arranger on some of Havens's early records. "I remember working with him with a conga player, and I think it was only natural that he should work with drums and with electric instruments. Because he was *that* strong in that rhythm. He was really phenomenal. His guitar was like a whole electric orchestra, very sophisticated rhythmically and very swinging."

Havens's low, hoarse voice—he had told *The New York Times* in the late '60s that the magnificent jazz-pop-blues vocalist Nina Simone was the only singer he claimed as an influence—had an earthy soul most singer-songwriters couldn't reach. He was particularly effective on imaginative covers of Beatles and Dylan songs that he was able to recast as his own. "He's infuriating because he won't sing the way you write it," says Bob Lind (the early folk-rocker famous for the hit

"Elusive Butterfly"), more in admiration than frustration. "Richie is one of the few guys who can take a song and show it to you a different way. And it's not conscious. Richie is all instinct."

As a songwriter he was less original, his own compositions sometimes acting as filler around the covers, rather than the other way around. While his first album, *Mixed Bag*, had tapped some of the usual New York session Mafia (bassist Harvey Brooks, keyboardist Paul Harris) to fill out the sound, he quickly proved capable of weaving all manner of instruments into his arrangements, including electric sitar (on "Run, Shaker Life"), conga, tabla, and flute. The personnel and instrument lineup on his double album *Richard P. Havens, 1983* worked toward a folk-rock-world-music fusion of sorts, though one grounded in the sort of bluesy folk he, Fred Neil, Dino Valenti, and others had pioneered in the Village back in the early '60s. But Havens's idiosyncratic style, according to *1983* producer Elliot Mazer, did not easily lend itself to accompaniment, since "Richie was not very interested in learning the chords for the songs. He made up his own, and it was a challenge for musicians to play with him."

"He's one of the sweetest, nicest guys I ever had as an artist," says Schoenbaum. "I used to hear him sing Dylan songs, and he would put [an] African-American side to it. They were terrific performances, I thought, some of the best interpretations outside of Dylan himself; they were completely different. He was not a great picker of a guitar player; he did a rhythm thing. But in talking about his producing, it was very hard to reach him. I wasn't trying to get him to do songs that were out of his milieu, but to get away from bongos and rhythm instruments that he used as backup, and get him a producer who understood what I was saying, and try to convince him to go . . . I don't think it was wise to get him off in a completely different direction, but to be a little more concerned about the production values and the type of songs. And he resisted it. I don't think he was ever produced correctly, in my opinion. He ended up with [MGM executive] Mike Curb, who completely didn't understand what was going on with Richie Havens."

Nico's sole Verve album, *Chelsea Girl* (1967), was wholly devoted to work by other singer-songwriters, at a time when that approach—perfected by Judy Collins, who was by now starting to write some of her songs—was less in vogue, as singers were now expected to write at least some of their material. It might seem inappropriate to peg the ex–Velvet Underground singer's debut as a folk-rock album. For one thing, it has no drums, and not many loud electric guitars. Yet, in a far darker and more avant-garde fashion than LPs by Judy Collins and Tom Rush, it was a sterling showcase for songs by emerging folk-rock composers. Most of the ones on the cleverly selected *Chelsea Girl* were otherwise unavailable at the time of the LP's release, including compositions by the teenage Jackson Browne (who played on the *Chelsea Girl* album), Tim Hardin, Lou Reed, and John Cale.

For Nico *was* really, at this point, a folk singer. She had done a little-known cover of Gordon Lightfoot's "I'm Not Sayin'" to launch her career, and top British session drummer Bobby Graham has remembered backing her on an unreleased 1965 French-language EP that included a Joan Baez cover. Her early solo gigs at the Dom in the Village (where a smitten Leonard Cohen was often in attendance) were accompanied by just one guitarist, a chore that fell to folk-rock luminaries Hardin, Browne, and Tim Buckley, as well as to Cale, Velvet Underground guitarist Sterling Morrison, and

Ramblin' Jack Elliott. For years she had been trying to record a Dylan song that the composer had yet to release, "I'll Keep It with Mine," which she said he had written for her during a brief fling in Europe in 1964. Among the memorabilia from Dylan's 1965 British tour auctioned at Christie's in London in 2002 was a letter from Nico to Dylan, declaring her intention to sing "Mr. Tambourine Man" on *Ready Steady Go* "for you especially" (a broadcast that apparently never took place). "Please, please, you promised to write me songs and I want to sing your songs," she gushed. "They are the only ones that make sense for me and my life depends on them."

Judy Collins released "I'll Keep It with Mine" before Nico could, but it was one of the songs on *Chelsea Girl*, and probably the least successful track on the album. Otherwise, it was a much-underrated gem of folk-baroque, the lovely folk-orchestral arrangements featuring graceful strings and flute as well as folky guitar. While "It Was a Pleasure Then" sounded like a drumless Velvet Underground outtake with its shrieks of electric guitar feedback, "Chelsea Girls" remains a hidden masterpiece of Warholian depravity, unsurprisingly since it was co-written by Reed and Morrison of the Andy Warhol–managed Velvet Underground. Tim Hardin's crushingly morbid "Eulogy to Lenny Bruce" dispensed with all accompaniment but a solitary guitar. Some listeners, however, could not get past Nico's low moon goddess voice, which often wavered into flatness. Nico was distraught with Tom Wilson's production, particularly the flute, taking a page from the Tim Hardin school of post-production hindsight when she moaned (in Richard Witts's biography *Nico: The Life & Lies of an Icon*), "I cried because of the flute .... There should be a button on record players, a 'No Flute' button." Unwilling to dip further into the experimental folk-pop well, Nico wholly transformed her music into pre-gloom-doom meditations on gothic harmonium, starting with her next album, *The Marble Index* (on Elektra, as it happened).

As a label that was artistically bold in its signings (folk-rock and otherwise; it also had the earliest albums by Laura Nyro, the Mothers of Invention, and the Velvet Underground), and also benefited (unlike Elektra and Vanguard) from major label distribution (by MGM), Verve's rock division seemed set up to become a major presence on the market. Its sharp decline in the late '60s, and simultaneous near-total withdrawal from the folk-rock field, was attributable to an about-face in attitude from the very hand that fed it. According to Jerry Schoenbaum, who ran the Verve/Folkways and Verve/Forecast imprints, "MGM at that time was Connie Francis and a whole bunch of middle-of-the-road stuff. The people involved at the A&R, promotion, and marketing level had no idea [of the newer rock market] until they settled upon, quite accidentally, the Animals."

Already in his mid-forties when he started signing folk-rock acts in late 1965, Schoenbaum was still hip enough to take his cue from his teenage son's love of Dylan: "I was taken with the lyrics and said, 'If that happens, it's gonna be widespread, very commercial, very marketable, and very playable on the radio.' Verve/Forecast was really an attempt, from an A&R viewpoint, to try to develop what was happening in the street." Although Janis Ian has said that she suspects the label was begun as a tax loss for MGM, Schoenbaum refutes that, and also recalls how he worked closely with Howard Solomon of Greenwich Village's Cafe Au Go Go in breaking acts: "The acts that I asked him either to open for somebody else, or to play, he did." Indeed, he remembers bailing out the Cafe

Au Go Go when that key venue got into financial hot water. "Howard got into trouble with tax people, came to me, and says, 'They're putting the furniture out and they're closing me down.' I went to see Arnold Maxim, the president of MGM. I said, 'Listen, I need a couple thousand dollars. This guy is very important to us in terms of New York City and promoting the artists that I'm interested in. He said, 'Go ahead, give him more money.' We did, and we saved his ass."

But overall, Schoenbaum feels Verve's rock divisions were never adequately supported. "I was the only executive at Verve/Forecast. I had no staff. I didn't have my own A&R people, I didn't have promotion people. I depended solely on MGM's marketing and promotion ability. Their attitudes were still in the Connie Francis phase, so it was hard to explain to them what was going on. They resisted it in many ways. Big changes took place at MGM. Mike Curb"—notorious for dropping many acts with supposed underground/drug affiliations from the label, and steering the roster toward wholesome acts such as the Osmonds—"and the rest took over, all these people were let go. Then they came to me and said, 'You know, we should have listened to you.'"

But actually Verve/Forecast's decline had predated the worst bloodletting of the Mike Curb era, and Schoenbaum had been gone for some time by late 1970, when Curb announced the termination of 18 MGM acts who (as reported in *Rolling Stone*) "advocate and exploit drugs." According to Schoenbaum, such pseudo-witch hunting had dogged Verve/Forecast even while he was still with the label. "I got a lot of criticism from the board of the old MGM. They got calls from a very conservative think tank telling them that there may be Communist influences in the people I signed. Of course it was far-fetched." Specifically such fears might have inhibited MGM's promotion of Janis Ian's hit "Society's Child," which wasn't getting played on radio until Leonard Bernstein featured it on his 1967 CBS television special on rock music. It was only that highbrow endorsement that broke the barricade, as "we got a call from our distributor in Los Angeles that some disc jockey there said, 'If Bernstein could put this girl on national TV, then I could play the record.' We had a big change from the promotion department." (In a less controversial imbroglio, Schoenbaum also blames the MGM promotional department for the failure of Laura Nyro's "Wedding Bell Blues" to become a national smash after it had become a regional hit in late 1966 on the West Coast; three years later it would be covered for a #1 single by the Fifth Dimension.)

Ultimately "there was a change in presidents, and the guy that took over was, I hate to use this word, one big asshole. He had no idea. He was a copycat. 'We need our Sinatra, we need our Barbra Streisand,' which is completely idiotic in terms of what was happening. The president had a board meeting, and a friend of a friend who was on the board said, 'He really put you down. He suggested that they get rid of you.' When he said that, I started to look around." The upshot was that Schoenbaum left Verve around 1969 and "went to Atlantic, and was not very successful."

Subsequent to Schoenbaum's departure, Verve went into an even greater tailspin, as "the Mike Curb thing was a disaster. They finally got rid of him. I can't explain the man, except that he's duplicity at its highest form. He tried very hard to negate whatever I had done." Verve/Folkways/Forecast had come to a most ignominious end. But for a while, it was almost as daring and innovative as any mid-to-late-'60s label that played a major part in folk-rock, though in contrast to Elektra or even Vanguard, its role has generally been undervalued and overlooked by history.

ut in Los Angeles, the Verve/Folkways concept of special subsidiaries devoted more to LP sales and artistry than quick hits had infected the majors. In late 1966, Nik Venet had discussed the formation of a Capitol subsidiary, FolkWorld, in *Billboard*. Venet, like Lou Adler, was a producer whose early successes had been in clean-cut pop-rock, his credits including the Beach Boys, Bobby Darin, the Lettermen, the Four Preps, and Glen Campbell. Folk-rock had opened his eyes to more message-oriented music. He'd already lost out to Lou Adler in a bid to sign the Mamas & the Papas, and had produced one of the Leaves' attempts to record "Hey Joe" (although the version that became a hit didn't bear his production credit). The FolkWorld label, he said, would work "with the concept of creating albums by these [folk-based] groups, which are an extension of their artistry and may not necessarily be tied to an initial single."

While FolkWorld never got off the ground as a major imprint, in the late '60s Venet produced numerous singer-songwriter-oriented folk-rock acts for Capitol that served as antecedents of Southern California country-rock and soft rock. These included records by Fred Neil, the Stone Poneys, Hearts and Flowers, John Stewart (formerly of the Kingston Trio), Mary McCaslin, Vince Martin, and Karen Dalton. Some of them never could have recorded for a major label, or perhaps wouldn't have recorded at all, had Venet not been in a position to help. Martin's 1969 album, *If the Jasmine Don't Get You the Bay Breeze Will*, was recorded in a few hours after the door had been opened by his participation in a Fred Neil session. It came as little surprise that the record by Martin, Neil's ex-duo partner, was something like a featherweight counterpart to Neil's own *Sessions* album, with a similar musical milieu but less force. Dalton, a Billie Holiday–with–a–twang Village folk singer who was a peer of Neil and Dylan in the early '60s, had been totally ignored by the folk and folk-rock boom on record, much as she had totally ignored contemporary trends. Dalton was never comfortable in the studio, and Venet virtually had to trick her into making her 1969 debut album by asking her to record a cover of Neil's "Little Bit of Rain" for his private collection, building upon that to coax an entire LP of songs out of her.

Dalton's album, like most of Venet's folk-rock productions, had a dry ambience that crossed the line from low-key to laidback. "Nik wasn't a strong producer," says Larry Murray, who was produced by Venet as part of Hearts and Flowers. "He hired incredible musicians to play on sessions. He would hire some kind of obscure people. Like Cyrus [Faryar] wasn't your basic studio player, but he had a style, played a lot of kind of peculiar instruments, and knew what to do with them. He played on a lot of our stuff. But all of a sudden, the chemistry of that session really didn't work out. It was kind of vanilla, you know?"

As the MC of Monday night hootenannies in L.A. at the Troubadour, Murray had met Mary McCaslin and brought the young guitarist-vocalist to Venet's attention. "Nik used the same players on almost all the sessions," says Mary McCaslin, who did a sedate 1967 folk-rock single for Capitol under the producer (other unreleased Capitol sessions from 1967 and 1968 were issued in the late 1990s). "You could hear a similarity a lot of times. Voices were recorded without much in the way of EQ to give it a little wetness and depth. He was good at discovering people; he brought a lot of people to Capitol. He wasn't good at working with them once he discovered them. He quickly disappeared from the picture as these artists' careers progressed." McCaslin's quick to stress that her

Capitol material is mostly demos, often rushed and recorded at the end of others' sessions, and that "I wasn't devastated by the fact that they didn't do an album." In any event, she'd get to do a modest, respectable soft-folk-rock album under better circumstances for Andy Williams's Barnaby label in 1969, with Murray producing, though he admits, "I don't feel that album tapped into what Mary was capable of." She really didn't find her voice until the 1970s, when she began to write much of her material and devise devilishly ingenious reworkings of Beatles, Supremes, and Who songs for folk arrangements, finding her success on the folk circuit rather than the rock one.

Still, Venet was able to work folk-rock territory with much more commercial results than he got with uncompromising projects like Dalton's album, which became an instant collector's item, or McCaslin's sessions, which mostly lay unreleased. Foremost among his clients were the Stone Poneys, with a young Linda Ronstadt. Although a group, at least at the start, the Stone Poneys had strong links to the singer-songwriter style in their low-volume, acoustic-flavored sound, their original material, their cover choices, and the ultimate singling out of their frontwoman that would see her become one of the foremost solo interpreters of contemporary folk-rock composers.

Their charming first LP (*Stone Poneys*, released early 1967) was in a way one of the first "back to basics" folk-rock albums, streamlining the instrumentation so that it sounded like coffee-house folk with far greater color and rhythm. Several of the same musicians who had made *Fred Neil* such a triumph were also on board for *Stone Poneys*, and the set combined strong originals by Stone Poneys acoustic guitarists Kenny Edwards and Bob Kimmel with well-chosen covers of songs by Neil, Tom Campbell, and Linda Albertano. It was an album that was rather like Peter, Paul & Mary, but with a fresh vigor that drew from the best of folk-rock's advancements, rather than coming off as a forced-sounding attempt to keep up with the times (as Peter, Paul & Mary's late-'60s folk-rock tracks often were). It was running against the general bigger, louder grain of the era; when the Stone Poneys played the Cafe Au Go Go on an early tour, laughs Edwards, "The air conditioner was louder than we were."

Continues Edwards, "Nik Venet was trying to jump on that bandwagon, and we were the ideal sort of vehicle for him as far as he was concerned. There was a time, right about there, that the folk music thing was somewhat associated with almost like a jazz, late-night cocktail feeling. I think he related to that. His personal taste was more towards the smoky jazz-folk, like Odetta, that kind of feeling. I know with the Fred Neil record, he liked the sort of contemplative side of that whole sound. Much more laidback, not aggressive.

"The first record was just basically bass, drums, and us: the live representation of what we did, with the addition of a rhythm section. I don't think that we had *any* radio play. In fact, the band sort of briefly broke up in between the first and second record. Then Nik Venet said, 'We can make another record, we can make this happen. If we're going to do anything with this, we gotta make something that sounds commercial and get on the radio.' I probably was the least pleased with that approach, 'cause I had a kind of more of a purist approach at the time, although he was probably right. He did get something on the radio."

That song was "Different Drum," a Mike Nesmith song that ended up being a bigger hit than anything he wrote for the Monkees. The Greenbriar Boys had already recorded their slower, more

The Stone Poneys, from a photo session for their first album.
Left to right: Bob Kimmel, Linda Ronstadt, and Kenny Edwards.

whimsical version of the the tune on 1966's *Better Late Than Never!*, after hearing Nesmith sing it in the Los Angeles folk club the Ash Grove before he joined the Monkees. "We actually learned that song off of a bluegrass Greenbriar Boys album," reveals Edwards. "We cut a version very much like that, with mandolin, kind of a jug bandy, bluegrass-lite version. That's when Nik Venet sort of took an executive position and went, 'This could be a hit song, and we need to sort of have an arranger arrange it.' So none of us actually played on the record version of that." As originally recorded by the Greenbriar Boys, Edwards adds, it was "a very kind of a tongue-in-cheek, funny song. I think one of the things that makes Linda's version of it so interesting is that it's this angst, and a driving vocal, expressing this lyric that is kind of whimsical and noncommittal. There's an interesting dissonance that actually helped it out."

The Top 20 success of "Different Drum," however, also signaled the breakup of the Stone Poneys as Ronstadt was groomed for a career as a solo artist. "Nik Venet, when he first heard us, the thing that drew him was her," says Edwards. "She was cute, a great singer, and a natural star. From the record company's point of view, immediately they wanted to push Linda as a solo artist. And frankly, Linda's taste in songs was really growing away from what Bobby [Kimmel] was writing. He was four years older than us, but seemed more mature, and he had fleshed out his artistic vision a lot more than we had at the time we all got together. By the time we'd met these other writers, I think her taste was, 'I want to do the songs I want to do, and here's people writing them.'

"So there was a spontaneous growth toward her being a solo artist, and by the time the third record came out, the band had really broken up. I don't even know how much I took part in any of the third record." Singer-songwriter Steve Gillette, who sang on the Stone Poneys' cover of one of his songs, was an eyewitness to the others getting frozen out: "While we were in the studio and just after having finished the duet vocals of Linda's and my version of 'Back On the Street Again' there was a scuffle and some noise just outside the door. When we opened it, there was a sad and for some, tearful scene in which it became clear that Kenny and Bobby had not been notified of the session, and had heard about it indirectly and showed up full of anger at the betrayal. Capitol really did try to break the group up."

Edwards's high opinion of Ronstadt's gifts is undimmed by such incidents (or indeed Linda's dismissal of the group in *Rolling Stone* in the early '70s, when she complained, "The Stone Poneys tried to combine the roots with rock and roll, and we were miserable"). "She had—and she still does—a great sensitivity to great songs. She was just beginning to form that then. She can pick songs, in the same way [as] Emmylou Harris, that are perfect for them, as if they'd written them. Almost as an art form, of finding people who write songs that are saying what you want to say. I don't think that people now, or even before then, had those kind of personal relationships with the songwriters."

Indeed the second and third Stone Poneys albums were dotted with covers of songs by several talented singer-songwriters who hadn't quite gotten the breaks that would have allowed them to be widely heard via their own releases: Nesmith (a star with the Monkees but not yet able to record as many original songs as he would have liked, or always record in the way he liked), Gillette, Tom Campbell, Pam Polland, John Braheny, and Tim Buckley (*Stone Poneys Vol. III* had no less than three Buckley songs). In a yet folkier vein, there was even a cover of the Greenbriar Boys–penned "Up to My Neck in High Muddy Water," taken from the same album on which the Stone Poneys had found "Different Drum." Ronstadt thereafter abandoned any pretense of being a part of the Stone Poneys and began a solo career, becoming the preeminent pop-rock singer of the 1970s who advanced to superstar solely on the basis of her interpretations of other people's songs.

Gillette puts Ronstadt's empathy for the vibe of a tune in quite colorful perspective: "I played guitar on the session where we recorded 'A Number and a Name' [which he co-wrote with Tom Campbell, and Ronstadt recorded on her first solo album]. I still remember with some excitement that Linda removed her blouse in the dimly lit studio, to get into the right mood for the song. Linda had the ability to be sensually present in a perfectly natural and honest way. It wasn't a ploy, just good fun. Something that is almost always overexploited in these soulless days in which we now abide."

The tight in-crowd of young, reflective, easygoing Southern California songwriters steeped in acoustic roots music was an incestuous scene that saw many of the acts covering each other's songs. In addition to those Ronstadt interpreted, there were also, from Orange County alone, Jackson Browne (whose early works were done by Tom Rush, Nico, and the Nitty Gritty Dirt Band), Steve Noonan, and Greg Copeland. Even Gregg Allman, then struggling in Hollywood with the Hourglass prior to the formation of the Allman Brothers Band, got in on the action, penning a beautiful, tender folk-rock ballad for the Sunshine Company, "Sunday Brought the Rain." ("Gregg *really* liked that whole folkie sort of traditional and contemporary acoustic music," confirms the Sunshine Company's Maury Manseau.)

Today Los Angeles seems like one unholy ribbon of superhighways in which no one walks and everyone drives, and interpersonal contact is kept at a minimum. It can be difficult to imagine a simpler, funkier time and town, when many of the singers and songwriters actually lived within walking distance of each other in communities like Venice, dropping by unannounced to jam, smoke joints, or try out songs on each other. "The old Ocean Park area [near the Santa Monica–Venice border] and the old Venice Canal area were the world's chicest slums, if you will," says Roy Marinell, then playing with the Gentle Soul. "There were these wonderful old homes that were built as beach houses that you could rent relatively cheaply, right on the beach. There were a couple of coffeehouses in the area. Ocean Park wasn't developed like it is now. Main Street is now one Starbucks after another. But in those days, it was all soup kitchens and bums sleeping in doorways." Some of that overflowing communitarian spirit seeps into the photograph on *Stone Poneys Vol. III*, where a couple dozen or so friends, kids, and dogs pose in front of Ronstadt's house in Venice, including Tim Buckley and his then-girlfriend Jainie Goldstein.

"My kids say, 'Well, how did you know Don Everly and these people?'" chortles Larry Murray, who knew almost everyone in the scene as the MC of the Troubadour's Monday hoot nights. "I said, 'Because they lived in the neighborhood, and we went to the same places, and we picked guitar and played.' They can't grasp that. It doesn't lend itself to any kind of interfacing humanity anymore. It was always people kind of hanging out, getting loaded, and jamming. People were really accessible. It was a lot of exchange of ideas on a one-to-one basis. We weren't necessarily listening to one another's records. We were really listening to one another, actually hearing them play it, and say[ing], 'What do you think of this?' Then you would leave and say, 'Well, that's pretty good, but I can do better. I'm gonna write a song just like that and go back and play it!'" They would play on each other's sessions as well, with, for instance, Linda Ronstadt and Kenny Edwards of the Stone Poneys appearing on the first album by Murray's band, Hearts and Flowers, and both bands sharing Nik Venet as producer.

The carefree California hippie vibe spilled over into the young singer-songwriters' records. Yet their lack of volume and assertiveness, and their sheer numbers, made it impossible for all of them to get the attention they deserved. Steve Noonan's sole Elektra album, recorded when he was 20, was bland and nervous, and he in fact never put out another. Gillette made just one modest album for Vanguard, with Bruce Langhorne on electric guitar. "I think I did kind of fit at Vanguard," he acknowledges. "Because [I] was a kind of an artsy folk throwback traditional songwriter, but songwriter working with traditional context, traditional elements. Very much like what Ian & Sylvia had been doing at that point." But he, like several, found Vanguard had shortcomings in artist development: "I never felt that Maynard Solomon really understood who I was, or what I did, or what merit there might be in the work that I was doing. I actually declined to make a second record, very foolishly." Especially because it turned out Vanguard was able to tie him up anyway, as his release from the label "wasn't actually a release at all. It gave them four options for future albums, and they wanted to call them in. And of course, when I went to Capitol with that, they said, 'Oh, well, there's no way we can do anything with you.' So that was a great mistake on my part, to sign that."

Jackson Browne was already skilled at crafting precariously delicate songs ("The Fairest of the Seasons," recorded by Nico on *Chelsea Girl*, was the best of them). But he never even got to make his first record in the 1960s, and a wealth of unreleased publishing demos he recorded as a teenager in 1966 and 1967 unveil the cause. His voice was timorous and callow, rendering the songs not so much into works of delicacy as the sound of a man scared of getting eaten alive by the studio microphone, let alone able to color his voice with enough feelings as the songs contained. Marinell remembers telling Browne that Jackson wasn't going to be able to join the Gentle Soul on a permanent basis, softening the blow by advising the dejected youngster to do his own songs with his own band: Browne later told Roy "it was the best advice of his career," according to Marinell.

Browne was even part of a costly Elektra experiment, overseen by Frazier Mohawk, to develop a band at Paxton Lodge, an isolated dwelling in the Northern California mountains. "The concept was to get rid of all of the stresses that were on these people, so that they would be free to create," explains Mohawk. "What I didn't realize at the time was that those stresses were in fact the motor that made them go. As soon as we took the pressure away and took care of everything for them, a lot of the creative juices didn't need to flow. So it didn't work. The creative juices that make for great songs weren't there.

"The people who were there were urban people. This was a country environment, and sometimes when that 60-cycle hum of the city goes away, people's motors wind down. Some people need New York, and they need some evil influences. Otherwise they have nothing to write about. Everything is beautiful, everything is fine. So who cares? That's kind of what happened." Although an album called *Baby Browning* resulted from the communal band, it wasn't released since, as Jac Holzman bluntly states, it "sucks. It really wasn't very good." It took about five years, and a considerable improvement in his vocals, before Browne made his album debut; it wasn't until the mid-'70s that he became a star.

"He wasn't a very good singer in the '60s," confirms John McEuen of the Nitty Gritty Dirt Band. "It was always comical: 'Yeah, Jackson's gonna sing?' But he took singing lessons. He was like the first guy that anybody knew [to do that]. His lyrics were so complicated, his chord changes were new. His singing caught up to his other talents." When he was informed that Browne had a record deal, McEuen laughs, "I says, 'Oh yeah? Who's he gonna have sing for him?' But he shocked everybody. It came out really cool."

The Gentle Soul, of whom Browne had briefly been a member (as he had in the Nitty Gritty Dirt Band), got the shaft more than any other talented act in the L.A. soft-folk-roots-rock scene. Its sole album, *The Gentle Soul* (1968), was rather like the Stone Poneys, though even more understated and at times bluesier and rootsier, perhaps more along the lines of what Kenny Edwards would have liked to have done as part of Linda Ronstadt's group. The close harmonies of songwriters Pamela Polland and Rick Stanley were embroidered with tasteful dreamy orchestration by Byrds producer Terry Melcher. And they were on the Byrds' label, Columbia (albeit on the Epic subsidiary). Judging by how impossible it is to spot an original copy today, it seems doubtful that its circulation even got into the four figures. Epic did little to further endear itself to the duo by neglecting to name Polland or Stanley on the cover, but nearly ten session men, including Ry Cooder, were duly credited.

Polland had been a cashier at the Ash Grove in L.A. (the roots-oriented folk club where Kenny Edwards had worked as a guitar salesman) when she met Cooder, whom she played with for a couple of years. "But while I was doing that, I also was writing my own songs," she says. "When I first started writing that kind of music, there was no such thing as 'folk-rock.' I was often turned away by record execs for being 'too rock to be folk, and too folk to be rock.' They had no bin to put me in. But by the late '60s, the Byrds had changed all that, and suddenly there was a place for my music." A place, in fact, with the producer of the Byrds' first hits, although Polland feels "Terry was a decent producer, but in retrospect, I don't think the orchestrated approach was right for the Gentle Soul. It's the more acoustic cuts that I like the most.

"For some reason, Columbia just gave up on us . . . and I never knew exactly why. It could have had something to do with Terry, it could have been because we [were] not a cohesive performing act by the time the album was released. Or maybe they just drew names out of a hat when it came time to decide who was going to be the tax write-off du jour. That was a sweet album for its time and I think we could have gone somewhere with proper promotion. Instead, because they let us die, Rick and I just gave up and went our separate ways."

"The Gentle Soul stuff was a nightmare, in terms of the recording sessions," expounds Marinell. "Terry Melcher at that time was going with Candy Bergen. It was a pretty cushy deal for us on some level. They rented us a house on Marmont Lane, right across the street from the Chateau Marmont. They gave us a food allowance, and they gave us a pot allowance. And every so often Terry would say, 'Okay, c'mon, let's go in the studio.' We'd be there for a couple hours and Candy would get a headache or something, and Terry would say, 'Oh, Candy's got a headache and we're gonna go.' I don't know if he just thought we were terrible, but it took forever to get anything done. Terry wasn't doing a great job of bringing us along musically. He was definitely too busy, and I don't think he had the foggiest idea of what to do. He did a great job with the Byrds, no question about it. But I've always really wondered just how good a producer Terry was, seeing what an artist is about and bringing that out. I'm not so sure that had his parents not been who they were [Melcher was the son of Doris Day, one of Columbia's biggest pre-rock stars], he would have gotten out of the starting gate."

The Gentle Soul was not the only victim of Columbia and Melcher's overextension. Another Melcher-produced band on the label, the Rising Sons (with Ry Cooder and Taj Mahal), had gotten a runaround that saw them eke out just one single for the label. Larry Murray says he and Jennifer Warnes recorded some folk-rock as part of a Peter, Paul & Mary–meets–the–Byrds trio at Columbia, after being offered a contract with Melcher, that never saw the light of day. In 1969, says Polland, after the Gentle Soul had dissipated, "Terry came up with a brilliant idea—he asked me and Ry to make an album of the blues music we had done as a duo some years earlier. He wanted us to take the train to New Orleans and record live at Preservation Hall with the authentic players of the day who were still alive, though dwindling. Ry was thrilled beyond his wildest dreams, and I thought it was a great idea too, but I didn't want to give up my career as a singer-songwriter (not labeled as such yet, but I knew I wanted to continue recording my own songs).

"Terry had the whole thing set up, but no matter how many times I asked him, 'And when do you think I'd be able to get back to recording my own material?,' he never had a clear answer for me.

So, I went to the top. I called the president of CBS, Clive Davis. I told him about the blues project, which he thought sounded great, then I told him about my desire to also pursue my singing/writing career. He gave me the following advice: that if I went to New Orleans, and the end result was a popular album, the record company would consider me obliged to continue in that vein, to follow suit with other albums in that ilk. He said if I really wanted to pursue my career singing my own songs, that I shouldn't even go to New Orleans, that I should just do that (record my own songs) and stay on one track. This was not an easy decision for me, as you might imagine.

"After a lot of painful grappling with my own heart, I called Terry and told him I didn't want to do the blues album, I wanted to record my own songs. Both he and Ry were so pissed off at me that to this day, Ry has not spoken to me (although I'm sure he's forgotten all about it by now), and Terry would not produce me as a solo artist. So I wound up being signed to this label with no producer and no one else really knowing what to do with me." Polland did make one obscure solo album for Columbia in the early '70s. But her stunted career was, like that of her friends the Rising Sons before her, another illustration of the dark side of the apparent advantages of signing with the giant that had fostered the Byrds, Simon & Garfunkel, and Bob Dylan. (Polland being asked to record blues in New Orleans, incidentally, was hardly the worst option Columbia gave its folk-rock artists. Chester Crill of Kaleidoscope remembers an Epic executive suggesting that the band record Bobby Vinton songs.)

s a result of the singer-songwriter movement, there was now room for cult oddballs with tenuous connections to folk-rock whose unconventional, uncommercial songs and voices would have stood little chance of securing ambitious full-length albums before 1967. Among them were Van Dyke Parks, known mostly as the lyrical collaborator for the Beach Boys' aborted *Smile* album before the release of his *Song Cycle* LP, and David Ackles, whose self-titled 1968 Elektra debut fell somewhere in a netherworld between Randy Newman, Tim Buckley, and Kurt Weill. "They weren't coming out of the folk scene at all," says David Anderle, who co-produced *David Ackles* and had gotten Van Dyke Parks signed to MGM before Parks went to Warner Brothers. "They were almost musical comedy theater or something. You can't really bag those guys." Yet at the same time, he agrees, Ackles, Parks, and Newman had their own place in the singer-songwriter movement: "These weren't rock 'n' rollers. They saw themselves as singer-songwriters. But they all wanted *big* success!" And Ackles and Parks never got it, their works condemned to an esoteric cult audience, though Newman did become a star, sort of, after about a decade of releasing albums whose massive critical acclaim went hand-in-hand with low sales figures.

Before the 1960s were over, the flexibility in image and repertoire afforded by the rise of the singer-songwriter also allowed several veterans of folk and pop to make unsuspected moves into folk-rock, shedding a square image for a relatively hip one. Bobby Darin had done so with "If I Were a Carpenter," and back in 1965 had made a relatively unnoticed stab at vague social protest, "We Didn't Ask to Be Brought Here," with a standard 12-string electric folk-rock riff on a single that bubbled under the Top 100. In 1969, he went as far as billing himself for one album only (*Commitment*) as "Bob Darin," growing a moustache and donning a jean jacket for the cover shoot. He even did Dylan, Tim Hardin, Leadbelly, and Beatles songs with acoustic guitar, harmonica, and a four-piece band at L.A.'s Troubadour club around this time. But other than that, Darin never did make folk-rock his sole focus, and although Neil Young has cited Darin as an unlikely inspirational role model for Young's own chameleon-like genre-jumping over the years, it's hard to imagine Neil devoting an entire album to songs from the musical *Doctor Dolittle*, as Darin did in 1967, just months after his first pair of folk-rock-influenced LPs.

Some of Darin's folk-rock-influenced tracks were produced by Nik Venet, who had made Vince Martin another of his reclamation projects. He also produced ex–Kingston Trio member John Stewart, who blossomed into a respectable folk-rock-country singer-songwriter with far earthier concerns than he'd unleashed with his old threesome. Stewart had actually made an almost incognito landing on top of the hit parade right after leaving the Kingston Trio, when the Monkees had made his "Daydream Believer" a #1 hit at Christmas in 1967. Davy Jones sang it with such preteen sentimentality that even years later, many familiar with Stewart's other work had no idea he was the author. "I was opening for him in 1972, and he sang 'Daydream Believer,'" remembers an amused Mary McCaslin. "Because I rearranged rock songs [into folk settings], I thought that was pretty cool. He gets offstage, and I said, 'Oh, what a nice thing for you to do, "Daydream Believer." I've always liked that song. What a good idea.' And he said, 'Well, I'm glad you like it, Mary, I wrote it.' At the time, I did not know that. It's a good thing I didn't say, 'Why are you singing *that*?'"

Around the time the Kingston Trio was breaking up, Stewart also recorded demos with the then-little-known John Denver, including versions of "Daydream Believer" and Denver's "Leaving on a Jet Plane" (to become a #1 hit for Peter, Paul & Mary in 1969). Fortunately for Stewart's credibility, perhaps, the demos met with little response, and Stewart ended up making his first post–Kingston Trio album as part of a duo with his wife Buffy Ford. *Signals Through the Glass*, issued in 1968, served as Stewart's belated folk-rock debut, and was something of an anomaly in his long career, not only because he shared vocals with Ford. The record was an odd mixture of the Kingston Trio's troubadour folk, luscious orchestrated sunshine pop (arranged and conducted by John Andrew Tartaglia, known for jingles, soundtracks, and his work with the easy listening Mystic Moods Orchestra), and the first stirrings of the dark and stark Americana for which Stewart would become known in his subsequent solo career. "July, You're a Woman" was pop-friendly enough to generate cover versions by Pat Boone and Robert Goulet, and "Holly on My Mind" was delicious candy folk-pop.

Yet on the same album, "Nebraska on My Widow" was a chilling portrait of loneliness. "Draft Age" was a downright spookily weird cinematic narrative of a day in the life of one Clarence Malloy, the hook being that this was the day he became eligible for the draft and death in Vietnam, the impending doom contrasted with a mocking cheery sing-along melody and ghoulishly apposite scenes of wholesome everyday American life. "Draft Age" and other songs on the LP, particularly "Mucky Truckee River," gave the sense of a lagging-behind-the-times, clean-cut folkie awakening with a jolt to the most unpleasant realities of late-'60s America and desperately making up for lost time. Perhaps the shift was partially due to Stewart's campaigning on behalf of presidential candidate Robert Kennedy, who was assassinated in mid-1968; perhaps Stewart was just seizing musical and lyrical opportunities not available to him in the more constrained format of the Kingston Trio. Obscure, long out-of-print, and not even especially highly rated by Stewart's own cult of fans, *Signals Through the Glass* is one of the most worthy curiosities in all of late-'60s folk-rock.

Most of those Stewart fans rate his second album, 1969's *California Bloodlines*, as his true masterpiece. Nik Venet took the production reins for this recording (*Signals Through the Glass* had been handled by Kingston Trio producer Voyle Gilmore), and it was his idea to cut Stewart in Nashville, although initially the singer-songwriter was reluctant. In keeping with Venet's usual modus operandi, the sound was stripped back and basic. Melodically it was blander than *Signals Through the Glass*, or for that matter "Daydream Believer." But it did establish the heartfelt, if sometimes mundane, Americana for which Stewart would become known, allowing him to reinvent himself as a critically respected contemporary singer-songwriter, a task at which virtually everyone else who first rose to fame in Kingston Trio–like groups failed. To ensure that the backing was as heartfelt as the singing, Venet even went to the extent of (falsely) telling the Nashville session cats that "Mother Country" was about Stewart's father, and furthermore (also falsely) that Stewart's dad had just died of cancer.

"His interpretations are so honest," said Venet in summarizing Stewart's appeal to Pete Frame of *ZigZag*. "He doesn't dress his songs up or sell them short . . . he sings them naturally but he was worried about *California Bloodlines* inasmuch as it wasn't glitter, it wasn't glamour, and it wasn't slick. I understand his worry, because he was trying to get a hit album, and he was almost ready to sell down to have a hit on the basis that a hit would enable him to go on and do what he wanted. But I said, 'No, just keep doing what you want to do . . . who knows, you may not have a hit record until after you're dead.' [Indeed Stewart wouldn't have a hit single until 1979.] But in your lifetime you can't sell down and really be happy.

"But he was worried that the album wasn't commercial enough, whereas I thought that was its whole charm. If he wants to have hits and make a lot of money, maybe he should call [hit producer] Richard Perry; personally I can only capture the artist. I don't guarantee top tenners, though I have had big hits. I wanted to capture John Stewart and if nothing else, with *California Bloodlines* I gave him a basis from which his solo recording career could evolve."

By far the most impressive transformation from passé early-'60s pop star to respected late-'60s folk-rocker was undergone by Dion, although he'd made some solid folk-rock with producer Tom Wilson in the mid-'60s that had passed unnoticed. In 1968, recovering from a serious drug habit and absent from the hit parade for five years, Dion was listening to Tim Hardin, Laura Nyro, and Robert Johnson. That year he made a stunning comeback with "Abraham, Martin and John," written by Dick Holler just after Robert F. Kennedy was shot in mid-1968. The gentle folk-rock rumination, with allusions to the assassinations of the Kennedys and Martin Luther King, Jr., made #4, its lush production managing to effectively counterpoint the song's sad mood instead of overwhelming it in gratuitous sentiment. "Those middle '60s years were watershed years for me," Dion explained to Kingsley Abbott in *Record Collector*. "I played some folk houses and intimate rooms. I *talked* to people properly and it brought me out. I found my voice. Some of my doors had been locked, but I began expressing. I guess 'Abraham, Martin and John' was the culmination of that time, with its nylon strings and finger-picking style."

The concurrent *Dion* album found him writing antiwar songs ("He Looks a Lot Like Me") and thoughtfully interpreting work by Fred Neil, Joni Mitchell, Leonard Cohen, Bob Dylan, and Lightnin' Hopkins. His 1970 album *Sit Down Old Friend* was an unplugged album before its time, finding him writing most of the material and recording with only his acoustic guitar as accompaniment. Although lacking a classic on the order of "Abraham, Martin and John" (which in fact would be his last hit), it was quality, wistful folk-blues that found his voice reaching unsuspected gradations of soul-baring, and deserves rediscovery.

While Dion had been recording in New York for more than a decade, new and much younger singer-songwriters continued to emerge from the region in the late '60s. Melanie Safka, billing herself by her first name only, made some underrated singer-songwriter albums with a low, husky voice tinged with childish vulnerability and innocence. Her critical reputation suffered irreparable damage when her kiddie pop early-'70s hit "Brand New Key" went to #1; her 1970 Top Ten smash "Lay Down (Candles in the Rain)" had stereotyped her as the ultimate Woodstock naif hippie. To this day, one risks serious ostracism from critics to utter any words of praise on Melanie's behalf in public. But unprejudiced listeners might find some of her early work a surprisingly earthy, sensual, and serious mixture of folk-rock with soul, pop, and a bit of Broadway, heard to best advantage on her 1969 album *Melanie*.

Melanie.

Like many folk-rock singer-songwriters of the '60s, Melanie had begun playing on the streets and in the coffeehouses-cum-basket houses of Greenwich Village, listening to records by old-school folkies Pete Seeger, Jean Ritchie, and Ewan MacColl. Also like many of them, her route to a recording contract and stardom would not just be unconventional, but almost accidental. While auditioning for a theatrical production in the Brill Building, she had stopped in an office to ask for directions, and went back afterward to thank the secretary. The office turned out to be that of Hugo & Luigi, aka Hugo Peretti and Luigi Creatore, the production team and Roulette Records executives who had worked on pop hits by Sam Cooke, the Isley Brothers, the Tokens, and numerous others. Hugo & Luigi invited her to come back, and she met Peter Schekeryk, who was working for their production company. "They said to Peter when they first were talking about him meeting me, 'She sounds like someone singing underwater,'" Melanie remembers. "'But maybe you have something you could do with her.'" When Schekeryk's garage-pop-psych production of the Balloon Farm's "A Question of Temperature" rose to the Top 40, she continues, the producer traded his financial interest in the single "just to get me out of the deal [with Hugo & Luigi], because they had signed me for everything."

Schekeryk would become both her producer and her husband. An early stop at Columbia worked out badly for label and performer, with a couple of flop singles and artistic disagreements with executive Clive Davis. "Clive didn't see it," states Melanie. "He mentioned Michele Lee, who was a very pop, slick singer. I was horrified, because I didn't *see* me in that at all. Also, he didn't see me doing my own songs. My sense of myself . . . I had very little, but I did have some sense of myself as something. I had a style, I had a thing. And I didn't sense it being in the direction of Michele Lee. She had a toothpaste commercial! And I'm just saying, oh my God."

It was only when she moved to Buddah, a label known mostly for pop-rock (though it issued a fair pop-folk-rock LP by singer-songwriter Penny Nichols in 1968), that she found her voice as a recording artist. At Buddah she was free to record with Schekeryk's eclectic and sometimes elaborate arrangements, though she had never played with a band before recording. "I didn't have any experience in anything," she emphasizes. "I wasn't the upper echelon of Greenwich Village, even. All of the sudden I'm in the studio with Larry Coryell, top session musicians, and all the top New York guys, [like pianist] Roger Kellaway, who came from classical jazz roots. I had a strong sense that this was bigger than me. It almost couldn't be stopped."

In spite of the frequent full arrangements on her early albums, Melanie often continued and continues to be called, to her bemusement, a folk singer. "At sixteen, I was trying to be the old wise woman that I am now," she laughs. "My voice was so odd, and my songwriting style was drawing from Kurt Weill and Billie Holiday. I just liked all this stuff, and I wanted my voice to project this old, wizened woman. I played the guitar, so I didn't have the musical training to be able to pull off those kind of songs. I think my style was mostly going out to be Billie Holiday, and getting it wrong. I didn't really have a sense of, 'I'm a folk singer.' Except that's where they put me because I played guitar! And I had long hair and looked right for that, so I was always called a folk singer. In fact, I was at Montreaux Jazz Festival, and I won jazz singer of the year; this was when I had just released 'Lay Down (Candles in the Rain).' That was good to a degree, and bad to a degree. 'Cause people didn't know exactly where to put me."

Due to the whimsicality of some of her more celebrated songs, critics and listeners often didn't put her in a serious light. Yet examination of her lesser-known early album tracks yields some surprisingly serious efforts, like the bittersweet, almost pained melancholy of "Leftover Wine." "I was at odds with my image my entire early career," she notes. "I was a very dark person, and a pretty dark writer mostly. The ones that seemed to emerge were the lighter moments. I wanted to be perceived as a serious singer-songwriter, and here would be these mega-hits that were silly and whimsical. [Even 1971's 'Brand New Key,' she says, had started out as "more like a Cajun swamp thing" than the romp into which it turned.] Coupled with my physical appearance of being cute, round-y-faced, when a camera pointed at me I smiled ... I wasn't one of those angst-ful long, angular people. It just didn't look the right part to be a person of any consequence, writing about social commentary or anything. I was doomed to be cute.

"My audiences kept me okay, because that was the only time I found true happiness, on stage. I kept being me, and people saw who I was. The whole thing: the funny songs, the sad songs, and all the different styles and using different genres. 'Leftover Wine'—my real fans, when I did shows, those were the songs they wanted to hear. In fact, 'Tuning My Guitar' and the darker songs became much more well known in Europe." Her quite dramatically different, languorously slow interpretation of the Rolling Stones' classic "Ruby Tuesday" even won the admiration of one particularly celebrated European musician. According to Melanie, the Stones "were very happy that I recorded it. In fact, I have a picture of Mick Jagger wearing a big button saying, 'Hear Melanie's "Ruby Tuesday" any day.'"

Bonding with one of the biggest audiences of all time—at Woodstock—would spark the creation of her first big hit, 1970's "Lay Down (Candles in the Rain)," which testified to the increased eclecticism of both Melanie and folk-rock in general with its use of the Edwin Hawkins Singers as backup vocalists. Bringing in a gospel group for such a song, as Melanie remembers, "was unheard of at that time. I couldn't have been happier with that, because I've always felt that music should transcend categorization."

An older Village vet made the transition to the singer-songwriter era in the studio with an approach that in a way stripped back to a core rather than dramatically expanding the ingredients. Jerry Jeff Walker, who had put some little-known Byrds-like folk-rock on a few tracks by the wide-ranging sorta-psychedelic New York band Circus Maximus, started a solo career with much more pronounced country and folk leanings. "We always seemed to bump heads," says Walker of Circus Maximus now. "We didn't know what we were doing. We were five guys who came from different backgrounds, who were trying to make something. We didn't know what it was. It was jazz, and basic rock, and folk, and trying to mix it together. We were always a little bit out of kilter, too wordy; we weren't hippie enough. I had all these songs from the road, but that didn't fit into Circus Maximus; we were going more in the psychedelic direction. It was [virtuosic folk multi-instrumentalist David] Bromberg that really kind of pulled me back to the folk circle, him and Izzy Young [proprietor of the Folklore Center in Greenwich Village], when I got into the city."

Walker, born Ron Crosby in Oneonta, New York, was more the storytelling troubadour than most singer-songwriters, in part because much of his own life had (unlike many who adopted the pose) been spent on the road. Indeed he'd spent so much of the early '60s picking up singing jobs where he could (often in New Orleans) that, as he writes in his autobiography *Gypsy Songman*, he had very little awareness of the tremors shaking pop and rock music at the time Beatlemania hit and many folkies went electric. The folk-rock groundswell was strong enough, though, to catch him in its slipstream when he went electric himself and joined Circus Maximus around 1966. It was one of his experiences as a young hobo of sorts, though, that would form the basis of the title track of his 1968 debut album, *Mr. Bojangles*.

"Mr. Bojangles," inspired by talks with an elderly tap dancer he met during a weekend stint in a New Orleans jail, told a character-based story in the best folk ballad narrative tradition. Indeed when Walker was first performing it, as he remembers, "I did so well in my job, they were sure it was a song that had been around for many years." It would eventually became a huge Top Ten hit, in a circuitous route somewhat analogous to how ancient folk ballads had been shaped by the folk process. As Walker remembers, "The Circus Maximus guys decided in '67, I guess it was, to go up to New York. We were going in bits and pieces, and got to Washington, DC. We went over one night to open mike night at the old Cellar Door. I couldn't get in, but I heard some band onstage singing 'Mr. Bojingles' [sic]. It was Emmylou Harris. Somehow, she had gotten a recording, probably from some club or something. I could have even made it at somebody's house, for all who knows. She couldn't hear the lyrics very clearly, so she thought it was 'Mr. Bojingles,' not 'Mr. Bojangles.' By that point I realized we better gas that car up and get it going to New York before the damn thing gets there ahead of me."

Walker would not record it on either of Circus Maximus's two albums for Vanguard. On a whim, one evening he and David Bromberg popped over to Bob Fass's all-night radio show on New York's noncommercial Pacifica network affiliate, WBAI. When they played "Mr. Bojangles" live over the air, Fass taped it and began to play it so often that listeners started to ask for it in New York record stores. Walker made a demo in his apartment for Vanguard (issued more than 30 years later on his *Best of the Vanguard Years* compilation) with Bromberg, drummer N.D. Smart (who would later play with Ian & Sylvia's Great Speckled Bird, Gram Parsons, and Emmylou Harris), and bassist Gary White. "That was my acoustic rock sound," says Walker. "Norman [N.D. Smart] plays the spoons on his legs at the end. But Vanguard nixed the whole idea, said they didn't want to have any idea for me to do that. They [gave] me a release to go to Atlantic." Walker has recalled that Vanguard's Maynard Solomon found the song a bit racist, though in fact the guy who'd inspired the number back in a New Orleans jail cell was white.

Atlantic wanted to record "Mr. Bojangles" badly, and by this time, according to his autobiography, a Walker recording of the tune had also appeared on a single as a rare thousand-copy giveaway item in Austin, Texas. But there would be some disagreements over how to back Walker now that he was a solo singer-songwriter. "They wanted something very commercial. I had to sort of use what was available to me when I finally got a chance to make a recording. But I also had Bromberg's ear, and he was telling me that we could get all these players that were around, [like] Jody Stecher on fiddle. I knew a dobro player from Ohio that I used to sit up and jam with; I said I'd like him to come and be part of my first record. He wouldn't come into New York. I think he drove as far as New

Jersey, and we had to send a car to go get him: 'I'm not bringing my car in there!' I even had Ron Carter play bass on one song; I'd seen him two nights before play with Miles Davis.

"Memphis, that's where [Atlantic] had their success, so they flew me down to cut 'Mr. Bojangles.' I came back, and they said, 'How do you want to make the rest of the album?' And I thought, 'You know what would be neat, is to take the Memphis rhythm section and put some of the Nashville acoustic guys on top of it.' Sort of like Ricky Skaggs meets Booker T. They went, 'We have no plans to mix Memphis and Nashville.' And I said, 'Okay.' There's a case again of somebody steering you. You're blown by the winds of chance; you take whatever you can do.

"I finally convinced [Atlantic] to take the strings off the single. They put that out without me knowing it, and then I took them off and went back to the organ, the way we recorded it. I said, 'I can't have an album that's got ten songs that are kind of acoustic dobro-y, and then have this thing come out with all these strings.' They went, 'Oh, okay, that makes sense.' So we put the organ back in. The way that it comes out on the album sounds more like it than the single did." In the meantime the single peaked at a mere #77 in the charts, hurt by a forgotten competing version by Bobby Cole.

Yet "Mr. Bojangles" was already on its way to becoming a standard, covered by such nonfolk-rock singers as Harry Belafonte, Harry Nilsson, and Neil Diamond (a 1970 cover by Bob Dylan even surfaced on the outtakes collection *Dylan*). In 1971, it would finally reach the Top Ten via an imaginative arrangement—and a few humorous lyrical misreadings—by the Nitty Gritty Dirt Band (a story told in a later chapter). Walker's song had made a long journey since he had played it for Ramblin' Jack Elliott around 1967 at the Village singer-songwriter hangout the Kettle of Fish, where Elliott (according to Walker's autobiography) tersely commented, "Too many words in it. Strange words."

Other less celebrated songs in a storytelling frame of mind, such as "Gypsy Songman" and "Little Bird," would appear on the three albums Walker made in the late-'60s. (In a strange contractual pay-off, Walker had to return to Vanguard to give the company that had rejected "Mr. Bojangles" his next album before returning to Atlantic for his final 1960s LP.) Some of that material was as dust-dry as his voice; "The Ballad of the Hulk" was much like the most verbose of Dylan's mid-'60s epics. But a thread that Walker sees running through his work, as exemplified by songs like "Mr. Bojangles," is the creation of new songs that could have actually been mistaken for ancient folk ballads. "Tom Paxton, you could say, was a guy who could play pretty traditionally, and then wrote on top of it," he muses. "Dave Van Ronk would get a new song by somebody and interpret it, only it *sounded* traditional at the time. I think about that point we decided, lookit, we can probably *write* one that sounds pretty traditional. That was the best thing about the tradition of folk music. It told you how to write a song that sounds timeless. That was the goal, to write a song that sounded like it could have been written yesterday or maybe a hundred years and a day [ago]."

Like many of the singer-songwriters coming to the fore around this time, Walker didn't have a commercial, conventional, or versatile voice. But by now folk-rock had changed the climate of acceptance within the industry to such an extent that for select artists such as himself, vocal personality was starting to matter more than standard chops did. "I was pretty uncertain of my own ability to play and sing. You find out as time goes by that even though you don't have the best ability or technique, you do have something individual to offer. I had many sessions where guys that I thought were great players would come over and say, 'Man, that's cool what you're doing there in that song. That gave it its whole feel.' I'd go, 'Really? I thought I was blowin' it!'" he laughs. "But the good accompanists look for some little body language 'phlump' of yours, and that's what they enlarge upon."

Arlo Guthrie, like Melanie and Richie Havens, would ride a Woodstock appearance from cultdom to stardom. He brought more of a name to live up to, however, than any other folk-rock musician. As the son of Woody Guthrie, he was seen by some as the flame-keeper of an American folk legacy that revered his dad more than any other figure. It could have been a cross to bear, and it's a tribute to Arlo that he became a respected singer-songwriter in his own right with a tale-telling style that, while owing something to the folk tradition his father had symbolized, was entirely his own. Another cross to bear was his 18-minute live shaggy-dog story of an arrest for littering that enabled him to escape the draft, "Alice's Restaurant Massacree" (since referred to almost always simply as "Alice's Restaurant"). As huge a hit as an underground hit could be, taking up the entire first side of his 1967 debut LP, *Alice's Restaurant*, it was very much an acoustic talking-folk-narrative piece (a style also contemporized by a less well-known, similarly lengthy FM radio fave in the late '60s, Jamie Brockett's "Legend of the U.S.S. Titanic"). For a time, "Alice's Restaurant" overshadowed Guthrie's efforts to establish himself as a singer-songwriter with more versatile wares to offer than funny stories.

Guthrie's gradual changeover to electric music, at first under the guidance of producer Fred Hellerman (who had been in the Weavers), was more awkward than most. Even a few years beyond 1965, artists and labels still sometimes had little or no idea of what they were doing when they electrified. "I was much more of a traditionalist than Fred Hellerman," says Guthrie of his first two albums. "A lot of the very earliest synthesizers that were used on those records were brought in by Fred, not by me. Then I wanted to take more control over the recording. There was a little bit of friction, not just generationally, but personally, as it would have been with anybody."

For his second album, he continues, "I wanted to make a studio recording, because I felt I was embarrassed by some of the things on *Alice's Restaurant*. 'Alice' is fine, but I thought I could have done it much better. It was really a live recording, even if it was in a studio. Because 'Alice's Restaurant,' as for most part the other songs, *had* to be done live. You couldn't add canned laughter. We wanted to attract a live audience, have them laugh at real places. And unfortunately for us, everybody who came to the studio had already *heard* 'Alice's Restaurant.' Some of the other songs, I wasn't even singing in tune, you know? Or it was too affected. It was the first time I really had a chance to listen to myself, and I wasn't comfortable with myself on that record.

"So I was determined to do a studio record. I started working on it, and then one day the studio called me up and said, 'Arlo, a terrible thing happened. Haley's Comet came over and your tapes were on the machine and it wiped out all the stuff. And now the record's supposed to come out in two weeks, man, and so we have to go get some live recordings. Where are you playing?' I was under the influence at that time, probably, [of] some illegal substances. I believed 'em!" He cackles with laughter at the absurdity of his naivete.

"So they recorded two nights at the Bitter End, which were probably the worst two nights of my life, and they put 'em on out on *Arlo*, which was the second one. It was terrible! I mean it was so embarrassing to me, I just wanted to crawl away and hide. I wasn't concerned whether it was folk-rock or folk. It was just lousy. So I left after that to get out from working with [manager] Harold [Leventhal] and with Fred Hellerman. I decided to go out to the West Coast and started recording for Warners directly." It was only at the very end of the 1960s that Guthrie would become fully comfortable with a fully arranged rock sound.

The most startling injection of new blood into the folk-rock singer-songwriter mainstream in the late '60s came not from New York or California, but from Canada, even if the performers recorded and often lived in the US. Ian & Sylvia had been pioneers in this regard since the early '60s, and one of the songwriters they were among the first to discover and record material by was fellow countryman Gordon Lightfoot. Canadians Leonard Cohen, Joni Mitchell, and Neil Young (although the latter wouldn't begin his solo career until after doing three albums with Buffalo Springfield) would soon follow Lightfoot's path to Stateside success. So would the four-fifths-Canadian group the Band, though as with every mini-movement there were forgotten flops from the region, like Elyse Weinberg, or singer-songwriters who were already recording but wouldn't get international recognition until after the 1960s, like Bruce Cockburn. Those with the ambition to match their talent knew that going South was necessary to mount a sustained musical career. "It's very difficult to make a living in Canada, let alone be a star," complained Mitchell in a 1968 radio interview for KRLA in Los Angeles.

It's difficult to pinpoint a vision that's particularly common or unique to Canadian folk-rock performers, but Mitchell tried, in a 1969 profile in *The New York Times*. "We Canadians are a bit more nosegay, more Old-Fashioned Bouquet than Americans," she speculated. "We're poets because we're such *reminiscent* kind of people. I love Leonard [Cohen]'s sentiments, so I've been strongly influenced by him. My poetry is urbanized and Americanized, but my music is influenced by the prairies. When I was a kid, my mother used to take me out to the fields to teach me bird calls. There was a lot of space behind individual sounds. People in the city are so accustomed to hearing a jumble of different sounds that when they come to making music, they fill it up with all sorts of different things."

A certain reserve and unhurried room to breathe were certainly characteristic of many of Gordon Lightfoot's songs, which had become popular cover choices among folk and pop artists as early as 1965 (although his first album wouldn't come out until 1966). In folk-rock, however, he would always have something of a borderline role. He was certainly not nearly traditional enough to be confined to the folk category, yet he never had the need to use full, rounded rock backup. (His songs, however, were sometimes covered by full-blooded rock musicians.) Although Lightfoot had done a misguided rock cover of Dylan's "Just Like Tom Thumb's Blues" on a 1965 single, folk, pop, and country were closer to his heart. As Phil Ochs wrote in *Broadside*, Lightfoot was "destined to become a pivotal figure in bridging the gap between folk music and country and western." Indeed when Jerry Jeff Walker started to span a somewhat similar breach in his solo career, as he recalls with some amusement, in his initial Toronto appearances "I was being billed as the Gordon Lightfoot of the States."

While Lightfoot's restrained, clipped vocal style was important to his appeal, his chief strength lay in the expansive yet sober romanticism and straightforward, easy-on-the-ear folk melodicism of his songs. Chief among them were "Early Mornin' Rain," "I'm Not Sayin'," "The Way I Feel," "For Lovin' Me," and "Ribbon of Darkness," all of which were on his 1966 debut, *Lightfoot*. All were extremely attractive choices for other acts looking for cover material, with Peter, Paul & Mary and Ian & Sylvia both recording "Early Mornin' Rain" and "For Lovin' Me" on 1965 albums; Nico putting "I'm Not Sayin'" on her flop 1965 pre–Velvet Underground single; and, much later, the British folk-rock band Fotheringay (with Sandy Denny) doing "The Way I Feel" on their sole LP in the early '70s.

Lightfoot, however, was not immune to the times. By his second album, he'd done an electrified remake of "The Way I Feel" and used some of the same musicians that had played on *Blonde on Blonde*. On 1968's *Did She Mention My Name*, he worked with John Simon (also producer of Leonard Cohen, the Band, and Big Brother & the Holding Company) to put some of his songs to subtle, graceful orchestration, most outstandingly in "Pussywillows, Cat-Tails." "He was surprised by the strings I added after the basic session, but I think he was comfortable with them," says Simon. "This was all very natural—no big deal. It's critics and analysts who make a big deal out of these things like Dylan going electric."

Although one of the least political of 1960s folk singer-songwriters, Lightfoot also made a worthy foray into topicality with the ominous "Black Day in July," penned in reaction to the terrifying 1967 summer Detroit riots. Unlike his admirer Ochs, he felt no need to be politically consistent. Not long before, in March 1966, he had barked in *Hoot* magazine, "What most people don't realize is that if they don't fight in Vietnam now, they'll be fighting in the US in ten years," adding for good measure that topical songwriters "have a lot of questions but no more answers than anybody else. They think they understand the problems of today but they don't." By the time of "Black Day in July" he'd obviously changed his tune somewhat, not just on record but also in *Rolling Stone*, where he declared, "What happened in Detroit is going to happen all over this country if we don't make some very radical changes."

Lightfoot had been performing and writing songs since the 1950s, and recording since the early '60s, before making an international name for himself. By contrast, Montreal's Leonard Cohen's birth as a recording star could have hardly been more sudden. Cohen was already an established, famous poet and novelist in Canada, and fooled around with playing folk music informally, as seen in the 1965 film documentary *Ladies and Gentlemen . . . Mr. Leonard Cohen*. It wasn't until 1966, already in his early thirties, that he decided to seriously pursue a music career, the principal motivation being the same consideration that had spurred poet-turned-folk-rocker Ed Sanders of the Fugs in New York: money, or at least earning enough money to support himself.

"A lot had to do with poverty," he confessed to *Rolling Stone* a few years later. "I was writing books (two novels and four volumes of poetry) and they were being very well received . . . and that sort of thing, but I found it was very difficult to pay my grocery bill. So then I started bringing some songs together. And it really changed my whole scene." A move to New York's hallowed artist haven, the Chelsea Hotel, brought him in much closer contact with the folk-rock scene and the industry. He caught his big break when Judy Collins covered what's still his most recognized song, "Suzanne," on her *In My Life* album in late 1966. That LP also included his "Dress Rehearsal Rag," and three more Cohen compositions made the cut for Collins's *Wildflowers* album the following year.

By 1968, Cohen was recording his own songs for Columbia. *Songs of Leonard Cohen* exposed the world to the most poetic and literate—in the real sense, not just an abstract one—songwriter in all of folk-rock. His droning sing-speak voice mirrored the morose gloom of much of his work, peopled with lost or unattainable women and an abiding sense of romantic futility. Nonetheless his melodies, though simple and downbeat, meshed attractively with his words, and his forlorn persona was ably backed by suitably moody acoustic guitar, flecks of spooky electric reverb, spectral female backup vocals, and classical string arrangements. These were songs for playing over and over again on disconsolate lonely nights, an ambience furthered on his similar if less impressive follow-up, *Songs from a Room*. Cohen was well aware of the effect it had on people, and not exactly eager to ease the pain, he described the latter album to *Rolling Stone* as "very bleak and wiped out. The voice in it has much despair and pain in the sound of the thing. And I think it's an accurate reflection of where the singer was ... at the time. I mean very, very accurate. Too accurate for most people's taste. But as I believe that a general wipe-out is imminent and that many people will be undergoing the same kind of breakdown that the singer underwent, the record will become more meaningful as more people crack up."

Leonard Cohen, folk-rock's most literary poet.

Particularly influential on his debut album was "Suzanne," referred to in *Broadside* by Joni Mitchell as the kind of "character sketch song" that had affected her own writing: "I wrote 'Marcie' [from her own debut album, *Joni Mitchell*] and thought that it wouldn't have happened if it hadn't been for 'Suzanne.'" The Suzanne of the song was as mysterious as any of the goddess-type women, like *Blonde on Blonde*'s "Sad Eyed Lady of the Lowlands," that Dylan had served paeans to in the mid-'60s. Yet Cohen's object of affection had an even more dreamlike and mystical quality, with its intermingling imagery of tea, oranges, rivercraft, and above all, the blissful ecstasy of touching Suzanne's perfect body with one's mind. These were heightened by the track's effective contrast between Cohen's stock-in-trade deadpan vocal, the gliding melody, and the gates-of-heaven strings and female backup vocals.

Cohen, sometimes reluctant to discuss his music in fine detail for the media, provided a surprisingly thorough account of its composition for a 1994 BBC radio interview, doing much to explain the images of tea, oranges, and touching Suzanne's body with his mind that had hooked listeners. "The song was begun, and the chord pattern was developed, before a woman's name entered the song. And I knew it was a song about Montreal. It seemed to come out of that landscape that I loved very much in Montreal, which was the harbor, and the waterfront, and the sailors' church there, called Notre Dame de Bon Secour, which stood out over the river. I knew that there're ships going by, I knew that there was a harbor, I knew that there was Our Lady of the Harbor, which was the virgin on the church which stretched out her arms towards the seamen. You can climb up to the tower and look out over the river, so the song came from that vision, from that view of the river.

"At a certain point, I bumped into Suzanne Vaillancourt, who was the wife of a friend of mine. They were a stunning couple around Montreal at the time, physically stunning, both of them, a handsome man and woman. Everyone was in love with Suzanne Vaillancourt, and every woman was in love with Armand Vaillancourt. But there was no . . . well, there was thought, but there was no possibility, one would not allow oneself to think of toiling at the seduction of Armand Vaillancourt's wife. First of all he was a friend, and second of all as a couple they were inviolate. You just didn't intrude into that kind of shared glory that they manifested. I bumped into her one evening, and she invited me down to her place near the river. She had a loft, at a time when lofts were . . . the word wasn't used. She had a space in a warehouse down there, and she invited me down, and I went with her, and she served me Constant Comment tea, which has little bits of oranges in it. And the boats were going by, and I touched her perfect body with my mind, because there was no other opportunity. There was no other way that you could touch her perfect body under those circumstances. So she provided the name in the song."

Unsurprisingly, considering Cohen's inexperience as a musician in any context, even the minimal studio arrangements of his debut LP took a good amount of struggle to perfect. While John Simon is credited as musical director and producer, as he remembers it, "the album had three producers: John Hammond did the couple of tunes with guitar only, I did a bunch of them, and Leonard Cohen did the ones with the oud sound. Cohen was chomping at the bit to record; Hammond would have to cancel sessions too often for Leonard's taste. It was great for me, because for the first time I experimented [with] using female voices for orchestral parts." (One of the female voices—to add to the large gallery of "how'd *they* get in here?" bit-role players in early folk-rock—was Nancy Priddy, whose daughter Christina Applegate starred in the TV series *Married . . . with Children*. Priddy also inspired Stephen Stills's gorgeous Buffalo Springfield song "Pretty Girl Why.")

"John Hammond was particularly generous in the way that he read a newspaper continuously while you were struggling in the studio," said Cohen in his 1994 BBC radio interview. "A lot of people felt that this was an expression of indifference or even boredom with the whole affair, but I cherished it because he gave you the feeling that you weren't being scrutinized at every moment. He had this newspaper laid out, and he seemed to be entirely indifferent to what was going on. I loved the atmosphere he provided, 'cause you could make mistakes, start over, do another take, and it seemed to affect him not at all. There was a remarkable, unusual generosity that prevailed in the studio, given the fact that people like me didn't know what the hell was going on. I didn't even know where to stand in relation to a microphone, I'd never used one before. So he created a very hospitable atmosphere. For instance, I'd always played in front of a mirror at home, I felt most comfortable looking at myself in a mirror while I played, just some sort of chronic narcissistic enterprise that was the foundation of the whole affair, so he arranged to have a full-length mirror set up. He indulged me completely. He was a very, very generous man."

One of the musicians who played on what Simon calls the "oud" part of the record was likely Chris Darrow, who had met Cohen in New York, when Darrow's group Kaleidoscope was playing at the Scene club. Darrow says that the brilliance of the settings on *Songs of Leonard Cohen* were, like those on many other early folk-rock records, the product of as much accident as inspiration: "One night, this guy comes up to me. He's a real pale guy and he's got short, short dark hair, and he's wearing a black leather jacket and carrying a briefcase. He says, 'I think you guys are great. I'm doing an album, would you be interested in playing on my record?' I said, 'Sure. See that guy? That's our manager over there, go talk to him.'

"So like the next day, we're up at this guy's motel room. I have no idea who this guy is. Of all the guys that I would have thought would have looked like a guy who was going to be making a record, he looked like an accountant or something. I mean, there was nothing that read rock 'n' roll. And I wasn't familiar with who he was. I didn't know of him as an author. Of course it was Leonard Cohen.

"This guy was basically having a lot of problems with the record. All these guys were trying to produce him, and they were bringing all these musicians in. And because he really wasn't a musician, he was having a hard time making anybody understand how his songs went. So they'd bring in a series of musicians, and then some guys would get it, and some guys wouldn't get it. So they were spending a lot of time on this stuff. For some reason or other, it was really easy for us to figure out how this stuff went. Because we were folk musicians, and his limited guitar playing was like . . . I mean, I taught guitar, and I had students that were better than he was.

"It was one of those things where you could sort of figure out what a guy was trying to do. So we ended up playing on a bunch of the stuff on the record. On 'Suzanne,' that's Chester [Crill] and David [Lindley] playing the twin violins. We put [it] together for him, because he didn't know what he was doing, and he admitted it. It was like, 'I don't know what to do. Help me here.' He was very open." Lest anyone get the impression he thought Cohen was a no-talent, Darrow not unreasonably hails *Songs of Leonard Cohen* as "one of the classic records of all time . . . that record and [James Taylor's] *Sweet Baby James* are probably the two most important single singer-songwriter records." (Darrow might not be the least-biased judge of the matter, as he also played on *Sweet Baby James*.)

Cohen was a unique talent, not easy to imitate with derivations. There would be no armies of new Leonard Cohens, as there were constant supplies of new Dylans. His overall contribution and influence were more subtle. It was nearly unprecedented for a major poet, whose significant credentials were literary and not musical, to enter rock. As he told *NME* in 1970, "Every time I pick up a pen to write something, I don't know if it is going to be a poem, a song or a novel." This blurring of lines between poetry and rock was yet another dimension to popular music that folk-rock had made possible. Jim Morrison of the Doors, Tuli Kupferberg and Ed Sanders of the Fugs, even minor figures like David Meltzer of Country Joe & the Fish—like Bay Area band the Serpent Power—all were poets who probably never would have entered rock 'n' roll if its realms for serious lyrical expression hadn't been opened by folk-rock.

By the same token, folk-rock gave an admission ticket to nonsinging, nonperforming poets to make important contributions as lyrical collaborators. Larry Beckett did this with Tim Buckley, as did Robert Hunter for the Grateful Dead, but there were other poets starting to do so for rock bands outside of the folk-rock world: Keith Reid for Procol Harum, Peter Sinfield for King Crimson, and Pete Brown for Cream. Most likely that would have never happened either, had not folk-rock raised the bar for popular song lyrics to a new, higher level. As a cumulative result, rock 'n' roll lyrics were themselves starting to be taken as poetry on their own terms. By late 1968, *Village Voice* critic Richard Goldstein was holding a panel discussion on rock lyrics at the New School for Social Research, dubbing rock 'n' roll the "poetry of this age" in *The New York Times*. In August, the same paper had reported that record labels were advertising the latest singles of Jerry Jeff Walker and Laura Nyro by running the complete texts of their songs in full-page ads in the music trades. Even if some listeners and critics then and now felt that taking the words so seriously was draining some of the fun out of rock 'n' roll—the fun that had helped define the music since its inception—it would have been unimaginable even two or three years previously for rock lyrics to have been deigned worthy of such serious scrutiny.

side from Neil Young (who had already tasted acclaim as a member of Buffalo Springfield), the greatest Canadian singer-songwriter of the 1960s was Joni Mitchell. Like Cohen, she made her initial reputation as a songwriter whose works were covered by others. Foremost among those were Judy Collins of course, but also Tom Rush, Fairport Convention, Ian & Sylvia, Dave Van Ronk, Buffy Sainte-Marie (whose cover of "The Circle Game," released as a single, was her most determined effort to crack the folk-rock-pop market), and George Hamilton IV. All of them had released Joni Mitchell covers before Mitchell's self-titled debut came out in 1968. But unlike Cohen, Mitchell had been trouncing around the folk circuit in the States and Canada for years, developing unusual guitar tunings and writing precious, fablelike songs with pleasing but uncommonly angular chord progressions. Her high, swooping vibrato vocals, which as Rush aptly noted were heavily influenced by

Judy Collins in Mitchell's early years, were a perfect match for the woman Lillian Roxon described in her *Rock Encyclopedia* as "tall, pale, slim, frail, the very model of a lady folk singer."

While Mitchell would soon eclipse the standard image of the genteel, high-voiced folkie Madonna with the modern and at times even avant-garde originality of her songwriting, guitar playing, and vocal phrasing, she did have some roots in the far more traditional folk scene. She told Gene Shay in a March 1967 radio interview that she'd gotten her first job because she sounded like Bonnie Dobson, the by-then-nearly-forgotten precious Canadian folk singer who wrote "Morning Dew." As she told *Broadside*, "I'm very Judy Collins–influenced because for the first year and a half of my career I memorized her albums. That's what I sang—my sets were her sets."

But even by a November 1966 interview with Barry Bird, about a year and a half before her first album was released, she was distancing herself from her roots. "In the beginning I had a soprano voice so everyone compared me to Baez," she allowed. "But I just decided that the only way I was going to be able to differentiate myself from any other of the singers was to have original material. Every time I'd find a song, I'd find out afterwards that Judy Collins or somebody—Joan Baez had recorded it. So then with my new material I thought I was fairly safe. And then I discovered some lower register tones that I didn't know that I could use before." That in turn affected her songwriting, as she told *Melody Maker*'s Karl Dallas in 1968: "Since I started writing songs, the range of my voice has extended downwards something like two octaves, which gives me a lot more freedom in the sort of melodies I'm writing."

At least at first, Mitchell would prove too idiosyncratic to mesh with accompanying musicians, either live or in the recording studio. It's not well known that a couple of years or so before her debut album, she'd done some full-band demos in Chicago produced by Corky Siegel and Jim Schwall of the Siegel-Schwall Band, a white electric blues group with a style and repertoire similar to that of the early Paul Butterfield Blues Band. "We felt, artistically, it would be interesting to approach with a little bit of a classical flavor," remembers Siegel. "Jim Schwall mostly provided this touch with his string and brass writing, which was really great stuff, way ahead of its time for bringing classical idiom into folk and pop. There was violin, trumpet, drums, bass, and cello. Two of the pieces were by Joni and the other two were performed and written by [her then-husband] Chuck Mitchell. With regard to other aspects of the arrangements, which were more my effort or fault, you could actually see the bell bottoms and the paisley and maybe even some white go-go boots."

It's doubtful this intriguing session will ever see release, although the two Joni Mitchell songs that were cut, "Night in the City" and "The Circle Game," were re-recorded by her on her early official albums. "The Circle Game" (an "answer" song to the farewell-to-adolescence ballad "Sugar Mountain" by Neil Young, whom Mitchell had met in late 1965 when both were unsigned struggling singer-songwriters) was lumbered with a squeaky trumpet fanfare and a plodding rhythm section, with no guitar presence to speak of. "Night in the City" is yet stranger, with violin, cello, mandolin, and a chorus that breaks into a rhythm falling somewhere between polka and square dance call.

It would be quite a while before Mitchell would attempt to record with musicians again. Even as early as a March 1967 radio interview with Philadelphia DJ Ed Sciaky she remarked, "I made the mistake once of orchestrating ["The Circle Game"] and getting a blues band ... who are also fine classical musicians to do an arrangement.... And I tried to do a rock version of it and I lost everything. It's strictly a ballad.... If you put a rock beat to it, it would really, really be a hit, but it doesn't work." That didn't keep several other artists from trying to cut folk-rock versions of "The Circle Game," including Ian & Sylvia, Tom Rush, Buffy Sainte-Marie, and (in England) the Ian Campbell Group. But Mitchell told Sciaky that in her estimation, "It didn't work out well because 'Circle Game' is not ever going to be a rock 'n' roll song. Ian & Sylvia found that out with their version, and I tried to do the same thing. It has to be kept down. It has to be a ballad. It's very tempting."

Bruce Langhorne, who played with more folk-rock singer-songwriters than just about anyone back then, also met Mitchell around this time. He feels her music sounded better unaccompanied for a reason: "I was used to just tuning into people and playing their material. And Joni— I couldn't really play with her. Because she was so creative and so wonderfully unpredictable, and her music was so sophisticated, that I couldn't just tune in and start playing and have it work."

Joel Bernstein met Mitchell as a teenage fan at one of her shows in a Philadelphia club in 1967, and soon afterward began to work with her as both a photographer and guitar technician. "When she first learns from Eric Andersen how to play in open G tuning, she uses the chords he taught her in her own compositions," he explains. "Eventually she comes up with her own unusual chords for those tunings. Look at the guitar chords for 'Marcie' [from Mitchell's first album], for example, which *nobody* is playing. The opening chord—nobody is playing that chord in an open tuning." Part of the reason she told so many stories at her early shows, as unreleased tapes attest, was to hold the audience's attention as she retuned between each song.

"When she's at home with her guitar and making her way from open G to open E, she gets lost on the way and realizes that the guitar is now tuned to a more unusual, more complex chord than a simple major like G or E, and starts to explore playing in that tuning, using shapes she has learned in standard and open tunings," Bernstein continues. "As soon as she comes into that, it's like going through the little door in *Alice in Wonderland*. She's opening out into new horizons of composition, because she's getting things that just were not possible in standard tuning. Even by the first album, 'The Dawntreader' is stunning. It's orchestral in its composition, it's chords nobody has come up with, a tuning nobody has come up with, chords within that tune that are amazingly inventive, with beautiful tension and release. As time goes on, her tunings get to be more complex, her chords less so, and her right hand tends to be more broadstroke, and loses that filigree thing."

In 1966 and 1967, Mitchell slowly built a following as a solo acoustic club and coffeehouse artist, particularly in the Northeast. As such she was bucking the trend toward electrification among singer-songwriters, which hurt her at the very outset. "The year Dylan went electric," she told *The New York Times* in 1969, "the folk clubs started closing all over the country. It was like an epidemic. The only people being hired were people who had records out. I was always bringing up the rear. In those days, if you only played acoustical guitar, club owners treated you as though you were a dinosaur." Yet in the long run, perhaps this made her stand out, particularly around 1967, when amps were getting cranked so loud that a singer-songwriter with a solo acoustic guitar could seem anomalous. That was particularly true of a singer such as Mitchell, whose songs were not nearly as much an outgrowth of traditional folk lyrics and melodies as those of most singer-songwriters of her generation. "Now everybody's branching out and there's room for all styles," she explained in the same article. "People are playing where they feel their music. I feel my music with a solitary voice and a solitary guitar."

The buzz was building about Mitchell throughout 1967, when she performed at the Newport Folk Festival. She strengthened her appeal by separating from her husband, Chuck Mitchell, with whom she had been touring. Joni had quickly overshadowed Chuck, who, judging from an unreleased recording of the time ("Winter Lady"), had a sub–Scott McKenzie sound that was both incompatible and far inferior to that of his wife. Joni also made friends with high-ranking established musicians such as Judy Collins, who has noted being called in the middle of the night by a fellow artist (variously remembered as Tom Rush or Al Kooper) who had Mitchell play her a song over the phone (variously remembered as "Both Sides Now" or "Michael from Mountains").

Yet it took a surprisingly long time for Mitchell to sign a contract and record an album, in part because she was far fussier about artistic control and fair terms than most artists in her position would have been. "No one paid much attention to folk music three years ago," she told *Melody Maker* in 1970, "and the record companies wanted to change my music, so I had to wait until I was in a position so that I could play as I wanted." Mitchell turned down Vanguard, calling their offer a "terrible contract" in a 1995 *Goldmine* feature; without naming names, she'd told Shay in a 1967 radio interview that "the most complained-about label is the one that wants me the most." Tom Rush, as previously noted, had tried to interest Jac Holzman in Mitchell without success, and subsequent feelers from Elektra petered out when Joni insisted on designing her album covers. Reprise was willing to grant her the unusual degree of artistic control (particularly for a new artist) she sought, and put out her first album in early 1968.

Having already made a big name for herself touring the folk circuit, and an increased Stateside presence after living in New York for a while, Mitchell opted to make *Joni Mitchell* almost wholly acoustic. This begs the question as to whether it has the right to be considered a folk-rock album at all. Mitchell herself, however, didn't see her own material as folk music. As early as November 1966, in one of her first interviews (on WRTI in Philadelphia), she was thinking of her songs as suitable for the pop field, with arranged orchestration; in March 1967, in a radio interview with Philadelphia DJ Ed Sciaky, she declared, "'Both Sides Now' is a rock song, given the beat and the emphasis."

And *Joni Mitchell* was at the very least far too contemporary in both material and production to be flagged as a folk album. Even upon its release, it was championed by the rock and pop audience at least as much as it was by folk enthusiasts, if not more so. David Crosby, then on the rebound from getting his pink slip from the Byrds, produced the LP, whose stark, restrained vocals contrasted splendidly with a haunting, cavernous reverb. As Mitchell explained it to Shay in a 1968 interview on WHAT in Philadelphia, "He had me sing into a grand piano with the ringing pedal down, and so you got these incredible... every note I sang repeated itself on the strings."

There was a crystalline austerity to the songs, making them a kinder, gentler counterpart to Leonard Cohen in that they lent themselves equally to repeated plays in solitary bedrooms. Mitchell was more prone to storybook imagery, however, and enchanting melodies, getting into occasional upbeat swinging rhythms in "Night in the City" and cinematic urban narrative on "Marcie" and "Nathan La Freneer." It is a captivating, underrated record, with an ethereal mystery missing from any of her subsequent releases. It's also a record that could have taken a much different shape, as she cut well over an album's worth of outtakes at the sessions—there were more outtakes from those sessions, in fact, than there would be over the course of her entire subsequent recording career. It was the era of concept albums, however, and Mitchell selected and organized the tracks to fit into an LP side titled "I Came to the City" and another titled "Out of the City and Down to the Seaside," although the ostensible concept/story of moving through urban experiences to freer realms was a loose one.

"If I'd recorded a year ago," Mitchell told *Rolling Stone* in 1968, "I would have used lots of orchestration. No one would have let me put out an acoustic album. They would have said it's like having a whole paintbox and using only brown . . . . In music today I feel that I can put down my songs with an acoustic guitar and forget the violins and not feel that I need them." She did make an exception for "Night in the City," using Stephen Stills on bass because "he came up with a beautiful bass line that I just couldn't deny." She'd continue to play unaccompanied live for quite some time too; an early Canadian TV appearance with orchestral arrangements found her at one point playing in 3/4 time against 4/4 accompaniment, and may have helped put her off the whole concept.

For all its relative simplicity, *Joni Mitchell*'s production was fraught with difficulties. David Anderle, who wasn't even working for Reprise and had barely started to do his own productions for Elektra, remembers being called in by Mitchell and Crosby to help remove some noise from a track. The process that took off the hiss from the album, she told Shay in the same 1968 WHAT interview, "took off a lot of the highs, which is the reason it sounds like it's under sort of glass . . . under a bell jar, that's what Judy [Collins] said. So you really need the words inside the book to follow my diction, which is pretty good, usually." Part of the problem could be traced back to Crosby's ingenious miking of piano strings as Joni sang her vocals into a grand piano, which created unforeseen difficulties later in the production process. "I wanted to try and get the overtones that happen from the resonating of the piano and, of course, it recorded at way too low a level," Crosby told Wally Breese of the JoniMitchell.com Web site in 1997. "If you use those mikes at all you get a hiss, so we had to go in and take those things out."

Joni Mitchell, often called *Song to a Seagull* because of lettering of those words formed by a flock of seagulls on the cover artwork, was at first glance a commercial flop, reaching only #189 during a brief stay in the charts. However, like several other folk-rock albums that charted low or not at all—*Forever Changes*, *Oar*, or *Fred Neil*, for example—it had a large influence totally out of proportion with its initial sales. "When that first album came out," asserts Mary McCaslin, "a light bulb went on in a lot of women's heads saying, 'Look at this. You're the woman singer-songwriter. If she can do it, I can do it.' It's so obvious that she was pretty much in control; David Crosby produced it, but to me, it was not intrusive in the album at all.

"She changed a lot of people's lives. There have been a lot of people since then who have been writing their own songs and out there doing it. I think it's directly because of Joni Mitchell.

There weren't that many women writing songs; the only other woman folk singer I can think of that wrote songs at all was Buffy Sainte-Marie. It's amazing to me how many people think her first album is *Blue* [Mitchell's fourth album, released in 1971]. It infuriates me." There were even a few obscure Joni Mitchell–like records almost straightaway, such as Mary Catherine Lunsford's self-titled 1969 Polydor LP and, to a lesser degree, some of Nancy Michaels's *First Impressions* the same year (on Mitchell's label, Reprise). Those albums were mediocre, and Linda Perhacs proved it possible to make a much more imaginative variation of aspects of Mitchell's sound on her haunting and mystical 1970 album *Parallelograms* (discussed in chapter two). "She was and still is an exceptional composer and performer who opened the doors for many others," praises Perhacs. "I loved her first albums."

While he wasn't yet a solo act, the most commercial folk-rock singer-songwriter of the era remained Paul Simon. Simon & Garfunkel remained big stars in 1967, touring (a fine January concert at the New York Philharmonic was finally issued in 2002 as *Live from New York City, 1967*), appearing at the Monterey Pop Festival (for which Simon served on the board of directors), and issuing a couple of decent-sized hit singles, "At the Zoo" and "Fakin' It." Unlike Bob Dylan, they were still very much in the public eye. Like Bob Dylan in 1967, though, they were taking an eternity to come up with their next album. A year and a half doesn't seem like much of a gap by twenty-first century standards, but when 1967 ran out, no Simon & Garfunkel LP had appeared since *Parsley, Sage, Rosemary & Thyme* had been issued in the fall of 1966. In part this was due to Simon's less-than-lightning pace of songwriting; the albums Simon & Garfunkel had put out in 1966 were a false barometer of Simon's speed, as nine of their songs were actually re-recordings of compositions from his UK-only 1965 solo acoustic album, *The Paul Simon Songbook*. In part this was also due to the painstaking perfectionism of the duo in the studio; eventually, it was reported, they would take 100 hours to record a single track (1969's smash single "The Boxer").

John Simon (no relation to Paul) had been working at Columbia for several years before his production of the Cyrkle's bouncy 1966 hit "Red Rubber Ball" (co-written by Paul Simon and Bruce Woodley of the Seekers) put him in line for sessions with the more prestigious Simon & Garfunkel. He co-produced some of the 1967 sides that would end up on the duo's subsequent *Bookends* album, and points out that its relatively drawn-out gestation was due in part to the extraordinary freedom, and funding, that the pair was granted in the studio. When Simon & Garfunkel first signed with Columbia as an acoustic folk team back in 1964, he explains, the label "had acts who were signed as folk acts, and had an unlimited budget. Because it was assumed that they would just be two guys and a guitar, one person and a guitar. They're all cheap recording to do. So the recording company paid for the budget, and it was not an advance against the artist's royalty.

"I started doing Simon & Garfunkel on the beginning of *Bookends*. The first thing we did was 'Fakin' It.' I was amazed because they said they wanted strings that sounded like violins, only lower and softer, so I got muted violas. Then they had these brass punctuations they wanted, and some percussion they wanted. So I booked the session like any normal session, with about an hour for the strings, and I asked Paul and Artie to sit with me and work on some parts they wanted to play.

So I authored the strings, horns, and percussion, which would have been three hours for one song, which was plenty of time in those days; we used to do four songs in three hours with regular acts.

"In the studio, there were about twelve violists after they all called their answering services to make sure they were in the right place. Because there had never been twelve viola players, and no violins and cellos, in the same room before. After they did that, they ran down the chart, and started tuning up, just doing some runs. I was in the studio rehearsing them, Paul and Artie were in the control room, and a voice snaps over the speaker from the control room—'What was that?' I said, 'What was what?' They said, 'What was that sort of tuning up kind of sound?' I said, 'Well, that was people tuning up and getting into tune.' They said, 'We like that. Forget the chart, we like that.' We spent three hours trying to get that again, and meanwhile, back in the lobby, the brass players were backing up, the percussion players were backing up. Everyone was just delighted because they were getting overtime.

"We went into six hours looking for the tune-up sound, and then bringing new people in," Simon finishes. "But it turned out to be incredibly expensive. I wondered why it was, and I asked Paul afterwards. And he said, 'Oh, we have a contract that we don't pay for our recording sessions. Columbia pays for them. So we don't care.' That was something that changed pretty darned quick after folk-rock, I think. They had [that budget] because, I think, most artists who were just plain old folk artists had that kind of budget, where the company paid for the recording. [Because the label was expecting it to be] nothing."

Yet while Simon & Garfunkel were radically expanding the boundaries of what was permissible in the studio, their commercial fortunes escalated in a far more conventional cross-marketing fashion. In 1968, they catapulted to even greater sales tallies than they or anyone thought possible when some of their songs were used in Mike Nichols's classic film *The Graduate*. *Bookends*, their #1 album of that year, contained the chart-topping song named after the film's bewitching "Mrs. Robinson." While its chugging acoustic guitars and impossibly infectious chorus gave it legs on AM radio, its lyrics were the sound of an America losing innocence and faith. It needed all those legs to get as much airplay as it did, as its references to God and particularly one to Jesus were still uneasy prospects for many radio programmers.

Paul Simon had initially made his name as a protest songwriter with "The Sound of Silence," even if it was a protest against depersonalization rather than a specific social issue. Now, like many of his peers, he was more the storyteller and painter of moods than an advocate of or generational spokesperson for specific actions and attitudes. "Nobody is talking for this generation," he emphasized to *Time* in 1968. "Nobody says, 'If you want to know what I think talk to Simon & Garfunkel.' Everybody has got his own ideas." Later that year he elaborated in *The New York Times*, "I try to avoid cliches—not always successfully. But I don't try to say anything I think the kids want to hear. You can't do anything real that way. I try to take an emotion or feeling I've had and capture it in one incident. And don't worry about the message of the song. I worry about entertaining—not boring—an audience; that comes first. Whatever else I get: great. If people see it my way: great. But I don't write for anybody else's feelings, or to convince them of my point of view."

Simon & Garfunkel, with Art Garfunkel on the left.

(He did nonetheless make his feelings clear on at least one hot-button political figure, dedicating "America" at the Forest Hills Music Festival in 1968 "to the idiot who's running for Vice President," Spiro Agnew.)

As big as they were, Simon & Garfunkel's artistry was still occasionally constrained by the period's narrow mindset. Simon, one of the most painstakingly slow craftsmen in pop, had not been able to write anything for six months at one point before *Bookends*. Three- or four-year gaps between albums were nothing for men and women of comparable status a few decades on, but the push for product meant that *Bookends* wasn't as much of a tour de force as it could have been. The record was envisioned as a concept album of sorts telling the story of birth to death; Garfunkel had mentioned this as early as February 1967, in *Newsweek*. But as it turned out only side one was true to that concept (and only vaguely so); side two was filled out with hit singles (albeit very fine ones) from 1966 and 1967. "It certainly didn't turn out to be any concept, except that one side," affirms Simon & Garfunkel's engineer/producer Roy Halee. "'Cause with Columbia Records, once you had a hit, they would be *screaming* for the next one. So I'm sure there was a lot of pressure and arm-twisting at that point; you know, 'Why is it taking so long? Come on, you guys.'"

With neo-concept albums, soundtracking one of the most popular and timely films of the late '60s, and endless sessions with orchestras, Simon & Garfunkel had certainly come a long way from the duo who had quickly cut an album of acoustic folk songs in 1964 that were strongly grounded in the folk tradition. If those links to the folk tradition seemed fainter throughout singer-songwriter folk-rock as a whole by the end of the 1960s, they were nonetheless still present. Singer-songwriters were still addressing headline-making crises, particularly the war in Vietnam and turbulent race and political riots within the United States. Even some artists accused of narcissistic obsession-confession did so, as Joni Mitchell did on "The Fiddle and the Drum."

But they were also recording impressions of their drug experiences and a shifting American psyche, and telling stories of characters whose lessons were not so much timely as universal, in the vernacular of the day (and of their generation) rather than the stilted folk phrasing of the past. At times they went back to the Bible for their grist, as Leonard Cohen did in his riveting "The Story of Isaac." "I would speculate that Dylan has not written anything about Vietnam because he shares the feeling of many people that the war is only one visible aspect of a basic chaos in American society and in the world," Tom Phillips wrote in *The New York Times* in 1967. "He is still a social critic, but Dylan's dissent today runs much deeper than politics."

Even *Time*, fairly clueless in its coverage of folk-rock's depth as late as mid-1966, picked up on this overall expansion of folk-rock themes in a February 1968 piece, finding that "today's troubadours are turning away from protest. Their gaze is shifting from the world around them to the realms within . . . . The result is that race, war and politics are becoming peripheral themes. What counts more is the intensely personal vision that deals with a romantic quest for love and 'self-realization.'" Works by Tim Hardin (who forthrightly declared "I'm too involved with my personal life to write about the world"), Richie Havens, Leonard Cohen, Tim Buckley, and Janis Ian were all cited as harbingers of the new folk-rock song. Lyrics from Buckley's "The Magician" (actually written by his collaborator Larry Beckett), Havens's "No Opportunity Necessary, No Experience Needed," and Cohen's "Suzanne" were all quoted with a seriousness and respect that would have been unimaginable in the pop music section of a mainstream magazine just a couple years before. The following year, *Time* would note similar qualities in Joni Mitchell, observing, "Her evanescent tunes and lyrics primarily evoke moods, emotions and changes of scenery, instead of proclaiming social messages of political protest. They are songs about love or about a country girl's cool-eyed reaction to urban life." (In early 1968 Mitchell had joked to the *Saskatoon StarPhoenix*, "I've written only one protest song. That was 'Urge for Going,' which was a protest song against winter. And it certainly isn't going to stop winter.")

Even the hand-wringing love songs, so loathed by gritty realist-oriented critics, were reflecting the changing, more complex dynamics of romance, sexual identity, and relationships between the sexes. "There are just so many big controversial social topics you can cover before you run out of topics," believes Janis Ian. "Part of it was also that all of us were listening to pop music, particularly the Beatles, and love songs suddenly didn't seem so trite. And part of it was dope— everyone was doing dope to try and get in touch with their inner selves, and to reach out more fully toward others."

It was a breakthrough in its own right for women singer-songwriters like Mitchell to be singing about romance with a fiercely independent feminine perspective, at a time when women's liberation was only just starting to become an issue. *Newsweek*'s Hubert Saal even highlighted "a new school of talented female troubadours" as a developing trend in July 1969, singling out five newcomers. Three of them (Mitchell, Melanie, and Laura Nyro) were well on their way to varying degrees of stardom; two, Elyse Weinberg (whose eccentric, shakily sung late-'60s album had some backup guitar by Neil Young) and Lottie Golden, are now almost totally forgotten. "What is common to them," theorized Saal, "are the personalized songs they write, like voyages of self-discovery, brimming with keen observation and startling in the impact of their poetry."

Yet as Melanie admits, "I didn't think of the social impact of being a woman, and being a singer and a songwriter. We were so different. It didn't matter to me that we were the same sex. I was probably more similar to Bob Dylan than I was to Janis Ian or Joni Mitchell—voice, style, everything. I used to be called the female Bob Dylan."

Sadly, the rise of women singer-songwriters did not have as much as an impact on the sexism within the music business itself as one might have imagined, according to Ian, who notes, "Folk people were no better or worse than any other music group in terms of treatment of women. Many of the female singers and songwriters of that era got their first cuts or starts because they were sleeping with the guitarist/bandleader/singer, etc. The youngest of the men, and the best of them (I'm thinking specifically of Jimi Hendrix and Tom Paxton), always saw someone like me as a fellow player and songwriter. The male artists who had strong enough egos not to be threatened always did (I'm thinking of Dave Van Ronk), but they were the exception rather than the rule." For her late-'60s albums, Mitchell was subjected to ad campaigns emblazoned with slogans that no one would have forced upon a male singer-songwriter: "Joni Mitchell is 90% virgin," "Joni Mitchell takes forever" (referring to the gap, which actually wasn't very long, between her album releases), and "Joni Mitchell finally comes across." (Warner Brothers at least didn't wholly adhere to double standards in marketing singer-songwriters as sex symbols, advertising an Eric Andersen release in 1970 with the slogan, "Anyone who looks as good as this: shouldn't sound as good as this. But Eric Andersen does.")

"It was very unfair that there was a rule about how many women they could actually play on radio," feels Melanie. "I don't know if it was written or not, but it was a rule. You'd have to have a certain amount of men and then they would play a woman. It's a horrible, horrible thing, because then every woman is your competitor, because there's no way you can all be on the radio, right? If they had played my record on the radio that week or month or whatever, they wouldn't have played Joni Mitchell. So there weren't that many women doing it. They certainly weren't being given the opportunity. That was just the way the game was played at the time. It didn't make me angry or anything. I just thought, that's the fact."

Still, even if some of the ideals wore better in song than in practice, the values that had given birth to the folk revival of the early '60s were still very much in play, albeit in a much different guise. Happy Traum, by then the editor of *Sing Out!*, was canny enough to recognize this in a major May 1969 piece titled "The Swan Song of Folk Music" in *Rolling Stone*, the young rock magazine that was the first major national forum for lengthy, critically astute reviews of singer-songwriter albums. "There are also many young singers and songwriters," Traum wrote, "who, although called 'folk singers,' actually defy any such classification. They are, though, worthy heirs to the title and should be treated in any discussion of what's happened to folk music; people like Jerry Jeff Walker, Arlo Guthrie, Joni Mitchell, Tim Buckley and Richie Havens, who are successful both in terms of a larger market and in terms of maintaining their independence of identity. They have successfully fused the folk and the pop worlds with their own personalities, and have created a new individual kind of folk music. Different, perhaps, than we used to imagine it, but real and very much alive, nonetheless."

4

in thyme

british folk-rock finds its voice

n July 30, 1967, the United States was in the throes of the Summer of Love, a full two years after the Byrds had topped the charts with "Mr. Tambourine Man" and Bob Dylan had gone electric at the Newport Folk Festival. In the United Kingdom, however, *Melody Maker*'s "Focus on Folk" column was still inquiring earnestly of a young Al Stewart whether "folk-rock, the hybrid musical form that arose from the demise of the American folk scene and manifested itself in the shape of the Lovin' Spoonful, the Byrds, and the electric Dylan, may happen here?"

Great Britain had led the way for so much innovation in mid-'60s rock music. It was the Beatles, after all, who were more responsible than anyone for inciting legions of young American folkies to go the electric route in the first place. Yet the mother country was still lagging behind in the cultivation of its own thoroughbred, distinctive folk-rock scene and sound. Transatlantic ping-pong, in the media even more than among musicians, was slower in the days predating e-mail, faxes, and satellite communications. *Melody Maker* itself had already posed essentially the same question as it asked Al Stewart 15 months earlier, when a headline mused, "Will folk rock be the next big influence on the pop world?" Yet with the notable exception of Donovan, no British performer had convincingly blended some of the best aspects of folk and rock music to make a major contribution to the international pop world.

Even as Donovan continued to score smash hits in 1967, a larger community of British folk-rock musicians was slowly coagulating. Like the singer-songwriters starting to emerge in the States, and the American country-rockers that would surface only slightly later, they largely drew on a rootsier base than the psychedelic folk-rockers who had risen to temporary prominence in the hippie heyday. Sometimes they drew upon explicitly American singer-songwriters and folk-rock groups in the process of finding their own voice. But the differences between the North American and British Isles folk traditions eventually gave birth to an entirely different spire of the folk-rock tower. It would be a long and gradual process, usually embracing electric amplification far more tentatively than their American cousins, although it would take the intercession of several American producers, managers, and songwriters to make it happen.

ven in 2003, a Yankee may find that talking with UK fans, musicians, and journalists about the unwieldy mass of music crowded under the umbrella of "folk-rock" will give new meaning to the cliché of America and Britain being separated by a common language. Some British observers go as far as to view folk-rock as an essentially British genre, with artists commonly hailed as central folk-rockers Stateside, such as Neil Young, dismissed as mere rock singers. Some interpret the term in its narrowest sense, as traditional folk songs played with some rock instruments. Muddying the waters further, others in the UK are in total agreement that the lion's share of significant folk-rock came from across the pond, enthusiastically hailing, say, Neil Young and Buffalo Springfield as prime exponents of the form. To unearth the reasons for these differing lines of thought, and for British folk-rock's relatively late start as an entity unto its own, it's necessary to retrace steps and examine some of the differences between the British and American folk scenes in the days just before folk-rock came together in the mid-'60s.

As purist-minded as some factions of the American folk community were, in Britain there were often yet purer standards of purity, and even more rigid borders erected between different styles. The man most often singled out for fomenting such attitudes is singer and songwriter Ewan MacColl. Like many of the figures responsible for reviving interest in folk music in the 1950s, MacColl was a Marxist and proponent of hard-Left politics. In the mid-'40s he had co-founded the Theatre Workshop, which presented revolutionary theater. In the '50s he threw himself into resuscitating folk music of the British Isles, as a presenter of BBC radio shows and an organizer of folk clubs in London. (American readers take note: In Britain a "folk club" does not so much designate an actual venue devoted to folk music, as it does an organization that will put on regular or occasional folk nights, at one or more establishments.) Strict guidelines were often laid down governing the performances and the repertoire. British singers were expected to sing only British songs; American troubadours American tunes; and so forth. Electric instruments were, as they say in Britain, "right out."

"Folk music is, and has always been, more a part of the British lifestyle than it has been in America," says Carolyn Hester, who did quite a bit of performing in the British Isles in the early '60s. "In the UK, the narrative ballad is as popular as the jig and reel. They appreciate their folk served straight. When I played at Ewan MacColl and Peggy Seeger's Singer's Club in London in the early '60s, the only stipulation put forward was that they preferred that we Americans present only American folk songs. They could do without us singing 'our versions' of 'their songs.' Fair enough." MacColl's format, certainly planned with the intention of popularizing folk music, nonetheless made it hard for some with the best of intentions to get involved. For instance, when Britishers Peter Asher (later of Peter & Gordon) and Andy Irvine showed up at MacColl's events, says Asher, "We could never sing anything at the hootenanny because our favorite songs to sing were American folk songs."

MacColl was a man of contradictions that cast aspersions on his absolutist postures. His dogmatic rules were enforced to preserve authenticity, yet he himself had changed his name from Jimmy Miller to Ewan MacColl. He said he was from Scotland, yet it's now thought he was born and raised in Salford, England, near Manchester. He promoted an almost nationalistic adherence to British songs, yet recorded more often for American companies than British ones. As a songwriter, he was famous not only for the biting realism of "Dirty Old Town" (written in 1950 and eventually covered by the Pogues), but also the straightforward love song "The First Time Ever I Saw Your Face," which in the 1970s became an American #1 single for Roberta Flack. This staunch advocate of purist British folk performers was also married to an American folk singer-songwriter, Peggy Seeger (half-sister of Pete Seeger), and had sung with jazz bands. Observes Robin Williamson of the Incredible String Band, "He started out as an actor, and he created a role for himself, and a world for himself. Like a lot of people do." As did (should this be considered a peculiarly British tic) plenty of figureheads on the American folk scene, like Bob Dylan and Ramblin' Jack Elliott.

Williamson adds that MacColl "didn't approve of using instruments," which might strike many Americans as extraordinary, given the usual image of folk as a music played on a solitary guitar or banjo at the very least. "The British folk tradition is not an instrumental tradition," muses Joe Boyd, the American who would become the preeminent British folk-rock producer on records by Fairport Convention, Nick Drake, the Incredible String Band, Fotheringay, and others. "It's primarily an unaccompanied tradition. The folk scene that I found in Britain when I arrived in 1964, if you went into a pub on a folk night, I would say that 90 percent of the music that you heard was unaccompanied. It was either solo unaccompanied, or harmony unaccompanied. The stars of that scene were Louis Killen, Anne Briggs, the Watersons, that kind of thing. The Ian Campbell Folk Group, with [future Fairport Convention member Dave] Swarbrick on violin, was considered a sellout." There were also far fewer jug band revivalists in the Jim Kweskin Jug Band mold than there were in America, with exceptions like Vernon Haddock's Jubilee Lovelies (whose rare 1965 Columbia LP was produced by early Donovan managers Peter Eden and Geoff Stephens) and the Purple Gang (half of whose late-'60s album was produced by Boyd himself).

"This tradition never really existed in America, of unaccompanied singing," Boyd continues. "It just wasn't something that people really did much. If you had a field holler on an old Lomax recording, that was only because they were in prison and couldn't get out their guitars." In Britain, he goes on, "The idea of singing with accompaniment was already, in and of itself, untraditional. People who were interested in tradition accepted the likes of Dylan and Phil Ochs because there was a political edge that they responded to, and because it was America, therefore it was natural. The authentic American performance was Woody Guthrie: a guy with a guitar, or a guy with a banjo. But in Britain, [unaccompanied singers] Jeannie Robertson, the Young Tradition, the Copper Family, Shirley Collins: that was authenticity, this was all the real stuff. So therefore, the presence of instruments just in and of themselves takes it away from authenticity. In America, everybody was used to seeing Earl Scruggs and Lester Flatt, and instrumental virtuosity. It was recognized and very authentic. From there, there wasn't *such* a big leap to electric guitar."

But it was a yet larger gulf for British folk musicians and listeners to cross, particularly when electricity was introduced into the equation. Purist outrage in Britain against electric instruments dated from long before Bob Dylan's 1965 rock albums. When Muddy Waters made his first British tour in 1958, audiences, apparently totally ignorant of his large body of classic electric full-band

Chicago blues recordings for Chess Records, were legitimately astonished when he showed up with an electric guitar. As Waters recalled in James Rooney's *Bossmen*, "They thought I was a Big Bill Broonzy—which I wasn't. I had my amplifier and [pianist Otis] Spann and I was going to do a Chicago thing; we opened up in Leeds, England. I was definitely too loud for them then. The next morning we were in the headlines of the paper—'Screaming Guitar and Howling Piano.' That was when they were into the folk thing before the Rolling Stones."

The image of the American bluesman as one who accompanied himself with just a single acoustic guitar—as Big Bill Broonzy had done in his European shows although even he had recorded in bands as early as the 1930s—was apparently so indelible that all American bluesmen were expected to conform to that format. As an ironic footnote, when Waters returned to Britain in 1962, as he told Rooney, "I went back—took my acoustic with me—and everybody's hollering, 'Where's your amplifier?' I said, 'When I was here before they didn't like my stuff.' But those English groups had picked up on my stuff and went wild with it." Meaning English groups such as the Animals and Rolling Stones, who would be so important in inciting many American folk musicians to turn to rock music.

But the young guys in the Animals and Rolling Stones were not representative of British folk's hardcore constituency. It not only frowned on electric amplification and (often) instruments, but also did not even always welcome the likes of Dylan and Ochs, or the whole idea that folk could become something that was a commercial commodity. MacColl, again, had a large part to do with the more pedantic wing of resistance. Interviewed by *Melody Maker*'s folk columnist Karl Dallas in September 1965, he unleashed a remarkably vicious tirade against the folk boom in general and Dylan in particular.

"We're going to get lots and lots of copies of Dylan—people who have one foot in folk and one foot in pop," he warned. "Dylan is to me the perfect symbol of the anti-artist in our society. He is against everything—the last resort of someone who doesn't really want to change the world. He doesn't say anything President Johnson could disagree with. He deals in generalizations—that's always safe. Who talks about peace more than Lyndon Johnson?" As for the increased popularity of folk itself, he hoped, "The best thing would be for the folk boom to end as quickly as possible, and that the clubs should continue their steady development." MacColl wasn't done with Dylan, chiding in *Sing Out!*, "Only a completely non-critical audience, nourished on the watery pap of pop music, could have fallen for such tenth-rate drivel. 'But the poetry?' What poetry? The cultivated illiteracy of his topical songs of the embarrassing fourth-grade schoolboy attempts at free verse? The latter reminds me of elderly female schoolteachers clad in Greek tunics rolling hoops across lawns at weekend theater schools ... [Dylan] exemplifies contemporary American songwriting, a movement where journalism is more important than art, where flabby sentimentality and shrill self-pity take the place of passion."

The extremity of his purple fury leads one to suspect that MacColl, the theatrical ex-actor, might have been overexaggerating to make his point. But if this was any reflection at all of the view of the man considered to be at the forefront of the British folk revival, it goes a long way toward explaining why small minorities were so vocal in their jeers at Dylan during his 1966 British tour.

Here was a former folk star who was committing the double sins of being commercially popular and playing electric rock, loud. Sometimes it was deemed treasonous enough just to become popular. As Marianne Faithfull, then not a songwriter, told *NME* in April 1965, when she returned to the folk clubs where she used to play, "They really hated me. They said I had done a great disservice to folk music. I had committed the unforgivable sin of becoming a success."

"In the UK there was a huge battle, huge ugly rows, between the purists, the not-so-purists, and the hardly-purists-at-all," laughs Nat Joseph, who had to be conscious of the factions as the head of Transatlantic Records, which was developing a substantial British traditional and contemporary folk catalog. "The cliques were a pain in the ass. And from a marketing point of view it was a nightmare. You had to be very careful what you said. Some people managed to cross the whole spectrum, but they would pretty much reckon that somewhere along the way, in each spectrum, there'd be attacks from the outside—'Why have you added instruments, why don't you go on singing traditional music the way it should be sung?' Then there were the ones who thought that the pop influence was medium terrible, [and] the ones that thought it wasn't terrible at all so long as they got part of the gravy train. The critics never were really able to make up their minds. In one sense, you could say it was a rich diversity, which was really good. And in another way, you could say it inhibited people from time to time. Not the great artists. I mean, people like Bert Jansch and Paul Simon took what was there and did good things with it."

At the same time, if MacColl and like-minded British folkies felt that their vigilance would ensure the growth and preservation of a uniquely British folk culture, they were only partially correct. He and others like A. L. Lloyd had done much to increase interest in British folk; by 1965, there were hundreds of folk clubs throughout the British Isles. But the consequences of their narrow guidelines, and suspicious insularity against anything that smacked of widespread popular acceptance, were similar to those that were being felt in the United States. Droves of young people, sincere in their love of folk music but uninterested in being preached to about what they could and couldn't play, were being frozen out of the very folk revival in which they'd been enlisted. Their only alternative was to create a more flexible framework for pursuing the music, even if its eventual incorporation of electric rock would be far more drawn-out and tentative than it was in the States.

"A lot of places wouldn't book us, see, in London, after the first year I went down there, because Ewan MacColl didn't like what we were doing so much," explains Robin Williamson of the Incredible String Band. "That's why we ended up running our own club in Edinburgh. Me and Bert [Jansch] and Clive [Palmer, a member of the first Incredible String Band lineup] ran a club in the back room of a bar, which ran every Thursday night. That was really how we were making money about 1961, '62, '63. We started to book people ourselves."

The importance of American influence on the burgeoning British scene in the early '60s—something the likes of Ewan MacColl would have viewed with an ambivalent attitude at best, a virulent, disparaging one at worst—cannot be overlooked. "In England in the early '60s there were very few record labels or journals specializing in folk music of a contemporary nature, and information about the artists was mostly picked up from the American publication *Sing Out!* or by word of mouth," says Mac MacLeod, a folk guitarist who would play with Donovan and move into electric rock by the end of the 1960s. "I'm not sure how I first got to hear of Jack Elliott, but I managed to get hold of a 10-inch vinyl release on Topic records (a very much 'do it yourself' English label) called *Jack Takes The Floor*. After hearing it I was very much hook, line and sinkered as I could relate to the style of playing, the rambling concept, and the fact that he was taking Woody Guthrie–type songs and early blues and giving them a contemporary feel.

"I was not alone in this adulation and amongst acoustic players of the period, Jack's version of 'San Francisco Bay Blues' soon became an anthem. Although Derroll Adams [another American, who played and traveled with Elliott] was also an influence, it was Jack who was the main man, primarily because the acoustic guitar was very much the instrument of the time. Other white American influences performing in these early days would include Pete Seeger, Guy Carawan, and Tom Paxton, the only one to spend much time here. Prior to Jack Elliott, and apart from Woody Guthrie, the main source of American material and inspiration came from the early black country blues artists such as Big Bill Broonzy, Leadbelly, Blind Boy Fuller, and Snooks Eaglin amongst others."

The British folk boom was indeed on in a big way in 1965, though again "folk boom" meant something different in the UK than it did in the US. Folk records, even folk-pop ones, rarely troubled the charts or got much press in the national music periodicals. Specialty folk labels like Transatlantic, founded by Nat Joseph after he'd established himself in the market by importing Folkways releases into England, and Topic made even less of a commercial impact than comparable US indies like Elektra. It was more of a grassroots deal, in which a country with just one-fifth as many people as the United States could support a staggering quantity of well-attended folk clubs, particularly considering the music got relatively little exposure in the media.

Actually the folk boom in the United States was over, having peaked in 1963, but when Paxton arrived for his first British tour in 1965, he found its British counterpart thriving: "There were literally hundreds of folk clubs around the British Isles. When we went over there, my first album for Elektra wasn't even released. It was being imported, it was getting around, and people were learning the songs. So I had a built-in audience already. And the important thing was that every night was like Saturday night at home. Whatever night it happened to be, the club, the room, would be packed. It wasn't like at the Gaslight [in Greenwich Village] where, like a Monday night in January, there would be six or seven people there. A Monday night in Birmingham, the place would be jammed, because that was the night the folk club was. So I went from jammed room to jammed room."

The most fabled clubs, as one would guess, were in London, particularly Les Cousins (often referred to colloquially simply as "the Cousins") and the Troubadour. "The Pentangle started in a basement club in Soho called Les Cousins," says top British folk guitarist John Renbourn, who would found the band with fellow acoustic guitar virtuoso Bert Jansch. "Bert and I used to play there regularly, and it became a bit of a scene. Lots of different musicians showed up, including Americans. Jackson Frank, Spider John Koerner, Danny Kalb, Dorris Henderson, Paul Simon, and so on. In fact around '66 it seemed as if the American players were listening more to what we were doing. The British guitar stuff had moved on from the copying stage (country blues and finger picking), and some of the young American visitors were picking up on that."

There were a number of American folk singers who took up permanent or temporary residency in England in the 1960s, having been preceded in that regard by Jack Elliott and Derroll Adams in the 1950s. Although Elliott went back to the States, Adams stayed, proving to be one of the most open-minded of the scene's veteran singers. He befriended Donovan, and told *Sing Out!*, "People who argue about the purity of folk music sicken me . . . I believe it's inevitable that pop and folk music will come together." Paul Simon, of course, had lived in England for a while in the mid-'60s and recorded his rare first solo album there in 1965, though it took a fluke placement of a dozen BBC studio recordings of his songs on a BBC religious radio program to gain him that opportunity with CBS London.

There were others, though, who still remain unknown in their homeland, and are not much better remembered abroad. Julie Felix, more noted as a television host than as a recording artist, nonetheless recorded many albums in a sub–Joan Baez vein. Jackson C. Frank made a rare, legendary cult album in 1965, produced by Paul Simon, and featuring several songs that would be covered live or on record by his one-time girlfriend, Sandy Denny. Shawn Phillips did a couple acoustic folk albums and worked with Donovan. Dorris Henderson, an African-American singer-autoharpist from Los Angeles with a love for Appalachian mountain ballads, defied several stereotypes at once; she recorded a decent album with Renbourn, and covered Simon's "Leaves That Are Green" on a single. Ben Carruthers, a friend of Dylan's, had set one of Dylan's poems to music on the early folk-rock single "Jack o' Diamonds" in 1965, produced by another American, Shel Talmy. (A few years later, James Taylor would start his solo career in London too, though he soon returned to the States.)

The American songwriters brought a fresh perspective to the British folk clubs, as well as an example to follow for those who were thinking of writing their own material and perhaps even entering the electrified folk-rock market. There were even a few, if not many, UK folkies with little-known rock 'n' roll pasts. Danny Thompson, later of the Pentangle, had played electric bass on Roy Orbison's first British tour; the Incredible String Band's Mike Heron had played R&B with Scottish band the Abstract (who had an electric banjo); Renbourn had played electric guitar in a school band; and Al Stewart had played in various rock groups. The table seemed ready to turn for many of the more open-minded folkies from acoustic to electric music, even if a bit belatedly in comparison to the firestorm that had already swept the States.

For various reasons (discussed in the section on Donovan in this book's predecessor, *Turn! Turn! Turn!*), this electric shift didn't take place, with Donovan having the British folk-rock field pretty much to himself for the next year or two. The split between folk musicians and pop-rockers, and between the folk scene and the "commercial" one, was deemed very cut-and-dried, with even Donovan's early, pre-electric work dismissed as pop by many folk critics and devotees. Whether because they felt intimidated about picking up electric instruments as a result, or because they were just not inclined to play loudly or absorb rock influences, many of Donovan's peers remained in the acoustic folk sphere, even if they were penning a good number of original songs. Even Donovan, says Fairport Convention guitarist Simon Nicol, wasn't seen as someone who'd mixed folk and rock as the Americans had: "It wasn't straightahead kind of rock. His musical director [John Cameron] was a guy who was much more used to sort of setting film music, and it was like tinkly harpsichord-y oboes, string sections. It wasn't the same sort of hard-nosed thing that Dylan did in Newport with a rock band, and what the Byrds and Buffalo Springfield did with their much more direct electric approach."

John Renbourn, one of the established acoustic folk musicians who did not electrify in the mid-'60s (and never did play much electric guitar, even after forming his folk-rock group of sorts, the Pentangle), feels that folk-rock "appeared old hat when it did arrive. The folk scene in England had been preceded by skiffle and also R&B, so when electrified folk appeared it wasn't anything amazing. In fact it was a step back. Even in skiffle the bands were playing with a straight beat, and later on, Lonnie Donegan had Les Bennetts on electric guitar. When the R&B stuff came in, all the bands were electric, and by the time the Animals came out with 'House of the Rising Sun,' that stuff was already considered as being a bit of a joke. I don't think many musicians at that time took [Animals singer] Eric Burdon too seriously."

Some mid-'60s albums seen as important to the genesis of British folk-rock were in fact less of a folk-rock synthesis than a general opening of British acoustic folk to influences from jazz, pop, world music, R&B, and (just a bit of) rock. Foremost among these were the albums by Davy Graham, who gave folk a rhythmic swing on his 1964 collaboration with Shirley Collins, *Folk Roots, New Routes*. Collins's smoky vocals were similarly far more emotional and stirringly phrased than those of the typical British folk vocalist of the time. Her discography stretched back to the mid-'50s; she had even accompanied folklorist Alan Lomax on trips to assemble field recordings in the American South in the late '50s. Her combination of upper-register power and haunting grace would echo in several of the high-voiced female vocalists who would rise to the fore of British folk-rock in the late '60s and early '70s, such as Sandy Denny, Jacqui McShee of the Pentangle, Maddy Prior of Steeleye Span, and half-forgotten figures like Polly Bolton of Dando Shaft.

Almost totally unknown in the United States and not often credited as a foremother to those singers, Collins maintains that "I never felt that my vocal style was an influence on other women singers as my style was so personal. What they might have got from me was repertoire, or at least the knowledge that there was a huge repertoire of English material to find if you were prepared to look for it. I think my dedication to finding good and interesting material was one of my strengths. I sometimes felt other singers were skimming the surface." Traditional folk singers sometimes weren't even particularly aware of the impact they were having on the folk-rock repertoire. When asked about the Pentangle's cover of her composition "The Time Has Come," Anne Briggs once told writer Colin Harper, "I'm not sure that I've ever listened to it. I wasn't particularly interested in what they were doing. That record must have been out for a couple of years, or a year at least, before I was even aware that there was a song of mine on it."

Nonetheless, it would be the dedication to both rediscovering interesting English folk songs and reinventing them that would ultimately become one of British folk-rock's distinguishing trademarks. That was still a few years down the road in 1964, yet "*Folk Roots, New Routes* was an important album because it showed what could be done with an arrangement of a song," believes Collins. "Thanks to Davy Graham and his remarkable and innovative guitar playing, the possibilities opened up. He was a great influence on John Renbourn and Bert Jansch in this country. The song "Nottamun Town' was picked up by Fairport Convention, and I believe that [Fairport guitarist] Simon Nicol has acknowledged that they learned it from *Folk Roots, New Routes*. I, of course, learned it from Kentucky's Jean Ritchie."

"Davy Graham was playing some great stuff, as was Bert [Jansch], and Paul Simon learned directly from both of them," enthuses Renbourn. "About the only American player I can think of who was doing comparable stuff was Sandy Bull, and we liked his early Vanguard records a lot. *Folk Roots, New Routes* pretty much single-handedly opened the way for song accompaniment and also purely instrumental ideas."

Graham and Collins did not pair up again on record. But Graham pushed the boundaries of British folk further on his January 1965 album *Folk, Blues and Beyond*, which boasted a lean, snazzy, full jazz-blues rhythm section, including drums, and melded blues, folk, jazz, and Middle Eastern music together in an invigorating fashion. Graham would continue to mine this world-folk-fusion on other obscure, more erratic 1960s albums, making sure to throw in imaginative covers of Beatles songs. But they weren't quite rock records, lacking the brash electrified guitars and rock-slanted material that would push them over that border, even as they were akin in some respects to the risk-taking of many of the era's folk-rock and psychedelic musicians. (It did not help, either, that Graham's vocals were colorless and adequate at best.)

Also cited as influential in prying open the folk repertoire to more contemporary material was the Ian Campbell Folk Group. "The Campbells really were playing some of the root music that would begin to move toward folk-rock, and were very influential," offers Nat Joseph, who would make a Campbell album the first folk release for his new label, Transatlantic. "Particularly in using the instrumental combination that they did, and also using contemporary, or more or less contemporary, material on occasion. I tried to figure out what fusion folk-rock had, and the Campbells had all of the three elements that I came up with: good tunes, relevant lyrics, and virtuoso instrumentals. That's a sort of qualifying mark of what folk-rock had to offer. The Campbells had it all, except they didn't have much of the rock, and it was sort of rather artificially put on at the end in the recording studio, such as when they did a very successful version of 'The Times They Are A-Changin'' [which made #42 in the pop charts in 1965]."

Although Campbell would eventually make an album with rock-ish instrumentation in the late '60s (with future Fairport Convention bassist Dave Pegg), there really virtually was no "rock" in their approach prior to that. The move from flexible folk to something that truly began to push British folk closer to a more identifiably British brand of folk-rock would largely be made by slightly younger, less experienced musicians than Campbell, Graham, or Collins.

In the studio, a lot of the credit for midwifing the maiden outings of the first and best post-Donovan British folk-rock artists goes to another two American expatriates, producers Shel Talmy and Joe Boyd. Talmy would work with the Pentangle and Roy Harper, both of whom, incidentally, were managed by yet another American, Jo Lustig (who also handled Ralph McTell, Julie Felix, and other more obscure contemporary folk performers, such as the Dransfields and Gillian McPherson).

Boyd's Witchseason management/production company oversaw Fairport Convention, the Incredible String Band, and Nick Drake. The producers' gifts were for enabling their charges to thrive in settings that preserved the best of their folk roots, filling out their visions with sympathetic arrangements that enhanced rather than drowned their acoustic textures. If this folk-rock fusion was never as hard, electric, and reckless as it was in America, its delicate wistfulness held its own considerable charms.

Folk-rock was never as big a business in the UK as it was in the States, and at times it seemed that well over half or so of the major acts had ties to Witchseason, Lustig, and/or Transatlantic Records. Transatlantic had already established itself as a leading British folk label in the mid-'60s with albums by Bert Jansch and John Renbourn; it was the natural home for the group Jansch and Renbourn formed in 1967, the Pentangle. While Transatlantic never duplicated the surprising commercial success it had with folk-rock through the Pentangle, it kept trying, putting out folk-rock or at least folk-rock-tinged releases by Ralph McTell, the Johnstons, Mr. Fox, the Humblebums (the duo of future rock star Gerry Rafferty and now hugely successful comedian and screen actor Billy Connolly), the Purple Gang (the jug band whose Joe Boyd–produced single "Granny Takes a Trip" found some off-the-wall popularity in the British psychedelic underground), and Sallyangie (the brother-sister duo of Sally Oldfield and future progressive rock icon Mike Oldfield). All the while it kept issuing more traditional folk as well by the likes of Dave Swarbrick, Ireland's Sweeney's Men, and Irish pub song specialists the Dubliners, who according to Nat Joseph sold "in incredible quantities, at least equal to Pentangle, if not more, if my memory serves me correctly since it's a long time ago and I don't have access to the actual sales records."

The Witchseason/Transatlantic folk-rockers would have likely made less commercial inroads than they did without the aggressive efforts of Joe Boyd and Jo Lustig. While Boyd was at least as much of an artistic force as a business one, with great aesthetic sympathy that enabled him to collaborate closely with his clients on musical matters inside and outside of the studio, Lustig was far more the conventional hustler. The brusque New Yorker had first come over to the UK to do publicity for Nat King Cole, and worked in film public relations as well as music management. Not particularly a folk or folk-rock enthusiast, "Jo was a shrewd PR-turned manager, who was after every act that he thought would make it," says Joseph. "The first success he had was with Julie Felix, who had TV shows. He used the TV show, which obviously he had influence over through her, to introduce quite a lot of folk talent. I think she probably said, 'We ought to have group X on,' and he probably nodded and said, 'That sounds like a hell of a good idea.' And then rushed off and signed them, knowing that there was going to be exposure on a television show, which was very rare in the folk world in those days in England."

"Lustig was like something from a Damon Runyan story," says Renbourn, who first met the manager when he was playing guitar for Julie Felix. "He came from some tough area in New York and had previously worked for the Mafia. He never told any of us why he was in England, and we never asked. Jo stopped us playing at [the club] the Cousins and did the things managers do, including antagonizing the record company."

Lustig also played an underacknowledged role in getting folk-based musicians such as the Pentangle out of the folk ghetto and into the mainstream media, though sometimes his schemes seemed fanciful or even unrealistic. Perhaps drawing upon his background as a public relations man in the film world, he made some surprising plans, many unrealized, to put the Pentangle into the public eye via television and films. One that would never go beyond the planning stage was a television show with the Pentangle and the Brian Auger Trinity in which the Pentangle would exchange singer Jacqui McShee for the Trinity's Julie Driscoll. Another unlikely and unfulfilled project had the group scoring a film featuring Orson Welles and Sharon Tate. A yet more unlikely and intriguing matchup that didn't take was a leading role for the group in a movie (never filmed) starring Dustin Hoffman called *Whatever Happened to Harry Kellerman*, in which, *NME* reported, "Hoffman is cast as a record producer, and Pentangle would portray the group on which he pins all his hopes." The Pentangle did manage to contribute some songs to the soundtrack of a little-seen film directed by Roddy McDowell, *Tam Lin*, based on the Robert Burns poem of the same name. (Oddly, it included a musical adaptation of "Tam Lin" by the Pentangle that sounded nothing like the far more famous version that Fairport Convention put on its *Liege & Lief* album around the same time.)

But, as Joseph points out, Lustig was not wholly insensitive to the artistic end of the equation: "The recording of Pentangle, putting it in the hands of a commercial producer, Shel Talmy, was certainly a move towards the commercial folk-rock that was beginning to burgeon around us. It wasn't my idea to get Shel Talmy. I think that was Jo's, and that proved to be a very good idea." Talmy, who with typical candor labels Lustig as "#1 of my most unfavorite people in the whole world," immediately qualifies: "However, as I have discovered along the way, there have been many jerks, crooks, scumbags, who have a talent for both discovering talent and promoting it. And Lustig was one of the best PR people I've ever known. If he'd been a straight shooter, he would have had his place in history, I think. That wasn't the case, but it didn't stop him from being a hell of a PR guy. He certainly put me into Pentangle."

For those who care to debate such issues until they're blue in the face, it's a matter of some contention as to whether the Pentangle should be considered folk-rock at all. "My own thoughts are that about the worst thing you can do to a folk song is inflict a rock beat on it," says Renbourn. "Some of the old tunes from the British Isles will stand it, but not many. Most of the old songs that I have heard have their own internal rhythm. When we worked on those in the group, Terry Cox worked out his percussion patterns to match the patterns in the songs exactly. In that respect, he was the opposite of a folk-rock drummer. We were lucky to have him aboard." Pentangle bassist Danny Thompson, who also played as a session musician on numerous other early British folk-rock records by Drake, Donovan, the Incredible String Band, Davy Graham, and others (as well as live with Tim Buckley), doesn't see the Pentangle as a folk-rock act either. "Without question, it was a folk-jazz band. It was *never* a folk-rock group. We had sitars and banjos. I mean, what rock band, even today's, got a banjo? We played traditional songs with some improvised bits, quite sort of modern for the time. I don't think [by] any stretch of the imagination can [the Pentangle] be called a folk-rock band."

Nevertheless, it was, and not just by Americans, but by British authorities like *Melody Maker* folk columnist Karl Dallas. The Pentangle would often play gigs and festivals with out-and-out rock bands such as Canned Heat, the Grateful Dead, Alice Cooper, and the Jimi Hendrix Experience, as well as singer-songwriters like James Taylor, John Sebastian, and Tom Paxton. And when singer Jacqui McShee looked back on the Pentangle's genesis in *Melody Maker* in 1969, she remembered how, after gigging with guitarist John Renbourn for a while and meeting his friend Bert Jansch, "John told me they were starting a rock-and-roll band." In a more general conceptual sense, as McShee told author Colin Harper, "I think we paved the way for people who had been solo artists, or who had been playing in duos, to actually form bands."

In 1966, Jansch and Renbourn had already established themselves as the best, and probably most popular, acoustic folk guitarists in Britain. Jansch was the gloomier and more original of the pair, and his complex folk-blues guitar stylings have been cited as primal inspiration by both Neil Young and Jimmy Page (both of whom have been quoted to the effect that Jansch did for the acoustic guitar what Jimi Hendrix did for the electric). His 1965 albums *Bert Jansch* and *It Don't Bother Me* also unveiled a seductively moody songwriter, one who summoned considerable darkness on the drug death lament "Needle of Death," but also engaging boisterousness on "Do You Hear Me Now?" (covered that year by Donovan). He had also recorded some material, more instrumental and traditional in nature, with Renbourn. Now they were ready to expand into a group situation, though Jansch and Renbourn would continue to record solo albums.

The rhythm section was poached from a band that had just started to be organized by Duffy Power, called Duffy Power's Nucleus. Although it only played once, Power had used the musicians—Thompson on bass, Terry Cox on drums, and John McLaughlin on electric guitar—for some excellent folk-R&B-blues-jazz recordings that wouldn't see release until 1970. Thompson and Cox's long resumes also included a stint with British blues god Alexis Korner. Even after the Pentangle started, Thompson would continue to play in a jazz trio with McLaughlin for some time.

Cox and Thompson's recruitment into the Pentangle, where Thompson played acoustic standup bass rather than electric bass, would give the group a rhythmic swing that, if not exactly straight rock, was certainly alien to the folk world. Power points out that they could have thrived in the more electric context his band would have offered, had he been able to organize it: "With Danny and Terry Cox, I was disappointed that it wasn't me, because they were there for the asking. If I hadn't have been so ill, I think, psychologically, and had a bit more luck, I could have made them my band. I thought they should have been my rhythm section. After all, they'd taken it and they were doing it with folkies, and they were doing it well. It's taken me years to get used to using somebody else."

Despite their somewhat dissimilar musical backgrounds, to Renbourn, it seemed logical for him and Jansch to team up with their new rhythm section. "Davy [Graham] made a groundbreaking EP with Alexis Korner, with 'Anji' [famously covered by Simon & Garfunkel] on it," he explains. "That was totally influential. Bert and I played a bit like that down at the Cousins. Alexis himself liked to come down and play, and he usually brought Danny and Terry, who were in his band. 'Round that time I also played with Dorris Henderson, who had a regular TV spot [on the children's

The Pentangle. Left to right: John Renbourn, Terry Cox, Jacqui McShee, Danny Thompson, and Bert Jansch.

show *Gadzooks! It's All Happening*, of all places], and Alexis had the band for that show. So I used to hang out with Danny and Terry.

"It was a fairly natural progression to all hook up at the Cousins. The weekend gigs ran all night and could be a big slog for anyone booked to play. You really had to stretch it out, and wound up playing just about anything you could think and improvising a lot. It was great playing with Danny and Terry, and gradually we got some coherent ideas together." The fifth point of the Pentangle was its principal singer, the high, diamond-sharp-voiced Jacqui McShee. She had already performed with Renbourn at the Cousins sometimes as a duo, and had sung on three of the songs on John's second album, 1966's *Another Monday*.

"Pentangle came together around the time that musicians in America were getting together and forming groups that were drawing on a wider range of influences," recalls Renbourn. "Not just folk, and not just rock. We listened to jazz composers like Mingus and Charles Lloyd, and early pre-classical composers Guillaume de Machaut, as well as traditional players. I don't remember the band ever discussing that stuff with a view to using it as a concept. It was just a part of the pleasure of playing together.

"I think it is a mistake to assume that Bert and myself conceived of the group and consciously created the sound. Certainly much of the music was an extension of our ideas, but the format was always loose. The group could sound very untogether at times, but was fantastic when it gelled. Everybody was expected to, and did, chip in with ideas. What was happening in America was similar. Bluesy/folky/potsmokey players were forming bands that went in for long improvised sections: Jorma [Kaukonen], Jerry Garcia, [the Blues Project's] Danny Kalb."

As a key difference, however, the Pentangle never played as hard and electric as those American guitarists, even on the occasions when Renbourn (and to a much rarer extent, Jansch) used electric guitars rather than amplified acoustics. "Bert and I both played amplified with a kind of crossover amp set up on stage. There really was no big deal. Going electric was not an issue. I had been playing in R&B bands since being at school. I also played a bit of sitar which we acquired through Alexis. We used recorders, glockenspiel, dulcimer, and even concertina. Sitar and banjo sounded good together. I played a bit of piano, too. Essentially we used what we had to make the arrangements, but there was no overriding master plan."

The Pentangle in a way were the Beatles of British folk-rock, in that its blend of diverse talents was greater than its parts, egging each other on to heights that none of the musicians could have achieved as a solo act. Yet for all its skill and experience, the new quintet didn't jell right away. "The first impressions of Pentangle were not positive," says Ian Anderson (not the Ian Anderson of Jethro Tull), now the editor of Britain's leading roots music magazine, *fRoots* (formerly *Folk Roots*), and in the 1960s a young folk-blues musician and fan. "Bert and John set themselves up in a club in [London's] Tottenham Court Road. They had a residency for some months. Basically, it was experimental. I don't think they really rehearsed what they were doing very much, and it was very untogether. Bert and John were well into that free-range guitar noodling on acoustic guitar. Which was fine, because they had the skill to do it. But then trying out bass and drums and this singer who was up in the stratosphere, on top of that—it was not always successful. I think that was actually quite a good idea, doing a residency. By the time they recorded, it was okay."

Although the Pentangle had first played live in early 1967, its first album, *The Pentangle*, didn't come out until May 1968. By that time, any lingering awkwardness must have been worked out. There were sterling updates of age-old traditional songs ("Let No Man Steal Your Thyme" and "Bruton Town"); irresistibly swinging McShee-sung folk-blues ("Hear My Call," "Way Behind the Sun"); showcases for the guitarists' instrumental virtuosity and jazzy improvisation ("Waltz"); and quality original material. If it was more a folk-jazz-blues stew than it was folk-rock, it certainly rocked with a beat, and was executed with vocal harmonies, vocal and instrumental solo trade-offs, and a daring, irreverent spirit that immediately connected with rock-oriented listeners. And rock listeners, rather than folk ones, probably comprised the majority of the Pentangle's audience. The album stopped just short of the British Top 20.

If upsetting folk purists is one of the first criteria for qualifying as a folk-rock band (which it shouldn't be), the Pentangle succeeded on that score too, much to Thompson's displeasure. "It wasn't just jazzing up folk tunes. The reason I remember the fact that it was innovative is that we had death threats, because we started to use amplifiers. Letters saying 'You're gonna die,' from folk fans. 'What you've done to Bert Jansch is terrible. Leave Bert alone. Don't electrify him.' We thought, 'How are we gonna let people hear what's going on?'" Yet as Joseph points out, such troublemakers were, as is often revealed by inspection of overblown feuds between folk-rock enthusiasts and folk purists, "a minority. The music was so good, it was generally accepted fairly quickly." It certainly wasn't alienating the folk audience that was Transatlantic's prime constituency: "If you were to speak to our sales manager at this point and say, did you have a dip when [the Pentangle's Top Five 1969 LP *Basket of Light*] came out, the guy would look at you and say, 'Are you crazy?' It was the most successful Pentangle record, and one of our most successful records that we released at Transatlantic."

Shel Talmy, principally known for producing 1960s hits by the Kinks and the Who, sees the Pentangle as "probably the most rewarding stuff I ever did, because we did everything from medieval chants to modern jazz, and all the stages in between. [Jansch] was particularly interested in eighteenth and nineteenth-century English ballads, which were fun to do. Every session was a new session. They all brought all these amazing musical influences together, which is why we ended up doing such an eclectic mix of music. They were the best, I thought, of their representative fields.

"I think [Jansch] actually got a lot from the group. Because when I did his solo album [1969's *Birthday Blues*], there was something missing, even though we used some of the same musicians. He and John Renbourn really played well together; they fed off each other. When he was doing his solo album, that really wasn't the case."

Although he was known for the groundbreaking feedback, distorted guitar solos, and power chords on his early Who and Kinks sessions, Talmy had plenty of prior experience recording acoustic guitars with the Irish folk-pop-country band the Bachelors, Chad & Jeremy, and some of the Kinks' folkier recordings. This served both him and the Pentangle well when it came to capturing their sound, particularly Jansch and Renbourn's, with presence and depth. "I have evolved a way of recording acoustics that I know nobody else quite does. The concept I was striving for, and on which I did a lot of experimentation, was to record an acoustic sound that had both space and clarity. Today that sounds like a no-brainer, but in the '60s it was another Everest to climb, given the level and limitations of the gear available.

"What evolved was a combination of mike placement, the type of mike used and enhancements I added from the board, fairly primitive at that time, but it worked. It also changed the sound to some degree, it made it more bell-like, from the method I evolved in both recording and, of course, mixing it. Also as far as the Pentangle in particular were concerned, I was recording two of the best acoustic players in the country, making everything a lot easier."

The Pentangle maintained its peak on its follow-up *Sweet Child*, a double LP combining a live disc and a studio one. Had it been entered in the unofficial competition for who could offer the most wide-ranging body of material among folk albums in the early '60s, *Sweet Child* might have won hands down. There were spirituals, blues, Charles Mingus covers, a children's Christmas song, traditional Scottish folk, traditional British folk, a tribute to Moondog, a cover of Anne Briggs's "The Time Has Come," Jansch and Renbourn's most riveting instrumental duet ("In Time"), and original songs drawing from all of these ingredients and more. It was the late '60s now, though, and the record had far more verve than any early-'60s single-artist folk album attempting such an assortment of tunes would have boasted.

"Pentangle covered songs from the Appalachians to Scottish fishing songs to the usual things about brothers," says Thompson. "But we didn't have electric bass, and we didn't have a big rock drummer. The drummer was more of a percussion player. I played double bass. We played Mingus things and we played traditional tunes. It was a great opportunity, because I was able to, with the use of traditional music—which happened to be our own music, European music—use all the influences for improvisation. Not jazz, particularly, but improvisation. I keep telling people that improvisation never started with Charlie Parker. It's been in world music since we were chucking rocks at each other. So I don't like to call it jazz, really, but it's certainly improvised music. Now I can look back and say, there wasn't any other band like it.

"Each individual was successful in their own right. Bert was definitely a writer, a songwriter. John Renbourn was a researcher. Jacqui was kind of our lead trumpet, if you like. She didn't waver at all. We could all sort of take a tune and muck about with it, but she was the reference point every time.

"Everybody played different every night. There was never a night where you played the same things, or the same solo the same way. Things varied. Like now with Richard Thompson, you go onstage and a tune can go anywhere, you know? That was happening with Pentangle, in order to keep your enthusiasm up. I mean, it would have driven you mad to go onstage every night, back-to-back tours in the States and Australia, to play exactly the same thing every night."

The band's third album, *Basket of Light* (1969), was its best, making the British Top Five and even yielding a small hit single, "Light Flight" (primarily due to its use as the theme for the first BBC dramatic television series broadcast in color, *Take Three Girls*). Never again would the group spark off each other in as heady a manner. It was another set of boundless variety, from the peerless updates of the traditional songs "Once I Had a Sweetheart" and "Lyke-Wake Dirge" to the buoyant near-pop of "Light Flight" and "Springtime Promises," as well as a surprisingly fine cover of the Jaynetts' girl-group classic "Sally Go 'Round the Roses." The already dense colors of the group's instrumental palette kept expanding, with "Once I Had a Sweetheart" using sitar, glockenspiel, and multitracked vocals. Subsequent albums were less exciting, and the group petered out a few years later. The reasons for its decline are hard to pinpoint. Perhaps it was just too much to ask of any musicians to keep so many disparate influences glued to each other for too many years, and Jansch and Renbourn had the distractions of ongoing solo recording careers as well.

"I left when it started to get a bit like cabaret," says Thompson. "When you go onstage and when one of the blokes says to you, 'You got to admit, it's good money, but it *is* boring'.... When someone says that, you say, 'No wonder I'm having a hard time onstage.' When we stopped playing darts together and drinking together and socializing together, it started to be more of a business. I don't want to sound like a real romantic, but when I walked away from Pentangle, they'd just signed a deal with Warner Brothers, which would have meant quite a few quid, and which we needed at the time. I said, 'No. I'm not in it for that.'"

The Incredible String Band was another group that put together elements of folk and world music into something that was called folk-rock, in part, because it couldn't be called anything else and it certainly couldn't be called folk. Again, inspiration for what some view as quintessentially Scottish whimsy came from America. "What we were doing in '65 was something quite different," says Robin Williamson, who with Mike Heron would be the principal mainstays of the ISB's shifting lineup. "What I was doing, as a good place to start, is carrying on in a direct line from

[Beat Generation author] Jack Kerouac in one way, and from traditional singers in Britain, as well as old-timey American music: a kind of mixture of those things. The folk scene in Scotland wasn't a revival, exactly. It was still all there, as it was in Ireland. It had never gone away. So when we came in with a new take on it, we were taking it right from the source, rather than from the revival. I liked Jeannie Robertson, the Scottish singer, and a number of other people that were tradition-bearers in Scotland and in Ireland.

"But I worked with Tom Paley from the New Lost City Ramblers when he came over to Britain. That's why I first began playing fiddle, really, was with him. So that was an old-timey element as well. Because I wanted to be a writer, really, rather than a musician at first, my main role model was Jack Kerouac, because I wanted to try and write like that spontaneously. So I was in a curious never-never land between the tradition of the Celtic heritage on one hand, and the spontaneous writing of the beatniks in another.

"It seemed to me it was a good idea to break down the barriers between performer and audience, and to break down the idea of a virtuoso, by having a go at playing instruments that one couldn't play at all, to try and create a sort of naive music or an innocent music, like naive painting. And it struck me that in those days, before the Moog synthesizer had really got going, the only way to make interesting sounds easily was to get interesting instruments. I later found out that Harry Partch had been doing this on the West Coast in the '40s. I didn't know about him in those days. It proved to be, in a way, kind of self-destructive with the beginnings of the synthesizer and it being easy to make those noises.

"What I feel I contributed to the period 1964–65 was kind of like fools rushing in where angels feared to tread," Williamson continues. "I wanted to be the one over the hill rather than the one that built the city. I wanted to have a go at a number of different things. It struck me that you could write a spontaneous, free-form lyric, à la Jack Kerouac, and then you could link it up with spontaneous free-form music, drawn from the various regions of the world. So you have like an Indian bit, a Spanish bit, a light opera bit, an African bit. You could use all those things like tonal colors, and have a bit of a go on various instruments, and so on. Plus then, of course, the whole notion of guitar tunings was a very important thing in Britain, with Bert Jansch and John Renbourn and Davy Graham, who had opened up the world of DADGAD tuning. We began, in the String Band, to use a lot of minor tunings and different kinds of modal tunings.

"More than folk-rock, what I was trying to do then was try to open up the whole subject of folk music into a different, and wider, sphere. Not necessarily a rock sphere, but more of a sort of literary and world music sphere. In fact, the term 'global village' was first coined by a New York reporter to describe an Incredible String Band concert in the '60s. [We] didn't do too much electric at first, it was more like odd instruments from Africa, or India, or somewhere like that."

The Incredible String Band's self-titled 1966 debut album was the first British folk-rock-related recording produced by Joe Boyd, who had worked in both the American and British folk scenes in various capacities. In 1966 he was running Elektra's British division, a position that would be short-lived. Boyd was actually at least as interested in signing cutting-edge British rock artists like Pink Floyd, the Move, and Eric Clapton as he was the folk-based ones that, in 1966, were still the backbones of Elektra's catalog. Boyd was also moving away from the standard folk milieu by co-running the UFO club in London, which became the leading outlet for underground psychedelic rock, presenting early shows by Pink Floyd, the Soft Machine, Tomorrow, Procol Harum, and the Crazy World of Arthur Brown.

In Jonathon Green's *Days in the Life: Voices from the English Underground 1961–1971*, Boyd recalled that Elektra president Jac Holzman "got more and more alarmed at my spending my time promoting groups instead of promoting Tom Paxton. He didn't want them. So virtually a year after I arrived at Elektra in London, Holzman and I had one of those 'You can't fire me. I quit' conversations." In 2000, Boyd clarifies that Elektra's resistance was not due so much to unwillingness to sign rock bands as because "Holzman was nervous about a young, inexperienced person 3,000 miles from home acting like a loose-cannon A&R man."

Boyd's subsequent concentration on the cream of the new wave of British folk-rock artists, he adds, "wasn't a conscious decision. Obviously I would have liked to form Witchseason Productions in order to record the Pink Floyd [whose first single Boyd did actually produce], which wasn't a particularly folky band. I would have been very happy to produce the Pink Floyd, Cream, the Soft Machine, the Move, T. Rex, and Arthur Brown. All those were people that I had worked with at various sessions. I didn't have prejudice against that. But I think that maybe two things sort of helped steer my work in a certain direction. One is that maybe my background, inclination, and taste were better suited to recording people who had a bit of an eye on the folk element, just in terms of having the right instincts, as opposed to being a Phil Spector or something, who had an instinct for teenagers hanging out on the street corner in working-class districts of urban centers. My instincts were probably more in the ground what my background had been, in terms of listening as I grew up.

"And also, there may have been elements of, dare I say it, class, in the sense that I probably was better suited to working with reasonably educated, middle-class people than street kids that in a way responded better to somebody who was used to working with them, and who came from the same milieu. I wasn't [Animals/Donovan/Lulu/Herman's Hermits producer] Mickie Most, I wasn't an Andrew Oldham [manager-producer of the Rolling Stones], I wasn't some of the wild boys that were in the London scene at that time. They were characters that just had things in terms of a way of dealing with people that I might never have. It may have been, simply, that the chemistry worked better with the likes of a bunch of kids from [the London neighborhood] Muswell Hill, or a Nick Drake, who went to Marlborough [a well-to-do, fee-charging English public school, the equivalent of an American prep school]. I come from Princeton, New Jersey, went to Harvard, and I'm just a middle-class guy." (Incidentally, while this was going on Boyd didn't abandon purely traditional folk entirely, producing albums of traditional material by Shirley Collins and Dave Swarbrick in 1967.)

"Joe was American, you see," figures Pete Frame, the avid rock fan and folk club organizer who in the late '60s founded *ZigZag*, Britain's first magazine devoted to hip rock criticism. "So he could see what was good. He had a better perspective. He'd grown up worshiping the great American talents. In fact, there's a copy of some magazine where Joe Boyd lists the 100 albums you must have. This would be about '64, and it was all Woody Guthrie and the early Dylans and Lead-belly and so on. It was a real incredible, seminal list.

"When he came over to England, he obviously saw a niche. He had an eye that other people in England didn't seem to have, and ears that people in England didn't seem to have. He had the coolest roster, just amazing. Anyone that was on Witchseason was just automatically in a league of its own." (Boyd, incidentally, also played an overlooked role in Joni Mitchell's early career, bringing her over to play support on a British Incredible String Band tour in autumn 1967 before she had a recording contract, helping her get a British publishing deal, and introducing some of her songs into Fairport Convention's repertoire.)

A vital associate in many Witchseason productions, and quite a few other British folk-rock records of the era, was engineer John Wood. Many Boyd productions, and for that matter other significant British folk-rock records, were done at Wood's Sound Techniques studio in London. Boyd and Wood had met while Boyd was still working for Elektra, which had used Sound Techniques for some of its recording, including Judy Collins's landmark *In My Life* album. The first project Wood did with Boyd was, of all things, a singer-songwriter who was a Cambridge don. But soon Wood and/or Sound Techniques would record numerous folk-rock sessions for acts on both the Witchseason and Transatlantic rosters.

Wood makes no great boasts for cultivating a trademark sound in his studio, but does note one key advantage it had for predominately acoustic musicians looking to expand their arrangements: "I never worked anywhere else where I could get such a good string sound from such a small section." On a more general level, though, Wood proudly states, "If there is one thing that distinguishes Witchseason's productions, the division-one status of the musicians we've worked with is an important component of the records we've made. Joe's always had a great love of both players and playing. It has also meant that there are very few records that Joe and I have ever made together which have any gimmickry or trickery on them. Because the object has always been to make sure the music speaks for itself." Plus, adds Nat Joseph, Wood was easier to deal with than some other figures of a similar eminence in the music business: "He was also a business man, so he dealt with things efficiently and didn't sit on the floor smoking pot."

The Wood-Boyd team was well suited for the needs of folk-rooted musicians chafing to break out of the British folk scene's more close-minded conventions. "Most of the generation that came in around [the time of] the Incredible String Band were looking to different horizons, and weren't quite so precious or dyed-in-the-wool about what they did," feels Wood. "The generation that was earlier were much more purist. They weren't interested in other influences. Heron and Williamson were interested in Chinese music, Indian music, American blues, jug band music. They had a very wide musical interest, very eclectic, as did Fairport [Convention]. Other people who previously had been in either folk or jazz in Britain were very insular."

lthough handled by Witchseason, the Incredible String Band releases did come out on Elektra. Clive Palmer was still part of the trio that made *The Incredible String Band*, which, though more expansive in its instrumentation and freewheeling in its ambience than British traditional folk, was still basically a folk record. Palmer left after its release, and the ISB briefly went on hiatus, regrouping as a Williamson-Heron duo with more exotic instruments, some of which Williamson had brought back from Morocco.

Gimbri, sitar, tamboura, flute, and oud mandolin are all heard in addition to the expected guitars on 1967's *The 5000 Spirits or the Layers of the Onion*. As the title suggests, the lyrics had taken a turn toward the far-out as well, with songs about hedgehogs, mad hatters, a dialogue with a floating cloud, and "Way Back in the 1960s," written (right at the heart of the decade's most psychedelic phase) from the point of view of an old man looking back on the madness many years down the line. For all its weirdness, its most popular song was a relatively cogent romantic one, "First Girl I Loved," which found its greatest Stateside audience through a cover by Judy Collins.

The instruments multiplied yet further on *The Hangman's Beautiful Daughter*, with hammer dulcimer, harpsichord, pan pipe, Jew's harp, water harp, chahanai (an Indian oboe, more commonly spelled shenai), finger cymbals, and more adding to the clamor. Both this album and its predecessor put growing emphasis on melismatic, vari-pitched vocals, creating a wavering drone that would either charm listeners into hypnotic bliss or drive them up the wall. "The catalogue of world musical influence that the group incorporates would read like the international section of the Schwann catalogue," marveled *The New York Times* in its review of the band's November 1968 appearance at the Fillmore East. "An eastern flavor seems to predominate, but, then, when you're settled into a raga mood, it turns American mountain or Chelsea hippie."

Although extremely varied in both vocal and instrumental arrangement, the sprawl could lack focus. It also lacked, strictly speaking, much rock to its folk-rock. There were no electric guitars on their early records (though, interestingly, they did have an electric guitar at their Fillmore East show). But as with the Pentangle, rock listeners would be the Incredible String Band's core supporters, sending *The Hangman's Beautiful Daughter* to #5 in the UK. It was an amazing placing for such an adventurous record and a band whose very format made hit singles out of the question, and whose airplay was limited to a few adventurous DJs. For that, the Incredibles and other like-minded underground acts had to rely upon longtime BBC rock DJ John Peel, who once played *The 5000 Spirits or the Layers of the Onion* in its entirety on one of his shows, although it was at midnight.

"The psychedelic aspect, well, that was common to all of us in those days," reflects Williamson when asked what set the group apart from anyone else on the British folk *or* rock scene. "I think we were the first to have a go at the world music aspect of it. We'd become a lot more urbane, because we'd been all over the world by the time we got to the third record or fourth record. I never made a very easy transition into rock, really only using electrical musical instruments after about 1969, '70. And it was a bit uncomfortable for me, really, after 1970, '71. I was playing electric violin by that point, and we had a drummer and a bass player. It was kind of just conceivable, but it wasn't an easy niche."

Incredibly (no pun intended), for a band that had staked out such an unusual niche with its first releases, by this time the Incredible String Band had actually spawned imitators, or at least deviators. Forest, the Fool (produced by Graham Nash, but more famous for its mural painting on the building that housed the Beatles' Apple-run boutique), and the Irish band Dr. Strangely Strange all released albums in the late '60s and early '70s that were strongly informed by the ISB's exotica, without approaching their models' imagination or popularity.

In Williamson's estimation, Joe Boyd's greatest contribution was that "he didn't interfere, really. He was more of an enabler than a director. If you said to him, 'Well, I would like such and such,' he would get it for you, but otherwise, just let you get on with it. Early on, the first record we made was all standing around one microphone, a 1950s-type technique. By the time we got to the second record, we were jumping tracks. And by the time we got to the third, there was a 16-track facility, so you could actually play things. It came to be like painting, and that was a wonderful opening of a door. Because I always loved the idea you could sort of put something on and rub it out, and try something else. That really began to be born in the studio. Things you could do in the studio, we'd then try to re-create live."

I n a way the Incredible String Band would be the British version of acid folk (a term that, of course, didn't exist in those days), a nest that was also filled, with a far heavier use of electric rock, by Donovan. "I was very happy when the Incredible String Band came along," said Donovan in *Disc* in 1968, "because they have the same feel for music as my songs—but, of course, they're not the same."

And, he could have added, the two acts' level of international success was not the same either. The very notion of the Incredible String Band getting a hit single with even the most accessible of their songs was faintly preposterous. But from the time he fully embraced electric folk-rock in the summer of 1966 with the "Sunshine Superman" single and album of the same name, Donovan went on a roll of several Transatlantic hits, if anything becoming a little more popular Stateside than he was at home. There were almost a dozen Top 40 hits before the end of the decade, in fact, from the giddily playful ("Epistle to Dippy," "There Is a Mountain," "Mellow Yellow") and blissful flower-power ("Wear Your Love Like Heaven") to dainty love songs ("Jennifer Juniper," "Lalena") and even a bit of low-key Vietnam War protest ("To Susan on the West Coast Waiting").

None of his albums during this period were as astonishingly and consistently innovative as the folk-rock-psychedelic-medieval brew of *Sunshine Superman*. Some of them have been derided as insubstantial, with too high a proportion of the fairy-tale-like evocations and gentle acoustic-dominated love and happiness ballads of which the bard was so fond. Still, for those who bothered to wade through them, there were some scintillating highlights, like the exhortations to get stoned (in those exact words) on *Hurdy Gurdy Man*'s "Get Thy Bearings"; several surprisingly biting observations of Swinging London on the verge of waning on *Mellow Yellow* cuts like "Young Girl Blues," "Hampstead Incident," and "Sunny South Kensington"; and the prime psychedelic pop freakout of *Barabajagal*'s "Superlungs My Supergirl," with its fishbowl vocals, go-go horns, and crunching, wiggly fuzz guitar. The spare, jazzy backup arrangements he used on his 1968 *In Concert* LP considerably reinvented highlights of the *Sunshine Superman* and *Mellow Yellow* albums such as "Celeste," "The Fat Angel," and "Writer in the Sun."

Donovan was also capable of summoning far more ferocious wattage on occasion than many have acknowledged. In 1968 and 1969, he made his best fusions of playful folk-rock and psychedelic hard rock on the singles "Hurdy Gurdy Man," "Atlantis," and "Barabajagal," the last of which was recorded with the Jeff Beck Group. The 1968 classic "Hurdy Gurdy Man," the best and biggest hit of the three, even had backing by a proto-Led Zeppelin of sorts, with Jimmy Page on smoking guitar, John Paul Jones on bass, and John Bonham on drums (Allan Holdsworth also added electric guitar, and Clem Cattini drums). Yet it remained at heart a storytelling folk song, introduced by Donovan's best memorable a cappella hum-scatting, and spinning the enigmatic portrait of a hurdy gurdy man singing songs of love—a portrait that could have applied to Donovan himself.

Donovan was quoted in *NME* in 1968 as saying that the song had first been written with a mind to having it recorded by Hurdy Gurdy, a band featuring his old friend Mac MacLeod, "whom I looked to in the early days to learn how to pick the guitar. I wrote the song especially for them but then we got into a disagreement over how it was to be produced. I wanted to do it one way and they another. So I said, 'Right then—I'll do it myself because I think it's good enough for a single.'" Elaborates MacLeod, "The Hurdy Gurdy's approach to music was loud and electric and very much towards improvisation. Don's idea for his song was not in this vein, and he did state that he was thinking more in terms of a quiet ballad with vocal chorus and celeste. We left it at that and some weeks later traveling to the West Country to find the proverbial cottage in which to work, I was most surprised to hear Don's single over the radio with a backing not quite as he had portrayed."

According to Donovan, he'd actually hoped to have "Hurdy Gurdy Man" cut by an entirely different artist. "I had written the song in India when I was there with the Beatles [in] early 1968 to meditate with the Yogi Maharishi. My close spiritual chum George Harrison had written another verse, but I did not record it as the powerful electric solo took up all the playtime. In those days singles were strictly three minutes in duration for the radio. On return to England I met my producer, Mickie Most, and said 'The Hurdy Gurdy' was for Jimi Hendrix to record. I had met Jimi the first week he arrived in London to form his three-piece with Noel Redding and Mitch Mitchell. A good friend of [Donovan's friend] Gypsy Dave and mine, Chas Chandler of the Animals, had just brought Jimi over. I heard this powerful Celtic-rock fusion for 'Hurdy Gurdy Man' and thought Hendrix was the guy to record it.

"Mickie Most disagreed and said it was my next single. I then suggested Hendrix to play on my next single. Mickie called Chas Chandler to find Jimi was doing one-nighters and couldn't make the session. Mickie said, 'We will get Jimmy Page,' and so we went into the studio. John Paul Jones, who had arranged 'Mellow Yellow,' also arranged 'Hurdy Gurdy Man' and played bass. John Bonham on drums, with Clem Cattini, and second guitarist Allan Holdsworth made up the band. And I never knew that was the birth of Led Zeppelin till later.

"My memory seems to say I met a Danish band called Hurdy Gurdy, and it's possible the title came from meeting them. They were friends with a folkmate, Mac MacLeod. There is a misquote in the music mags that I wrote the song for the Danish group. Not so. Certainly the lyric was from India, perhaps the title came from meeting the Danish group."

Donovan has a lot to say about "Hurdy Gurdy Man" and how it defined a particular folk-rock tributary. "I am considered folk-rock and as a genre it covers many styles. But I would describe my kind of fusion as being from the folk root, but of a deeper level. I invented the title 'Celtic-rock' to describe my own fusion. I dove deep into the ancient Celtic root for my exploration, whereas most American and British folk artists studied the folk ballads, jigs and reels, blues and jazz of the last 300 years or so. You could say I plumbed the depths of a deep worldbeat which is most apparent in the groove of 'The Hurdy Gurdy Man.' This record had as players John Bonham, John Paul Jones, and Jimmy Page, three British artists who would go on to create the most popular and true Celtic-riff-rock band in the world, Led Zeppelin. Page knew he wanted to go where I walked and rocked—down that Celtic-rock road.

"I would call my sound Celtic-rock, as the merging of drums, bass, and keyboards which British and Irish/Scottish/Welsh bands play is not American folk-rock at all. The 'drone' which I introduced into my fusion was continued by many UK/Irish bands who played the excitement of pop, but with a Celtic bravado which is not related to the folk-R&B style Dylan began in the USA. We in the UK and Ireland were drawing on our Celtic-classical roots, which meant that the drums were closer related to the Celtic round skin drum called the bodran."

Just as Donovan was a virtually singular figure among British folkies in his full embrace of electric folk-rock in the mid-'60s, so was his journey from folk-rock to psychedelia a mostly solitary one in his homeland (although it was already a well-traveled road back in the US). Marijuana had been

Donovan,
Celtic-rock bard.

ingested by folkies in the UK before 1965, and they would take acid later. But drugs had more audible influence on straight-up British rock than they did on British folk-rock, and whether chemically inspired or not, there was little folk-rock-psych in the British Isles. Even those who imbibed made different footprints on the genre than their US counterparts. In common with British psychedelia as a whole, both Donovan and the Incredibles were more playful and storybook-flavored than the American space cowboys, evoking a psychedelic-tinged world riddled with fantasy, mythology, and medieval relics. "The only way to make the world into a paradise is to behave as if it WAS paradise," stated Williamson in *Disc* in 1968.

Today Williamson has tempered his views somewhat: "I'm not sure that I believe that in quite the same way. I've become more realistic, more pragmatic, and more kind of oddly religious as I get older. I'm not a Christian or any other religion, but I do have a profound sense of awe for the wonder of the universe, and a respect for whoever created it, the mysterious origins of it. I'm more interested now in throwing my soul at eternity rather than pumping chemicals into my system."

Donovan is keen, however, to discuss the mythological aspects of his and the ISB's music as reflections of a spiritual quest that is serious, not naive. "The direct influence of mostly Celtic mythology on my work is a rediscovery of our true Northern European spirituality which existed before the Christian Roman invasions," he states. "The myths and legends are a form of psychological journey which Carl Jung describes in his studies as a path to wholeness, which is the pagan way to enlightenment. The ISB and I knew this intuitively and promoted the Western way to self-knowledge, in contrast to the Christian Middle Eastern way and the then Far Eastern Indian and Chinese yoga sweeping the West. Tales of myths and legends and fairy folk are not frivolous children's fantasies, but real and meaningful ways to understand the inner world and thus overcome the shadow which threatens the human race in every time throughout history. In presenting this inner journey through song, I am again a bard, and have left folk-protest and entered the field of true change." (Such lyrical inclinations, incidentally, were not exclusive to the British side of the folk-rock pond; flights of Tolkienesque fantasy are certainly found in Pearls Before Swine's music and some of Joni Mitchell's early songs, as well as some songs on the Beau Brummels' *Triangle* album.)

Aside from Donovan and the Incredible String Band, the only other act to ride the British folk-psych train (with an honorable mention to the early-'70s solo albums of original Pink Floyd leader Syd Barrett) was Tyrannosaurus Rex, the duo of acoustic guitarist Marc Bolan and bongo player Steve Took. Bolan had actually been in the rock band John's Children, purveyors of mod-psych mayhem on a brief 1967 German tour with the Who. Tyrannosaurus Rex was a gear shift in reverse, with Bolan's distinctly warbling vocals espousing a Tolkienesque lyricism embodied in the tongue-twisting title of their 1968 debut, *My People Were Fair and Had Sky in Their Hair . . . But Now They're Content to Wear Stars on Their Brows*.

As with Donovan and ISB, there was a bit of never-never land about its music. "I suppose it's escapist," Bolan surmised in *Record Mirror*. "Civilization now is very plastic, people have the wrong sets of values. So I write about different lands—places where the good things ARE good, and not just because we've been brought up to accept them that way." Bolan's minimal melodicism could wear thin quickly, and his fantasy-ridden imagery could sometimes make the Incredible String Band seem staid in comparison. After a few solid-selling albums he would discard Took, beef up his pop hooks, and plug back in to become T. Rex, the British glam rock sensation of the early '70s.

John's Children singer Andy Ellison thinks he knows why Bolan unplugged for a few years. After their infamous tour with the Who, he remembers, "All our equipment was confiscated, and there we were sort of being deported from Germany, very sadly shifting our way out through the back roads in Simon's [manager Simon Napier-Bell's] Bentley. On the way, we dropped off at Luxembourg and spent a couple of nights there, where we saw Ravi Shankar in concert. I always remember that Marc was really taken by just seeing these guys sitting there onstage with sitars and bongos. He was very quiet after that concert, and seeing as when we got back to England we had no equipment, Marc disappeared. He didn't have money—the easiest way to start making music was to sit there, grab his old acoustic guitar again, and things went on from there. He started having success that way, but I feel that he really still wanted to do the electronic thing again. Because he had such wild abandon and excitement with John's Children."

he Pentangle, Donovan, and the Incredible String Band had all made important contributions to folk-rock, albeit—in the Pentangle and the ISB's cases—often in tangential ways that did not employ the electric guitars that were rock's most defining instruments. Prior to 1968, rather incredibly, there was not a single British rock group that played electric folk-rock consistently and well. It is thus not too surprising that the band to become roundly acclaimed as the best British folk-rock group, Fairport Convention, took its initial inspiration from American folk-rock, particularly the guitar-oriented California sort.

It could be said that Fairport Convention was the first true second-generation folk-rock band, in that its initial repertoire and model came not from folk songs, but from imported folk-rock records. In our days of worldwide simultaneous releases and block-long music megastores, it can be easy to forget that in 1967 even LPs on Vanguard and Elektra could be hard to come by in England. To learn songs by Love, Richard & Mimi Fariña, and Jim & Jean commanded the same kind of obscurist archivism that American teenagers of the late '50s and early '60s needed to locate Alan Lomax field recordings, Library of Congress LPs, and Folkways releases.

This is what Fairport Convention, formed in North London by guitarists Richard Thompson and Simon Nicol and bassist Ashley Hutchings, did to master a repertoire that likely was unduplicated anywhere in the British Isles in 1967. Over the next few months the lineup was filled out by drummer Martin Lamble, singer Judy Dyble (who also played what she believed, she once told *Melody Maker*, might have been the only electric autoharp in the country), and singer Ian Matthews [who now goes by the spelling Iain Matthews]. Except for Hutchings, all were still in their teens (Nicol was only 16); except for Matthews, who'd been on a 1967 pop-rock single by the Pyramid, none of them had played on any records.

"When I received the invitation to 'check out' Fairport I knew absolutely nothing about them," recalls Matthews. "All I knew was that they were beginning to establish themselves as an underground favorite, by playing regularly at the UFO club. But the crowd I was running with at the time were listening to a completely different genre of music. The day I met the band for the first time they had gathered in a small studio in south London called Sound Techniques, to record their first single. I was between homes at the time and I walked in with my suitcase and a dozen albums under my arm: Tim Hardin, Richie Havens, Tim Buckley, Byrds, etc. I believe these albums got me the job, because it was coincidentally exactly what they were all listening to, plus Dylan, Joni, and Richard Fariña, of course.

"At the time no one in the band was writing with any seriousness, so we dug deep into that type of approach for inspiration and for stage material. I don't think anyone apart from possibly Joe Boyd had any vision of where the band was headed, or what we might become. We were developing something and placed no boundaries on it. At the back of our minds American folk-rock was the happening thing, both musically and inspirationally. We loved the Airplane, and the two-lead-vocalist approach appealed to us. Because of our name and our scruffy onstage presence, lots of people around that time thought we were American, and considering the possible rewards, we were not about to attempt to dispel that presumption."

"Wherever Fairport played when we started in '67, there were groups playing improvisational music to a large extent," says Hutchings. "They'd start out on a chord formation and maybe sing a few words, and that would just be the vehicle to go off and paint colors instrumentally, for long stretches. There was really almost no one else tackling the best singer-songwriters and what one might loosely call contemporary folk music. Eclection were the only band I can think of right now touring England at that time who impinged on our territory. Why that is, I don't know. It's just how it was.

"And I'm glad it was, really, because we wouldn't have stood out. And we *did* stand out as a band. In the early days, we weren't that good. But we stood out because we played these short, intelligent, rather lovely songs, and no one else was doing them. Pentangle came from a whole different area. We didn't consider that we were anything like Pentangle. They played acoustic instruments, but also they came largely from the jazz side. They *swung* the folk. We *rocked* the folk."

Actually the band occasionally delved far more into psychedelic improvisation than many realize. Joe Boyd's interest in the group was initially piqued by Thompson's guitar work during its half-hour cover of the Paul Butterfield Blues Band psychedelic instrumental "East West." On French TV in 1968, it did a radical seven-minute rearrangement of Richard & Mimi Fariña's "Reno Nevada" (now available on its archival box set *Fairport Unconventional*), Thompson taking the helm with several uninterrupted minutes of explosive jam-soloing. In the studio, however, concise songs would initially be the order of the day, though those early psychedelic jams looked forward in some respects to the lengthy updated folk epics that would appear in the group's later incarnations.

The band's first album, 1968's *Fairport Convention*, is often dismissed as an irrelevant curiosity due to its dissimilarity to the group's later, more British folk-fueled efforts. To the contrary, it was a highly credible and enjoyable, if derivative, West Coast–styled folk-rock album, owing much to the early Byrds and Jefferson Airplane, particularly the Airplane's male-female vocal harmonies and vocal solo tradeoffs. In fact, in Fairport's very early days, some of the UK media even dubbed the band "the British Jefferson Airplane," and Fairport were once billed as "England's Top West Coast Group." The songs the musicians covered would have been obscure to almost anyone on either side of the Atlantic: Joni Mitchell's "I Don't Know Where I Stand" and "Chelsea Morning" (both of which she had yet to release), Jim & Jean's "One Sure Thing," the Merry-Go-Round's "Time Will Show the Wiser," and Ben Carruthers's "Jack o' Diamonds," the last of which was a true affidavit to their record-collecting prowess, as it's doubtful the original 45 could have sold more than a few copies. More importantly, the band showed itself capable of writing strong original material in the same mold.

"We were quite fortunate really, because in Joe and his direct link to Warners at the time, we had a private source to whatever American material we wanted," points out Matthews. "He was responsible for many of our early influences. Were it not for him, I may not have listened to Moby Grape, or Buffalo Springfield, for quite some time. Joni Mitchell too, Joe had a direct line to her publishing demos and supplied us with whatever we could handle. I'm sure the Joe pipeline was how Sandy [Denny] got [her composition] 'Who Knows [Where the Time Goes]' to Judy Collins. [Boyd also gave the band access to demos of unreleased Bob Dylan material.]

"I was not one of the driving forces behind the early Fairport direction. Most of this was engineered behind the scenes by Joe. He was very good at dropping subtle ideas and Richard, Ashley, and to a lesser degree Simon were very open and good at picking up the idea and running with it. I was simply a singer at that point, struggling to find direction. Richard was one to never even consider the possibility of simply recording a soundalike cover. He was constantly searching for an alternate way to interpret these great songs. In retrospect, I see that he was a fine influence on my own ability to do that too. If we couldn't somehow add to the original, in some way, then we inevitably abandoned the song."

The art of interpreting American folk-rock songs would provide Fairport's foundation for quite some time. Setlists from the era included additional covers of the likes of Love, Phil Ochs, Jefferson Airplane, Eric Andersen, and Leonard Cohen (as well as yet more early Joni Mitchell songs that never made it onto their albums). On the BBC, it went yet further, with interpretations of songs from Gene Clark's first solo album (a flop even in the States), Richard & Mimi Fariña, and two particularly unacknowledged Everly Brothers gems. Some of the best of these, with Sandy Denny rather than Dyble on female vocals, were assembled on a collection of 1968–69 BBC sessions, *Heyday*. Fairport's arrangements, in the manner of the best folk-rock covers, gave a bright rock lift to outstanding songs that made them both different than and equally worthy as the originals. In some cases, they exceeded their models. Certainly there is no better Leonard Cohen cover than Fairport Convention's "Suzanne," with its dramatic alternation of Denny and Matthews solo vocals and entirely restructured tempos that both stutter and glide, investing it with a tension missing from Cohen's typically downbeat rendition. The remake of Richard & Mimi Fariña's "Reno Nevada" was similarly brilliant, with its close harmonies and Thompson's customary versatile, imaginative guitar riffs.

If it seems strange that a repertoire based around American folk-rock verged on the exotic in England in 1968, it should be remembered that some of the American folk-rock artists, particularly the album-oriented ones, were far less celebrated in the UK than in their homeland. "Grateful Dead, Jefferson Airplane, Country Joe, all those people—I don't think they meant a lot to English bands," explains Pete Frame. "I mean, Country Joe & the Fish, you couldn't read about them in *Melody Maker* or the *New Musical Express*, apart from maybe a mention and a line here or there. When Jefferson Airplane came over, there were limited audience[s] for it. Because you couldn't hear the bloody things on the radio. No one was playing them," apart from John Peel. And though some big bands like the Byrds and several singer-songwriters, from Judy Collins to Tim Buckley, toured Britain in the 1960s, some major folk-rock artists, like Buffalo Springfield, never made it to the UK at all.

"The Americans carried the ball as far as I was concerned, no contest," feels Matthews. "All the great songs from that era came from the USA. The British scene was so very different, different attitude, different social structure and very different things to say. To me the American writing was so much more glamorous and worldly. I related to it much stronger than anything Al Stewart or Bert Jansch had to say."

However, just as R&B-inspired British rock groups such as the Rolling Stones and the Yardbirds could not have sustained themselves indefinitely on covers of American artists like Chuck Berry, Bo Diddley, Jimmy Reed, and Muddy Waters, so was it only a matter of time before Fairport's well of American folk-rock covers both ran dry and marked the group as passé. The missing piece of the puzzle that transformed it into a more original band with a distinctly British style was supplied by Sandy Denny, the greatest British folk-rock singer, who replaced Judy Dyble in the spring of 1968.

Although she had appearances on only two poorly distributed LPs before joining Fairport Convention, Denny brought a more substantial resume and higher reputation to the band than any of the other members. She'd been singing in folk clubs since the mid-'60s, with a high voice that initially owed much to both Judy Collins and Shirley Collins. In addition to the upper-register clarity and power of the Collinses, however, Denny had a knowing, oft-searing emotional passion to her vocals. She particularly excelled at haunting, minor-key songs with a peculiarly British ambience, her voice floating above the song with the all-enveloping chill of a fog covering the English moors. She was also comfortable with both traditional and contemporary material, and with both acoustic ballads and rock songs. Her voice pulsed with an uninhibited life that no band could overpower.

Denny had actually already recorded about four or five albums worth of material before joining Fairport, though few of the songs had been released. A couple dozen unreleased 1966–68 home demos, eventually coming to light on the CD bootlegs *Dark the Night* and *Borrowed Thyme*, are superb by any standard except (at times) the fidelity. With just a guitar as accompaniment, she filled the room with poignant longing and regret on traditional British and American folk songs; interpretations of recent work by Fred Neil and Jackson C. Frank; and her own compositions, which were rapidly ripening into tunes with a brooding magnetism similar to the covers she favored. Jo Lustig had suggested Sandy Denny to John Renbourn as a replacement for Jacqui McShee in the early days of the Pentangle, although Renbourn spurned the idea.

In 1967, while a singer in the Johnny Silvo Folk Four, Denny participated in a couple of acoustic folk albums on the small Saga label, one credited to Alex Campbell and Friends (on which she variously took lead and backup vocals), the other to Sandy Denny and Johnny Silvo. Although her singing was excellent (ten of the tracks have been compiled on the CD *The Original Sandy Denny*), the simple folk arrangements, on both traditional tunes and covers of songs by Tom Paxton and Frank, were often old-fashioned and outmoded. Denny was better served by a band, and took many of the lead vocals on 1967 mild folk-rock sessions with the Strawbs. Mostly comprised of originals by Strawbs guitarist Dave Cousins, this batch also included her first recorded composition, "Who Knows Where the Time Goes," the song that Judy Collins would cover on her 1968 album of the same name. Denny proved adept at putting her vocals onto more upbeat, pop-slanted material than she had leaned toward on her folk recordings—"And You Need Me," with a melody redolent of the Beatles' "If I Fell," in particular was a heartbreaker. Unfortunately these cuts weren't released at the time, though they did finally come out in 1973.

"I don't really think that you could classify Sandy, in her early folk days, as a folk singer," maintains Cousins. "She sang in folk clubs, but she was singing songs like Jackson Frank's 'Blues Run the Game.' And the odd folk song, but she was also doing lots of Dylan-type songs as well. Although she could sing folk songs magnificently, she was equally at home with pop music. If you listen to 'On My Way' on the Sandy & the Strawbs album, which is the first track we ever put down, we were trying to be the Mamas & the Papas. That was the sort of song that we were doing at that time. The trouble was that my voice was nowhere near the quality that Sandy had on those early records. My voice was very nasal. It's warmed up over the years. It sounded pretty naff at the time."

Shortly after joining Fairport, Denny explained to *Melody Maker* that "I wanted to do something with my voice. Although I can play guitar adequately I was feeling limited by it. It was a kind of stagnation. I was developing but the guitar was restricting. I always had it in my mind to join a group. I joined the Strawbs last year but I wasn't really ready for it but now I feel free to sing how I want to."

Joe Boyd had known Denny for about a year before she joined Fairport. "I think Sandy was a completely different person than Judy, a much more powerful singer, a much stronger voice for a start. I think the band became less tentative with Sandy, because Judy was a delicate singer. There might have been a little bit of a feeling of holding back or hesitancy about being too aggressive in the band because the vocalist was so tentative, frail.

"But with Sandy, you had a powerhouse. I think she boosted the band's confidence in a way because she was quite well known as a solo artist. The fact that she chose to join Fairport boosted all of their confidence level in themselves as a band. She brought her own songwriting, great songs. Then, I think she was really the key person ultimately responsible for introducing them to English folk music, because she had a large repertoire of songs that she used to sing with the band on the road or in hotel rooms after concerts and things."

"I think she focused our attention on it, that's absolutely true," counters Hutchings. "But what people often forget is that all the members of Fairport in the early days—Richard, Simon, Judy, and myself—used to go to folk clubs, and traditional folk clubs as well, in London, on a regular basis. So we were very familiar with Ewan MacColl, Bert Lloyd, many of the American visitors, in the folk clubs from the mid-'60s. So Sandy was really reminding us about that material. She wasn't introducing us to it for the first time." When Fairport eventually made such material a major part of their set, he allows, "It was still a shock to people. It was a shock to us! But I'm anxious to point out that we were au fait with traditional music from years back before then."

The shift was evident, though only in part, on early 1969's *What We Did on Our Holidays*. Like the Byrds, Fairport crafted a near-ideal balance between imaginative reworkings of traditional folk songs ("Nottamun Town" and "She Moves Through the Fair," the latter actually a 1916 poem by Irishman Padraic Colum that the band set to music); quality covers of contemporary folk-rock singer-songwriters, some quite obscure (Joni Mitchell's "Eastern Rain," Bob Dylan's "I'll Keep It with Mine"); and original folk-rock material by various members. The self-generated cuts were the most variable. Certainly Denny's mournful "Fotheringay" and the Matthews-Thompson collaboration "Book Song" were melodic folk-rock of the highest order, yet there were also more forgettable songs, and the cloddish blues-rock of "Mr. Lacey."

This balancing act was preserved, with slightly less impressive results, on mid-1969's *Unhalfbricking*, which went to town (in another parallel with the Byrds) with obscure Dylan covers, none of which had showed up on Dylan's LPs. These included the ballad "Percy's Song" (with heartstopping vocals by Denny), "Million Dollar Bash" from Dylan's then-unreleased 1967 Basement Tapes, and a fittingly eccentric Cajun cover of "If You Gotta Go, Go Now," translated into and sung in French as "Si Tu Dois Partir." This became perhaps the most eccentric folk-rock hit single of all, stopping just outside the British Top 20; the French lyrics were obtained when (according to Nicol in *Record Mirror*) the group appealed to the audience for a translator at one of its shows at the Middle Earth club.

"The scene at Middle Earth was that you'd do two sets, and they'd be separated by quite a considerable time while other bands did their thing," verifies Nicol. "I think the boredom factor was one of the reasons we came up with this wacky idea. Three or four punters joined us in the dressing room; they were either French visitors or students of French working in London, and happened to be there that night. Sandy and Richard between them had fairly good school-level French. That's how we sort of thrashed it out. But nobody would pretend that the translation of that lyric would have passed muster at the Strasbourg court of justice." "If You Gotta Go, Go Now" had at this point only been released by Dylan on an obscure European-only single, although Manfred Mann had taken it to #2 in the UK, in English of course, back in 1965. Nicol admits that had the song been better known, they might not have been quite so reckless in turning it upside down: "If it had been on [Dylan's 1964 LP] *Another Side of*, maybe we wouldn't have been so libertarian with it. 'Cause he was on a pedestal at that time."

Unhalfbricking also featured Fairport's own recording of Denny's "Who Knows Where the Time Goes," and Sandy offered another illustration of her peerless aptitude for folk-rock melancholy on "Autopsy." The band would have been better served at this point to focus more on Denny songs than those by Thompson, who had emerged as Fairport's other principal composer, particularly with the unceremonious departure of Matthews. Ian left the band in early 1969 after appearing on just one song on *Unhalfbricking*.

Part of the reason the band felt that Matthews no longer fit in was his tepid interest in its growing focus on remoldings of British traditional folk songs, epitomized by *Unhalfbricking*'s 11-minute epic "A Sailor's Life." (This tune had already been recorded by folk notables like Martin Carthy, who put it on his second album, and Judy Collins, who did it way back in 1962 on her debut LP.) "They were exploring the trad side of things heavily at that time, and the end of my tenure came when I discovered accidentally that they were in the studio without me," says Matthews. "Joe wanted to move on to phase three quickly and sentiments had no place in his plan. I was asked to leave and dumped on the same day. Presuming that he meant soon, I got in [the] van to go to the show. Ashley turned to me and said, 'Where do you think you're going?' Sandy, bless her, turned to him and said, 'You heartless bastard.' I got out and away they sped." The animosity, incidentally, couldn't have run that deep; Hutchings played on Matthews's first post-Fairport solo album, and *NME* even reported in late 1970 that Ian had approached Ashley and drummer Gerry Conway with a mind to form a new group, though that didn't come to pass.

"I think it would have been impossible for him to have gone with the direction the band went in," says John Wood. "When you listen to *What We Did on Our Holidays*, all the tracks with Ian are much smoother. There's almost a desire to have more polish on them, and to double-track; he liked to double-track. It's a very different form, really."

"What everyone has to remember is, we were very young," responds Hutchings when asked for his take on Matthews's departure. "I suspect that at the time, we weren't aware of how good a combination Sandy and Ian were, vocally. If you listen in particular to the *Heyday* album, to the radio sessions, the voices blend incredibly well. I suppose it was inevitable that once we moved onto the traditional material, Ian would leave. In those days, he wasn't really interested in folk music; I think he would agree with that. So his days were numbered. There wasn't really a decision to make, once we got on the road to traditional material.

"In retrospect, I think we could have worked harder in trying to make it work as a group. It would have been interesting to see what would have happened had Ian stayed, and somehow got through *Liege & Lief* [Fairport's late-1969 album, and its first to focus almost wholly on material with or derived from British traditional folk roots]; whether it would have evened out, panned out.

Fairport Convention shortly after Sandy Denny joined. Left to right: Ashley Hutchings, Simon Nicol, Richard Thompson, Martin Lamble, Ian Matthews, and Sandy Denny.

We'd have pulled it more back into the mainstream with Ian singing a lot. Because if you listen to the early Matthews Southern Comfort [Matthews's first post-Fairport band], they started to do some traditional songs; they tended to be American ones. I wonder what the combination would have been like, doing a mixture of traditional song, maybe American and English, with Sandy, with Ian, with the band."

Over the years, a sort of party line has developed among many rock and folk historians that Fairport Convention did not reach its peak, and truly develop its own vision, until it recorded the *Liege & Lief* album later in 1969. This view holds that prior to this, Fairport was too imitative of West Coast folk-rock, and found its identity when it decided to focus primarily on electrified English traditional folk. To those who value diversity, innovation, and quality original material matched with great singers and players, this view is, of course, nonsense. It's arguable, but Fairport was never better than during that brief period when Denny and Matthews were both in the band.

"Even in retrospect, I find early Fairport neither derivative nor unfocused," offers Matthews. "Most critics seem to have a hard time resisting labeling anything, even if it's unlabelable. Fairport was such an act, original from the get-go. OK, they found a niche that no one else had explored with *Liege & Lief*, but I challenge anyone to show me a band from that era and be able to say 'that sounds like early Fairport.' I believe *Liege* was a huge turning point in the band's identity and acceptance, and I respect the many stylistic changes they made for that album. But listening back, my favorites were *Holidays* and *Unhalfbricking*, and let's not forget the oft-overlooked *Heyday*— not sonically the best, but what great material and drive, you can taste the enthusiasm." Another personnel change in 1969, this one born of far more tragic circumstances, would cement Fairport's new British trad folk direction.

efore that took place, very few British folk-rock groups of note followed Fairport Convention, and maybe it wasn't a coincidence that the best two of them had Fairport connections. The first, and one that still draws blank stares even from many folk-rock buffs, was Eclection. Although the band was based in England, only one of its five members was British. Principal songwriter Georg Hultgreen (now known as Georg Kajanus) was from Norway; the band's other songwriter, Michael Rosen, from Canada; singer Kerrilee Male from Australia, where she had sung in the mid-'60s with Dave's Place Group, featuring ex-Kingston Trio guitarist Dave Guard; and Trevor Lucas, also from Australia. Lucas had already recorded a couple of rare folk albums, and would eventually marry Sandy Denny, playing in some of her bands as well (including a mid-'70s incarnation of Fairport Convention). Drummer Gerry Conway, like Danny Thompson and Terry Cox, was a veteran of Alexis Korner's band, though much younger than the pair who comprised the Pentangle rhythm section, only just leaving his teens when he joined.

Perhaps it was their largely non-British background that allowed them—unlike virtually everyone else in the UK—to make a quick transition to electric instruments despite acoustic folk backgrounds and to quickly coalesce into an ensemble, much as several folk-rock artists had grouped together in California after growing up in widely dispersed regions of the US. Kajanus had, he admits, been "a purist fighting the acoustic battle versus the electric demons creeping into the scene," but would end up buying a Fender electric 12-string from the Who's Pete Townshend, "who for some reason wanted to sell the guitar rather than destroy it in his usual manner." Likewise Lucas, adds Kajanus, was "initially unhappy about playing bass rather than playing his favorite acoustic Fender six-string. He grumbled a bit but finally gave in."

Rosen's friend Joni Mitchell, who spent some time in London in 1967, was the one who named them Eclection, according to Kajanus: "There is, of course, no such word as Eclection, but her idea for the name was based on the eclectic nature of our nationalities as well as our diverse musical backgrounds." It was also through Mitchell and Rosen, thinks Kajanus, that the band contacted Elektra's Jac Holzman, and Eclection soon became one of the few British bands on its roster: "We were flabbergasted when he did sign us, considering the icons he already had on his label."

Given the disparate nationalities, it's perhaps unsurprising that the band's sole album, 1968's *Eclection* (on Elektra), didn't sound that British at all. Actually, it sounded very much as if it could have been done in California. There were echoes of the Mamas & the Papas and Jefferson Airplane in both the stirring choral male-female harmonies and the soaring, orchestrated sunshine-speckled production (by Ossie Byrne, who produced Bee Gees albums during the same period). Although very pleasant and well produced, and guitarist Rosen's occasional quasi-classical trumpet was an unusual touch in a straightforward folk-rock band, it was not quite on the level of Fairport Convention's earliest efforts. Perhaps the material wasn't quite distinct enough to demand success; maybe the group lacked a singer with the personality of a Sandy Denny, Jacqui McShee, or Bert Jansch, though Male had an interesting Seekers-with-guts flair.

"The musical direction of the group was probably closer to American folk-rock than anything else," agrees Kajanus. "The most influential artists for me at the time were people like Dylan, the Byrds, Fred Neil, Simon & Garfunkel, the Beach Boys, the Mamas & the Papas, and Gordon Lightfoot." (In fact Kajanus and Rosen had met when Kajanus was going table-to-table in a London sausage restaurant singing a Lightfoot-heavy repertoire.) Although Kajanus is "in some ways surprised that I ended up the principal songwriter since I certainly did not think of myself at the time as an accomplished composer," he allows, "I was very prolific and had a good ear for melody. Other powerful influences on me at the time were classically orientated music as well as the French chanson, i.e. Jacques Brel and Georges Bressens, so an interesting combination was created. As to my lyrics, English was my third language (after Norwegian and French), so that should give me license for some of my poetic obscurities.

"Eclection's mixture of musical backgrounds and influences were in vast contrast to our contemporaries in England at that time. Also our producer, Ossie Byrne, was instrumental in utilizing the string arrangements that lifted the tracks away from the current sounds. We weren't even sure of the idea when he first suggested it, but we were all pretty pleased with the result. I listened to it recently and I was struck by the mood created by the vocals generally, and some of the inventiveness of the vocal arrangements. Basically, I liked the naive and wistful flavor of the album. I was also saddened that Kerrilee Male's voice was so tragically underused. Her voice was exceptional, and I wish that we had found a way through our arrangements to create more lead vocals for her. This was one of the main reasons why she finally left the band."

"Once we started playing live, it was very soon apparent that Kerrilee didn't want to stay with it," says Conway. "Once she left, the band slowly but surely changed, with different members leaving. We ended up sort of a half-a-million miles away from what we started with." The band did recruit the estimable American (ex-)folk singer Dorris Henderson to add a soulful dimension, but only made one single with her in the lineup before splitting.

"Unfortunately, the musical direction of the group then shifted to a much more jazz-orientated approach due to numerous guest musicians passing through," amplifies Kajanus, who would resurface in Sailor, who had several rock hits in the UK in the mid-'70s. "I was feeling more and more trapped in an alien musical environment and I finally had to leave. Also, the fact that nothing happened with the album was a bit of a blow to all of our egos. As far as America was concerned, there was no promotion that I can remember. Perhaps it was the fact that we were based in the UK and signed to a US record company that presented a major logistical problem. Of course, the Incredible String Band did make the Atlantic crossover, but I guess we didn't catch the same boat."

"I loved that group," says a wistful Jac Holzman of Eclection. "They were a fascinating group, a wonderful band, and I thought the records were wonderful. I think our mistake was not bringing them to the States, because they really needed to get out of England. There was too much other stuff competing in England, and in the States, we might have had an easier time. I don't know why we didn't bring 'em. I think, had we got 'em the right venues and gotten them some help with their show, it would have worked."

The other Fairport-related group would prove far more durable. After suffering the loss of Sandy Denny, the Strawbs kept their shoulders to the wheel, landing a contract with the then-young American label A&M. By that time their sound had evolved quite a bit from their origins as the Strawberry Hill Boys, the trio of guitarist-banjoist Dave Cousins, guitarist Tony Hooper, and mandolinist Arthur Philips, who played folk clubs in the London area. To most Americans, someone such as Cousins, who learned to play banjo from Weavers records in order to play bluegrass and ran the White Bear folk club—where artists such as the Strawbs, Renbourn, and Jansch performed—would qualify as a "folk" musician. Cousins is keen to wash his hands of that label, which seems partly attributable to fine semantic distinctions between how the term "folk" is applied in America and Britain. It's less important to quibble about exactly what makes one a folk musician or not than to emphasize that he was not from the *English* folk tradition. "Although we played in the folk clubs as the Strawberry Hill Boys, we were playing more American-type music," he stresses. "We only did the odd British folk song."

As the Strawberry Hill Boys evolved into the Strawbs, they incorporated more original material, mostly penned by Cousins. That was enough in and of itself to further distance them from the sometimes draconian behavioral codes of the British folk community. "While the likes of Bert Jansch and John Renbourn, heavily influenced by Davy Graham, were using tunings to translate English folk songs, I was using them as a basis for writing new songs," he observes. "For example, 'Tell Me What You See in Me' [included on both the *Sandy & the Strawbs* album and the Strawbs' A&M debut] was written in a D modal tuning." Many of his new songs, sometimes quite poppish in ways reminiscent of Donovan, the Seekers, and the Mamas & the Papas, show up on both *Sandy & the Strawbs* and *Preserves Uncanned*, a 1991 double CD of unreleased 1966–68 recordings.

By the time of *The Strawbs*, released on A&M in May 1969, the band was focusing more on somber, at times over-earnest story-songs with a bittersweet, almost Elizabethan base. Production-wise, it was strides ahead of the far sparser folk-rock of *Sandy & the Strawbs*, embellishing the acoustic guitar with recorder, Gregorian backup vocals, and orchestration. This gave the music an almost medieval ambience well-suited for material like "The Battle," a six-minute piece that used a chess game as a metaphor for war. "The Man Who Called Himself Jesus," inspired by a man who'd been thrown out of a shop for insisting he was the Second Coming, was less a retelling of an incident than a question as to whether anyone would believe that Christ was who he said he was if he got resurrected. The medieval-Gregorian feel was never more to the fore than on "Where Is This Dream of Your Youth," which Cousins had written as a possible single for the Young Tradition, the traditional English folk harmonizing group who often recorded a cappella: "I was trying to write them a pop song."

Continues Cousins, "The interesting thing was, I didn't really listen to music at that time. I just played music. The only records I maybe listened to were the Mamas & the Papas, Simon & Garfunkel, and the Beatles. I'd given up listening to the old folk records. I was listening much more to pop music at that time. So we were much more of a pop group in our early days than we were ever a folk group. However, because of the playing in folk clubs, we've been lumbered as folk-rock musicians. In the UK, we were never considered to be really part of the folk mainstream. We became very much more part of the underground music scene. We were playing acoustic music, but we had cellos with us and things like that. Where I was writing long songs such as 'The Battle,' 'The Man Who Called Himself Jesus,' these were not really of a folk origin. These were much more ... long, that's what they were!"

The Strawbs' first attempt at an album had actually been rejected by A&M, who had signed them on the basis of a couple of Cousins's lighter, more accessible songs, "Oh! How She Changes" and "Or Am I Dreaming." The label was surprised to receive a grandly produced extravagance including guest appearances by the 36-piece Ted Heath Orchestra, a five-member Arabian band, and stalwart session men Nicky Hopkins and John Paul Jones. "It was a pop album," says Cousins. "We were much more interested in the Beatles and the Bee Gees [than folk]. They said, 'Well, what's this crap?' 'Cause it was us being the Bee Gees, if you like. It was probably the third-most expensive album at the time ever produced in Britain, after the Beatles' *Sgt. Pepper* and the Bee Gees' big albums. Some of it is awful. Dreadful. There was an unappreciated tribute to [A&M co-founder] Herb Alpert on one of the songs." (Some tracks from the rejected LP appear on *Strawberry Music Sampler No. 1*, circulated to publishers in 1969 and issued on CD in 2001.)

"My early songs are very much pop songs," summarizes Cousins. "It was only when Donovan started to rise, I thought, 'Christ, if he can write, so can I.' Then I started to get into more of the folk-type imagery, if you like. It turned into much more ... for want of a word, gothic seems to suit it better. I've devised a different phrase for it now, which is baroque 'n' roll. Which is where things like 'Tears and Pavan' [from their 1973 album *Bursting at the Seams*] came from. I don't know of any other band that ever played anything like it. 'Cause it is medieval-sounding, and yet it's rock music."

Even back in a 1970 *Melody Maker* interview Cousins acknowledged, "I suppose my songs are old-fashioned, out of date, but then again they aren't. I don't deliberately set out to write a song to sound as though it were from some different age, it just comes out that way." His present-day reluctance to be classified as a folk musician to the contrary, he went on to state in the same piece, "I really want to write A FOLK SONG you know that people will be singing for 50 years or more. Or maybe pick it up in 50 years, and sing it as a folk song. For me that would be the ultimate achievement." Cousins differentiated the Strawbs from other British folk-rock groups, however, by pointing out that "we'll play every instrument we can. One minute we've got dulcimers and pianos and tablas, and the next something completely different . . . Fotheringay [Sandy Denny's early-'70s group] said we sounded great and all we needed was an electric guitarist and drummer. Great, but we would have sounded like everyone else." As an extension of their instrumental eclecticism, the Strawbs would move into a harder progressive rock sound in the 1970s, with Rick Wakeman playing keyboards for them prior to joining Yes, and ultimately have big British hits in 1972–73 with "Lay Down" and "Part of the Union."

The Strawbs' switch from acoustic music to rock was undoubtedly easier to navigate in light of their never having been strict traditional English folk musicians in the first place. Very few groups that had started their recording careers as purveyors of indigenous British Isles music followed a similar course, and if they did, they did so with trepidation. In Ireland, the Johnstons alternated straightforward acoustic treatments of folk songs with rather nice folk-pop covers of songs by Joni Mitchell, Leonard Cohen, Dave Cousins, Gordon Lightfoot, and the like. The use of rock instruments and pop orchestration was restrained to the point of daintiness. But those looking for an early Fairport Convention-lite could do worse than to check out their late-'60s Transatlantic albums *Give a Damn* and *Bitter Green*. The latter had an especially outstanding cover of Leonard Cohen's "The Story of Isaac," giving his dour original a bright, melodic sheen, much in the way Fairport Convention had made Cohen's "Suzanne" and "Bird on a Wire" far more engaging and palatable to pop ears. Two of the Johnstons, Paul Brady and Mick Moloney, subsequently went on to become two of the most internationally lauded Irish folk musicians as solo performers.

"Transatlantic's vision of us was to replace the Seekers, who had just broken up," says Moloney. "We were clean-cut, we were two fellows, two girls, you know? We were doing traditional material. The two sisters [Adrienne and Luci Johnston] had been doing material by Ewan MacColl, and were interested also in songs that sounded poppy, like Tom Paxton songs. [Brady and I] were more traditional, although Paul had a rock background. We would not have been part of the folk-rock movement, in the sense that we were playing acoustic instruments all the time. But when we started to perform together, we were interested in all different combinations of traditional and contemporary. Transatlantic decided to sign us with the idea that we would be a full poppy-type group, but could still continue playing traditional music—they had no problem with that.

"We went over to London with a sense of adventure. Transatlantic immediately started to expose us to new songwriters. They would inundate us with songs by songwriters who were to become very famous, like Joni Mitchell, Leonard Cohen, and Gordon Lightfoot." Moloney, in fact, remembers sifting through literally hundreds of such tapes. "We liked some of those songs, so we ended up saying, yeah, we'd do them. But from that moment onward, it seemed that a lot of the artistic control was out of our hands. We were very naive about it. We would record tracks with, say, a bass and drums, and we would go back two weeks later and hear a whole orchestral track that had been scored and recorded in our absence. We would have listened to the finished product with a sense of wonderment, almost like, 'Is this really us?'

"At the same time, we never vetoed anything either. So to be fair to Transatlantic, they came up with the notion, and we were a party to it, but a very naive party. It's only looking back with wiser heads that myself and Paul especially would look back and shake our heads and say, 'I wonder why we didn't exert more control there.' The orchestration has dated the songs, and made them experiments that didn't really work. Our version of 'Both Sides Now,' for instance, just categorically, is nowhere near as good as Judy Collins's version. We just didn't get inside the song. We were outside the material. I think, in the long run, it shows."

Although it's been virtually forgotten, the Johnstons had a brief opportunity to beat Judy Collins to the punch with an American hit cover of "Both Sides Now," which they also released as a single in 1968. "I personally thought their record was at least as good as Judy Collins's," claims Transatlantic's Nat Joseph, who had known the head of Collins's record label, Elektra's Jac Holzman, for years before both versions were released almost simultaneously. "Jac had this thing about breaking Judy Collins, and would have done anything to make sure she broke with something. 'Both Sides Now' came out first from the Johnstons [in the US], on a new label called Tetragrammaton, an independent with, supposedly, a lot of money and clout behind it from the publisher Artie Mogull. That started breaking, and we were all celebrating. And Jac rushed out the Judy Collins version, and at that point they had more bucks than Tetragrammaton. Jac completely outspent Tetragrammaton. We were all devastated, because we'd thought we'd got the jump on them by a couple of weeks, and all of a sudden, Judy was in the Top Ten.

"I'm not putting down her version; I've always respected her greatly as an artist. It was just a huge disappointment for us with the Johnstons, who went on to make a lot of very good records that were kind of medium sellers. But after that, the impetus seemed to have gone." Actually, the Johnstons' "Both Sides Now" made just #128 (for a week) in *Billboard*, by which time Collins's version had already entered the Top 100. More crucially, it wasn't nearly as magnificent or imaginative an interpretation. But as noted in the previous chapter, Holzman did later write that he moved quickly once he heard a version by a group across the Atlantic was in the offing.

"I thought that the future would be with a group like the Johnstons, adapting folk or ethnic music with more of a pop sound," says Joseph. "I think I was probably wrong. That was a development that I should have known wasn't going to make it that strongly. Because it was an artificial graft-on, rather than the natural folk-rock that came out through a lot of the American groups in particular. On the Johnstons' records, there's nothing unique. It was unusual, however, that you had solo instrumentals, solo unaccompanied voice, huge orchestral stuff, and small folk-rock things, all on one LP. One side of them was nearest to being potentially pop in America, although a lot of people said they were too like Peter, Paul & Mary, which curdled my blood.

"There were people, including me from time to time I will admit, who desperately had chart hunger. There was a dichotomy between the people who had chart hunger, and the other people who said, 'Look, there are these people who are also extremely talented at playing Irish instruments, or singing traditional songs, and they should have stuck to the same marketing strategy as we used with the Dubliners, who were basically an ethnic group.' We tried to do both, and didn't really totally succeed at either."

In hindsight Joseph sees that the British folk and pop climate was simply not as conducive to blending of the best of both worlds as the American music scene was: "I didn't think you were going to get many Pentangles. Fairport Convention, Steeleye Span—they came through naturally. But a lot of stuff went on around that core which wasn't really folk or folk-rock at all. You didn't have the same influence from country music as you had in the States. You didn't have, really, any parallel pop influence that you had in the States, that produced people like Neil Young who moved to what is now generally known as folk-rock. I think British folk-rock wasn't going to ape American folk-rock and be successful."

Joseph was correct that the more successful, or at least more distinctive, path for British folk-rock would lead away from imitation of American sources. For British musicians, this would come via a reappreciation of their country's own deepest folk roots. In this respect, though, they were again—if only unconsciously—lagging slightly behind their American counterparts, who were undergoing their own return to a basic indigenous form in the late '60s. And as with many of folk-rock's mutations, that path would be cleared by the Byrds and Bob Dylan. At the beginning of 1968, the most iconic of all singer-songwriters was finally returning after an 18-month absence to a music world that had seen many changes, but would once again find itself stood on its head by a new Dylan album.

5

the new dylan
and country-rock

he death of Woody Guthrie on October 3, 1967, after a long and agonizing deterioration at the hands of Huntington's chorea, was to many folk-rockers both a reminder of where they had come from, and an invitation to re-embrace those roots. Two benefit concerts, billed as a "Tribute to Woody Guthrie," for the Committee to Combat Huntington's Disease took place at Carnegie Hall on January 20, 1968. That gave some of the best of the old and new guards—including Judy Collins, Arlo Guthrie, Richie Havens, Tom Paxton, Odetta, Ramblin' Jack Elliott, and Pete Seeger—a chance to acknowledge their debt to a man who still cast a long shadow over all of folk and folk-rock music.

The events are most remembered, however, for the first concert appearance by Bob Dylan since his mid-1966 motorcycle accident. A very different-looking Dylan led the Band, still without an official name and still months away from the release of its debut album, through jaunty rock versions of three Guthrie songs (later released, as were other extracts from the shows, on the *Tribute to Woody Guthrie* compilation). "I thought it was great fun myself," says Paxton, who was sitting right next to Dylan and the Band as they performed onstage. "It wasn't as if he lost any sense of what Woody's songs were about."

The preceding 18 months had been a time of serious retreat and reassessment for Dylan, whose life with his new wife and growing family in Woodstock was so reclusive as to be almost invisible. Prior to a short, vague interview he gave reporter Michael Iachetta in May 1967 for a *New York Daily News* article, he had not talked to the media since the accident, lending more credence to rumors of his retirement or incapacitation. His punishing pace and lifestyle had been burning him out, and he was now content to sit out the psychedelic revolution, recharge his batteries, and change his priorities.

Part of that involved starting to distance himself from his manager Albert Grossman, and sorting out his recording contract, re-signing with Columbia on July 1 after fielding another tempting offer. "I went up to Woodstock one day, and he showed me a million-dollar check he had from

MGM," says his producer of the time, Bob Johnston. "He said, 'You want to come to MGM, do all this?' I said, 'No, I got too many artists [at Columbia], and I don't want to leave that, because MGM, they're kind of out-the-back-door people anyway.' And he said, 'Oh, really?' And he put it back up on the mantle, and that's the last I ever heard, he never went to MGM. I don't think it was because of me. I think he just decided he didn't want to go. He sat up there with a million-dollar check on his mantle, which would be about $20 million today." It was a trophy, perhaps, of just how badly the industry wanted him to get back on the playing field.

ylan, unbeknownst to all but a few, *was* writing and recording in 1967, in fact at a highly pro-lific rate. With the Hawks—the group that had backed him on his 1966 world tour and had yet to be renamed the Band (although drummer Levon Helm didn't rejoin until November 1967)—he was making home recordings of more than 100 songs, including both originals and covers. This is the material that has come to be known, and canonized, as the Basement Tapes, largely recorded in the basement of a house, nicknamed "Big Pink," that the Hawks were renting near Woodstock. The songs that emerged on the 1975 double album *The Basement Tapes*, mingled with some Dylan-less Band cuts (some overdubbed or wholly recorded in '75), represent but a fraction of what the musicians recorded together in mid-to-late 1967. The actual circumstances under which the tapes were cut, and what their purpose was, are still shrouded in some mystery.

What's more important is how the tapes show Dylan's excavation into his deepest roots, often predating the birth of rock 'n' roll, for his latest fit of inspiration. He referred to those roots in a

Bob Dylan with the Band at the "Tribute to Woody Guthrie" concert on January 20, 1968. Left to right: Rick Danko, Bob Dylan, and Robbie Robertson.

mid-1968 interview with *Sing Out!*, where he cited Scrapper Blackwell, Leroy Carr, Jack Dupree, Lonnie Johnson, Jelly Roll Morton, Buddy Bolden, Ian & Sylvia, Tom Rush, Charley Pride, Porter Wagoner, and the Clancy Brothers as some of his then-current faves—all names that, with a couple exceptions, would have been unfamiliar to all but a handful of rock enthusiasts in 1968. The covers that have shown up on the mammoth five-volume bootleg series *The Genuine Basement Tapes* are a further testament to the deep reservoir of Americana that Dylan and the Band were exploring, whether for kicks or for other unknown reasons. There were songs that had been done by Ian & Sylvia, Johnny Cash, and Elvis Presley, "The Bells of Rhymney," and traditional folk numbers that would have been extremely obscure even when Dylan was making trad folk the basis of his setlist in 1961.

More notable, though, were Dylan's own songs. Whether incited by his brush with serious injury on his motorcycle or not (although "This Wheel's on Fire" certainly seems to allude to it), they often had the feeling of a man who has faced down his inner demons and crossed to the other side of a particularly treacherous canyon. "I Shall Be Released," "Tears of Rage," "Nothing Was Delivered," and "Too Much of Nothing" all had the aura of Biblical mountaintop sermons. But at other times there was merely the sense of a man, relieved of especially onerous burdens, letting loose and enjoying himself, as on "The Mighty Quinn" and "Million Dollar Bash." The Band fleshed out the compositions with empathetic, ensemble interplay that drew heavily on gospel-like vocals, organ, and piano, as well as rousing choruses.

It wasn't long before some of these songs started to get released, but only via covers. Indeed, hitting the studio with unreleased Dylan songs from this cache became something of a cottage industry for a year or two. Peter, Paul & Mary were first off the mark, putting out "Too Much of Nothing" as a November 1967 single, followed by Manfred Mann's terrific hit cover of "The Mighty Quinn." Julie Driscoll, Brian Auger & the Trinity made the British Top Five with "This Wheel's on Fire"; the Byrds did "You Ain't Going Nowhere" and "Nothing Was Delivered" on their 1968 album *Sweetheart of the Rodeo*; Fairport Convention did "Million Dollar Bash"; Ian & Sylvia did "Tears of Rage." The Band did "I Shall Be Released" and a couple of others on their debut album. Flatt & Scruggs even took a shot, with "Down in the Flood." Coulson, Dean, McGuinness & Flint, with ex–Manfred Mann bassist Tom McGuinness, put no less than seven *Basement Tapes* covers on their 1972 album of obscure Dylan songs, *Lo and Behold*.

The availability of this material, even as heard by interpreters, couldn't help but fuel demand for the originals. If the circulation of cover versions wasn't enough, *Rolling Stone* editor Jann Wenner stoked the fire with a page-one article in June 1968 headlined "Dylan's Basement Tape [sic] Should Be Released," containing extensive rundowns on the most prominent songs to arise from the sessions. The demand was met, though in a tatty fashion, in 1969 by *Great White Wonder*, the first popular rock bootleg. The double LP cobbled together seven of the more notable Basement Tapes tracks with various other unreleased '60s Dylan performances, some dating back to 1961.

Conspiracy theorists have wondered whether the trickle of Basement Tapes bootlegs was Dylan's own way of helping to build a mystique around the sessions. But there seems little doubt that at least at the outset, he wasn't intending the tapes for public consumption (although presumably he had no issues with making some demos available to other artists, whose cover versions were a nice source of publishing income). In late 1969, Columbia even announced its intention to take legal action against *Great White Wonder*, huffing in *The New York Times*, "We consider this record an abuse of the integrity of a great artist. They are at one time defaming the artist and defrauding his admirers." At the end of the year, *Rolling Stone* reported that Dylan was suing a Vancouver pressing plant for manufacturing the LP. (Dylan wasn't the only folk-rock star to tussle with the pirates, with Atlantic Records filing suit against retailers and the manufacturer for selling a bootleg of 1969 Crosby, Stills, Nash & Young live material, *Wooden Nickel*; Neil Young would slag it as "a capitalist ripoff" at one of his concerts.)

Ultimately, however, the distribution of *Great White Wonder* proved mostly unstoppable. A never-ending stream of other Basement Tapes followed, both in the late '60s and through the following decades. The hunger for unreleased Dylan material was so insatiable by 1970 that producer Bob Johnston told *Melody Maker* he'd had all his tapes moved from New York to a vault in Nashville. "A lot of Dylan's material we're recording I'm destroying because I don't want things to get out," he added.

When it finally came time to cut his much-anticipated follow-up to *Blonde on Blonde*, though, Dylan opted not to record any of the Basement Tapes songs in a proper studio, or even to use the Band. Instead he wrote an entirely new set of a dozen songs for *John Wesley Harding*, all cut in a mere three days of sessions in October and November 1967 in Nashville. *Blonde on Blonde* veterans Charlie McCoy (on bass) and Kenneth Buttrey (on drums) were the only musicians to back Dylan's guitar and harmonica, although Pete Drake added steel guitar on a couple tracks. In 1969, Robbie Robertson would tell *Rolling Stone* that Dylan had asked him to add lead guitar, and Garth Hudson to add organ, after recording half of the album, an offer which they declined.

In his 1969 *Rolling Stone* interview, Dylan cited Gordon Lightfoot's 1967 LP *The Way I Feel*, also recorded in Nashville with the participation of McCoy and Buttrey, as the inspiration for his decision to record there with the same players. "I'd used Charlie and Kenny both before, and I figured if he could get that sound, I could. But we couldn't get it," laughed Dylan. "It was an attempt to get it, but it didn't come off. We got a different sound . . . I don't know what you'd call that . . . it's a muffled sound." (Ironically, according to producer Elliott Mazer, when Lightfoot returned to Music City in September 1968 to cut *Back Here on Earth*, "We had booked Charlie McCoy and Kenny Buttrey and when we got to Nashville, Gord decided to cancel them. We paid them anyway.") "I didn't want to record that album," claimed Dylan of *John Wesley Harding* in *NME*. "I was going to do an album of other people's songs, but there weren't enough of the right quality."

The album was cut in much the same expedient haste as it was written, remembers McCoy. "The whole *Blonde on Blonde* experience, I felt like he was maybe just a little uncomfortable. But the next time he came back, for *John Wesley Harding*, he was like a different person. I noticed a really marked difference in his whole demeanor the second time around." Dylan was more relaxed, and though he'd always charged through his sessions with the patience of a bull in a china shop, on *John Wesley Harding* he outdid himself. "We did *John Wesley Harding* in nine-and-a-half hours, the whole record!" McCoy exclaims. But "it wasn't [quick] for normal Nashville country music. For us that were used to the four songs a session, we thought, 'How in the world can these people [like the Beatles] spend this much time?' We couldn't identify with these monstrous recording budgets, because *nobody* in Nashville at the time had a monstrous recording budget."

Although they had been cut with lightning speed, the songs on *John Wesley Harding* were extremely well crafted. As many have noted, the LP was packed with Biblical references, Dylan's crazed surrealism and yelping vocals receding under stern, concise lyrics (oddly devoid of choruses) and far more restrained, calmer singing. Although not lacking some tension, the record was extremely subdued, as if the singer and musicians were consciously keeping their emotions and energies in check. Occasional tracks like "All Along the Watchtower" (the album's standout, totally reworked into a hard rock hit single by Jimi Hendrix) and "As I Went Out One Morning" had interesting minor-key progressions and a hint of urgency to the rhythms. But overall it was melodically basic, even bland, with an evenness to the strumming that reconnected Dylan's music with his just-fallen icon Woody Guthrie.

"I was always with the traditional song," Dylan responded when *Newsweek*'s Hubert Saal asked him about his return to an acoustic guitar-and-harmonica-driven sound shortly after the album's release. "I just used electricity to wrap it up in. Possibly I wasn't ready yet to make it simple. It's more complicated playing an electric guitar because you're five or ten feet away from the sound and you strain for things that you don't have to when the sound is right next to your body. Anyway it's the song itself that matters, not the sound of the song."

ven at the time, *John Wesley Harding* was hailed as a "pull out the plug" antidote to electronic, psychedelic, and spiritual excess as more and more cosmic trickery enveloped contemporary rock. Dylan went on record as criticizing the most acclaimed album of 1967, the Beatles' *Sgt. Pepper's Lonely Hearts Club Band*, as unnecessarily overproduced. To reduce *John Wesley Harding* to a conscious jolt that brought rock back to its senses, though, is an oversimplification. Dylan was working within his own limitations; he lacked the studio know-how or electronic ambition to make a *Sgt. Pepper*, or even an "Eight Miles High." *John Wesley Harding* is not so much an indictment of the overindulgent reach of psychedelia as it is a reaffirmation of Dylan's love for earthy, basic folk and country music. The country component of his sound was more to the fore on *John Wesley Harding* than it had ever been. It was the first widely acknowledged landmark in a new genre, country-rock, that was largely rooted in the folk-rock of the mid-'60s.

Dating the exact origination of this folk-rock subgenre is—like finding the one person responsible for coining the folk-rock and singer-songwriter appellations—impossible. Certainly critics were starting to think along those lines by the time Jon Landau wrote a full-page piece in *Rolling Stone* in September 1968 titled "Country & Rock" (sans hyphen), focusing exclusively on the country-leaning rock of the Byrds and Buffalo Springfield. Poco was referred to as a country-rock group in a May 1969 concert review in *Billboard*, and country-rock had definitely become a label by the time the headline "The New Sound of Country Rock" was plastered on the cover of the January 12, 1970 issue of *Time*, although the article centered around the not-wholly-country-rock emissaries the Band.

During this time, it's sometimes been forgotten, there was also a sort of "pop-folk-country-rock fusion," as Robert Shelton termed it in a late-1968 *New York Times* article, when artists like Bobbie Gentry, Glen Campbell, Johnny Cash, and John Hartford had some mainstream success with blends that could be heavier on country and pop than folk and rock. RCA Nashville in particular got on a folk-country kick aimed at the mainstream market with records by George Hamilton IV, Hartford, Bobby Bare, and Waylon Jennings, putting a "Folk Country" logo on Hamilton IV's *Folksy* album (with his country hit cover of Joni Mitchell's "Urge for Going"), and issuing a record actually titled *Folk Country* by Jennings in 1966. Hamilton IV and Hartford even appeared at the 1968 Newport Folk Festival, although ultimately this sort of music was not only too mild to qualify as folk-rock, but also only mildly influential on the popular music mainstream. Socially conscious and creative folk-rock singer-songwriters, however, could certainly identify with the thought-provoking ambitions of a song like the classic chart-topper "Ode to Billie Joe" by Gentry, who told *Newsweek*, "I use the story as a vehicle to point up indifference. The tragic event is discussed at the dinner table where Billie's suicide is no more important than passing the black-eyed peas."

You can also get carried away and find strong strains of country-rock (as you can with folk-rock) dating back to the beginning of rock itself, when Elvis Presley and many others mixed country with R&B to produce rockabilly. The specific country-rock style of the late '60s and early '70s, however, largely grew out of mid-'60s folk-rock. And even more so than mid-'60s folk-rock, the country-rock movement would be centered in Southern California. As in several other crucial phases of folk-rock's development, the Byrds were at the forefront of its incubation.

The group's *Sweetheart of the Rodeo* stunned listeners in the summer of 1968 who had been expecting another Roger McGuinn–captained test of folk-rock-psychedelia's outer limits. Instead they heard a modest country-rock record, largely bereft of the dense electric 12-string chime that had been the group's single most defining characteristic. Much of the record's country influence has been ascribed to the input of newcomer Gram Parsons. But it's vital to point out that country music had always been an ingredient in the band's mix, particularly its harmonies, but also in some of its material. On their second album, the Byrds covered mainstream country star Porter Wagoner's moralistic homily "A Satisfied Mind," and on *Fifth Dimension*, McGuinn's "Mr. Spaceman" had put a goofy cosmic twist on country-folk-bluegrass. Coming from a bluegrass background, Chris Hillman had the strongest affinity for country of anyone in the Byrds. Two of his songs on 1967's *Younger Than Yesterday*, "Time Between" and "The Girl with No Name," were country-rock before the term had been devised, with a bluegrass lilt to the harmonies and tempos, and solos by guest guitarist Clarence White, who earned his stars in the bluegrass band the Kentucky Colonels. White was also heard on one of the highlights on *The Notorious Byrd Brothers*, "Wasn't Born to Follow."

For the Byrds' follow-up to *The Notorious Byrd Brothers*, McGuinn had planned an ambitious double album that would, in five chronological parts, cover the entire history of twentieth-century popular music, from the most traditional folk, country, and bluegrass to the latest in electronic gadgetry. A small sampling of what the final leg of that journey might have sounded like, the outtake "Moog Raga," was eventually issued more than 20 years later. There was no rock *or* country in this instrumental experiment by McGuinn to fuse Indian ragas with the latest (although it now sounds primitive) in synthesizer technology. His double-album dream would be unfulfilled, however, as both Hillman and David Crosby's replacement, Gram Parsons, lobbied successfully for an all-out country album.

"That was more Roger's deal," says Hillman of tracks like "Moog Raga" and *Younger Than Yesterday*'s "C.T.A.-102," which had matched another proto-country-rock track with weird electronic simulations of space alien voices. "I would play on it, but it wasn't something I was involved in, other than as the bass player. He had that side of him, musically, that was not my style of music. It really wasn't something that I loved that much. But I was a player, and that's his piece of material, so I supported it. But I sort of dragged him into the country stuff, so it works both ways. And he performed quite well with that [country] stuff."

Hillman, unlike McGuinn, has no regrets that the double-album history of twentieth-century music never happened. "With all due respect, I didn't want a bunch of 'C.T.A.-102's or 'Moog Raga' or whatever that stuff is. He had that Moog synthesizer; then, it was like owning a computer in 1955. It took up the whole room. It made a lot of noise. It wasn't really musical. It was like a toy, a gadget. But it was interesting. I respect him; he was following something that intrigued him, and he likes electronics.

"It didn't work for me, and I'm glad it didn't happen. 'Cause it would have made no sense at all. Although there weren't that many strong parameters then; you could sort of do those kind of projects, record company budget willing, on that end. But to put the two of them [traditional and electronic styles] together would have been a little crazy. It would have been an interesting separate project, but either I didn't understand what he was doing, or I just didn't like it. I'm glad we did the *Sweetheart* as it was."

"I couldn't get anybody to support me on that," acknowledges McGuinn. "Chris was behind Gram, and Gram wanted to do straight country, and that was it. It would have been fun if we could have pulled it off. I agree it was extremely ambitious, and it's almost doubtful that we could have done it. But I would love to have tried, at that time. Basically, we *did* do it, not just in one album, but in a series of albums. We've done old-time music, and almost every genre you can think of."

Parsons's influence over the Byrds during what was actually a short stint in the band (lasting less than six months) has been overestimated, and the impression some accounts have given of a country musician virtually hijacking the Byrds' plane is not quite accurate. Parsons, like most folk-rock musicians, was primarily tutored in rock and folk, not in country. As a teenager, he'd played rock 'n' roll in the Legends with Lobo and Jim Stafford. He then tried his hand at folk for a while, making some demos (issued only posthumously, in the 1970s) in March 1965 with the folk group the Shilos. Solo acoustic demos from 1965 and 1966, recently unearthed for the *Another Side of This Life* compilation, reveal a competent but ordinary coffeehouse folk singer, Parsons's repertoire mixing traditional material, the odd original, and covers of songs by Fred Neil, Buffy Sainte-Marie, Tim Hardin, Billy Wheeler ("High Flyin' Bird") and Hamilton Camp ("Pride of Man").

After briefly attending Harvard, Parsons formed the International Submarine Band in Boston, which soon moved to New York. The band was one of countless acts to get lost in the Columbia shuffle, its sole single for the label passing into instant rarity. One side of that 45, "One Day Week," finds country-rock and even folk-rock far from Parsons's mind, sounding far more like the Dave Clark Five than the Byrds. One side of their only other single (for Ascot), the Dave Dudley–meets–rock of "Truck Drivin' Man," was far more indicative of a growing immersion in country music.

By 1967 the International Submarine Band was in Los Angeles, recording its only album, *Safe at Home*, for producer Lee Hazlewood's LHI label. This has occasionally been pinpointed as the first all-out country-rock album, a title that's highly questionable. As heard on this LP, the band was more a straight country band in the Merle Haggard style—and not a particularly exciting one—than a blender of the best of country and rock, in the manner the Byrds had fused the best of folk and rock. The band's, and particularly Parsons's, contributions were that it presented country music played by musicians who *looked* like rock musicians, like hippie rock musicians even. By the time *Safe at Home* came out, Parsons had joined the Byrds, coming to Hillman's attention as a result of sharing the same manager at the time, Larry Spector.

"Being with the Byrds confused me a little," Parsons admitted in 1970 to *Melody Maker*. "I couldn't find my place. I didn't have enough say so; I really wasn't one of the Byrds, I was originally hired because they wanted a keyboard player. But I had had experience being a front man and that came out immediately. And Roger (McGuinn) being a very perceptive fellow saw that it would help the act and he started sticking me out front."

Whether an experienced band led by a very established singer-songwriting guitarist who was a star in his own right was really looking for a frontman, or seriously thinking of using Parsons as a keyboard player rather than a singing guitarist, is highly debatable. But McGuinn and the Byrds, for all their infighting, had always been good at spotting and highlighting the strengths of their individual members while integrating them within a team framework that never let any one musician overshadow the others. "I'm a country musician by upbringing, and I used to write little songs in that vein for the band, but the rest of the band always shouted me down," Hillman told *Melody Maker*. "Then Gram joined and I had an ally, so we managed to turn Roger's head toward our kind of music."

Nonetheless, Parsons's tenure in the Byrds was short and not so sweet. A conservatively shorn band (with Hillman's cousin, and ex–Rising Son, Kevin Kelley on drums) played as a country-oriented act at the Grand Ole Opry on March 15, 1968, shortly after Parsons joined. It was a breakthrough as the notoriously old-fashioned Opry was reluctant to feature a rock group, and Parsons dampened the occasion somewhat by deviating from a plan to sing two Merle Haggard songs. Although he did sing the first of the pair, he then led the band through a spur-of-the-moment substitution of one of his own compositions, "Hickory Wind" (actually written with former New Christy Minstrel Bob Buchanan), which axed any prospects of a return visit. Still, the new incarnation of the Byrds was well received in concert, where their country direction was solidified by nonmembers Jay Dee Maness on pedal steel and Doug Dillard on banjo.

For the *Sweetheart of the Rodeo* album (recorded in both Los Angeles and Nashville), the Byrds did offer one typical feature: two Bob Dylan songs, both from his Basement Tapes ("You Ain't Going Nowhere" and "Nothing Was Delivered"). Otherwise the Byrds were getting more traditional, and more country, than they'd ever been, with covers of the Louvin Brothers' "The Christian Life," Woody

Guthrie's "Pretty Boy Floyd," Gene Autry's "Blue Canadian Rockies," Merle Haggard's "Life in Prison," William Bell's country-soul classic "You Don't Miss Your Water," and Parsons's own "Hickory Wind" and "One Hundred Years from Now." McGuinn incurred Parsons's wrath by re-recording some vocal tracks, substituting his lead vocals for those of Parsons, when LHI (to which Parsons was still under contract) threatened to sue Columbia. After all that, a couple of lead vocals by Gram did end up on *Sweetheart of the Rodeo*, and in the 1990s some versions of the album's songs with Parsons's original vocals surfaced on CD.

Although critically acclaimed, the record was not as much of an innovative accomplishment as any of the Byrds' previous albums. The idea was certainly fresh, but the execution was more competent than exciting, lacking the risk and variety that had typified the group's previous realizations of McGuinn's concepts of albums as electronic magazines. "It wasn't my favorite Byrd record," reflects Hillman. "But as far as a legacy, it opened the door for so many people who got into country music, or started to discover country music, through that album. All the controversy over Gram's vocals or Roger's vocals . . . some of Gram's vocals that we didn't use weren't as good as people think they were. Roger might have gone a little overboard on 'Christian Life.' I think he was an actor, he was doing a part, he just was overacting on the accent a bit. But it's okay, it worked out alright. I think there's a lot of good things on there."

While Parsons and Hillman were instrumental in steering the Byrds into country music, McGuinn was a willing passenger. "It's a departure for the Byrds, but not a departure from my music," he emphasized in a lengthy interview he gave John Cohen of the New Lost City Ramblers for *Sing Out!* at the time of the LP's release. "I was interested in this kind of music ten years ago." *Sweetheart of the Rodeo* was also consistent with the eclectic flight pattern that had been even more of a compass to the Byrds' aesthetic than the 12-string guitar. "You have to keep moving or you're a sitting duck," he noted tersely in *Melody Maker*.

"It was something in the air, almost like the earth was passing through a cloud," says McGuinn of the nearly coincident moves of the Byrds, Dylan, and some other folk-rock vets into country-rock. "I think it was a direct result of psychedelia, the sort of chaotic . . . the noisiness of it. People wanted to return to—this is, I believe, subconscious—but they wanted to return to a simplicity that country music presented, with basically three-chord songs and melodies and stories, as opposed to the, you know"—here he breaks off to mimic an acid rock guitar solo. "You can only do that so long before you get tired of it, like anything else. It was a simultaneous thing that Dylan was doing, and we didn't have contact with him at that point. We had no idea he was going there. I'm sure he wasn't influenced by us at that point, when he was doing *John Wesley Harding*."

It was a course the Byrds would follow to some degree, but without Hillman or Parsons. After completing a British tour, Parsons left the Byrds, without prior notice, on the eve of a South African tour in the summer of 1968, saying he objected to playing in a country still under apartheid rule. Hillman has said that he believes this was more an excuse for Parsons not to make an arduous trip, enabling him to stay in London to hang with his new buddies in the Rolling Stones. The group was left to struggle through a semi-disastrous and controversial jaunt across South Africa, using one of its roadies to fill in for Gram. Parsons was replaced with Clarence White as soon as the group returned to the US, but only a couple months later, Hillman left. McGuinn was now the only remaining original member of the group he had co-founded less than five years before.

White, along with some other musicians, had been making some obscure forays into primordial country-rock that played a vastly overlooked role in creating the kind of sound associated with the Byrds/Flying Burrito Brothers axis in the late '60s. For one or two years before joining the Byrds, he'd been gigging and recording with drummer Gene Parsons (no relation to Gram, he could also play an assortment of instruments), guitarist-fiddler Gib Guilbeau, and bassist Wayne Moore in a loose aggregation that eventually came to be known as Nashville West. Unlike the others, White had been a big name in the folk world as the virtuosic guitarist in one of the most respected mid-'60s bluegrass bands, the Kentucky Colonels. Like many of the folk and country musicians to play significant parts in folk-rock, he shared with the Byrds an association with Jim Dickson, who had approached White about recording "Mr. Tambourine Man" before suggesting it to McGuinn's group.

Respect did not translate to cash, and White's switch to electric music was motivated, as it had been for several important folk-rockers, by sink-or-swim financial straits as well as personal taste. As Gene Parsons remembers, when he first met Clarence around 1965, White "had just decided to start playing electric guitar, much to the dismay of his bluegrass family, initially. He realized that he wasn't gonna be able to raise a family and make enough money to get along on what he was able to make in bluegrass at that point. James Burton [the great rock session guitarist, most known for his work on hits by Ricky Nelson] took him under his wing. When I first met him, he still used a capo on the electric guitar. He hadn't been playing it that long."

White did most of his bluegrass work in open tuning with a capo, and if it seemed naive of him to use it on an electric guitar, it should be noted that Roger McGuinn had done the same thing when he first started playing his electric 12-string Rickenbacker. Advised to remove the capo by Dickson, McGuinn had done so and figured out how to play the new scales in every key in a week or two. Likewise White, according to Parsons, threw his capo away within a couple weeks, and took to his new electric "like a duck to water. It seemed like the Telecaster was made for Clarence White."

Over the next two or three years, White, Parsons, Guilbeau, and Moore would record, sometimes with other musicians and in various combinations, a bewilderingly large and scattered body of virtually unheard singles and albums in Southern California. Often produced by Gary Paxton, and often released on Paxton's Bakersfield International label (and sometimes on others, including Capitol), these recordings form one of the most significant but poorly lit corners of the entire 1960s folk-rock discography. Paxton, since landing a fluke #1 novelty record in 1960 as the singer on the Hollywood Argyles' "Alley Oop," had beavered away at the margins of the rock and pop world ever since. In Parsons's view, "Because he was so musical and such an artist in his own right, a lot of the business just escaped him." Partially because of that, barely anyone got to hear many of those early records with White and Parsons.

On these rare recordings (some still unreleased), an unusual and sometimes off-the-wall blend of country, folk, rock, and pop was coalescing, sometimes when the musicians were employed as session men backing up no-names like Richard Arlen, Dennis Payne, and Darrell Cotton. Guilbeau and Moore had already tried their hand at a Peter & Gordon–like folk-rock sound in the mid-'60s (as Gib & Wayne) on "World of Dreams." They, White, and Parsons used their studio work as opportunities to blend winsome, low-key folk-country-rock with weird touches like mellotron (on the Gosdin Brothers' "There Must Be Someone," which the Byrds would cover after White and Parsons joined them), electric sitar, marimbas, and guitars fed through a Leslie speaker for a whirling effect. Guilbeau's LP *Authentic Cajun Songs By Gil Guilbeau* had a Cajun-folk-rock blend heard nowhere else in California. The Spencers' 1968 single "Make Up Your Mind," fronted by an unremarkable husband-wife vocal duo, was backed by goofy Byrdsy cosmic acoustic/electric country-rock with overheated fuzz guitar that reverbed into the stratosphere on the fade. Gram (not Gene) Parsons is the figure most often cited as an avatar of "cosmic American music," a term he dreamed up on his own for the kind of country-rock he played, but the Flying Burrito Brothers and the country-rock incarnation of the Byrds didn't spring out of nowhere. Much of the same flavor can be found in the disperse body of pre-1969 White-Parsons-Guilbeau-Moore sessions, if in embryo.

"I was coming from a folk background, Clarence from a bluegrass background, Gib from a Cajun background, and Wayne from a bluegrass and country background," remarks Gene Parsons. "We were taking some different ingredients and mixing 'em where they might not have been mixed before. I think if anyone in the bunch of us was responsible for any permanent changes in world music, it would have been Clarence. The way that he played guitar was absolutely revolutionary."

It became even more revolutionary when White and Parsons innovated a true country-rock guitar tone with the stringbender. Combining properties of the rock electric with the pedal steel, the device was invented by Parsons when he and White were working together in their gigging band. Initially they were called the Reasons or the Wonderful Reasons, and eventually they were referred to as Nashville West, after the club where they became the house band (though apparently they never billed themselves by that name while they were an active unit). The stringbender, actuated by a shoulder strap and placed inside the guitar itself, enabled White to coax a pedal steel sound from an electric six-string guitar. In 1968 Parsons, White, and original Byrds co-manager Eddie Tickner even patented the device, which Parsons continues to custom-install for guitarists today. "I don't consider it to be an effect; I consider it to be an actual instrument," claims Parsons. "A lot of people tried to emulate that stringbender sound, and didn't even realize there was a stringbender being used."

Nashville West never did release anything during its short lifetime. Pleasant live country-rock recordings of the group were eventually issued in the late '70s, although these were, as Parsons puts it, "simply to document Clarence's guitar playing before a stringbender." They also give a rather distorted picture of the band, focusing more on its instrumental chops than its vocals. Had the musicians been able to record a proper studio album, Parsons believes it might have sounded rather like the Gosdin Brothers' 1968 country-rock LP *Sounds of Goodbye*, on which he and Guilbeau played. But rock musicians, including some in the Byrds, were checking out the band live, where, as Parsons says, "They heard country songs played with extra rhythm. Clarence would lay down this incredible rhythm on the guitar and do all these wonderful embellishments around it that no one else has done, and the rhythm section was going right along with him. So it was more than just boom-chuck boom-chuck, or boom-ba-boom, boom-ba-boom. He was doing added notes, chords, runs and stuff, not just to be doing added stuff, but this whole other realm of expression people hadn't heard before. They would sit with their mouths hanging open and watch Clarence play, and listen to the band." It wasn't long before White and Parsons made the leap from the bandstand to the band of the most illustrious members of the audience, the Byrds.

Although McGuinn did say in a *Sing Out!* interview just after *Sweetheart of the Rodeo* that "our next album is going to be all electronic music," that project remained unrealized. Gene Parsons came into the Byrds alongside White, guaranteeing that the group would continue to play with a country slant, which pleased McGuinn: "I wanted to harness that energy they had and keep going in that direction. They loved the stuff, and I was having fun with it." Parsons has recalled that he, White, Guilbeau, and Gram Parsons recorded two or three songs at sessions while this rapid game of musical chairs was at its most transitional, though ultimately he and White threw in their lot with the Byrds.

Hillman was replaced by John York almost immediately after Gene Parsons joined; indeed, Chris smashed his bass on the floor and quit after Gene's very first show. Had Hillman stayed, speculates Parsons, "I think it would have gone in the direction the Burritos ultimately went. Which was very, very country, or what we thought was very country in our own West Coast sort of younger-than-a-lot-of-the-musicians-in-Nashville kind of way. Chris was really into Jerry Lee Lewis, and trying to sing like Jerry Lee Lewis; Jerry Lee Lewis was just coming out and singing country at this point [in 1968, the former rockabilly singer had launched a comeback as a mainstream country star with the single 'What Made Milwaukee Famous']. I think one of the reasons Chris was so anxious to get out of the Byrds and go with Gram is because I don't think Roger was capable of being *really* country. And, you know, they'd been in the group long enough together. There was a lot of problems."

Nonetheless, Hillman's departure marked the end of the Byrds as a major force in rock music. McGuinn may have been the pilot of the band, acknowledged by Gene Parsons as "the stabilizing force all the way through with his 12-string, the glue that kept that whole thing going." But at the same time it was very much a unit on its great 1964–68 recordings. All those personnel changes couldn't help but take their toll. None of the various additional musicians who flitted in and out of the band over the next five years were, with the possible exception of White, as creative or aligned with McGuinn's vision as were the original Byrds. They made some intermittently good music, country-rock or otherwise, on their final albums, usually when McGuinn was at the fore. Sometimes they came up with outstanding tracks, like "Jesus Is Just Alright," "Chestnut Mare," and "Drug Store Truck Drivin' Man" (co-written by McGuinn and Gram Parsons, recorded after Gram's departure, and performed by Joan Baez on the *Woodstock* soundtrack). But McGuinn was not an especially prolific or consistent songwriter. The shortage of first-rate material from his colleagues, or of the dynamic friction with David Crosby, Gene Clark, and Chris Hillman that had sparked the Byrds' greatest achievements, consigned many of their later recordings to journeyman rank.

Ironically, as their live work had always been considered their Achilles' heel, they were at their best onstage, developing into a consistent, accomplished concert attraction and putting some of the best post-Hillman Byrds recordings on the live portion of their 1970 *(Untitled)* album. "The road managers told us, 'Wow, this is a real band. This is fantastic,'" enthuses Gene Parsons. "Not to belittle what the other guys did, because they hadn't had the experience that we'd had, playing in bars night after night after night. They brought their own magic to the first group. But live, the general comment was, 'You sound much more together than the original band.' At least the technical playing part of it. Some of the best playing I ever heard of Clarence's was far and away better than anything that was recorded." Better, he agrees, than the tentative tracks unearthed for the 2000 CD *Live at the Fillmore February 1969*, which was actually never intended for release, and taped as a sort of soundcheck for a live album Columbia was recording of the bill's headliners.

The Byrds' later country-rock outings were outshone by the group that Hillman and Gram Parsons founded in late 1968, the Flying Burrito Brothers. As with *Sweetheart of the Rodeo*, there was really more country than rock in their debut, 1969's *The Gilded Palace of Sin*. While it has sometimes been hailed as a breakthrough meeting of the hardcore country of George Jones and Merle Haggard with a hippie rock aesthetic, in reality it was freaky only in relation to mainstream country music's rigid, narrow conservatism. At its core, it was solid country music, most of it from the pens of Hillman and Parsons, with a greater flexibility and unpredictability than Nashville or Bakersfield permitted, due no doubt in part to some of the musicians' rock experience. Sneaky Pete Kleinow's pedal steel was used as a lead instrument, but with a fuzztone that added some rock recklessness. The two covers, of the soul songs "Do Right Woman" and "Dark End of the Street," did R&B with country feeling. Lyrically Hillman and Parsons reflected the counterculture they were still, somewhat, a part of, as "My Uncle" was inspired by Parsons's draft notice; "Sin City" by Hillman's disillusionment with the seedy L.A. music business; and "Christine's Tune" by a member of the infamous conglomeration of rock super-groupies, the GTO's. "Hippie Boy" was a poke at both hippies and the religious sanctimony common to many country warblers. "Hot Burrito #1" remains the best-known showcase for Parsons's vocals, limited in power but exuding boyish earnestness.

"In the Burritos, when Gram was a coherent guy—I mean when we first started working together, before I lost him—we had this wonderful vision," says Hillman. "We were sharing the house together, had both come off a couple of unpleasant relationships, and took solace in each other as friends. But we also wrote some great songs. It was like I was starting over. I was hungry again. And I don't think I could have gotten to that place, staying in the Byrds. Although in hindsight, I regret not working with Clarence a little more, 'cause he was an old friend from the bluegrass days. The Burritos had a whole other insight into the thing, which was really quite interesting at the time. A lot of it was Gram's vision, which is good. But he got me thinking a little harder on what I was doing, and it was *really* good.

"That first album was great, the first year was great, and like I say, I lost him. Lost him to all the indulgent fantasies that he was going after, and that's where it ends. He had talent, not any more than anybody else, and he had a lot of charm. But he just got taken by all of the trappings that didn't mean anything." Parsons did stick around for a second, less impressive album, *Burrito Deluxe*, which included a cover of Mick Jagger and Keith Richards's "Wild Horses" that predated the Rolling Stones' own release of the song (the Stones had originally sent it Gram's way in hopes that he could get Sneaky Pete Kleinow to put steel guitar on the track). The Burritos introduced yet another ex-Byrd into the lineup when Michael Clarke took over the drum seat from Jon Corneal, as well as adding future Eagle Bernie Leadon on guitar. Parsons was let go in spring 1970 after skipping rehearsals and shows, pursuing an erratic recording career (and indulging in some of his fantasies by hanging out with Keith Richards) for a few more years before dying of drug- and alcohol-related complications in 1973.

Just as the Byrds had spawned one of country-rock's most notable groups, so did the second-greatest of the Los Angeles folk-rock bands, Buffalo Springfield. Richie Furay had been simultaneously finding himself as a composer and crawling onto the country-rock juggernaut on the Springfield's final album, *Last Time Around*, on which he wrote and sang the country-rock classic "Kind Woman." That cut had been graced by the pedal steel of Rusty Young, and co-produced by Jim Messina, who had joined Buffalo Springfield in its dying days as bassist. Furay and Messina were the members most responsible for touching up *Last Time Around* for release, and together with Young founded Pogo. (The band later changed their name to Poco, after feeling pressure from cartoonist Walt Kelly, creator of Pogo, the worldly-wise opossum.) The new group would allow both Furay and Messina far greater creative freedom and songwriting presence than they could have possibly hoped to attain in Buffalo Springfield, as well as a means to tap further into the country-rock that had been infatuating them of late.

"The first time I recall any conversation about the idea of putting country into the music was between Richie and I in the back seat of a cab in Nashville," remembers Messina. "I believe the group [Buffalo Springfield] was still on the road at that time. The next thing I recall was trying to finish [the Springfield]'s 'Kind Woman' and getting Rusty into the studio and Richie and I going, 'Wow, he's cool, wouldn't he make a nice member of a band.'"

"Certainly the one instrument we sought to include and incorporate in our music was the steel guitar," picks up Furay. "We were blessed to hook up with the finest innovator of the instrument, Rusty Young. He was always ready and willing to take the instrument to its limit while being able to 'make it cry' in a traditional sense. At first this was Jimmy['s] and my vision—bridge that gap, make country music accessible to a wider audience." By the time the band's debut album, *Pickin' Up the Pieces*, appeared in 1969, its name had been changed to Poco. Also gone by that time was original bassist Randy Meisner, who had quit while the album was being mixed, although some of his bass and vocals are heard on the record. Meisner later joined the Eagles.

It's never had the hip cachet of *Gilded Palace of Sin* or *Sweetheart of the Rodeo*, but *Pickin' Up the Pieces* is at least as important as those records, and more accessible to the rock-oriented listener. In contrast to those other albums, *Pickin' Up the Pieces* is a rock album with country influences, rather than the work of musicians bringing rock sensibilities into country music. "The Burrito Brothers were a little more like a country bar band, but more sophisticated," comments Messina. "Our focus was on harmonies, with emphasis on songwriting and lots of vocals. We never wanted to be a country band. That wasn't our goal. We just wanted to bring country music into our style. Quite honestly, I think that's what we were doing in Buffalo Springfield, when we were doing 'Kind Woman.'

The Flying Burrito Brothers. Left to right: Bernie Leadon, Michael Clarke, Gram Parsons, and Chris Hillman.

'I Am a Child,' with Neil Young [also on the Springfield's *Last Time Around* album], was bringing country into his music."

Much of Buffalo Springfield's most ingratiating qualities—stellar melodies, impeccable musicianship, and a rollicking joy—survived intact on Poco's debut, albeit with a more wholesome, country-dabbed, cheery bounce. The harmonies glowed, and Furay's tenor singing was never better. One of the most upbeat albums of the 1960s, folk-rock or otherwise, *Pickin' Up the Pieces* is perhaps too optimistic to find favor with jaded modern critics who thrive on darkness and subterfuge, even of the relatively subtle sort found in songs like the Flying Burrito Brothers' "Sin City." Poco's later albums were harder-rocking and less consistent, and the band, like so many in the genre, eventually mutated into something nearly unrecognizable after musical chairs of lineup changes. Furay himself left in 1973.

While veterans of the Byrds and Buffalo Springfield were proving it was possible for folk-rockers to move into country-rock, some of their buddies were also demonstrating it was possible for bluegrass and folk musicians to make a similar leap. The Dillards, a pure bluegrass group when they began recording for Elektra in the early '60s, had long moved within the orbit of both those bands. Early Byrds co-manager/producer Jim Dickson had taken on similar duties for the Dillards before he even met the Byrds; the Dillards' mandolinist Dean Webb helped organize the Byrds' harmonies on "Mr. Tambourine Man"; the Dillards had shared the same bills with the Byrds at some shows in the mid-'60s; Doug Dillard had played banjo with the *Sweetheart of the Rodeo*–era lineup on stage; and drummer Dewey Martin had briefly been in the Dillards before joining Buffalo Springfield.

The Dillards also made some rare mid-'60s recordings, four released on Capitol singles and a couple on an archive compilation on the Together label, including a cover of Tom Paxton's "The Last Thing on My Mind." These found the group aiming for a Byrdsy sound, though inevitably some shades of bluegrass could be heard too. In Chris Hillman's estimation, "The Dillards, at the time we did a little tour with them, had made that mistake in hindsight of plugging in. They felt they had to start playing electrically to compete, and sort of lost the whole magic of what they were doing at that time." The Dillards reverted to an acoustic lineup around the time Dewey Martin joined Buffalo Springfield, with Byrds co-managers Jim Dickson and Eddie Tickner loaning the newly launched Springfield the electric instruments that the Dillards no longer needed.

Yet the Dillards' wishes to expand beyond the strictures of bluegrass—which are about as strict as any in popular music—dated from long before the heyday of folk-rock. They had left Elektra, in part, because the label didn't seem sympathetic to their more progressive inclinations. Webb remembers that the band had wanted to update a song called "Hey Mr. Banjo" into one called "Hey Mr. Five-String," noting that "Elektra was horrified at the idea. It just wasn't folky enough for them. Too commercial. On some of these tours with [the Byrds], we were starting to experiment with plugging in our instruments. I was playing electric mandolin. Douglas [Dillard] had an electric 12-string guitar, and started finger picking it. Curly Walters signed us [to Capitol], seemed to understand exactly what we wanted to do, and we never saw the guy again. Then they started putting us with all these other producers. I don't know how many we went through. And none of 'em seemed to understand the kind of material we wanted to do."

By 1968 both the Dillards and Elektra were older, wiser, and working together again, Herb Pedersen having replaced Doug Dillard. Explains guitarist Rodney Dillard, "We asked for a release [from Capitol], 'cause they didn't know what to do with us either. Elektra seemed to understand what we wanted to do at that point." Agrees Webb, "By the time we re-signed with them, they had already signed the Doors. They were going that route already."

Their first album from their second tour with the label, 1968's *Wheatstraw Suite*, exceeded all expectations of those who had known the Dillards primarily as a leading bluegrass band or from their frequent guest appearances on the *Andy Griffith Show*. It was something like a bridge between the Byrds and the Eagles, though with far deeper shades of country-bluegrass than either of those groups ever boasted. The rhythm section was electric, the orchestral arrangements (by Al Capps) Los Angeles pop, the harmonies very much country, and somehow it all clicked. The material was incredibly varied, from covers of Tim Hardin's "Reason to Believe," the Beatles' "I've Just Seen a Face," and ex–Rising Son Jesse Kincaid's wonderfully eccentric "She Sang Hymns Out of Tune," to quality original songs, some of them remakes of ones they had first cut between their stints with Elektra. It was hard to market to either the rock or country audience, but was an unqualified artistic triumph.

"I wanted to take what I'd learned in my root music, what I grew up with, and apply that in a broader rhythmical sense and structure," says Rodney Dillard. "I wanted to change rhythmically, but still maintain those instruments that gave the identity to that mountain stuff that we did. When you do that R&B-meets-bluegrass, you come up with some other kind of thing. It's either really horrible or moderately successful." As for the orchestration, "We tried to keep it subliminal, yet give it a depth that the music might not have had. You had to have the basic tracks and the heart and the content. Any kind of sweetening, you do just the salt, you don't overuse it. I think that's a secret to that particular project. It was where the organic raw met the orchestrated structure, and that happened to be a good combination. It didn't come out like Muzak, because you heard the guitar and you heard the squeaks. You know, there's a few mistakes on the *Wheatstraw Suite* album on rhythm, that are left in. It was okay."

The approach was successfully replicated on *Copperfields*, released at the beginning of 1970, although it wasn't as stunning as *Wheatstraw Suite*. It was just as diverse, however, in its fusion of bluegrass, rock, pop, country, and folk, from the a cappella cover of the Beatles' "Yesterday" to the burningly poignant orchestrated ballad "Touch Her If You Can," which actually had some hit single potential had anyone thought to market it aggressively as such at the time. "Brother John" had a sense of adventure similar to that heard on many 1966–67 Byrds releases, putting Dave Brubeck–like jazz tempos to McGuinn-type guitar picking. Rodney Dillard's loathe to dwell too much on analyzing what the group had in mind with such experiments, seeing them as just a natural, organic expression of what they wanted to play: "Herb had written this great song, we just thought it was fun, and we got to goofing around with it one day and decided to record it that way. Besides, I'd never been able to play jazz guitar before." He does feel that Elektra wasn't as effective as getting the music to listeners as it could have been, and both *Wheatstraw Suite* and *Copperfields* had little impact in the pop field, though they were hugely appreciated by some critics and in-the-know fans.

The Dillards. Front row, left to right: Rodney Dillard, Dean Webb. Back row, left to right: Herb Pedersen, Mitch Jayne.

An equally quirky band that drew from country and rock, and eventually did make a pop break-through, was Long Beach's Nitty Gritty Dirt Band. It had made the middle of the Top 100 in 1967 with a pleasant folk-rock tune given sunshine pop orchestration, "Buy for Me the Rain," penned by Steve Noonan and Greg Copeland. The song wasn't typical of the group's albums, if only because nothing was really typical of the Nitty Gritty Dirt Band's early records. "The music at the time was jug band/eclectic," says John McEuen, one of the group's several multi-instrumentalists. "It was 'Buy For Me the Rain,' it was [Jackson Browne's] 'These Days.' It was 'Shimmy Like My Sister Kate,' 'Euphoria,' drug songs from the '30s. A real mish-mash of material. In reality, the band rarely knew more than 18 songs. When a new one would come along, we'd either forget or throw out an old one. When there was new songs, it was more like along the lines of, 'What can we do to this?' If it was an in-strumental, I probably brought it into the group. If it was a ballad, it might come from Jeff [Hanna]."

The band's sound wasn't as well integrated as that of the Lovin' Spoonful or some of the many others who used jug bands as a springboard for a certain folk-rock eclecticism, and the group even broke up for a while in 1969. "1969, with the inclusion of Jimmy Ibbotson into the group, is when the Dirt Band truly found the focus of its folk-rock schooling," continues McEuen. "The *Uncle Char-lie & His Dog Teddy* album was us making our statement of 'This is what we've learned. We're gonna make a new kind of country-folk-rock.'"

"We started rehearsing and looking for material and realized there was really no style we couldn't do," observed Hanna in *Rolling Stone*. "Anyone that we hear that we like, we'll attempt. We can do jug music, country, pure acoustic mountain music, Cajun, folk-rock, just anything. On the *Uncle Charlie* album, we tried everything from bluegrass to hard rock and for once the FM stations appreciated it."

The record's top achievement was integrating folk-associated instruments, particularly man-dolin and banjo, into a rock context in a way that felt natural rather than forced. Well-chosen cov-ers of songs by Randy Newman, Mike Nesmith, and a young Kenny Loggins helped. None helped as much as Jerry Jeff Walker's "Mr. Bojangles," perhaps the last great folk-rock rearrangement of the 1960s (recorded in 1969, says McEuen, although the *Uncle Charlie & His Dog Teddy* LP came out in 1970).

Walker's original had been relatively sparsely arranged and nonchalantly delivered; the Dirt Band dressed it up with mandolin, calliope, accordion, harmonica, and vocal harmonies. In his autobiography *Gypsy Songman*, Walker wrote that Ibbotson told him he had first come across the song when "a good witch" gave Jimmy the "Mr. Bojangles" single while he was packing his car for his move from Indiana to California, uttering "I know this will mean a lot to you" before walk-ing away. It wasn't until a few months later, mulling over what songs to record for *Uncle Charlie* after having joined the Nitty Gritty Dirt Band, that Ibbotson remembered the gift and dug it out of his trunk. Walker also made sure to note that the Dirt Band, like Emmylou Harris a few years be-fore, had changed some words in a liberal manner that echoed the folk process, perhaps due to the waterlogged condition of the single after all those months in the trunk. "He spoke right out" was changed to "the smoke ran out"; "he laughed-slapped his leg a step" became "he laughed and clicked his heels and stepped."

According to McEuen, "Jeff came into the rehearsal one day and said, 'I heard a song I want to do last night on the radio, about a guy, a dancer from the '30s, and his dog.' Ibby then jumped up and shouted, 'I have that! In my record collection!,' which consisted of only that record, given to him by a definitely strange witchly type, but not so uncommon in those days. Jeff took it into the other room and learned it by himself, and then came back and taught it to us. In that way, we who had not heard it were not influenced by Jerry Jeff's version.

"We went to see him in Philly at the Main Point coffeehouse. We had already recorded it, and told him (like many others) that it was coming out as a single. He told me a couple of years ago that this was the trip where he decided to quit music, and headed to Florida a bit dejected, rejected, and uncollected. On the way, [he] pulled over in a rest area on I-95, somewhere like Virginia. Around 5:00 A.M. his traveling buddy said, 'Hey Jerry! Isn't that song on the radio yours? Isn't that the Dirt Band's "Bojangles"?' It was, and being treated like a hit that it was to become. He said he pointed the car to Austin that day [where Walker would continue a long-running career as a country-folk-rock musician that endures to this day], and never looked back."

It would take until early 1971 for the song to make the Top Ten. "When we played the album for the record company, we threw out our suggestions—'Yeah, this'll be a good single, well here's another one that's a good single,'" recalls McEuen with some amusement. "We played 'Bojangles' last. We said, 'Now, this is just an album cut. I mean, it's in waltz time, the title doesn't appear till the middle, and it's really long. But we think it's a pretty cool piece of art.' When that was over, several of the people at the meeting said, 'That's the first single!' And we were really depressed. We thought our career was over. It's not going to get played, Jerry Jeff already had it out, it wasn't a hit, it's too long for people... stuff like that. But it wouldn't go away, and I think a lot of it had to do with the novel sound of the instrumentation, from calliope and accordion to mandolin, harmonica, acoustic guitars." The record's intricate tale of a tap dancer, feels McEuen, gave listeners something else to hang onto: "It was a story, like 'Yukon Railroad' was a story, and other things." The Nitty Gritty Dirt Band would not have any other big hit singles in the 1970s. But the song was its springboard to an extremely durable career that found it attracting a sizable country audience, particularly after recording with country and old-time folk heroes like Mother Maybelle Carter, Earl Scruggs, Doc Watson, and Roy Acuff on its ambitious 1972 triple album, *Will the Circle Be Unbroken*.

s throughout all avenues of 1960s folk-rock, there were numerous country-rockers who made fine records that never reached the ears of a national audience, and sometimes not even a cult audience. Among the best was Hearts and Flowers, who made a couple of albums under Nik Venet at Capitol. *Now is the Time for Hearts and Flowers* was little-heralded at the time of its release in 1967, but did much to anticipate the melting of walls between folk-rock, pop, bluegrass, and country that would be amplified by the Dillards, Nitty Gritty Dirt Band, and others. Original material with well-constructed, bluegrass-colored harmonies was smartly juxtaposed with clever covers of songs by Tim Hardin, Kaleidoscope, Goffin-King, and Donovan.

The later *Of Horses, Kids and Forgotten Women* was more of the same, with a little more orchestration. The 1968 album also featured new member (and future Eagle) Bernie Leadon, who had played bluegrass with Chris Hillman and principal Hearts and Flowers singer-songwriter Larry Murray way back in the early '60s in the Scottsville Squirrel Barkers. The LP's "Ode to a Tin Angel" was a highly atypical, and quite entrancing, detour into all-out psychedelia, with its hypnotic distorted vocal harmonies, wind chimes, and over-the-top orchestration. (Composer Murray's explanation for that left-field experiment: "I got off into that symphonic kind of genre there for a while, and got that out of my system. That was like the test run on a lot more to come, but just kind of faded away.")

More typical of the record was an outstanding cover of Jesse Kincaid's "She Sang Hymns Out of Tune," one of the best folk-rock songs never to get a wide hearing in the 1960s, though several tried, including Kincaid himself on a rare single. "It was part of everybody's repertoire," notes Murray. "I don't know what it was about the song; it was just a simple little waltz-time, visual thing about a crazy old lady." Ultimately, though, the group's unhurried, placid approach didn't have enough idiosyncratic traits to blazingly distinguish itself from several other artists treading the same territory, other than its frequent and deft use of autoharp.

"If we were playing at certain clubs, you'd see Hearts and Flowers play all acoustical country roots music," reminisces guitarist Murray. "We would do a lot of Merle Haggard stuff, but we would do it kind of in the folk-pop style. The very next gig we would have, we'd play a lot of folk-rock stuff. That's why we got a lot of different kind of reviews. We would see ourselves reviewed someplace that would talk about how country we were, and how could we survive playing in L.A.? But that wasn't who we were. That was just one facet of what we were doing.

"I think the eclectic nature of the group came out strongest on the album[s], and it was to our detriment. Basically, there wasn't a focus on either one of them. I often look back and say, we should have gone one hard direction or the other. A lot of comments and reviews that we got on the first album were, 'Well, it's clever.' That kind of stuff. I remember when a tune of ours was getting a lot of airplay on rock 'n' roll radio, and I was listening one time, and the song ended, and the disc jockey says, 'Geez, they should save up their money and buy an echo chamber!' And I was going, 'You know, he's right.' We cut that stuff really dry. Nik Venet was a little responsible for that.

"I think [Venet] saw something in us and didn't know what to do with it. He was always trying to find a handle on Hearts and Flowers, and never could. We were so eclectic that it would confuse him. It would confuse the *players* a lot of the times. Consequently we came up with something that just didn't fit the mold at the time." Murray also feels that Venet submerged the group's country leanings somewhat: "Nik knew that in clubs, we were doing pretty much like uptown bluegrass, and did a lot of traditional country songs in a kind of updated way. We just kind of brought 'em up to 1965. Nik wasn't really happy about us wanting to do an album that consisted of that stuff. Nik would let us do maybe one kind-of-country track on every other session, just to kind of get it out of our system. But they got all shoved to the back." Indeed the dozen outtakes that surfaced on the 2002 compilation *The Complete Hearts and Flowers Collection* were among their more country-oriented songs. Murray also recalls that the group wanted to record country star Mel Tillis's "Ruby, Don't Take Your Love to Town," but the hit went to Kenny Rogers & the First Edition, after the band taught the song to Rogers and another member of the First Edition in the parking lot of the Ledbetters club in L.A.

There were others who, like Hearts and Flowers, would find a greater cult appreciation among historians and collectors than they enjoyed at the time. It was a close-knit country-rock family in Southern California, and unsurprisingly several of them had strong-to-passing affiliations with the Byrds' circle. Gene Clark plunged deeper into country music, and commercial obscurity, as part of Dillard & Clark (with Doug Dillard). Their first album, 1968's *The Fantastic Expedition of Dillard & Clark*, was a pleasing, likable effort (with Bernie Leadon and Chris Hillman among the instrumental supporters), and has amassed an avid cult following in excess of its modest charms. Clark simply was not within miles of the brilliance of his early Byrds songs, a problem more evident on the far less impressive follow-up, *Through the Morning, Through the Night*, in which Dillard & Clark were turning into a run-of-the-mill bluegrass-folk act.

A&M Records briefly harbored a few early country-rock pioneers, and Clark and Gram Parsons played on the 1969 album by fellow A&M artist Steve Young. *Rock, Salt & Nails* was yet another low-key blend of country, (a little) rock, folk, and traces of blues, swamp pop, and even soul and gospel. Young had a darkness and seriousness, however, that many similar singer-songwriters lacked. The Flying Burrito Brothers had made concerted attempts to cross country with soul on tracks like their cover of Aretha Franklin's "Do Right Woman," but there can be few other country-soul hybrids as effective as Young's "Love in My Time," with its stirring soul-gospel female backup vocals. Judicious dramatic strings capped a worthy debut, but Steve Young's name is still unfamiliar to the general public, except as the author of a song (included on *Rock, Salt & Nails*) eventually covered by the Eagles, "Seven Bridges Road."

Like Parsons, and unlike most of the other Southern Californian country-rockers, Young was actually from the South, where country music had started before establishing beachheads in Bakersfield and Los Angeles. The Alabaman had moved to California in the mid-'60s, where he took the common route from the folk revival (writing songs on a 1964 folk-bluegrass-country LP by Richard & Jim) through folk-rock (briefly playing with Stephen Stills and Van Dyke Parks in a pre–Buffalo Springfield group, the Gas Company) and a bit of pop-psychedelia (as part of the group Stone Country). The little-known Stone Country album, issued on RCA in 1968, is one of the most schizophrenic records with any ties to late-'60s folk-rock, at times sounding like a blend of Jay & the Americans with the Byrds (as difficult as that is to envision). It was only on a couple of his own songs, particularly the graceful yet gutsy orchestrated folk-rock of "Woman Don't You Weep Me," that there was a sense that Young was expressing something of himself. Songs like that would form the entire menu on *Rock, Salt & Nails*.

"There was just more of a mixture there," responds Young when asked what might have made his brand of country-rock different from the cheerier SoCal norm for the genre. "More folk influence, more blues influence, more rock influence. But at the same time, my sound, some of it is almost traditional. The way I see it, people like me or Gram Parsons or Doug Dillard were actually Southerners. We had lived with it for all our lives, and it was a natural part of us. I had more raw roots showing. It was more serious." This could often result in a rather grave if dignified atmosphere on *Rock, Salt & Nails*, "and that can be said of my whole musical career. It's pretty hard for me to lighten up."

When the album was recorded, according to Young, producer Tommy LiPuma "wanted to capture something kind of pure. LiPuma really wanted A&M to promote this. He thought it was great. He played it for 'em, and they all kind of scratched their heads. 'God, I don't know. What is this?' So they sent it to Nashville, and of course Nashville said, 'Well, we don't know what it is, but it's not really country, so we're not interested in it.' It was that same old story."

Even harder to find than *Rock, Salt & Nails* was the 1968 Capitol album by the Gosdin Brothers, *Sounds of Goodbye*. Vern and Rex Gosdin had been associated with Chris Hillman and Jim Dickson before the dawn of the Byrds with the bluegrass band the Hillmen, and both Gosdins had supported Gene Clark on his debut LP (Vern Gosdin also added some guitar to the Byrds' "The Girl with No Name"). Whether due to their proximity to Clark or not, *Sounds of Goodbye* is undoubtedly the best Gene Clark–like record you'll ever hear, though with a greater country influence than Clark's first album had shown. Its country-rock owed much more to the sound of the 1966–67 Byrds than to *Sweetheart of the Rodeo*, with a downbeat but appealingly melodic air of staid heartbreak. Aiding the pair as session players were the ubiquitous Gene Parsons (on drums, banjo, harmonica, and harmonies) and Gib Guilbeau.

"We were trying to do kind of a Byrds feel, 'cause I always thought it was great, what they had," says Vern Gosdin. "I just loved it. My brother and I didn't get into that, because they were doing such a great job. But later on, we thought we might kind of touch on it anyway and have some luck with it. We tried it, and it didn't work." Gosdin, without his brother, became a major country star in the 1970s and 1980s, and concludes, "I think my thing was country all along, so I finally got where I belong."

"Some of the finest music of the period came from Vern and Rex, and I think Gene Clark took a lot of his inspiration from that," offers Parsons. "I think he's the best songwriter in the bunch of the Byrds, and spoke the same language as Vern and Rex. [It's] haunting, more than slightly melancholy, and Gene's got that same quality: honesty in the music. It's not an affected style. It's plain, honest, and straight from the heart. There were a lot of younger musicians [who] would come and listen to Vern and Rex, and get pretty excited when they'd hear them sing. They were never real strong stage personalities. They were into the music; they weren't into the showmanship."

Although *Sounds of Goodbye* came out on a major label, it must have sold virtually nothing, considering how difficult a copy is to come by today. "I don't think Capitol ever did anything with it," reckons Parsons. "It was right in the gray area that didn't fall into any playlist category, either on the rock stations or the country stations. It was a little too out there for the country stations, and a little too out there in another way for the rock stations." The Gosdins' stab at country-folk-rock over, they split and Vern withdrew into purer country music. "I know they were frustrated about not having commercial success," adds Parsons. "Both these guys were trying to raise families, and it was difficult. They were getting a little older, and a little desperate about what direction they should go to have some monetary success. That might have been one of the factors that influenced them."

lready in his thirties when *Sounds of Goodbye* came out, Gosdin was not quite the unlikeliest veteran to make his way into the California country-rock scene. That honor probably belonged to Rick Nelson, who had always had some country in his music, dating back to his early Hollywood-produced rockabilly records; the well-traveled Clarence White had played on Nelson's *Bright Lights & Country Music* and *Country Fever* albums, released in 1966 and 1967 respectively. Nelson's laconic vocals were heard on a low-charting country-rock cover of Dylan's "She Belongs to Me" in 1969. His Stone Canyon Band, featuring steel guitar and (between his stints in Poco and the Eagles) Randy Meisner, made country-rock that was sleepy even by the genre's laidback standards, culminating in his surprise self-penned 1972 hit "Garden Party." The Everly Brothers were fellow 1950s rock stars who matured into the country-rock motherlode, particularly on their 1968 album *Roots*, which put covers of Merle Haggard and Glen Campbell side by side with songs by Randy Newman and the Beau Brummels' Ron Elliott.

Some would see Michael Nesmith as the unlikeliest country-rocker of all, given his pedigree as a member of the Monkees. In fact his true pedigree was not the teen pop-rock hits for which the Monkees were most famous, but country music and the early-'60s folk revival. He'd done a rare, plaintive folk single in 1963, "Wanderin'"/"Well, Well," in which his droll sense of humor was already well in evidence. Even before he'd joined the Monkees, he'd played on a nicely Byrdsy (and similarly rare) single, "How Can You Kiss Me?," as part of Mike, John & Bill. He'd also put out some pre-Monkees solo records (sometimes under the name of Michael Blessing), including a cover of Buffy Sainte-Marie's "Until It's Time for You to Go," and bad satires of both draft dodgers ("The New Recruit") and Bob Dylan–like folk singers ("What's the Trouble, Officer?"). He emceed Monday night hoots at the Troubadour club in L.A., and tended to be the writer of the Monkees' most credible original material, usually in a country-influenced folk-rock style. The Greenbriar Boys, who'd done the original version of Nesmith's "Different Drum" before the Stone Poneys' hit, had even sent on a tape of Mike's recordings to Vanguard Records, though the label passed.

But for all the Monkees' record sales, Nesmith had had relatively little opportunity to showcase his rootsiest and more ambitious singer-songwriting on record. His first solo album, 1968's *Wichita Train Whistle Sings*, was a peculiar one-off instrumental orchestral enterprise that only came about as a tax write-off. He'd also produced unreleased, and very good, recordings by one of the finest unknown Californian folk-rock bands, the Penny Arkade. Penny Arkade drummer Don Glut, as noted earlier, believes this was an attempt to gain Nesmith at least some credibility and respect for his musical abilities in a community inclined to dismiss Mike as just a manufactured cog in the Monkees' machine.

By the end of the 1960s, *The Monkees* TV show was off the air and Nesmith was free to be himself, rather than squeeze in little hints here and there on Monkees LP tracks that few serious post-adolescents ever heard. "It took him a few months after the collapse of the Monkees," says John Ware, drummer in Nesmith's first country-rock group, Michael Nesmith & the First National Band. "He had gotten bad financial advice and went into bankruptcy. When I joined the Stone Poneys, he was just this guy with this curly long beard who rode a Harley, who sat in the corner of the rehearsal hall. We got to be friends, so when the Monkees collapsed, we were already hanging out together. The First National Band was my idea, and it was only because I thought that Mike needed something to do. He was writing really good songs, and they were getting recorded by a lot of interesting people. The guys who were producing at RCA wouldn't let it go that direction.

"So I talked him up and he said, 'Well, it ain't gonna happen because Red Rhodes is not gonna join that band. He's not gonna leave the Palomino.'" Rhodes was a top steel guitarist who played as a session man on some key folk-rock records, like the Byrds' *The Notorious Byrd Brothers* and James Taylor's *Sweet Baby James*. He also led the house band at the Palomino, a North Hollywood club that served as the leading venue for country music in the L.A. area, and was gradually opening its stage to country-rockers such as Linda Ronstadt and the Flying Burrito Brothers. Perhaps Nesmith felt that Rhodes was out of his league, but Ware was undeterred: "I said, 'Give me a chance.' So I called Red and went over, had a few beers with him, and he said, 'Sure!'"

Michael Nesmith and the First National Band's debut album, 1970's *Magnetic South*, was in Ware's judgment "cerebral country. The difference between that and other country-rock bands is, most of them wanted to be outlaws and play like they were country ramblers. But Mike was trying to paint a picture about America and his place in it. I think the First National Band were so far away from the rest of the L.A. country-thing that it's a difficult conversation." Nesmith gave his memorable take on it in a 1970 *Melody Maker*: "My music is kinda doped-up L.B.J., kinda acid country."

"It was such a bizarre and thoughtful collaboration of musicians, and that's what he encouraged every day at the studio," continues Ware. "He'd bring in all these strange African instruments, and that's what I played. It only took us, I think, 14 days to do the entire album, including mixing and mastering. Almost everything you hear on that record is live, with the exception of the yodeling." That yodeling was heard on the album's hit, the wistfully blue "Joanne," which stopped just outside the Top 20, though according to Ware, "he was so embarrassed by that. He called me up after he finished the vocals and says, 'You're gonna hate me, 'cause I *yodeled* on it.' And I *loved* it." But for the most part, the public didn't hear the album from which it hailed, which peaked at #143. The First National Band would continue for a couple more albums, but have more success in England, where Nesmith's past as a Monkee was less of an albatross to bear.

Climbing up the ladder to fame while Nesmith descended past her was the woman who'd had the first hit with a Nesmith composition, "Different Drum." Linda Ronstadt was now a solo artist, and one of the few women in country-rock, which would be perhaps the most male-dominated branch of folk-rock. For whatever reason, there were few other female country-rock performers of note, though some others dabbled in it to little commercial effect, such as Sylvia Tyson (as part of Great Speckled Bird) and Barbara Keith. Ronstadt put part of the blame on sexism, telling Ben Fong-Torres of *Rolling Stone*, "It's almost impossible for a girl singer to put a good band together. First, women are just not taken seriously. They have to shout around to get people to listen. Women just are not encouraged to make a living doing this kind of thing. People relate to us to differently." As for the indifferent commercial performance of her early solo albums, she blamed part of it (again to Fong-Torres) on recording the second of these, *Silk Purse*, in Nashville instead of California. "I was working with Nashville musicians and I don't really play country music," she claimed. "I play very definitely California music, and I couldn't communicate it to them."

ot everyone felt the same way. While early country-rock was centered around Southern California, several folk-rock survivors were, perhaps inspired by Dylan's example, wading into the music by traveling to Nashville to record country-rock in the city's studios. Eric Andersen, Buffy Sainte-Marie, Ian & Sylvia (who soon formed the country-rock group Great Speckled Bird), Joan Baez, and Leonard Cohen (whose *Songs from a Room* had precious little country, but *was* recorded in Nashville) all recorded there in the late '60s. So did also-ran folk-rock singer-songwriters like Jake Holmes. So did David Blue, who was actually finally getting beyond his embarrassing Dylan fixation (as heard on his 1966 self-titled Elektra debut) to become a respectable if minor brooding, country-influenced singer-songwriter by the time of 1970's Nashville-cut *Me, S. David Cohen*. The Beau Brummels, who'd regained control of their work on 1967's haunting, understated *Triangle*, recorded their more country-tilted 1968 album *Bradley's Barn* at the Nashville studio of the same name. John Stewart did his second and most critically respected folk-rock album, *California Bloodlines*, in Nashville. Country Joe McDonald even cut his 1969 solo tribute album to Woody Guthrie in the city, and some other folk-rockers noted for pretty radical sounds and images would record there around that time, like Pearls Before Swine and the Holy Modal Rounders.

Not everyone making folk-country-rock in Nashville was seasoned by the early folk-rock wars. Newcomer Townes Van Zandt, his approach yet to lower into the less-chipper registers of his more renowned later work, recorded an impressive debut, *For the Sake of the Song*, that put a droll spin on the moody cowboy folk-rock of writers like Steve Young. The odd touches of ghostly female choirs and organ were abetted by co-producer Jack Clement, who had engineered and produced Sun Records artists like Johnny Cash and Jerry Lee Lewis back in the 1950s.

Bob Johnston, who produced Dylan and Cohen in Nashville, valued the city's less-pressurized atmosphere, which gave him and his artists more license to create without interference by the suits. "Whenever the powers to be would start over [to] the studio or something," he says, "I had people, and one guy would call me and tell me they were on the way over. So most times we'd leave the studio, lock it up. They'd come in, wait for an hour. Then they'd leave, then I'd get a call, and we'd go back. That kept 'em out of the loop. So they didn't know a goddamn thing." Dylan himself declared his preference for Nashville studios in *Newsweek*, where he explained, "I've cut seven albums in New York. You have to put up with all that taxicab nonsense and that big-city confusion which disables you a lot. It's always cold and you can't go outside when you want, you get a boxed-in feeling. And, though New York has top-quality people, musicians sure know how to play in Nashville."

Eric Andersen sees a particularly straightforward advantage to cutting sessions in Nashville: "It was cheap to record there at one time, very cheap. And very fast. So if you wanted to have musicians, you could do it cheap, really quick. Their musicians, they didn't need chord sheets, nothing. They just played numbers on matchbook covers. We would put two, three songs on a matchbook cover, just using the number system. Nashville understood songwriters. Everything about country music's all around the song. Nashville had their own formulas, but it was based around the singer, the song, the personality."

Andersen adds that the benefits flowed both ways: "Pete Drake, the great steel player, he jumped in on my project with [the album] *Stages*, and he started doing things he never ever did before. And he had a blast. 'Cause it wasn't the straight country lick stuff. It was a time when they were simpatico, and they were looking for a change too. Maybe *Nashville* was looking for a change. And they got it." John Stewart saw how this could work to his advantage when he recorded *California Bloodlines*, telling *ZigZag*, "On those sessions, their playing was inspired—they played with their hearts, for a number of reasons, not the least being that they were so glad to be participating in something other than straight country and western music."

Those looking for the same kind of to-the-bone Nashville production that had graced Dylan's return to the record shelves did not always have their expectations met, however. When Steve Young recorded in Nashville for Reprise, "There was a funny kind of clash between me and some of the Nashville players, even though I was a Southerner. It's like some of them just didn't know where I was coming from, or they thought I was strange. They didn't understand some of these songs." When Jerry Jeff Walker made his second album, *Driftin' Way of Life*, "We flew right to Nashville, and that wasn't actually the approach I wanted to do. I wanted do more like what Dylan was doing with *John Wesley Harding*. But I wound up getting that full Nashville treatment, where they're all in little cubicles. I don't remember how many guys were playing, that's how many there were. You go in the room, and it's like they're all over behind some post and around behind some baffle." But there were no complaints about their efficiency: "We cut it in two days, and mixed it in three." It was really not until Walker moved to Austin in the early '70s, in his estimation, that he hooked up with musicians that comprised a truly simpatico band: "By the time I got here in '71 or so, it was no longer, like, folk and rock. It was folk-country-rock, because our crowds were crossing over."

Speculates Charlie McCoy, who played on many of the folk-rock and country-rock records cut in Nashville, "It was almost like, 'Oh, okay, if Dylan went there, then it must be okay.' It was like the floodgates opened after he came." Elliot Mazer, who produced albums in Nashville by Gordon Lightfoot, Ian & Sylvia, and Linda Ronstadt during the period (and would in the early '70s produce Neil Young's chart-topping *Harvest* LP in the city), agrees: "Everybody that went to Nashville after Bob did so because of Bob. Kenny Buttrey's drumming was the driving force. Kenny played *songs* on drums, Kenny listened to the singers, watched their left hands to anticipate the rhythms. He was magnificent."

Sylvia Tyson qualifies the rush to follow Dylan somewhat: "It wasn't that we [Ian & Sylvia] were copying Dylan, but just that we thought that was a really good idea. Because there were wonderful players down there. There were writers down there that we admired, producers. We got to record in the studio that Elvis Presley recorded in. How great is that, you know? I mean, we got to play with people like Jerry Reed. What a guitar player, holy shit.

"We were using the young hot players. We certainly used some of the older players, some of the best ones. But what we, I think, had to offer them was a chance to do something other than country. Because our music was the music we wrote, and it wasn't certainly traditionally country." It likely helped, too, that Ian & Sylvia were not Johnny-come-latelies to country, with a country undercurrent to their harmonies even on their earlier folk albums, which included a cover of Johnny Cash's "Come on Stranger" (on 1965's *Early Morning Rain*). Now they were using their Nashville sessions to take chances with their music, doing country-rock versions of a couple of Dylan's Basement Tapes tunes on 1968's *Nashville*, and putting strings and choir on some of the material on *Full Circle* the same year. They'd go further in 1970 with their country-rock band Great Speckled Bird, which included a drummer, pedal steel guitarist, and guitarist Amos Garrett, who came up with a way to bend two or three strings at a time.

I n contrast, to all appearances, as time went on Bob Dylan seemed to be using Nashville as a means of making his music more conservative and *less* adventurous. *Nashville Skyline*, though recorded in 1969 with the same musicians who had played on *John Wesley Harding* (as well as guitarists Norman Blake and Charlie Daniels), contained his purest country outings to date. That in itself wasn't a cause of distress to his fans, and indeed caused little if any harm to its sales, as it reached #3. Many longtime Dylanites, however, were aghast at the simple, sometimes cliché-ridden love songs that were now his main diet. Also shocking, though not unwelcome, was his new, almost unrecognizably low and sweet vocal croon. An outstanding Top Ten hit single from the album, "Lay Lady Lay," softened the blows on all fronts. Even some who faithfully bought the records, though, were wondering whether the emperor was getting caught without his clothes on.

Dylan, as ever, was unfazed by the surprised and sometimes dismayed reactions to his new persona. He went as far as to claim that the latest new Dylan was closer to who he really was than any of the previous models, though with someone who changes faces as much as he has, it's arguable whether any certain style represents the "real" Dylan. "These are the type of songs that I always felt like writing when I've been alone to do so," he said when *Newsweek* interviewed him about *Nashville Skyline*. "The songs reflect more of the inner me than the songs of the past. They're more to my base than, say, 'John Wesley Harding.' There I felt everyone expected me to be a poet so that's what I tried to be. But the smallest line in this new album means more to me than some of the songs on any of the previous albums I've made."

But Dylan was running into a trough as a songwriter. He had only four songs when he arrived at the *Nashville Skyline* sessions. Even the final album was filled out with an instrumental and a duet with Johnny Cash on a remake of "Girl from the North Country." He and Cash had been good friends for years, and Cash had covered Dylan material since before it was fashionable to do so, going back to his 1964 album *Orange Blossom Special* (which included a cover of "It Ain't Me Babe," complete with mariachi brass). There were also rumors of a Dylan-Cash tour, which never took place.

At the *Nashville Skyline* sessions, the pair even recorded an entire unreleased album's worth of material together (since bootlegged), including Carl Perkins on guitar. They remade a few old Dylan and Cash tunes, as well as running through covers of rockabilly standards like "Matchbox" and "That's All Right Mama" and miscellaneous country songs. Bob Johnston later claimed in *Melody Maker* that he'd been offered $300,000 for a Dylan-Cash tape, presumably by bootleggers on the hunt for another *Great White Wonder*. It might have been a good time for everyone involved, and its rockabilly-cum-country-rock treatments are fun to hear. But the execution was on the slipshod, perfunctory side, with Cash's vocals and songs far more to the foreground than Dylan's.

For the first time in his career, perhaps, Dylan was seriously struggling as to where to take his music next. In 1970, there were plans for the Byrds and Dylan to record an album together, news of which would have probably been greeted as one of the ultimate meetings of the gods in 1966. Neither act held such iconic stature four years later, though, and the project, never set in stone, fell through. Clive Davis blamed the Byrds in his autobiography for not showing up at the session, although McGuinn has said the group was contacted too late to participate, and in any case he wasn't enthused about the Byrds being used as a backup group to a Dylan album. The one McGuinn-Dylan collaboration to escape onto record in the period was the title track of the Byrds' 1969 album *The Ballad of Easy Rider*, although Dylan insisted that his name not be placed on the songwriting credit. It was a placid and beautiful piece that both musically and lyrically reflected the contemplative full-circle aura of late-'60s country-rock, though it's better heard as the acoustic McGuinn solo track that ends the *Easy Rider* film than the Byrds' more orchestrated version. McGuinn, incidentally, has stressed that Dylan's contribution to the song was minimal, involving only a line or two.

It took his one-time backup band, the Hawks, to bring the stew of Americana Dylan had sung on *The Basement Tapes* to a full boil. The Hawks, called the Band by the time of 1968's *Music from Big Pink* (named after the house where many of the Basement Tapes had been recorded), would have almost surely never gotten to where they were going without having their songwriting consciousness raised by their intensely close working relationship with Dylan in 1965–67. Toughened by years of backing minor rockabilly singer Ronnie Hawkins, they were a good bar band, but not, based on the rare singles they made in the mid-'60s before renaming themselves the Band, a particularly original one. And as with many of Dylan's career decisions that turned out for the best, the Band's association with the singer originally came about as much through fortuitous accident as conscious strategizing. When Dylan was looking for an electric band back in 1965, he told *Rolling Stone* four years later, he originally wanted to get a group together with Hollywood session aces James Burton (on guitar), Joe Osborn (on bass), and Mickey Jones (on drums; Jones would indeed play with the Hawks on Dylan's 1966 tour as Levon Helm's temporary replacement). It was only through the staunch advocacy of a Canadian secretary in Albert Grossman's office, Mary Martin, that the Hawks were introduced to Dylan and became his band—without which it seems highly unlikely that this particular band would have become *the* Band.

It's not quite accurate to call what the Band did in the late '60s folk-rock, country-rock, or even Americana (especially considering that all but one of them were from Canada). It was all of the above, really: a smorgasbord of North American roots music, evoking rural life in both the twentieth and nineteenth century, but using words (most often by principal Band songwriter Robbie Robertson) that could approach Dylan in their learned-yet-ambiguous tone.

Part of the Band's sound—different from anything else going yet in many ways rooted in music that predated rock by decades or even centuries—could be attributed to their relative isolation from contemporary music trends during the year or so they worked with Dylan on the Basement Tapes. As Dylan noted in interviews during the time, his personal listening booth was running to pretty anachronistic and esoteric playlists. Since he and the Band were spending so much time together, it's likely the group was listening to such old-time music as well, and picking up a lot of influence and how-to guidance from Dylan himself. "From Bob, Robbie learned to write songs," says John Simon, who produced both of the Band's late-'60s albums, *Music from Big Pink* and its 1969 follow-up, *The Band*. "The only things they listened to were very, very old. Never listened to current radio or other artists." By contrast, he notes, his fellow clients Simon & Garfunkel "used to listen to the radio a lot, compare themselves to other people, and try to be on the cutting edge of things. But the Band was the total opposite.

"I'm sure they were sharing things with Dylan too, and then he'd give them things to listen to. They were very close, so they traded favorite things. The guys in the band didn't know who Allen Ginsberg was until Dylan told them. I think [drummer] Levon [Helm] was a little more into the Delta black blues, and [bassist] Rick [Danko] was more into country, bluegrass, the Stanley Brothers, the Osborne Brothers, and anybody like Hank Williams and Jimmie Rodgers. There were even hymns that Rick was into. Robbie was pretty much a sponge and picked up a little bit from everybody."

"[Dylan] was a man with a lot of words we weren't even aware of before," said Robertson of the Band-Dylan symbiosis in *The New York Times* in 1969. "We were just a rock and roll band. But, as time went along, things fell together, and we found out that the same things that meant a lot to us meant a lot to him, too, that the same songs we still liked, he did, too. What we learned from him was that a rock song doesn't have to be a nitwit song, that you have to work on it to make it hold up. And we taught him what we know about rock and roll." To *NME* in 1970 he added, "We were a scrounge road group when we met [Dylan]. We'd had one of his albums, and we all liked it, but it didn't snap on us like that, you know. And we had no idea he was as strong as we later found out he was. The first [album] was reflective of the fact that we were trying to shake off the years of wildness on the road and trying to cool it in our lives and in our music." The mood and the playing on the first two albums, Robertson summed up, "reflect directly the feeling and nostalgia of the time."

The Band played as an ensemble, not as flashy soloists, with gospelized harmonies, an especially rich organ-piano blend, and Helm's slow, emphatic half-time drumbeats. *Music from Big Pink* and *The Band* might not have sold as much as Dylan's records from the time (although they sold quite well). But they were more influential, particularly on Eric Clapton, who cited the Band's first album as one of the reasons he quit Cream to pursue less amplified music, and on George Harrison, who would put Band-like sentiments (and a bit of country-rock) to superb, epic pop-rock melodies and production on some of his 1970 solo debut, *All Things Must Pass*.

Yet country-rock, despite *Time*'s cover story "The New Sound of Country Rock" in January 1970, never did become a huge commercial deal, as folk-rock once had. Just as it would take huge dollops of pop to give singer-songwriters a huge audience in the early '70s, so it would take massive infusions of pop to put country-rock over in a big way in that decade, through Linda Ronstadt and the Eagles (two of whom had once played in Ronstadt's backing band). Both of those acts had strong roots in 1960s folk-country-rock—Ronstadt in the Stone Poneys and the Eagles in Poco (with whom Randy Meisner had played), while Eagles guitarist Bernie Leadon had been in both the Flying Burrito Brothers and Hearts and Flowers. Both live and in the studio, Ronstadt's bands had schooled numerous players who made light or heavy imprints on country-rock, including future Eagles Glenn Frey and Don Henley, as well as John Ware and Red Rhodes. "If you wanted to be a team player in L.A. country-rock, you had to have played with Linda," says Ware. "It's amazing how many great players went through her, and what good ears she had for that stuff."

There were also those who kept burrowing away with individualistic, uncommercial country-rock in the early '70s, like Mike Nesmith (though even he had managed a hit in 1970 with "Joanne"). But as with singer-songwriters, the country-rockers' commercial breakthrough was, unfortunately, made possible by smoothing out the edges of the style's earliest, freshest manifestations with blandness that all but flattened its most exciting features.

"Country music is an anathema to a lot of people," says Chris Darrow, who also played in Ronstadt's band for a while, in reflecting on how country-rock differed from earlier folk-rock forms in consumer appeal. "Nobody likes the twangs, a lot of people don't like steel guitars, a lot of people don't like the subject matter, and it sounds cornball to a lot of people. Country-rock is much more of a musician's kind of music. Folk-rock was more strummy; country-rock is a more steel guitary, lead guitary kind of thing. Folk-rock had a much more melodic, prettier, accessible ring to it than country-rock did. That's one of the reasons that country-rock took time to develop, until it came out of the voices of people like Linda Ronstadt. The Eagles, they're the Byrds of the '70s."

As unusual as it seemed for so many folk-rockers to go country in 1968 and 1969, the musical reasons are not so difficult to detect. They'd always liked country music, and with the more open musical environment that folk-rock had helped to create, they had the opportunity to explore it to their satisfaction. In California in particular, a good number of folk-rock and country-rock musicians were well-acquainted with country after playing bluegrass in their formative years: Chris Hillman, Chris Darrow, David Lindley, Larry Murray, Bernie Leadon, Clarence White, and others. Even some time after that in the mid-'60s, as Jim Messina points out, "I recall Buck Owens and the Buckaroos really starting to take off; Merle Haggard was happening, starting to pull more into our generation's listenership. You gotta realize that Buck Owens was the greatest country-rock band that ever was, when he was in his heyday. [Buckaroos lead guitarist] Don Rich was incredible; the band was hot, and it was rockin'. Biggest mistake I think [Owens] ever made was doing *Hee Haw*. 'Cause he ruined the credibility of his music."

A thornier question to answer is why back-to-basics country-rock found an audience. Country music was, not quite fairly, often viewed as the province of the kind of stereotyped Southern rednecks that shot hippie motorcyclists Peter Fonda and Dennis Hopper at the end of *Easy Rider*. Folk-rock had always been far more identified with, and an expression of, the counterculture than the status quo. So it could come as a shock to read someone at the forefront of the back-to-basics countrified folk-rock movement like Robbie Robertson, for instance, tell *Newsweek* in late 1969, "Where we come from, we don't hate our parents. We're not going to write songs about what a drag they are or what a drag they made the world. Hell, they just made us. We're not at too many peace rallies. Our music's not concerned with that."

One theory that's often mooted is that country-rock, and for that matter laidback singer-songwriting, was the soundtrack to a young America exhausted by the struggles of the Vietnam War, the civil rights movement, and the generation gap. The country's youth was further demoralized by police brutality against demonstrators at the 1968 Democratic Convention, and the subsequent election of Republican Richard Nixon as president. Young people, the theory goes, got fed up with trying to change the world, and were now trying to change themselves.

At the same time there was a rise in the back-to-the-land ethos that led to the kind of communes also found, as it happened, in the movie *Easy Rider* (which used period music by the Band, the Byrds, and Dylan on its soundtrack). Joni Mitchell, whose early songs included hymns to the dazzle of city life inspired by her time as a resident of New York (most famously in "Chelsea Morning"), had by the summer of 1969 changed her tune, venting her disillusionment in *Newsweek*: "I'm a little in awe of cities, being raised in a prairie town in Saskatchewan. I thought then that cities were beautiful. I judged them by their neon. Then in New York I found that cities are really vulgar. I saw their dirt, found they were plastic and in a rush for the dollar. Now I'm ruralizing myself again. I owe it to myself to live where there's greenery." (Albeit "ruralizing" herself apparently meant taking refuge not in a remote farm, but in the greenery of Laurel Canyon in the hills just above West Hollywood, where Mitchell was living at the time of the quote, and which was just a few minutes from Sunset Strip and major L.A. recording studios.)

As with most generalizations about the era's music and culture, there's some truth to these speculations, but plenty of holes as well. In fact, countercultural dissent and turbulence was if anything greater in 1969 than it had ever been. The 250,000-strong National Mobilization Against the War demonstration against US involvement in Vietnam on November 15 was the largest antiwar protest in American history. Increasing militancy among African-Americans, particularly the Black Panthers, was exacting savage, violent repression from government agencies. Student unrest on American campuses was at a new height, again resulting in some tragic retribution from authorities, culminating in the slaying of several students by the National Guard at Ohio's Kent State in 1970. The women's rights and ecology movements, addressing issues that even the Left had only recently recognized as important, were getting their first serious national attention. Open-air music festivals, many of them antiestablishment in posture, gave the youth places to gather in forces of hundreds of thousands, Woodstock being just the most famous of these.

How did country-rock, the Band, and *Nashville Skyline* fit into all of this? Ed Ward put it eloquently in his piece on the Band in *The Rolling Stone Illustrated History of Rock & Roll*: "I was living in Ohio at the time, in a room with two windows, one overlooking a saloon and the other facing north, where there was nothing but fields and a farmhouse. I could sit for hours, playing *The Band* and looking out one of those two windows. If my experience is anything like typical, I would say that *The Band* helped a lot of people dizzy from the confusion and disorientation of the '60s feel that the nation was big enough to include them, too."

Chris Hillman, then with the Flying Burrito Brothers, made a similar connection in a 1970 interview with *Melody Maker*. "When we started kids in this country did not want to listen to country music," he admitted. "But the music over here is becoming a lot softer and melodic now, I don't like loud music and 20-minute-long guitar solos, I find it tedious. A lot of it has to do with politics. It's loud and nasty on the streets so people want to listen to music that is going to soothe them. There is a big following here now for groups like us and Poco."

There was some audience flow in the other direction, too. "What happened was, it all started to melt there for a while," offers Poco's Jim Messina. "We could bring folk lyrics into country music. Being in the South with the Buffalo Springfield, having long hair was not a good thing. We got bad, bad looks and bad, bad remarks made toward us. We could have said, 'These people are creeps. We're not gonna share anything with 'em.' Instead, we chose to say, 'Let's share our lyrics with 'em. Let's write country-rock music. Hopefully, we can bridge the gap.' And I think we did. If you listen to country music now, it's what Richie [Furay] and I and the Burrito Brothers and the Eagles first started doing."

It wasn't necessary to be living in the countryside to gain some solace from rustic Americana, either. In her memoir *Growing Up Underground*, Jane Alpert, who spent four years in hiding for her role in New York bombings by radical groups, remembers playing *Nashville Skyline* over and over again in 1969. Perhaps she found in it a mirror of her own hoped-for-journey to the end of the rainbow after the revolution had eradicated global injustice. As she observed, "In the beginning of his career he [Dylan] had struggled so hard to be himself that his voice had always been strained, his lyrics contorted and difficult.... Now, at 28, he was a survivor, had fallen in love again, had discovered that life could be startlingly, lyrically easy."

eatherman, America's most notorious underground organization of the late '60s, may have taken its name from a line in Bob Dylan's "Subterranean Homesick Blues," but Dylan himself wasn't going to lead any revolution. In fact, he would not even declare himself against the Vietnam War, which by 1968 was not even that controversial a position among many middle-aged suburbanites. In his interview at that time with *Sing Out!*, as editor Happy Traum recalls, "I tried very hard to engage him politically, and he wouldn't go for it"; at one point Dylan even muttered, "How do you know I'm not, as you say, for the war?"

Perhaps Dylan, as ever, just did not want to be pinned down as a spokesman for any cause, or pinned down to any definite position on anything. With his new visual and musical image as country squire in *Nashville Skyline*, he wasn't going to be capturing the zeitgeist of the twenty-something generation either. That role fell to—as much as any rock musicians in 1969 could have assumed such a role—the veterans who formed folk-rock's first and still most celebrated supergroup: Crosby, Stills, Nash & Young.

6

folk-rock superstars
and supergroups

I t was no surprise that most of folk-rock's ultimate supergroup rose from the ashes of the two most inventive and fractious Los Angeles folk-rock bands, Buffalo Springfield and (the first incarnation of) the Byrds. Nor was it a surprise that this supergroup would not be named after an animal or an airplane, but simply be a string of the featured players' last names: Crosby, Stills, and Nash (and, a bit later, Young). Individual members of several of folk-rock's biggest mid-'60s groups were by the end of the decade being driven to go out on their own or into new, looser alliances that promised greater individual freedom. Their new choices were fired both by their egos and the chance for unbridled (or at least more) space for their songwriting talents. Jon Landau (later manager of Bruce Springsteen) even singled out "the return of the solo artist" as one of the chief trends in rock music in a *Rolling Stone* state-of-the-rock-scene summary at the end of 1970. "The elimination in many instances of the banks of amplifiers and the breaking of the group bond returns the accent to a single person's feelings and thoughts," he wrote. "In many ways it allows for a far greater range of emotional expression. The soloists are without a doubt the new auteurs of popular music."

John Sebastian of the Lovin' Spoonful, for instance, certainly put up with a lot of hassle to get his solo recording career off the ground with his 1970 solo debut. A protracted contractual tangle had held up its release, with MGM and Warner/Reprise suing each other over the rights and MGM putting out an LP with identical music around the same time it appeared on Reprise. MGM then put out a live album, recorded without Sebastian's knowledge or consent, performed and taped on primitive equipment in a desperate attempt to milk him for all he was worth before the legal ink dried.

Yet asked how it felt to go out on his own, John Sebastian immediately exclaims, "In a word, delightful. I was having a wonderful time. This isn't to minimize the output and the good efforts of the Spoonful, but it was a time when music was changing, and I'd been playing with some pretty good musicians who were very often now off on their own, beginning to be visible. The singer-songwriter setting for an album was like complete freedom. Because, you remember, the Spoonful were adamantly against using studio musicians.

"So here was an opportunity to play with a fabulous drummer that was very different than my experience in the past. Vocalists with tremendous flexibility. Background singers. All of these people that, to me, were just like instruments. They were things that I wanted to interact with and to be able to use. The singer-songwriter can just kind of call up any mood he wants. He wants to play a little baroque brass ensemble, or a little flute and recorder, he can do it."

olk-rock's biggest duo, Simon & Garfunkel, was feeling the strain of solo ambitions and divergent interests as the decade waned. As Paul Simon wrote all of their original material and had more input into studio production (with help from Art Garfunkel and engineer/producer Roy Halee) than anyone, it was only a matter of time before he would feel it necessary to sing all of his songs alone. For the time being, however, he remained a part of the duo.

With Garfunkel distracted by a new acting career, the only Simon & Garfunkel release to appear in 1969 was the hit single "The Boxer," whose lilting scat vocal chorus and lyric (about Bob Dylan, some thought) were touched by the rare hand of effective melodrama in the thundering drums and arching strings of the long fadeout. Much of the duo's energy that year was directed toward a one-hour television special for the Bell Telephone Hour on CBS. When much of it featured images of the recent turbulence that was both redefining and eating away at the soul of America, including newsreel footage of Robert Kennedy, Martin Luther King, Jr., Cesar Chavez, Vietnam, and Woodstock, sponsor AT&T balked. The special was only aired, according to Simon, due to pressure from CBS (which owned Simon & Garfunkel's label, Columbia); AT&T, which had paid $600,000 for the show, sold it to Alberto-Culver for a mere $170,000 and swallowed a huge loss.

On their final studio album, 1970's *Bridge Over Troubled Water*, Simon seemed itching to break away from folk-rock barriers, branching into gospel on the title track, Peruvian music on "El Condor Pasa (If I Could)," and calypso rhythms for "Cecilia." Weirdly, "Bridge Over Troubled Water," now among the most overplayed standards of the twentieth century, might have become a Blood, Sweat & Tears hit had things worked out differently. Simon, according to Roy Halee, "thought that it might be nice for [Blood, Sweat & Tears singer] David Clayton-Thomas, and perhaps the band. We played it for Clayton-Thomas, who at the time didn't care that much for it. Maybe it might not have evolved that way, because if Clive Davis at the time had heard the song, he might have insisted that we do it. But I do remember, in the control room, him playing that tune for Clayton-Thomas."

Simon, like the folk-rockers who had gone psychedelic, was just too eclectic to be contained in a folk-rock format. He would not go psychedelic, but in a solo career that began in the early '70s, he would become more of a pop-ethnic-world music dilettante than any other mainstream pop star. This came as no surprise to Halee (who continued to work with Simon on several of the singer-songwriter's solo albums, up through *Graceland* and into the 1990s), "'cause he was always looking for something new to get involved with. He was always interested in all types of music. Anything that came along that was fresh and interesting, he would jump into." Aside from

Bob Dylan, Paul Simon would become the only folk-rock singer-songwriter who was about as big a star in the mid-'70s as he was in the late '60s (and, in the mid-'80s, would be for a time more popular than he'd ever been).

The loss of Garfunkel's harmonies—"vestigial" was the favorite word among critics to pinpoint Art's contributions—cut Simon's strongest links to the folk and folk-rock music with which he'd first made his name as a songwriter. (Contrary to some reports, Garfunkel does seem to have had a definite role in the studio as a co-producer of their later work; an extended *New York Times* profile of the duo in 1968 described him "in the glass-enclosed booth rejecting takes, suggesting changes in intonations, approving or disapproving of Simon's 'feeling.'") Although he'd established himself with hymns of social alienation like "The Sound of Silence," Simon had never seen himself as a topical songwriter in the early-to-mid-'60s finger-pointing tradition, telling *NME* shortly before Simon & Garfunkel broke up, "People read things, messages, into my songs, but I don't set out to try and make people see my point of view. I worry about entertaining, then if people see it my way, that's fine."

Simon was ultimately best suited toward a solo career in which he called all of the shots, rather than a partnership or a band. Crosby, Stills & Nash (Young would come later), however, were originally conceived as a means for the singer-songwriters to enjoy the best of both worlds: the camaraderie and stimulus of a working group, yet also the freedom to play and even record elsewhere, as a soloist or with others, as the mood struck. In a way it could be viewed as an expression of the era's rising communal values, a pooling of resources that would nevertheless allow much latitude to do your own thing. In time that flexibility would cause as many problems as it deterred. But for all three founding members, initially at any rate, it was a whole new ballgame, with more room to move than their old bands had afforded. And not quite the same as a one-off jam by big names, as Stephen Stills had recently participated in (on the *Super Session* album) with Mike Bloomfield and Al Kooper. "A supergroup, to me, means a group that plays super," clarified Stills in *Record Mirror*. "Supergroups are a different matter [than super sessions]. These are the second- and third-generation groups made up of friends who have left their former outfits. They don't mean to be 'super,' but they quickly acquire that tag."

That David Crosby and Stephen Stills would want a higher profile is unsurprising. Both were known for their high estimation of their own talents, and had already formed a strong friendship and professional bond. Crosby had sat in with Buffalo Springfield at the Monterey Pop Festival back in June 1967, and sung backup vocal on their recording of "Rock & Roll Woman." By mid-1968, they were already doing a three-song demo together, broadcast in the L.A. area by B. Mitchell Reed (the same DJ who'd smuggled out the unreleased nine-minute version of Buffalo Springfield's "Bluebird" for radio play), who attributed the cuts to the Frozen Noses.

Although Graham Nash had been the most adventurous songwriter in the Hollies, and a fine high harmony singer, his recruitment was more of a surprise. The Hollies might have covered Paul Simon songs; Nash even came to some Simon & Garfunkel sessions to observe, and Simon had turned Nash on to Bulgarian folk choral vocals. Nash had also become pals with John Sebastian and Cass Elliot. The Hollies had even penned some moderately psychedelic tunes like "King Midas in Reverse." But they were in 1968 still considered very much a British pop group.

The Hollies' plans to record an entire album of Dylan songs pushed Nash over the edge. On December 8, 1968 he did his last show with the group; two days later he was in America to rehearse with Crosby and Stills. "I quit the Hollies because of the *Sing Dylan* album," he told *Melody Maker* in mid-1969. "It was just that I knew they would turn his songs into big commercial rock-riffed, hit single-type album tracks. I dig Dylan, man, but this—to me—is not how you treat his songs." It's ironic that, in the space of just four short years, a strategy that had at one time been groundbreakingly radical—a rock group covering Dylan songs, as the Byrds had done to launch their career—was by late 1968 dismissed as the ultimate in unhipness.

The Hollies offered this rebuttal, also in *Melody Maker*: "All of Graham's songs are very slow, and very boring. He wants to go all soppy, artistic and beautiful. But we just want to stay as the Hollies." Everyone got their wish in the end, most likely. The Hollies did record their erratic album of pop-rock Dylan covers, which made #3 in Britain. Nash was free to chase his more esoteric pursuits (which, in truth, were not that far-out) with Crosby, Stills & Nash. An unusual sports-like trade of contracts freed Nash from Columbia to record for Atlantic, who in exchange gave up Richie Furay so he could record as part of Poco for Columbia.

"It all started over a year ago in Los Angeles," Nash told *Disc* at the end of 1968, long before the release of CSN's debut. "One day David and I wondered what it would be like to blend high-pitch voices like mine and Cass [Elliot] and his with McCartney. Stephen came to us around then— unknown to us he'd been sitting thinking roughly the same thing . . . . This is a gamble in a way, but we all knew we had to leave the groups we were with because they wanted to stay safe and warm where they were, and we couldn't.

"We're not starting another group. For a start we're all signed to different labels. But we're pioneering. We may come together on a more permanent basis . . . . We're going to make record companies change their ideas. We're not their private property. There's no reason why they should compete with each other, and no reason why people from different companies shouldn't play together if they're happier and making better music not staying in a rut."

As that comment reveals, their format was far from set in stone as they began to work together. As Cass Elliot revealed to *Record Mirror* in 1969, "A year or so ago, I worked out what would be my ideal group: Dave Crosby, Steve Stills, Graham Nash and myself. When we all eventually got together, I discovered that the three of them were so good that they just didn't need me." For a while John Sebastian was considered as part of the equation. "I was friends with all of those guys, as they were putting together their band," Sebastian says. "They needed a place to record, they needed a way to kind of focus in on what the group really was. 'Cause, as hard to imagine as it is now, there were still members that didn't know whether they were really in it or whether they were just accompanists. [Bassist] Harvey Brooks was playing along, Paul Harris was playing keyboards with them occasionally. A lot of the fine tuning had yet to be done.

"I had a house in Long Island. I said, 'You guys, come out to Long Island, it's easy to rent a place out there and we'll use my garage as kind of a place to play, and we can get something go-

Crosby, Stills, & Nash with some famous friends. Left to right: John Sebastian,
Stephen Stills, Graham Nash, Joni Mitchell, and David Crosby.

ing.' The guys came out to Sag Harbor, started playing both in my house and eventually in a house that they'd rented, set up the equipment, and they were at a point where they were starting to feel like they wanted to have drums as part of the group. I was, and remain, an amateur, strictly capital A, drummer. The extent of my visibility is on a few fills on Spoonful records. But because I think there was this kind of communality of idea and intent there at a certain point, Stephen, who was becoming the acknowledged leader of the band at that stage, said 'John, instead of us sweating and auditioning 80 million drummers, why don't you come along and play drums? We don't need Sam Lay [drummer in the Paul Butterfield Blues Band]. We need somebody to just kind of keep the time, and you would add another voice and another songwriter, which would be really cool. It would make for vast quantities of songs available,' and so on.

"You have to remember the way that the sequence of events had gone for me. I had kind of run the course with the Spoonful, gotten off on my own solo career, then been held up by MGM with a record for a year and a half. I was sitting on that first solo record, trying to get it released, while they were trying to pressure me to put it out as a Spoonful record. And I was saying, 'Hey guys, this would be really dishonest, I'm the only Spoonful on this record.' So being in this kind of limbo made me particularly afraid [of] yet another move. And I felt like, somehow or another, I'd managed to keep my audience from the Spoonful through to this John Sebastian character thing, and I don't think I dare make a third move to yet another group." Crosby, Stills & Nash even tried playing with musicians who had worked on Sebastian's debut solo album, including a couple (the aforementioned

Harvey Brooks and Paul Harris) who had been among the most frequently employed session men in 1960s New York–produced folk-rock.

Crosby, Stills & Nash, completed with support from several other musicians (including Dallas Taylor, who had also played on Sebastian's solo LP and was now the act's permanent drummer), was a Top Ten hit that immediately rocketed them into rock's elite. Reassessed after years had passed, its imperfections were more noticeable. Although the harmonies were astonishingly close and powerful, there was also a certain saccharine, calculated cleanliness, viciously slagged by John Morthland in the first edition of *The Rolling Stone Record Guide* as "limpid 'adult bubblegum' rockers and ballads of numbingly ersatz sensitivity." It was far worthier than that, but at the same time, there were no songs, except Stills's "Suite: Judy Blue Eyes" (about his affair with Judy Collins), that stood up to the best tunes Stills and Crosby had written for their former groups.

But the album did capture the essence of folk-rock in its harmonies and acoustic-electric guitar textures, as well as what the lifestyle and values of folk-rock's original audience had matured into by 1969. There were wrenching love songs that played out like multichapter stories (the aforementioned "Suite"). Graham Nash tapped into hippie utopianism at its most wide-eyed on "Marrakesh Express," one of the songs that had been rejected by the Hollies, and the one that most aptly fit the "adult bubblegum" description. In Crosby's "Long Time Gone," there was ham-fisted anger at the 1968 assassination of presidential candidate Robert Kennedy, who'd shown signs of maturing into an idealistic politician on the side of justice rather than power. "Wooden Ships," also recorded (more effectively) by Jefferson Airplane, was apocalyptic antiwar allegory. It was even reported in 1970 that the band would make a movie based on the song, with a screenplay by science fiction writer Theodore Sturgeon and hopes to snag Stanley Kubrick as the director, although nothing came of it. Stills, perhaps in emulation of his own strange '60s journey from military academy pupil to hippie, told *Rolling Stone* "the character I picked out for myself was a military man evolving into being a freak."

This was also a group that could switch at the drop of a hat from totally acoustic, dew-crusted ballads like "Helplessly Hoping" and "Lady of the Island" to relatively hard-rock cuts like "Wooden Ships" and "Long Time Gone." In a little-noticed parallel with Bob Dylan's mid-'60s shows, the first parts of their concerts would be acoustic. One of their finest tracks (recorded in 1970 after Neil Young had joined) was the acoustic "Find the Cost of Freedom," an elegy for blood shed and lives lost in warfare. Delivered with the solemnity of a graveside farewell, it was consigned to a non-LP B-side (although a live version shows up on *4 Way Street*).

"Our music is going in every direction that I've been able to figure out," boasted Crosby in *Melody Maker.* "One song comes out like Motown, one comes out South African, one comes out folk and one comes out like a Bulgarian harmony. There's no way I can tell in what direction we're going in—we're going in so many directions at once."

Two women who were closely involved with Crosby, Stills, and Nash both professionally and personally would do much to consolidate their own stardom around the time CSN were getting together. One was Joni Mitchell, who, though no longer produced by David Crosby, was coming into her own as a recording star, rather than a writer of songs covered by others (though her ex-lover-producer and his new bandmates would soon have a big hit with one of her tunes). The other was Judy Collins, who discarded her characteristic baroque-folk arrangements to record her final album of the 1960s, *Who Knows Where the Time Goes*, with full rock accompaniment, including then-boyfriend Stephen Stills on electric guitar.

"The combination of musical backgrounds is what really makes this feeling of what we all tend to call folk music, whatever that hybrid is," Collins said when discussing the album with Karl Dallas of *Melody Maker*. "What we do might be the combination of a classical influence with a folk one with a country-western flavor to it sometimes with a very blues influence, but it all makes sense, it all interrelates together." To *Record Mirror*, she elaborated, "I felt for a time that I had to be in a rock group. In fact, it was good for me as I learned a lot about changing my voice and controlling it better. I was beginning to sound a little lamented on a lot of things."

The producer of *Who Knows Where the Time Goes* was David Anderle, another Elektra staffer who found himself in a position to work with the label's top veteran star without much of a studio resume. Many of the arrangements used on *Wildflowers* had been devised in Anderle's house in Los Angeles, where he was working as the director of Elektra's West Coast office. It was around that time, he remembers, that he saw her play a few club shows in L.A.'s Troubadour. "I went down every night and watched the whole show. I was sitting upstairs in the balcony, and I would look down and watch all these date people falling in love, girls putting their heads on their boyfriends' shoulders, and people nudging each other at certain moments in songs. It was so warm, and there was so much love generated in the audience.

"So I said to her at one point, 'You know what? You should make an intimate record, something with like just a rhythm section, and I think it would be fantastic. Because people fall in love at your concerts.' And she thought that that was a good idea. She went back to New York and put a little band together, but they were mainly classical musicians. They came out here and were recording some demo stuff, and one night I said, 'The idea is right, but you got classical people in there trying to do it. And it's completely wrong.'

"So she called Jac Holzman and said, 'I want David Anderle to produce my record.' I had never produced a record before!" he laughs. Although he'd actually worked on Elektra albums by David Ackles and Diane Hildebrand, he clarifies, "those were the only two things I ever did. And [Jac] said, 'Are you fucking kidding?' And she said, 'Well, I'm not gonna do it unless he does it.' And so he let me do it. I called Stephen Stills [then at loose ends just after the breakup of Buffalo Springfield], Van Dyke [Parks], and some other people. [To] Stephen I said, 'You gotta help me, man, I need to produce a record and I don't know what I'm doing. But I know what I want to *hear*.' He got [steel guitarist] Buddy Emmons and [famed rock 'n' roll session guitarist] James Burton in there, and I got [drummer Jim] Gordon [later of Derek & the Dominos] in there, and Van Dyke and some other people. And of course I got [engineer] John Haeny to save my butt in the control room.

"She had made such *perfect* records up to that point, in terms of her pitch and so forth," he continues. "I was just going for feel. As a matter of fact, I remember Jim Gordon saying to me one night, 'This is the first time since I've been in L.A. that I've actually played sessions where the singer is singing at the same time.' We had a great time. [Blues guitar great] Lonnie Mack, people like that, were around Elektra at the time, and they were coming up to me and going 'Man, I never really got into this folk stuff, but I really love this record.' I was under a lot of heat, 'cause I went over budget a little bit, and it wasn't Judy's perfect vocals, and all that kind of pristine stuff. But I thought it worked. And I still do."

Collins had played a strong role in folk-rock's journey throughout the 1960s, perhaps stronger than any artist who had actually been established as an acoustic folk star before folk-rock began, with the exception of Bob Dylan. Yet *Who Knows Where the Time Goes* is really her only all-out rock album, as opposed to the baroque-folk of *In My Life* and *Wildflowers*, though she had cut isolated tracks (like her covers of Richard Fariña's "Hard Lovin' Loser" and Dylan's "I'll Keep It with Mine") that rocked fairly hard. And Collins would never come as close to straightahead rock again, though *Who Knows Where the Time Goes* did pretty well. "I don't know if she ever says it, but I think she was really disappointed in that record in the beginning," believes Anderle. "She got back to New York and I think she took a lot of shit from her snooty friends back there. If you listen to it, some of the stuff is really kind of strange vocal stuff. Later on, she did call me; she was putting a best-of record together. And she said, 'I've had a chance to go through everything and I really hear what you did, and I want to just thank you for what you did.'"

The continuity with the earlier Judy Collins was there, however, in her typically astute choice of cover material. Leonard Cohen's "Bird on a Wire" and "Story of Isaac" were selected after Cohen played them to Anderle and Collins following a rollicking lunch. Ian Tyson's "Someday Soon," a Nashville steel guitarist would tell Anderle years later, had "the part every steel player has to learn before he can move on," played by Buddy Emmons. The album also extended her reach to the championship of new British folk-rock composers with covers of songs by Sandy Denny (the title track) and the Incredible String Band's Robin Williamson ("First Boy I Loved"). Denny, who at that point had only just joined Fairport Convention, in particular was totally unknown in the US, and "Who Knows Where the Time Goes"—eventually viewed as her signature song of sorts—had not even appeared on any official release before the Collins album. (Oddly, Collins cut two versions of "Who Knows Where the Time Goes." One was the full-band production with key change that appeared on the LP. The other, a far sparser, drumless arrangement sans dramatic upward key change, was only on the B-side of "Both Sides Now" and the film soundtrack of *The Subject Was Roses*, though it later showed up on the greatest hits collection *Colors of the Day*.)

On both *Who Knows Where the Time Goes* and *Wildflowers*, to her surprise, Collins was also discovering her own songwriting talent on tracks like "My Father." "I was never interested in the writing aspect," she says. "Then I sat down at the piano, and then I met Leonard Cohen, and then it all kind of came together. And I started to write, thank God."

"At one point I gave her in one way the worst, and in one way the best, advice that I've ever given anyone," says Bruce Langhorne, who sometimes accompanied her on guitar on live gigs. "She came up to my house one time, and she'd been fooling around with songwriting. She played her songs for me. I listened to them, and I didn't really hear anything in her songs. They didn't get to me. So I told her that I didn't really like what she was doing. I gave her some advice about what to try to write about. I think I told her, 'Why don't you try writing about a relationship?' It was really poor advice for me to give to someone who was as sophisticated as she was. But it was all I could come up with at the time.

"I read in a subsequent interview with her that had been a really significant moment for her, that what I had said had really hurt her. Fortunately, she didn't let me discourage her," he laughs. "She went on and wrote some really great songs, like 'My Father.'" Which, of course, was about one of the most important relationships in Collins's life, among many other reasons, she says, for "the meticulous lessons of choosing great songs, which my father had taught me. My father *always* chose the great songs that were gonna last."

Writing songs, of course, was never a problem for the woman who had written Collins's biggest hit. Joni Mitchell had such a staggering backlog of quality compositions that there would be no danger of her falling prey to the dreaded second-album-letdown syndrome. As unofficial live recordings from the late '60s illustrate, there were a fair number of good Mitchell songs she never put on wax herself, though one, "Eastern Rain," at least made it onto Fairport Convention's second LP. By Mitchell archivist Joel Bernstein's count, she had no less than 52 songs written before recording her first album, and was by that time able to perform three consecutive sets, with more than 30 compositions, without repeating a single one. Even "Both Sides Now," along with her nearly as celebrated "Chelsea Morning," would have to wait until her second album, *Clouds*. "Urge for Going," one of her most exquisite melancholy ballads, had been vital to starting her career when it was covered in 1966 by Tom Rush and (for a country hit) George Hamilton IV, yet she only put her own recording on a non-LP B-side—and waited until 1972 to do so. "The Circle Game," one of her most well-loved concert tunes for years, wouldn't come out until 1970's *Ladies of the Canyon*.

By then she'd just about finally crossed the bridge to electric rock music. Like her self-titled 1968 debut album, 1969's *Clouds* had been acoustic, though the pristine Judy Collins–influenced phrasing of her debut had widened into something more identifiably Mitchell. Too, her guitar playing became more rhythmic (particularly on "Chelsea Morning"), and her use of multitracked vocals more frequent and proficient. In *Time* magazine shortly before the release of *Clouds*, Mitchell had prepared listeners for something of a gloomfest, promising, "My next album will be even sadder. It gets into the pain of the heart."

There were still the breed of character-sketch songs she'd so admired in Leonard Cohen, with "For Free" stirred into being by a London street clarinetist, and "Willy," more famously, about her lengthy romance with Graham Nash. It could leave the impression that Mitchell was sharing an almost verbatim diary of her innermost life with her listeners, though she cautioned readers not to take the lyrics 100 percent literally in a 1970 *Melody Maker* profile. "There is a certain amount of my life in all my songs," she admitted. Yet she added, "They are honest and personal, and based on truth, but I exercise a writer's license to change details." Her skill for capturing detail in song was so exacting, though, that it would soon convince millions that she had been at the biggest countercultural celebration of the twentieth century, though she had not even been present as a spectator, let alone a performer, at Woodstock.

Like James Taylor, Linda Ronstadt, Jackson Browne, and others entrenched in the Hollywood session production milieu, Mitchell would not peak commercially until the mid-'70s. By that time, her music had expanded way beyond the principally acoustic guitar and piano accompaniment of her earliest records. As she'd predicted in *Melody Maker* in 1970, "I guess there will just come a time when I'm hearing more music than I'm able to play and then the change will come about naturally." If she was not thought of as a folk-rock singer anymore by then, it was consistent with her declaration way back in September 1966 in *Hoot*: "I only hope that I never have to be categorized—just to feel that I am a musician."

The chart performances of Judy Collins's *Who Knows Where the Time Goes* and Joni Mitchell's *Clouds* were almost identical, the former peaking at #29, the latter at #31. Collins was still far more famous than Mitchell, whose only prior album, after all, had struggled up to only #189. Yet Mitchell was on her way to becoming a bigger star than Collins, largely without the aid of hit singles. Their different levels of success in the 1970s were naturally partially attributable to changing tastes, in which confessional songwriters such as Mitchell were far more in vogue than singers such as Collins who leaned heavily on interpretation (with exceptions like Linda Ronstadt). Their differing successes were also partially attributable to changing record company politics. Collins's label, Elektra, which had done more for folk-rock than any other independent company, was about to change hands and get swallowed up in a corporate merger. Mitchell, on the other hand, would be allied with labels and management that were crowding into the elite power circles of the record business, and making folk-rock-based music into a slicker, mass-marketable genre that would dominate much of the 1970s.

As noted before, Mitchell had experienced her share of snafus in getting a deal, getting promoted tastefully, and recording her albums without embarrassing technical glitches. It would really not be until the early '70s that singer-songwriters and the industry fully came to grips with each other. The industry *had* to—even if the singer-songwriters (Mitchell was a great example) were more determined to gain creative control of their sessions and packaging than most artists had been in the pre-folk-rock era. There was just too much money to be made.

Young, hungry managers were horning in on the scene as well. One was Elliot Roberts, who became manager of Neil Young and Joni Mitchell, getting steered to Mitchell when Buffy Sainte-Marie gave him a tape of Joni. Roberts gained Mitchell's trust by offering to accompany her on a four-week tour, on the spot and paying his own way, after seeing her perform in Greenwich Village in 1967 when she was still without a record deal. Another new mogul on the scene was Roberts's mentor David Geffen, who helped Crosby, Stills, Nash & Young get their deal with Atlantic, and would sign budding late-'60s folk-rockers-turned-'70s superstars Mitchell, Jackson Browne, and Linda Ronstadt to his Asylum label in the early '70s.

Although the independent labels Elektra and Vanguard, and the MGM-distributed Verve/Folkways/Forecast, had been responsible for inking many of the best singer-songwriters in the mid-'60s when folk-rock took off, bigger majors like Columbia and Warner Brothers were adapting and scooping up a larger share of the available talent by the late '60s. Vanguard didn't help its cause by its reluctance to adapt to the changing needs of contemporary recording artists. Producer Denny Bruce was doing West Coast A&R for Vanguard at the time and remembers how, when he wanted to do an album with John Fahey for the label that figured a few other musicians into the budget, "My asking for $4,000 was the beginning of World War III. No matter what I wanted for Fahey the answer was 'No, he's a solo guitarist.' The company's hot-headed bottom line was, 'We didn't have to give Joan Baez a nickel, she wanted to be here.'"

"There was a lot of competition for these artists," says Verve/Forecast chief Jerry Schoenbaum. "It wasn't just Vanguard, Elektra, and Verve/Forecast. Warners got involved, Columbia [got] involved, and a whole host of big companies run very professionally were competing with me. Clive Davis seemed to have a great affinity for getting a hold of the artist that, for whatever reason, left Verve/Forecast. Janis Ian, [Tim] Hardin, he signed these people. Sometimes I wish he had signed me!"

Davis, who became vice president of Columbia in the mid-'60s, takes a good deal of credit for getting the label in tune with the rock trends of the day in his autobiography *Clive: Inside the Record Business*. To some degree, this is likely self-aggrandization: the Byrds, Bob Dylan, and Simon & Garfunkel had all been signed to Columbia before Davis's reign, and in print he's far more likely to bask in the reflected glory of the hit records than mention the numerous Columbia folk-rock recordings that didn't sell much, even if they were good albums. As noted a while back, he had tried to edge Melanie in an inappropriately middle-of-the-road direction during her brief stint with the company. Melanie saw the corporatization of the business rearing its ugly head even then, musing, "When I signed to Columbia, there were still ears running record companies as far as A&R people. It was just at that moment, it seemed, that they became Clive Davis and lawyers." Still, Davis did make Donovan his first signing (to the subsidiary label Epic), and Columbia took on eccentric talents like Leonard Cohen, who had barely made any professional music before his debut LP, while continuing to churn out blockbusters for Dylan and Simon & Garfunkel.

"They were a pop label that didn't really want to get involved in it," says producer/engineer Roy Halee, who was, along with Simon & Garfunkel, one-third of the production team for the duo's late-'60s albums and had worked on some sessions by the Byrds and Dylan. "They wanted to look the other way when Dylan walked in the studio. Then all of a sudden, they started to make huge amounts of money from these acts. So they were kind of forced into it." Davis's role was indeed important, and not just from a business angle, according to Halee: "He was aggressive, sending people out, hearing acts, getting involved and signing acts. And he had pretty good ears. It got to the point where it got to be a little too much, where he was picking singles, telling producers how to edit their singles."

Even in the late '60s, though, outdated ways of making records could throw big obstacles in the path of the folk-rockers Columbia signed. Jim Messina of country-rock pioneers Poco produced the band's 1969 debut album *Pickin' Up the Pieces*, and remembers how the group was still required to use CBS studios if it lived within 90 miles of the facility. Poco did, and Messina was saddled with an engineer who had worked with the likes of Andy Williams and Teresa Brewer, with no experience in either rock or country music. Messina was also not allowed to touch the board because of union legalities, even though he was a member of the union. After complaints from him and other producers and artists, Messina recalls, Davis "went to bat for us, told them they had to make changes because the artists were upset." Eventually CBS's Los Angeles studio was closed, making way for artists like Messina to use more sympathetic ones in California like Wally Heider's or Sunset Sound, though that wouldn't happen until several years down the line.

The major label that became most identified with the singer-songwriter movement, however, was Warner Brothers and its sister label Reprise. Originally begun in the late '50s as an offshoot of the Warner Brothers film company, Warner Brothers Records had until the late '60s been one of the more middle-of-the-road majors. It didn't totally ignore the folk or folk-rock market, as Peter, Paul & Mary were mainstays of its roster; the Mugwumps had done a 1964 single for it before three of their members found fame in the Lovin' Spoonful and the Mamas & the Papas; and the Modern Folk Quartet had recorded for the label in both its wholesome folk and early folk-rock days. When Warners first merged with Reprise in the early '60s, if anything that might have tilted its balance more toward middle-of-the-road pop, as Reprise was founded by Frank Sinatra, who naturally was the company's main star. As late as 1966, Warner Brothers seemed at sea with how to handle innovative folk-rock bands like the Beau Brummels, forcing them to record an album of Top 40 covers as their first Warners LP.

Under the influence of Warners executives like Joe Smith, Mo Ostin, and Lenny Waronker, Warner-Reprise began to move in more progressive directions by 1967. Waronker himself produced the Beau Brummels' far more serious and artistic follow-up *Triangle* that year, and the label, it seemed, began to snap up blossoming singer-songwriters right and left. Some were right off the folk circuit and primed to move into folk-rock on their first recordings, like Joni Mitchell and Arlo Guthrie; others, like Van Morrison and Waronker's friends Randy Newman and Van Dyke Parks, were not predominantly folk-rooted. The label also went after established folk-rock singer-songwriters whose contracts with other companies were expiring, like Neil Young, James Taylor, Eric Andersen, John Sebastian, and Gordon Lightfoot (as well as some groups with singer-songwriters, like the Fugs and the Youngbloods). By mid-1970, *Billboard* ran a feature headlined "WB-Reprise Push in Singer-Songwriter Mart" that proclaimed: "Warner Bros–Reprise is developing a strong hold on the singer-songwriter market. In addition, the label complex has also pioneered the 'new thing' in the pop scene, the individual disk artist as opposed to the group concept which held sway, more or less, since the advent of the Beatles six years ago."

Warner-Reprise has received a lot of credit for being an artist-friendly organization that not only gave temperamental talents leeway to be creative and experimental, but also exhibited a great deal of patience, sticking with singer-songwriters for years until their sales finally matched their reputations. In many cases, this was true. Joni Mitchell's debut album barely made the bottom of the Top 200, and Neil Young's first solo LP missed the charts entirely, but within a couple of years both were superstars. Gene Parsons, who recorded for Warners as a solo after leaving the Byrds, calls it "a very supportive record company. I mean, they kept people on like Randy Newman and Ry Cooder when they weren't making any money on 'em. But they believed in 'em, and they stuck with 'em and hung in there. For *years!*"

As in every company of significant size, though, there were two sides to that coin. Steve Young, who moved to Reprise after cutting one of the finest overlooked late-'60s country-rock records for

A&M (*Rock, Salt & Nails*), was extremely discouraged by his experience with the company, which as he remembers almost didn't release his sole LP for the label. Barbara Keith, who did one album for Reprise in the early '70s, wasn't completely happy with the result and gave back her advance money; Warners, she has recalled, pulled the record off the market right after its release. Tom Rapp, Tom Paxton, Nancy Michaels, David Blue, Nico, and the post-Fugs Ed Sanders all made singer-songwriter albums for Reprise that were barely noticed, and probably barely promoted considering how hard it is to find copies.

Overextended rosters of underpromoted singer-songwriters, of course, were hardly unique to Reprise. When asked by *Rolling Stone* in 1971 why Verve/Forecast had signed minor folk-rock singer-songwriter Patrick Sky, whose two late-'60s albums for the label were heard by barely anyone, Dave Van Ronk (who'd made his own obscure folk-rock LP for Verve/Forecast, *Dave Van Ronk & the Hudson Dusters*) half-joked that labels "all go through a seven-year itch of signings—they'll pick up anybody who isn't nailed down." Even with its superstars-in-the-making, however, Reprise made some surprising gaffes. Joni Mitchell's first album went through convoluted engineering problems that cut off highs and lows and washed it in reverb. Neil Young's debut was subjected to a bizarre mastering process, Heico-CSG, that tried to make stereo sound better when played on mono equipment (the album was later issued in a remixed form, at Young's insistence).

Others, though, appreciated the high level of professionalism that Warner Brothers–Reprise did bring to many of its projects, particularly those recorded in Los Angeles with a plethora of top session players. One was Arlo Guthrie, whose integration of rock instrumentation didn't fully take until his third album, *Running Down the Road*, recorded with creme-de-la-creme L.A. session cats like Ry Cooder and James Burton. The drug-smuggling tale "Coming in to Los Angeles" gave the album its notoriety, though actually much of it is far tamer country-rock. As noted earlier, Guthrie had undertaken his real-life journey to Los Angeles to record directly for Warners in the first place in order to get away from the manager and producer that had hindered some of his earlier attempts to do things his own way.

"The first real record that I was involved with was *Running Down the Road*, and that was all electric," he says. "We were still a little too crazed to make a decent record. It took another few years. But I started putting together a real good team at that point, with Ry Cooder coming in, and some other great players. And when we got to make *Washington County* (1970), it was really my first, what I would call, good record. It had elements of very traditional stuff—we did some old Doc Watson stuff—singing-wise, and we really combined elements of modern rock 'n' roll. Not just in the sound of it, but in the technique of it, of overdubbing and stuff like that, cutting tape, playing with stuff, being creative. I mean, the Beatles had done some incredible things in the studio, and we wanted to play too."

Guthrie even took a page out of the 1965 school of re-recording acoustic songs for the pop market by doing a 45-only rock version of "Alice's Restaurant." Retitled "Alice's Rock & Roll Restaurant," it was neither too hard-rocking nor too effective, losing much of its impact when cut down from its epic length to fit onto a single. "Warners came to me and said, 'Arlo, you can't play "Alice's Restaurant" on the radio,'" he recalls. "'You have to shorten it for the radio.' In those days, nothing

Arlo Guthrie performing "Alice's Restaurant" at the 1967 Newport Folk Festival.

over two-and-a-half minutes could get played. So when somebody shows up with a 20-minute piece, you can imagine, right? So we tried to think it through. There was no way to do it. The whole *point* is that it takes that long to tell that tale! I finally came up with making up, basically, lurid and graphic lyrics to the chorus, so that they would leave me alone, 'cause I knew they wouldn't put it out. We had a great time doing it. It wasn't like it was bad.

"So they edited 'Alice's Rock & Roll Restaurant' after I had left town. They edited the lyrics, changed around the music, and put it out anyhow." The song proved much more adaptable, in a way no one could have predicted, to the silver screen, providing the basis for *Bonnie & Clyde* director Arthur Penn's *Alice's Restaurant* movie in 1969, starring Guthrie himself. Released on the heels of his successful Woodstock appearance, for a moment there might have been hopes that it would launch him into superstardom; there was even a cover story on him and the film in *Newsweek*. Although the film did well, only one of his subsequent albums (1970's *Washington County*) made the Top 40, putting him into the same respectable-but-not-huge early-'70s commercial niche occupied by the likes of Richie Havens.

Both the song and movie of "Alice's Restaurant" were based on an actual experience of Guthrie's—getting drafted and devising or at least toying with creative ways to wiggle out of going to Vietnam—that was common to most American men between the ages of 18 and 21. (Guthrie has emphasized, however, that the film contained a lot of fictionalized alterations of what actually took place.) Understandably, many listeners identified with the song and its songwriter as something of a mirror image of themselves. As fan Ron Kowalke told *Newsweek* while waiting in line to see *Alice's Restaurant*, "Arlo has the same problems and he's going through the same things we are." This identification could be taken to extremes, and sometimes singer-songwriters issued cautionary statements explaining that their lyrics were not always based on actual incidents or to be taken too literally, but were made-up stories and characters like those in most plays and novels. But such identification was nonetheless central to the appeal of the major singer-songwriters reaching stardom as the 1960s turned to the 1970s, often with the aid of state-of-the-art Los Angeles production and session musicians in support.

The man with the canniest touch for shaping the sprawl of Southern Californian singer-songwriting talent into a high-selling product for Warners was producer/manager Peter Asher, who had done his bit for helping light the way to folk-rock in 1964 as half of the British duo Peter & Gordon. By the late '60s he was an A&R man at Apple Records, the label founded by the Beatles at the height of their psychedelic altruism. Asher didn't work there long, but was able to sign James Taylor to the label and produce the singer's first album in London. Taylor had been part of a New York rock band, the Flying Machine, also including one-time Fug and eventual leading L.A. session guitarist Danny Kortchmar. Gigging for months in 1966 at the Night Owl Cafe, the group only managed to release one single on a small label before breaking up, though demos were later issued as well. Both songs from that 45, and another from the demos, would end up being re-recorded for *James Taylor*, which also featured "Something in the Way She Moves," whose title line helped inspire George Harrison's "Something."

The Apple LP, recorded with session men including Paul McCartney, introduced the world to the calmest, most introspective of the major singer-songwriters to make their first major work in the 1960s. Taylor's extremely serene confessions of his inner anguish, bonded together by his reassuring voice and accomplished acoustic guitar playing, would do more than any other performer to set the tone for the singer-songwriter sound of the 1970s. In particular, 1970's *Sweet Baby James* was singer-songwriting that everyone from hippies to suburban moms could enjoy, even if some of the songs had buried undercurrents of depression. These were sometimes inspired by Taylor's own battles with drug addiction and mental illness, which had periodically led to hospitalization and institutionalization.

There were still folk dimensions to Taylor's sound, and live he was even covering Woody Guthrie songs as late as 1970, according to one *Melody Maker* report. But *Sweet Baby James* was far more pop-friendly than anything Woody Guthrie did, or that Arlo Guthrie did, for that matter. Subsequently the album, and the door it opened for Carole King and Carly Simon, would be condemned by revisionist critics as the smug, self-satisfied blandness that punk needed to blast into obsolescence. As Jon Landau accurately predicted in *Rolling Stone*, "He is establishing the style of the genre in the early '70s. Contemplative, reflective, natural to an often painful degree, unpretentious, not inordinately humble."

Taylor's musical and lyrical intimacy created a facsimile of one-on-one communication. It, like some of the aforementioned work of Arlo Guthrie and Joni Mitchell, was mistaken by some listeners as a diary of real-life incidents, though Taylor too warned against taking them verbatim, allowing in *Melody Maker* that "yes, I s'pose you could say I've used my own experiences for songs, but my songs are not actually about things that've happened to me." (Much earlier, Janis Ian had also cautioned against impressionable listeners assuming that a singer-songwriter's compositions and life were synonymous, emphasizing in *Newsweek* in mid-1967 that "Society's Child" was "definitely not from personal experience.") *Sweet Baby James* was, indeed, the touchstone of what would come to be called the "confessional" school of singer-songwriting, though less sympathetic critics would castigate it as "self-absorbed."

At the time, however, *Sweet Baby James* was showered with overwhelming praise and sales. Both it and its single, "Fire and Rain" (sparked by the suicide of an old friend of Taylor's, despite its placid surface), made the Top Three. By now Taylor was on Warner Brothers, the Beatles having munificently released Taylor from his contract, despite resistance from Apple's new business manager, Allen Klein. Too, Asher and Taylor were recording in Southern California, using an elite group of session players to craft a professional sound both slick and engaging. Asher would also manage Taylor, and act as manager/producer for Linda Ronstadt, using a similar approach in the studio to facilitate her big breakthroughs.

"The whole idea was to take James, the song, his vocal, and frame it precisely," says Asher. "In both James and Linda's case, they were certainly the focus and the centerpiece, and everything else was there to make them sound good. The arrangements came from experimentation and discussion. James is more of a mish-mash in a way, because yes, he owes something to the folk era, undoubtedly. But also, his take on music has always been kind of R&B. And what you hear a lot in his singing is that, even though he plays sort of finger picking guitar, he tends to sing more like Sam Cooke. Even when he sings his own songs, there's an awful lot of classic R&B in his phrasing and singing. Whereas Linda clearly comes more from her sort of country and Mexican heritage, and considerably less from rhythm and blues. But undoubtedly, folk-rock plays a great role in both their music."

The transitional folk-rock-to-pop singer-songwriters like Taylor—many of them, though not all of them, recording in Southern California—were making it possible for another advancement that would help lead to the end of the 1960s-style folk-rock road. The way was now clear for other singer-songwriters with no real folk background to write their own personal songs and sing them, even if they had previously been consigned to behind-the-scenes roles of supplying songs for other artists. Carole King, Randy Newman, and Harry Nilsson were the most successful, none of them reaching their pinnacles until they'd stepped from behind the curtain to start doing their own records. Laura Nyro, who'd started on Verve/Forecast although she was never really a folk artist, was another who mixed pop, soul, and singer-songwriter aesthetics into a personal style. There were other, more blatantly commercial composers who never were bracketed into the "singer-songwriter" tag, more because they didn't find as much critical favor than due to a wholly different aesthetic. As Jerry Jeff Walker points out by way of illustration, "Neil Diamond was a singer-songwriter uptown. He was managed by the same office that I wound up with, the people that owned the Bitter End. Then this guy writes an article about singer-songwriters in Greenwich Village. Diamond goes, 'Singer-songwriter? That's what we all are!'"

T he wider scope of singer-songwriting in the 1970s also created opportunities for 1960s performers who'd made false starts at the edges of folk-rock without getting far. There was Jackson Browne, of course, but also Warren Zevon, who'd been placing songs with the likes of the Turtles in addition to making folk-rock-poppish singles as half of Lyme & Cybelle in 1966. There was Harry Chapin, who'd recorded extremely obscure, unremarkable pop-folk-rock in 1966 as part of the Chapin Brothers. There was Canadian Bruce Cockburn, who'd briefly been in the pop-folk-rock group 3's a Crowd, which included Neil Young's old bandmate Ken Koblun on bass and whose sole album was co-produced by Cass Elliot. Jennifer Warnes had made her first albums in the late '60s, long before becoming known both for adult contemporary hits and interpretations of songs by Leonard Cohen. Robin Lane sang backup vocals on Neil Young's second album in 1969, a full decade before issuing her first album as the leader of one of the more neglected new wave-pop crossover bands, Robin Lane & the Chartbusters.

There were others. In the 1960s Carly Simon, who'd briefly tasted minor fame in the middle of the decade as half of the folk duo the Simon Sisters, had been managed by Albert Grossman; been produced by Bob Johnston; recorded an unreleased version of "Baby, Let Me Follow You Down" with rewritten lyrics by Bob Dylan and featuring Mike Bloomfield, Al Kooper, Robbie Robertson, and Rick Danko on backup; briefly been a duo with Richie Havens; and sung with Elephant's Memory, later to serve as John Lennon's backing band. In Levon Helm's autobiography *This Wheel's on Fire*, the Band's Danko said Grossman's organization was trying to make Simon "into the female Bob Dylan." All of this had gotten her pretty much nowhere. In the 1970s she became James Taylor's female confessional counterpart superstar, and his partner in marriage. Mary McCaslin, however, proved it was possible to go in the other direction, finding a measure of widespread success as one of the most popular artists on the 1970s folk circuit, especially famed for her unusual folk arrangements of rock songs.

And there were, finally, several shining lights among singer-songwriters who were simply unable to ride the gravy train into the 1970s, even if they were among the previous decade's most important innovators of the entire genre. Four of them were Fred Neil, Tim Hardin, Tim Buckley, and Phil Ochs. All but one of them would be dead within a dozen years of the dawning of the '70s; all of them had their careers curtailed by mental problems and/or substance abuse; and all of them possessed volatile artistic temperaments incompatible with the demands of the industry. And all of them were about as good as the best of the '60s singer-songwriting veterans who became big stars (or bigger stars) in the '70s. Yet all are nearly forgotten today by the mainstream pop audience, their lives and demises offering sobering reminders that talent alone wasn't enough to survive and thrive in the music business.

The first to fade from the scene, though the only one to live until the twenty-first century, was Fred Neil. Neil was certainly not industrious following his 1967 album *Sessions*, releasing just one more album of live material and outtakes before retiring permanently from the studio. "Fred was probably the greatest 12-string player alive," says his one-time manager, Howard Solomon. "And the uniqueness of his basso profundo voice, I don't think anybody has ever achieved that quality of sound. Like Frank Sinatra is to his idiom, that's what Freddie brought to the folk idiom, a kind of phrasing that nobody's ever been able to duplicate. And he loved to sing and play. But he did not love to sing and play for the money, particularly. He would play and sing for the money when push came to shove and he had to pay for something. But he loved to be free, playing to the dolphins or sitting around the pool with John Sebastian and Harvey Brooks and a whole retinue of people." In fact he rarely performed or was seen in public between the early '70s and his death in 2001.

"When he was in L.A., we used to all hang out," says Barry McGuire. "He would sit there and sing, and we would just melt. We all wanted to be like him, and he couldn't get a hit record! It just never seemed to open for him. He was very involved in this drug abuse. I think that kind of scared everybody away. I was very laced with drugs myself, but Fred seemed to be even more so than me."

"Freddie couldn't handle people giving him any kind of adulation," feels his friend Denny Doherty. "You had a Fred Neil session happening in L.A., and the world would show up. Freddie would go, 'What are all these people here for?' 'They love you, Fred!' 'I don't want 'em around.' 'Fred, get 'em all to sing.' And Freddie's just going, 'I just wanna play with these three people, and what are all these people in the studio?' The studio would be *jammed* full of people. 'Cause here was this icon. All he ever wanted [was] just to play his music and be left alone. But nobody would leave him alone 'cause he was so great. He didn't want to be watched when he was creating, or working, or trying to make records.

"So the big party turned into the big party, and Freddie turned into the big partier. And nothing was accomplished in a lot of those sessions. So he just sort of backed off and tried to get away from everybody, and in so doing, found a little peace and quiet, and said, 'It's this or that? I'm taking *this*. That other shit's crazy. I can't handle that Hollywood recording scene, that's too nuts for words. I want to go back to the Grove [Coconut Grove, in Southern Florida].' And he did."

Tim Hardin, like Fred Neil, never matched the songwriting of his first two albums. Unlike Neil, he hung around and tried for years. *Live in Concert* (1968) was mostly comprised of material he'd already recorded in the studio, but offered a stunning new work in the seven-minute eulogy for Lenny Bruce, "Lenny's Tune" (covered by Nico the same year on her first album, where it was actually titled "Eulogy to Lenny Bruce"). On *Suite for Susan Moore and Damion: We Are One, One, All in One*, Hardin's first album after leaving Verve, his talent for compact songs seemed to have deserted him (as it had with Neil for *Sessions*). It was replaced by an interesting but turgid fog of stream-of-consciousness lethargy, the somnolence enhanced by liquid jazz keyboards, tremolo guitars, and somber poetry recitation. "Unfortunately Tim Hardin was never captured on record as he was," bewailed Phil Ochs in *Rolling Stone*. "I still think he was the best singer of the '60s. In his youth he shamed everybody else on stage, in terms of singing and the geometry of singing and timing and tones and musicianship; he was just not to be believed."

There were occasional bright moments on subsequent albums for Columbia in the early '70s, but Hardin's career, like his art, was slipping into obscurity. His ongoing drug habit didn't help. Few people remember that he appeared at the Woodstock festival, where a chance to open the proceedings was blown as, according to festival co-producer Michael Lang (speaking in Joel Makower's *Woodstock: The Oral History*), the singer was "a little too blitzed." (Hardin did sing at the event, but the opening slot went to Richie Havens, whose blistering performance passed him into legend.) He also didn't seem to be in good shape a few weeks earlier in concert in Manhattan's Central Park, where he had performed with, according to *New York Times* reviewer John S. Wilson, "a soft, mumbling manner of singing that made his lyrics difficult to follow even at relatively close range to an amplifier. He was soon being interrupted by cries of 'louder!' from the bleacher seats but he seemed unable to adjust his delivery or his volume in a satisfactory manner."

"Very few people ever said, 'I saw Tim Hardin's concert, it was just terrific,'" stresses the producer of his best work, Erik Jacobsen. "He would go and pass out. That's what he was famous for." Adds Jerry Schoenbaum, "Very often when he was in California he called me up, told me his wife was pregnant, blah blah—the usual excuses that drug addict[s] will give you in order to get more money. I loaned him hundreds of dollars, and I knew where it was going. It's a sad story. He could have been a giant in the business." Hardin would die of a heroin overdose in 1980, shortly before his fortieth birthday.

Tim Buckley, in contrast to Neil and Hardin, was becoming more artistically ambitious as he reached the 1970s. He lost his audience, however, as he fell under the influence of ever more avant-garde jazz singers and contemporary classical composers. *Lorca*, his fourth and final Elektra album (1970), presented long tracks in which Buckley often dispensed with conventional rock- or folk-song-based chord progressions. The lyrics were so abstract, the voice so bone-chillingly operatic and anguished, that it sometimes sounded as if he were speaking in tongues. Elektra dropped Buckley after *Lorca*, president Jac Holzman telling *Musician* two decades later, "He was really making music for himself at that point. Which is fine, except to find enough people to listen to it."

Buckley would continue to evolve at faster rates than his listeners could assimilate over the next few years, following a retreat into sun-baked jazzy ballads (*Blue Afternoon*) with his most challenging album, *Starsailor* (1970). It mixed liver-being-torn-out vocalizing, contemporary classical music accompaniment that made labelmate Frank Zappa's excursions seem tame, the French chanteuse mock-up "Moulin Rouge," the lusty jazz-folk-blues raveup "Down By the Borderline," and the actual folk-rock song "Song to the Siren" (which he'd performed back in late 1967 for, of all things, the final episode of *The Monkees*). The potpourri was emblematic of the kind of no-holds-barred approach that has guaranteed him a strong cult following into the twenty-first century. At the time, though, it was inaccessible to the rock audience, including those who had fallen in love with the gentler, song-anchored folk-rock Buckley of his first Elektra albums. Commercial pressures led Buckley to try increasingly generic L.A. funk-rock on his final releases, before his death at the age of 28 in 1975 from a heroin overdose.

"Tim was ready at any point to put out a five-album set," claims Larry Beckett, who wrote lyrics for many of the songs on Buckley's first pair of albums (and collaborated with him intermittently throughout the rest of his career). "He loved so many kinds of music, and was so good at it, that limiting him to the two sides of an LP was almost ridiculous. Even in public, like you see on the live stuff as it starts to [get released], he would start to diverge. In private, he would diverge even farther, and play and sing all kinds of stuff, either covers or originals, that had nothing to do with anything. I mean, they're just out from left field."

Buckley at least got to release a few more albums on his way to commercial oblivion. Phil Ochs would record barely anything after the 1960s, not so much for lack of will as lack of muse. Ochs had performed and demonstrated at the 1968 Democratic Convention in Chicago, witnessing brutal repression by the city's police force, and some sourness began to seep into his impressions of an America crumbling into moral decay on 1969's *Rehearsals for Retirement*. Here Ochs moved to a fairly straightforward folk-rock approach that eliminated some of the highs of the successful risks on his prior, far more varied orchestral-folk-rock albums for A&M. But it did make for more consistent listening, with a reasonably strong set that reflected his disillusionment with idealistic left-wing activism.

"Eventually I found myself in a stale position," Ochs reflected in *The New York Times* in the spring of 1970. "I could go on and be a sort of Pete Seeger. But after Chicago I was so depressed, so full of despair that I just went crazy and didn't care anymore. I decided to do just what I wanted to do." But *Rehearsals for Retirement* was another low-charting LP, and Ochs's muse began to retreat as he found less causes to extol and ran up against writer's block. His final studio album, 1970's sarcastically titled *Greatest Hits* (not a compilation but a set of new material), had just one outstanding track, the funereal, too appropriately titled "No More Songs."

At Carnegie Hall in March 1970, Ochs attempted to reinvent himself as a gold lamé-covered performer alternating reworkings of solid original compositions from his catalog like "I Ain't Marching Anymore" and "Tape from California" with covers of hits by Buddy Holly, Elvis Presley, and Merle Haggard (the arch-conservative "Okie from Muskogee"). The performance was Ochs's version of Dylan at Newport in 1965, arousing jeers of outrage from an audience wanting more of his political commentary (though strangely, according to *Rolling Stone*'s review of the show, "Okie from Muskogee" got cheers). Ochs himself claimed in *The New York Times* a few days later that "during the second half, the audience completely turned around to an extent that never happened to me before. By the end, when I was doing my Elvis Presley medley, they were jumping on the stage and shaking my hand. It was like an old time '50s rock concert—total ecstasy." To *Billboard*, he claimed, "Ultimately, my act can be taken as a political act since it is a use of American mythology, and Presley is part of this. The show could be called 'The Phil Ochs Experience: Elvis Presley meets Che Guevara.'"

Yet there would be no eternal debates à la Dylan's 1965 Newport set about how well Ochs's new sound went over at his 1970 Carnegie gig. Captured on the live album *Gunfight at Carnegie Hall* (not released until the mid-'70s, and then only in Canada), it didn't result in drawing the huge new

Phil Ochs, folk-rock's social conscience.

audience that Dylan did when he turned his back on his past. It wasn't so much unwillingness on the part of his audience to accept a new persona as it was dissatisfaction with the quality of the content. Notes Gene Shay, hardly a close-minded folk radio programmer, "I was disappointed when Phil Ochs decided to go the gold lamé. I thought it was actually a novelty." The whole idea of reconciling old and new into an Elvis Presley–meets–Che Guevara persona was misbegotten, not least because he wasn't a notable interpreter of Presley or Holly.

Ochs, unsurprisingly, felt otherwise, and in 1971 railed against A&M's decision not to release the album in *Rolling Stone*. "They don't see the point of putting out the rock medleys when people can buy *Buddy Holly's Greatest Hits*," he fumed. "They don't like my old songs being on it, they think my fans would feel gypped. Also they just think it's terrible. I had a cover ready and everything. And they just said, 'No.' It's sort of shocking. I'm afraid it may be the end of my career." It was, sadly, an accurate prophecy. In the last five years of his life manic depression got the better of him, and there were no more albums before he hung himself in 1976.

"I think his problem, why he dried out so badly on the writing level, was that basically he was not a craftsman," postulates brother-manager Michael Ochs. "He couldn't be a Neil Sedaka or a Jeff Barry or a Barry Mann [all hit songwriters from the Brill Building school]. He couldn't sit down and just churn 'em out. The songs just came to him in an inspirational way, and he really had very little control over that. The thing I noticed the most drastically, as far as a change in Phil's look, was when Nixon resigned and there was a party, and it was the most lost I'd ever seen him. It was like all of a sudden, the dragon was slain. Phil got his inspiration from conflict, really, and it was usually external conflict. If it was internal conflict, like a Leonard Cohen or a Dylan, Phil could have written more personal songs a lot easier.

"But the problem was that he was so stimuli-driven. So when you take away the two biggest dragons, the Vietnam War and Nixon, all of a sudden he was really at a loss. And it was so hard to keep his stimuli up in L.A. In New York, you can't escape the stimuli. It's everywhere you go. You're always on the cutting edge in New York, and in California, you're on the bleeding edge, unfortunately. It was horrific out here back then. You'd ask people who the president was, and almost half of them wouldn't know, other than the super-rich and the movers and shakers."

"Phil wanted to be a big popular star," summarizes his close friend Judy Henske. "I think that he was always hoping that he'd get a record that would go on popular radio, and he'd just be a big recording star, instead of more of an obscure character, the way he was. Bob Dylan became a big hit, writing heavy songs, and I think Phil thought, 'Well, I can do this too.' Phil was much more intellectual than Dylan. But he didn't have the touch that Bob Dylan still has. It's a very common popular touch that goes from his pen to your ear, and you want to hear it again."

Plenty of singer-songwriters envied Dylan's talent, of course, but Ochs was the only one who truly seemed to let it eat him up. The shame of it was not only that he might have been unable to accept himself as a valid talent with something to say, but that he was in fact making a deep impression on other artists of great stature, perhaps unbeknownst to him. In a little-heard 1969 interview with KSAN in San Francisco, Neil Young, after admitting that he didn't own a Dylan album for fear of being too influenced by him, went on to cite Ochs as a big influence, particularly on his melodies. Furthermore, he placed Ochs on the "same level as Dylan," adding, "I think he's a genius."

"But he was really, truly insane, and his insanity killed him," adds Henske. "It wasn't politics that killed him. 'Oh, he's all upset about this political stuff'—that's bullshit. He was sick. And then he also got very crazy, where he mixed himself up with Elvis and he went to see Elvis a couple of times in Vegas. He was mentally ill, and his mental illness killed him. It was sad, 'cause he *didn't* have to die. But he wouldn't go to a doctor, he wouldn't take his medicine, because he had these enormous highs, and low, low, lows. He wouldn't give up the huge, crazed highs."

For a very brief time, it might have seemed like Neil Young—with one flop album to his credit in early 1969 after jumping ship from Buffalo Springfield—was also destined to fade away like Fred Neil, Hardin, Buckley, and Ochs, if not ignominiously burn out in as disastrous a fashion. Fate, however, played its own cards in the middle of the year, almost immediately vaulting Young to the inner pantheon of folk-rock's hottest properties. Rather like Bob Dylan, Crosby, Stills, & Nash had decided to open their concerts with an acoustic set, and plug in for fairly loud rock 'n' roll for the second half, when they prepared to start touring. (Young, incidentally, had been doing this when touring with Crazy Horse as well, as early as February 1969.) When it came time to go on the road, it was thought advisable to beef up the sound, particularly for the electric portion of the show. Bruce Palmer of Buffalo Springfield was considered for the bass slot, but didn't pass muster, the position going to 19-year-old Motown session man Greg Reeves. The additional guitarist, Neil Young, seemed like both an obvious choice on purely musical grounds and asking for trouble if the band wished to remain a stable unit. Young and Stills, after all, had sometimes tried to blow each other off the stage with mind-frying guitar volume in Buffalo Springfield, even if they were also capable of mind-blowing guitar duels.

But CSN (soon to be abbreviated CSNY) could use an extra singer-songwriter, particularly one with a much grainier sensibility and greater aptitude for hard rock than Crosby and Nash possessed. And Young needed the exposure that a supergroup could give him—more, actually, than CSN needed him. Hard as it might be to imagine today, now that Young is acclaimed as the '60s rocker superstar who has aged with more grace than any other, in 1969 his solo career was only just starting to get noticed. In late 1968 he was still playing coffeehouses—his early B-side "Sugar Mountain" that spurred Joni Mitchell's "answer song" "The Circle Game" was recorded at Ann Arbor's Canterbury House—and he was billed below Mitchell for some shows at New York's Bitter End. In early 1969 he was still at the bottom of some bills even after starting to tour with Crazy Horse. We've had 30 years to get used to his one-of-a-kind-voice, but when his solo debut *Neil Young* came out at the end of 1968, it was not uncommon for listeners to mistake his high, trembling pitch for that of a woman.

Neil Young was more countrified and folky than many would have expected, often bolstered by orchestrations from multipronged talent Jack Nitzsche. Some of the songs were outstanding, like "The Loner," which helped define his outcast, underdog persona, and the nine-minute "The Last Trip to Tulsa" was undeniably his most Dylanesque moment on disc. It didn't even make the Top 200, though, and as a solo artist Young was already in trouble.

There was an underlying nervousness in Young's vocals that, while appealing, was also taken as a sign of an artist unsure of himself. "When I was with the Springfield, I held back," he admitted in *Rolling Stone*. "I was paranoid about my voice. So on my own first LP I buried my voice intentionally. The second LP I brought it up more. I had more confidence. That's what working with Crazy Horse has done. It's given me confidence. That's why I want to continue as a single. But I won't be singing that much with the new group [CSNY]. Mostly just playing a lot." In an interview in late 1969 on his 24th birthday with San Francisco radio station KSAN, he confessed that it "took about six or seven albums" before he could sing as good as the next guy.

To *NME* he elaborated, "When the Springfield broke up I felt I couldn't work in a group context—and I certainly never realized I'd be in a group with Steve again, even though I guessed that we'd probably be playing together sometime. Now I think I've reached just about the perfect state. I'm part of the group, which I really dig, and I can also express myself as an individual through my own things. And I need very badly to make my own music, partly because it boosts my ego to the required dimension."

Crazy Horse backed Young on his second album, *Everybody Knows This Is Nowhere*, issued around the time of *Crosby, Stills & Nash*. Feeling that he'd overdone the overdubbing on his debut,

Young was now opting for a more live sound, with Crazy Horse's raw spontaneity counting more than polished virtuosity. This was not only one of his finest records, but the record that established the knack for which he's still unsurpassed: the ability to alternate between jagged hard rockers and wistful acoustic-flavored country-folk-rock with equal facility. The hard rockers did not lack folk elements either: "Down by the River" certainly had the epic narrative thrust of any ancient folk murder tale. It, like the similarly lengthy "Cowgirl in the Sand," would be done by Young in concert as either an acoustic folk ballad or twisted rocker, as the mood suited him.

Young's choice of Crazy Horse for a backup band, and a ragged-but-right feel to both his live shows and recordings, has often been seen as a reflection of his preference for spontaneity and feel over slickness and polish. According to Jim Messina, who played bass on some of *Neil Young*, that's an attitude that predates *Everybody Knows This Is Nowhere*, even given Young's subsequent complaints that his first solo album suffered from too much production. "I remember coming back to do an overdub on something," he says. "I listened to the music, and wrote out a chord chart on it. I went out in the studio and said, 'Run it, so I can see if my chart's right.' I played, and I recall feeling like I had missed something, or it didn't quite flow right. So when it was over, I said, 'Okay, I'd like to do one now. I think I need to change something.' And they said, 'Oh no, it's fine.' I said, 'Are you sure? I'm almost positive I made a mistake.' They said, 'No, it sounded great.'

"Either I was a much better player than I thought, or they settled for less. I don't know," he laughs. "It just felt looser than I would have preferred. But it's up to the artist to decide what it is that's right or wrong about their music."

Young's songs were far more troubled, and stacked with deviously ingenious and surrealistic images, than those of any of his new compatriots in Crosby, Stills, Nash & Young. It was really as a live musician that he made his principal contribution to CSNY, continuing his career as a soloist without interruption. He had more success with releases bearing his own name than anyone else in the band did, particularly after 1970's *After the Gold Rush* made the Top Ten. Although he did play on the only studio album CSNY recorded before they broke up (the first time), 1970's *Déjà Vu*, he offered just a couple of songs (and one collaboration with Stills). Some have viewed his involvement with the band as a temporary aberration or even a careerist move to boost his own profile, although in his KSAN interview his enthusiasm for the venture seemed genuine enough. He even called *Crosby, Stills & Nash* a better album than the Beatles' own just-released smash, *Abbey Road*, and described the middle section of "Carry On," a cut from CSNY's then-upcoming *Déjà Vu* LP, as the best vocal arrangement he'd ever heard on record.

That second album, like the first, reflected a wide-lens portrait of hippiedom at the close of the 1960s, whether in Nash's odes to beatific domesticity ("Our House" and "Teach Your Children," the latter with steel guitar by Jerry Garcia); their cover of Joni Mitchell's "Woodstock," her depiction of the festival as a garden of Eden; another disgruntled let-my-freak-flag-fly blast from David Crosby, "Almost Cut My Hair"; and Stills's plug for the dawn of a new love-suffused era, "Carry On." In this context Young's inscrutable if irresistibly melodic "Country Girl" sounded downright exotic, like a comet streaking across a clear blue sky.

oung also wrote CSNY's 1970 non-LP hit single "Ohio," a moving if blunt response to the killings at Kent State, with the Bill of Rights printed on the back sleeve. ("You'll never hear it on the air," predicted Nash, inaccurately, when introducing the song at a show at New York's Fillmore East.) While folk-rock had done much to liberate songwriters from the confines of protest and topical songwriting over the preceding five years, it's crucial to point out that the leading folk-rockers did not abandon politically and socially conscious statements, either in their music or in their public life. Judy Collins is not the first performer who comes to mind when critics single out political singer-songwriters, yet in the late '60s she was quite active in left-to-radical affairs. In early 1970 she was called as a defense witness for the Chicago Seven, who were standing trial for inciting a riot at the 1968 Democratic National Convention. Collins attempted to sing Pete Seeger's "Where Have All the Flowers Gone," which defense attorney William M. Kunstler argued, according to *The New York Times*, "was not entertainment but a protest against young men's deaths in war and was directly relevant to the protests during the convention."

She was cut off after just one line by Judge Julius J. Hoffman, who also refused to let Phil Ochs sing "I Ain't Marching Anymore," or Arlo Guthrie to sing "Alice's Restaurant," or Country Joe McDonald to sing what *The New York Times* reported as "Vietnam Rag," most likely a mistitle of "I-Feel-Like-I'm-Fixin'-to-Die Rag." One can only imagine the apoplexy that might have ensued had McDonald been allowed to start that off with the Woodstock version of his F-I-S-H cheer, which changed F-I-S-H to F-U-C-K. McDonald actually did run into legal trouble over that chant later that year, getting fined $500 for leading the infamous rallying cry in Worcester, Massachusetts, and then getting fined $5,000 for doing the same thing at Phoenix Coliseum, in violation of that venue's antiobscenity clause. As Coliseum manager Jim Jones was quoted in *Creem*, "Five or six times he yelled, 'What does it spell?' and they roared out the answer. That was enough for me."

The old struggles against censorship of controversial folk-rock songs were alive and well in the new decade. When Collins made critical remarks about the Chicago Seven trial on *The Dick Cavett Show*, they were blipped out of the broadcast, inciting her to send a written appeal to the chairman of the FCC to investigate the incident. (Earlier Joan Baez had been similarly blipped on CBS TV when she tried to speak on behalf of her then-husband David Harris, who was jailed for draft evasion.) Perhaps because the dignified, stately tone of her music was less avowedly inflammatory than, say, Country Joe's, Collins made some surprisingly forthright remarks in the media without suffering a fallout. "I think LSD has great potential for saving the world," she even proclaimed in a 1967 piece in *The New York Times*, though this was prefaced by some cautionary remarks about playing too seriously with that particular fire.

Yet Collins differed from the protest folk singers of the early '60s (some of whose songs she had sung during that era) in that she didn't see her music as a doctrinaire vehicle. "I don't think protest music, as such, has a place anymore, because it has the sense of lecture instead of the sense of life," she said in the same 1967 *New York Times* article. Music, as she elaborated in a 1969 *Newsweek* item, had the power to be progressive while transcending specific party lines. "I was at Oberlin last fall," she stated by way of illustration, "where the student body was politically split, not just between left and right, but within the left itself, and some of the differences were pretty bitter. Well, I gave a concert there and everyone got very excited. The music created a feeling of togetherness. It changed a split group into a sensitive, feeling, unified one. Sometimes, the time and energy with which we pursue our political interests tends to undermine our feeling of being people. I try to make my audience feel their common humanity."

The tension between artistic freedom and an urge to link arms with the counterculture was a difficult balance to maintain. Singer-songwriters realized they were powerful spokespersons for progressive change, yet were uneasy with the burdens and expectations that entailed. Understandably, they felt a little torn by conflicting impulses. "At Denver some kid came up to me and said, 'Please don't split up, we need you,'" Graham Nash told *Melody Maker* as CSNY's popularity crested. "That really made me think, and I wondered if I wanted that kind of responsibility. If I wanted to be somebody people could look up to? Because in our music we never try to give answers, just to tell how it is so that people are aware and can take it from there." In the very next paragraph, though, Nash was proclaiming, "I really feel America needs me."

There were also idealistic murmurs of transcending petty politics altogether as a new age peeked over the horizon. "All political systems are on the way out," said Arlo Guthrie, already ensconced in a 260-acre rural property in western Massachusetts, in his *Newsweek* profile. "We're finally gonna get to the point where there's no more bigotry or greed or war. Peace is the way. And you don't seek peace, you use it. In 20 years, all that stuff'll be over. People are simply gonna learn that they can get more from being groovy than being greedy. And when they find out, it's gonna be the biggest surprise party of all time. I'm not interested in converting people. Reality converts people and my songs are about reality.

"I don't get involved in the world outside, man," he added. "I create my own. I stay with my friends. We're in the same boat and don't believe we should get out of the boat. Too many people have been too concerned about everyone else. It's nice to be your brother's keeper but first you have to learn to keep yourself." If Guthrie's insularity and unfulfilled predictions sound naive, it must be remembered that, for all his fame, he was still just 22 years old. Far from retreating into an apolitical cocoon, he would do much work for antinuclear, ecological, and other progressive causes over the next few decades.

"When I think of Vietnam or [the 1969 violence between protesters and the National Guard in] Berkeley, I feel so helpless," Joni Mitchell told *Newsweek*. "I've never been political. I still haven't made my own moral decision of what I feel is right for man and for the world. My mind will not give me these answers. I just write about what happens to me. I leave out some parts and leave in some, tell some literally and trip out on others." Still, only a month later Mitchell was singing her own antiwar statement, the chilling a cappella piece "The Fiddle and the Drum," in front of a huge national television audience on *The Dick Cavett Show*.

Giving voice to progressive causes and dissent had became much more complicated than it had been when Bob Dylan, Joan Baez, Pete Seeger, and Peter, Paul & Mary had joined hands to sing "We Shall Overcome" at the 1963 Newport Folk Festival. Yet even battle-scarred spokespersons for social change through music saw some continuity between the more explicitly political folk revival of the early '60s and the unforeseeably wide kaleidoscope of rock music at the end of the decade. In a mid-1970 *Melody Maker* article, Peter Yarrow of Peter, Paul & Mary—still active at the beginning of the 1970s, if no longer huge hitmakers—offered "a distinction between the place of music today and yesterday, and of the movement today and yesterday." As he saw it, "The two are linked quite inextricably. The music [in 1970] articulates all the dimensions of the new emphasis on spirituality as opposed to a change inside the prevailing system. Most of it came from the hippie movement, acid-rock or whatever—but that's really a misnomer because the lifestyles of these people were very loving towards one another, very non-competitive and with a strong sense of the universal brotherhood of man.

"The songs of the early '60s talked in amorphous terms about answering questions that were still unanswered, but the writers of today's songs are willing to specify what is wrong, and who is wrong, and exactly what should be done to correct it. They'll mention Nixon by name"—perhaps here Yarrow was referring to CSNY's "Ohio," the only big hit of the moment to do so critically— "that's an example of how they've become far less guarded, far less afraid. There's no more 'How many roads must a man walk down, before they can call him a man?'.... The energy is now used in a commitment to spirituality rather than to a change in political form. In other words, it's now about a total way of life." (Yarrow himself was still trying to advance specific political causes in his work in the late '60s, writing a song for antiwar, Democratic presidential candidate Eugene McCarthy's campaign, "If You Love Your Country.")

Just as some fans identified too closely with the work of singer-songwriters like Joni Mitchell and mistook some of her compositions as portraits of real situations, so did some admirers take the all-for-one ethos of CSNY songs to heart and imagine that band to be a high-profile commune of sorts. Onstage they could strike an ideal pose between the individual and the collective. That was particularly so during the acoustic half, which featured the foursome in every possible combination, sometimes performing solo, sometimes joined by others over the course of a particular number. As Vicki Wickham gushed in a *Melody Maker* review, "It was like watching a beautiful moving kaleidoscope."

In fact, CSNY were prey to the same complex emotional dynamics that sowed discord in all social groups, including many of the communes that sprung up in the late '60s. "We are four individuals with huge egos, who have an incredible love/hate relationship," Nash admitted in *Melody Maker.* "We know each other so well that we know exactly how to push each other's trigger. We can and do incite love or hate, and we can cool each other out. But we dig, respect and need each other's music. We get off on that. There's a lot of music we can only make together, that can really excite us, though we all know we could go out on our own, we need that. If our heads aren't quite together, the music's not." And for all CSNY's musical adventurousness and antiestablishment attitude, they could still find themselves in some surprisingly compromising positions to promote their product. In October 1969, they somehow ended up playing "Long Time Gone" on network television's *The Tom Jones Show,* with the host usurping lead vocal duties, complete with a James Brown–like scream at one point. "I don't understand how that happened," mumbled a dumbfounded Neil Young

Joni Mitchell with Graham Nash.

when interviewed a few weeks later on KSAN in San Francisco, promising listeners that nothing of the sort would take place again.

For all their similarities with their audience, CSNY's superstardom gave them a far greater amount of wealth, privilege, and adulation than almost any young people of roughly their age. They were in the odd position of being viewed both as spokespersons reflecting the best aspects of their generation, and as a sort of Rock Aristocracy Central, holing up in hilly L.A. hideaways like Laurel Canyon and the slightly more remote Topanga Canyon (and relocating to plush abodes in Northern California, England, and other regions as the mood took them), pulling other icons into their orbit while remaining the center of the action. Joni Mitchell's career had been closely intertwined with CSNY all along, with Crosby producing her first album, Stills playing on it, and the group covering her "Woodstock" for a huge hit. Mitchell's "Willy," as was no secret even at the time, was about her romance with Graham Nash, and Neil Young wrote "Sweet Joni" about her, but, in keeping with his inscrutable attitude toward issuing his huge backlog of unreleased material, his performance is only available on live bootlegs.

Other auxiliary members of the CSN/CSNY in-crowd, the hippie version of the Rat Pack perhaps, were John Sebastian, who had helped the group in its infancy and played mouth harp on the title track to *Déjà Vu*; Judy Collins, with whom Stills had a long romance and played on her *Who Knows Where the Time Goes* album; and Cass Elliot, whose generous friendship had helped bring Nash to the US and bring CSN together. Other interrelationships included the Grateful Dead's Jerry Garcia, who played steel guitar on *Déjà Vu*'s "Teach Your Children." CSNY returned the favor by advising the Dead on recording harmony vocals for *Workingman's Dead*. Jefferson Airplane covered Crosby's "Triad," which the Byrds had recorded but not released in 1967. Paul Kantner had co-written "Wooden Ships" with Crosby and Stills (the song was recorded by both CSN and the Airplane).

These interconnections were an extension of the communal vibes that had been shared by folk-rock artists since the time they were struggling acoustic folkies, whether it had been Kantner sharing a Venice, California house with Crosby, David Freiberg, and Sherry Snow, or Sebastian meeting Zal Yanovsky at Cass Elliot's apartment when they all gathered to watch the Beatles on *The Ed Sullivan Show* in early 1964. Inevitably, though, the musicians were now further removed from the street scene that had nurtured their grassroots followings in the mid-'60s, and there was grumbling that they were growing out of touch with their humbler constituents. When CSNY came to Greenwich Village in 1970, it was not to hang out with their guitars in Washington Square or the intimate clubs at Bleecker and Macdougal. It was to play the renowned Fillmore East a few blocks away in the East Village, where they demanded not only a Persian carpet to play on, but also that it be recentered periodically during the performance.

CSNY's *Déjà Vu* went to #1 just a month after the Beatles broke up, and "Woodstock," "Teach Your Children," and "Ohio"—a three-song primer to the quartet's varying moods, if such a thing could ever exist—were all hit singles in the spring and summer of 1970. At that time they did a phenomenally successful tour of the United States, captured on the sprawling double album *4 Way Street*. Like their shows, the album was split between acoustic and electric material, sometimes performed solo and sometimes by partial combinations of members, and sometimes doing songs that only showed up on their various non-CSNY albums.

"The main strength was their ability to play very well acoustically and electrically," notes Joel Bernstein, who was photographer for the *4 Way Street* sleeve and saw the 1970 Fillmore East shows, which comprised part of the record. "In their case, unusually, you have four songwriters in the band, where each person was contributing no more than 25 percent to the setlist at that point. They're at or near songwriting peaks for all of them, so you're able to have a very honed set. What Neil Young is playing with CSNY, he only has to pick five or six songs; he's not doing a 20-song setlist. They're not counting on one songwriter in the band to pull it off.

"I remember CSNY opening a show at the Spectrum [in Philadelphia] where I was out in the audience shooting, and they had not yet figured out that they should come out electric, and then do an acoustic set, and then do an electric set. They started off with an acoustic set that was nearly drowned out because the audience was more in a Beatlemania kind of mode. At the Fillmore East, they could do that successfully, but not at an arena."

For a moment, it might have seemed as if CSNY were indeed poised to take the Beatles' place. It didn't happen, in part because the very wish to create a structure for informal music-making on which CSNY was founded would help lead to their dissolution. Eventually there were spats among the members about artistic direction and conflicts of interest between their commitment to the group and their own solo projects, just as there had been in Buffalo Springfield and the Byrds. Even in the midst of their spring-summer '70 tour they broke up temporarily and replaced the rhythm section. They split up a couple of months later without having even made another studio album, though they've since intermittently reunited onstage and in the studio.

In a way, it was Buffalo Springfield and the Byrds all over again on a more massive scale. Musical conflicts, solo ambitions, and internecine bickering worked against long-term stability, even as the individual members sparked each other to heights they (save Young) couldn't reach alone. Young's lukewarm commitment to the group was another obstacle. "For the other three guys, CSNY is still the biggest thing they've ever done," muses Bernstein, who still works for Young as an archivist. "For Neil, even while he was doing it, it was not like, this is *my* band. It was an interesting project. But because he wasn't in control of it, having had his head-to-head with Stephen in the Springfield, he was only going to do that again in a limited way. The other guys always gave 110 percent to making CSNY happen. I think Neil did—*when* he was in it."

For just a bit, though, they'd been folk-rock's ultimate extension into the mainstream of popular music, both on record and as one of the featured attractions at the Woodstock festival. It made sense that their biggest hit was "Woodstock," the song that summarized folk-rock's headiest ideals. As an electrification of a song performed acoustically by its composer, Joni Mitchell, it echoed the format that had gotten folk-rock started just five years before with "Mr. Tambourine Man." Like many of the best folk songs, it was the story of a real-life event, albeit one that Mitchell had not personally witnessed (just as Stills had not witnessed the riots depicted in Buffalo Springfield's "For What It's Worth"). Before the year was out, in fact, "Woodstock" would get to #1—but not by CSNY, and not in America. Matthews Southern Comfort, featuring an ex-singer from Britain's leading folk-rock group, made it a chart-topping single in Britain. That might have been the final flourish of the folk-into-rock process in the 1960s, but it was still very much alive indeed.

7

liege & lief

a truly british folk-rock

he first (literally) British folk-rock LP ever," announced Island Records' full-page ad for Fairport Convention's *Liege & Lief* in *Melody Maker* on December 4, 1969. That's almost five years after the Byrds recorded their "Mr. Tambourine Man" single, and three and a half years after Donovan did *Sunshine Superman*. To those surveying the whole of folk-rock for the first time—and to many who lived through the era, on both sides of the ocean—it does not seem possible that a style whose birth is so identified with the 1960s could not have taken root in Britain until the dying days of the decade. Yet in a way, Island Records was right. *Liege & Lief* was not the first British folk-rock album, but it *wasn't* until the very end of the 1960s that an entire school of distinctly British folk-rock performers rose to put their own stamp on what had been a primarily American hybrid. In so doing they were responsible for the last major branch of folk-rock to flower in the 1960s.

Rocked-up renditions of British traditional folk songs with electric guitars and a fiddle—as Fairport Convention pioneered on *Liege & Lief*—were a big part of this. But its dominance of British folk-rock as the '60s turned into the '70s has arguably been overplayed. As in every mini-movement, there were many facets of British folk-rock in this period, with singer-songwriters and original material playing a strong role as well, though never as strongly as it did in the States. Just one of the major early British folk-rock singer-songwriters would become an international star, and not until the 1970s. Just one of them would have an international hit single, and then only with a cover of a song by a major American singer-songwriter already covered for a hit in the US by the biggest folk-rock group. And just one of them would become a major icon among critics and fans, but not until about a quarter-century after his death.

y the late '60s, there were enough acts recording in a folk-rock fashion in Britain that a more identifiable studio sound was beginning to emerge for the genre as a whole. In part that was because there was a relatively small clique of players who seemed to pop up on sessions all over the place. That had happened in the mid-'60s in New York folk-rock, would again happen to a varying extent in mellow Los Angeles singer-songwriter rock of the late '60s and early '70s, and was also taking place on a smaller scale in London, where virtually all British records of all sorts were recorded. The Pentangle's Danny Thompson kept a particularly prolific session log, especially considering he was in a top group himself, playing on records by Donovan, the Incredible String Band, Nick Drake, John Martyn, and others. "He was the session guy for anything that was jazzy or sort of rocky," proclaims Transatlantic Records chief Nat Joseph. "There was a [bassist] called Brian Brocklehurst, who did a lot of our sort of lighter, poppier stuff; I think he did all the Johnstons stuff."

When it came to solo singer-songwriters, as in every other department, British folk-rock lagged far behind the States in quantity, but did produce some acts of quality. Certainly the most famous of them, although it would take until the mid-'70s for him to attain international stardom, was Al Stewart. His prior experience in rock bands before his entry into the folk circuit equipped him to record with electric instruments and orchestral accompaniment as soon as he began cutting discs as a soloist. (Prior to that, incidentally, he had played second guitar on Jackson C. Frank's self-titled, Paul Simon–produced 1965 album.) His 1967 debut *Bedsitter Images*'s orchestral-folk approach was inspired by Judy Collins's *In My Life*, though where *In My Life* sounded magisterial, *Bedsitter Images* came off as twee. He wasn't the only one in the UK to move into folk-baroque in 1967; Bert Jansch had done so as well on a rather nifty solo period piece the same year, *Nicola*, the only album on which he played both electric and acoustic guitar, and half of whose tracks had orchestration. *Bedsitter Images* nonetheless did introduce Stewart's gift for narrative songs of autobiographical romance and everyday British life, shown to its best advantage when the orchestra was given the day off for the finest song, "Beleeka Doodle Day."

It was shortly after *Bedsitter Images* was recorded that *Melody Maker* asked Stewart, "Does this mean that folk-rock, the hybrid musical form that arose from the demise of the American folk scene and manifested itself in the shape of the Lovin' Spoonful, the Byrds, and the electric Dylan, may happen here?" "Pop and folk are moving closer together," he responded. "Within the next year a whole stack of folk singers are going to switch to electric guitars." That stack wouldn't be a large one, but certainly Stewart went much farther into straightforward folk-rock on 1969's *Love Chronicles*, which featured backing by several members of Fairport Convention and contributions from Jimmy Page (who was only then getting Led Zeppelin together).

"It's folk-rock, which I suppose is an outdated phrase," he told *Melody Maker*. "On *Bedsitter*, the orchestra drowned everything out. On this one the group just drift in and out. The group are good and the backing is so much better." He also defended his finely chiseled songs of experience on these grounds: "I'm not ready yet, to say anything of value outside my own immediate scene. I don't want to write yet another song against the bomb or the war in Vietnam. What does that prove? I can only write about things I really know about, and I'm in no position to set myself up as a leader. I don't even know if people need telling what to do."

Love Chronicles inevitably got its most attention for its 18-minute title track, due both to its length and the use of the word "fucking," though just once, amidst its autobiographical recount of serial love affairs. (That was enough to get it withdrawn from the American market before its initial projected release, but the songwriter vowed not to change the lyrics of "Love Chronicles," written for his girlfriend of the time, Mandi.) Stewart had developed into a troubadour of tentative but definite talent, however, with a voice that was like Donovan in its burr, yet thinner and more fragile. His minor-key melodies hovered over his vignettes like eternal rainy days, most poignantly on his best early song, "Ballad of Mary Foster." Its jaunty, sardonic depiction of bourgeoisie family life in the provinces dis-solved into an entirely different second section in which he assumed the voice of the wife and mother, ruminating over a troubled life that had found her trapped in a loveless marriage. Far more than the over-arching "Love Chronicles," it was a knockout blend of drastically shifting perspectives within one song, and remains one of British folk-rock's least acknowledged high-water marks. In time Stew-art's preoccupation with world history would come to dominate his work, and though some find his more grandiose efforts in that mode pretentious, it was certainly an outgrowth of the storytelling drift found in many a traditional folk song.

While Stewart would eventually become (other than Donovan) the most famous British folk-rock singer-songwriter who began his career in the 1960s, the one to garner the greatest wealth of retroactive critical acclaim was a Joe Boyd/Witchseason act, Nick Drake. At the time, though, Drake was a cult taste, in part because he rarely played live and gave only one interview. On his 1969 debut *Five Leaves Left*, he was something like a darker Donovan, well acquainted with the folk-blues structures that were pillars of both Donovan and Bert Jansch, but with breathier, more measured vocals. The lovely baroque orchestration of his fellow Cambridge student Robert Kirby enhanced the foggy, muted despair, an attractive surface concealing underlying despondency.

Although *Five Leaves Left* was promising, Drake's vision really came to fruition on 1970's *Bryter Later*, with its classical-influenced orchestral arrangements, female soul backup vocals, and three members of Fairport Convention among the instrumentalists. The songs espoused a be-mused yet melancholic despair. "Hazey Jane II," "Poor Boy," and "At the Chime of a City Clock" were so soothingly melodic and gorgeously arranged, however, that the album did stay on the side of music to contemplate by, rather than music to bum out by.

An underrated factor in *Bryter Later*'s brilliance was the high quality of the backup musicians. In the early days of British folk-rock, these could be Achilles' heels on albums such as Al Stewart's *Bedsitter Images*, whose orchestration could have clearly been more sympathetic to the needs of the singer and the songs. "In the '60s, when you had to bring in string players, most of the time, they would take a very elitist view of what they were doing," criticizes John Wood, who engineered all three of Drake's albums (and produced Drake's final LP as well). "They would look down their noses at the people they were working with. You would have the same thing if you wanted a jazz player to play on a pop record, unless you tended to go out and look for young players. If you wanted a jazz musician to play a tenor sax solo, they would regard it as rather beneath them and wouldn't be par-ticularly interested in what they were doing. They'd be there for the money, and that was that. Danny [Thompson] was just about the only bass player you could use at the time. He was about the only person who was open-minded, and had the technique.

"The players on *Bryter Later* were people in their late twenties, early thirties, and they were a different generation. When we were booking string sections for the Drake records, one of the reasons the strings sound like that is that they didn't come from normal journeyman musicians. We used players from the symphony orchestra, an English chamber orchestra, who interestingly enough had a better attitude."

The featured performer was himself no slouch at his instrument. "Nick was an extraordinary musician with very, very strong technique," notes Boyd. "The guitar playing was incredibly clean and accurate and inventive. The way he developed his tunings, some people still haven't figured out some of his tunes. With Nick, I think I was, as a producer, certainly very influenced by the first Leonard Cohen record. I was very impressed with that, I thought that was a really beautifully produced record. The voices on 'Poor Boy' are definitely a nod, a tip of the hat, in the direction of [Cohen's] 'So Long, Marianne.'" Of Drake's records, he adds, "I think *Bryter Later* is the most successful production. It's one of those albums that I can listen to without ever thinking 'I should have done this better.'"

At the time, they certainly could have done better in the stores. Drake's low sales were a cause of great distress to the already sensitive, reclusive singer-songwriter. "The reasons he wasn't successful during his lifetime were a combination of fairly simple things," theorizes Boyd. "First of all, he didn't build up a live following or tour. The example who I guess could be a kind of parallel to Nick in some ways and did do well [was] Leonard Cohen. His records were released in North America at the height of the boom in FM radio, when people were playing a lot of album tracks. He didn't tour either. He didn't perform until well after he had become a famous person.

"Because Nick's records weren't released in America until the early '70s, it was really down to England to make him a star. He fell, unfortunately, in the period between the demise of the pirates. Really, all you had was BBC Radio One, and there wasn't really much room for album tracks or for artists like Nick on radio in Britain. Eliminate live performances, radio exposure— I mean, there isn't a lot there to get what he did across. But at the same time, it's also true that I think the music doesn't reach out and grab people by the lapels. It takes a bit of getting used to, and it's also very English. I think for America at that time, a kind of unassertive introspective English musician wasn't necessarily going to get a lot of attention."

Drake made one more album in 1972, this time without Boyd (who had moved to Los Angeles to work for Warner Brothers). *Pink Moon* was his starkest work by far, featuring just him and his guitar save for one piano overdub. The sound of a man unable to express his despair with many words, it was his last release, as he died in late 1974 from an overdose of antidepressant medication. Yet as with Love's *Forever Changes* and Skip Spence's *Oar*, the cult around Drake's work— all of it, not just one album in particular—just kept growing and growing in the quarter-century after his death, picking up many influential musicians of subsequent generations along the way. In 1999, the same kind of resurrection Skip Spence was undergoing was also granted to Nick Drake, though perhaps to the tenth power, after Drake's "Pink Moon" was featured in a Volkswagen commercial. Sales of Drake's catalog multiplied by several hundred percent. *Pink Moon*, which had sold less than 5,000 copies while Drake was alive, was suddenly selling that many copies within a few weeks; his best-of compilation *Way to Blue* reached the 100,000 mark in the UK alone. There

Nick Drake, the ultimate cult folk-rock singer-songwriter.

was even an excellent film documentary on his life, *A Skin Too Few*, quite a feat to pull off given that no performance or interview footage with Drake as an adult is known to exist.

"The reason why it's successful now is because it's too good *not* to be," says Boyd. "There are a lot of things which feel like they're a part of their time, and they have a fascination for that reason. But Nick's music doesn't really feel that way. It feels kind of outside of time in a way, and so it doesn't date. People, once they sit down quietly and listen to a Nick Drake record, very rarely lose interest after that."

"If you played most people *Bryter Later* and asked them, 'When was this record made?,' I don't think any of them could tell you," agrees Wood. "I don't think anybody would say 32 years old, or whatever it is. Few people would make a record that you couldn't somehow date. In a way, Dylan's easier to date, stylistically and lyrically. Some Randy Newman records would be hard to date as well; I sort of put him in that vein. I always thought the first time we ever recorded it, it was exceptional. For some reason it's taken everybody else 30 years to find out."

ick Drake was, over the course of time at least, the most popular of a peculiar breed of British folk-rock songwriters whose eccentricity, obliqueness, and relatively temperate use of rock and pop flourishes consigned them to a cult audience. By and large most of them have remained cult tastes. Boyd at one time produced John Martyn, who, after starting his recording career as an ordinary acoustic guitarist in the mold of Jansch and Renbourn, put Echoplex on his electrified acoustic and added hues of jazz to his folk-rock-blues mix, doing some recording in Woodstock with members of the Band (and often singing in partnership with his wife Beverley). "By '72 John Martyn was playing free-form amplified guitar solos that made anything Fairport was doing sound reactionary," opines former *Melody Maker* reporter Andrew Means. "'Don't put me on the folk page,' he used to beg. Even though he was still in the clubs, [he] was just starting his electric experimentation and sounded more like a one-man Pink Floyd than anything tradition-based."

Initially Martyn had been scooped up by Witchseason, according to John Wood, because Boyd "had always wanted to record a girl called Beverley [who went by just her first name and had been on the folk and folk-pop scene since the mid-'60s, even landing a spot on the Monterey Pop Festival through her friendship with Paul Simon]. Joe and I spent a couple of evenings trying to record stuff with Bev in Sound Techniques, and Joe never felt we could get the musicians to do it. It just didn't really jell. So he put together an idea of recording in the States. The priority was to ship Bev out to Woodstock and work with Paul [Harris, keyboardist and session man on many 1960s American folk-rock records], and then go into the studio in New York. This is all set up and ready to go, and then Bev married John. So he had to be part of the record, basically."

On that record, 1970's *Stormbringer*, most of the Martyns' supporting cast were veterans of the earliest 1960s New York folk-rock sessions—not just Harris, but also bassist Harvey Brooks, drummer Herbie Lovell, Band drummer Levon Helm, and Band producer John Simon (on keyboards). Consequently it might have boasted the most American textures of any British folk-rock record of the time, though the genteel pleasantry of the sound was definitely British. It was too genteel to be truly striking, in fact, though there was a slight overlay of restrained brooding on the more ambitious lyrics ("Stormbringer," "John the Baptist"), and some fetching femme folk-blues from Beverley Martyn on "Sweet Honesty." "There was always tension, really," judges Wood, "because if you listen to the record you can tell very much whose is whose on it. There is a distinct division between what's John's, and what's Beverly's. But I think that experience got John more interested in the wider horizons of other players, and other styles. He'd just also started playing around with Echoplex. He tended to go mad with it. Then they did a second John and Bev album [1970's jazzier, more mundane *Road to Ruin*], which was probably more tense."

Martyn's subsequent flip-flopping between idioms has made him too esoteric even for those whose tastes are inclined toward inaccessible cult rockers. "After that record, Witchseason and Joe had to depart company for financial reasons," continues Wood. "He said, 'Could I possibly produce a record with John Martyn for around 2000 pounds?' That was [1971's] *Bless the Weather*, and although that's got some folky stuff on it, it's also got a bluesy feel to some of it. Then [1973's] *Solid Air* has a much more bluesy jazz feel. After that he got interested in reggae, and he got interested in hip-hop. In a way, he never really had enough self-confidence, almost, to go down one route and stick with it. It's almost as though he was always really looking for something else. He never really seemed to be very satisfied with anything he did."

Influenced by Bert Jansch and John Fahey, and more rock-oriented than either, Michael Chapman was darker, gloomier, and more passionate than Martyn. He was ultimately even harder to get a handle on, too, lacking the more tangibly direct, emotional impact of a Jansch even as he explored similar states of mind, as well as numerous guitar tunings. Like Martyn, Chapman too seemed reluctant to be binned in the folk section and came to view himself as a contemporary rock musician, sometimes to the point of abrasiveness. "I want to get out of the folk clubs right away," he told *Melody*

Maker shortly after he began releasing albums. "I've only been on the folk scene because it was the only place you could play with an acoustic guitar. I don't know anything about folk music—it bores me to tears. What I'm doing's got f*** all to do with folk music. I'm not interested in the guitar alone now. I want a more complete sound for the songs I'm writing and that's why I'll be working with a group.... I don't want to be considered an acoustic guitar freak."

Other, even more obscure UK folk-rock singer-songwriters of the time included Welshman Meic Stevens, who varied between sub–Dylanisms and some fey, foreboding work that seemed to wish to approach the mysticism of someone like Donovan or original Pink Floyd leader Syd Barrett, yet seemed incapable of articulating his inner muses as captivatingly. (Stevens eventually would concentrate on Welsh-language recordings.) Duncan Browne was early Rolling Stones manager-producer Andrew Oldham's venture into folk-baroque production, pretty but ultimately insubstantial and unmemorable. Vashti Bunyan, one of Joe Boyd's most obscure clients, had done some recording for Oldham in a sub–Marianne Faithfull style in the mid-'60s. Robin Williamson and a couple Fairport Convention members were among the backup musicians on Bunyan's 1970 album *Just Another Day*, sad rainy-day folk with a threadbare wispiness, like a feather that if blown upon would crumble to pieces. Ralph McTell sometimes had his lilting, amiable storytelling folk embroidered by light rock backup and orchestration, though not on the first recording of his most famous composition, "Streets of London." Originally released in 1969, when his tale of the London homeless was re-recorded in 1974, it went to #2 in the British charts.

Common to all of these artists was a certain self-effacement that did not, as Boyd might say, grab you by the lapels. More importantly, they did not disturb or provoke as Drake or Jansch could, though on the surface Drake or Jansch might seem as calm as the others. At least the most notorious British folk-rock eccentric, Roy Harper, could never be accused of reticence and self-effacement. Harper had spent time in mental institutions and prisons as a young man, and a bitterness against social regulation, as well as a manic unfocused intensity, were the distinguishing traits of his early releases. *Sophisticated Beggar* (1966) was like hearing the usual Jansch-Donovan-type folk-blues through a dyslexic filter. Mostly acoustic, it made bows to rock experimentalism with its reverb and backward effects, and an uncharacteristic all-out rocker, "Committed," that recalled Syd Barrett at his looniest. For his next two albums Harper hooked up with producer Shel Talmy to put some electric rock backing and orchestration to his fractured compositions.

As with numerous diatribes from both left-wing ideologues and mental patients, these left no doubt that Harper was stirred up about *something*, but left much mystery as to what exactly that something was. He was prone to trying to jam way too many verbose, often stream-of-consciousness observations into too little space. His songs rambled on too long and his voice and melody wound all over the map. He might have been well advised to take on a collaborator who could have helped shape the numerous shards of appealing tunes and striking phrases that were buried in his work into something more coherent. Especially befuddling was 1969's *Folkjokeopus*, whose impenetrable spew exhausts the patience of all but the most determined listeners, though Harper's acoustic guitar work was, as always, incongruously stellar. It was not until 1971's *Stormcock* that Harper, by now produced by early Pink Floyd co-manager Peter Jenner, marshaled his resources into folk-rock opuses that were more focused and affecting, with help from fan Jimmy Page (who contributed guitar under the pseudonym S. Flavius Mercurius).

"I don't belong to any group or 'ism' at all and [the] only thing I am is me," declared an unrepentant Harper in *Melody Maker* back in 1967. "I'm a person who was stolen by me from the state and given back to myself. When I was young I saw all one side, then I went over to complete anarchy. I saw that was only another 'ism' and finally landed nowhere near either side. In fact, I landed back inside myself. Some of the songs do this. They start out nice and suburbia and suddenly swing violently across to anarchy. Then at the end finish in mid-air on a question which can only be answered when the opposites are seen for what they are." Ambitions for his musical backup could cut an equally wide swath, as he revealed in the same magazine in 1968, "I'm writing an operetta with the Nice and a group called Jethro Tull .... What I'd really like to do is form a 30-piece band with the Mothers, the Floyd, the Nice, Tyrannosaurus Rex, the Scaffold, the Liverpool Scene, Peel and Me, and have the total PA all arranged in a big, free space somewhere and just play for two days solid." (Needless to say, the grand plan never came off.)

Shel Talmy, as usual, doesn't mince words when asked how it was to work with such an up-and-down talent. "Roy Harper was not a bed of roses. He was basically a card-carrying anarchist and revolutionary and all those good things, and all I wanted to do was produce records. I didn't want to hear some political bullshit spiel. So it was fractious. He doesn't sell millions, he sells [to] a few groups of people. And he always will, because of the type of stuff he does. [BBC rock DJ] John Peel's sort of offbeat show is the kind of stuff that Roy Harper appealed to. I'm talking about the days when John Peel would only play really oddball stuff that nobody else would play. Which, quite frankly, doesn't appeal to me on a regular basis. I can take some of it.

"The best thing you can say about [Harper] is that he hasn't compromised himself. Apart from the stuff I did with him, of course!" Talmy laughs. "What I did was make him sound a hell of a lot more professional than he is, or was, or will be. And I think he resents that, quite frankly.

"I liked a lot of his stuff. A lot of his stuff I thought was absolutely crap, which I pointed out, and I'm sure that didn't go down real well either. It was self-indulgent, and it was not particularly musical. He's basically an unstructured artist, and I tried to apply some structure to it. I'm not wild about long, rambling things with no beginnings and no ends, and this is more or less where Roy was at, at that time. We had professional musicians; Danny Thompson, for openers. But these were guys who wanted to make a record for god's sake, you know. And Roy had another agenda."

as the agenda of the singer-songwriter as a class welcomed by the British folk world? Not always, going back to the tired root cause of lack of respect for tradition and unwritten guidelines for what constituted folk music. "Folk, like its close neighbor country music, is heading for disaster at the hands of a bunch of ruthless individuals who have totally disregarded the basic code of folk music," scolded Brian Chalker in an extraordinarily cross column in *Record Mirror* in May 1968. "Can we honestly accept *Alice's Restaurant* and *Bedsitter Images* as folk music? The list of artists specializing in and performing traditional material is decreasing weekly .... The day is fast approaching when we shall have no choice of musical styles—they will be one type—Pop!" One could feel him shudder at the very mention of the dreaded P-word.

"Once upon a time a folk song was held to be one that had no known author and had virtually been passed down through history," Chalker continued. "Today, just about anything can earn the title 'folk' without so much as a whisper from the reviewers or critics—do they earnestly believe that bongos, trumpets, drums and Hammond organs will keep the folk sound separate from music. If we must commercialize folk music at all, let it be by way of amplified conventional instruments; heaven forbid that we ever have to face a Vox amplifier on the end of a Jew's harp, but that would be better than some of the things that are currently being put out as 'folk music.'"

Chalker stuck his foot further down his throat with what amounted to a call for a blacklist: "If we are to save what is left of British folk music then we must kick the following list of people out of the folk clubs—Arlo Guthrie, John Renbourn, Roy Harper, Al Stewart, Tom Rush, Antoine, Alexis Korner and all the other pseudo-folk types who would have you believe that folk music ends with them." Suspicions of some sort of conspiracy to dilute and kill folk music blossomed into borderline paranoia when he further asserted, "As the months tick slowly by it is becoming increasingly apparent that pressure is being applied to folk artists who sign recording contracts—just as soon as they step into the studio, that's it, suddenly they're nonentities amidst the clutter of the studio—they are told basically what to sing, how to sing it and what chords to play on their guitars."

A swift rebuttal from Wally Whyton, compere of the BBC Radio One program "Country Meets Folk," pointed out the inconsistency of Chalker's positions with laconic wit: "Dylan singing his own compositions is OK. Tom Rush singing the blues is not. Tom Paxton is all right but not Alex Campbell singing a Tom Paxton song. Joan Baez passes the whiteness test but not Tim Hardin although Joan frequently sings Tim's songs."

Hairline distinctions between folk and folk music that was, um, not quite folk could get pretty silly at times. The Ian Campbell Folk Group, for instance, dropped the "Folk" from its name when it recorded, with augmented musical arrangements, songs by Ewan MacColl, Joni Mitchell, Tim Hardin, and Gordon Lightfoot on its 1968 album *The Circle Game*. This included, incidentally, the most obscure Mitchell cover ever in "Dr. Junk," which Joni never recorded herself, featuring whimsical drug satire that was highly atypical for a Mitchell composition, complete with Bo Diddley beats and dabs of psychedelic quasi-sitar, Pink Floyd–ish organ, and psychedelic reverb on the fade.

Although the songwriters Campbell covered were often considered folk musicians, or at least (in Mitchell and Lightfoot's cases) heavily folk-influenced popular musicians, he felt obliged to explain himself in the music press. "Why the omission of the word folk?," Campbell asked in *Melody Maker*. "The question answers itself. Most of the songs on the record are not folk songs in any sense of the word. We don't wish to add to the confusion there already is about the word. We agree with A.L. Lloyd on this point. It's time we stopped the misleading habit of calling everyone who plays an acoustic guitar a folk singer.

"This record reflects what is happening on today's scene. People are now conditioned to this sort of thing. When you can have a so-called folk concert featuring Julie Felix, who has nothing to do with any kind of folk music, Tom Rush, who is more influenced by Bo Diddley than anything else, the Incredible String Band—what have they got to do with folk?—and perhaps one solo folk singer or true folk group, if audiences are prepared to accept this sort of thing then why should we have to be classified?"

ZigZag magazine founder Pete Frame dismisses the fallout of such purist wrangling as so much hot air: "There were always debates raging in the *Melody Maker* or in the folk clubs about what constituted folk music, but most rational people ignored them." Sighs Nat Joseph, "We used to get thoroughly fed up with, 'Is it a folk-rock band?' Well, it's *music*. That was always my answer." At any rate, critics such as *Melody Maker*'s own folk columnist Karl Dallas were proving to be far more openminded than the party-liners. *Melody Maker* had always given folk music more space for serious coverage than any of the other major British music papers, and Dallas took a catholic approach, continuing to cover traditionalists along with new British folk-rockers like Fairport Convention and visiting American singer-songwriters like Judy Collins. "Karl's an old Commie," says Arlo Guthrie, who'd known Dallas well since staying at his apartment after running out of money as a visiting teenager in 1965. "So his point of view was, these were people singing songs of the proletariat. But he loved the music, and he loved all the aspects of it. He never got caught up in the sort of fundamentalist attitudes that some of the individuals did. Karl was open to it, because first of all, from a practical point of view, for a journalist who gets to go to all of these places with an expense account, you don't want to lock yourself out by saying something too stupid."

Still, the more hard-line attitudes of the time went at least some way toward explaining both why there were relatively few folk-rock singer-songwriters in the UK in the late '60s, and why some performers recognized by Americans as pop-folk-rockers weren't considered as folk-rock in the least by many British circles. One such artist was Mary Hopkin, who had one of the biggest singles of 1968 with "Those Were the Days" (itself an English-language adaptation of a Russian folk tune, with lyrics by a former Columbia University architecture teacher). Hopkin actually far preferred Donovan-type pop-folk to the pop records on the Beatles' Apple label for which she's most famous. Indeed she had recorded folk songs in Welsh on obscure EPs prior to signing with Apple, and had originally been inspired by Joan Baez, Judy Collins, and Bert Jansch. She had come to the attention of Apple, in fact, when she sang the core folk-rock classic "Turn! Turn! Turn!" on the British television show *Opportunity Knocks*; Twiggy saw the program and recommended Hopkin to Paul McCartney, then scouting for acts to put on Apple. Her cover of "Turn! Turn! Turn!" likely earned Pete Seeger as many royalties as the Byrds' hit had, since it appeared on the flipside of "Those Were the Days." Apple took some pains to remove her from those role models; as Peter Asher told *Disc*, "Paul [McCartney] saw that Mary had a really good voice but she wasn't Mary Hopkin. She was a mini–Joan Baez."

Never taken seriously by critics then or since, Hopkin's high, trilling voice actually handled serious folk material well. Though her Apple debut album *Postcard* was burdened with some pre-rock pop standards, she also did three Donovan songs, and Donovan played on the LP. "I'm determined to remain more of a folk singer," Hopkin huffed in *NME* in early 1970. "I've nothing against pop, but it's not really me." And after some pop singles like her hit cover of McCartney's "Goodbye" and the less successful ditties "Que Sera Sera" and "Knock Knock, Who's There" (which was selected in 1970 to represent the UK in the infamously vapid annual Eurovision song contest), she *did* get more seriously artistic with her final Apple album, *Earth Music*. The respectable, dignified record included instrumental support from Ralph McTell, Dave Cousins, and Danny Thompson, plus David Bowie producer (and, for a while, Hopkin's husband) Tony Visconti, though at this point Hopkin's career was floundering, as was the Apple label itself.

There were few other such folk-rock-pop interpreters in Britain, and they usually lacked the frilly finesse Hopkin proved capable of projecting given the right material. Californian expat Julie Felix had done electric folk-rock cuts as early as 1966 on *Changes*, which had a horrendously stiff cover of Ian & Sylvia's "Gifts Are for Giving," and put a Judy Collins–like mix of Mitchell, Dylan, Donovan, Paxton, Ochs, and Mike Heron covers on her later album *This World Goes Round & Round*. As a vocalist she was colorless, though, which made such LP projects pointless.

Al Stewart's "whole stack of folk singers [who] are going to switch to electric guitars" likewise did not include many other relatively straightforward folk-rock-pop singer-songwriters in their ranks. One, however, was Peter Sarstedt, who went to #1 in 1969 with "Where Do You Go My Lovely?," and took some of the most pretentious, smug qualities of folk-rock minstrelsy tunesmiths. His ersatz eclecticism was like a caricature of Donovan that had been created for some TV movie, bloated by some exceptionally fruity orchestration, though there's a morbid fascination in hearing James Bond soundtrack horns collide with Al Stewart–like vocal phrasing on his "Mary Jane."

More likable was Matthews Southern Comfort, formed around Ian Matthews after the singer-songwriter's 1970 debut solo album (called, confusingly, *Matthews Southern Comfort*, though the group by that name only formed afterward). On the three 1970 albums credited to either him or Matthews Southern Comfort, Matthews went into more laidback, countrified folk-rock than he had sung with Fairport Convention, though he used a couple guys from his old band as session musicians on his first post-Fairport album. He too would have a British #1, with a worthy 1970 cover of Joni Mitchell's "Woodstock" that was at once far more wistful than Crosby, Stills, Nash & Young's version, and yet had a far more full-bodied folk-rock arrangement than Mitchell's own recording. Matthews told *NME* that his band originally did the song on a BBC broadcast "strictly a la Joni Mitchell," which created enough interest to encourage the group to devise its own arrangement. "I felt quite very guilty when I met Joni, because I had changed the melody of the song," he added. "Funnily enough she said that she thought it was better the way I did it! I told her the only reason I altered the melody was because I couldn't reach the high notes." Most of the material Matthews recorded on the three 1970 albums bearing (in one way or another) his name owed far more to American folk-rock and country-rock than other British folk-rockers of the period, and he was indeed about the only major British folk-rocker to take a lot of inspiration from country-rock.

Filling out the thin ranks of British folk-rock singer-songwriters were likable also-rans like Al Jones, whose 1969 album *Alun Ashworth-Jones* had traces of Donovan, Roy Harper, Al Stewart, John Renbourn, Bert Jansch, and Nick Drake, but ultimately not enough Al Jones to stand out from the pack. And there were few British women folk-rock singer-songwriters whatsoever, with some exceptions like Sandy Denny, Vashti Bunyan, and the Nico-in-tune, deep-voiced Bridget St. John (whose songs were as reticent if not more so than Nick Drake's, but folkier and blander). "I don't really think there's sympathetic ears for the contemporary songwriter over here," John Martyn told *Melody Maker* in 1970. "In America, people like Nilsson and Laura Nyro are important. The casual listener over the past ten years has been addicted to a particular kind of music. There's a whole section of the industry devoted to giving the public its daily fix." As noted earlier, Martyn and his wife Beverley had done some recording in America around this time, giving him more basis than most had for comparison.

There was, perhaps, another reason why there weren't loads of British folk-rock singer-songwriters. Homegrown folk-rock just wasn't that big a commercial deal in Britain: far less so, for instance, than the British blues boom, which saw Fleetwood Mac, Chicken Shack, John Mayall's Bluesbreakers, Ten Years After, and others make high-charting electric blues-rock albums in the late '60s. By 1970 even Donovan would fade from the upper tier of the charts, failing to enter the Top 40 ever again after the summer of 1969's ebullient and eccentric "Barabajagal."

In one parallel with folk-rock's American course, the British singer-songwriting school would have its greatest successes with artists who poured a lot of confessional pop into it in the early '70s, when Cat Stevens and Elton John became worldwide stars. (In the mid-'70s, Al Stewart and Gerry Rafferty, who'd once been half of a subdued, somewhat folk-rock duo with folk singer-turned-comedian Billy Connolly in the Humblebums, did the same.) John, interestingly, was once engaged (in July 1970) by Joe Boyd to record publishing demos, since bootlegged, of songs by Nick Drake, Mike Heron, and John Martyn. Even Leo Sayer had done some time in folk clubs and as a street busker in the early '70s before rising to mainstream pop stardom.

S tevens and John were a couple of examples of how British folk-rock made its influence felt in the larger pop and rock world. "There was a lot more connection between the folk scene and the pop scene in the '60s than there has been ever since," says *fRoots* editor Ian Anderson. "It is unusual now for people on the rock scene to know anything about the people who were working in the folk scene. In the 1960s, you can be sure that most of your major rock guitarists would also know about Bert Jansch and Davy Graham. And not only that, they mixed up together. A lot of people from the rock scene used to go down to Les Cousins in Soho. So quite often, you'd get people like Cat Stevens who'd come down to do a floor spot at the Cousins and try out a song. Well, he would never be seen in any other folk club in the country. It was not unusual for people like Long John Baldry to come down. And that was where you got this sort of fusion between the bluesy side of things and the folk side of things, which produced, in the end, things like Pentangle.

"I think that's why the music got so exciting, 'cause everybody listened to everybody else. So, although you might choose to just play one thing, at the same time, you had an open mind for something else. So you had, for example, the Young Tradition, who were [an] a cappella, hard-line traditional harmony singing group, who would be just as likely to go and see a blues band, free jazz, or whatever. That applied from any direction. I certainly, as a blues player, opened for some of the early folk-rock bands, like Fairport and Pentangle, things like that. Al [Stewart], very often, used to take me out with him when he went to gigs so I could do a floor spot. John Renbourn did it with my friend Al Jones. The only people who seemed to be really heavily into competition, to my memory, were Roy Harper and John Martyn. Those were the guys who were keen on being stars."

"We played with people like Fairport Convention, Fotheringay, and Sandy Denny," points out longtime Elton John lyricist Bernie Taupin of John's early gigs. "We [also] played with Eric Clapton and Derek & the Dominos, Leon Russell, the Byrds, the Kinks. People weren't so apt to pigeonhole. Whether it was Cat Stevens or the Kinks, it was really all rock 'n' roll. With the mists of time, people forget that when we first started, we were really thought of as kind of a folk act, sort of like a Cat Stevens or James Taylor. As bad as it was, our very first album, all that stuff was total folk. It couldn't be more folky. It was all bad interpretations of everybody from Fairport to Leonard Cohen to Joni Mitchell. It wasn't very good, but it was certainly folk music. Bad folk music, but folk music all the same."

Purists quail at the notion of traditional folk having any significant bearing on the direction of major British rock stars of the time, such as Elton John. Yet it's undeniable that folk-rock influences, of both the American and British variety, can be heard in some of their work. Even as unknowns in the late '60s, soon-to-be-stars John and Taupin were among those rabid collectors scarfing up import folk-rock albums by the likes of Love, Leonard Cohen, and Pearls Before Swine (whose "Rocket Man" helped inspire the 1972 Elton John hit of the same name), even waiting for the 8:00 P.M. deliveries of LPs from the States at Musicland on Berwick Street in London. "Elton and I clicked with each other on a musical level, and that level was the fact that we were interested in every kind of music, whether it be jazz, blues, folk, rock, pop," stresses Taupin. "There was no musical bigotry involved in anything. I think that's why, to our credit, our music in those early days really lent from everything. There were touches of folk, country, rock. We just soaked it all up, and it went into one big melting pot."

On a rootsier level, Rod Stewart was very vocal in his admiration of folkies such as Ramblin' Jack Elliott, Hamilton Camp, and British folk singer Wizz Jones. His first solo album, 1969's *The Rod Stewart Album*, had a cover of Ewan MacColl's "Dirty Old Town," and some of his best work of the early '70s was folk-rockish, such as his cover of Tim Hardin's "Reason to Believe" and the megahit "Maggie May." David Bowie was a fan of the Fugs and Love back when it was hard to even get their albums in the UK, and a very good bootleg exists of an early 1969 session with him and John Hutchinson on acoustic guitars. With their closely interwoven harmonies, they sounded something like a British Simon & Garfunkel, committing to tape unplugged versions of "Space Oddity" and several of the better songs he would record in full rock versions on his 1969 *David Bowie* album (aka *Space Oddity* in the US). That year, Bowie even claimed in *Disc* that he sang like "Dylan would have done if he'd been born in England." Terry Cox of the Pentangle contributed drums to *Space Oddity*, and as late as April 1971, Bowie would tell *Melody Maker* that he was working with Cox, though that didn't result in an enduring association.

Traffic's 1970 cover of the traditional British song "John Barleycorn" certainly rates as one of the finest, and most famous, rock adaptations of a British folk number, learned via a recording of the tune by British trad folk group the Watersons. Although it was atypical of Traffic's catalog, folk-rock was certainly instrumental in elevating its lyrical aspirations. Back in 1967, original Traffic member Dave Mason had gone as far as to brag to *Melody Maker*, "I changed my whole idea about life about a year ago, listening to a Bob Dylan LP one night in the flat of a Birmingham club owner."

Folk-rock even made serious inroads into the formative work of some leading progressive-art-rock bands. King Crimson seems like one of the last groups you'd associate with folk-rock, but had a direct connection to Fairport Convention. In mid-1968, recently ousted Fairporter Judy Dyble briefly joined and recorded a few songs (eventually released on rarity compilations) with the embryonic King Crimson, then struggling under the name of Giles, Giles & Fripp. A heavier, fuller art-rock version of one of those songs, Ian McDonald's "I Talk to the Wind," shows up on King Crimson's debut album *In the Court of the Crimson King*, which still—through McDonald's presence—bears traces of folk-rock in the lilting, melodic, storytelling songwriting of most of the tunes. It's also interesting to note that the early King Crimson included Joni Mitchell's "Michael from Mountains" in its rehearsals, and played Donovan's "Get Thy Bearings" live. (As a much more obscure folk-to-prog connection, Sonja Kristina of the prog-rock band Curved Air had sung briefly with the Strawbs as Sandy Denny's replacement.)

Echoes of the '60s British folk era were felt several years later in the work of Mike Oldfield. Five years prior to *Tubular Bells* he had been, with his older sister Sally, the 15-year-old half of the quaint, overly precious folk duo Sallyangie, his acoustic guitar work heavily influenced by John Renbourn and Bert Jansch. The Oldfields recorded an album for Transatlantic in 1968 after being recommended by Renbourn himself. The album was quiet, even twee, acoustic folk, but Sallyangie did try a fey baroque-folk-rock approach on the obscure 1969 non-LP single "Two Ships"/"Colour of the World," as well as at least a couple of electric band tracks that have yet to be released. Nat Joseph attributes part of the label's failure to develop the group as "a failure by our A&R department to recognize Oldfield's potential. My A&R department didn't seem to relate to either of them and deemed his sister to be far more marketable."

Pink Floyd, Britain's most famous acid rock group, actually used jaunty fairytale British folk-isms fairly often, particularly on its first album, under the stewardship of its original leader, Syd Barrett. Barrett had left the band due to mental disintegration as he became an acid-dropping casualty, and the folk in his acid folk asserted itself more strongly on his two solo albums (both from 1970). Often acoustic in feel, these frequently seemed like a reclamation project bestowed upon a benign busking lunatic, albeit one with a knack for catchy tunes and affecting if scrambled wordplay. Though not as consistent or brilliant as Skip Spence's *Oar*, Barrett's albums *Barrett* and *The Madcap Laughs*, along with the outtake collection *Opel*, endure as some of the best acid folk put to posterity by psychedelic rockers who may have been folkies at heart, but whose minds got fried before they'd quite made it back from their trips. Pink Floyd itself reverted to Barrett-like spaced-out folkiness from time to time on its first records following his exit, and the Roger Waters–penned "Grantchester Meadows" (from 1969's *Ummagumma*) is certainly rural British folk-rock at its most enchanting.

And, folk would once again come to the fore on some of the Beatles' late recordings. The group didn't stay in the *Rubber Soul* folk-rock bag, or indeed any bag, for too long. But it isn't often observed that the folk influence made something of a comeback on *The White Album*, on songs such as "Dear Prudence," "Blackbird," "I Will," "Julia," and "Long, Long, Long." This may well have been an afterglow of their trip to study transcendental meditation with the Maharishi in early 1968 in India, where only acoustic instruments were available. Also on that meditation course was Donovan.

"While the Beatles and I were in India they wrote the *White Album* songs," Donovan recalls. "It was obvious *The White Album* would have a distinctive acoustic and lyrical vibe. Paul, John, George, and I all had our acoustic guitars with us. George would later say that my music greatly influenced *The White Album*. I played all my styles, and the Beatles were exposed to weeks of Donovan. [Incidentally, their friendship dated from long before this junket; Donovan had contributed the lines about blue sky and green sea to "Yellow Submarine."] John was influenced to write romantic fantasy lyrics on the two songs he wrote, 'Julia' and 'Dear Prudence,' after my teaching him my finger-style guitar method. He was a fast learner." Just prior to the *White Album* sessions, the Beatles did a couple of dozen or so "unplugged" acoustic demos of *White Album* material that might qualify as a lost Beatles folk-rock album of sorts, complete with a campfire sing-along version of "Revolution." Some of the songs were released on *Anthology 3*, the others showing up on bootlegs.

Known largely as one of the world's most successful hard-rock or early heavy metal bands, Led Zeppelin, as Donovan previously noted, incorporated a good deal of acoustic folk and folk-rock influences into its works, although these tended to show up on lesser-known tracks. Far from being a dilettante, Jimmy Page's interest in folk and folk-rock was deep before Led Zeppelin. Not only was he a big fan of acts like Bert Jansch and Kaleidoscope, but as already detailed he also played on late-'60s sessions by Donovan and Al Stewart. Rising Sons bassist Gary Marker remembers Page, even before joining the Yardbirds, being impressed enough with one of Ry Cooder's 12-string acoustic arrangements to ask the L.A. guitarist to tape it for him.

Page had already made an explicit venture into folk-rock in his Yardbirds days with the instrumental acoustic guitar showcase "White Summer," based on the British Isles traditional folk standard "She Moves Through the Fair." On Led Zeppelin's debut album, another folky guitar showcase, "Black Mountainside," was similar to the arrangement of the traditional Irish folk song "Blackwater Side" heard on a 1966 Bert Jansch LP. On both "White Summer" and "Black Mountainside," Page used the DADGAD tuning that is one of British folk's most distinguishing traits, as popularized by Davy Graham, Jansch, et al. Also on *Led Zeppelin I* was the band's riveting adaptation of obscure American folk singer Jake Holmes's "Dazed and Confused," and its reworking of "Babe, I'm Gonna Leave You." The latter folk-rooted song had already borne various writing credits and been given quite different cover treatments by several rock bands, including Quicksilver Messenger Service, the Association, and the obscure British band the Plebs.

The folk-rock connections go on and on, actually, with Led Zeppelin, into the 1970s. *Led Zeppelin III*'s "Hangman" was close to a 1965 version of the traditional number "Hangman" by Dorris Henderson. On *Led Zeppelin IV*, Sandy Denny contributed vocals to Led Zeppelin's "Battle of Evermore," which in a sad irony marked the only time most mainstream American rock fans heard her voice. It has also been reported that Page and Robert Plant were big fans of such folk-rock artists as the Incredible String Band, Fairport Convention, Joni Mitchell, and Love.

Today Robert Plant shares bills with artists such as American cult folk-rocker Tim Rose, whom John Bonham backed on a British tour before joining Led Zeppelin. Plant's 2001 setlist included vintage folk-rock classics, some quite obscure, such as "A House Is Not a Motel" and "Bummer in the Summer" from Love's *Forever Changes* and Tim Buckley's "Song of the Siren," alongside "Hey Joe," "Morning Dew," and "Season of the Witch." Several of those songs also ended up on his 2002 album, *Dreamland*, affording him a chance to revisit folk-rock roots that he revealed as early as a 1970 interview for *Melody Maker*. In it he heaped praise upon Buffalo Springfield's debut album: "It was the kind of music you could hare around to or you could sit down and dig it, and I thought, 'This is what an audience wants—this is what I want to listen to.'" He went on to confess that Love's *Forever Changes* had literally moved him to tears, as "three years before I was shuddering to listen to [blues great] Sonny Boy Williamson, and three years after that I was sobbing to Arthur Lee and *Forever Changes*, and I thought there must be something wrong with me! For something to get at me that much, I mean." In other interviews of the period he raved about Poco, the Youngbloods, Neil Young, Fairport Convention, Matthews Southern Comfort, and, again, *Forever Changes*: "No one can deny the beauty of [that album's] 'The Old Man' or 'Andmoreagain'," he told *Melody Maker*.

I t is a testament to British folk-rock's low profile that many general rock fans have only been exposed to it in a second- or third-hand manner, via groups such as Led Zeppelin. In part this was attributable to a level of containment, reserve, and detached narrative- and character-based songs that permeated much of the genre. With exceptions such as Sandy Denny, British folk-rock did not have nearly as many of the soul-baring or boisterous qualities that were found in much of American folk-rock. It is not satisfying to blame this, as some have tried, on stereotypical assumptions that it was a natural outgrowth of a cold, remote British national character. There were plenty of British extrovert rock bands in the 1960s who took exhibitionism to unprecedented levels, such as the Who and the Rolling Stones.

It could be that there was less of a sense of both social consciousness and confessional urgency to British folk-rock because the United Kingdom was not involved in the Vietnam War or an equivalent, and far less torn by racial conflict and the civil rights struggle. That is not to say that British folk or folk-rock musicians were necessarily apolitical. A large ad in *Melody Maker*, headlined "Folksingers and the War in Vietnam," attracted signatures of nearly 100 figures concerned about the escalation of the war, including Bert Jansch and Denny. Back in 1965, Donovan had marched alongside Joan Baez in an anti–Vietnam War protest in Trafalgar Square.

But British musicians, unlike their American male counterparts, did not face the very real threat of conscription into the armed forces to participate in a war they found immoral. The absence of threats to immediate survival might have made it easier to dwell on mythology, medievalism, and the like. When revolutionary commentary found its way into late '60s rock, it tended to be by British rock bands such as the Rolling Stones ("Street Fighting Man") and the Beatles ("Revolution"), among others. Mick Jagger, Keith Richards, Brian Jones, John Lennon, and George Harrison might not have not had the draft to worry about, but they did have to face off with the establishment due to assorted drug busts.

Simon Nicol, only in his teens when Fairport Convention started to record, emphasizes, "You're talking about the actions and thoughts of juveniles." At the same time he does see the burning issues of the day making an impact, if only as a general mindset that lent itself to encouraging musical experimentation: "The whole Summer of Love thing was tangible. There were possibilities, social revolution in the quiet and positive manner, that did seem achievable at that time. We [Fairport] were doing nothing about that politically or socially; I've never had those kind of goals myself. But in our way, we were riding a wave which was very much part of its time." Countercultural exhortation and agitated activism, though, rarely found its way into British folk-rock. The Johnstons' Mick Moloney thinks the British Isles folk-rock groups "were mostly apolitical, in contrast to the American bands. There was the odd political song that made its way in there. But they were just trying to develop new sounds, in an artistic vision rather than a social vision."

A final consideration was that British folk-rock, far less so than the American version, had no real definite strain that was idiosyncratically, definitively British in character. The album most responsible for changing this was Fairport Convention's *Liege & Lief*. This, too, launched the music that was most responsible for the different perceptions of what precisely constitutes folk-rock that persist in the British Isles to the present. Ian Anderson, who's had to give thought to such questions for years as editor of *fRoots*, summarizes the distinctions as follows:

"In America, there seems to be this general acceptance since the 1960s that a singer-songwriter with an acoustic guitar is folk. Whereas over here, there's much more implication that it has some kind of roots in traditional music, and that is actually quite a profound difference. If you read a review of, say, Nick Drake, in a mainstream newspaper here, they would describe him as folk. But most of the people in the folk scene wouldn't. It's not that they don't like him, or say he's not any good, or anything like that. But it doesn't come into the radar as what's considered folk. And therefore, in this country, most people believe that folk-rock started with Fairport Convention. Because they were, in essence, along with Pentangle and Steeleye [Span], the first people who actually took traditional songs and put [them to] a rock band rhythm section and electric guitars.

"Basically, British folk-rock was based on traditional music, and American folk-rock wasn't. Simple as that. And also, because of that, it always had fiddles, whereas American folk-rock always seemed to be jangly 12-string guitars and things like that. Keyboards? British folk-rock never had much in the way of keyboards."

Picking up the same thread, Fairport Convention's Ashley Hutchings adds, "Folk-rock over here means traditional folk music rocks up. Music that has been called folk-rock in America, we don't consider to be folk-rock at all over here. Although we [Fairport Convention] were heavily influenced by the Byrds at the very beginning, a few steps down the line, the Byrds weren't folk-rock anymore. I love them, I've got every single record they ever made. But folk-rock to me, to be folk-rock, has to have folk music. It's no good it just being someone who sings songs, strums an acoustic guitar, and he or she is backed by a rhythm section. Artistically speaking, I think we've made, on balance, better contributions to the furtherance of traditional music over this side, by sticking with traditional music and experimenting with it."

Some have seen a hint of the "traditional folk music rocks up" aesthetic in the Irish group Sweeney's Men, who, like their Transatlantic labelmates the Johnstons, included future luminaries of Irish folk. One of them, Andy Irvine, was only with them on the first of their pair of late-'60s Transatlantic LPs, which was average Irish folk; on the second, reduced to a duo of Johnny Moynihan and Terry Woods, they went into slightly moodier and bluesier material that nonetheless fell far short of folk-rock. In between those albums, however, they'd augmented the lineup onstage with electric guitarist Henry McCullough, who'd been in the Irish rock band Eire Apparent and would go on to play with Joe Cocker and Paul McCartney's Wings. The electric incarnation of the band caused enough outrage among purists, in a scenario which by 1968 had become old hat, to incite penny-throwing attacks from listeners displeased at them for committing sacrilege.

Rather incredibly, more than one critic has built upon this undocumented (on record) phase of an Irish traditional folk band going electric to hail Sweeney's Men as the first folk-rock group, or the one credited with inventing folk-rock. Only if the very narrowest definition of the term folk-rock is applied, and only if the folk component of folk-rock is considered to be of British Isles origin exclusively, does this hold any water at all. Which is to say that it *doesn't* hold any water at all, though one of Sweeney's Men's alumni, Terry Woods, would have an influence on 1970s British folk-rock as a member of Steeleye Span. Another, Johnny Moynihan, would (like Irvine and both Mick Moloney and Paul Brady of the Johnstons) eventually take a more traditional approach to contemporary Irish folk music, in Moynihan's case as a member of Planxty.

It makes far greater sense to credit Fairport Convention as the prime originators of a folk-rock strain based largely on British traditional folk idioms. Fairport Convention's shift to traditional English folk songs, begun with "A Sailor's Life" on *Unhalfbricking*, had accelerated in May 1969 after the group's van was involved in a serious road accident that claimed the life of drummer Martin Lamble and Richard Thompson's girlfriend, Jeannie Franklin. "The defining event which led to the *Liege & Lief* period, which made Fairport what it has come to be ever since, was the car accident, where Martin Lamble was killed," believes Joe Boyd. "The group at first was very unsure that they would play together again. When they began to consider the possibility of reforming, they were very, very clear that they would never perform the old songs that Martin had played on. They would have to start from scratch with repertoire. They wouldn't go back and try to redo things they'd done with Martin.

"That led to the question, 'What kind of repertoire *will* we do?' That all happened around the time [the Band's] *Music from Big Pink* came out, that was a big influence on them. They were very stunned by that record. It was so rooted in American traditions that they felt that if they could come up with a kind of music which was as English as that record was American, that it would justify reforming as a group. They also wanted to get the same snare drum sound." Dave Pegg, who would join Fairport on bass just before the year was out, confirms that "when we lived at the Angel [the converted pub in which the band dwelled in the early '70s], it was like all you heard was the Band, every room you went into, either *Big Pink* or *The Band*. It was more or less the petrol." As an aside, the Band's influence on British artists was not limited to Fairport; as Ian Anderson tells it, "I remember John Martyn coming down the Cousins one night with a copy of *Music from Big Pink*, insisting that it was put on the record player immediately. That was like bringing the Band right into the center of the den of folk-rock."

"Fairport decided to stop being an American-type folk-rock band, and become an English-type folk-rock band," Boyd continues. "It had already begun to be interesting during *Unhalfbricking* with [its 11-minute version of the traditional folk tune] 'A Sailor's Life,' but it hadn't really occurred to them to just go completely over to that other direction. They were really interested in following that strand when the car accident happened. And if they had gone and made a kind of *Liege & Lief*–type of record, with Martin Lamble in the drum chair, the whole history of folk-rock might have been very, very different, because of the different drum style."

Instead the group carried on with drummer Dave Mattacks and, in a more crucial announcement of its new trad leanings, fiddler Dave Swarbrick (though it's interesting to note that Nicol had played electric violin with the band on occasion before Swarbrick joined). Swarbrick had recorded traditional British folk both on his own and with guitarist Martin Carthy, and guested on "A Sailor's Life" (the first time he ever played with an amplifier) before being made a full member for *Liege & Lief*. This was in itself a shock to the more trad-bound segment of the British folk audience, in whose eyes, says Nicol, "if anyone was a turncoat [Swarbrick] was. He had established himself as a gifted figure, working in the tradition, alongside the incredibly gifted and scholarly Martin Carthy. He was totally respectable. And here he is, throwing his hand in with a bunch of long-haired greasy dope-smoking guitarists." As this was going on, Ashley Hutchings undertook some dedicated research into discovering traditional songs at the Cecil Sharp House in London, named after the esteemed folk song collector who had founded the English Folk Dance Society in 1911. In a way it was an extension of the archivism Fairport had already applied to digging out obscure American folk-rock songs, but now steered to a far larger, more ancient, and avowedly British body of work.

"The archivist mentality, it's always been there with me personally, and it remains there to this day," says Hutchings, who would in the 1980s write and perform a one-man stage show based on Sharp's life. "I think I kind of pulled the rest of the band along. I mean, they were happy to do the material that we agreed on. But I was always the one that did the most research whether it was needed or not, when we got into *Liege & Lief*. In fact, by the time I moved on to Steeleye Span [at the beginning of 1970], I could hold my own with people like Martin Carthy and [Steeleye Span]'s Tim & Maddy [Prior], who'd been steeped in the folk tradition in Britain for some years. Simply because I'd thrown myself into it so wholeheartedly; in a very, very short time, I'd done all that research and all that listening.

"I wonder whether, if I hadn't have been in Fairport, it would have gone the same way. Maybe Fairport needed someone in the lineup to push, to beaver away, because that was a large part of what we did." Yet it wasn't wholly alien territory to the others by any means. Sandy Denny had already been familiar with such material for years, including some of the very songs Hutchings was discovering, and as a performer, Swarbrick was more steeped in this kind of thing than anyone else in the band. Denny promised "heavy traditional music" in *NME*, adding, "the next album is going to be completely different. It will be based around traditional British folk music, which we may put new words to if necessary. We're not making it pop, though. In fact it will be almost straight; only electric."

Armed with this repertoire, Fairport devoted *Liege & Lief* primarily to energetic rocked-up traditional material, with a few originals (and only half a song by Denny) chucked in. Some echoes of its prior harmonized folk-rock could be heard on "Farewell, Farewell," which Hutchings says Thompson built out of Sweeney's Men's arrangement of the traditional number "Willy O' Winsbury." (Further tangling this particular passage through the folk process, Sweeney's Men's Andy Irvine had actually matched the wrong tune to the words, owing to a mix-up in Child ballad numbers.) But the accent was now on traditional epics, with Swarbrick's fiddle the most vital link to a distinctly British folk lineage. ("There's nothing like a good long murder ballad to get them going!" exclaimed Simon Nicol cheerily in *Disc* at the time.) "Tam Lin," the Halloween tale that's probably the most familiar Fairport track to Americans, was the best of these, with Thompson's ominous guitar, Mattacks's chunky drums, and Swarbrick's spooky fiddle counterpointing one of Denny's most powerful, eerie vocals.

Although, as Nicol now acknowledges, "the album was a milestone in the band's career," at the time the group wasn't fully conscious of this. It was still, after all, somewhat in shock at the death of Lamble and Franklin. For a few months the remaining musicians got themselves together, mentally and physically, in a country house rented by Boyd for the band near Winchester. "My feelings at that time were more dominated by the rebirth of the band after the crash, and the reconstruction with this new direction," explains Simon. "That seemed more significant to me than the actual album. What was more significant to me was that we'd overcome the shock of losing Martin, and proved that we could repair ourselves, individually and collectively, and come back with a stronger band."

I t was a risk to tilt *Liege & Lief* at such a pronounced angle, given the fine balance the group had mastered with its previous two LPs. But it was a hit, reaching the Top 20 and remaining in the charts for 15 weeks, though by the time it entered the listings, Denny and Hutchings had left the band.

Only in August, Denny had told *Record Mirror*, "It's like we're going along a completely different road now; what we'll do when we reach the end we don't know. It's really put a new breath of life into us . . . we were all lapsing into apathy. We weren't even sure that we'd ever start playing again." The band's plunge into English folk hadn't necessarily portended a permanent focus. At a concert at the Royal Festival Hall around the time of *Liege & Lief*'s release, it broke up traditional songs from the album such as "Matty Groves" and "Tam Lin" with two selections of jigs and reels, originals, and a cover of the Byrds' "Ballad of Easy Rider" (the last of which had actually been recorded by the band during the *Liege & Lief* sessions, an outtake eventually surfacing on Richard Thompson's *Guitar, Vocal* compilation).

But Denny was being pulled in a different direction, both by a romance with Trevor Lucas and a need for a more flexible format, in part to make sure there was room for her own compositions. The romance with Lucas culminated in not just (several years down the road) marriage, but also the formation of Fotheringay, featuring Denny, Lucas, and one of Lucas's bandmates in Eclection,

Gerry Conway. "We love traditional music, and after all Trevor and I were originally folk artists," she explained to *Melody Maker*. "But we've got a lot of contemporary music we want to do, and that's very important to us." Denny also told the press she wasn't keen on continuing to force herself through the incessant traveling and American tours that Fairport was undertaking to build their international profile. Meanwhile Hutchings wanted to go yet deeper into traditional British folk, even more so than Fairport's new concentration upon such material would allow. In fact, Hutchings had floated the idea of expanding Fairport radically, and taking the band far deeper into traditional folk, by adding folk musicians Martin Carthy, Bert Lloyd, and Terry & Gay Woods (soon to join Ashley in Steeleye Span) to the lineup. This was wisely rejected by the remaining Fairporters as inadvisable.

As with the Byrds, the constant rotation of personnel, while guaranteeing fresh blood and ideas for the first few albums, had also begun to change the group's dynamic so that its sound was almost unrecognizably different. It is not understating matters to note that Fairport Convention's *Liege & Lief* set the direction for British folk-rock to this day. But the loss of a singer-songwriter such as Denny wasn't easy to dismiss. If there is one trait that Fairport possessed more than almost any other rock band of comparable status, however, it was the ability to persevere, reorganize, and continue in the face of never-ending lineup changes and the lack of a dominant frontman or frontwoman. It was almost as if the band was a concept that overshadowed the presence of any specific musicians. As Nicol told *Melody Maker* shortly after the departure of Denny and Hutchings, "The point is that it has never been down to one person to dominate the band's whole style. If someone leaves it is only the approach that changes." Denny gave *NME* her own valediction: "I look upon Fairport as the mother group. They've had a lot of people dropping out but they still go on and will be a popular unit for a long time to come."

They weren't an institution of that sort, however, when Hutchings and Denny abandoned ship. As the 1970s began, their immediate concern was to somehow keep afloat. Dave Pegg, formerly in Birmingham rock bands (he'd even played with John Bonham in one of the drummer's pre–Led Zeppelin outfits, the Way of Life) and then in the Ian Campbell Group during Swarbrick's final days in that ensemble, replaced Hutchings. Their first album with the revised personnel, *Full House*, was in Nicol's estimation "a hugely important record, because it was a hard act to follow *Liege & Lief*. Peggy came in with all this fantastic fundamental power, which we'd never had before with Ashley; it was all more cerebral with him. But we now had real balls in the engine room. And we had to survive without Sandy up front."

"Obviously, it was different without Sandy and Ashley," says Pegg. "They were pulling in different directions. Sandy wanted to write her own songs, and Ashley wanted the band to do completely traditional music. Neither of them saw eye to eye over that, and I think that's why they split up. So when I joined the band, it was Richard and Swarb who were doing most of the writing; they'd started writing together, and came up with some really good stuff. We didn't have a lead singer; the band were very strong instrumentally, but there was quite a bit of nervousness about who was gonna sing. We'd rehearsed this stuff for about three weeks, all the songs that eventually went out on *Full House*, and some of the stuff from *Liege & Lief*.

"We were just literally playing backing tracks, and nobody was singing," he laughs. "It was a couple of days before the first gig when, literally, it was whoever drew the shortest straw got to be the lead vocalist. Luckily it wasn't myself or Dave Mattacks, otherwise it would have been hell. The group didn't really have an out-front singer; Richard and Swarb developed as singers really quickly, and later on Simon had to do more and more vocal work. But it made up for it with its instrumental prowess, which was very good, the *Full House* lineup. We were a very powerful band." Onstage they had to develop an almost entirely new repertoire from the one they had just mastered with the release of *Liege & Lief*, in front of audiences that had just (or never) gotten used to hearing the songs from that album. Yet against the odds, like *Liege & Lief*, *Full House*—mixing the kind of fiddle-heavy trad British folk covers heard on *Liege & Lief* with Thompson/Swarbrick originals in the same mold, with a somewhat heavier rock attack—made the Top 20 in England.

In America it was a different story, as it was for most British folk-rock, with none of their first five albums even making the charts. Fairport did well with American audiences as a touring act, but usually as a support band to groups like Traffic. *Rolling Stone*'s Ed Ward, though, did recognize how the group was doing for English folk music what some more celebrated bands were doing for American roots music in his review of *Full House*, where he raved, "England has finally gotten herself her very own equivalent to the Band . . . . By calling Fairport an English equivalent to the Band, I meant that they have soaked up enough of the tradition of their countryfolk that it begins to show all over, while they still maintain their roots in rock."

lthough Richard Thompson hung on for a little longer before starting his own acclaimed solo career and Fairport made a few more hit British albums, it never reclaimed the peaks of its 1960s work. Nor was Sandy Denny ever as good after leaving Fairport, though she made some fine music in the 1970s, starting with Fotheringay's sole, self-titled 1970 album. *Fotheringay* was a return to the diversity that had characterized Fairport, with original material (largely by Denny), covers of songs by Gordon Lightfoot and Dave Cousins, a Basement Tapes relic by Dylan ("Too Much of Nothing"), and a traditional wartime epic, "Banks of the Nile," that rivaled anything of a similar nature on *Liege & Lief*. Fotheringay was not as strong or unique a collection of talent as Fairport had been, however, and split up partway through an unfinished second album when Denny went solo.

Some have suggested that Joe Boyd, who produced *Fotheringay*, was less interested in developing the group than encouraging Denny to start her own career. Fotheringay guitarist Jerry Donahue says Boyd would "be there in the studio, but he was usually reading a newspaper with feet on the desk. The engineer was doing all the work." By the time Denny did step out on her own, she and Boyd would in any case not be able to work together any longer, and nor would other longtime Boyd clients be able to continue collaborating with the producer. The whole Witchseason operation—which had pretty much been the axis of British folk-rock—was winding down, as Boyd sold the management/production company and moved to Los Angeles to supervise film scores for Warner Brothers.

"Basically, financially, Witchseason overreached themselves, " summarizes John Wood. "To some extent, it was probably by overindulging artists. I never saw any sort of time limits or budgetary control on records, really. They were also touring bands and publishing. At the end of the day, the financial side of it got out of control. So Island Records took on Witchseason and met its liabilities. Certainly the recording liabilities to Sound Techniques were fairly large. Joe was very straightforward and frank about it, and we never had a problem over it."

Though Witchseason was not a label (even if many of Boyd's productions were placed with Island), it had been instrumental in supporting many of the best British folk-rock acts in both management and the studio. There was also a house sound of sorts that was cultivated by frequent moonlighting between acts, with Fairport's Richard Thompson, for instance, playing on albums by Nick Drake; Dave Pegg on albums by Nick Drake and John Martyn; Simon Nicol on the album by Vashti Bunyan; and Robin Williamson on albums by Bunyan and Shirley Collins. With Boyd's departure, a major straw stirring the drink was lost. As for Denny, she never was as effective on her own as she was with a group, and after years of worsening personal and alcohol problems, she died in her home under mysterious circumstances in April 1978.

oyd has intimated, as well, that his parting of ways with the Witchseason roster he fostered wasn't solely due to financial frustrations. Although British folk-rock musicians generally have a far more genteel image than most other rock acts, at times even they could be a handful to manage, as Boyd had found with the Incredible String Band. By the end of the 1960s, the Incredibles' sound had softened somewhat as Rose Simpson and Licorice McKechnie took larger roles in the vocal and instrumental arrangements. Arguably they were putting out too much material in too short a space of time—an astonishing eight albums were issued between 1966 and 1970, two of them double LPs—and there was a sense that they were running over too much of the same territory too often. In a 1997 article for the *Guardian*, Joe Boyd pinned part of the group's decline on the Church of Scientology, writing that in the two years after they joined the church in 1968, "ISB's output lost its inventiveness, its charm and the wild beauty of its melodies. They were more efficient in the studio, but there were fewer moments of surprise and inspiration. Songs began to sound much the same. Was this a natural decline after years of tremendously original output? Or was it Scientology?

"Soon after, other things changed too. Together with other residents of the Row [eight cottages rented by the band on a Scottish estate], the group organized a pageant called *U*. They wanted to take their new creation on tour, but I was unsure: with a cast of ten dancers and musicians, plus sets and costumes, it was going to be an expensive show to take on the road. Many of the songs had meanings even more obscure than those of their opaque masterpieces in the past.

"Promoters who had earlier been happy to book the ISB were dubious about *U*. Guarantees were reduced, the group was financially at risk everywhere, and audiences began to level off. Poor reviews and responses to *U*'s first few performances made me beg them to call off the rest of the tour and rebuild ISB. They would hear none of it. Their confidence was impossible to dent—they were sure *U* would work. It didn't, and we lost a great deal of money. The saga of *U* helped me decide what to do next: I sold my production company and moved away from London."

Described by Williamson in *Melody Maker* as "a surreal parable in song and dance," *U* hooked the Incredibles with the unclassifiable performance ensemble Stone Monkey. In their cottages on the

Tennant estate, the large team worked up a hard-to-define combination of music, drama, dance, and pantomime, with sets that were colored slides projected from the front and rear. "I'd been pushing for a while to get a visual element into what we were already doing musically," says Williamson. "I liked the notion of everybody having a go, regardless of their particular abilities; using all people at their various levels. This was something the Stone Monkey had already imbibed in the notion of street happenings, getting people to generally explode. These people were already doing Indian movement ideas, Indian street theater ideas, Japanese, Burmese, and Thai kind of puppet notions. For better or worse, we tried to flush all those things in there."

As one might suspect, the plot was kind of secondary to the vibe. "Everything is evenly balanced, and because the framework of the story is thin, there's plenty of opportunity for adding sketches as we feel like it," Malcolm LeMaistre of Stone Monkey told *Melody Maker*. Or, as Williamson puts it, "The vague notion was, a soul incarnates out of nowhere, lives, and then vanishes again at the other end. Hence the idea 'U,' manifesting into matter and then reascending back into the great finale. It was such a forgiving plot line. We liked to engage in all sorts of asides, which

The Incredible String Band. Left to right: Licorice McKechnie, Mike Heron, Robin Williamson, and Rose Simpson.

includes robots, call girls, space characters, a pirate or two, some highwaymen, and a number of other bits and pieces."

Actually the accompanying soundtrack double album of sorts was one of the Incredible String Band's better, and certainly more overlooked, efforts, covering an even more astonishing amount of ground than usual. Considering its track record, that made it one of the most eclectic releases by anyone of the period, folk-rock or otherwise. At nearly two hours it might try the patience of less-forgiving listeners, but those willing to persevere are rewarded by a potpourri of psychedelic instrumentals led by sitar and piercing fuzz guitar, charming minstrel folk with a wicked undercurrent, old-time Americana, and one tune with a string arrangement by sometime Grateful Dead keyboardist Tom Constanten.

But the endeavor wasn't sustainable as a traveling road show, though a live production of *U* ran for about ten days at London's Roundhouse in April 1970, and then for about five days right after at the Fillmore East. As a story-less production running for more than two and a half hours with more than 20 songs and about 15 performers, it was apt to draw the ire of established media critics as well. "The performances in Britain and America were rapturously received by the crowds, but absolutely panned by the press," says Williamson. "Most of the press just insisted on viewing the dance as not really being technical. It totally missed the point. It wasn't *supposed* to be technical. It [the press] said it had no structure; the whole idea was to allow it to occur. But we ran into dance critics who said the dance isn't dance, and the theater critics who said, 'This isn't theater.' Of course, it wasn't either dance *or* theater. That wasn't what we were trying to do."

It was a definitely 1960s concept, even if it was a few months into the 1970s already, and the upshot was that "after we'd done the Fillmore East, we ran out of money. The String Band took the remains of the show, just with the four of us, to the West Coast and did a few more dates on the West and elsewhere, but without all the dancers." The dream of a traveling folk-rock troupe of sorts was dying, as were other dreams of all sorts that had seemed possible, if only briefly, in the mid-to-late '60s. The family-type, artist-friendly atmosphere of Witchseason may have been less utopian than *U*. But it was likewise an outgrowth of the decade's noblest aspirations, even if the balance sheets ultimately got too unbalanced to keep it operating for as long as its architects had hoped.

The most traditional wing of the divergences that had led to Fairport Convention's reshuffling was helmed by Ashley Hutchings, who made his intentions clear to *Melody Maker* as he was helping to form a new band at the end of 1969: "I want to develop along the same lines as Fairports did. They searched the surface, now we want to take traditional British songs and adapt them to an electric setting, creating an unmistakable British sound. With Fairports, we found that this was far more successful than when we played our own material. But Fairports are still basically a rock group, and we would be folk musicians going electric . . . . I hope we will be even more British, by virtue of the concertina, mandolin, dulcimer and so on.

"I believe that virtually all rock music is based on American forms. We've got a number of fine bands, but they seem to end up taking American music back to America—it's the same with any music. What we are trying to do is get people interested in British forms. I personally like all sorts of music, but I'm particularly interested in British music. I just hope that the new group will achieve this by reverting back to the roots, and doing traditional material."

The group ended up being called—at the suggestion of Martin Carthy, from the chorus of a folk song he'd just learned called "Horkstow Grange"—Steeleye Span. Also in the band were Maddy Prior—who had been singing in folk clubs alongside the likes of Mac MacLeod back in the mid-'60s—and Tim Hart, with whom Prior had been performing and recording in a folk duo. Hutchings, Terry Woods of Sweeney's Men, and Woods's wife Gay filled out the group on 1970's *Hark! The Village Wait.* (Andy Irvine and Johnny Moynihan of Sweeney's Men had been in the very first lineup, but backed out after a just a bit of rehearsal.) Like Fairport Convention, the musicians holed up in a country house to get their music and an album together, though this particular lineup never played live and broke up right after the record was finished.

As Hutchings promised, the album was comprised wholly of traditional British folk, played on electric rock instruments (though no drums) as well as fiddle, harmonium, autoharp, concertina, mandolin, and electric dulcimer. The guitars, banjo, and bass were electric; "The only reason we didn't amplify the mandola," Hart told *Melody Maker*, "is because the pickup falls through the sound hole." Steeleye Span was the kind of rare rock band, then or since, that could comfortably appear on a television show where its performance would be interrupted by the host's five-minute demonstration of dulcimer construction, as actually happened during a Steeleye gig on Anglia TV in 1970. With *Liege & Lief,* not only had a whole new path for British folk-rock been established—it would soon become the dominant direction.

"One would have thought that first of all Fairport would make a traditional folk album, rocks-up," says Hutchings now. "And then after a year or two, they would start to write songs which were influenced by the tradition and put them in the set. But bang, in one go, we did the whole thing on *Liege & Lief.* So in a way, we were stepping back with Steeleye. We were taking one step back further than Fairport, because it was wholeheartedly British traditional folk songs and tunes, in an electric context. That meant a bit more time and effort went into researching the songs, getting the right songs."

So the first half of the 1970s, a time that saw folk-rock recede from the American pop scene, was actually a golden age of sorts for folk-rock in the British Isles. Britain had always run behind the States in grappling with the folk-rock fusion, even as it had set the pace for several other branches of '60s rock, starting with the Beatles and the British Invasion. It was fitting that it would not only harvest the last significant strain of 1960s folk-rock, but also carry the concept forward into the next decade with far greater presence than the music maintained in Britain's former colonies. In the autumn of 1970, Fairport Convention, the Incredible String Band, the Pentangle, and Fotheringay were at the peak of their drawing power, all of them undertaking tours that season, even if they weren't at their peaks in the recording studio. Steeleye Span showed that purist outrage was hardly a '60s phenomenon when Martin Carthy (who had already rejected invitations from both Ashley Hutchings and Dave Swarbrick to join Fairport Convention) joined on electric guitar in 1970 following its first album, to much outcry from folk hard-liners; the band eventually made the Top Ten in 1975 with

"All Around My Hat." The more pop-oriented, folk-rockish Lindisfarne was briefly one of the most popular groups of any kind in Britain in 1971–72. By the end of 1971 Hutchings had left Steeleye Span to pursue yet more obscure and traditional electrified English music with the Albion Country Band, which at times also included his wife, hallowed British folk singer Shirley Collins, and Carthy.

The enlistment of top folk veterans such as Carthy, Collins, and Swarbrick in folk-rock bands could be seen as the ultimate validation of British folk-rock. Conversely, in the eyes of some purists, it could be viewed as the ultimate betrayal of British folk music. As had been the case half a decade earlier in the States, the gulf between electric folk-rockers and supposedly outraged folk purists has sometimes been overemphasized by historians for dramatic effect. "Of course some people made a fuss about both me and Martin Carthy 'going electric,' as they did with Bob Dylan," reflects Collins. "But the integrity of my Southern English singing style was entirely unaffected by the accompaniments, and most people recognized this. In any case, I always trusted my own judgment and instincts."

Carthy himself offhandedly shrugged off any stigma for electrifying in *Melody Maker* shortly after he joined Steeleye Span. "I got bored with playing chords several years ago. So playing electric guitar, which is a melodic rather than a harmonic technique, is in the same line of development. I didn't have any special reason for going electric, but just liked Tim and Maddy. I don't think it matters how you play music. The language stays the same." Martin added that he thought the only reason folk musicians hadn't electrified before was that they couldn't afford the electric equipment, which indeed was a greater obstacle in Britain than America, the UK's standard of living being somewhat lower. In Fairport Convention, Dave Swarbrick distanced himself a little from the whole debate, telling *Melody Maker*, "We are not a folk group, and we don't play folk music."

For the main issue was not acoustic versus electric, or folk versus rock, but a simple matter of expanding musical possibilities with different arrangements, as Collins had done back in 1964 with Davy Graham on *Folk Roots, New Routes*. She admits that "I never had a huge interest in folk-rock—the 'folk' part was where my passion lay." Yet to her, a similar sensibility was at work on her collaboration with sister Dolly Collins on the medieval-sounding 1969 album *Anthems of Eden*, featuring instruments associated with centuries-old early music styles, and her 1971 electric folk-rock LP *No Roses* (backed by the Albion Country Band): "As with the use of early instruments on *Anthems in Eden*, where the songs were so sympathetically arranged by my sister Dolly, on *No Roses*, the songs were enhanced by the variety of instruments both acoustic and electric. I wouldn't have agreed to do it if I'd thought otherwise. Most people were open-minded about it as far as I remember—lots of them even enjoyed it! I know I had a great time making *No Roses*." It also needs to be pointed out that such new electric projects did not necessarily prevent folk-rock musicians from continuing to do some live work in clubs without electric backing, as Carthy, Hart, Prior, and Bob & Carole Pegg (of Mr. Fox) were all still doing in late 1970.

"Because *Liege & Lief* appearing was a dramatic moment, chroniclers have tended to polarize: 'there was this faction, there was that faction'," surmises Hutchings. "But certainly over here there were a lot of people who thought, 'Oh, wow, that's interesting!' They didn't necessarily leap to its defense and say, this is the *only* way forward. But people like Bert Lloyd, for example, said, 'This is very interesting.' As far as I know, Bert didn't say, 'Wow, this is fantastic'; he never said that. But he had an open mind, and said, 'I'd like to hear it again.'

"There *were* people who were disgusted. [This was nothing new to Fairport, even before their switch to a traditional British folk-rock-based repertoire; back in August 1968, an angry *Melody Maker* reader had complained about being 'subjected to a neo-pop group called Fairport Convention' at an event billed as a folk concert.] I remember people walking out of gigs [with] Fairport and Steeleye. I remember later on even with the Albion Band at the Royal Albert Hall, some guy standing up in the middle of the hall and shouting at the top of his voice, 'This is not folk music!' But I would say it was no more than 20 percent who felt that way. Basically, I think, because we did it so well, because Carthy in Steeleye Span and Swarb in Fairport did it so well, and certainly as far as Steeleye is concerned, with good taste, that allayed many people's fears."

"At that time, it was only 60 years after the publication of Cecil Sharp's early work," points out Nicol. "It was within living memory. There were people around who made a direct connection back to those days when the music has been rescued by Child and Sharp, and in its way had been scholarized and put under glass. It had been preserved in a kind of respectful and scholarly manner. What was being done to it before people like Fairport came to it was more interpretive and recital-based, rather than treating it as raw material. Fairport were perhaps a vanguard of a movement which felt that you *could* take these songs, and you could interfere with them. Yet you wouldn't destroy their innate qualities. The substance would survive any amount of tinkering."

"The Fairports, you have to remember, that we were 19-, 20-, 21-year-old kids," adds Pegg. "Most of our gigs were played to audiences of the same age group. Our musical influences were very similar to the kids that we were playing to, really, in terms of we all came from rock 'n' roll, or R&B. The only traditional musicians in Fairport, really, were Dave Swarbrick and Sandy Denny, who'd grown up amongst the folk tradition and earned their living by going around touring and playing in folk clubs acoustically." And even when Fairport played at Ian Campbell's Birmingham folk club when Pegg joined, "we had a really good night. I think the Fairports were the first electric group to ever play there, certainly with drumkit and stuff. And people really enjoyed it."

In a similar way to how things had played out in the States about five years before, the ire of miffed traditionalists was more than offset by the addition of substantial numbers of new, younger listeners who might not have gone within a mile of anything folk-related before the likes of Fairport suckered them into it. *NME*'s Nick Logan was one such listener, as he confessed in a 1970 piece that dubbed Fairport's sound "rock and reel." He vented that "I, for one, still find it hard to believe that I can be brought to the edge of my seat by old English jigs and reels reminiscent, in content but not at all in delivery, of the stuff that used to bore the pants off me in school song and dance lessons and on those dreadful Robin Hall–Jimmy McGregor TV folk shows."

"The emergence of British folk-rock didn't have the shock value of Dylan going electric at Newport," summarizes Andrew Means, who as a 20-year-old in 1970 was beginning his stint as a *Melody Maker* reporter, often covering the folk-rock beat. "When Fairport began adapting traditional song for their rock group format, it did generate discussion as well as excitement. *Liege &*

Lief was certainly a watershed. Although Fairport had recorded traditional material before, they hadn't devoted an entire album to it or done it with such finesse. But the development wasn't as polarizing as one might expect.

"In fact, both traditionalists and contemporary fans had reason to salute *Liege & Lief.* The trads could say that Fairport were showing the relevance of traditional forms to modern life (always a big talking point), and the contemporary people could draw validation from the instrumentation and concert settings. *Liege & Lief* influenced folk singers, who were already familiar with this material, to pick up electric instruments. The distinction between the more orthodox rhythmic dynamics of Fairport and Fotheringay, and the melodic polyphonic Steeleye, led to some observers, notably Karl Dallas, tagging the former 'folk-rock' and the latter 'electric folk.'

"If there's one enduring failure of British folk-rock of that era in my mind, it is its failure by and large to pick up the challenge posed by Ewan MacColl and write new songs in the traditional musical vein, but with lyrics focusing on contemporary viewpoints. The exception is Richard Thompson, and Sandy Denny's remarkable work as a soloist in the early '70s."

The influence of Fairport Convention, its moderate pop chart album success to the contrary, remained pervasive, and as with every rock genre, "spawned a number of groups that weren't that good," as Ashley Hutchings notes. The group most prone to clone Fairport were the far less memorable Trees, who likewise mixed traditional folk songs and originals and put many of those to way-long electric-guitar-heavy arrangements. They also had their own Sandy Denny in Celia Humphris, one of several women sporting superficial similarities to Denny, but possessing none of the indelibly arresting chill-charm Sandy stamped over all her vocals. ("The new Sandy Denny?" read one headline of a *Melody Maker* item on another Denny-like singer-songwriter, Shelagh McDonald.) *Melody Maker's* Karl Dallas did see the importance of Trees as indicative of a sort of second-generation blurring of lines between the camps: "Their inspiration goes back independently to the folk and rock scenes of a few years ago, indicating that the long-awaited, long-needed reconciliation between the folk and pop movements is actually beginning to happen. Also, in the person of singer Celia Humphris, this new amalgam is beginning to produce its own singers, who have never sung either pure folk or pure rock."

The swing toward rocked-up, extended interpretations of traditional material—almost as a British parallel to the back-to-the-basics ethos that had led to country-rock in the States—was felt in far more established bands too. Although it probably wasn't due to influence from Fairport, it turned out that the Pentangle, its best work already in the past, devoted all of its fourth album, 1970's *Cruel Sister,* to traditional folk songs. Again it was most likely coincidence, but like *Liege & Lief,* this included an epic reworking of a traditional folk song, a marathon 18-minute workout of "Jack Orion." And as with *Liege & Lief, Cruel Sister* differed from standard folk interpretations (such as the one John Renbourn and Bert Jansch had given "Jack Orion" in 1966 for the title track of Jansch's third album) in its use of electric guitar, with Renbourn's increasing use of fuzzy (if low-volume) electric tones. By this time the Pentangle had spawned its own somewhat sound-alike band, Dando Shaft, though that group differed from the Pentangle in its greater emphasis on original material with pastoral lyrics, Bulgarian-influenced tempos, and an almost bluegrass-like interplay among speedy guitar, mandolin, and fiddle lines.

Among the second-division, just-post-Fairport British folk-rockers who *weren't* that bad was Mr. Fox, who put a hard-edged gypsy gloom-drone into its most interesting work, the rock rhythm section backing organ, melodeon, whistle, fiddle, woodwinds, and cello. Like Fairport Convention and Steeleye Span, Mr. Fox were consciously trying to "preserve the British roots, rather than going back to the American roots," as the group's Carole Pegg told *Melody Maker*, though her husband and bandmate Bob Pegg immediately acknowledged in the same story that the group's rhythm section had an American flavor. Like many UK folk-rock bands, they had a link to Fairport Convention through a friendship with Ashley Hutchings, who had talked with the Peggs about being in the band that evolved into Mr. Fox in the spring of 1970 before getting lured back into Steeleye Span. Unlike Fairport and Steeleye, however, the Peggs wouldn't be digging into the black hole of the British traditional folk archive. "There are electric groups which concentrate almost entirely upon folk material (Fairport, Steeleye Span) and there are others whose songs are almost all contemporary (Fotheringay, Dando Shaft)," observed Karl Dallas in *Melody Maker*. "Mr. Fox are different, in that they play almost entirely original stuff, but treat it as if it were traditional."

"Fairport took familiar material and transmuted it to folk-rock from folk," speculates Nat Joseph, whose Transatlantic label released Mr. Fox's two early-'70s albums to nothing more than cult acclaim. "[Mr. Fox] were creating the illusion that you were listening to folk music. Bob and Carole Pegg were very interested in murder and death in the folk idiom. When we first heard the album, I remember everybody in the company being very enthused by what they were getting, because they weren't expecting anything so tough and earthy. Unfortunately, not enough people really liked it. It got critical acclaim, but it didn't catch on."

British folk-rock tenaciously held onto an influential corner of the pop scene over the next few years, spreading its influence in some small ways without ever becoming a commanding force. In Ireland, Clannad used a similar approach with Irish folk, although as its fine, underrated 1973 debut album *Clannad* demonstrated, the musicians were certainly influenced by the likes of the Pentangle when the group first recorded. More specialized subniches were dug by acts such as Amazing Blondel, who played several dozen instruments in its excursions into medieval music, and Comus, whose arty and ominous folk-rock sometimes sounded like a soundtrack to a witches' coven. Veterans like Thompson, Harper, Martyn, McTell, Jansch, and Renbourn kept slogging 'round the circuit with more or less steady, large cult followings.

There was even, as there were in the States, a wealth of eccentric, sometimes privately pressed British folk-rock that is only now being discovered by cult collectors, as heard on the Kissing Spell *History of UK Underground Folk-Rock* compilations. It was a chummy scene that saw acts gigging on both the rock and folk circuits, and came crashing down commercially in the late '70s when the British punk and new wave explosions blasted folk-rockers out of both financial and critical favor.

The core audience that has enabled some of them to continue to perform and record through the early twenty-first century came largely from the folk world, not the pop one.

Across the water in the States, British folk-rock never has been more than a minority cult taste, even when Fairport Convention and the Pentangle were at their peaks. Nat Joseph dealt with American executives like Mo Ostin, Jac Holzman, and Maynard Solomon often when licensing Transatlantic product for US distribution, and contends, "One always felt that the Americans thought to themselves, quite reasonably, 'We've got so much talent in what we call the folk-rock area, we don't really need the more traditional variety,' which was usually what they were being offered." Americans who *are* British folk-rock aficionados are as vociferous in their zeal as any. One of the leading US folk magazines, *Dirty Linen*, is named after a song on Fairport's *Full House*. For years, Richard Thompson's wife, Nancy Covey, has run special British package tours for Americans centered around the Cropredy Music Festival, an event in turn always centered around performances by various current and former members of the still-alive Fairport Convention. For most pop-weaned American ears, however, British folk-rock's a taste they can't acquire. Much as country-rock's audience was limited by those who couldn't abide twangy voices and steel guitars, many Americans couldn't get past the sharp fiddles so prominent in the British folk-rock of Fairport Convention and others.

"I think the average person has a great deal of trouble listening to or enjoying music which is devoid of African influence," speculates Joe Boyd, who has lived and worked in both Britain and the United States for extended periods. "African-inflected rhythms are the currency of courtship, the currency of fun, and the currency of every kind of popular music, really. So when you have a music such as Northern European folk music, which is pretty devoid of that influence, of that color, that flavor, it's *always* going to be a very, very minority interest. It will never be a broad popular interest. Whereas the Band playing with Dylan, or the Byrds, or Buffalo Springfield, is full of blues, black influence, all through. In the rhythms, and the textures of the melodies, and the way of singing, and everything. It's much sexier music. And therefore, it's always going to be more popular."

Boyd looks back on the belated British folk-rock flare with mixed feelings. "I think everything that happened in so-called folk-rock in Britain after *Liege & Lief*, and after the Pentangle … that was really in a way the *beginning* of something. Whereas in America, it began a good deal earlier, in a way influenced by Britain again, but by a different group of Britons, a different scene of British groups playing American music, like the Spencer Davis Quartet doing Leadbelly songs.

"The problem is, with a lot of things that were great when they were started, as they get descended in the generations, they get reduced to their simplest elements and become cartoon images of themselves. And so you have things which I find unlistenable, which are obviously very influenced by early Fairport. You know, I'm at a folk festival and I hear that kind of lickety-split jig-and-reel being played, I head for the beer tent. I can't stand it. Partly out of guilt, perhaps," he laughs.

"Like anything innovative, [Fairport] opened up a lot of Pandora's boxes. What they did was so strong that it's impossible in a way for a Northern European rock band to address its own traditional music in a rock context without quoting, in some way, from Fairport. Usually I find it depressing to listen to because to me, it's a kind of pale copy of what Fairport were doing. The same thing goes for women singers singing traditional music, particularly of the British Isles, in a modern context. You hear echoes of Sandy [Denny] in an awful lot of contemporary female singers who have a feeling for tradition of some kind."

Back in the days of *Liege & Lief*, though, Fairport Convention had not just popularized a whole new approach to folk-rock. In Britain, its musicians were the chief agents for, if only tentatively, bridging the infighting factions that have ferociously protected folk from any sort of contemporary pop influence—in the 1960s and, to a degree, up to the present day. "Two years ago, folk-rock was something of a dirty word," wrote Karl Dallas, possibly the United Kingdom's most widely read folk critic, in *Melody Maker* in early 1970. "Folkies didn't understand why so many of their heroes were going electric, and your true rocker didn't like anything that didn't pound along like a thundering herd. Today, thanks to Fairport Convention, the word could become respectable again. For if what they are playing is not folk-rock, then the term has no meaning."

With Fairport Convention's *Liege & Lief* there was, at last, one album, and one group, on which all of Britain—where dozens of perspectives on folk-rock clashed—could agree. *This* was folk-rock. Probably.

folk-rock from
newport to woodstock

I n July of 1965, Bob Dylan took the stage at the Newport Folk Festival with an electric rock band in front of 15,000 people, and got—for at least part of the time and from at least part of the crowd—booed, or, at the very best, a mixed reception. A little over four years later, he took the stage at the Isle of Wight Festival in front of 200,000 people, again with a rock band, and no one thought anything of it.

Just a few days before that, musicians who had started as folkies, and were now established as folk-rock or psychedelic stars, comprised about half the bill at Woodstock. They played before half a million people in what will likely remain history's most famous rock festival, and probably the most famous mass gathering of any sort. Again, no one complained or even took special note of performers using electric instruments and amplification. Indeed, the audience reveled in them.

How, exactly, had so much managed to change in a mere four years, expanding the attendance at such events by tenfold and twentyfold while eliminating any outrage over the mix of folk and rock? Much of the answer lies, of course, in the records made during the five-year folk-rock revolution that had preceded the summer of 1969. Records and songs, however, don't tell the whole story, even when coupled with explanatory comments by musicians at the time, and their retellings of the events from memory several decades later. A lot of the story lies in how the music was presented live, and how those audiences changed along with them.

T he Newport Folk Festival was the most prominent model for the pop music festivals that had multiplied all over the Western world by the late '60s. It's not well remembered that Newport had not just folded up its tents and vanished into the obscurity of its own purity after the furor generated by Dylan's controversial 1965 set. To the contrary, Newport immediately began to open up its roster to rock artists and folk-rock singer-songwriters, while also retaining the more traditional, acoustic folk artists that had been its base. Dylan did not return to the Newport Folk Festival, although, interestingly, *Melody Maker* had reported that he was scheduled to appear there the following summer, on July 24, 1966, but canceled "because he will be filming." It would have been fascinating to see how he would have been received, almost certainly playing with a group (the Hawks aka the Band) that was both far tighter and far louder than the thrown-together outfit that had backed him at Newport '65. The Festival didn't get Dylan in 1966 (or, for that matter, perennial folkie favorites Joan Baez and Peter, Paul & Mary), but it *did* get the Lovin' Spoonful, who were actually, if anything, selling more records.

So how did the Newport audience react to an electric folk-rock band that was certainly more pop in inclination than Dylan had been? "No problem, was the reaction," states a bemused, emphatic John Sebastian. "They accepted us fully," confirms Steve Boone. "We got a good reception at Newport, and I really enjoyed that show." The remaining holdout purists, Boone feels, "went into the background, realizing it was a wasted cause to keep railing against electricity, more or less like the Flat Earth Society." Still, there was one carryover from Dylan's woes in 1965. "The public address system was so bad that they couldn't be heard properly," reported *Melody Maker*. "Everyone thought if they stopped the concert to fix the PA things might get out of hand, so they carried on regardless." The same magazine reported that as about 8,000 people couldn't get in, about 1,000 started climbing fences behind the stage, causing them to collapse, though Sebastian and Boone have no memory of this. (*The New York Times* placed the figure of turnaways at 6,000, noting that only "a few caused trouble by trying to break through the wood fence, but prudent police action kept them in check.")

"On one level the festival reflected the growing acceptance of folk-rock and other amalgamations of contemporary folk songs with electric instruments," acknowledged Robert Shelton in his *New York Times* report. "This was dramatized by the appearance of the Lovin' Spoonful, a bizarre op-art rock quartet that scored a spiritual triumph for modernity in folk music." Unfortunately no footage exists of the Spoonful's performance, though Murray Lerner was on hand to assemble clips for his *Festival* documentary. "We had trouble with the sound, unfortunately," he explains, adding that "there were people who were very negative about the idea of my filming them. I think the only controversy [about their appearance] would have been among people organizing the festival." The Lovin' Spoonful aside, the big change he noticed was offstage. "The *audience* changed, I thought, in '66. There was more physical movement. You didn't see much getting up and dancing during concerts at Newport to the rhythm, to the beat of the performers. But you began to see that in '66, especially [during] Howlin' Wolf"—a clip that did make it into *Festival*. "And he was electric."

Also at Newport in '66 were a number of other acts who were either playing electric rock or, even if they played acoustic at the festival, were in the process of entering folk-rock on record: the Blues Project, Chuck Berry, and singer-songwriters Richie Havens, Judy Collins, Phil Ochs, Tom Rush, Tim Hardin, Eric Andersen (accompanied by Harvey Brooks on electric bass), Tom Paxton, and Buffy Sainte-Marie. "I organized something I called a New Folk Concert," says Peter Yarrow of the festival's increasing attention to folk-rock-affiliated singer-songwriters. "I virtually said I was going off the board [of directors] unless Newport recognized the new singer-songwriters, whose styles were not necessarily trying to recapitulate the exact style of folk. I said, 'Look, I just want to create a Sunday afternoon concert, and I'll book it.' Lots of people like Eric Andersen, who was already going in that direction, were accommodated, and it became kind of a platform for their recognition."

Predictably, at least one pundit was, if not outraged, adamant that folk-rock had no place at such an occasion. "Folk-rock does not belong at Newport," declared Ralph Earle in *Boston Broadside*, justifying his reasoning with logic that seems tangled now, but did reflect the opinions of a sizable chunk of the audience at the time. "For two reasons, one aesthetic, one practical. The former stems from the fact that folk-rock incorporates a wide diversity of influences. It does not represent the indigenous music of an easily delimited group of people. Rather, it combines traditional harmony and melody, the blues, rock 'n' roll, jazz, poetry, and gimmickry in varying admixtures. In this sense, which is the sense of folk music at Newport, it does not belong at the festival.

"The other reason is its rapid growth. Folk-rock is growing fast enough to stand by itself. The Lovin' Spoonful didn't need to be there and didn't belong there. More than once the question was asked, 'If [Newport co-founder] George Wein wants rock 'n' roll, why doesn't he hold a festival for it?' The question was more than angrily rhetorical. Folk-rock should address itself to the task Richard Fariña ascribed to it. It should seek to elevate rock 'n' roll, its closest relative in the family of music, from the status of electrified pabulum to something meaningful enough to deserve being called popular culture."

Of course folk-rock was already doing that, although rock 'n' roll was hardly mere "electrified pabulum" and was certainly already worthy of designation as popular culture. However Earle, and perhaps other similar observers, seemed unaware that folk-rock was at the same time changing, and many would say elevating, the tastes of folk fans too. Beyond festival grounds, folk and rock audiences were also coming together at clubs and venues that had previously specialized almost exclusively in folk music.

Sing Out! editor Irwin Silber caught on to the changeover early on, noting in July 1966, "More than half the coffeehouses that featured folk singing less than two years ago are now strictly rock and roll or Folk Rock." In a *Billboard* article headlined "Record Companies Battling for Underground Artists" three months later, Verve executive Jerry Schoenbaum saw it too. Asked to comment on the scene that had spawned the Fugs, Paul Butterfield, the Blues Project, Mothers of Invention, and the Velvet Underground, Schoenbaum observed, "You could refer to it as the coffeehouse underground. Because that's where these groups are performing—the Poor Richard in Chicago, Le Cave in Cleveland, the Unicorn in Boston, Cellar Door in Washington, the Village and Riverboat in Toronto." Even Izzy Young, proprietor of the Folklore Center in Greenwich Village, crossed over to folk-rock by co-sponsoring (with Angry Arts for Life and Against the War in Vietnam) and emceeing two shows billed as "folk-rock concerts" at the Village Theatre in spring 1967. Actually these were more shows that featured both folk and rock artists rather than emphasizing folk-rock per se, but some overlap was present nonetheless.

A particularly important club in the transition from live folk to live rock was Greenwich Village's Cafe Au Go Go, where musicians such as Fred Neil, Tim Hardin, the Blues Project, Richie Havens, the Fugs, John Sebastian, Eric Andersen, the Youngbloods, and others performed. Some performers, like the Blues Project, even recorded live albums at the club. Owner Howard Solomon sees the shift not just as a result of their changing approaches to songwriting and recording, but also the availability, for the first time, of quality electronic equipment that could put the music over in a club without sacrificing the message of the words. "The folk idiom was the basis of the Cafe Au Go Go, which later developed into all-electric music," he says. "It seemed to be the natural evolvement as soon as we began to get equipment from Fender. We were the first ones to use Fender equipment and the tube amps, and the use of the B-3 organ and the first Ampex 440Bs all seemed to happen simultaneously in '64, '65. We were given the use of them, complimentary. We had a good close relationship with the electronic manufacturers.

"People like John Sebastian came through the picture and picked up on the mere fact that there were amplifiers onstage for anybody's use, with an organ, an acoustic piano, and for its day [a] state-of-the-art sound system. You were not being blasted with sound, you were incorporating *into* the sound. And though it was a small venue, people could play loud, which became the way of the day. People could come in and actually record on the first Ampex four-track system.

"See, when a person like Tim Hardin went electric, it wasn't rock 'n' roll. It was just more impact, I would say, to his music. It wasn't really rock-heavy. It leaned to folk. People [like Hardin] still played understandable lyrics and memorable musicality, where you could walk out of the place, and still remember the music. It wasn't gone at the end of the song. The lyrics had impact, they had meaning."

Barry Melton and Country Joe McDonald played the Cafe Au Go Go in their just—pre—Country Joe & the Fish days, opening for the Blues Project. Melton's eager to point out how such venues and bands helped break down an unspoken barrier between musicians drawing from traditional folk music who were going electric, even if some of the groups were more blues-rock than folk-rock. "Somehow on the folk circuit, African-American musicians were given sort of permission to amplify if they wanted to," he feels. "It wasn't necessarily extended to white musicians, and particularly young white musicians. Whereas when African-American people did it, it was like that was a permissible extension of where the blues could go. You could have B.B. King and Albert King records, and still have an authentic record collection. Lightning Hopkins was really big on the folk circuit, and you didn't know when he came into town to play your club whether he was going electric that night or acoustic. No one said boo when he would come amplified."

For the folk circuit, Melton continues, "One of the things that really authenticized electric music was the Paul Butterfield Blues Band and its neighbors. The Blues Project [had] guys who had really been well-noted folkies: Danny Kalb, Steve Katz. Part of the reason why they got away with being electric and being allowed to be right there in the middle of Greenwich Village, playing at the Cafe Au Go Go, was because they were the *Blues* Project."

In the same manner as the Paul Butterfield Blues Band had helped open folk clubs to the concept of electric music in general, Solomon also gives the Cafe Au Go Go credit for an indoor festival of sorts that helped mix up electric and acoustic sounds around Thanksgiving 1965. "The thing that launched all of this, that changed the folk scene, was the Blues Bag. It just vaulted everything off into another dimension. I brought together the most amazing retinue of artists over a five-day period that had ever been experienced in New York. This was before big concerts or outdoor arenas or anything like that. We're talking about a 350-seat club that sold out two performances every night for five days, and was recorded by MGM. And it brought together not only the electric folk scene, but the chitlin circuit blues players, who were basically all acoustic, except for Muddy Waters. It brought the black and the white together, so to speak, in New York City."

Here as in so many areas, the debt modern rock owes to folk-rock has yet to be fully acknowledged. It was not until the intellectual, arty appeal of the coffeehouse venue was merged with the visceral volume of rock that a strong circuit was built that would allow touring rock bands to play to appreciative, informed audiences of their own age or slightly younger, rather than get bundled up into Dick Clark nationwide bus tours. And the fact was that rock was edging folk out of its longtime strongholds in the second half of the 1960s, forcing many one-time coffeehouses and folk clubs to modify their booking policies as a sheer matter of economic survival. As Art D'Lugoff of the Village Gate admits, "There was a paucity of [folk] singers that could draw. If they depended only on folk, it was kind of difficult, unless they started turning toward non-acoustic music, electric music." D'Lugoff himself had difficulty adjusting to staging rock shows, although the Village Gate swung with the changing times by putting on the Byrds in October 1966, complete with a light show. "The rock thing was too new for me to go with it. Of course, later on, I got a handle on it, [when] I put on Talking Heads and Patti Smith and Blondie in the '70s."

This didn't mean that the musicians were always able to handle the switchover from acoustic to electric seamlessly, in part due to the limitations of the technology of the day. "If we'd have had all the stuff that the bands play with now back in '62–['65], I think the transition would have been a lot better," believes Jerry Jeff Walker. "When we would rehearse at my apartment in New York, we had Gary White playing bass, real soft; N.D. Smart, the drummer, would play brushes; and [David] Bromberg and I played two acoustics [guitars]. It sounded real nice. But we had no way to amplify that or send that out. PAs weren't very good. You had to use, basically, an electric amplifier to amplify it, which was real brittle, hard-sounding. I remember breaking strings 'cause I was playing so hard.

"They'd use to do these things in the parks [in New York], just an afternoon of five bands. There was some bands that were electrically loud, that excited the crowd, but didn't have good songs. But they had good energy. We were trying to figure out how to get that energy in a sort of acoustic rock-folk combination. We just didn't have the equipment. There wasn't electric that sounded like acoustic; there wasn't acoustic that sounded like electric." This didn't stop Walker from getting gigs in both coffeehouses and rock clubs, as well as festivals such as Newport, though as Jerry Jeff qualifies, the Newport setup "in all fairness could not repeat people walking out, and sitting down, and playing over and over and over, fairly quickly and have 'em sound good. The workshops, oddly enough, always sounded better to me than the main stages."

S till, the Newport Festival continued to grow more flexible as the decade waned. The 1967 event included Arlo Guthrie (whose "Alice's Restaurant" ended the festival), the Incredible String Band, Joni Mitchell, Gordon Lightfoot, and Leonard Cohen. Buffalo Springfield was supposed to play, but had to cancel when Richie Furay came down with tonsillitis. In her autobiography *Singing Lessons*, Judy Collins, then on Newport's board of directors, remembers lobbying for a "singer-songwriter concert" at the '67 festival, writing that she "finally convinced the board to have an afternoon concert that turned out to be historic," including not just Cohen and Mitchell (who had yet to release records), but also Janis Ian, David Blue, Mike Settle, Tom Paxton, and Eric Andersen.

In 1968 the envelope was pushed much further with Kaleidoscope, Tim Buckley, Sandy Bull's electric guitar improvisations, and Big Brother & the Holding Company, the latter of whom were "unquestionably the hit of the festival," according to Jon Landau's report in *Rolling Stone*. "All the repressed quality of a folk concert where one sits and passively listens gave way to the spontaneity and excitement of rock and roll, as the stage was being set for their performance. People were now free to move their bodies and one could see in an instant why folk music could never have remained the music of the young: It isn't physical enough."

Landau actually went on to give the performance a highly critical, even harsh review. But he did single out for praise one song, "The Cuckoo"—dedicated by the band to old-time Appalachian folk singer Buell Kazee—that linked Big Brother and Janis Joplin with the traditional folk music that was the festival's ostensible foundation. (For that matter, Kaleidoscope and Taj Mahal also performed "The Cuckoo," also known as "Coo Coo" or "Coocoo Bird," at Newport.) "Some members of the festival do not place their faith in novelty or new talent to pump life into these festivals, but most of the listeners do," concluded *The New York Times*. "They were rising to their feet repeatedly this afternoon to show their appreciation for the up-and-coming younger performers who upped and conquered." The paper of record went on to hail Kaleidoscope as "superb. The combo turned from a Buck Owens country tune to a chilling modernistic variation on the Dock Boggs lament, 'Oh Death.' As a finale, this super-eclectic group did a Turkish dance that had overtones of electronic experimentation along with the string effects of a Middle Eastern band."

Pressure from the city of Newport, rather than the festival itself, forbade rock at the 1969 event, according to Jan Hodenfield's report in *Rolling Stone*, which noted that "Taj Mahal, promised as the closing act, didn't show and there were rumblings that the Newport City Council had considered including him in the post–Jazz Festival ban on rock." Apparently the edict was primarily directed at rock groups, as there had been several rock bands, and some unruly audience behavior, at the Newport Jazz Festival earlier that year. Nonetheless the 1969 Newport Folk Festival bill included Joni Mitchell, the Pentangle, Van Morrison, the Everly Brothers, James Taylor, Arlo Guthrie, Steve Young, and Jerry Jeff Walker, all of whom more listeners would probably have judged as "rock" or "folk-rock" than "folk." The ban on "rock" seems not to have been fully enforced in the end, with John S. Wilson's *New York Times* report noting that Buffy Sainte-Marie switched from acoustic instrumentation to electric rock during her set, though he felt "the individual qualities of her voice and the throbbing intensity of her singing were largely lost" when she and three accompanists pumped up the volume. Although attendance had slackened off from 73,000 in 1968 to 51,000 in 1969, support for the event still seemed robust. It was puny, however, in relation to the hundreds of thousands of young people that would in 1969 turn up at the summer's biggest rock festivals.

ssentially, what had happened was that instead of relying upon folk festivals such as Newport to continually broaden its reach into electric rock, folk-rock artists were starting to share the stage with rock artists of all guises. This mirrored the collective, if probably unconscious, decision folk-rock itself had made when it first got popular in 1965. Just as folk-rockers' messages were going to reach far more people if they shared space on AM radio next to the British Invasion, Motown, and Herb Alpert, so were they going to reach far bigger live audiences by sharing bills with the likes of the Who, Jimi Hendrix, and Sly & the Family Stone instead of stretching the allowable boundaries of folk festivals.

There *weren't* any such festivals before 1967 that put such a concept to use. All-star shebangs in Britain like the *NME* Pollwinners Concert and the Richmond Jazz & Blues Festival (which actually by 1965 was featuring British Invasion rock bands and evolved into the still-thriving Reading Festival) were important, overlooked prototypes. Another overlooked precursor was an odd week-long series of concerts produced by New York DJ Murray the K in 1967 at the RKO 58th Street Theater in New York, which found the likes of Jim & Jean, the Blues Project, Phil Ochs, and Simon & Garfunkel sharing bills with the Who (in their first American appearances), Cream (also making their Stateside debut), the Miracles, Mitch Ryder, and Wilson Pickett. Such affairs, allowing each act just a few songs and oriented toward screaming teenyboppers, were not keeping pace with the growing physical and intellectual maturity of folk-rock's (and all of rock's) audience. At the Murray the K gig, for instance, there were five shows a day, in which the Who had to trot out and do the same two or three songs each time.

The festival that changed this, and set the format emulated by rock festivals for the rest of the '60s (and still to an extent today), was the Monterey Pop Festival in Northern California in June 1967. Like many, and perhaps most, of the festivals that followed, Monterey if split in half could have been billed as a folk-rock festival. There were the Mamas & the Papas, the Byrds, Buffalo Springfield, Simon & Garfunkel, and the cream of the new folk-into-psychedelic San Francisco bands: Jefferson Airplane, Big Brother & the Holding Company, Country Joe & the Fish, Quicksilver Messenger Service, and the Grateful Dead. Plus the festival was co-produced by Lou Adler and John Phillips, figureheads of the most commercial folk-rock coming out of Los Angeles as the producer and leader respectively of the Mamas & the Papas. Adler and Phillips also bought out the initial organizer of the festival, Benny Shapiro (who had helped recommend the Byrds to Columbia Records in 1964), with the help of fellow folk-rock movers and shakers Paul Simon and Byrds producer Terry Melcher, as well as Johnny Rivers.

But there was much more at Monterey than folk-rock: the Who, Jimi Hendrix (in *his* first American appearance as leader of the Jimi Hendrix Experience), the Electric Flag, Booker T. & the MG's, Otis Redding, Lou Rawls, Hugh Masekela, the Animals, Laura Nyro, Ravi Shankar, and about 50,000 in the audience. "It was a goal, actually, to be very eclectic and to spread across all genres what we considered pop music at that time," says Adler. "To go from the Association to Lou Rawls, Johnny Rivers, Simon & Garfunkel, Hendrix, Joplin . . . we just went with whatever music we felt either had ebbed as an influence, or was a new influence. We were just presenting music, and never told one artist what they could do or what they shouldn't do, or not take an artist because of what they did. And the audience was drawn for all of those acts. So someone that came to see the Association or Simon & Garfunkel was being exposed to Hendrix and Joplin, and accepting it. And accepting Otis

Redding in a way that no white audience had, though he had never appeared before a white audience of that size. We accomplished what we set out to do. That was to expose the audience to all of that music, and expose the artists to each other. Some of those artists had never heard some of the other artists, in person."

An ironic consequence of the festival was that it gave a huge boost to many acts, including several from San Francisco alone, that would render the poppier sounds of the Mamas & the Papas (then not long away from splitting anyway) passé. "We were well aware that in order to validate the festival, and also to expose the groups that were on the so-called cutting edge, we had to have the San Francisco groups," adds Adler. "What was considered underground certainly exploded and became aboveground. There was a tremendous mining of the San Francisco groups, as far as the ones that were unsigned, and even some that were signed. The San Francisco groups benefited by it. Some of those contracts and deals that they made, I don't know if it would have been possible at that time, except for the exposure of Monterey."

Monterey was in a way an extension of the communitarian spirit that had given birth to the Newport festivals, but without its insularity. Folk-influenced music, albeit wholly of the folk-rock sort, could now stand on equal footing with psychedelia, hard rock, soul, and Indian ragas as just one of several great popular styles, rather than as something separate, aloof, even elitist in its view of itself as more ideologically correct than the pop devoured by the great unwashed. As a consequence folk-derived music made far greater inroads into the American mainstream. Record companies like Vanguard and Elektra had voraciously scouted Newport for talent. But it was quite another level to have Big Brother & the Holding Company, then stuck on the small and negligent Mainstream label, whooshed to superstardom on the backs of CBS and a new management deal with Albert Grossman, in large part due to Janis Joplin's explosive performance at Monterey.

As D.A. Pennebaker's classic rockumentary *Monterey Pop* convincingly illustrates, the environment at these events was changing and expanding as quickly as the musicians were. It was as if the best qualities of Murray Lerner's *Festival* and the teen-oriented, indoor-staged mid-'60s extravaganzas *The T.A.M.I. Show* and *The Big T.N.T. Show* had been combined, overlaid with color, much longer hair, and far more flamboyant wardrobes. Asked to compare Monterey with Newport, Pennebaker fires back, "A totally different place and different kind of audience. Newport audiences, I can't imagine ... it's such a different audience. First of all, they tend to be folkies, a lot of them. And they're very stylized in what they accept. I think at Newport, the idea was, 'Well, we're getting all these wonderful musicians here for you to appreciate.' Because they were all famous and they're big names out of the past. It's kind of like if somebody gathered a museum appearance of some sort, of these people that they'd brought in from some archeological dig. Therefore, they *had* to be appreciated.

"At Monterey, every act was a big surprise. Nobody knew what to expect. Particularly if they were from Los Angeles, they really hadn't heard Janis before. I hadn't. So you were there kind of like [at] a dawn of a new age, and there was not the feeling of antiquity at all. I think that that's what made it work. People didn't feel they had to force up all this reverence for something. They just could sit there and smoke pot and dig it."

Buffalo Springfield performing at the Monterey Pop Festival in 1967, with David Crosby sitting in for Neil Young. Left to right: David Crosby, Richie Furay, and Stephen Stills.

"Monterey, it's kind of the end of the folk era and the beginning of the rock era," adds Barry Melton, who played at Monterey as part of Country Joe & the Fish. "An enormous number of those performers had been on the folk circuit. They understood in some ways that the difference between acoustic and electric music was that content was more important than the medium. It was the *content* of what you were doing that mattered.

"But the pop festival was extraordinarily different from the folk festival in one major way," stresses Melton, who had attended folkfests at Newport and Monterey itself a few years earlier in his teens. "All the folk festivals I went to, a significant part of the audience was people who played and sang themselves. They would line the exterior of whatever the festival was. Hundreds of people, playing guitars, playing together. Rock music never had that participatory element.

"One thing I remember in Monterey that was a hangover from the folk tradition is they had the main stage show, but they also had these little stages that were set outside of the main arena that were forums for sort of like smaller bands or unpaid bands to play. They kept that part of the folk tradition as part of the festival: a place off the main beat, where people could play, in keeping with the folk tradition. I jammed with somebody in a little place, and it was a big deal, 'cause I was one of the main stage guys, coming to the little place to jam. Monterey had that because it was part of the folk festival tradition, to provide a forum for the nonstar players, to put a place outside the grounds where people could get together and less accomplished folks could play music. We played many, many festivals between Monterey and Woodstock. But that part of it dropped away. It ceased to exist."

If they drew far less amateur musicians than the folk festivals had, they also drew many thousands of listeners who had never and would never have gone to a folk festival. By the same token, folk musicians crossing over to rock were drawing listeners at concerts way off the folk circuit who wouldn't be coming to either folk *or* rock festivals. "The reason why so many performers, particularly young performers, made that transition from folk to rock was accessibility," says Melton. "They wanted to reach a wider audience. When electric music gained some authenticity and acceptance even among the folk audience, they got to take those people with them. And then, of course, got to carry it to the much wider audience that was just going there to dance. I realized, as I was making the transition, it made it a lot easier to survive playing music. Because once we started playing rock 'n' roll, all of the sudden we were in venues where people could care less what we were saying or what we were doing. As long as the backbeat was there, they were happy. And they were too drunk anyway to know what we were doing, exactly.

"But it allowed us to book ourselves in proms and dances, where the content of what we were doing didn't matter one bit. We began picking up work at, like, the armory in [the Oakland suburb] Concord or whatever, playing the rock 'n' roll dance. Maybe two kids who had been to the city before and had some idea of what was going on there would come up and tell us that they actually appreciated us. We had no expectation that any of them really cared anything about what we were doing. They didn't care that we were folk musicians, or how authentic it was."

Monterey set the ball rolling for rock and pop festivals that sprouted across the country within a couple of years. It must be emphasized that this proliferation hardly heralded the death of the folk festival—far from it. Newport kept at more or less the same attendance level in the late '60s, and there were numerous others that kept staging regular events. As Happy Traum noted in his rather misleadingly titled 1969 *Rolling Stone* piece "The Swan Song of Folk Music," these varied in scale from the Old Time Fiddlers' Convention in Union Grove, North Carolina, which had attracted 10,000 people, to the Smithsonian-sponsored Folk Life Festival in Washington, DC, which half a million had attended (not all at once, of course).

And several established folk festivals were, like Newport, putting some folk-rock and just plain rock bands on the bill, whether as a concession to popular tastes or a genuine outreach to bridge the gap between the ever-narrowing folk and rock worlds. Joni Mitchell, John Sebastian, the Incredible String Band, the Flying Burrito Brothers, ex-Beau Brummel Sal Valentino, and Crosby, Stills, Nash & Young played at the 1969 Big Sur Folk Festival, with footage of CSNY and others (including one scene in which an irate Stills leaves the stage to scuffle with a heckler) showing up in the rarely seen documentary *Celebration at Big Sur*. Van Morrison, James Taylor, the Pentangle, Steve Young, the Incredible String Band, Tom Rush, and the Sir Douglas Quintet played the 1969 Philadelphia Folk Festival (Fairport Convention played there the following year). The Berkeley Folk Festival presented Jefferson Airplane and Country Joe & the Fish, complete with psychedelic lighting, back in 1966, with Marty Balin (according to *Broadside*) pointing to an acoustic guitar and labeling "the instrument 'an antique.'" Kaleidoscope and eccentric Texas psychedelic band the Red Krayola played the same festival the following year. "When we got into doing folk festivals, we could really work the room," boasts Kaleidoscope's Chris Darrow. "We were good at festivals, because we could *project* that weird stuff across for 20,000 people outside on a Saturday afternoon drinking beer and doing acid."

Arlo Guthrie, a frequent performer at such folk festivals, says that any remaining purist outrage at the mixing and matching of folk to rock in concert had largely vanished at this point. "There were a few holdouts at the festivals. But for the most part, I think most people were delighted. [Folk singer] Oscar Brand and all those guys, they were delighted with what was going on. The inclusion of all the new sort of ways that music could be played and heard made everybody, I think, very happy. We were *all* having a good time. It wasn't just me. For the most part, at these festivals, we were having a great time. We were partying, we were just smiling for like days. I don't remember seeing anybody mad at *anybody*."

But the rock festivals were the ones drawing the big numbers, and getting the major media attention, as the 1960s drew to a close. In the summer of 1970, *Rolling Stone* estimated that about two and a half million young people had attended approximately 30 festivals in the intervening three years since Monterey. There were rockfests in Seattle, Denver, Miami, Atlanta, Toronto, and in Orange County near Los Angeles (for the Newport Pop Festival, which despite the name wasn't anywhere geographically near the Newport folk and jazz festivals in Rhode Island). Many of them featured folk-rockers, or sometimes just plain folk musicians. The biggest of them, of course, was Woodstock, in mid-August 1969.

oodstock, like Monterey, could have been a folk-rock festival had it been divided in half along such lines. The opening day, in fact, was dominated by folk-rock singers, starting off with Richie Havens, and also featuring Country Joe McDonald, John Sebastian, the Incredible String Band, Tim Hardin, Melanie, Arlo Guthrie, and Joan Baez. The next few days also saw several rock bands with clear folk-rock roots take the stage: Jefferson Airplane, Janis Joplin, the Grateful Dead, Country Joe & the Fish, the Band, and, in only their second show ever, Crosby, Stills, Nash & Young (though *Crosby, Stills & Nash* had been released two months earlier). As at Monterey, these performers stood shoulder-to-shoulder with some of the loudest, most raucous acts on the planet, like Jimi Hendrix, the Who, and Ten Years After, as well as an assortment of other new stars like Santana, Joe Cocker, Creedence Clearwater Revival, Canned Heat, and Sly & the Family Stone.

But, as with Monterey, the point was not that it *could* have been divided among folk-rock and other-rock party lines, but that it *wasn't*, even in its sequencing. The idea probably never occurred to anyone. "Folk-rock educated the mass audience to folk music, and created an acceptance of folk music that probably hadn't existed previously," speculates Barry Melton, who played Woodstock as part of Country Joe & the Fish. "The popularization built the modern genre of musician that can slip back and forth between the two mediums, and it's perfectly okay. People understand it. The rumored appearance throughout the festival was gonna be if and when Dylan was gonna show up, because we were in the neighborhood [of Dylan's Woodstock home]. I don't think it would have made a bit of difference if it had been acoustic or electric, or there would have been any expectation one way or the other. We're fortunate today, because those distinctions have been abolished."

Murray Lerner got as close a view, literally, as anyone of the changing perceptions of rock and folk's interaction at such occasions. He had filmed the Newport Folk Festival from 1963 to 1966 (including Dylan's 1965 Newport appearance), and would go on to direct the *Message to Love* documentary of the 1970 Isle of Wight Festival, whose bill put Jimi Hendrix, the Doors, the Who, Miles Davis, and the like alongside Joni Mitchell, Leonard Cohen, the Pentangle, and Donovan, as well as Woodstock vets Melanie, John Sebastian, and Richie Havens. At festivals like the Isle of Wight, playing electric music and mixing folk, rock and pop, observes Lerner, simply "wasn't an issue anymore. It was much more diverse, and people weren't worried about it. I can see the value of working hard to not make folk music an extinct species. But I can't see the value of saying, 'Because of that, we shouldn't have this other stuff.' That wouldn't work anyway."

"My experience with festivals was that it was almost an anything-goes thing," says Melanie. "Today, something like that would never happen. The marketers would figure out their demographics and who're they're appealing to, and get the groups that were appropriate and wore the right jeans. Everything would be homogenized to be right: the look, the sound, the style. Now there seems to be, like, a stylist involved in the production of shows.

"I didn't think this was something that was just gonna be reduced to a style or a trend. To me, this was the beginning of renaissance on Earth. We believed that we were going to change the planet, and the music was where it began. To me, this was revolutionary. That's what the festivals felt like."

Those folk-based musicians who had kept apace enough to qualify for inclusion at such festivals could appreciate how the changing times, and changing context, were working to their benefit by bringing them rock fans that never would have come to Newport. Enthused Tom Paxton to *Record Mirror* after his appearance at the Isle of Wight Festival in 1969, "These days people are willing to listen to more than just one category of music. A great many rock and roll fans are willing to listen to good folk." He added to *Disc*, "It was absolutely fabulous, apart from my own success. I think much of the reason for my success was the contrast. There had been many loud, hard rock groups that afternoon, and the difference made them listen." Along the same lines, Bert Jansch would comment to *NME* the following year that when the Pentangle toured America with the likes of Canned Heat, "We thought that because we were so un-amplified, the kids wouldn't listen. But they did. Today's market will accept anything."

Woodstock's audience consisted of about half a million people, almost all of them younger than 30, some quite a bit younger than that. There have been estimates that up to a million-and-a-half tried to get to the festival at some point, many giving up or turning back when they ran up against miles and miles of immobile traffic. Remarkably, particularly the first day and night, several performers got their message across to a crowd as large as all but one or two cities in New York State with little more than—or sometimes nothing more than—an acoustic guitar. At times the chaotic overspill, combined with the need to improvise as artists and organizers combated numerous logistical foul-ups, created what amounted to an impromptu hootenanny.

Tim Hardin had initially been approached to go on first, but finding him somewhat incapacitated at show time the organizers turned to Richie Havens, who, he recalled in his autobiography, had been expecting to go on fifth. The crowd was getting impatient, though, and Havens agreed after personal entreaties from young festival co-producer Michael Lang. Accompanied only by fellow acoustic open-chord guitarist Paul "Deano" Williams and conga player Daniel Alexander McCloud

Richie Havens performing at Woodstock in 1969.

(bassist Eric Oxendine didn't make it due to the unprecedented traffic snarls), Havens began what he thought was only going to be a 20-minute set. Every time he went offstage, Lang cajoled Richie into going out yet again, promising that the next act was on the way, asking for just one more or three more songs.

Havens started off with "Handsome Johnny," an antiwar lament by Lou Gossett, more famous now as an actor but at one time a Greenwich Village folk singer. "Handsome Johnny" could have been a traditional folk song, and had originally been written about conflicts stretching from the Civil War through World War II. But as part of the venerated folk process, Havens added new verses with explicit references to the Vietnam War, and the civil rights "war" or struggle in Birmingham, to give it contemporary relevance. The references to other wars through the ages made it clear that this was not a song about Vietnam exclusively, but about the cost of *all* war, whether the conventional kind or the sort that denied basic rights to African-Americans.

Havens then dug into his repertoire for the expected Beatles covers and one of the most seminal proto-folk-rock tunes, "High Flyin' Bird." Running out of ideas and songs, he improvised a chant-song, "Freedom," around the spiritual "Motherless Child," which he'd heard sung to him by his grandmother while growing up. It was this galvanizing, heavily rhythmic performance that, more than any other, defined Havens's music to the world, and (via its inclusion in the subsequent *Wood-stock* film) endured as an apotheosis of the Woodstock festival and the entire 1960s counterculture.

"I had to perform for almost three hours," reminisced Havens in *Goldmine*. "No one else was there to go on, and I had to go back out about seven or eight times, and at the end I didn't know what the heck I was going to sing, and the first thing that went through my mind was that we already had the freedom that we were supposed to be looking for. What are we talking about, we already got it! So I started singing the words 'freedom, freedom,' and then 'Motherless Child' came back to me, which I hadn't sung in, like, eight years.... I had gone through every song in my repertoire, and by that point, I really knew a lot of songs, but I couldn't think of many after almost three hours of performing. It's kind of interesting that the tune I'm most known for was totally improvised on the spot."

It would not be exaggerating matters to see his Woodstock set as an extension of what he'd done as a struggling folkie in Greenwich Village, now amplified to the thousandth power. "The Au Go Go may not have survived if it weren't for Richie Havens," remembers Howard Solomon. "Because Richie Havens was always there when you needed him. He used to triple and quadruple out the basket houses of the Bitter End and the Au Go Go and the Gaslight and Manny Roth's place downstairs. When he started to play the Au Go Go, he started to build a following. He played there almost every night, for years. And for $5 for food, later on for a couple thousand a week, he just built his reputation and built a following." Now Havens was doing the ultimate yeoman service, pulling triple duty to help save the day for a crowd bigger than the whole of Greenwich Village. No one knew it yet, but the Woodstock festival would need plenty of spirited determination like Havens's to make it through the next three days—the crush of people, shortage of basic facilities, and downpours threatened power lines and turned the fields into a mud bath.

There still wasn't anyone else ready to go on after Havens finally finished, though. In keeping with the spur-of-the-moment spirit Country Joe McDonald, booked to play with the Fish but not as a solo act, was convinced to take the stage, using an acoustic guitar that had been tied up with rope and a matchbook cover for a pick. McDonald, like Havens, had to dig deep into his folkie roots to summon the performance for which he (and to some degree, Woodstock) remains most known. It was the "I-Feel-Like-I'm-Fixin'-to-Die Rag," the song that he'd recorded as a jug band tune for Arhoolie Records in mid-1965, and that the Fish had made into a psychedelic anthem. Now he stripped it back to its folk core, with an important exception of course, though one that could be considered a valid part of the folk process. The opening F-I-S-H cheer became the F-U-C-K cheer. And the half-million-strong crowd shouted and sang along against the Vietnam War, in what may have been the largest mass sing-along in history.

And *still* the proper show wasn't set to get started. So John Sebastian, not even expecting to play Woodstock but wandering around backstage, was next in line to be connived into going onstage with nothing but his acoustic axe (borrowed from Tim Hardin) and no setlist. Sebastian was stoned on acid, and his ensuing performance, punctuated by rambling flower-power speak, was subsequently the cause of considerable embarrassment to the singer. Nonetheless that set would include the low-key, utopian ballad, "I Had a Dream," which was the highlight of his debut solo album, as well as "Darlin' Be Home Soon" and "Younger Generation," both favorites of his Lovin' Spoonful days.

And thus did both the acid and the acoustic folk-rock flow through day one of Woodstock. Tim Hardin got the chance to do his own version of his own song that had, to his bitter resentment, been made into a hit by Bobby Darin, "If I Were a Carpenter." Hardin's performance, however, would not make it onto the Woodstock soundtrack, again denying him some of the recognition he sought (the recording was eventually released in the 1990s). Melanie kept the spontaneous volunteer brigade on the move by subbing for a worried Incredible String Band after the rain starting pouring down, the scene inspiring the composition of one of her best-known songs, the 1970 Top Ten hit "Lay Down (Candles in the Rain)." Looking back on that day more than 30 years later, Melanie reminisces, "I went to Woodstock in a helicopter, and I didn't even know what it was when I was up in the air. I said, 'What is that? Oh my god, it's people!' It was amazing, and terrifying."

She also testifies to the chaotic, world's-biggest-hootenanny disorganization backstage. "I was lower echelon, totally not even to be reckoned with. Every hour, somebody'd come up and say, 'You're on next!' I'd get all ready, feeling I was gonna die, and cough. I had worked myself into a coughing fit, and thought I had no voice left. I'd get all ready, and then they'd say, 'No no, we're not on. Somebody else is on.' And this went on *all day long*. By the end, I was a piece of Jell-O. It was gone, all hope of it being called off. I was so hoping somebody would say, 'It's over, you don't have to do this. Somebody else is gonna take your spot.'" She laughs. "But it didn't happen, and I finally did go on."

Arlo Guthrie kept several threads of the folk-to-Woodstock continuum alive in his performance (with a backup band): the narrative tale, this one bound to find favor with drug-using hippies ("Coming in to Los Angeles"); the obscure Dylan cover ("Walking Down the Line"); and the spiritual "Amazing Grace," probably the one song more than any other apt to be sung at momentous occasions by people of all ages and political and religious beliefs. Joan Baez, unsurprisingly, was the strongest link to the days of Newport yore and the pre-rock folk revival. She had remained one of America's most vocal and visible celebrity dissenters, with her then-husband, David Harris, in jail for draft evasion at the time of her Woodstock performance. Her set included "We Shall Overcome" and "Joe Hill," an ode to the labor leader who had used folk to rally the masses back in the 1910s, long before virtually everyone in the Woodstock crowd was born. Yet even when Baez took the stage, the imprint of the changes folk-rock had wrought reverberated strongly in her rendition of the Byrds' "Drug Store Truck Drivin' Man," the sardonic yet subtle Roger McGuinn–Gram Parsons putdown of a Ku Klux Klan racist.

British folk-rock was represented by the Incredible String Band, whom few remember as being at Woodstock, since their performance was absent from both the soundtrack and the film. "Somebody described Woodstock in advance to us, I think it was Joe Boyd, as the little upstate folk festival," says Robin Williamson. "That's what he thought it was gonna be. He was wrong on that one." The Incredibles' experience proved that not all went magically right on day one. They'd already set up when the downpour started, and concerned that their sitar, bowed gimbri, rugs, and assorted other equipment would get damaged, they opted not to play until the next morning.

"Woodstock wasn't a very good gig for us," Williamson admits. "We got rained out. We had a gig in New York City that night, the Saturday night, in a stadium, which we couldn't get out for. So we had to sleep in a tent, we did a morning gig, and then we ended up going out by helicopter to get to this stadium, flying over New York City in a small plane. Open-air large festival gigs were always a bit hard for the String Band. We were basically an acoustic band at that time, so getting enough volume out of things . . . generally feedback and sound problems were part of the gig. Unfortunately, the film cameras ran out. Maybe that's a blessing, maybe not."

Yet all those acoustic folk-rock acts on day one of the Woodstock festival were not that much of an off-the-cuff, unrehearsed anomaly. Many artists who recorded with full folk-rock backing in the studio were still touring with either drastically pared-down setups in the late '60s, or sometimes with nothing other than the acoustic guitars, harmonica, and maybe piano they would have relied upon before 1965. Touring with a band was expensive, for one thing. Inadvertently, perhaps it helped some of them retain their stodgier, less rock-inclined fan base. Says Michael Ochs of his brother Phil, "He didn't perform with a band, and he would still do 'I Ain't Marching Anymore.' And he could do 'Pleasures of the Harbor' and that's fine. A folk artist is allowed to be poetic, and allowed to be personal, as long as he doesn't bring musicians on stage with him, god forbid. Or maybe he could bring a bass player, at best."

Other late-'60s folk-rockers with pop crossover appeal who had to worry little about folkie backlash nonetheless preferred to play live as a solo acoustic singer. Melanie used full rock and orchestral arrangements on even her earliest records, but told *Melody Maker* in 1970 that "I don't miss the big arrangement when I'm on stage though. The most I would ever want would be a bass or something to keep me from being lonely." In 2002, she reflects, "I think that was my salvation, because I could present myself exactly the way I was. I didn't feel like a chick singer with a backup band; I just didn't feel like I could pull it off. It felt too glitzy, too showbizzy. I just sat on a straight-back chair, not even a high stool. That was another thing—they'd always bring out a stool, because a folk singer, if they sat, used a stool. They would always have this stool ready, so eventually I had to write in my [contract] rider: 'straight-back chair.'"

Even Simon & Garfunkel, who surely could have afforded to take a full band and maybe even an orchestra out on the road, rarely played with any accompaniment other than Simon's acoustic guitar. When they toured in late 1969 with musicians who had played on their records, Simon told *Rolling Stone* a few months later, "It worked out badly. First of all we came out on stage with the band, and people would yell: 'Get the band off, we just want to hear you!' I would say: 'Oh, that riff is so old; you said that about Dylan. Christ that's four years ago that this happened; what are you talking about? Everybody has a band. We're the only ones around without a band.' . . . We didn't rehearse it to the point of real tightness. But they were soft. That's one good thing; they didn't blast out." On their November 1969 Carnegie Hall concert, they would use the Dylan-pioneered acoustic-electric vision of sets, using piano, guitar, bass, and drums only in the second half.

Residual resentment of Simon & Garfunkel's use of a rock band seems odd in light of how their hit singles and albums virtually always boasted full rock production. Yet Simon's comments to the contrary, by 1969 rock audiences seemed quite tolerant of mixing acoustic and electric music. That tolerance to some degree could account for the success of most of the acoustic folk-rockers in Woodstock's opening hours. Even one such act that didn't go over as well, the Incredible String Band, realized this. "The audiences in America were fantastically patient in '67, '68, '69," praises Williamson.

"We were supposed to do a gig once either in Fillmore West or somewhere in Berkeley, I can't remember. The equipment had been loaded off the plane without us knowing it in Canada somewhere, so we arrived in San Francisco with no instruments. All I had was a three-string North African instrument called a gimbri and a bow. So the audience sat for three hours, going 'HMMM,' which I played along with. I actually got this on tape. I can't imagine any audiences being a) that patient and b) that kind of blissed out much later than that [1969]. They seemed to be actually *enjoying* the experience of waiting."

There was much more waiting to be endured on days two, three, and "four" of Woodstock, with rain and various other calamities causing multiple delays. (There wasn't technically a day four, but due to lagging schedules it wasn't until Monday morning that the last of the weekend's acts hit the stage, climaxing with Jimi Hendrix.) After day one the program would be far less acoustic-oriented, but even so, echoes of folk-rock's legacy abounded. Jefferson Airplane did Fred Neil's "The Other Side of This Life," the song having evolved from its Village folk origins to an arrangement with extended, elastic bursts of psychedelic guitar. The Band played "Tears of Rage" and "This Wheel's on Fire" from Dylan's Basement Tapes, which were also tapped for Joe Cocker's reading of "I Shall Be Released." The Paul Butterfield Blues Band, some of whom had backed Dylan back at Newport '65, kicked off day four, although the group's lineup—like Country Joe & the Fish's—had almost totally altered since 1965. Canned Heat made an indirect nod to the old Delta bluesmen who had surfaced at the Newport Folk Festivals with its blues-rock cover of "Going Up the Country" (originally recorded in the late '20s by Henry Thomas, whose "Honey, Just Allow Me One More Chance" had been covered on 1963's *The Freewheelin' Bob Dylan*). And Jimi Hendrix roared through "Hey Joe," that most-covered of folk-rock songs of mysterious origin.

All facets of folk-rock's most contemporary face were present in the middle-of-the-night set by Crosby, Stills, Nash & Young, making only their second public appearance. "This is the second time we've ever played in front of people, man," announced a shaky-voiced Stephen Stills from the stage, a moment captured for posterity on both the film and soundtrack. "We're scared shitless!" The quartet came through, however, with a strong if sometimes wavering set that epitomized the flexibility of what was now acknowledged as folk-rock's supergroup. There were wholly acoustic songs, most notably "Suite: Judy Blue Eyes" (performed without Neil Young and with just two guitars), and all-out electric ones, like "Wooden Ships." There were complex love songs (again, "Suite: Judy Blue Eyes"), hymns to the hippie lifestyle ("Marrakesh Express"), and strains of social consciousness ("Find the Cost of Freedom"). There was room for unexpected covers (the Beatles' "Blackbird"), a nugget from the glorious past of Buffalo Springfield (Stills and Young dueting on an acoustic "Mr. Soul"), and vehicles for the group's solo aspirations (Young's "Sea of Madness," never released in a studio version by either Young or CSNY). "Many have remarked that their music is perfect, but sterile; that night it wasn't quite perfect and it was anything but sterile," wrote Greil Marcus in his lengthy report on the festival for *Rolling Stone*. "They seemed like several bands rather than one."

"I saw this about eight months ago," says Jim Messina of CSNY's scenes in the *Woodstock* film, "and I just got that heart feeling like a fan gets when you go, 'Whoa! Jesus, these guys take the cake! Listen to that. Listen to those harmonies.' It's just one guitar and three voices, and they just blew the hell out of everything. They were so together and so musical. At times, god, it was an orchestra of harmony. It was mind-blowing. And that was watching it, what, 30 years later?"

Still riding the high of Woodstock, Crosby and Stills, as well as Jefferson Airplane and Joni Mitchell, appeared on *The Dick Cavett Show* the next day. Within the limited amount of time granted by national network talk shows, it too presented the varying faces that folk-rock sported by 1969. Stills, on acoustic guitar, performed a cut from CSNY's forthcoming *Déjà Vu* album, "4 + 20." The Airplane was now at its psychedelic apogee, calling for revolution on "Volunteers" and for unity on "We Can Be Together," Grace Slick somehow getting away with singing "up against the wall, motherfucker" on national television. Crosby, always eager to sit in with other groups, bashed a tambourine and sang backup on "Somebody to Love." He also managed to slip in a condemnation of the major environmental damage wreaked by seven major car and oil companies, four of which, Cavett immediately rejoined, were among his sponsors.

Mitchell, still not working with a band live, played "Chelsea Morning" on guitar. She moved to the piano for a couple of songs, including one, "Willy," about her then-boyfriend Graham Nash. Then she delivered an a cappella rendition of her antiwar ballad "The Fiddle and the Drum," introduced as "a song I wrote for America, as a Canadian living in this country"—notwithstanding a comment to Cavett that "I sing mostly about love, and things that I can understand. I don't understand politics." Perhaps the British purists would have been proud to see this throwback to a folk music that had not even allowed itself to be sullied by instrumentation. It was quite something different, however, to sing unaccompanied traditional ballads in British pubs, and to sing a pointed, freshly written anti-imperialist critique of American warmongering to millions of television viewers. True, the musicians' revolutionary messages were regularly interrupted by commercials for bras, girdles, and cigarettes. It was nonetheless unimaginable that young people could have sung and said such strong stuff on a national broadcast without the five preceding years of musical and social change, in which folk-rock had played such a large part.

As noted earlier, Mitchell had not only not performed at Woodstock, she had not even been there as a spectator. She was supposed to accompany CSNY to the festival grounds, but decided against it for fear of missing the Cavett appearance should the troupe not make it back to New York City in time. Her experience of Woodstock, like most Americans, was limited to the media coverage, seen on television while cooped up in her hotel room. It's ironic, then, that she would pen the song, "Woodstock," that would become the festival's retroactive anthem. Crosby, Stills, Nash & Young put it on *Déjà Vu* and made it a hit single; this recording was used on the soundtrack to the *Woodstock* film as well. Stephen Stills had notions of writing an anthem himself, telling *NME* in 1970 that on the plane back from Woodstock, "I was trying hard to think of something to write about the festival. We told Joni of our plans and I kept working out some ideas. Just as I was on the verge of getting it together, Joni came over and played us her song. She got there first, I said that I couldn't top it."

"The deprivation of not being able to go provided me with an intense angle on Woodstock," Mitchell told Dave Zimmer in *Crosby, Stills & Nash: The Authorized Biography*. "I was one of the fans. I was put in the position of being a kid who couldn't make it. So I was glued to the media. And at the time I was going through a kind of born-again Christian trip—not that I went to any church, I'd given up Christianity at an early age in Sunday school. But suddenly, as performers, we were in the position of having so many people look to us for leadership, and for some unknown reason, I took it seriously and decided I needed a guide and leaned on God.

"So I was a little 'God mad' at the time, for lack of a better term, and I had been saying to myself, 'Where are the modern miracles? Where are the modern miracles?' Woodstock, for some reason, impressed me as being a modern miracle, like a modern-day fishes-and-loaves story. For a herd of people that large to cooperate so well, it was pretty remarkable and there was tremendous optimism. So I wrote the song 'Woodstock' out of these feelings, and the first three times I performed it in public, I burst into tears, because it brought back the intensity of the experience and was so moving."

"Woodstock" portrayed the festival as a garden of Eden of sorts, and viewed through the most rose-colored of glasses it might be seen as the ultimate fulfillment of the progressive, humanitarian ethos trumpeted by the folk revival of the early '60s. Yes, many of the young musicians who had entered the folk revival back then were now playing electric instruments. But the folk foundations of their music were still strong, and now the message was not just reaching small cliques at university coffeehouses and Greenwich Village clubs, but hundreds of thousands of people at once (and many millions more through the *Woodstock* soundtrack and film). The music and the values that had informed folk-rock were no longer cultivated in isolation but presented alongside popular music of widely differing sorts, both disseminating more freely and influencing more heavily all kinds of other musicians—and popular culture as a whole.

The generation that had been weaned on folk music was now at the forefront of great waves of social change: an antiwar movement that eventually helped get the United States out of Vietnam, a civil rights movement that made life better for African-Americans, and extensions of that movement into advocacy for women's rights and a cleaner environment. Its music was not dogma, as much of the early folk revival had been, but a clarion call that demanded that life be enjoyed on all levels, rather than couching itself in dry terms of organized labor gains and radical political ideologies.

Woodstock and similar gatherings were descendants of folk festivals of the first half of the 1960s that were also important countercultural statements. Woodstock would not have been possible without the smaller-scale folk community that had supported the Newport Folk Festivals, the archetype for such events that, starting with Monterey, had grown steadily bigger. But an event of Woodstock's magnitude could never have happened if folk-rock had not widened the audience for socially conscious and lyrically ambitious music many times over what acoustic folk music could have assembled, and if the audience had not been willing to put the ethos of folk-rock into social action. Folk music alone would not have attracted an audience of such proportions and devotion.

Folk-rock was necessary to enact this transformation, and in turn could not have been supported without a transformation in the rock and pop listenership as a whole. The Woodstock crowd had itself become part of the spectacle, for the most part coping heroically with conditions that had made the region declared a disaster area. It became as much the focus of media commentary as the onstage performers, shaping the course of the weekend as no audience could have at the comparatively regimented Newport. Sebastian made the Newport-Woodstock contrast in a little-noted remark during his set, exultantly announcing to the audience, "This is really a mindfucker of all time, man. I've never seen anything like this, man. I mean, you know, like, there's Newport, right? But they *owned* it! It was something else."

So much, unquestionably, had been gained on the road from Newport to Woodstock. What, though, had been lost? Representation of the most authentic folk roots artists, for one thing. The more intimate, one-on-one communication between artist and audience in both performances and workshops, for another. And a diversity in age range among both performers *and* audience. The vast majority of those at Woodstock were between the ages of 15 and 30, and though Newport had always been slanted toward young adults, there were certainly more older people in the crowd and on the stage.

The Hobart Smiths, Doc Watsons, Georgia Sea Island Singers, and Son Houses that had filled the bills at Newport in the mid-'60s might have been able to keep gigging at specialized folk festivals. But they never would reap the larger audiences, record sales, media exposure, and (in at least some cases) fees that young, almost exclusively white, usually middle-class folk musicians turned folk-rockers did, at Woodstock and elsewhere. "The traditionalists will go on forever, working the summer festivals whenever possible and picking up enough bread from faithful record buyers to sustain them, but the vital youthful attention that put the fire back in Doc Watson's fingers and the tears back in Blind Gary [Davis]'s voice is missing," wrote John Lombardi in his *Rolling Stone* review of the Philadelphia Folk Festival a few months after Woodstock. "And its absence has an obvious effect on performance."

"I did notice that after Woodstock happened, the festivals right after that . . . you suddenly had a new and younger audience of people who were not particularly folkies at all," says CSNY–Joni Mitchell photographer Joel Bernstein, then still in his teens and very much a part of that audience. "It was"—he breaks off to mimic a stage MC shouting—"'the Philadelphia [drops to a mumble] folk [rises to a shout again] Festival!' It wasn't so important to them what the music was, but just the whole experience. The expectation was of a much bigger thing, and attracted a whole other audience. Younger people are attending the Newport Festival in '69. You have a sense of the peak of things having been, say around '64; not commercially, necessarily, but for the folk part of it."

Bernstein was one of those younger people in the audience at Newport '69, when he was still in high school. "A lot of people in the audience were there for the more contemporary artists. There might be [folk] acts who they suffered through, or didn't get entirely." At the same time, he acknowledges, veteran traditional folkies did stand a chance of catching a much bigger slice of the young audience than they would have if folk-rock had not been bringing in a more pop-rock-minded demographic. "There were acts who would unexpectedly completely turn on the bigger 20,000-seat audience. The Georgia Sea Island Singers were electrifying to this white audience, for example. There was no sense of, 'Well, this is gospel, and I'm not into that Jesus stuff.' The collective power of the group in one voice was really exciting. Nobody in that audience had ever heard of them, or knew the history of Georgia Sea Islands, or knew about Alan Lomax's recordings [with the group]. Many of them would have been there to see other acts."

Still, such opportunities for crossovers to young white audiences that would have never otherwise heard the likes of the Georgia Sea Island Singers were limited. African-Americans, rural lower-class citizens, the elderly, the Third World—all were poorly represented at festivals like Woodstock, if at all, in either the artist lineup or the crowd. The revolution was real, but it had been largely a young, white, and middle-class one as well, rather than one that truly united and uplifted all peoples. After that brief moment circa the summer of 1963 when it seemed like folk might become the nation's dominant popular music, its most authentic practitioners had retreated back into the small folk festivals and folkloric recording sessions from whence they came. Harsh critics might lambast this ghettoization as the equivalent of the reservations the American government had parceled out to Native Americans after claiming their territory.

Many white middle-class folk musicians and enthusiasts, if not as economically depraved, still felt themselves shut out of the folk-rock revolution, unwilling or unable to adapt to the new order. "For a while I became decidedly not with it," Mike Seeger of the New Lost City Ramblers told Karl Dallas of *Melody Maker* in the early '70s. "That was at the time that Bob Dylan went electric and Vanguard dropped all acoustically-accompanied people from their label apart from Doc Watson. They were hard times, though we still managed to work here and there. But the coffeehouse circuit that provided us with our daily bread had turned over to rock and roll." Even so, Seeger immediately acknowledged that within a few years, the double-edged sword of folk-rock had flipped and perhaps even helped expose him to new audiences: "Now, things are much nicer. The other night I played in support of the Quicksilver Messenger Service, and I was a little worried. I did just the same things as always, old-time fiddle tunes, an unaccompanied ballad. They seemed to love it. That couldn't have happened a few years ago. Today people seem much more ready to listen to other types of music and things have become much looser."

If the occasional sorrow over those that had been left behind seemed like a token crocodile tear, the sense of loss, felt most keenly by traditional folk performers but also by many on both sides of the fence, was nonetheless often genuine. "I wouldn't minimize the tragic effect on artists, as well as on audiences, of taking these narrow musical stances," reflects John Sebastian. "Because I always felt that there were an awful lot more people that were totally capable of taking the next step, whatever we name it. Some simply were afraid because their friends told them they would be forever wrong after that. There were very unthought-out reasons for all of this. In the same way that a lot of the great country bluesmen moved to Chicago and electrified their style, it was fairly logical that a few middle-class white boys might do the same kind of a thing."

The most famous of those middle-class white boys who had moved from folk to rock, Bob Dylan, was not present at Woodstock. Even if the festival wasn't far from his home in the town of Woodstock—it actually took place at Max Yasgur's farm in Bethel, about 60 miles away—Dylan had other plans. Just a couple weeks later, he would perform at the second Isle of Wight Festival, backed by the Band. It would be his first full concert since his motorcycle accident in July 1966.

The Isle of Wight, like Woodstock and Monterey, again could have been halved into a folk-rock festival in its own right. On the program were Eclection, Tom Paxton, the Pentangle, and Richie Havens, as well as the fresh-from-Woodstock Joe Cocker and the Who, and British rock bands like the Moody Blues, the Pretty Things, and the Nice. Dylan was to close the final night of the proceedings. Three of the four Beatles came over to attend the festival, all of them hanging out with Dylan, who was staying at a nearby farmhouse. George Harrison in particular enjoyed a strong rapport with Dylan at this point, playing songs like "Mr. Tambourine Man," "Lay Lady Lay," and "Blowing in the Wind" with him in the dining room. There was even a game of doubles tennis matching Dylan and John Lennon against Harrison and Ringo Starr. The world at that point had no way of knowing that *Abbey Road*, which had just been completed, was the last album the Beatles would record. Paul McCartney—the Beatle who would make the split official by announcing his departure on April 10, 1970—was absent, and understandably so, as he and his wife's first child, Mary, was born the day before the festival began.

It had been only three years since some wag shouted "Judas!" at Dylan's electric set in Manchester during his spring 1966 world tour. But no one now seemed to expect anything *other* than an electric concert. That battle, silly and unnecessary as it sometimes was, had been won, leaving Dylan to do as he wished in peace. The question of whether he was going to play with a band or not didn't even come up at a press conference two days before the festival, though Dylan's enigmatic persona was still intact, if in a muted fashion befitting his more subdued post-accident behavior. Why had he come to the Isle of Wight? "To see the home of Alfred Lord Tennyson." Were his days of protesting over? "I don't want to protest anymore . . . . I never said I am an angry young man." What songs would he be doing? "I'm not going to do anything new . . . things you will have heard before but with new arrangements." What about the Beatles? "George Harrison has come to visit me. The Beatles have asked me to work with them. I love the Beatles and I think it would be a good idea to do a jam session." If indeed anything of the sort had ever been discussed, the Beatles would never make it back into the studio as a foursome, let alone with Dylan in tow, though Dylan and Harrison would do some unremarkable low-key recording together in 1970.

"Isle of Wight was interesting since Bob and the Band were at the end of their relationship," says Elliott Mazer, who with Glyn Johns recorded the subsequent performance. "Rehearsals were very informal, and mostly they talked and hung out rather than play. Bob would suggest a song, they would play the opening and the end, and move on. George Harrison and John Lennon came to our house in the Isle and watched all this unfold."

Dylan's slot on August 31, 1969 was preceded by a set from the Band. His one-time backup musicians were now stars on their own, carrying enough weight to delay their appearance by an hour and a half as they tinkered with the sound system, in turn delaying Dylan's own highly anticipated performance. Even Dylanologists don't rate his hour-long show at the Isle of Wight highly, finding it perfunctory and certainly lacking the fire he had regularly whipped up with the same musicians in 1966. Rather than dividing the show into discrete acoustic and electric halves, as he had in '66, he opened with a couple of songs with the Band before going solo for a few numbers, such as the folk song "Wild Mountain Thyme," but largely comprised of originals, including "Mr.

Tambourine Man." Then the Band returned for the remainder of the show, revisiting old songs like "One Too Many Mornings" and "Like a Rolling Stone," tackling recent cuts from *John Wesley Harding*, and even dusting off a Basement Tapes relic, "The Mighty Quinn." "There was not one so-called 'protest' song," wrote Ray Coleman in *Disc*. "But then, to expect him to perform early epics like 'Masters of War' or 'Talking World War III Blues' would be rather like asking the Beatles to do 'Please Please Me' or 'She Loves You.' It's an era gone, if not forgotten."

Four of the songs, including "The Mighty Quinn" and "Like a Rolling Stone," would appear on his 1970 album *Self Portrait*, the double LP of misbegotten covers, outtakes, and half-formed ephemera that would alienate far more fanatics than his conversion to electric rock 'n' roll ever did. The Isle of Wight audience was expecting a performance of three hours or so, and was taken aback when Dylan and the Band took permanent leave of the stage after only one hour, ending with "Rainy Day Women #12 & 35." There were no catcalls, as there had been in Newport and Manchester. Instead the unsated crowd shouted for more, for 20 minutes, to no avail.

"There were no new songs as such and the event was predictable," reported *Record Mirror*. "But it was a big success. Dylan had appeared, he had been there and he had entertained. The show had been a good one, and Dylan's act had been thoroughly professional and musically near-perfect."

What had caused such outcry, "tears of rage" as Dylan had titled a recent song, at Newport back in 1965 when he first played folk-rock before a live audience was now just considered part of the norm. The folk-rock revolution that Dylan had done much to launch had driven most of that shift in musical and cultural attitude. Now, it was clear, folk-rock's most controversial—yet also its most exciting—days were over.

epilogue

....

folk-rock's legacy

By the beginning of the 1970s, folk-rock had woven itself so intricately into the very fabric of rock music that it was rarely thought of as a separate category anymore. This was a victory inasmuch as the whole controversy over whether folk and rock should mix had been decisively settled, and folk had done its job in helping elevate rock into an entirely different art form. As is the way when any new innovation gets absorbed into the mainstream, however, folk-rock had lost much of the brash boldness that had done so much to jolt popular music in the first place.

There was some influential, and sometimes very good, folk-rock made in 1970, even if it was rarely called folk-rock any longer. Much of it was from singer-songwriters: Neil Young's *After the Gold Rush*, Joni Mitchell's *Clouds*, and James Taylor's *Sweet Baby James*. Crosby, Stills, Nash & Young released *Déjà Vu*, and the Grateful Dead issued its best and most folk-oriented albums, *Workingman's Dead* and *American Beauty*. British folk-rock saw the continued success of Fairport Convention, the first album by Steeleye Span, and the Sandy Denny–speared *Fotheringay*. There were also quirky singer-songwriter albums that would find a much greater cult following in subsequent decades than they attracted in 1970, such as Nick Drake's *Bryter Later*, the Syd Barrett solo LPs, and even fine, still virtually unknown releases like Linda Perhacs's *Parallelograms*, which sounded like a spaced-out Joni Mitchell.

Bob Dylan, after the critical disaster of *Self-Portrait*, restored himself to grace somewhat with the far more straightforward *New Morning*, although it wasn't on the level of his best 1960s work, despite a build-up in *Melody Maker* from Al Kooper (who called it Dylan's "best album") and producer Bob Johnston (who called it "a goddamn mindblower"). The singer was also awarded a controversial honorary doctorate in music from Princeton that year, a sign of respect unimaginable in 1965, yet also a sign that such folk-rockers were no longer ultimate symbols of antiestablishment sentiment. Already Dylan's zenith was seen as something from the past: Ralph Gleason's *Rolling Stone* review, headlined "We've Got Dylan Back Again," inaugurated off-and-on celebrations of the singer's artistic comebacks that have persisted into the twenty-first century.

There were even, hard as it was to believe at the time, occasional conflicts between folk purists and artists seen to have sold out by electrifying. Ian & Sylvia were taking their country-rock band Great Speckled Bird on the road and still, says Sylvia Tyson, sparking "some very adverse reaction. We had some situations where the minute people saw pedal steel onstage, they would get up and walk out. They thought of us as folk music, as the acoustic thing, and the idea of an electric instrument on stage was an anathema to certain people who, for whatever reason, just couldn't deal with it. The folk

Nazis." Phil Ochs was booed for putting Buddy Holly, Elvis Presley, and Merle Haggard songs into his Carnegie Hall show in March 1970. Martin Carthy disappointed British traditionalists by playing electric guitar after joining Steeleye Span that same year. There was even a public debate, chaired by respected British folk musician Ian Campbell, before Steeleye Span's 1971 appearance at the Keele Folk Festival as to whether amplification was desirable or not for such music.

But folk-rock's golden age was done, even as its influence continued to hover over much of what was heard on both AM and FM radio. Much of the combination of forces that had been so striking and radical in the mid-'60s had by now become formulized to an extent, moving closer to the pop center. That was most apparent in the boom of laidback confessional singer-songwriters, particularly Taylor, Carole King, Jackson Browne, Cat Stevens, and Carly Simon, as well as mellow country-rock stars the Eagles and Linda Ronstadt. In his "Absolutely Frank" column in *Guitar Player*, the ever-lovable Frank Zappa (who had once posed in an ad for Hagstrom Guitars bearing the logo "Folk Rock is a Drag") went as far as to blame "folk-rock 12-string swill" as "the predecessor of the horrible fake-sensitive type artist/singer/songwriter/suffering person, posed against a wooden fence provided by the Warner Bros. Records art department, graciously rented to all the other record companies who needed it for their version of the same crap." In *Rolling Stone*, Ben Gerson was almost as nasty in his estimation of Warners superstar James Taylor's 1971 album *Mudslide Slim and the Blue Horizon*. "He is a purveyor of a fashionable soft sound," sniped the reporter. "He represents no political challenge or challenge to a life style."

Some of the most successful singer-songwriters of the early and mid-'70s, of course, were veterans of 1960s folk-rock: Neil Young, Joni Mitchell, Paul Simon, Bob Dylan, and indeed Taylor and Browne. Other singer-songwriters who had been stars in the 1960s struggled much harder to maintain a similar profile, such as John Sebastian. "Folk-rock became commercial music," says the former Lovin' Spoonful leader. "Some of the people that made commercials imitated us and our contemporaries so heavily that there were times when I said, 'God, I should just shut up and move to New York and make Alka Seltzer commercials.' There was this big transition to hard rock and heavy rock, and studs and codpieces rock. Meanwhile, stuff that was selling products was all kind of imitations of the Spoonful and the Mamas & the Papas and James Taylor. It was a funny time."

There was not only competition from other singer-songwriters, but also from new styles of rock music: heavy metal, glam rock, progressive rock, funk, and jazz-rock fusion. Many of the great groups from the '60s, whether folk-rockers for part or all of the time, had broken up in the early '70s: the Byrds (whose original members did reunite for a dismal 1973 reunion album), Crosby, Stills, Nash & Young, Simon & Garfunkel, Jefferson Airplane, and of course the Beatles. The initial success of CSNY had led some to predict that temporary supergroup or super-session alliances would become common in the future, yet some such folk-rock projects in 1970 came to nothing, like an unexciting Dylan session with George Harrison on guitar (bootlegged but never released, though one song showed up on an archival Dylan box set), or a Dylan-Byrds album that never got off the ground. The music business, taking advantage of the huge demographic for rock that folk-rock had done much to help create, became more corporate and less inclined to take risks. Some of the labels that had taken the biggest risks were either gone, like Verve/Forecast; fading drastically in commercial viability, like Vanguard; or changed beyond recognition, like both Elektra, which president Jac Holzman sold to Warner Brothers in 1970, and the Witchseason management/production stable, sold by founder Joe Boyd to Island Records.

Rock festivals had petered out, cowed by the violence in December 1969 at Altamont (which had its own echoes of folk-rock with appearances by Crosby, Stills, Nash & Young, Jefferson Airplane, and the Flying Burrito Brothers). In August 1970, as *Rolling Stone* reported, only 18 of 48 festivals planned since Woodstock had actually come off. The Pentangle was so disillusioned with the downturn in the festival vibe that it was announced in 1970 that the group would play no more such open-air events (though that stance was eventually modified). Pentangle manager Jo Lustig, noted *NME* in its report on the decision, "felt that people were now attending pop festivals more as a social event than to hear the music."

The huge crowds, disorganization, and drug use were dumbing down the general tone of the events. Sometimes it even spilled onstage to abuse the performers, as seen in Murray Lerner's *Message to Love* documentary of the 1970 Isle of Wight festival, where Joni Mitchell's mike was commandeered for revolutionary rhetoric by a crazed-looking hippie she'd met in Greece. As 18-year-old fan Alan Boyce told *Rolling Stone*, "You can't go to a festival anymore and enjoy it. Not if you're thinking." In 1970, the magazine had done an eight-page spread on festivals; by the following year, that coverage was reduced to an article limply anticipating the summer's extravaganzas with the headline "A Leaky Handful of Festivals."

Off festival grounds, rock concerts were moving from ballrooms and auditoriums into increasingly larger and impersonal arenas, obfuscating the audience-performer bond that in folk-rock's case had started in small coffeehouses. In the last week of 1969, *Rolling Stone* reported that the Cafe Au Go Go, arguably the most important New York venue in the folk-to-electric folk-rock transition, could no longer "make a go of it," according to new owner Moses Baruch. "I tried to do it and even took in Richie Havens as a partner. But it's impossible. The big groups go to the Fillmore East and personally, if I wanted to see them I'd rather go there since you see a show and it's not too expensive. I just can't cover the costs." The Cafe Au Go Go, where Havens and so many others had gone electric in folk-rock's early days, was now the Cafe Caliph, "serving up Middle Eastern entertainment and fare."

And for all the progress that seemed to have been made in opening the Newport Folk Festival bills to electric rock since Dylan's flaming 1965 set, the 1970 event was canceled, with festival co-founder George Wein declaring, according to a May 1970 Associated Press report, that the next Newport Folk Festival "will not include any rock music.... He said foundation members would work to produce a festival in 1971 to show that 'folk music can communicate to youth in the same way that rock music has.'" It smacked of the desperation of the purist-of-the-pure back in 1965, when some guardians of the folk flame viewed folk-rock as a passing fad, although at this point there was no turning back that clock. What's more, in the early '70s the Newport Folk Festival, once such a big part of popular music and indeed popular culture, would go on a 15-year hiatus before resuming in the mid-'80s, never again to command as much media attention as it had in the 1960s.

As has always been the case in its evolution, rock and pop music were moving on, spawning new genres and artists, often generated by a need to appeal to a younger age group as established stars grew older and more set in their ways. Naturally there was still no shortage of folk-rockish singer-songwriters. Indeed there was a whole army of new Dylans in the 1970s, from Bruce Springsteen to Steve Forbert. Most couldn't hope to measure up to the comparison; luckier ones, like Springsteen (signed, as Dylan had been, by John Hammond and initially recorded as a folky singer-songwriter), managed to establish a wholly separate identity. Plenty of new singer-songwriters in the folk-rock idiom emerged to critical acclaim and modest sales, among them Loudon Wainright III, Steve Goodman, Joan Armatrading, and John Prine. There was a mildness to their character, and their sound, that kept them from sending any major shock waves through the entire pop scene.

In part that was because, although many '70s singer-songwriters were accomplished, intelligent, and witty, they did not face such obvious and urgent sociopolitical issues as they had in the '60s. American involvement in the Vietnam War finally de-escalated, the draft ending in 1973, American troops withdrawn the same year, and the war ending entirely in 1975, without an American victory. The worst abuses of segregation and anti-African-American discrimination had been ameliorated, with blacks and other minorities starting to assert themselves more strongly in politics and economics. President Nixon had resigned in the aftermath of the Watergate scandal.

There was still (and still is) just as much to get upset about as ever: environmental destruction, multinational corporate exploitation of Third World resources, continued sexism and racism at home and abroad, the dangers of nuclear power and weaponry. These were complex, insidious, and in many ways more subtle concerns, however, and harder to get immediately and viscerally worked up about in the eyes of many. These issues needed years of concerted, dedicated, often tedious working-within-the-system efforts to address, and did not lend themselves as well to the concise strictures of popular song.

Indeed many of these issues would be addressed by punk and new wave musicians, who often shared with 1960s folk-rockers a disillusioned alienation from the status quo. They differed, however, in their use of harsher, more militant lyrics, more abrasive music, and a greater emphasis on do-it-yourself ethos. They would often try to work outside the system to subvert it, via independent record labels, and a network of alternative clubs and college radio stations, rather than be as concerned with getting their messages across to the masses. And they felt no need to pay homage to roots music, often favoring buzzsaw guitars, chilly synthesizer blasts, shouted vocals, and overtly cultish stances of outsider rebellion, without clear antecedents in folk music.

These younger generations of musicians also were simply not as aware of or plugged into the folk traditions that had given rise to both the folk revival and about half of folk-rock. This was not due to any shortcomings or inherent inferiority in their musical or intellectual abilities. It was inevitable as pre-1965 folk recordings receded further into the past, rarely played except on specialty, noncommercial radio programs. For punk, new wave, and alternative rock musicians, and for many others, folk was not their folk music; *rock* was their folk music. Some punk and new wave celebrities were hardly unaware of folk-rock. Patti Smith had sung with Eric Andersen at the party announcing Dylan's mid-'70s Rolling Thunder Revue touring ensemble. When Bruce Botnick, the co-producer of Love's *Forever Changes*, happened by chance to meet the Clash, the English group raved about the album. Closer to the pop-rock center, Tom Petty had obviously learned many lessons from Roger McGuinn and the Byrds, in both his vocal and guitar styles. But folk-rock was just one of many rock traditions to be mined now, and not often one of the principal ones.

In the 1980s echoes of folk-rock became more distant. More and more bands who would be referred to as "folk-rock-influenced" by critics were in fact only emulating certain sonic aspects of folk-rock, rather than truly capturing its essence or propelling the form into a new era. The whole school of 1980s alternative jangle-pop bands, led by R.E.M., owed much to the Byrds in their ringing guitars. Around 1987 it seemed that every other week saw another album by R.E.M. imitators who might have been imitating the Byrds' 12-string guitars without ever having even heard the Byrds. But otherwise, R.E.M. and the so-called paisley underground neo-psychedelic bands of the early 1980s were really not too similar to the Byrds, or embodiments of the folk-rock spirit. More successful at falling into the folk-rock continuum, though not so much at gaining a significant international audience, was the "rogue folk" movement in Britain, in which groups like the Oyster Band played folk-based dance music with a rock-influenced energy. In Ireland, the more punk-oriented Pogues took that approach to make greater inroads into the pop audience, though not enormous ones.

Periodically singer-songwriters emerged who combined the personal and the political in musical settings not far removed from those used by the early folk-rock singer-songwriters. Suzanne Vega, Tracy Chapman, and Billy Bragg all fit that description, and were all huge critical favorites, sometimes selling huge numbers of records, as Chapman did with her first album in 1988. But they were just part of rock's increasingly fragmented landscape, not a dominant or trend-setting one. They weren't the only ones addressing political issues, either: plenty of alternative rock bands and new rap/hip-hop acts were as well, if not always in as politically correct a fashion as the older generation would have preferred.

The concept of mixing acoustic sets into rock music, as 1960s concerts by Dylan and CSNY had, made an unexpected comeback starting in the late '80s with MTV's long-running series of "Unplugged" showcases. These allowed all manner of stars and mid-level artists to present material in a predominantly acoustic format. Both veterans like Neil Young and new idols like Nirvana took advantage of this to release *Unplugged* albums. It was not unusual for an act like, say, Nirvana to reveal some unsuspected affection for and familiarity with folk songs on such occasions, as Kurt Cobain did when he sang Leadbelly's "Where Did You Sleep Last Night?" Such excursions, however, were more detours than main courses. That's not to accuse a group such as Nirvana of being dilettantes, but only to observe that such covers serve as more illustrations of how features of folk and folk-rock were now accepted parts of rock's mosaic, if no longer unusual or groundbreaking ones.

The 1990s did see, however, a resurgence of young musicians interested both in American roots music of all ages, and in trying to shape it into something that was individual and noncommercial. The performers grouped under the No Depression heading, so-named for the 1990 Uncle Tupelo album of the same name, combined alternative rock with vintage country and folk music.

Not many of them made a big impact on the mainstream, but they usually weren't preoccupied with doing so anyway. Uncle Tupelo spin-offs Wilco and Son Volt, quirky singer-songwriter Will Oldham (aka Palace), and critics' darling Lucinda Williams, the last of whom had actually started recording in the late '70s, were all doing their part to move folk-rock along in this fashion, even if they weren't calling it folk-rock at this point.

Folk music itself, incidentally, had not died out by the early twenty-first century. Indeed there were plenty of folk festivals in the US and overseas, perhaps more than ever. It could be that there were more bluegrass and old-time music festivals than there were of any other kind in the States, nearly all of them emphasizing the participatory workshops and dances that had been staples at Newport. The Newport Folk Festival itself, for that matter, had made a successful comeback from a 15-year hiatus and was still very much up and running in 2001. Its lineup that year included plenty of commercially viable and alternative singer-songwriters with some debts to folk-rock: Joan Osborne, the Indigo Girls, Nanci Griffith, and Emmylou Harris, who had gotten her start as a recording artist in Gram Parsons's band in the early '70s. In the summer of 2002, Bob Dylan made worldwide headlines by returning to the scene of folk-rock's single most controversial concert and playing the Newport Folk Festival for the first time since his 1965 electric debut. Again he mixed acoustic and electric material, including the two songs most pivotal to launching the folk-rock revolution, "Mr. Tambourine Man" and "Like a Rolling Stone." The last time he'd tried playing "Like a Rolling Stone" with an electric band at Newport, he'd been greeted with a maelstrom of boos, cheers, and cacophonous confusion; this time his performance was showered with unanimous cheers from the 10,000-strong sellout crowd.

Overseas the Cropredy Festival, begun in the late '70s as mainly a Fairport Convention concert plus guests, has grown to become the biggest event of its kind in England, drawing more than 20,000 listeners for a weekend of Fairport and other folk- and folk-rock-related acts. Many other long-running festivals, from a resurrected Woodstock to WOMAD, owed something to forerunners such as Newport. An event like WOMAD, which mixed traditional and contemporary music from around the world with rock-based performers, owed much to the more wide-ranging, tolerant aesthetic that folk-rock had fostered (as did the far greater popularity of world music as a whole in the West at the end of the twentieth century).

Folk performers continued to issue numerous albums, and folk programming was rampant on public radio, sometimes on popular national syndicated shows such as *A Prairie Home Companion* and *Mountain Stage*. In the late '90s and early 2000s, there was a small swell of interest in the folk music that had served as such an inspiration to folk-rockers in their formative years: the re-release of Harry Smith's *Anthology of American Folk Music* to enormous critical acclaim; the restoration of numerous volumes of Alan Lomax–assembled recordings on CD; the movie *Songcatcher*, portraying a woman folklorist immersing herself in mountain music and culture at the beginning of the twentieth century; and the Coen Brothers' film *O Brother, Where Art Thou?*, whose soundtrack featured surprisingly vibrant facsimiles of rural folk and blues music of the early '30s. Documentary filmmaker D.A. Pennebaker, who had captured important moments in early folk-rock on celluloid, was one of the directors of *Down from the Mountain*, which presented an evening of traditional folk music at

Nashville's Ryman Auditorium in May 2000. The *O Brother, Where Art Thou?* soundtrack's sales had, unbelievably, topped five million by mid-2002, the album peaking at #1 in the charts; a *Down from the Mountain* tour, featuring most of the performers heard on that soundtrack, spawned a live recording of its own. And Art D'Lugoff, who ran the now-defunct Village Gate, is trying to raise money for a folk music museum to be established in Greenwich Village, aided by a 2000 benefit concert featuring performances by Judy Collins and John Sebastian.

Folk-rock, too, had to some degree changed folk music. For more artistically liberal folk performers such as Mary McCaslin—who had her own brush with folk-rock in the 1960s—the same radical approach early folk-rock groups had used to electrify traditional songs could be applied in reverse. Even after directing her focus to the folk world, she's never thought it a big deal to reinvent rock classics like the Who's "Pinball Wizard" or the Beatles' "Things We Said Today" into acoustic folk arrangements. "The thing is, all those folk songs have been done and been done and been done," she points out. "It's great, it's a wonderful thing, it should be preserved, and it's nice to bring them back every now and then. But you have to move forward. Steeleye Span and Fairport Convention, they took folk songs and did them rock. I took rock songs, and I did exactly the opposite. I find it real interesting when I hear somebody take a song that is known as a rock song, and use a more folk approach to it." Open-mindedness was one of folk-rock's chief legacies, and it was a lesson that could be applied within the very folk circuit from which many folk-rock greats had escaped.

Yet there was not nearly as much of an interaction between folk and rock as there had been in the mid-to-late '60s. That was an unrepeatable phenomenon, as all wonderful supernovas of popular music are. Traditional folk music was again largely in its own world, isolated from the most popular currents of the most popular music in the English-speaking world.

And what of the original 1960s folk-rockers? Almost without exception, all of them continued to work and record over the last 30 years. Most of them still do so today, even if many of them no longer have a recording contract, and some of them primarily play and record for their own pleasure rather than for a living. Richard Fariña and Fairport Convention drummer Martin Lamble were the only major folk-rockers cut off in their primes during the 1960s, but, sadly, many others have passed on since, starting with Gram Parsons and Clarence White in 1973 (not to forget Janis Joplin in 1970, who owed at least something to her folk beginnings). Cass Elliot, Nick Drake, Tim Buckley, Phil Ochs, Sandy Denny, John Lennon, Tim Hardin, Mike Bloomfield, Gene Clark, original Byrds drummer Michael Clarke, Richard Manuel and Rick Danko of the Band, Dino Valenti, Jerry Garcia, Bryan MacLean of Love, Skip Spence: all made substantial contributions to the evolution of folk-rock, and all died before their time, with depression and/or substance abuse sometimes playing a strong role.

At times it seemed that David Crosby, ravaged by years of drug abuse, was destined to join that list, but with a transplanted liver he remains very active in 2002, with both CSNY and his band CPR. During the writing of this book, John Phillips, Tim Rose, Zal Yanovsky of the Lovin' Spoonful, Fred Neil, and Mimi Fariña, lamentably, did join the list, Neil and Fariña passing away during the same month. Saddest of all, in late 2001, George Harrison succumbed to cancer. It was his

12-string electric guitar in *A Hard Day's Night* that had, if inadvertently, inspired Roger McGuinn of the Byrds to create the sound that is folk-rock's most lasting trademark.

There have been others who have died whose contributions have been more peripheral and cultish, or on the business or production side, but nonetheless important: Paul Butterfield, David Blue, Nico, Trevor Lucas, Val Stecklein of the Blue Things, Rex Gosdin of the Gosdin Brothers, Dave Van Ronk, Adrienne Johnston, Michael Stewart of the We Five, and Sonny Bono; producers Tom Wilson, Paul Rothchild, Nik Venet, Felix Pappalardi, Jack Nitzsche, John Hammond, Moe Asch, Harry Smith, and Alan Lomax; and managers Albert Grossman and Jo Lustig.

Yet the list is not all that long considering how many people were, for a few years, part of the 1960s folk-rock crusade. Just as that movement almost immediately began to fragment into psychedelia, singer-songwriting, country-rock, and more, so has it fragmented yet more in the ensuing 35 years. With public taste too fickle to allow it, no one quite managed to remain a superstar for all that time, though some, like Paul Simon, came close. Some, again like Simon, did better than others by unveiling an unsuspected versatility that took them far beyond folk-rock-related music. As had been the case back in 1966 when many folk-rockers started to go psychedelic, this was another extension of the eclectic restlessness that had brought them to folk, and then to folk-rock, to begin with. Simon dipped into reggae, gospel, and then South African pop music, becoming more popular than ever when he recorded with South African musicians for *Graceland* in the mid-'80s. Joni Mitchell, having by the mid-'70s become a general pop superstar, almost completely erased those commercial gains by turning to jazz, though her personal artistic satisfaction in doing so probably could not have been measured.

Neil Young flitted back and forth between country music, folk-rock, all-out hard rock assaults on the eardrum, and detours into rockabilly, electro-rock, and bar-band blues. His iconoclasm frustrated critics and listeners, and sometimes cast him way out of commercial favor, but ultimately won him respect as the most relevant and durable '60s rock musician of any kind. Far beyond the commercial radar or her acoustic folk origins, Buffy Sainte-Marie concentrated on computer-generated electronic music (a field she'd started to investigate around the end of the 1960s on her album *Illuminations*, which had a great deal of electronically altered vocals and sonic textures). "The word computer or electronic might frighten a loyal guitar fan, but for an artist it's always been just another tool," she maintains. "A computer doesn't replace a guitar any more than a piano replaces a violin or oil paints replace water colors."

Some went to the other extreme and re-embraced their roots. Ian Tyson of Ian & Sylvia became a big straight-up country star in his native Canada. Chris Hillman became a mainstream country star as part of the Desert Rose Band in the late '80s. Dan Hicks continued to play the wryest of Western swing with His Hot Licks. Others went on to continued success as record producers, most notably Peter Asher, but also Joe Boyd (who worked with R.E.M. and Billy Bragg, and helped bring Bulgarian music to Western ears with the Trio Bulgarka), Lou Adler (who produced Carole King), and Erik Jacobsen (who produced Chris Isaak). Ry Cooder and David Lindley made their names as the hottest of L.A. session guitarists, and pursued individual projects that allowed them to indulge their interests in (by American standards) esoteric world music. To the surprise and sometimes dismay of some of their original fans, some found inspiration, and along with it a new artistic direction, in born-again Christianity. Bob Dylan was easily the most visible of these, particularly in the late '70s and early '80s, just after he had embraced the Christian faith.

Then there were those who chalked up some of their greatest achievements entirely outside of the music field, bringing the best of folk-rock's humanitarian ideals to the world at large. Ed Sanders of the Fugs won the 1988 American Book Award for his *Thirsting for Peace in a Raging Century: Selected Poems 1961–1985*. Mimi Fariña founded and was, for a quarter-century, the driving force behind Bread and Roses, the Marin County, California-based organization that stages several hundred annual musical performances at prisons, old-age homes, homeless shelters, children's hospitals, and AIDS hospices. Barry Melton of Country Joe & the Fish is now the public defender of Yolo County in California; Tom Rapp of Pearls Before Swine got an Ivy League law degree in the 1980s and got into "what I call '60s law: civil rights, employment discrimination, First Amendment stuff." The church in which the Alice of "Alice's Restaurant" lived was bought by Arlo Guthrie and now houses the Guthrie Center and Guthrie Foundation. The nonprofit organizations support progressive causes ranging from health care and the environment to raising money for a cure for Huntington's chorea, the disease that killed Arlo's father, Woody. Fred Neil was such a recluse that few knew he had co-founded the Dolphin Project, an organization dedicated to stopping the capture, exploitation, and trafficking of dolphins around the globe.

For the most part, though, the folk-rock veterans kept close to the music that had first pushed them into the public eye in the 1960s, continuing to record and perform, sometimes producing work of quality and integrity. Some eventually got a bigger audience after years of slogging through the trenches, such as Richard Thompson, but usually they played to diminishing audiences. Some rely on the folk circuit for much of their schedule now; others have gone onto oldies tours. Others remain major concert draws, but can't sell nearly as many records as they did in their prime. Pop is not kind to those in middle age, and there are many, many younger and hungrier artists with whom to compete.

Far from being embarrassed at the prospect of continually re-examining his past onstage, Denny Doherty built an entire theatrical production (*Dream a Little Dream*) around it, telling the story of the Mugwumps and the Mamas & the Papas to Toronto audiences night after night in 2001. "It seems like it's full circle," he reflects. "And I don't know how many times in a life you get a chance to finish something, or to at least feel that something is being finished or brought to a conclusion. It's a nice feeling."

In their late middle age, some musicians now working on a much smaller scale than they had as mid-'60s stars are taking the opportunity to go back to their deepest traditional folk roots. John Sebastian is playing jug band music as leader of John Sebastian and the J Band, recording with original country-blues legend Yank Rachell (then in his eighties) shortly before Rachell's death. In 2002, Arlo Guthrie was working on a compilation of songs by his father with the Dillards as guests. Roger McGuinn's 2001 CD *Treasures from the Folk Den* was comprised almost entirely of traditional folk songs, with guest contributions from Judy Collins, Joan Baez, Pete Seeger, Odetta, and Tommy Makem.

Even as McGuinn devotes much of his current repertoire to the same traditional folk songs with which he began his career as a teenager, he does so in a way consistent with the merging of acoustic folk and electronic futurism that was so characteristic of his innovations with the Byrds. Many of his renditions of traditional tunes—some recorded back in the late '50s, when he *was* a teenager—are available to hear as MP3s on his Web site. In July 2000, he gave a statement before the US Senate Judiciary Committee hailing the artistic freedom and economic advantages granted by MP3 technology. He wrote a foreword to the *Complete Idiot's Guide to MP3: Music on the Internet*. He's still a gearhead, still as devoted to traditional folk as ever, yet still as up on the latest technology as ever, and still finding those interests totally compatible with each other.

"It's just a continuation of what I do," he shrugs. "I *have* always regarded myself as a folk artist, even during the Byrds and even with the electric instruments." It's still unknown whether his music has been heard by benign outer space aliens, as he and David Crosby hoped 35 years earlier. But it *has* been heard in the highest echelons of government, as verified by a recent photo on McGuinn's site that shows him signing an autograph for British Prime Minister Tony Blair. Somehow it's hard to imagine George W. Bush making a similar request. (Though perhaps ex–Vice President Al Gore would have if he'd been declared the winner over Bush in the 2000 presidential election; when Bob Dylan played at the 2002 Newport Folk Festival, Gore was standing just offstage.)

A much odder and unexpected homage to one of folk-rock's giants was heard on May 22, 2002, when Labour Party MP Peter Bradley put an Early Day Motion into Parliament declaring "that this House pays tribute to the legendary Arthur Lee, also known as Arthurly, frontman and inspiration of Love, the world's greatest rock band and creators of *Forever Changes*, the greatest album of all time; notes that following his release from jail he is currently touring Europe; and urges honourable and especially Right honourable Members to consider the potential benefit to their constituents if they were, with the indulgence of their whips, to lighten up and tune in to one of his forthcoming British gigs." At Bradley's invitation Lee, who took advantage of his newfound freedom to tour both Europe and the United States in 2002, received the motion in person at the House of Commons the following month.

So folk-rock had reverberated, longer and louder, through all levels of the Western world, than anyone might have guessed back when the Byrds had recorded "Mr. Tambourine Man." What does the first generation of folk-rockers think now of folk-rock's legacy, both cultural and musical, 35 years later?

McGuinn: "It was a shot in the arm for rock. It gave rock more lyrical integrity, and I think rock has maintained that to some extent over the years in various forms. I think that's the legacy, is that the bubblegum rock of pre-'65 doesn't exist anymore. Well, it does on some level, like Britney Spears and all that. But, you know, the real rock bands, the grunge guys and all that, are still doing stuff that's more lyrically meaningful."

Arlo Guthrie: "Those days were so great. We felt like we were changing the destiny of the entire world, and that the music was somehow the background to all of that. But you have to understand that in the context of the entire world, it wasn't just the music that was being integrated. *People* were being integrated. We were black and white, and yellow and red and purple, and all different classes, all different religions. All of the traditional barriers, all of the groups that were run by traditionalists for countless centuries, had suddenly fallen apart. Their voices were sort of diminishing in the roar of this new world, where we were all gonna get along, we were all gonna stand up for each other, we were all gonna learn everything.

"The music was one little edge of an entire change in the world, and that change wasn't by any means in the big majority of people. It was enough to reach this critical mass that made it possible for other people to participate in it, even if they didn't believe it. And then the next week, *they* would be on the stop the war [movement], or ban the bomb, clean the air, fix the water, do this, do that. And the music was inclusive.

"The way it is today is the way it was before this time—where everybody's in their own little world, everybody's in their own little group, it's easy to market. We have not seen the likes of those days before or since those days. [Today] there are people who are making those sounds, singing with the same heart, communicating some of the same ideas. There are some people who we don't understand. But it is not the only form of doing it now, 30 years later. There are so many other ways to do that, that the force of the music itself is lost. Not because it's less powerful, but because it was all funneled *just* through the music years ago, and now there's a dozen other ways to communicate it."

Barry Melton of Country Joe & the Fish: "The music business has maintained its connection with progressive politics, and progressive politics has therefore maintained its connection with youth. And I think that's an outgrowth of the '60s. But by the same token, I think the '60s are an outgrowth of the '30s. What I mean is, there's no doubt of a connection between Bob Dylan and Woody Guthrie. There's no doubt of a connection between the Weavers, who were *the* Vanguard act, the act that put Vanguard on the map, and Country Joe & the Fish.

"I have some fundamental beliefs that have not changed. Certainly I thought the war in Vietnam was wrong, and I still think the war in Vietnam was wrong. As a matter of fact, it's been interesting watching all the people who were responsible for that war, like [former Secretary of Defense] Robert McNamara, saying it was a mistake, and agreeing with me over time. I like being vindicated. I'm not saying I wasn't an idiot in a lot of ways. We changed, and hopefully, our perspective widens. I'm a public defender, and I work on statewide criminal justice issues for indigent people. So people who know me know that actually I'm doing the same thing I've always done, just a different manifestation of it, and maybe in some ways a more age-appropriate manifestation of it."

Buffy Sainte-Marie (who was told long after the 1960s that Lyndon Johnson's administration had tried to suppress her work): "My life and career have been unexpectedly wonderful, and I've never let the loss of my American audience bother me much, except as a too-late unprovable censorship issue of the past. I invested my '60s singing money in my own nonprofit Nihewan Foundation for American Indian Education, and saw two of my grantees go on to found and preside over tribal colleges which continue to thrive. My concerts in American Indian communities in the US, and communities in a few other countries, continue to support the foundation's work in teacher training, curriculum development, the Nihewan Youth Council on Race, and the Cradleboard Teaching Project.

"The only part that really bugs me is that the work I was doing in the US through music should have been maximized to serve more people at the time, but I guess that was the issue. Therefore I continued and continue (through five years of *Sesame Street*, 20 years of digital art and music, speeches, articles, lectures and adjunct professorships at several colleges) to combine Native American studies and the arts in ways that teach me and others about alternative thinking and alternative expression. Moral: If grampa LBJ shuts you out of showbiz, find other ways to accomplish your task."

Pamela Polland of the Gentle Soul: "I truly believe the folk-rock era helped shape an entire generation of people who otherwise might have continued the legacy of the straight and narrow prejudices and mores of the '50s. My parents, for instance, brought into this world by parents with somewhat Victorian sensibilities, got very stuck in the rut of not questioning authority. They were brought up to lie about their feelings and to conceal who they truly were, bless their hearts. Not that they were inherently dishonest people—in fact, as parents go, mine were probably the hipper variety. But to this day, my mother lives to 'make nice nice' and 'not rock the boat.' And certainly not get angry, or at least not display anger.

"The '60s, and the topical music that came out of that era, exposed anger and other very real human emotions to the younger generation of that time. We took that ball and ran with it all the way into the 'me generation' of the '80s where self-help and personal transformation therapies became the springboard for the now so-called New Age Movement. And I can GUARANTEE you that any self-respecting New Ager can probably sing you at least the first verse of 'Turn! Turn! Turn!'

"The social change came FIRST, and the music reflected that. But the music 'announced' the changes to wider audiences—it heralded the changes, and in so doing, it educated a broader public. Just as rap now gives us a peek into inner city issues, music has a power to educate on a level that touches us more than a newspaper article."

Peter Yarrow of Peter, Paul & Mary: "I believe that the fusion of folk and rock into folk-rock was filled with meaning and passion, and it's a positive energy. It's important to look contextually at the meaning of folk music and folk-rock, not as a musical form, but a place of intent. For me, the place of intent and the sense of community that was created by that stream of commitment and consciousness still characterizes the best that's in America."

Robin Williamson of the Incredible String Band: "I think it is true to say that a lot of ideas which are now common words, like ecology and so on, were born in the '60s. And I like to think that we had something to do with the beginnings of all that.

"Things go three steps forward, two steps back. We saw that very clearly in the '60s. All of a sudden, not only were they opening the doors, they were blowing down the doorframe and taking away the wall. And then in the '70s and in the Thatcher era in Britain, people just became self-interested and greedy. They went right back to as bad as it had ever been before that in the '50s, and worse. So everything that had been gained in terms of kindred spirits and fellow feeling and an attempt to break down barriers and walls was put right back. But some things, as I say, didn't go away, because ecology came out of the '60s. The women's rights movement came out of the '60s. Respect for children came out of the '60s. A whole different attitude to education came out of the '60s. And some of those things have stayed with us, in spite of the idiocies of human folly, greed and pride."

Sherry Snow aka Halimah Collingwood, half of Blackburn & Snow: "It was part of a movement, of a new way of living. And a new way of thinking and feeling and expressing and being free and being liberated. However different people chose to experience it and express it and get there, it was a really happening experience. People wanted to leave the old style of security behind, discover something new, and find something that was much richer and more real. I think that whole philosophy and desire for truth is what propelled the expression of the music. You hear it in Bob Dylan. Bob Dylan exemplifies it.

"But we were *all* feeling it. It wasn't [like] I listened to Bob Dylan's music and it made me want to be like that. It was something that was churning and bubbling and coming to the surface in a whole lot of people in that generation all over the country, and it was exemplified in Cambridge and in San Francisco, [which] I think were the two really hotbeds of the activity. And maybe Bob Dylan helped us all to see that it was possible. But I always knew something was possible like that. It was just the time. The musicians and the political activists were the messengers of what everybody was feeling and thinking."

Bob Johnston, producer of Bob Dylan, Simon & Garfunkel, Leonard Cohen, and Dino Valenti: "Dylan was a prophet. It'll be three or four hundred years before anybody knows it, that he helped stop a war and changed everybody's attitude. That's why we're not hiding under the desk anymore, the children at school. I don't think they tore the Berlin Wall down and opened up China and Russia with politics. I think they did it with Levis and rock 'n' roll music. And I think Dylan was at the spearhead of it."

Tim Rose, speaking shortly before his death in 2002: "We've given freedom to musicians that wasn't there before. We were outside the mainstream. We did not come in through the traditional channels that the accepted music business understood. We were self-contained. 'The singer sings, the writer writes, the producer produces'—in the '60s, most of the major labels, that's what they understood. The musicians took control of the direction of the music, against the wishes of the music business itself. This is un-fucking-precedented in music.

"You don't have to be a highly trained musician to play this. What you have to do is have a passion to want to do it. You have to have a need to want your voice heard. And within the great scope of rock, there's a forum for you. The music we've written still gets recorded today. People are still recording 'Morning Dew,' 'Hey Joe,' 'Come Away Melinda' [all songs from Tim Rose's first album]."

Gary Marker of the Rising Sons: "Studios and engineers day after day constantly had their eyes on the clock and worried more about their quarterly budgets than producing groundbreaking, musically challenging records. And they also had the problem of trying to come up with something that would beat back the tide of English records and groups. That whole folk-rock thing on the charts around '65 changed all that, of course. Suddenly, the industry—almost overnight—fell into the hands of airy-fairy, artsy-fartsy brooding wandering minstrel types who spent endless hours noodling in the studio until some kind of inspiration hit them. This drove the profit-driven, bottom-line corporate types right out of their minds—and eventually out of the business. At least for a while. The bean counters are back and have seized control."

Chris Darrow of Kaleidoscope: "Most of the people who got into folk music in the '50s and '60s were reacting against an establishment of the bland and the normal, searching for a more real and down-to-earth ethic to attach oneself to. The advent [of the] folk-rock movement in the '60s allowed that a performer could mine the past for rich material that was both melodic and uplifting, or spiritual, if you will. Due to the state of the world at the time and the need to return to a simpler existence, songs of freedom and brotherhood like 'Turn! Turn! Turn!' gave an authenticity and depth to popular music that had not been heard before or since. The directness and elegant simplicity of traditional folk melodies paved the way for songs like 'Get Together' by the Youngbloods, [and] 'For What It's Worth' by the Buffalo Springfield.

"One of the things I think folk-rock music has, was a sense of 'languid time is possible in your life.' There is a certain kind of element of enjoyment of just your environment, your surroundings, and your thing which sort of permeates this music. It [doesn't] necessarily have to be about that, but this music has a rural sunny day, open-air kind of feeling. It's not like something that has come out of the post-punk era, where everything is sort of interior indoors and dark. It's a whole different kind of thing. I think that's why a lot of us cling to some aspect of it in our lives right now. It's an attitude that there may be a return of, because there might be a need to have something with an uplifting flavor coming out, as opposed to something that's so dismal."

Jerry Jeff Walker: "It's been a long strange ride. I still get quite a big charge when I play 'Mr. Bojangles' and look out and 30 couples are just waltzing all around the dance floor. Damn nice to see people holding each other, smiling at each other, and dancing while you play. They can still absorb the lyrics. I'd realized my songs were part of a fabric of their lives, and that it makes it worthwhile."

Donovan: "The result of all this conscious lyric and experimental music fusion in the '60s is obvious. All musical barriers are down and all audiences are free to appreciate any kind of music and idea which they want. Freedom has appeared: freedom to do whatever you feel, say and sing whatever you want, play and fuse however you dream.

"As to the musical styles of today, some say the young have gone techno and machines make the music. But when you deconstruct rap and study Moby, you hear once again the root of folk— it's Africa, it's dangerous, it's irreverent. Even though there are mechanical sounds out there, popular music must always return to the roots, the same roots which were suppressed as social folk music, suppressed as long-haired hippie music—the roots are folk wherever you go.

"Popular music means the music of the populace—the music of the 'folk' who live on the earth. We who brought pop back to its roots continue to play anything we want as we respect freedom and will not be told what to think, feel, or sing. That's real folk-rock, man!"

Are the old songs—and "Turn! Turn! Turn!" is now an old song, at least in the eyes of our fast-moving society—relevant today? Judy Collins thought so, putting Pete Seeger's song into the repertoire for her 2001 Wildflower Festival Tour, on which she shared the bill with fellow folk-rock vets Janis Ian, Richie Havens, and Roger McGuinn. McGuinn "and I and the others are singing 'Turn! Turn! Turn!' together, at the end of the show," said Collins in July 2001. "I didn't know how I'd feel about this, so I didn't ask him [Roger, to sing it], but he offered. It's so much fun. It's basically his and my voice, with harmonies. It's very funny, after 38 years, to come back around. The circle just is amazing."

"Turn! Turn! Turn!," the song that Collins had recorded in 1963 with McGuinn on guitar, and that McGuinn had taken to #1 with the Byrds two years later, had brought them together again. And it had endured as a classic into the twenty-first century, probably exceeding Seeger's wildest dreams when he wrote a plaintive folk plea based on Biblical verse. The folk process that had brought the song to life was alive and well. So were those who had shaped the folk-rock anthem's improbable journey, which has now ended more or less where it started, catching billions of ears along the way as the world and music continue to turn, turn, turn.

discography

T here were many albums and singles made between approximately mid-1966 and the early '70s that contained quality folk-rock. What follows is a selected list of the best and most important of those releases that include music discussed in this book, with some possible additional releases to explore mentioned in the capsule reviews. Bear in mind that this discography, in line with the rest of the book, covers the music made by the generation of performers that shaped 1960s folk-rock. The records listed here reflect the 1966–70 era in which folk-rock diversified and flowered from its roots in the initial mid-'60s folk-rock explosion. To keep the list within that focus, acoustic folk records from the 1960s by major folk performers such as Dave Van Ronk, Odetta, and Martin Carthy are not listed. Nor are post-1970 records strongly indebted to the innovations of 1960s folk-rock. (Of course, anyone interested in the roots of folk-rock—and the music early folk-rock itself has influenced—should investigate some such releases that fall outside this volume's boundaries.)

The record labels listed for these entries are the most recent known labels on which the albums have been reissued or maintained in print. For reviews of many folk-rock albums not listed here, and additional, detailed reviews of many folk-rock albums that *are* listed here, readers are encouraged to check out the largest online database of album reviews and artist discographies, the All Music Guide, at www.allmusic.com.

Links to Web sites with all sorts of weird and wonderful details about folk-rockers featured in this book, as well as some additional lists of wonderful and weird folk-rock recordings and other folk-rock miscellany, are found on the author's Web site, at www.richieunterberger.com.

Turn! Turn! Turn!: The '60s Folk-Rock Revolution (Backbeat Books, 2002), the prequel to *Eight Miles High*, has a critical discography of the most important folk-rock recordings from the 1964–66 era that celebrate the birth and rise of folk-rock. Some of the best-ofs and compilations in the following discography will include some of that music. It seemed inappropriate to be too rigorous in dividing such anthologies chronologically; the main purpose is to direct listeners to the best music described in the text, even if it sometimes shares space with tracks from an earlier vintage.

The complete discography of the author's recommended 1960s folk-rock recordings—covering the entire decade—can be viewed online at www.richieunterberger.com/folkrockdisc.html.

Eric Andersen, *Violets of Dawn* (1999, Vanguard). A sampler of the best of Andersen's early recordings, including his best early songs: "Violets of Dawn," "Close the Door Lightly When You Go," "Thirsty Boots," and "The Hustler." The track selection is almost the same as on Vanguard's *The Best of Eric Andersen*, but the sound on this CD is better.

The Band, *Music from Big Pink* (1968, Capitol). Folk-rock was only one of the tributaries drawn upon for the album that, more than any other, put Americana into folk-rock. It never would have happened without folk-rock, and specifically the Band's old bandleader Bob Dylan, who at the Basement Tapes sessions cut earlier versions of several *Big Pink* songs ("Tears of Rage," "I Shall Be Released," "This Wheel's on Fire") with these musicians. The CD reissue has the outtakes/ alternates that are almost de rigeur for such things these days.

The Band, *The Band* (1969, Capitol). A continuation of the music explored on its debut, this time with a total reliance upon original compositions. It includes the Band's most popular songs, "The Night They Drove Old Dixie Down" and "Up on Cripple Creek," and additional outtakes and alternates on the CD reissue.

Syd Barrett, *Crazy Diamond* (1993, EMI). A selection to make the purists howl, perhaps, but it's undeniable that much of the ex–Pink Floyd leader's zany solo output has an acid folk charm. This three-CD set has almost everything he did as a solo artist, including all the songs from his two 1970 albums, and plenty of outtakes.

The Beatles, *Unsurpassed Demos* (1991, Yellow Dog, bootleg). Twenty-four acoustic *White Album* demos, recorded in May 1968 at George Harrison's house, including songs the Beatles wrote in India while they and Donovan were studying with the Maharishi. This is the chance to hear the Beatles as an unplugged band, highly enjoyable as well as educational, and often boot-legged in part or whole under different titles as well.

The Beau Brummels, *The Best of the Beau Brummels* (1987, Rhino). A good 18-song survey of their 1960s tracks, though not perfect in its song selection, particularly with the omission of "I Want You." It does have their key hits "Just a Little" and "Laugh, Laugh," as well as stand-out lesser-known singles like "Sad Little Girl." There's much to enjoy on some other Beau Brummels releases if you like what you hear here, such as 1965's *Vol. 2*, Sundazed's three-CD mid-'60s rarities collection *San Fran Sessions*, and the more reflective 1967 album *Triangle*.

Big Brother & the Holding Company, *Big Brother & the Holding Company* (1967, Columbia/Legacy). While Big Brother & the Holding Company were already getting into hard psychedelic rock by the time they recorded their debut album at the end of 1966, much of the material was derived from folk and pre-rock blues and gospel sources, such as "Down on Me," "All Is Loneliness," and "Blindman." The CD reissue adds the non-LP single "Coo Coo," as crazed a psychedelic rock update of an overdone folk music standard as you'll hear.

Blackburn & Snow, *Something Good for Your Head* (1999, Big Beat). All four of the songs the duo managed to release on singles while active are here, including the David Crosby–penned "Stranger in a Strange Land," along with 16 previously unreleased outtakes. Among the most unjustly undiscovered folk-rock of the 1960s, the male-female harmonies and solid early folk-rock song-writing should appeal to anyone who likes the early Jefferson Airplane, though at the same time it's not so similar to the Airplane or other big-name folk-rockers as to sound imitative or derivative.

The Blue Things, *The Blue Things* (2001, Rewind). A reissue of the great lost folk-rock group's 1966 RCA album, with six bonus tracks from 1966–67 singles (including some very cool psyche-delic ones like "Orange Rooftop of Your Mind"). Highly recommended to anyone who enjoys the early Byrds and Beau Brummels, though it has an earnest longing appeal of its own. The getting-harder-to-find Cicadelic LPs *Story Vol. 1–3* fill out the picture with numerous outtakes and early singles, as do the Collectables CDs *Story Vol. 1–2*.

David Bowie, *The Beckenham Oddity* (Leisure Records, bootleg). Probably recorded in early 1969, this unreleased acoustic tape, since bootlegged (usually under the title *The Beckenham Oddity*), documents the brief period when Bowie, with singer-guitarist accompanist John Hutchinson, sounded something like a British Simon & Garfunkel. Bowie takes most of the vocal leads, with frequent harmonies by Hutchinson, the set including unplugged versions of several of the better songs that would show up on his 1969–70 recordings. Despite wobbly low fidelity, it's charming, tuneful, affecting, and, well, sincere—an adjective you wouldn't often use for Bowie's work.

Tim Buckley, *Tim Buckley* (1966, Elektra). Although it might have sounded a bit callow in relation to his subsequent music, *Tim Buckley* was a deft and delicate portrait of the teenage troubadour at his most folk-rock-soaked. The production was state-of-the-art early Elektra folk-rock, embellished by some sympathetic orchestral arrangements by Jack Nitzsche.

Tim Buckley, *Goodbye and Hello* (1967, Elektra). Buckley's most consistent album found him expanding his reach into art song and psychedelia, but never at the loss of the song-oriented material that he and Larry Beckett penned at the outset of the singer's career. Unpredictable melodies, grandiose arrangements, and great vocalizing were to the fore throughout, whether on the outstanding antiwar statement "No Man Can Stop the War," the eerie "Hallucinations," or the placid folkie ballad "Morning Glory."

Tim Buckley, *Happy Sad* (1969, Elektra). As much jazz as folk-rock, this was still a beguiling if low-key listen, as Buckley successfully inserted new yet accessible directions into his style. Although for the most part a languid set, it also built up a powerhouse of energy on the jazz-folk-funk workout "Gypsy Woman."

Tim Buckley, *Morning Glory: The Tim Buckley Anthology* (2001, Elektra). Almost everything Buckley did in the first five years of his recording career needs to be heard to appreciate the impossibly eclectic scope of his vision. This two-CD compilation is a good place to start, though, mostly sticking to his 1966–70 releases, and throwing in a previously unreleased solo 1967 version of "Song to the Siren."

Buffalo Springfield, *Buffalo Springfield Again* (1967, Atco). The band's most diverse and impressive album, even if it spun into psychedelia, country-rock, and hard rock from its folk-rock base. Stephen Stills's "Rock & Roll Woman" and "Bluebird" were among his very best songs, while

Neil Young's "Expecting to Fly" was his best early composition, and "Broken Arrow" one of his most ambitious.

Buffalo Springfield, *Last Time Around* (1968, Atco). The least impressive of the group's albums, not just due to the increasing fragmentation of the band, but also to a slightly lower standard of material. There were some great songs here, though, like Neil Young's "I Am a Child," Stephen Stills's "Pretty Girl Why," and Richie Furay's "Kind Woman."

Buffalo Springfield, *Buffalo Springfield Box Set* (2001, Rhino). This four-CD box set isn't quite definitive, and could have been done better. It's missing some tracks from *Last Time Around*, and disc four, comprised of songs from the first two albums in their original sequence, is a waste as all the tracks appear on other discs in the package. Still . . . it has almost everything the group issued, and dozens of cool demos, outtakes, and alternates, and as such must be considered a great collection of music.

The Byrds, *Fifth Dimension* (1966, Columbia/Legacy). Uneven, but essential for their pioneering outings into psychedelia on "Eight Miles High," "Fifth Dimension," "I See You," and "I Come and Stand at Every Door." Additionally, "John Riley" was one of the greatest rock updates of a traditional folk song. Like all of the Columbia/Legacy Byrds CD reissues, it's bolstered with several bonus tracks of rarities and previously unissued outtakes and alternate versions. Among those are the earlier RCA Studios version of "Eight Miles High" and "Eight Miles High"'s non-LP B-side, "Why."

The Byrds, *Younger Than Yesterday* (1967, Columbia/Legacy). Their best album other than *Mr. Tambourine Man*, not just for the hit singles "So You Want to Be a Rock & Roll Star" and "My Back Pages," but also for some of their best LP-only cuts, like "Renaissance Fair," "Everybody's Been Burned," and "Thoughts and Words." Chris Hillman's "The Girl with No Name" and "Time Between" were overlooked table-setters for country-rock.

The Byrds, *The Notorious Byrd Brothers* (1968, Columbia/Legacy). Like *Younger Than Yesterday*, another high-flying fusion of folk-rock, country-rock, and psychedelia, from the cover of "Goin' Back" and the buoyant optimism of "Natural Harmony" and "Tribal Gathering" to the futuristic "Space Odyssey." The bonus tracks include David Crosby's controversial "Triad" and Roger McGuinn's ultimate electronic excursion, "Moog Raga."

The Byrds, *Sweetheart of the Rodeo* (1968, Columbia/Legacy). Overrated, perhaps, but this was an early country-rock milestone, and the only album that Gram Parsons recorded with the Byrds. The bonus tracks include some takes with Parsons on lead vocals that didn't make the final album.

The Byrds, *Greatest Hits* (1999, Columbia/Legacy). You won't go wrong with any of the first five proper Byrds albums. But as an introduction, *Greatest Hits* covers their 1965–67 recordings in splendid fashion.

The Charlatans, *The Amazing Charlatans* (1996, Big Beat). Twenty-three 1965–68 tracks, most of them previously unreleased, were assembled for this important archival collection. The

Charlatans' good-time jug band–blues–saloon music take on folk-rock was more engaging than exciting, but once in a while it *was* exciting, as on Dan Hicks's giddy early psych-folk outing "We're Not on the Same Trip," and the ominous reading of the English madrigal "I Saw Her."

Gene Clark, *Echoes* (1991, Columbia/Legacy). Clark's 1967 debut solo album, *Gene Clark & the Gosdin Brothers*, was a letdown in comparison to his work in the Byrds. But it was okay, and not too dissimilar to vintage 1966 Byrds, though more subdued. The entire album, plus six early Byrds tracks to feature him as singer-songwriter and three previously unreleased early solo cuts, are compiled on this CD.

Leonard Cohen, *Songs of Leonard Cohen* (1968, Columbia). Cohen's debut boasted some of the best lyrics ever to grace a popular music album on songs like "Suzanne," "Master Song," and "So Long, Marianne." He made his extremely limited vocal range work for him rather than against him, his brooding songs counterpointed by attractive if muted acoustic-orchestral settings.

Judy Collins, *Wildflowers* (1967, Elektra). The commercial pinnacle of the baroque-folk mini-genre was highlighted by Collins's hit cover of Joni Mitchell's "Both Sides Now." Gorgeous orchestral arrangements graced the rest of the album as well, standouts being another Mitchell cover ("Michael from Mountains") and no less than three Leonard Cohen songs.

Judy Collins, *Who Knows Where the Time Goes* (1968, Elektra). By far Collins's most rock-oriented album, though this was more laidback than you might expect, given a supporting cast that included Stephen Stills, Van Dyke Parks, James Burton, and Jim Gordon. The title track cover of Sandy Denny's song was its shining moment, while the interpretations of Ian Tyson's "Someday Soon," Leonard Cohen's "Story of Isaac," and Robin Williamson's "First Boy I Loved" (originally "First Girl I Loved") were all notable, as was Collins's own composition "My Father."

Judy Collins, *Forever: An Anthology* (1997, Elektra). Certainly this suffers from a lack of chronological sequencing, and not all of it covers the 1960s. Still, the 35 songs include most of her key 1960s folk-rock recordings, among them "Both Sides Now," "Who Knows Where the Time Goes," "Hard Lovin' Loser," "Suzanne," "First Boy I Loved," and "My Father," not to mention her 1963 recording of "Turn! Turn! Turn!"

Country Joe & the Fish, *The First Three EPs* (1993, Sequel). The third of Country Joe's EPs, done in the early '70s, isn't worth noting, and nor are the two songs folkie Peter Krug did to fill out side two of Country Joe's first EP. But the other tracks, from the 1965 and 1966 EPs, make this an important early San Francisco Bay Area folk-into-psychedelia document, including the 1965 jug band version of "I-Feel-Like-I'm-Fixin'-To-Die Rag" and the awesome 1966 psychedelic instrumental "Section 43."

Country Joe & the Fish, *The Collected Country Joe & the Fish* (1987, Vanguard). A good best-of, running more than 70 minutes, that properly leans heavily on their first and best album. It also includes "I-Feel-Like-I'm-Fixin'-To-Die Rag," which is essential not just to any Country Joe & the Fish anthology, but to any overview of 1960s folk-rock as a whole.

Crosby, Stills & Nash, *Crosby, Stills & Nash* (1969, Atlantic). The first album by folk-rock's major supergroup, and a hugely influential one, though its contents have aged variably. Stephen Stills, if only in retrospect, was the main motor, and wrote the album's best song, "Suite: Judy Blue Eyes," while "Long Time Gone" and "Wooden Ships" showed their more aggressive, harder-rocking profile.

Crosby, Stills, Nash & Young, *Déjà Vu* (1970, Atlantic). Actually, Neil Young's songwriting contributions to this album were fairly light, but they did include the outstanding multipart suite "Country Girl." The core trio continued to write and play in a fashion similar to that essayed by its debut, coming to a peak on the cover of Joni Mitchell's "Woodstock." Unfortunately *Déjà Vu* doesn't include the 1970 non-LP singles "Ohio" and "Find the Cost of Freedom," both of which were among their finest moments. Incidentally, CSNY's live *4 Way Street*, though often ragged, was an intermittently worthwhile (and long) double-CD snapshot of their varied 1970 acoustic and electric live sets, the CD reissue adding some additional previously unreleased material.

Sandy Denny, *The Original Sandy Denny* (1991, Mooncrest). A compilation of acoustic folk tracks, taken from albums originally released in 1967. Other than the Jackson C. Frank and Tom Paxton covers, the material was running behind the times, but Denny's singing was already magnificent. For more such just-pre-rock early Denny, search for the bootlegs *Dark the Night* and *Borrowed Thyme*, which also have wonderful vocals on 1966–68 acoustic folk home demos and radio performances, though the fidelity varies from superb to marginal.

Sandy Denny & the Strawbs, *Sandy Denny & the Strawbs* (1991, Hannibal). Although slighter and less powerful than what Denny would record with Fairport Convention, these tracks (done in 1967 but not released until 1973) were charming if tentative early British folk-rock, highlighted by "And You Need Me" and the first version of "Who Knows Where the Time Goes." Note that the 1991 CD on Hannibal has some overdubs not present on the original 1973 release of these sessions, *All Our Own Work*, which is the preferred version, but very hard to find.

The Dillards, *Wheatstraw Suite* (1968, Collectors' Choice Music). One of the greatest country-rock albums, though country-rock might be too limiting a label to put on its fusion of bluegrass, country, folk, rock, and pop. Much of what the Eagles put to a pop polish could be heard in embryo here, though non-Eagles fans shouldn't let that scare them off, as this album was far earthier and quirkier.

The Dillards, *Copperfields* (1970, Collectors' Choice Music). Although not quite as groundbreaking as *Wheatstraw Suite*, *Copperfields* was a similarly eclectic, upbeat trawl through country-rock-bluegrass fusion, with surprising dabs of other influences thrown onto the canvas. "Touch Her If You Can" could have been a pop hit single, for instance, while "Brother John" uncovered an unsuspected knack for jazzy McGuinn-like guitar licks.

Dion, *Sit Down Old Friend* (1970, Ace). This doesn't have "Abraham, Martin and John," but it's the best album from the singer's folk-rock comeback period, wholly comprised of introspective, soulful folk-rock-blues, with Dion's acoustic guitar the only instrumental backup. On its CD reissue, it's paired with his less impressive 1971 album *You're Not Alone*.

Donovan, *Mellow Yellow* (1967, Epic). Although this tapered off from the highs of its extraordinary predecessor, 1966's *Sunshine Superman*, it was still a solid record. Not as eclectic as *Sunshine Superman*, it went deeper into jazzy swings and playful lyrics, particularly of course on the huge title hit. There were some wry, even dark musings on Swinging London life, though, in "Young Girl Blues," "Hampstead Incident," and "Sunny South Kensington."

Donovan, *Troubadour: The Definitive Collection 1964–1976* (1992, Epic/Legacy). The absence of "Celeste" from this two-CD best-of is inexcusable. But for the most part it does a good job in compiling his strongest material, including all of his hit singles, numerous standout album tracks, and a handful of previously unreleased cuts.

Nick Drake, *Bryter Later* (1970, Hannibal). The best of the three albums Drake put out during his lifetime contained his most captivating melancholic songs ("Hazey Jane II," "At the Chime of a City Clock," "Poor Boy"), as well as classical-influenced, orchestrated instrumentals that counterpointed the vocal numbers well.

Nick Drake, *Fruit Tree* (1985, Hannibal). Drake didn't record much during his short life, but virtually everything on his three albums was of high quality. All three of them—1969's *Five Leaves Left*, 1970's *Bryter Later*, and 1972's *Pink Moon*—are on this four-CD box set, which adds a disc of non-LP outtakes (available separately as *Time of No Reply*) that are well worth hearing too.

Bob Dylan, *The Basement Tapes* (1975, Columbia). The highlights of Dylan's recordings with the Band during 1967, including well-known and well-covered songs like "Too Much of Nothing," "This Wheel's on Fire," and "Tears of Rage." A good summary of that output for those who don't want to lay out the cash (and considerable legwork) for *The Genuine Basement Tapes*, the five-volume series of Basement Tapes bootlegs.

Bob Dylan, *The Genuine Basement Tapes Vol. 1–5* (bootleg). With 100-plus songs, this bootleg is too extensive for the average fan, perhaps, but it's a fascinating look at what Dylan and the Band were up to in 1967. Includes not just the famous songs from the official *Basement Tapes* release, but also some other outstanding originals like "I Shall Be Released" and "The Mighty Quinn," unreleased alternate versions, and lots of vintage (and sometimes off-the-wall) folk and roots music covers.

Bob Dylan, *John Wesley Harding* (1967, Columbia). The stately, subdued, philosophical back-to-basics record that marked Dylan's re-entry into the public eye after his mid-1966 motorcycle accident. Highlighted by "All Along the Watchtower," "As I Went Out One Morning," and "The Wicked Messenger," and very influential on the birth of country-rock, if skeletally arranged.

Bob Dylan, *Biograph* (1985, Columbia). This five-record box set covers Dylan's work through the early '80s, but not unexpectedly features much material from the 1960s. It's valuable not only for the inclusion of all his major hits and several vital LP tracks, but also a number of important non-LP folk-rock singles, live versions, and outtakes from the 1960s, like "Mixed Up Confusion," "Positively 4th Street," "Can You Please Crawl Out Your Window," and "Quinn the Eskimo" (aka "The Mighty Quinn"). Other important 1960s rarities appear on Columbia's three-CD *The Bootleg Series Vol. 1–3*, and too many Dylan bootlegs to count.

Eclection, *Eclection* (1968, Collectors' Choice Music). Perhaps the finest, way-obscure late-'60s British folk-rock album, though it actually sounded more Californian than British. Its harmonies, production, and song construction strongly recalled Jefferson Airplane, the Mamas & the Papas, and the Seekers, but the band split before doing any additional albums that might have carved a more distinct identity.

Fairport Convention, *Fairport Convention* (1968, Universal Island). Too often dismissed as derivative and inconsequential, this was in fact highly respectable Jefferson Airplane–Byrds– styled folk-rock. The only album the band did with Judy Dyble as its female singer, it included both fine interpretations of songs like Joni Mitchell's "Chelsea Morning" and "I Don't Know Where I Stand," and fetching, tuneful originals in the classic mid-'60s folk-rock mold.

Fairport Convention, *What We Did on Our Holidays* (1969, Universal Island). The first album the band did with Sandy Denny aboard was its best, whether on contemporary covers like Joni Mitchell's "Eastern Rain," traditional folk like "She Moves Through the Fair" and "Nottamun Town," or first-rate original material like Sandy Denny's "Fotheringay."

Fairport Convention, *Unhalfbricking* (1969, Universal Island). Not as strong as *What We Did on Our Holidays*, but still at a high level, especially on the French cover of Bob Dylan's "If You Gotta Go, Go Now" and Sandy Denny's mordant "Autopsy."

Fairport Convention, *Liege & Lief* (1969, Universal Island). The album that set the pattern for 1970s British folk-rock in its heavy emphasis on traditional material and the incorporation of fiddler Dave Swarbrick into the group, reaching its apex on the epic "Tam Lin."

Fairport Convention, *Heyday* (2002, Island). A great collection of late-'60s BBC sessions with the Sandy Denny lineup; the majority are covers never released on Fairport's official albums, like Leonard Cohen's "Suzanne," Gene Clark's "Tried So Hard," Richard Fariña's "Reno, Nevada," and Eric Andersen's "Close the Door Lightly When You Go." These recordings are not as representative of the band's scope as its studio releases are, but they're as good as anything Fairport Convention put out. Try to find the 2002 edition, which added eight extra tracks not on the original 1987 release. There are even more BBC Fairport sessions, though of dubious fidelity, from the late '60s (along with many other rarities from throughout Fairport's career) on the archival box set *Fairport Unconventional*.

The Flying Burrito Brothers, *Hot Burritos! The Flying Burrito Brothers Anthology 1969– 1973* (2000, A&M). You couldn't do much better for a survey of the early work by the Gram Parsons–Chris Hillman lineup of this leading country-rock band. This double CD includes everything from their first two albums, as well as some odds and ends from other compilations and a non-LP single. Note, however, that there's also a good amount of less impressive post-Parsons material on disc two. If you want more consistency, you don't lose much by opting for the single-CD *Sin City: The Very Best of the Flying Burrito Brothers*, whose 25 songs were all cut during the Parsons era, and include every track from the group's first pair of LPs.

Fotheringay, *Fotheringay* (1970, Hannibal). The sole album by Sandy Denny's first post–Fairport Convention project wasn't as good as late-'60s Fairport, but wasn't much worse either, hitting its high point on the lengthy reworking of the traditional folk number "Banks of the Nile." There's more Fotheringay, believe it or not, on bootlegs, *Poems from Alexandra* (with 1970 BBC performances and a few studio outtakes) being the best of them.

The Fugs, *It Crawled into My Hand, Honest* (1968, Edsel). One of the better folk-rock-into-psychedelia records, on both the 16-song suite that comprises side two, and the potpourri of folk-rock and psychedelic, gospel, and country pastiches on side one. It's not currently in print as a separate title, but is included in its entirety on the Rhino Handmade box set *Electromagnetic Steamboat*, a three-CD package including all of their late-'60s recordings from their erratic stint on the Reprise label.

The Gentle Soul, *The Gentle Soul* (1968, Sundazed). Like a mellower, rootsier Stone Poneys, this band's sole album was one of the better exponents of laidback late-'60s Los Angeles folk-rock, with fine harmonies, wistful songs, and some dreamy orchestration. The CD reissue on Sundazed adds nine bonus tracks from non-LP singles and outtakes.

The Gosdin Brothers, *Sounds of Goodbye* (1968, Capitol). A damned obscure, hard-to-locate LP, but a very good one, on the cusp between Byrds-like folk-rock and early country-rock. Anyone who likes Gene Clark's songs on Byrds albums and his first solo album will enjoy this as well, so similar is some of the reticent, vulnerable sadness to the material and its execution.

Davy Graham, *Folk Blues and All Points in Between* (1985, See For Miles). This well-selected overview of his 1960s work emphasizes his 1965 album *Folk, Blues and Beyond*, on which he combined blues, folk, Indian, Middle Eastern, and jazz music, working with a rhythm section. Though not quite folk-rock, it anticipated much of what colored arrangements by British folk-rockers like the Pentangle. The post-1965 material is good too, including blues, the Indian-heavy "Blue Raga," and a most idiosyncratic cover of Joni Mitchell's "Both Sides Now."

The Grateful Dead, *Workingman's Dead* (1970, Warner Brothers). The first Dead album with a folk-rock focus was one of its best, approximating the sound of Crosby, Stills & Nash on "Uncle John's Band," with the Jerry Garcia–Robert Hunter songwriting partnership hitting its Americana stride throughout the disc.

The Grateful Dead, *American Beauty* (1970, Warner Brothers). Although similar to its predecessor *Workingman's Dead*, *American Beauty* had more songs that became well-known staples of the group's repertoire: "Box of Rain," "Sugar Magnolia," "Ripple," "Truckin'," and "Friend of the Devil." For a more complete Grateful Dead experience, note that all of their studio albums and most of their live albums through the early '70s, plus a bunch of studio outtakes and live recordings stretching as far back as 1965, are found on Rhino's mammoth 12-CD box set *The Golden Road*, which speckles folk-rock throughout to varying extents.

Guilbeau & Parsons, *Louisiana Rain* (2002, Big Beat). A nifty 25-track scoop of odds and ends that Gib Guilbeau and Gene Parsons recorded, either as the duo Guilbeau & Parsons or on sessions credited to other artists, circa the mid-to-late 1960s. Much of this was recorded just prior to or around the same time the Byrds and the Flying Burrito Brothers were embracing country-rock, though it's gotten far less attention. And much of it sounds rather similar to the country-rock of the late-'60s Byrds, Gene Clark, and Flying Burrito Brothers, mixing folk-rock, Bakersfield country music, and some Cajun and R&B.

Arlo Guthrie, *Running Down the Road* (1969, Koch). Guthrie's first full rock album was an uneven mix of originals and Pete Seeger, Woody Guthrie, and Mississippi John Hurt songs, but included his most effective 1960s rock recordings in the skittering title track and the famous "Coming in to Los Angeles." The yet more famous "Alice's Restaurant Massacree" is on his 1967 debut, *Alice's Restaurant*.

Tim Hardin, *Hang on to a Dream: The Verve Recordings* (1994, Polygram). Hardin, for all his influence, only recorded three studio albums during the 1960s. The first and best two of those, *Tim Hardin 1* and *Tim Hardin 2*, are found on the first disc of this set; the second disc features mid-'60s demos, some from as early as May 1964, that are largely given over to blues, illustrating his first excursions into electric music. There is additional material of merit to be found on the various demo and live albums Hardin put out in the 1960s, as well as 1969's *Suite for Susan Moore and Damion: We Are One, One, All in One*. But the first disc of this set contains what is inarguably his most focused work, including "If I Were a Carpenter," "How Can We Hang on to a Dream," "Misty Roses," "Lady Came from Baltimore," and "Reason to Believe."

Roy Harper, *Stormcock* (1971, Science Friction). Although this is a little bit beyond the outer edge of this book's self-imposed chronological boundaries, it's worthy of note as it's similar to Harper's earlier work, but better and more focused. Consisting wholly of four lengthy tracks, the guitar playing on this moody set was extraordinary, especially on "The Same Old Rock," where the lead was taken by one S. Flavius Mercurius, who was actually Jimmy Page helping out under a pseudonym.

George Harrison, *Beware of ABKCO!* (1994, Strawberry, bootleg). Ever wonder what *All Things Must Pass* might have sounded like unplugged? This collection of 15 solo George Harrison demos, often on acoustic guitar, gives an indication. Many of these songs didn't end up on *All Things Must Pass*, actually, but they do often show the just-ex-Beatle at his folkiest and most Band-Dylan-influenced.

Richie Havens, *20th Century Masters—The Millennium Collection: The Best of Richie Havens* (2000, Polydor). A rather brief (12-track) but serviceable overview of his late-'60s work, including "Handsome Johnny," "High Flyin' Bird," and some Dylan and Beatles covers. There's no "Freedom," but that's better heard on the *Woodstock* soundtrack anyway.

Hearts and Flowers, *The Complete Hearts and Flowers Collection* (2002, Collectors' Choice Music). Both of their late-'60s albums and a dozen previously unissued outtakes are combined onto this double-CD set. For the most part it's decent early country-folk-rock, highlighted by their cover of Jesse Kincaid's "She Sang Hymns Out of Tune" and their out-of-character psychedelic tour de force "Ode to a Tin Angel."

Dan Hicks, *Early Muses* (1998, Big Beat). Previously unreleased demos from 1967 and 1968 that link the more psychedelic work of his first band, the Charlatans, with the droll faux Western swing of his solo recordings. These songs are as witty as any low-key psych-folk, with unusual, appealing minor-key melodies that spin off in unexpected tangents.

The Holy Modal Rounders, *The Moray Eels Eat the Holy Modal Rounders* (1968, Water). Folk-rock-psychedelia at its most fractured, on a recording that even the participants admit was disorganized in the extreme. In most cases, that leads to messy, hard-to-hear indulgence. In rare cases, such as this one, it led to inspired lunacy.

Janis Ian, *Society's Child: The Verve Recordings* (1995, Polydor). While hearing all of her first four albums at once might seem excessive if you're not a devoted fan, actually the price of this two-CD set—which has everything from those records—isn't that much more than a single-disc 1960s best-of would entail. These albums were better than some critics have made them out to be, too, with more shades of soul and blues than some have admitted.

The Incredible String Band, *5000 Spirits or the Layers of the Onion/The Hangman's Beautiful Daughter* (2002, Collectors' Choice Music). This double CD combines the group's most popular albums into one package. *The Hangman's Beautiful Daughter* (1968), a Top Five LP in the UK, had its most psychedelic-informed world-folk whimsy, though a reasonable argument could be made for preferring 1967's *The 5000 Spirits or the Layers of the Onion*, which included the Incredibles' most acclaimed song, "First Girl I Loved."

The Incredible String Band, *U* (1970, Collectors' Choice Music). Perhaps a double LP (now a double CD) adding up to almost two hours is too much to take even for Incredible String Band fans. Yet even though this only sprung into being as the soundtrack of sorts to the ISB's ambitious multimedia stage production *U*, it was actually for the most part among the band's most listenable material, rewarding patient admirers. While "The Juggler's Song" had the sort of medieval minstrelsy that audiences had come to expect, this album's more unexpected instrumental excursions with sitar and electric guitar counted among the ISB's most far-reaching and experimental endeavors.

Jefferson Airplane, *Takes Off* (1966, RCA). The band's first album was a bit thin-sounding, but certainly its most folk-rock-fueled, with good early originals like "It's No Secret" and "Blues from an Airplane," and a cover of Dino Valenti's "Let's Get Together." The CD reissue includes both the stereo and mono versions, and restores a song, "Runnin' 'Round This World," that was chopped off most pressings of the LP.

Jefferson Airplane, *Surrealistic Pillow* (1967, RCA). The greatest San Francisco 1960s psychedelic rock record also had a lot more folk-rock than is usually acknowledged, like "D.C.B.A-25" and the superb ballad "Today," alongside the hits "White Rabbit" and "Somebody to Love."

Jefferson Airplane, *Jefferson Airplane Loves You* (1992, RCA). Excellent three-CD box set includes most of the Airplane's top tracks, as well as some rarities, and rounds out the band's early folk-rock phase with its more psychedelic and hard-rock-oriented work. Some other good early folk-rock outtakes, like the late-1965 studio version of "High Flyin' Bird" and the Skip Spence composition "J.P.P. McStep B. Blues," can be heard on the rarities compilation *Early Flight*.

The Johnstons, *Give a Damn/Bitter Green* (1997, Castle). A two-for-one CD reissue of the late-'60s Johnstons albums to feature contemporary material, though 1969's *Bitter Green* did have some traditional folk as well. This Irish folk-rock group might not have had as much depth as Fairport Convention, but there were pleasing similarities in the way it interpreted writers like Joni Mitchell and Leonard Cohen, with its version of Cohen's "The Story of Isaac" rating as an overlooked gem.

Kaleidoscope, *Blues from Baghdad: The Very Best of Kaleidoscope* (1995, Edsel). A fine 78-minute compilation of the band whose folk-rock eclecticism was unmatched, including the best of both its relatively short, succinct tracks and its psychedelic–Middle Eastern jams. Unfortunately the best of those lengthy excursions, "Taxim," is missing here, but you can find it on Kaleidoscope's second album, *A Beacon from Mars*.

Gordon Lightfoot, *The United Artists Collection* (1993, EMI). Lightfoot might not have been among the more exciting 1960s folk-rock singer-songwriters, but he was very consistent, as demonstrated by this two-CD set, which contains all four of his 1960s studio albums. The early standards "Early Mornin' Rain," "I'm Not Sayin'," "For Lovin' Me," and "The Way I Feel" are all here, as are first-rate lesser-known tunes like "Black Day in July," "Ribbon of Darkness," and "Pussywillows, Cat-Tails."

Love, *Forever Changes* (1967, Rhino). One of the great 1960s rock albums, and the greatest folk-rock-psychedelic fusion, albeit with glimmering strings and horns rather than the usual masses of distorted guitars and effects. Arthur Lee's songs were magical and timeless, and Bryan MacLean's "Alone Again Or" was Love's best track. The Rhino CD reissue adds various peripheral bonus cuts, including a 1968 non-LP single and previously unissued alternate takes.

Love, *Love Story 1966–1972* (1995, Rhino). A double-CD compilation that includes everything from *Forever Changes*, most (but not everything) from the 1966 debut *Love*, and all of the good material from the band's second album, *Da Capo*, which was great music though it was less strongly folk-rock–based than the other recordings by the group's first incarnation. The post–Bryan MacLean–era material is a bore, though. The two Sundazed CDs of MacLean acoustic demos, *ifyoubelievein* and *Candy's Waltz*, are recommended further listening, though much of the material was recorded after the 1960s.

The Lovin' Spoonful, *Greatest Hits* (2000, Buddha). Though a major folk-rock group, the Lovin' Spoonful's albums were patchy enough to make a best-of the preferred point of entry. And *Greatest Hits* is the best best-of, its 26 tracks including all of their hit singles, as well as outstanding album tracks like "Younger Girl."

The Mamas & the Papas, *Creeque Alley* (1991, MCA). Like the Lovin' Spoonful, the Mamas & the Papas' best output can be succinctly boiled down to a good best-of that serves them better than their individual albums. The two-CD *Creeque Alley* does this, including all of their hit singles, outstanding B-sides and LP tracks like "Got a Feelin'," some pre–Mamas & the Papas cuts by the Big Three and the Mugwumps, and some post–Mamas & the Papas solo efforts.

Melanie, *Melanie* (1969, Castle). Her best individual album, worth risking glares from hipper-than-thou record clerks for the fairly strong combination of folk-rock singer-songwriting with earthy white soul, pop, and darkly comic, theatrical inclinations. For a more rounded view of her output, there's the Rhino compilation *The Best of Melanie*, with her Woodstock-inspired hit "Lay Down (Candles in the Rain)" and the highly underrated, anguished epic ballad "Leftover Wine."

Joni Mitchell, *Joni Mitchell* (1968, Reprise). Delicate to the point where its very fragility creates a tension of its own, this is not usually as highly regarded among critics as is her work of the 1970s. Yet it was a beautiful, entrancing, and haunting album, packed with good-to-great songs, including "Michael from Mountains," "Night in the City," "Marcie," and "Nathan La Freneer."

Joni Mitchell, *Clouds* (1969, Reprise). Mitchell's voice and production headed more toward the singer-songwriting mainstream on her second album, though still without standard rock accompaniment. Some of her best songs were here, like "Chelsea Morning," "Both Sides Now," and "I Don't Know Where I Stand."

Joni Mitchell, *Second Fret Sides: 1966–1968* (Wild Wolf, bootleg). There are plenty of late-'60s unreleased Joni Mitchell live tapes floating around, most of them quite good, if not always of the greatest fidelity. This two-CD bootleg has some of the best of them, including some songs she never put on her official albums (like "Eastern Rain"), and fine, more minimally and folkily arranged performances of familiar classics like "Both Sides Now," "Chelsea Morning," and "The Circle Game."

Fred Neil, *The Many Sides of Fred Neil* (1998, Collectors' Choice Music). This two-CD set contains all three of his Capitol albums, as well as half a dozen previously unreleased outtakes. Certainly the first of those albums, *Fred Neil*, stands as his greatest record, including "Everybody's Talkin'" and other wonderful songs like "The Dolphins." The rest of the material is not up to the standard of that LP, but is still worth a listen.

Michael Nesmith and the First National Band, *Magnetic South* (1970, Pacific Arts). Nesmith's first entirely serious full-length album statement was quality, dignified country-rock, with some of the finest steel guitar (by Red Rhodes) heard in the genre. If it got a little sleepy at times, there was also some sly breezy humor to cuts like "Calico Girlfriend," and of course the irresistible yodeling hit "Joanne."

Nico, *Chelsea Girl* (1967, Polydor). A high point in avant-folk-rock, even if there were few electric guitars, no drums, and the singer herself vehemently disowned it in subsequent interviews. Cool string arrangements, deep-voiced seductress vocals (though admittedly not for everyone), and good, often otherwise unavailable songs by Lou Reed, Jackson Browne, Bob Dylan, John Cale, and Tim Hardin.

The Nitty Gritty Dirt Band, *Uncle Charlie & His Dog Teddy* (1970, Liberty). The group's versatile country-folk-rock breakthrough was highlighted by its mega-smash cover of Jerry Jeff

Walker's "Mr. Bojangles," but also included worthy interpretations of songs by Mike Nesmith, Randy Newman, and Buddy Holly, all done with a multi-instrumentalist aesthetic that would do the New Lost City Ramblers proud.

Phil Ochs, *Farewells & Fantasies* (1997, Elektra). A bit pricey for an anthology, perhaps, but this three-CD box set does a good job of covering highlights from both his acoustic and electric periods. Some rarities are here too, the most important of them being the 1966 electric rock version of "I Ain't Marching Anymore," released only on a UK 45 and *Sing Out!* flexi-disc at the time.

Phil Ochs, *Pleasures of the Harbor* (1967, Collectors' Choice Music). Ochs's first and best rock album, though like all of his rock records, its eclecticism was inconsistent. "Outside of a Small Circle of Friends" was his most famous song (and should have been a hit single), while "The Party" was one of his most outstanding long narratives, and "Flower Lady" among his best melodies.

Tom Paxton, *The Best of Tom Paxton* (1999, Elektra). A smartly-chosen, good-value (26 songs) single CD compiling his 1964–71 recordings for Elektra. It's true that his late-'60s electric albums are lightly represented, but this does include the songs for which he's most famous: "The Last Thing on My Mind," "Ramblin' Boy," "I Can't Help But Wonder Where I'm Bound," "Victoria Dines Alone," "Bottle of Wine," and, yes, "Goin' to the Zoo."

Pearls Before Swine, *One Nation Underground* (1967, Abraxas/ESP-Disk). It's a pretty close call whether this debut or their second album, 1968's *Balaklava*, was the most vital Pearls Before Swine record. Optimally both would be combined onto one CD package. But *One Nation Underground* might have the edge for the inclusion of some of their best inscrutably fragile acid folk tunes, like "Another Time," "I Shall Not Care," "Ballad to an Amber Lady," and "(Oh Dear) Miss Morse," as well as the snarling antiwar screed "Uncle John." *Balaklava* was fairly similar in tone, with a little more production sophistication, though the songs were of a slightly lower caliber.

The Pentangle, *The Pentangle* (1968, Castle). On this fine debut, the Pentangle presented a fully realized fusion of folk, blues, jazz, and miscellany so unprecedented that folk-rock was the only label that fit. "Bruton Town" and "Let No Man Steal Your Thyme" were outstanding traditional folk interpretations, and "Pentangling" a mighty instrumental showcase for the band's virtuosos.

The Pentangle, *Sweet Child* (1968, Castle). This double album was divided between a concert set and a studio one, its range of repertoire probably unmatched by any other act of the time. It was the studio part, though, that was the better half, particularly on "In Time," one of the great guitar-based instrumentals by anyone, Bert Jansch and John Renbourn both flashing their best wares.

The Pentangle, *Basket of Light* (1969, Castle). The group's third album was its best overall, with the small UK hit single "Light Flight" and some of its best covers ("Once I Had a Sweetheart," "Sally Go 'Round the Roses") and originals ("Springtime Promises"). Like all of the Pentangle Castle CD reissues, it includes some non-LP bonus tracks and alternates cut around the same time.

Linda Perhacs, *Parallelograms* (1970, The Wild Places). One of the most obscure releases listed in this discography, and certainly one of the hardest to describe with any convenient reference points, other than to peg Perhacs as kind of an acid folk Joni Mitchell. Although perhaps too lyrically fanciful in a hippie sort of way for some hard-nosed listeners, it was an inventive record, particularly in its harmonics, with a lovely if subdued strangeness.

Peter, Paul & Mary, *Ten Years Together: The Best of Peter, Paul & Mary* (1970, Warner Brothers). Indeed this has the best of their records from both the early '60s folk boom and the later 1960s folk-rock era. From the former, we hear "Blowin' in the Wind," "If I Had a Hammer," and "Don't Think Twice, It's All Right"; from the latter, there's "I Dig Rock & Roll Music" and Dylan's "Too Much of Nothing"; and there are also the Gordon Lightfoot covers "For Lovin' Me" and "Early Mornin' Rain."

Poco, *Pick Up the Pieces* (1969, Epic/Legacy). Country-rock at its most folk-rock-influenced and wholesome, which is not a knock, but actually a hearty endorsement. This was also the best showcase for Richie Furay's talents as a singer and songwriter, with lots of help from his cohorts.

Quicksilver Messenger Service, *Quicksilver Messenger Service* (1968, Capitol). Although this album is more remembered for the lengthy psychedelic guitar showcases "The Fool" and "Gold and Silver," actually the majority of it was devoted to concise, melodic folk-rock with that peculiarly bittersweet San Francisco flavor. "Pride of Man" remains one of the greatest folk-rock rearrangements of a song originally written and performed (by Hamilton Camp) as a straightforward acoustic folk tune.

Tom Rush, *The Circle Game* (1968, Elektra). Rush's best moment on record was also an important forum for early singer-songwriters Joni Mitchell, Jackson Browne, and James Taylor, none of whom were well known when he placed covers of some of their compositions onto his final Elektra album.

Buffy Sainte-Marie, *The Best of Buffy Sainte-Marie* (1970, Vanguard). This 24-song survey of her early work includes most of the songs she's most famous for (and that were frequently covered, by folk-rockers and others): "Codine," "Universal Soldier," "Until It's Time for You to Go," "My Country 'Tis Of Thy People You're Dying," and "Now That the Buffalo's Gone." Plus there's her most concentrated effort to crack the folk-rock singles market, a cover of Joni Mitchell's "The Circle Game."

Satya Sai Maitreya Kali, *Apache/Inca* (2000, Normal/Shadoks). Although Satya Sai Maitreya Kali, as Craig Smith billed himself, put out these two albums in the early '70s, it's actually a mishmash of 1967 sessions cut by his folk-rock group the Penny Arkade and some later solo Smith recordings. It's quality acid-folk-rock, approaching a midpoint between Buffalo Springfield and the Monkees on the most accessible Penny Arkade tunes, reminiscent of acid folkies Skip Spence and Dino Valenti on the weird solo ones. Both albums are combined into one package on this two-CD reissue.

Simon & Garfunkel, *Live from New York City 1967* (2002, Columbia). A very fine selection indeed of 19 songs from their January 22, 1967 concert at New York's Lincoln Center that serves as a good document of how the duo sounded live, as an acoustic act. It includes hits ("The Sound of Silence," "I Am a Rock," "Homeward Bound," "The 59th Street Bridge Song (Feelin' Groovy)," "A Hazy Shade of Winter") and interesting, less iconic non-hits ("Leaves That Are Green," "Richard Cory"). Unfortunately it omits their version of "Red Rubber Ball" from this show, which surfaced on the box set *Old Friends*.

Simon & Garfunkel, *Bookends* (1968, Columbia). Their best, most incisive album, whether on the hit singles "Mrs. Robinson," "A Hazy Shade of Winter," and "Fakin' It," or the more deliberately constructed first half, with Simon's anthemic "America."

Simon & Garfunkel, *Bridge Over Troubled Water* (1970, Columbia). A little too slick for its own good in some of the arrangements, and certainly further removed from folk-rock than their earlier albums, *Bridge Over Troubled Water* still contained several outstanding songs. The gospel-powered title track was the most famous, but "The Boxer" was better, and "El Condor Pasa (If I Could)" and "Cecilia" hinted at the world music directions Simon would explore in his solo career.

Simon & Garfunkel, *The Columbia Studio Recordings 1964–1970* (2001, Columbia/Legacy). A well-packaged five-CD box set of all of Simon & Garfunkel's studio albums. Even if you have the old LPs, you might find this worth consideration due to the addition of a few bonus tracks, from non-LP cuts and previously unreleased outtakes, tagged onto the end of each album.

Alexander "Skip" Spence, *Oar* (1969, Sundazed). Not just a great cult rock album, but a great album, period, standing as the best fusion of pre-rock folk, blues, and country with psychedelia. Spence's life might have been tragic, but given the circumstances *Oar* was a surprisingly light and humorous record, though with dark undercurrents. The 1999 CD reissue on Sundazed adds numerous outtakes and alternate versions, though none of those are on the same level as the proper album. By the way, Spence billed himself by his given name (Alexander Spence) on this release, but virtually everyone refers to this recording as a Skip Spence album.

Steeleye Span, *Hark! The Village Wait* (1970, Shanachie). Steeleye's debut was less a musical milestone than it was an important indication of the path the more traditional wing of British folk-rock would head down in the 1970s. Of course Maddy Prior's frequent lovely upper-register lead vocals made these rocked-up traditional songs much more than a history lesson, with electric dulcimer, concertina, five-string banjo, and autoharp on hand in addition to electric guitar and bass.

Al Stewart, *To Whom It May Concern 1966–1970* (1993, EMI). All of his first three albums, as well as an early non-LP single, are compiled on this two-disc set. While overly precious at times (as was much of his 1967 debut *Bedsitter Images*, actually), the best songs are among the better late-'60s British singer-songwriter recordings, particularly "Ballad of Mary Foster."

John Stewart & Buffy Ford, *Signals Through the Glass* (1968, Capitol). Stewart fans would argue strenuously for his proper 1969 solo debut *California Bloodlines* as a point of entry. But this far less celebrated effort, with wife Buffy Ford contributing some vocals, was simply more melodic and intriguingly odd, if more uneven. Stewart, the just–ex–Kingston Trio folkie, caught up fast to the changing musical and social currents on mixtures of roots Americana folk, orchestrated sunshine pop, and even mild psychedelic touches with standout tunes like "Nebraska Widow," "Mucky Truckee River," and "Holly on My Mind." The devastatingly understated "Draft Age" captured the dread of Vietnam hanging over America's youth in an especially unnerving fashion.

The Stone Poneys, *The Stone Poneys Featuring Linda Ronstadt* (1967, Capitol). The first of the three Stone Poneys albums was really the only one to feature the band as it originally sounded: a Peter, Paul & Mary with more guts, embroidered by tasteful Nik Venet production and sympathetic session musicians. The other two Stone Poneys albums were solid too, though, particularly *Evergreen Vol. 2*, which had their hit "Different Drum."

The Strawbs, *Strawbs* (1969, A&M). The Strawbs' official debut got a little ponderously somber in songwriting and quasi-medieval arrangements at times, but was still an affecting, intelligent highlight of early British folk-rock, particularly on "The Man Who Called Himself Jesus" and the Gregorian-toned "Where Is This Dream of Your Youth." There's also much good, if folkier, early Strawbs to be found on the double CD of 1966–68 outtakes *Preserves Uncanned*, and the rare odds 'n' ends on *Strawberry Music Sampler No. 1* give us a chance to hear some late-'60s music that didn't make it onto *Strawbs*.

James Taylor, *Sweet Baby James* (1970, Warner Brothers). His 1968 Apple debut *James Taylor* may have been a little less slick. But this was the record that made him the superstar and defined the 1970s singer-songwriter movement, particularly on the hit "Fire and Rain."

Dino Valenti, *Dino Valente* (1968, Koch). Sun-baked hippie folk-rock mysticism shone at its brightest on Valenti's sole solo effort, misspelled *Dino Valente* [sic]. The judicious use of echo complemented the somewhat spaced-out lyrics well, and Valenti made the most of his limited vocal talents with his tender, inquisitive songs, the work of a troubadour trying to guide the hippie flock to both spiritual and sensual fulfillment.

Townes Van Zandt, *For the Sake of the Song* (1968, Rhino). Some would rather file this under country or folk than folk-rock. But for those unfettered by such boundaries, it's fine storytelling, laconically witty country-folk with some rock trimmings in the production. Some find the occasional backup vocals ostentatious, but actually they added a good amount of oddball color, particularly on "The Velvet Voices" and the gloomy, dramatic "Sixteen Summers, Fifteen Falls."

Jerry Jeff Walker, *Mr. Bojangles* (1968, Rhino). Walker's solo debut remains known for the original version of the title track, though it was only a very mild hit single in comparison to the Top Ten cover by the Nitty Gritty Dirt Band a couple of years down the road. Walker's knack for storytelling in song also came through in "Gypsy Songman" and "Little Bird," while "The Ballad of the Hulk" showed his debt to Dylan songs like "Desolation Row." Other interesting early Walker is found on *Best of the Vanguard Years*, which has a demo version of "Mr. Bojangles" and some of the folk-rock he did in his late-'60s band Circus Maximus, with "Oops I Can Dance" sounding especially similar to the mid-'60s Byrds.

Neil Young, *Everybody Knows This Is Nowhere* (1969, Reprise). The album that saw Young come into his own as a solo artist was far more confident than his rather laidback debut, *Neil Young*.

"Cinammon Girl," "Down by the River," and "Cowgirl in the Sand" remain among his best rockers, yet he proved equally capable of wistful near-folk, especially on "Round & Round (It Won't Be Long)."

Neil Young, *After the Gold Rush* (1970, Reprise). The album that made Young a solo singer-songwriter superstar was in much the same spirit as *Everybody Knows This Is Nowhere*, but mellower. "Tell Me Why," "Only Love Can Break Your Heart," and "Don't Let It Bring You Down" all rate among his best songs, and again he proved he could rock hard, if with a bluntness that verged on political incorrectness, with "Southern Man."

Steve Young, *Rock, Salt & Nails* (1969, A&M). One of the finest little-known late-'60s country-rock albums, in large part due to boasting far more serious hues than most records in the style. Young's original songs were convincing fusions of country-rock-folk with blues, soul, gospel, and swamp pop, though some of the covers were less interesting. "Seven Bridges Road," later done by the Eagles, is by far the most famous tune, yet "Holler in the Swamp" and "Kenny's Song" are on the same level, the subtle background strings adding drama without overdoing it. It's been only intermittently available on CD, though you may have better luck finding the 1994 reissue on Edsel than the original A&M LP.

The Youngbloods, *Euphoria 1965–1969* (1998, Raven). This 25-track Australian import might be a bit out of the way, but it's a good compilation of their better songs, among them "Get Together" of course. Numerous other cuts, though, like "Sunlight," "Darkness, Darkness," "Ride the Wind," and "All Over the World (La-La)," are almost as good.

Various Artists, *Casey Kasem Presents America's Top Ten: The 60s—The Folk Years* (2002, Top Sail). This sticks to Top Ten singles exclusively, but contains some of the folk-rock hits most important to spreading the folk-rock gospel to the mainstream: the Byrds' "Mr. Tambourine Man," Barry McGuire's "Eve of Destruction," the Mamas & the Papas' "California Dreamin'," the Lovin' Spoonful's "Daydream," the We Five's "You Were on My Mind," Donovan's "Mellow Yellow," Judy Collins's "Both Sides Now," Scott McKenzie's "San Francisco," and the Youngbloods' "Get Together." It also has the pre–British Invasion folk hit by the Rooftop Singers, "Walk Right In," and folk-pop and pop-rock hits bearing folk-rock influences, like the Seekers' "I'll Never Find Another You" and Harry Nilsson's cover of Fred Neil's "Everybody's Talkin'."

Various Artists, *Heroes of Country Music, Vol. 5: Legends of Country Rock* (1996, Rhino). This 18-song collection isn't an ideal introduction to early country-rock, as licensing restrictions prevented the inclusion of tracks by Buffalo Springfield, the Grateful Dead, Rick Nelson, and some other notables. Still, it has useful cuts by the Byrds, Flying Burrito Brothers, Linda Ronstadt, the International Submarine Band, Hearts and Flowers, Poco, Bob Dylan, Michael Nesmith, and the Nitty Gritty Dirt Band. There are also some country-flavored tracks by acts not normally associated with country-rock (the Lovin' Spoonful, the Everly Brothers, the Youngbloods), though the songs by Pure Prairie League and the Marshall Tucker Band extend and dilute the concept too far into the 1970s.

Various Artists, *The History of UK Underground Folk Rock Vol. 1 & 2* (Kissing Spell). Issued in the 1990s without release dates, these already hard-to-find discs compile mighty little-heard British folk-rock from 1968 to 1978, often from recordings privately pressed in minute quantities, concentrating on the earlier years of that time span. None of these names are familiar—Trees and Mellow Candle are probably the best known, and hardly anyone knows who *they* are. But for anyone who likes the Fairport Convention/Pentangle/Incredible String Band side of things, there are some very cool nuggets to be found here, sometimes in an acid folk state of mind.

Various Artists, *Monterey International Pop Festival Box Set* (1992, Rhino). A four-CD box set of recordings from the 1967 Monterey Pop Festival, including cuts by the Byrds, the Mamas & the Papas, Big Brother & the Holding Company, and Jefferson Airplane. Much of the rest of the set isn't folk-rock (which is not to say the other artists who are featured aren't on the same level), the sound and performances vary from good to mediocre, and there's nothing by Buffalo Springfield, Simon & Garfunkel, and Country Joe & the Fish, though some of their Monterey tracks circulate on bootlegs.

Various Artists, *Nuggets Vol. 7: Early San Francisco* (1985, Rhino). From Rhino's long out-of-print vinyl *Nuggets* series (not to be confused with its recent *Nuggets* 1960s garage box sets), this is a good overview of very early San Francisco folk-rock, with cuts by the Beau Brummels, the Vejtables, the We Five, and the Charlatans, as well as very early psychedelia by Country Joe & the Fish and the Great Society.

Various Artists, *Nuggets Vol. 10: Folk-Rock* (Rhino). An odd mix (from the mid-'80s, though it doesn't bear a release date) of huge folk-rock hits (the Byrds' "Mr. Tambourine Man," the Turtles' "It Ain't Me Babe," Barry McGuire's "Eve of Destruction," Scott McKenzie's "San Francisco"), pop-leaning minor hits (the Sunshine Company's "Back on the Street Again," the Nitty Gritty Dirt Band's "Buy for Me the Rain"), and rarities by Jake Holmes (the original version of "Dazed and Confused"), the Modern Folk Quartet, and the Deep Six.

Various Artists, *Songs of Protest* (1991, Rhino). Although it's only about half folk-rock, this is a good place to pick up on some major hits in the protest folk-rock bag. Barry McGuire's "Eve of Destruction," Sonny Bono's "Laugh at Me," Janis Ian's "Society's Child," Dion's "Abraham, Martin and John," the Turtles' "Let Me Be," Donovan's "Universal Soldier," Phil Ochs's electric version of "I Ain't Marching Anymore," and Country Joe & the Fish's "I-Feel-Like-I'm-Fixin'-to-Die Rag" are all here, as well as the notable early Dylan cover by Manfred Mann, "With God on Our Side."

Various Artists, *Troubadours of British Folk Vol. 1 & 2* (1995, Rhino). While it's true these two volumes span the mid-'50s to the mid-'70s, and are only partially comprised of folk-rock, they do include representative tracks by important British folk-rock figures Donovan, the Pentangle, the Incredible String Band, Fairport Convention, Fotheringay, Steeleye Span, Nick Drake, Roy Harper, Davy Graham, and Ralph McTell, as well as Traffic's "John Barleycorn." There are also important sides by folk performers who were major influences on British folk-rock: Ewan MacColl, Lonnie Donegan, Martin Carthy, Anne Briggs, the Young Tradition, Shirley Collins, and others.

Various Artists, *Washington Square Memoirs: The Great Urban Folk Boom 1950–1970* (2001, Rhino). Less than a third of this is genuine folk-rock, but this three-CD box set is a great way to follow the transition of urban folk from its just–post–World World II manifestation through the early '60s folk boom to the onset of folk-rock. Many major North American folk performers of the period, or folk-rock performers of the era with heavy roots in the folk boom, are represented here, including Bob Dylan, Ian & Sylvia, Judy Collins, Judy Henske, Richie Havens, Tim Hardin, Gordon Lightfoot, Richard & Mimi Fariña, Phil Ochs, Fred Neil, Tim Buckley, Buffy Sainte-Marie, Arlo Guthrie, Barry McGuire (as part of Barry & Barry), and Jesse Colin Young.

Various Artists, *Woodstock: Three Days of Peace & Music* (1994, Atlantic). After the appearance of the chart-topping three-LP *Woodstock* set in 1970, there have been enough subsequent packages containing additional/similar music to confuse even the most dedicated record-buyer. This four-CD box set has most or all of what you need, for performances both within and beyond the folk-rock style. Folk-rockers are amply represented, naturally, by Crosby, Stills, Nash & Young, Richie Havens, John Sebastian, Country Joe McDonald, Melanie, Arlo Guthrie, Tim Hardin, and Jefferson Airplane.

interviewees

．．．．．．．．．．．．．．．．．．．．．．．．．．．．．．．．

ight Miles High draws upon firsthand author interviews with the following musicians, producers, managers, journalists, venue owners, folklorists, filmmakers, and promoters (primary mid-to-late-'60s affiliations noted in parentheses). My thanks go to:

Lou Adler (producer, the Mamas & the Papas and Barry McGuire)

Peter Albin (Big Brother & the Holding Company)

David Anderle (producer, Judy Collins and David Ackles)

Eric Andersen

Ian Anderson (British musician, present-day editor of *fRoots* magazine)

Peter Asher (producer/manager, James Taylor and Linda Ronstadt)

Larry Beckett (songwriting partner of Tim Buckley)

Joel Bernstein (photographer, Joni Mitchell and Crosby, Stills, Nash & Young; guitar technician, Joni Mitchell; archivist, Joni Mitchell and Neil Young)

Steve Boone (the Lovin' Spoonful)

Bruce Botnick (engineer/producer, Elektra Records)

Joe Boyd (producer, Fairport Convention, the Incredible String Band, Nick Drake, John & Beverley Martyn, and Fotheringay)

Denny Bruce (producer, John Fahey)

Tom Campbell

Judy Collins

Shirley Collins

Gerry Conway (Eclection, Fotheringay)

Dave Cousins (the Strawbs)

Chester Crill (Kaleidoscope)

Chris Darrow (Kaleidoscope)

ED Denson (manager, Country Joe & the Fish)

Jim Dickson (manager/producer, the Byrds and the Dillards)

Rodney Dillard (the Dillards)

Art D'Lugoff (owner, the Village Gate club, New York City)

Denny Doherty (the Mamas & the Papas)

Jerry Donahue (Fotheringay)

Donovan

Gary Duncan (Quicksilver Messenger Service)

Kenny Edwards (the Stone Poneys)

Andy Ellison (John's Children)

Phil Elwood (music journalist, the *San Francisco Examiner*)

Cyrus Faryar (session guitarist, Fred Neil)

John Forsha (session guitarist, Fred Neil and Tim Buckley)

Pete Frame (administrator, Luton folk club, England; founder, *ZigZag* magazine)

David Freiberg (Quicksilver Messenger Service)

Barry Friedman aka Frazier Mohawk (producer, Kaleidoscope and the Holy Modal Rounders; mentor, Buffalo Springfield)

Richie Furay (Buffalo Springfield, Poco)

Steve Gillette

Don Glut (the Penny Arkade)

Arthur Gorson (manager/producer, Phil Ochs, Tom Rush, David Blue, and Jim & Jean)

Vern Gosdin (the Gosdin Brothers)

Stefan Grossman

Arlo Guthrie

Roy Halee (engineer/producer, Simon & Garfunkel)

Judy Henske

Carolyn Hester

Dan Hicks (the Charlatans, Dan Hicks & His Hot Licks)

Chris Hillman (the Byrds, the Flying Burrito Brothers)

Jac Holzman (president, Elektra Records)

Ashley Hutchings (Fairport Convention, Steeleye Span)

Janis Ian

Erik Jacobsen (producer, the Lovin' Spoonful, Tim Hardin, and the Charlatans)

Billy James (talent acquisition & development executive, Columbia Records; West Coast director, Elektra Records)

Bob Johnston (producer, Bob Dylan, Simon & Garfunkel, Dino Valenti, Leonard Cohen, the Byrds, and Johnny Cash)

Nat Joseph (founder, Transatlantic Records)

Georg Kajanus aka Georg Hultgreen (Eclection)

Jorma Kaukonen (Jefferson Airplane)

Carol Kaye (session guitarist and bassist, Simon & Garfunkel, Dino Valenti, and others)

Howard Kaylan (the Turtles)

Steve Lalor (the Daily Flash)

Bruce Langhorne (session guitarist, Bob Dylan, Richard & Mimi Fariña, Tom Rush, Fred Neil, Richie Havens, Gordon Lightfoot, Buffy Sainte-Marie, Eric Andersen, John Sebastian, and others)

Murray Lerner (director, Newport Folk Festival documentary film *Festival* and 1970 Isle of Wight Festival documentary film *Message to Love*)

Banana Levinger (the Youngbloods)

Peter Lewis (Moby Grape)

Bob Lind

Mac MacLeod (guitarist, Donovan)

Maury Manseau (the Sunshine Company)

Roy Marinell (the Gentle Soul)

Gary Marker (the Rising Sons)

Iain Matthews (Fairport Convention, Matthews Southern Comfort)

Elliot Mazer (producer, Gordon Lightfoot, Ian & Sylvia, Linda Ronstadt, Richie Havens, Jerry Jeff Walker, and Jake Holmes)

Mary McCaslin

Charlie McCoy (session musician, Bob Dylan)

John McEuen (the Nitty Gritty Dirt Band)

Roger McGuinn (the Byrds)

Barry McGuire

Andrew Means (journalist, *Melody Maker*)

Melanie

Barry Melton (Country Joe & the Fish)

Jim Messina (Buffalo Springfield, Poco)

Mick Moloney (the Johnstons)

Moondog (noted New York City street musician)

Larry Murray (Hearts and Flowers)

Simon Nicol (Fairport Convention)

Michael Ochs (manager, Phil Ochs)

Gene Parsons (the Byrds, Nashville West)

Tom Paxton

Dave Pegg (Fairport Convention)

D.A. Pennebaker (director, Bob Dylan documentary film *Don't Look Back*; cinematographer, Bob Dylan documentary film *Eat the Document*; director, 1967 Monterey Pop Festival documentary film *Monterey Pop*)

Linda Perhacs

Shawn Phillips

Pamela Polland (the Gentle Soul)

Duffy Power

Tom Rapp (Pearls Before Swine)

John Renbourn (the Pentangle)

Joshua Rifkin (arranger, Judy Collins)

Tim Rose

David Rubinson (producer, Columbia Records)

Tom Rush

Buffy Sainte-Marie

Jerry Schoenbaum (executive, Verve/Folkways and Verve/Forecast Records)

Richard Scott (the Blue Things)

John Sebastian (the Lovin' Spoonful)

Gene Shay (folk radio program host, WHAT and WDAS in Philadelphia)

Corky Siegel (the Siegel-Schwall Band)

Irwin Silber (editor, *Sing Out!* magazine)
John Simon (producer, the Band, Leonard
    Cohen, Gordon Lightfoot, Simon &
    Garfunkel, and Carolyn Hester)
Sherry Snow aka Halimah Collingwood (Black-
    burn & Snow)
Howard Solomon (owner, the Cafe Au Go Go
    club, New York City)
Peter Stampfel (the Holy Modal Rounders)
Shel Talmy (producer, the Pentangle,
    Roy Harper)
Bernie Taupin (lyricist, Elton John)
Danny Thompson (the Pentangle)
Happy Traum
Sylvia Tyson (Ian & Sylvia)
Jerry Jeff Walker

John Ware (Michael Nesmith & the First
    National Band)
Dean Webb (the Dillards)
Dick Weissman (session guitarist and banjoist,
    Scott McKenzie)
Frank Werber (manager/producer, Blackburn
    & Snow and the We Five)
Robin Williamson (the Incredible String Band)
John Wood (engineer, Fairport Convention,
    Nick Drake, the Incredible String Band,
    John Martyn, the Johnstons, and Bert
    Jansch)
Peter Yarrow (Peter, Paul & Mary)
Jerry Yester (the Lovin' Spoonful, Judy Henske
    & Jerry Yester; producer, Tim Buckley)
Steve Young

bibliography

Abbott, Kingsley. *Fairportfolio: Personal Recollections of Fairport Convention from the 1967–1969 Era*. Norfolk, England: SK Productions, 1997.

Alpert, Jane. *Growing Up Underground*. New York: William Morrow & Co., 1981.

Barker, Derek, ed. *Isis: A Bob Dylan Anthology*. London: Helter Skelter Publishing, 2002.

Beatles, The. *The Beatles Anthology*. San Francisco: Chronicle Books, 2000.

Brend, Mark. *American Troubadours: Groundbreaking Singer Songwriters of the 60s*. San Francisco: Backbeat Books, 2001.

Browne, David. *Dream Brother: The Lives and Music of Jeff and Tim Buckley*. New York: Harper Entertainment, 2001.

Brunning, Bob. *Blues: The British Connection*. Poole, England: Blandford Press, 1986.

Cable, Paul. *Bob Dylan: His Unreleased Recordings*. New York: Schirmer, 1978.

Colby, Paul, with Martin Fitzpatrick. *The Bitter End: Hanging Out at America's Nightclub*. New York: Cooper Square Press, 2002.

Collins, Judy. *Singing Lessons: A Memoir of Love, Loss, Hope, and Healing*. New York: Pocket Books, 1998.

Cornyn, Stan, with Paul Scanlon. *Exploding: The Highs, Hits, Hype, Heroes, and Hustlers of the Warner Music Group*. New York: Harper Entertainment, 2002.

DeCurtis, Anthony, and James Henke with Holly George-Warren, eds., original editor Jim Miller. *The Rolling Stone Illustrated History of Rock & Roll*. New York: Random House, 1992.

Doggett, Peter. *Are You Ready for the Country: Elvis, Dylan, Parsons and the Roots of Country Rock*. New York: Penguin Books, 2000.

Dunaway, David. *Pete Seeger: How Can I Keep from Singing*. New York: Da Capo Press, 1981.

Echols, Alice. *Scars of Sweet Paradise: The Life and Times of Janis Joplin*. New York: Metropolitan Books, 1999.

Einarson, John. *Desperados: The Roots of Country Rock*. New York: Cooper Square Press, 2001.

Einarson, John, and Richie Furay. *There's Something Happening Here: The Story of Buffalo Springfield: For What It's Worth*. Kingston, Canada: Quarry Press, 1997.

Eliot, Marc. *Death of a Rebel: A Biography of Phil Ochs*. New York: Franklin Watts, 1989.

Engelhardt, Kristofer. *Beatles Undercover*. Burlington, Canada: Collector's Guide Publishing Inc., 1998.

Fonda, Peter. *Don't Tell Dad: A Memoir*. New York: Hyperion, 1998.

Fong-Torres, Ben. *Hickory Wind: The Life and Times of Gram Parsons*. New York: St. Martin's Griffin, 1998.

———. *Not Fade Away: A Backstage Pass to 20 Years of Rock & Roll*. San Francisco: Backbeat Books, 1999.

Frame, Pete. *The Complete Rock Family Trees*. New York: Omnibus Press, 1980.

———. *More Rock Family Trees*. New York: Omnibus Press, 1998.

Gill, Andy. *Don't Think Twice, It's All Right: Bob Dylan, the Early Years*. New York: Thunder's Mouth Press, 1998.

Gleason, Ralph J. *The Jefferson Airplane and the San Francisco Sound*. New York: Ballantine Books, 1969.

Graham, Bill and Robert Greenfield. *Bill Graham Presents: My Life Inside Rock and Out*. New York: Doubleday, 1992.

Grant, Lee, with the Original Dillards. *Everybody on the Truck! The Story of the Dillards*. Nashville, TN: Eggman Publishing, 1995.

Gray, Michael, and John Bauldie, eds. *All Across the Telegraph: A Bob Dylan Handbook*. London: Futura Publications, 1988.

Green, Jonathon. *Days in the Life: Voices from the English Underground 1961–1971*. London: Pimlico, 1998.

Greenwald, Matthew. *Go Where You Wanna Go: The Oral History of the Mamas & the Papas*. New York: Cooper Square Press, 2002.

Griffin, Sid. *Gram Parsons: A Music Biography*. Pasadena, CA: Sierra Records & Books, 1985.

Hajdu, David. *Positively 4th Street: The Lives and Times of Joan Baez, Bob Dylan, Mimi Baez Fariña and Richard Fariña*. New York: Farrar, Straux and Giroux, 2001.

Harper, Colin. *Dazzling Stranger: Bert Jansch & the British Folk and Blues Revival*. London: Bloomsbury Publishing, 2000.

Havens, Richie, with Steve Davidowitz. *They Can't Hide Us Anymore*. New York: Spike Books, 1999.

Helm, Levon. *This Wheel's on Fire: Levon Helm and the Story of the Band*. New York: William Morrow, 1993.

Heylin, Clinton. *Bob Dylan: A Life in Stolen Moments: Day By Day: 1941–1995*. New York: Schirmer Books, 1996.

———. *Bob Dylan: Behind the Shades: The Biography—Take Two*. London: Viking, 2000.

———. *Bob Dylan: The Recording Sessions 1960–1994*. New York: St. Martin's Press, 1996.

———. *Bootleg: The Secret History of the Other Recording Industry*. New York: St. Martin's Press, 1994.

———. *No More Sad Refrains: The Life and Times of Sandy Denny*. London: Helter Skelter Publishing, 2000.

Hinton, Brian. *Message to Love: The Isle of Wight Festival 1968–1969–1970*. Chessington, England: Castle Communications, 1995.

Hinton, Brian, and Geoff Wall. *Ashley Hutchings: The Guv'Nor & the Rise of Folk-Rock*. London: Helter Skelter Publishing, 2002.

Holzman, Jac, and Gavan Daws. *Follow the Music: The Life and High Times of Elektra Records in the Great Years of American Pop Culture*. Santa Monica, CA: FirstMedia Books, 1998.

Hoskyns, Barney. *Across the Great Divide: The Band and America*. New York: Hyperion, 1993.

———. *Waiting for the Sun: Strange Days, Weird Scenes, and the Sound of Los Angeles*. New York: St. Martin's Press, 1996.

Humphries, Patrick. *Nick Drake: The Biography*. London: Bloomsbury Publishing, 1997.

———. *Paul Simon*. New York: Doubleday, 1988.

Jahn, Mike. *Rock*. New York: Quadrangle Press, 1973.

Jennings, Nicholas. *Before the Gold Rush: Flashbacks to the Dawn of the Canadian Sound*. Toronto: Penguin Books, 1997.

Kooper, Al. *Backstage Passes & Backstabbing Bastards*. New York: Billboard Books, 1998.

Lee, C.P. *Like the Night: Bob Dylan and the Road to the Manchester Free Trade Hall*. London: Helter Skelter Publishing, 1998.

Lefcowitz, Eric. *The Monkees Tale*. Berkeley, CA: Last Gasp, 1985.

Lewisohn, Mark. *The Complete Beatles Chronicle*. New York: Harmony Books, 1992.

Makower, Joel. *Woodstock: The Oral History*. New York: Doubleday, 1989.

Marsh, Dave with John Swenson, eds. *The Rolling Stone Record Guide*. New York: Rolling Stone Press, 1979.

McDermott, John, with Eddie Kramer. *Hendrix: Setting the Record Straight*. New York: Warner Books, 1992.

McDonough, Jimmy. *Shakey: Neil Young's Biography*. New York: Random House, 2002.

McNally, Dennis. *A Long Strange Trip: The Inside History of the Grateful Dead*. New York: Broadway Books, 2002.

Miles, Barry. *Paul McCartney: Many Years from Now*. New York: Henry Holt & Co., 1997.

Nadel, Ira B. *Various Positions: A Life of Leonard Cohen*. New York: Pantheon Books, 1996.

O'Brien, Karen. *Joni Mitchell: Shadows and Light: The Definitive Biography*. London: Virgin Books, 2001.

Perry, Charles. *The Haight-Ashbury: A History*. New York: Vintage Books, 1985.

Phillips, John, with Jim Jerome. *Papa John*. Garden City, NY: Dolphin Books, 1986.

Phillips, Michelle. *California Dreamin'*. New York: Warner Books, 1986.

Riordan, James, and Jerry Prochnicky. *The Life and Death of Jim Morrison: Break on Through*. New York: William Morrow & Co., 1991.

Roby, Steven. *Black Gold: The Lost Archives of Jimi Hendrix*. New York: Billboard Books, 2002.

Rogan, Johnny. *Crosby, Stills, Nash & Young: The Visual Documentary*. New York: Omnibus Press, 1996.

———. *Neil Young: Zero to Sixty: A Critical Biography*. London: Calidore Books, 2000.

———. *The Byrds: Timeless Flight Revisited: The Sequel*. London: Rogan House, 1997.

Rooney, James. *Bossmen: Bill Monroe & Muddy Waters*. New York: Da Capo Press, 1971.

Rowe, Barbara. *Grace Slick: The Biography*. New York: Doubleday & Co., 1980.

Roxon, Lillian. *Lillian Roxon's Rock Encyclopedia*. New York: Tempo Books, 1971.

Russo, Greg. *Mannerisms: The Five Phases of Manfred Mann*. Floral Park, NY: Crossfire Publications, 1995.

Scaduto, Anthony. *Bob Dylan: An Intimate Biography*. New York: Grosset and Dunlap, 1971.

Schumacher, Michael. *There But for Fortune: A Life of Phil Ochs*. New York: Hyperion, 1996.

Selvin, Joel. *Summer of Love*. New York: Dutton, 1994.

Shapiro, Harry. *Alexis Korner*. London: Bloomsbury Publishing, 1996.

Shelton, Robert. *No Direction Home: The Life and Music of Bob Dylan*. New York: Beech Tree Books, 1986.

Sounes, Howard. *Down the Highway: The Life of Bob Dylan*. New York: Grove Press, 2001.

Turner, Steve. *A Hard Day's Write: The Stories Behind Every Beatles' Song*. New York: Harper-Perennial, 1994.

Walker, Jerry Jeff. *Gypsy Songman*. Emeryville, CA: Woodford Press, 1999.

White, Timothy. *Long Ago and Far Away: James Taylor: His Life and Music*. New York: Omnibus Press, 2001.

Wiseman, Rich. *Jackson Browne: The Story of a Hold Out*. Garden City, NY: Doubleday, 1982.

Witts, Richard. *Nico: The Life & Lies of an Icon*. London: Virgin Books, 1993.

Woliver, Robbie. *Bringing It All Back Home: Twenty-Five Years of American Music at Folk City*. New York: Pantheon Books, 1986.

Zimmer, Dave. *Crosby, Stills & Nash: The Authorized Biography*. New York: St. Martin's Press, 1984.

acknowledgments

When I decided to write the history of 1960s folk-rock, I had the feeling that I would face the most daunting writing project I had ever undertaken. I was right. Over the three years it has taken to research and write *Eight Miles High* and its preceding volume, *Turn! Turn! Turn!*, dozens of friends, fans, fellow writers, and music professionals have provided vital contact information, assistance in setting up interviews, rare recordings and videos, leads to unearthed information, and just plain moral support. This book could not have been completed without their help.

Special thanks go to those friends who let me stay in their homes on my out-of-town research trips. Susan Mallett and Curt Lamberth cheerfully gave me accommodation and other amenities in their house in Oxford, England, as they have for other lengthy stays while I have worked on other books. In New York, Jason Gross and Bob Maresca were second-time-around hosts for book-related sojourns, as were Gordon Anderson and Lisa Kotin in Los Angeles. In London, Nora McCormick and Dana Mayer made me welcome to stay in their flats while I worked in that city.

In the San Francisco Bay Area, extra-special thanks go to these fellow folk-rock fanatics who spent many hours discussing, playing, and displaying items in their archives that I would never have heard or located otherwise: Joel Bernstein, Alec Palao, and Pat Thomas. In London, Ian Anderson of *fRoots* magazine generously allowed me to look through his office's large collection of 1960s folk periodicals. Jeff Davis of Flat Plastic Sound in San Francisco let me borrow numerous recordings, many of them out of print and hard to find.

Many thanks as well to all of the following individuals for their help with acquiring music, interviews, and other useful information, often going to great lengths to make sure I had copies of numerous rarities and the contacts I needed: Rene Aagaard, Gene Aguilera, Jim Allen, Bill Allerton of Stand Out Records in London, Ken Barnes, Mike Barnes, Joel Bellman, Bill Belmont, Jeroen Berkvens, Sean Body, Pirmin Bossart, Paul Bradshaw of Mod Lang Records in Berkeley, Denny Bruce, Ron Cabral, Richard Campbell, Phil Carson, Bruce Carter, Chris Charlesworth, Douglas Cooke, Jud Cost, Steve Davidowitz, Jeff Davis of Niagara, Fred Dellar, Gary Diamond, Dawn Eden, Bruce Eder, Ben Edmonds, Sean Egan, Joe Ehrbar, John Einarson, Tom Erikson, Peter Fields, Trudy Fisher, Don Fleming, Robert Foos, Tim Forster, David Gans, Bill Allen George of the Jackie DeShannon Appreciation Society, Charlie Gillett, George Gimarc, Thomas Gladysz, Joe Goldmark, Giorgio Gomelsky, Dick Greener, Mark Greenstein, Matt Greenwald, Ayelet Hacohen, Randy Haecker of Legacy Media Relations, Matt Hanks, Colin Harper, Karl Ikola, Richard Morton Jack, Jeff Jarema, Elliot Kendall, Alan Korn, Michele Kort, Harvey Kubernik, Teri Landi, Kristan Lawson, Spencer Leigh, Andy Linehan, Tim

Livingston of Sundazed Records, Jeff March, Tom McQuown, Stacy Meyn, Debi Moss, Mark Moss, Ric O'Barry, Michael Piper, Domenic Priore, Ann Rasmussen, Steven Rickards, Carol Rothman, Ben Sandstrom, Michael Scully, Will Shade, Doug Sheppard, Steve Silberman, Phil Smee, Pat Smith, Sid Smith, Steve Stanley, Mike Stax of *Ugly Things* magazine, Armin Steiner, Rick Storey, Anatol Sucher, Denise Sullivan, Jeff Tamarkin, Bryan Thomas, Jennifer Vineyard, Ed Ward, Steven Ward, Jeff Watt, Charlie Wilkinson, Kurt Wolff, Chris Woodstra of the All Music Guide, Reinhard Zierke, and Alan Zollner.

Janet Rosen of San Francisco, and her husband, Stuart Kremsky, provided especially valuable friendship and critical counsel from the book's inception through its completion, as did Lanajean Vecchione in the book's final stages. In New York, agent Sheree Bykofsky, and her assistant Janet Rosen (no relation to the San Francisco Janet Rosen!), provided professional and sympathetic representation. Agent Robert Shepard offered useful advice in the proposal's formative stages. My parents, Sue and Elliot, were again fully supportive of my endeavors.

As they have done with my books *Turn! Turn! Turn!*, *Unknown Legends of Rock 'n' Roll*, and *Urban Spacemen & Wayfaring Strangers: Overlooked Innovators and Eccentric Visionaries of '60s Rock*, Backbeat Books have eagerly applied their best resources to ensure the publication of a book that seeks to dig deep into the riches of rock history. Thanks need to be spread around to editors Dorothy Cox and Richard Johnston, and publisher Matt Kelsey; managing editor Nancy Tabor; production editors Amy Miller, Amanda Johnson, and Michael Baughan; marketing communications manager Nina Lesowitz; sales coordinator Kevin Becketti; copy editor Julie Herrod-Lumsden; text designer and compositor Leigh McLellan; cover designer Doug Gordon; and proofreader Larissa Berry. Also to these boosters at Backbeat UK: Nigel Osborne, Tony Bacon, Doug Chandler, and Holly Willis. And a special note of both thanks and remembrance to Backbeat Books sales manager Jay Kahn, whose unexpected death in 2002 shortly after the publication of *Turn! Turn! Turn!* was a tragic loss to his friends and colleagues. We will always miss him and mourn his passing.

The greatest thanks go to the more than 100 musicians, producers, promoters, and journalists who graciously granted the interviews upon which much of this volume is based. Folk-rock couldn't have happened without them, for which we should all be grateful. This book certainly would not have happened without their participation, for which I will be eternally grateful.

about the author

ichie Unterberger's books include *Unknown Legends of Rock 'n' Roll* (Backbeat Books, 1998), which profiles 60 underappreciated cult rock artists of all styles and eras. His *Urban Spacemen & Wayfaring Strangers: Overlooked Innovators & Eccentric Visionaries of '60s Rock* (Backbeat Books, 2000) contains more in-depth surveys of 20 underrated greats of the era, again drawing on dozens of firsthand interviews. Unterberger is also author of *The Rough Guide to Music USA*, a guidebook to the evolution of regional popular music styles throughout America in the twentieth century, and the travel guidebook *The Rough Guide to Seattle*. A senior editor for the All Music Guide, the largest online database of music biographies and album reviews, he lives in San Francisco.

The first half of the history of the 1960s folk-rock movement documented in *Eight Miles High* is covered in its predecessor, *Turn! Turn! Turn!: The '60s Folk-Rock Revolution* (Backbeat Books, 2002). It covers the birth and heyday of folk-rock from 1964 to mid-1966, with a chapter on the music's roots in the early-'60s folk revival. In *Turn! Turn! Turn!*, Unterberger portrays the immense influence of the Beatles and the British Invasion that sparked young acoustic folk musicians to electrify starting in early 1964; the birth of electric folk-rock in the hands of the Byrds, Bob Dylan, the Lovin' Spoonful, and others in late 1964 and early 1965; the folk-rock boom launched by the Byrds' #1 cover of Dylan's "Mr. Tambourine Man"; the ensuing struggles between folk purists and electric rockers as Dylan's "Like a Rolling Stone" became a huge smash and he "went electric" at the 1965 Newport Folk Festival; the rise to stardom of the Lovin' Spoonful, the Mamas & the Papas, Donovan, and Simon & Garfunkel in the Byrds' and Dylan's wake; and the initial diversification of folk-rock into the music of early singer-songwriters like Tim Hardin, Fred Neil, Janis Ian, and Richard Fariña, as well as the early ascension of California folk-rock bands like Buffalo Springfield and Love.

More information about Richie Unterberger, his books, and the music he documents (including the 1960s folk-rock covered in this volume) can be found on his Web site: www.richieunterberger.com. E-mail can be sent to him at richie@richieunterberger.com.

photo credits

index

WHEN IT COMES TO MUSIC, WE WROTE THE BOOK.

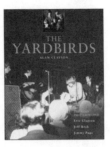

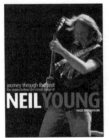